UNSPEAKABLE ACTS

UNSPEAKABLE ACTS

Jan Hollingsworth

CONGDON & WEED

New York • Chicago

A SUBSIDIARY OF CONTEMPORARY BOOKS, INC.

Library of Congress Cataloging-in-Publication Data

Hollingsworth, Jan.
  Unspeakable acts.

  1. Fuster, Frank.   2. Fuster, Iliana.   3. Child
molesting—Florida—Miami—Case studies.   4. Sexually
abused children—Florida—Miami—Case studies.
I. Title.
HQ72.U53H63   1986   364.1′536   86-16624
ISBN 0-86553-163-3

Copyright © 1986 by Jan Hollingsworth
Library of Congress Catalog Card Number: 86-16624
International Standard Book Number: 0-86553-163-3
0-8092-0163-3Z (Contemporary Books, Inc.)

Published by Congdon & Weed
A subsidiary of Contemporary Books, Inc.
298 Fifth Avenue, New York, New York 10001
Distributed by Contemporary Books, Inc.
180 North Michigan Avenue, Chicago, Illinois 60601

Published simultaneously in Canada by Beaverbooks, Ltd.
195 Allstate Parkway, Valleywood Business Park
Markham, Ontario L3R 4T8 Canada

For the children

Author's Note

Florida law prohibits disclosure of the identity of child sexual abuse victims. For this reason, as well as to protect their privacy, the names of all family members have been altered.

However, their story is true.

And the children's words are their own.

UNSPEAKABLE ACTS

Part I

THE BETRAYED

"I never cease to be amazed at the depths to which humanity will stoop."
—Christopher Rundle
Chief Prosecutor, Sexual Battery Unit

Prologue

Rachel Goldman knew from the moment she walked into Scotty's room that this was no ordinary nightmare. As she surveyed the scene, lit dimly, but not dimly enough to appease her anxiety, the plaintive cries that woke her in the wee hours of this Monday in May became more pronounced, etching memories with knifelike precision. Her almost-three-year-old son lay screaming in the rumpled bed, his head drenched in sweat, the sheets soaked in urine. Rachel felt a vague, gnawing chill form at the base of her spine.

"Give me back my pants! Give me back my pants!" Scotty thrashed about, pleading with frightening insistence.

Rachel quickly scooped up her son and cradled him, her arms forming a makeshift shield from the invisible enemy. But the child wouldn't be consoled. Caught in the fuzzy twilight between sleep and full consciousness, the little boy continued to sob as he envisioned a terror too real for his mother's reassuring embrace to dissipate.

Rachel rocked him gently, feeling increasingly helpless to comfort him, frustrated by why she could not. "I don't understand, Scotty. Who has your pants?"

"The man. The bad man took them." Scotty was shaking uncontrollably.

The bewildered mother felt the chilling dread creep up her spine. The hairs on the back of her neck stood on end. "What man? What does he look like?" Rachel wasn't so sure she wanted to know.

"A big black man . . . at nurs'ry . . . he took my pants, and he hurt me." Scotty was beginning to regain his composure. His mother, on the other hand, was about to lose hers. Something was very wrong here. In fact, something hadn't been quite right since last Thursday, when Scotty's teacher told her that her irrepressible son had fallen asleep sitting up in class—during a birthday party, no less. At the time it seemed an amusing anecdote; unusual, not alarming. But

3

Rachel had sobered when he conked out again driving the eight blocks from his temple nursery school to the family's Miami Beach condominium. It was the beginning of an inexplicable transformation that would take place over the next few days, culminating in the nightmare that so abruptly unmasked reality.

On Friday, his father would later recall, "Scotty just didn't want to go to school. He always looked forward to it. But that day he didn't, and I forced him . . ." His voice trailed off as paternal guilt overshadowed reason. He couldn't have known.

Over the weekend there were other signs. Small ones. Nothing that could add up to this, thought Rachel. Scotty's appetite hadn't been up to par. And he kept complaining that his "bumpy" hurt. But Rachel had checked him and found nothing out of the ordinary.

Then his sleep patterns went upside down: long, deep sleeps throughout the day; unmerciful wakefulness at night. The sleep that shut out the confused and frightening thoughts would not come 'round the clock. Yet even in slumber, Scotty couldn't escape his newly acquired demons. The vision he secreted so carefully spilled into his consciousness with a lifelike horror. It loosed his bladder, wetly defiling the warmth and safety of his bed. The parents wondered if he might be getting sick. Now this.

Rachel was beginning to think the unthinkable.

Quietly, she changed Scotty's pajamas and bedclothes, wiped his tear-stained face, and tucked him back into bed. She paused to gaze at the tiny face nestled deep in the pillow and wondered if this hadn't been some sort of bad dream—hers. Rachel searched for a pad and pen. She must document this; it would be too tempting to rationalize in the morning when reason might force her to confront her worst fears. She wondered if Scotty's words would elicit this much anxiety in the warm light of day. They did.

The next afternoon, as Rachel stood in the examining room at Jackson Hospital's Rape Treatment Center, the anxiety turned to disbelief, then to rage as the doctor regretfully informed her that her son had been raped. Not Scotty, she thought. Not beautiful, bubbly, trusting Scotty. But the child's injuries were unmistakable. His rectum was ruptured. She wanted to die.

It was a week before the family, accompanied by two Miami Beach detectives, visited the temple preschool the child attended. Scotty squeezed Rachel's hand tightly as they approached the building and passed by a young black man trimming hedges. "That's the bad man," he whispered. "That's the man that hurt me."

Stunned, Rachel said nothing as Scotty led the entourage to an elevator and pressed the button to the catering floor, a location that school personnel assured the detectives the child had never visited. There, in a men's room, he explained to the adults in three-year-old fashion what had occurred. What he described wasn't sodomy. This apparently was a separate, less intrusive assault.

Jabbering excitedly about a "secret room," Scotty toddled back to the elevator and directed the grown-ups toward his classroom. There, not ten feet from where he and a score of his classmates played, he led them to a door partially hidden behind a stairwell and slid it open to reveal a benign assortment of tools, buckets, brooms, and mops. A pair of worn coveralls hung from a rusty nail in the wall.

As she entered the room, Rachel felt the horrible dread return. The one-time bomb shelter (now a storage area and changing room for the temple's maintenance workers) was completely soundproof.

Scotty's parents and the policemen watched, transfixed, as the little boy stepped into the room and pointed to his penis and bottom. "Here," he said. "He hurt me here."

Remembers Rachel, "You just wanted to die when you saw him."

That was before she discovered that her only son also had gonorrhea of the throat.

Scotty Goldman was not to be a part of the events about to unfold. He was the catalyst.

1

About thirty miles from the Miami Beach temple, in the southwest Dade County residential development of Country Walk, the Vickers family was about to embark on a nightmare of its own.

Three-year-old Steven Vickers, freshly scrubbed, emerged from the bathtub, dripping puddles all over the shiny tile floor. His mother, Jill, wrapped him in a towel and began blotting off the remnants of his evening bath.

"Mommy," he ventured. "Kiss my body."

"Body" was what Steven called his genitals. Jill was annoyed. For a fleeting moment she wondered if this was some bit of wisdom imparted by his older sisters.

"Who told you that?" she demanded.

"Iliana*," he replied. "Iliana kisses all the babies' bodies."

Jill felt a knot forming in the pit of her stomach. Iliana Fuster was the trusted mistress of the Country Walk Babysitting Service. Dozens of the neighborhood children were left in her care.

• • •

The phone call came during one of those rare moments of tranquility that permeate a television newsroom. Deadline was several hours away, and the crews were still out on the streets. The police scanners crackled with routine calls; no major coke busts, no double homicides. A relatively dull news day by Miami standards. One had to die rather spectacularly to make the evening news.

The assignments editor cocked an ear toward the scanners as she shuffled through a newspaper, clipping articles for future reference. The razor edge of an Exacto knife sliced cleanly, silently along the border, leaving scraps of newsprint on the cluttered assignments

---

*Although Iliana Fuster's name is spelled "Ileana" in court documents, it is spelled throughout this book as it appears on her birth certificate.

desk. A moment's peace was hard to come by in this business; she should have known not to answer the phone.

"Hi. Joe and Laurie Braga here." The cheerful Boston accent that offered greetings belonged to Joe, but she could also sense Laurie's quiet presence on the extension.

Joe raced on, not waiting for a response. "Is this a good time to talk?"

This was a standard Braga introduction. No neophytes to the world of media, they were familiar with the diluted attention span of an assignments editor. If she was in the middle of one of the day's minicrises, their business could wait. They wanted both of her ears. She listened as the conversation proceeded in stereo. One rarely talked to the Bragas separately.

"We just heard that the McMartin case is going into preliminary hearings. Thought we'd let you know in case you were planning some kind of local tie-in story about the daycare system here in Dade."

Crafty little devils, she thought. They'd probably been waiting since January, when McMartin broke, to see the local media pick up on the story. Here it was May, and still not a murmur. They must have decided that someone needed a nudge, and that someone was her.

Typically, their story suggestion came solidly skewered on a news hook, one she'd been toying with herself for some time. The case of the "best little preschool in Manhattan Beach" was about to enter a California court. Seven adults, including the school's septuagenarian founder, faced more than a hundred counts of sexual abuse, the most horrific tale of crime against children in the nation's history.

Small wonder the Bragas were getting a little antsy, she thought. It was a prime opportunity for a blitz of sensational "Can it happen here?" stories. Not that she figured the pair would approve of handling the issue with typical "flash and trash" abandon. "Shocking tales of preschool sex . . . details at eleven" wasn't exactly their style.

The Bragas were many things, but sensational wasn't one of them. Unconventional, perhaps. Eccentric by some people's estimation, though they rather disliked that particular label. But they were responsible. Joe, with his silver midback ponytail, and Laurie, with her calf-length chestnut tresses, were periodically called upon by the local media for expert opinions on matters related to young children. An articulate, colorful pair, they exuded "good television."

More important, they possessed between them a store of knowledge about children's development that all the media combined couldn't begin to tap.

And they indulged in common sense, not psycho-babble. The Bragas' approach was so practical, their interviews so absorbing, that viewers quickly forgot that they might be (as one reporter suggested) "unreconstructed relics from the sixties."

Someone apparently forgot to tell them that idealism went out with love beads and fringed suede vests. And that commitment to a universal cause was now considered some kind of social aberration. So here, in 1984, they continued to embrace the notion that the Brotherhood of Man wasn't dead, just resting. And that children were the key to its resurrection.

This was the driving force behind their singular role as child advocates. Solidly credentialed in children's development and early childhood education, the Doctors Braga could just as easily have hung out a shingle and contented themselves with collecting a three-figure hourly rate for crawling around inside kids' heads. Instead, they used their gift of oratory to speak for those who could not speak for themselves—the community's smallest citizens. At times over the past two decades, their voices resembled the proverbial cry in the wilderness. Little did they suspect the price they would eventually pay to be heard. And only in retrospect would they recognize this phone call as the first piece in a puzzle of interlocking events destined to alter the course of their lives.

But on this sunny spring afternoon, the conversation and its circumstances seemed unremarkable. It was the Bragas' habit to contact the media occasionally in order to push children's issues into the public eye.

Their approaches to the media were judiciously selected. And if anyone in this town was in touch with the goings-on in the daycare community, these two were.

The assignments editor sensed a story.

She would look into it tomorrow, she told them. But tonight, she had a newscast to worry about.

● ● ●

Chad Herschel's hand grasped his mother's fingers tightly as she steered him up the walkway toward the red door that led to horrors still untold. Briefly, he considered wailing a firm protest. But that hadn't ever worked before. Mommy didn't understand.

"Normal separation anxiety," her friends had clucked.

"He's just fine after you leave," Iliana had assured her.

Everyone seemed to have an answer for his panicked reluctance to stay in this house.

Chad wished he could tell her a few things. Instead, he listened intently to his mother's usual parting words: "Now you be good and do what Iliana says, and I'll be back to get you a little later."

Chad nodded silently, then took an apprehensive step over the threshold. Maybe it wouldn't happen today. Maybe they would be tired. Maybe they would just let him take a nap, and he could bury himself under the blankets, safe and shut out from their world for a few short hours. And then his mother would take him home.

Chad Herschel's life had not been uneventful, right from the start. Born prematurely and deprived of oxygen for a precarious period of time, his first weeks were spent confined to an incubator as doctors maintained a vigil to assess any signs of brain damage that might have been caused by his difficult entry into the world.

But it wasn't until his second year that its toll became apparent. Chad suffered from a speech impediment so severe that only his therapist and his mother could clearly understand his communications. Compared to the host of other possibilities outlined by the doctors who attended him in his first weeks of life, his handicap was mild and ultimately correctable with proper therapy.

Encouragingly, the little boy had developed normally in every other respect, emerging as a bright and exceptionally curious child whose preoccupation with figuring out how things worked left a trail of dismantled toys, doorknobs, and household objects everywhere he went. But try as he might, he couldn't figure out the profane rituals that took place when he was sent to his babysitter's house.

"Mommy says it's OK," said Iliana, as she bound his thumbs together and secured them behind his head, beneath the halo of platinum curls.

Chad's mind swam. He could hear his mother's words: "Do what Iliana says." And now Iliana was reminding him that Mommy said this was OK. How could she? How could Mommy say it was OK for someone to hurt him—to frighten him this way? This was wrong. He sensed it from Iliana's furtiveness and from her incessant warnings not to tell anyone. If this was OK, then how come he would die if he told? How come Mommy and Daddy would die? Was this done to all little boys?

So far his "rites of passage" had included oral copulation, sodomy, mind-altering drugs, and systematic terrorism beyond description. Chad Herschel was not yet three years old.

Stripped naked, bound hand and foot, Chad became engulfed in his own speechless impotence. He watched in mute terror as Iliana slipped a tight rubber band around his penis. He could see it begin to swell. Iliana squirted lotion on his face. His body recoiled, repulsed by its familiarity. It was sickly white and sticky, like something else he'd seen many times before.

Chad squirmed, searching the room for a friendly face, someone who could help him. His eyes came to rest on the only other person in his line of vision—his friend, Joshua, who looked on in equally mute terror. There would be no rescue.

Joshua was littler than he was.

Suddenly, Chad couldn't see Joshua anymore. Or anything else. Iliana was putting drops in his eyes. Everything went blurry.

The horror was complete.

• • •

When the show ended at 10:30, the assignments editor pounced on the phone to make one last round of beat checks before the 10:55 update. It was a nightly ritual involving twenty-some calls to fire and police agencies throughout South Florida. Sometimes she got around to all of them. Some nights she didn't. Twenty-five minutes was just about enough time to make the rounds and write a fifteen-second reader or two on any breaking news she might come across. She figured if she really hustled she could wrap up the beat checks, crank out the overnight report, and be out of the station by eleven.

Ordinarily she didn't rush the process, but tonight she had some loose ends to wrap up on the home front. Her family had just moved into a new house, and there were still boxes to be unpacked and closets to be organized—the settling in.

It was half past eleven when she finally hit the ramp on State Road 836, heading due west. As she approached Miami International Airport, the semilit silhouettes of downtown skyscrapers began to fade from the rearview mirror. Just ahead, the Florida Turnpike cut a swath through a sparsely populated section of the county, one of the few signs of civilization for miles. Home was still ten miles away, just this side of the Everglades. She was beginning to think she should probably have her head examined for transplanting her family to the middle of nowhere.

But any second thoughts she was having were quickly dispelled as she pulled into the entrance of Country Walk and coasted by the familiar sign inviting passersby to "Own a Piece" of Arvida's country. It bore the development's logo, a barefoot Tom Sawyerish character snoozing up against a tree, with a cane pole in hand and a puppy snuggled on his shoulder. It was a study of innocence and simplicity, capturing the essence of the developer's marketing strategy. Country Walk was promoted as an oasis of tranquility, a refuge from the traffic jams, crime, and general urban madness of metropolitan Miami. It was the haven that she and her husband had long sought for their son—a planned, model community, patrolled by marked security cars, sheltered from the outside world by fences and shrubs. It was the perfect place to live if you had kids—or wanted access to them.

She braked as she approached the next sign instructing her to "Slow Down, Rabbit Crossing." A week of nocturnal homecomings had convinced her that this wasn't just Arvida's way of being cute. Rabbits, turtles, and other wildlife did, in fact, stroll across this street.

During the day, it was the dogs and kids she had to watch out for—loping retrievers and spaniels shepherding bands of little gremlins aboard motocross bicycles who roamed the roads like miniature Hell's Angels, thumbing their noses at the acres of bike paths that wound through the development.

One of the paths skirted a ten-acre lake stocked with bass and bream that were left to propagate unchecked. Rarely fished, its inhabitants had reached supernal proportions, both in size and in number.

Directly across the lake, the eastern quadrant housed the Country Center, the nexus of the development. Manned by a youthful corps of green-shirted Arvida employees, the huge barnlike structure was the hub around which all social functions revolved. On any given day or evening, the calendar of events might include Moms and Tots classes, aerobics, children's ballet, or karate. Weekdays, the center housed a half-day program for preschoolers. And nine months out of the year, yellow school buses lined up to deliver elementary students to the after-school program. During the summer, the Country Center was headquarters for an Arvida-run summer camp, a staple for the community's working parents.

Just past the Country Center was the beginning of the estate homes section. Townhouses and patio homes were available for residents who preferred to own a more urban "piece of the country," but the bulk of the development consisted of single-family dwellings set on spacious lots, each with several trees and a man-made hill. The obligatory mounds, interspersed throughout the community, created lush rolling meadows bordered by white rail fencing, a sharp contrast to the flat, barren topography outside the confines of Country Walk. Arvida's landscapers had somehow coaxed a glorious emerald carpet to thrive in the inch-thick layer of topsoil that covered a deep bed of solid coral rock. The deceptive fertility effectively obscured the fact that a spade couldn't be sunk deep enough to bury a canary.

The homes themselves, priced up to $200,000, were modeled after classic wood-frame Florida "cracker" homes. The quaint, clapboard homesteads, each topped with a weather vane, created a rustic charm in keeping with the country theme.

The operative word in describing Country Walk was *green*. Vast expanses of greenbelt, planted with stands of giant ficus, beckoned neighborhood climbers. Manicured hedges and sculptured shrubs were tended by a small army of gardeners. And clumps of wispy pampas grass, bearing a striking resemblance to sea oats, added a novel twist to the terrain, considering that the nearest ocean was more than twenty miles away. Someone had trucked a small forest out here to finish off Arvida's masterpiece.

All things considered, Country Walk seemed the logical southernmost extension of Walt Disney's Main Street U.S.A. Ironically, the development was a Walt Disney production of sorts, Arvida having recently been acquired by the massive Disney conglomerate.

The neat, respectable homesteads, lush foliage, and youthful, prosperous inhabitants combined to form a postcard village caught in a time warp curiously juxtaposed against Miami's space-age asphalt maze. There was a sense that one needed only the price of admission to partake of the God-given immunity from harm bestowed on the privileged class that resided within its gleaming white fences.

But the aura of security would prove to be little more than illusion.

For the time being, however, there was not a hint of Country Walk's impending reputation as paradise gone awry.

The assignments editor eased into her driveway. The house was still as she crept up the stairs to tuck the covers over her sleeping son.

He barely stirred.

Two doors away, in the cream-colored house on the corner, Steven Vickers slept fitfully, perhaps dreaming of secrets he could not share.

2

Christopher Rundle had done well for himself in the seven years since he transplanted himself to Florida from Great Britain; following a lengthy (and expensive) appeals process, he had been granted special dispensation to practice law despite his foreign credentials. Rundle promptly went to work for the state and became the recently appointed chief of the sexual battery unit, an irony underscored by the nature of the offenses he was charged to prosecute. Carnal crimes were neither prodigious nor prevalent in his native land, certainly not to the extent that made pursuit of violators a legal specialty.

Still, the appointment was a step up for the ambitious young Brit, a choice plum he would gratefully accept no matter how foreign the concept proved to his sensibilities. His enthusiasm for his new position, however, would wane considerably in the months to come. And even now, there was a hint of impending chaos, evidenced by the disheveled appearance of his work space.

Chris Rundle's office on the sixth floor of the Metropolitan Dade County Justice Building reflected more of the man and his job than the assistant state attorney would have cared to volunteer on his own. There was simply a sense that the office's occupant either had just recently taken residence there or was possibly on the verge of moving out. Both assumptions were reasonably accurate; no sooner had Rundle accepted his new post than he found that the entire sexual battery unit was to be relocated to the ninth floor of the building.

Chris Rundle was in limbo.

His staggering caseload was not.

"Where do you get your information?" The prosecutor's ruddy complexion flushed a deep crimson on this particular frying pan of a June afternoon, but not from the heat. Rundle had enough problems without this nosy reporter's prying into the confidential affairs of the Dade state attorney's office.

The party on the other end of the phone didn't answer. He knew she wouldn't. Rundle tried again. "You know I can't discuss open investigations with you."

Yes, the assignments editor knew. She and Rundle had been through this routine many times over the past few weeks, he trying to protect the integrity of his investigations and she trying to elicit confirmation of details she had managed to scrape up from various sources. They were both doing their jobs, but the process seemed to be getting stickier by the day. Rundle, alternately hostile and bewildered by her access to classified information, was convinced that someone in his office was leaking what he considered to be "state secrets." He was even more concerned that any day now he might "switch on the telly" and find them prominently displayed on the Ten O'Clock News.

She knew that day was still at least a month away. What had started out as a simple examination of local daycare regulations had by now developed into a full-blown series. Her research had turned up far more than she had bargained for: a daycare system so seriously flawed as to create an inherent potential for abuse and a judicial system so insensitive to child victims that they became fair game for those who chose to exploit them. The only operative "rule" seemed to be: if you're going to rape or molest children, make sure they're too young to make credible witnesses. Preschoolers seemed especially desirable in this respect. And it lent an ominous grain of practicality to an adage common in pedophile circles: "Eight is too late."

It seemed to be a well-known anomaly in social service and justice circles. But the "deep background" information she was getting from concerned insiders was so startling, she knew she needed to collect sterling verification. So she'd spent the past month checking and cross-checking people's stories, following a trail of obscure public records and filched private ones to an inescapable conclusion: there was a real problem out there, and John Q. Public was playing ostrich, partly because he wasn't privy to the facts.

And partly because he didn't want to be.

Despite an apparent conspiracy of silence surrounding the issue, she had managed to uncover several cases in which children may have fallen prey to their caretakers. Most were never turned over to the state attorney's office for investigation. Of the ones that were, none were prosecuted.

In one case, the accused admitted the "transgression" and was quietly dismissed from the daycare facility. But the case she found most disturbing was the one she'd been badgering Rundle about for weeks: the temple preschool.

Scotty Goldman, almost three, bearing the physical and emotional scars of last month's assault, had identified his attacker and submitted to two videotaped interviews with police investigators. The two suspects (the second of whom Scotty identified as a spectator, not a participant) had both failed police polygraphs. Suspect number one had even proffered a confession of sorts—but not the sort that was admissible in court. While vehemently denying that the incident could have possibly taken place at the temple, school officials had fired both workers, one of whom (the confessor) was currently applying for janitorial work at other local daycare centers. Yet there was no arrest, and it didn't seem likely that there ever would be.

The editor believed the whole affair smacked of a cover-up. Maybe, she suggested to Rundle, the state attorney's office didn't want to take on the powerful Miami Beach temple?

The prosecutor was indignant. "He's two years old, for Chrissake. Are we going to put him on the stand so he can say 'goo-goo ga-ga' to the jury? No judge will consider him a credible witness. We need corroborating evidence, which is what we're looking for. But without corroboration, the defense will simply attribute his testimony to the overactive imagination of a very young child."

She started doing a slow burn. "I'm sure any jury would agree it's somewhat difficult for a child to 'imagine' that his rectum is split wide open or that he's contracted gonorrhea of the throat."

Rundle sighed. There was no question that the child had been assaulted. The question was, by whom? The law, for the most part, didn't consider Scotty competent to supply that information. Rundle had spent the better part of a month trying to explain that to this "TV person," but it didn't seem to be sinking in.

He glanced at his calendar. In another week he would be on a plane, headed for a two-week holiday in England, where he could clear his head of this sort of thing—if only temporarily. All he needed was some hotshot reporter opening up this can of worms. She clearly didn't understand what he was up against.

Of the state's seventeen felony divisions, sexual battery was near the bottom of the totem pole. The five prosecutors in his unit could barely keep up with the host of unsavory deeds committed by and upon the good citizens of Dade County. These troublesome problems of women and children didn't warrant the manpower or attention paid big-time drug smugglers and gun-happy Mariel refugees.

Besides, sexual battery was unlike any other crime. It didn't generally take place in public, leaving the victim the sole witness to the assault. The preferred defense strategy put the victim on trial, making her reluctant to participate in the justice system at all. And in the case of a child victim, the system made it nearly impossible for him to prosecute; defense attorneys made mincemeat of them on cross-examination. It was a rare instance when he came across a child who would be considered a credible witness, declared competent for court purposes, and whose testimony would remain consistent throughout the judicial process. Kids weren't old enough for justice. That they were old enough for rape happened to be one of life's unfortunate ironies.

It was doubtful that Scotty could withstand the rigors of prosecution even if a court would consider him competent to testify, which it probably would not. At the very least, the defense would maintain that Scotty had erred in identifying his attacker, that to a two-year-old white child all black men looked alike. The case didn't look very promising, but the Miami Beach detectives kept plugging away at it. Their latest plan involved convincing temple officials to let them show Scotty's classmates an educational film called *Some Secrets Should Be Told* in case there were additional victims who might come forward to corroborate Scotty's story. So far, the school's director was resisting strenuously.

Rundle was concerned that, if the assault was made public, what was left of the case would surely fall apart. He was convinced that was the only reason the TV newswoman hadn't aired it already. Lord knows she had the information.

Where the hell was she getting this stuff, anyway?

• • •

The third-floor ladies' room at Channel Six was an improbable place to find the station's premiere news anchor taking a cat nap. The shabby little enclave boasted two stalls with plumbing of dubious capabilities; from one of them emanated an odor of suspicious origins, prompting speculation that something (perhaps a rat) had met its maker nearby. Along one wall ran a stained Formica counter bearing a toothbrush, a blow-dryer, and a vial of dark pancake makeup. In one of the sinks, a faucet extruded a perpetual drip of the sort employed in ancient China to extract information from unfortunate prisoners.

Oblivious to the dreary surroundings, Barbara Sloan sprawled half-asleep on what was once a couch—a torn vinyl affair that had passed its prime sometime during the postwar era. Barely five feet tall, the rumpled figure bore little resemblance to the larger-than-life image she projected nightly into tens of thousands of South Florida living rooms. Unlike many local television personalities, Barbara was acutely aware that real life did tend to diminish one's proportions. Right now she felt about two feet tall.

The assignments editor walked in and settled into the couch next to her, reluctant to disturb the weary anchor. The past several weeks had taken its toll on both of them. After two months of investigation (most of it on her own time), she had recruited Barbara to take the raw material and mold it into a coherent series on the daycare regulatory mess. Barbara pretty much had her hands full delivering a daily news fix to the station's viewers and rarely took on extra projects. But she was the obvious choice for the series. Barbara was one of the best writers on staff and really cared about kids. Divorced and childless, the anchor spent what little free time she had doing volunteer work for the Big Sisters organization.

The story would pique her interest enough to make her dig deeply and thoroughly. Yet she could be counted on for balance as well. Besides, the subject matter was important enough to warrant an anchor's attention.

Barbara stirred. She looked beat. After last night's show she'd worked past midnight putting the finishing touches on the series, then rose at the crack of dawn this morning to promote it on the station's public affairs show "Frankly Speaking." She'd really taken the subject to heart. Both of them had, for that matter. Somehow, dealing with the unimaginable magnitude of this particular crime was more emotionally draining than the murder and mayhem they encountered daily. Especially when the perpetrators were allowed to roam about, unchecked.

The anchor's eyelids fluttered, then opened. Barbara groaned. She was beginning to regret having let the assignments editor talk her into this messy project. "It's in the can," she said. "In the can, but not finished. This one'll never be finished."

Barbara had that one right. The three-part series ran a total of thirteen minutes—about seven times longer than the average news story. And it still seemed incomplete. Between the station attorney and time constraints, they'd been forced literally to wrench the guts out of it. There was a distinct discrepancy between what they knew and what they could tell. It was a fact of TV life.

The assignments editor made her way down the stairs to the second-floor editing room for one last look at the final product. She located an empty editing station, flipped on the power, and shoved in the tape. She instantly recognized the image on the screen. Barbara had started the series with an interview of Doctors Joseph and Laurie Braga:

> JOE: One in four females . . . one in six males will be molested or raped by the time they are eighteen. . . .
> LAURIE: Overall, in terms of child abuse, including sexual molestation, Dade County is much higher than the rest of the country. . . .

The statistics would have little impact. They were, after all, just numbers, not two- and three- and four-year-olds with bloodied diapers and recurrent nightmares; children who would face adulthood with a confused and frightened perception of human sexuality—some of whom would go on to repeat the cycle of abuse with their own children or someone else's. The studies were conclusive: child molesters weren't born; they rose from the ashes of molested children.

> BARBARA: It is the ugliest secret most of us could ever imagine. Last year more than a quarter of those treated at Dade County's Rape Treatment Center were under the age of twelve. Thirty-three of those children were infants. The terrible secret made national news this year when a seventy-six-year-old grandmother, members of her family, and the staff of the daycare center she ran were arrested in California on 115 counts of sexual abuse against children. The case hasn't gone to trial yet. . . . Could child molesting happen in Dade County's daycare facilities?

The assignments editor could picture the viewers resolutely shaking their heads. "Not at my kid's school." This sort of thing always happened to someone else, if, in fact, it ever happened at all.

> BARBARA: More than 35,000 children are enrolled in Dade County's

licensed preschool system. . . . There are 655 licensed daycare centers in the county. They are inspected by six counselors. Licensing standards and inspections by those six counselors are the primary safeguard against incidents of child molesting in local nurseries. . . . The court records we looked at showed HRS [Department of Health and Rehabilitative Services] took action on at least one complaint. It shut down a preschool last year when the owner was arrested for allegedly molesting a three-year-old child in his care. We won't mention any names because the case never got to court. Though the child was definitely abused by someone, the Dade state attorney's office says conflicting evidence would have made a case against the daycare operator extremely weak. He has since been relicensed and is open for business.

Well, parents, she thought, we would love to tell you who this guy is, but our attorney says we can't. Not to worry, though—he's probably not the guy running *your* kid's daycare center. Or is he?

BARBARA: Legal experts say even when the evidence is very solid, in general, child sexual abuse cases are difficult to nail down.

Enter Chris Rundle to explain the woes of the justice system.

RUNDLE: It is probably harder to prosecute an abuser of a child than most any other form of prosecution. The ability of a child to give you information and give a court information on a competent level is the first thing you have to deal with. The second thing you have to deal with is the effect of that child reliving those experiences and being able to go through those things again for a judge, or anybody else for that matter.

Herein lay the gaping hole in the series. The children's systematic exclusion from the justice process and the growing abuse problem in the mass-access daycare environment were two issues that were inextricably intertwined. And here they had given the court angle all of thirty seconds, another fact of TV life.

The reality remained that it was against the law to molest children, but the justice process rendered the law impotent.

BARBARA: The legal system wouldn't have to be tested if we had successful abuse prevention. Applicants for a daycare license in Dade County are screened through the Child Abuse Registry, an agency that's been heavily criticized because only nine counselors are available to handle the 86,000 complaints that come in every year. It's estimated another 25 percent of the complaints never even get logged because of the overload.

There was no time to mention the fact that last year more than fifty thousand files containing histories on known pedophiles had been sent out with the trash. The Tallahassee-based registry was short not only on personnel, but space. Of course the registry didn't have to worry about storing files on cases determined to be "unfounded." The term implies that a thorough investigation had been conducted and that the allegations against a particular individual were without merit. In reality, "unfounded" often translated into "I just got twenty new cases dumped on me today, and the guy says he didn't do it, and the kid's not ripped up, so let's move on to other things."

By Florida law, case files marked "unfounded" had to be destroyed within thirty days. Therefore, an individual could have dozens of complaints lodged against him or her over a period of months, years, or even decades, and if a caseworker couldn't do enough legwork to substantiate the allegations, there would be no existing record documenting a pattern of abuse that would "red flag" a file for closer scrutiny. The child molester was free to practice his aberration; his "rights" remained intact.

BARBARA: In the state of Florida, anyone who's eighteen and doesn't have a written record of alcohol, drug, or child abuse is eligible to open a daycare facility. Dade County's childcare system is regulated by minimum state standards. . . . But consider the case of [name deleted]. He owns and operates this daycare center in Miami. Several years ago he was charged with attempted first-degree murder in a shooting incident in which another man was wounded. The charges were later reduced. [He] was ultimately convicted of two counts of attempted manslaughter. Court records indicate his defense was insanity, that a combination of alcohol and stress put him in a psychotic state at the time of the shooting. Court records also show he served two years of a prison sentence and was on parole when HRS issued him a daycare license. [He] was relicensed this spring. How did his case slip through the cracks? Or did it? . . . In Florida, even a first-degree murder conviction is not, in itself, grounds for denying a daycare license.

The station attorney had a field day with this one. Among other things, he persuaded Barbara to leave out one small detail in the ex-con/daycare operator's saga; namely, that he recently had been charged with taking indecent liberties with a toddler in his care. The case was never prosecuted, and following a brief suspension, HRS reissued his license.

There were other interesting facets of his biography that, time permitting, Barbara could have gone into. Like the fact that he was an elementary schoolteacher at the time of the shooting incident. And that the Dade public school system, finding little use for what a court-appointed psychiatrist had termed a "psychotic alcoholic," decided it no longer required his services. But there was HRS, ready to welcome him with open arms into the daycare system. Barbara had asked HRS about that. They told her they considered the wayward felon to be "rehabilitated."

BARBARA: Do you think it's possible for somebody who's been convicted of, say, a felony, to open a daycare center in Dade County?
MOTHER: No, I don't think the government would permit that.

Barbara had asked a dozen mothers the same question and had received virtually the same response from all of them. The phenomenon was consistent with Americans' peculiar ambivalence toward government regulation—a rabid aversion to "Big Brotherism" tempered by an expectation that the government would regulate the "important" things. It created a false sense of security.

It was an invitation to tragedy.

BARBARA: . . . Florida's licensing and inspection system may not be flawless, but it's all there is. And it's still important that parents look for that license. That's because child specialists estimate hundreds of people are providing childcare illegally. With no license, no regulation at all.

The assignments editor viewed these revelations with no small measure of discomfort. Because of the nature of her job, she considered herself to be better informed and more cautious than the general public. Yet her middle-class smugness had made her guilty of the same assumptions. Surely the people charged with the responsibility of caring for the community's children were subject to microscopic scrutiny. And surely the premium she paid for her son's expensive private preschool was additional insurance of quality care. To believe otherwise would be downright un-American—or so she had thought.

BARBARA: Money doesn't buy the most closely regulated daycare. In fact, the opposite may be true. Centers where welfare children are enrolled are inspected seven times as frequently as those that don't receive federal subsidies. . . . Aside from state inspections, childcare operations with children receiving federal funds are also monitored and receive technical assistance from the Metro-Dade Division of Child Development Services. Such centers are inspected by that office twice a month and have stiffer personnel requirements. About a third of all daycare centers fall into that category.

She stopped the tape. There was more, but she knew what was there—and what was missing. Notable for its absence was any mention of the temple episode. After three months of investigation, the case was still open. She had decided (reluctantly) to hold the story as long as there was a shred of a chance that publicizing it might jeopardize the case. Her news director had concurred; Channel Six would not be responsible for a disclosure that might throw a wrench into the natural disposition of this case. Once the State closed the case—with or without an arrest—it would be fair game. But for now, Barbara's piece would have to air without it.

Although the series wasn't what it could have been, they had given it their best shot. If nothing else, the investigation had been a personal education for both of them. Hopefully, it would serve warning on the community's parents: Dade County's daycare system was a major accident waiting to happen.

What they didn't know was that it already had.

3

Apogee occupies just under an acre of prime Coconut Grove real estate—a little patch of Nirvana nestled almost dead-center amid the incongruous mixture of inner-city decay and urban elegance that characterizes the century-old bayfront settlement.

The Grove, as locals refer to it, suffers from an identity crisis: an irreconcilable blend of tawdry and sublime, where sleek Mercedes must glide past slums before passing through the iron gates that encase gracious estates—a fanciful lifestyle dogged by a persistent and sobering reality. The Grove is a mutation, its complexion radically varied from block to block—even door to door—the result of a curious transition that has spanned decades. Historically, the community has displayed the tolerance to embrace the most novel specimens of Americana, showcasing the countercultures unique to each generation.

During the course of the past three decades, Coconut Grove has weathered an evolution that transformed the one-time Bohemian stronghold into a bastion of Yuppiedom.

Sidewalk cafes and trendy boutiques may have replaced the psychedelic shops that once lined Main Highway during its sixties heyday as Greenwich Village South, but the cultural imprints of its past may never be entirely erased, contributing to the homogeneous disparity that is unique to Coconut Grove. There remains a hint of its artsy Bohemian flavor in the die-hard free spirits who cycle ten-speeds along the winding oak-laden roadways. And vintage Volkswagen microbuses sporting "Peace" bumper stickers can still be found parked next to the newcomers' BMWs.

Apogee was a bellwether for Coconut Grove's latest (and perhaps lasting) transition. Its creator, architect/developer Robert Davis, possessed the distant vision in the early seventies to foresee the area's upscale possibilities. Riding the crest of a spiritual high point in his life, the Harvard-educated businessman conceived a monument to his youthful exuberance—a townhouse complex of uncommon design. It would become, symbolically, his own personal apogee— the farthest from his orbit of convention that this otherwise traditional man would stray.

Davis built on his treasured tract ten multiple-story residences. The concrete-and-glass dwellings went beyond living space. They were, in essence, enclosed space. Robert Davis had created an avant-garde tree house with multiple levels of glass outer walls and skylights that eliminated the demarcation between indoors and out.

Inner walls and doors were nonexistent, the interior completely open from floor to third-story ceiling. The upper floors were defined as little more than expanded lofts accessible by an open staircase. Even the bathrooms were subject to a rather startling disenclosure, though recessed doors could be drawn from within the wall should the timid require a private moment.

The properties sold quickly to Grovites with a penchant for the unique. And ownership turned over just as rapidly when the couples who bought them came to realize that a lack of walls—and thus privacy—could be hazardous to a marriage. Over the years, a number of residents had defiled the architectural integrity by constructing their own barriers, partitioning off the abodes as though the absence of separation were an act of oversight, not design.

Such was not the case for the mistress of Apogee, who purchased the first unit, built in 1975. Dr. Laurie Davis Braga was intimately acquainted with her brother's creative intent. And a place without walls—a place that defied convention—suited her just fine.

• • •

Laurie Braga liked to compare the building of a house to the building of a person. "No matter what you put on the facade, the structure of the foundation is going to determine how sturdy that house is. The same is true of a human being. The foundation for a person's whole life occurs in his or her earliest years. And what happens in those early years determines what that child is going to be as an adult."

Based on that principle, one could only surmise that the foundation for the child who grew into the woman now known as Dr. Laurie Braga must have been laid in granite. Few people who knew her then or know her now are likely to dispute the supposition.

The circumstances surrounding the genesis of this particular human being are noteworthy in that they shed some light on an otherwise mystifying role that she and her lifemate, Joseph, would come to play in a convoluted drama they had no cause to suspect lurked on their horizon. Before it was over, who they were, and how they came to be, would loom significantly.

Ancestral blood may have been one source from which Laurie's strength of character was drawn. Hers was the legacy of self-made southern aristocracy, the roots of which still run deep in the city of Birmingham, Alabama. Laurie's great-grandfather, a turn-of-the-century penny merchant, parlayed a wagon full of pots, pans, and notions into the largest chain of department stores in the state.

Louis Pizitz was an imposing figure, a man of iron resolve who steamrolled over most of the people in his life. So it came as something of a shock (probably to the old man himself) when, as he neared his centennial, he began to exhibit a gentleness that few people suspected he possessed. The cause of this newfound docility could be attributed quite directly to the arrival of his great-granddaughter.

Louis Pizitz was smitten with little Laurie.

"Big Papa," as she called him, turned his empire into her own private playground. The apple of Louis Pizitz's aging eye had the run of the giant downtown store. So the ninth-floor confectioners quickly grew accustomed to the doe-eyed child who patiently watched them ply their trade, then politely sampled the finished product. It was here that Laurie developed a weakness for fine chocolate that carried into her adult years. And it was here that the first bricks were laid.

The store excursions usually wound up with a visit to the first-floor soda fountain, where Big Papa would command that the most enormous sundae possible be concocted for the little girl. Ordinarily a dour man, Big Papa would light up as he coaxed the child to shovel her way through it. The old man was captivated by this ray of sunshine that had arrived to cast an unexpected glow on his twilight years.

"He spoiled me rotten," she would say of him decades after his death. But the store clerks who knew her at the time recall a sweet, gentle child who seemed not the least bit tainted by Big Papa's endless shower of gifts and privileges. Perhaps it was because he supplied her with something she valued even more: unconditional love. "I think every kid should have someone who loves them that way," said Laurie. "It made me feel very special."

Laurie loved Big Papa dearly, but her mother held a special place in her heart that even Louis Pizitz could not attain. "She was such a gentle soul and very much childlike herself," Laurie remembers. "She had a real intuitive sense for kids." She was, in a sense, the neighborhood Pied Piper. Whenever parents on the block were missing a child, they had to look no farther than the Davis home to find it.

And over all children, Laurie's mother cherished the daughter she alternately referred to as "too good to be real" and "a kid from Mars." She prayed that no harm would come to this special child who required no discipline and who showed a concern for people and their feelings far beyond her years. At about the time other little girls were wishing for ponies, Laurie was blowing out her birthday candles with a pointed bid for world peace. "Are you sure you're from this planet?" her mother worried in mock exasperation.

Despite an upbringing awash in extraordinary warmth and devotion, Laurie grew to be a young woman possessed of a puzzling emptiness. Something was missing in her life. She just couldn't put her finger on it—not until she met Joe.

He was a first-year teaching fellow at Boston University—a young instructor who had not yet earned the title of "Professor." A smallish man with sharp, elfin features, Joseph Braga's chief ambition at the time was to compel his students to think. He taught psychology and philosophy; his students say he taught them well.

Fresh from three years spent teaching in the very proper Boston public school system, the young almost-professor found his life suddenly complicated by an instant attraction to one of his students. "I thought she was the most beautiful person I'd ever seen. There was something that radiated from her."

Laurie was equally enamored. "I had never met anyone like him before. For the first time in my life, I felt whole."

It was a match.

Boston was a splendid city in which to be young and in love. And it was in Boston, during the late sixties, that two young spirits began to grow as one. With typical Pizitz determination, Laurie had managed to coax Joe out of his initial teacher-student misgivings. That out of the way, he eagerly set out to help her discover every nook and cranny of his hometown. Discreetly (they thought), the couple prowled the streets of Boston; no eatery went unsampled, no historical site unexplored. They were inseparable.

Laurie became Joe's research assistant. A number of studies they conducted, particularly the ones that involved the interviewing of children, would come to play an important role many years later in a courtroom almost a continent away. But at the time, it seemed yet another academic achievement—one more opportunity to expand their collective mind.

The courtship blossomed. The couple made a pact: conservative Joe would let his unstylish crew cut grow out as long as Laurie agreed never again to scissor her own shoulder-length hair. The results of that agreement would someday give certain lawyers many serious hours of consternation.

Joe Braga had always been a collector of memorabilia. He never went anywhere or did anything of significance without squirreling away some prized souvenir—a ticket stub, a parking decal, a key. So when Laurie entered the picture, the collecting commenced in earnest. "His Story" became "Our Story," which, after a time, came to fill several immense albums. Among the cards, notes, and snapshots came to rest a Massachusetts driver's license that would also come to play a critical role in that distant courtroom. But in those early, innocent years, it was simply part of the bottled memories meant to be uncorked and savored in quiet moments of reflection. The Bragas were hopeless romantics.

Joe and Laurie knew from very early on that regardless of what they did with their lives, they wanted to do it together—"twenty-four hours a day, if possible." There occurred in the relationship a commingling of intellect in the most profound sense, the central bond derived from a strong identification with children. From this vantage, the couple carefully constructed a plan around which their personal and professional lives could evolve.

As Laurie neared completion of her bachelor's degree work in special education, Joe was finishing off his doctoral dissertation related to normal learning and human development. They began to cross-study each other's coursework. One day, Joe made an observation that would ultimately set the course for their life's work. "You know," he said, "you have so much developmental knowledge in your field that people who've studied normal learning don't have."

"Of course," said Laurie, "because we're looking at the same information, but through a different set of eyeglasses. We're looking at what went wrong and trying to remediate it."

The best way to understand normal learning (and thus, human behavior), they concluded, was to understand deficits and break-downs in learning.

It was decided that Laurie would, instead of pursuing a traditional psychology degree, continue her graduate studies in special
education—not just one or two specialties, but every area possible,
from mentally retarded and autistic children to the aphasic, the deaf,
and the learning disabled. "Our Story" contains pictures of Laurie's
"special children," each captured in the same soulful expression of
a child who feels understood. Laurie would someday be accused of
casting a spell over children. In a sense, her accusers would be right,
but not in the sense they intended.

She broke her back under the ponderous courseload, but it paid
off. Between the two of them, Laurie and Joe now had the "whole
picture" of human development. And since they traded off all of
their information, the whole became greater than the sum of its
parts.

Laurie has always considered the 1969 festival at Woodstock to
have been a celebration of her marriage to Joe. On the same day that
half a million flower children frolicked in the mud on Max Yasgur's
upstate New York farm, an historic wedding was underway—the
first and only to take place on the staid and hallowed grounds of
Boston University.

The bride wore traditional white and a dazzling smile upstaged
only by the trail of delphiniums intricately woven through her
thick, chestnut mane. The groom, equally luminous, was turned out
in a pinstripe suit, a Prince Valiant haircut his sole departure from
convention.

The event was an odd blend of old and new—a "rock 'n' roll
wedding" with all the time-honored trappings thrown in for good
measure. The theme, boldly engraved on the invitations and the
wedding cake, bespoke the era's rampant idealism: "All you need is
love." It was a sign of the times. Conversely, Joe and Laurie Braga
didn't reflect the times; the times reflected them. Their optimistic
ideology would remain with them long after disillusionment had
extinguished it from the rest of the tribe.

Those close to them realized that theirs was not a passing
commitment.

Mayor Richard Daley's Chicago was suffering the final throes of
the Days of Rage when the new Dr. and Mrs. Braga blew into town.
The Chicago Seven, the SDS, and the Weather Underground had
taken civil disobedience to new and violent heights.

The deceptively conservative Bragas (hair notwithstanding) continued to march to their own drummer. The way to literally change the world, they believed, was to make things better for the next generation—to set an example for the little ones who would eventually take charge. So they plunged into what they considered more constructive pursuits.

Laurie went to work on her doctorate at Northwestern, while Joe found himself a classroom on the sparkling new Chicago campus of the University of Illinois. When the young professor learned that an entire south-side neighborhood had been razed to make way for the facility where he was now employed, Dr. Braga conceived the strange notion that, when something is taken from a community, something ought to be given back in return.

Joe presented himself to the directors of the city's Division of Child Services. "Need any help?" he inquired.

The reception he received was worthy of a visitor from another dimension. Child Services couldn't *pay* people to work on childcare programs, and here was this weird professor *volunteering*! They took him up on the offer.

The first day Joe and Laurie showed up at Rockwell Gardens—a south-side no-man's land where local gangs amused themselves recruiting new members at the daycare center—they were greeted by a small mob of menacing youths. "Hey, honky, you in the wrong nayba'hood" and "Get you' white ass outa here" were eventually replaced by a chorus of "Leave 'em alone. They's the people that's helpin' the kids."

For the next five years, the Bragas worked closely with every group in the city involved with childcare and early childhood education, including the Chicago Housing Authority's model demonstration program and Cook County's Head Start. The aim was to coordinate the fragmented mishmash of children's services into a coherent network and to develop programs that would stimulate young minds.

Chicago's daycare centers became a working laboratory for the Bragas' research into new ways of optimizing children's growth and development. They also became Joe's classroom when he put his students to work in the model demonstration centers. Real children could teach them what books could not; real children could benefit from the bright young students as well. Joe made it a class assignment that each student must beg, borrow, or scavenge the highest-quality toys and educational materials that he or she could lay hands on. The students delivered by the truckload to hordes of cheering preschoolers.

Mayor Daley's office, not oblivious to the commotion the renegade doctors were wreaking, asked the Bragas to produce a child development training manual for the community's parents and childcare workers. Suddenly, the city of Chicago was in the publishing business. Daley's office was deluged with book requests from Oshkosh to New Zealand. The city of Chicago got out of the publishing business.

The Bragas did not.

They authored four books on child development and children's learning, aimed at an audience of teachers and parents. The Bragas' knack for reducing academic pontifications to everyday language prompted Prentice-Hall to invite them to edit a human development series spanning birth through death. This led to a stunningly successful collaboration with Elisabeth Kübler-Ross entitled *Death: The Final Stage of Growth*. It also led to a new sideline— counseling parents whose children had died.

This new vocation evolved by word of mouth. At first, nursery school teachers and social workers called them to lend support to bereaved parents. Soon, nurses were summoning them to hospitals in the middle of the night. They accepted money from no one. If the Bragas had their way, every individual would be issued a guardian angel at birth to help shuffle through the bad cards life would undoubtedly deal at times—whether he could afford it or not. In lieu of that, the Bragas were adept at dispensing coping mechanisms to help see them through the rough spots.

It was in much the same manner (and for the same reason) that the Bragas entered the world of child sexual abuse. And it was during this period that they began to see its victims surfacing with increasing—and unsettling—frequency.

The arrival of March is generally not cause for Chicago's inhabitants to celebrate the rites of spring. It would be another month before the icy winds gusting off Lake Michigan would subside to a dull numbing of the flesh. But on this particular March afternoon in 1974, the mercury shot up to a sultry eighty degrees and the sun broke through the leaden skies as if to light a path for the couple who pointed their new VW Beetle straight toward the Sunshine State. The Bragas were on the road once again, this time at the invitation of the University of Miami Medical School.

"It was really a strange day," Laurie still can recall. "Like an omen." A less auspicious embarkation may have more appropriately foreshadowed the disappointments that lay ahead for them.

Joe and Laurie sped toward Miami with a strong sense that the time had come for them to put down roots and do their life's work. Boston, Chicago, the years of experience, and the careful building of credentials had all been a dress rehearsal for the shining moment when they would "plant themselves to a rock" and educate the world about the importance of small human beings. Apogee seemed a most appropriate rock on which to plant themselves; a place without walls lent itself to the boundless ideals and aspirations of its new occupants.

With typical Braga zeal, the couple threw themselves into high gear. In addition to dual teaching responsibilities at the university and their trademark "good work" in the community, the writing and editing demands intensified. Their publisher sent them on a whirlwind author tour to promote the human development series. No one entertained the notion that the couple who "worked like a small crowd" might someday run out of reserves. That was before the world began caving in around them.

The first setback centered around a comprehensive study of the short-term, intermediate, and long-term needs of the community's children that the university commissioned them to conduct. They found that children's services in Dade County were either piecemeal or nonexistent. And the federal funds needed to remedy the situation had dried up since the Chicago days. In the strange logic of the post-"Great Society" era, children's needs were considered the most expendable. So the study, which the Bragas considered a mammoth testament to the diminutive value society places on its newest members, found its way into a dusty file cabinet—academic jettison.

The vision of what they once thought possible began to diminish.

By 1976, an overworked Laurie fell seriously ill, at one point spending a fabled "forty days and forty nights" in a Miami hospital. "Terminal," the doctors advised Joe, who could not be pried from her side. His health began to crumble along with hers.

Joe checked Laurie out of the hospital and took her home to Apogee, where they came to learn the most cold and sobering of life's lessons. The pillars who had always lent a sturdy crutch to those around them suddenly found themselves in a strange involuntary exile in their greatest time of need. Their friends clucked sympathetically, then quietly disappeared. They came to realize that the only people they could ultimately depend on were each other. And that they could no longer sacrifice themselves to help a world that wasn't all that interested in being helped anyway. As Laurie healed, she came to believe that the cause of her illness was not malignancy, but simply "fate's way of saying 'slow down and remember what your priorities are.' "

The shattering disillusionment was but a preview of the assault they would confront a decade later. In a way, it toughened and prepared them for what lay ahead. "Once you soberly face the world as it is and get beyond the disappointment and the hurt and the anger, it gives you a real strength to go on."

Laurie woke one morning to the profound realization that the sixties were over.

• • •

The thing about rainbows is that they always seem to emerge from the darkest clouds.

Laurie loved rainbows.

They were her trademark, appearing on the covers of the books she coauthored with Joe and sprinkled around Apogee in various forms: cloth, stuffed, ceramic rainbows; rainbow flags; and even tiny paper rainbows, which she carried in her pockets to share with small children (who she knew were the only ones who truly understood the importance of rainbows in this world).

It was the children who kept the rainbows in Laurie's life, allowing her to emerge from her illness and the bitter pill that had accompanied it a bit wiser but hopeful nonetheless. The unextinguished spark led Joe and Laurie to give their dreams another chance—this time within the scope of a smaller vision.

It started at flea markets, where the couple began selling some of the knickknacks they'd collected over the years to fund programs for the local daycare centers. Avid treasure hunters, they scoured the neighboring booths, searching for restorable refuse. A dollar bought a scruffy giant lion, which Laurie painstakingly stuffed and stitched into renewed regal splendor. The kids at the preschool they presented it to couldn't have cared less that it had seen better years; their toys were few and far between, and to them the big cat was pure magic.

But recyclable toys weren't the only booty they carted home from these weekly forays. Joe and Laurie's trained eye turned up numerous prizes among the discarded trinkets offered for sale. An endless array of priceless collectibles and antique toys found themselves converted into funds used to finance educational materials for the low-income centers that appeared invisible to the rest of the world.

By 1980, the Bragas had incorporated their efforts into the Center for Children, later to become the National Foundation for Children. A nation of two, they tapped into the local daycare system, spurred by the conviction that children whose needs are neglected become adults who do not care about the needs of others. They had already seen too much of that in their short lifetimes.

The vision began to grow again. It focused on their belief that an entire generation—their generation—would eventually rediscover its priorities. The children of the sixties—the ones who once thought they could change the world—had become today's doctors, lawyers, politicians, and journalists. Many, possibly embarrassed by their "establishment" lifestyle, now smirked at the ideals they had once held. Joe and Laurie believed that, if they could come to realize that they hadn't "sold out," that what they once valued wasn't just the product of youthful fancy, that smoldering social conscience might reignite. And if it did, they now had the power to act on it. And that's what the Bragas were banking on. The children of the sixties now had offspring of their own. They had a vested interest in the future.

This relentless faith in the evolution of the human condition was based less on blind optimism than on a more practical perspective. "It's not that we have such faith in them as they are," Laurie once explained. "We have faith in them as they are capable of being. And we have faith in the fact that the current trend toward materialism— the Volvos and the status symbols—is going to wear very thin after a while and is going to become very empty. At that point there will be a new fashion. And the new fashion will be reviving that part of them that has been asleep for the past twenty years.

"The way to literally change the world is to make things better for the next generation, which in turn makes things better for the generation after them, and on and on; particularly because in doing things for the next generation we set an example for those children. We show them what it means to be a human being. We really believe that. The only alternative is despair."

For the most part, the Bragas kept this cosmic view to themselves, practicing their philosophy rather than preaching it. But their cause remained invisible, and they lived with the growing fear that, when their energies were depleted, no one would pick up where they left off; certainly not the governmental bureaucracy that paid dog-catchers and garbage collectors far more than the daycare workers who were expected to raise society's future leaders.

Children, after all, were disenfranchised. They didn't vote. And unless there was a public outcry by those who did, the Bragas' dream of a child-centered society didn't stand a chance.

. . .

Apogee's visitor carefully picked her way along the tree-lined walkway, the coarse gravel beneath her size-ten feet producing an inelegant gait as she ambled up the rise. The angular, bespectacled figure paused for a moment, scanning the concrete and glass structures for the rainbow flag and brightly painted rainbow tree that would mark her destination.

As towering as a redwood, and as quietly intense, Janet Reno appeared distinctly fit to shoulder the burden of the largest criminal prosecution jurisdiction in the southeastern United States. That particular issue was currently the subject of hot debate as Dade County's state attorney faced what insiders were calling the closest race of her political career. Reno seemed unconcerned. But then, no one knew what Janet Reno was thinking unless she chose to tell them in no uncertain terms.

The woman was an enigma—a local legend as complex as the system of justice she was charged to administer. Alternately criticized as "a politician, not a prosecutor" and lauded as a "fair, honest, and just" lover of the law, she was, realistically, a little of both. She could not otherwise have reigned for six years over justice in one of the nation's most troubled communities.

Janet Reno's kingdom was a simmering cauldron of racial tensions and political turbulence. Dade County's criminals and its victims were, for the most part, either black, white, or Hispanic. Prosecuting a major crime that crossed over racial boundaries was a precarious high-wire act where a misstep might result in a violent eruption of volcanic proportions. Reno served, as one editorialist put it, "as a lightning rod" for much of Miami's "free-lance hatred and frustration."

The job came with a built-in controversy clause.

Despite this, ethnic boundaries curiously seemed to melt away during the last election. But Reno's universal appeal was ominously threatened this time around by former city attorney Jose Garcia-Pedrosa, who was currently orchestrating a nasty challenge to her throne. The Hispanic community was well known for its potent solidarity at the polls. That left, almost by default, Miami's ghettos a potential battlefield for decisive black votes.

Now, a short three months before the November election, the

Garcia-Pedrosa political machine was gearing up for the final onslaught, his hefty campaign coffers financing an aggressive attack on the incumbent's record. Reno had no political machine to speak of, her campaign a family-run affair, its meager funds supplied largely by a handful of loyal assistants who stood to be turned out on the streets should their queen be deposed. Garcia-Pedrosa had his own people waiting in the wings for appointment to key positions, some of them former Reno employees who took issue with their former boss's management style.

To work for Reno was to adore or despise her. There was no middle ground. The state attorney could heap on her prosecutors the most glowing of praise for a job well done and just as easily cut them off at the knees the following day with a few choice words about speedy-trial deadlines.

Of those who remained in her employ, she commanded at least a grudging respect. Though most courteously addressed her as Ms. Reno in her presence, other designations were used when she was safely out of earshot—some affectionate, some not. "The Boss" was most prevalent, though "Bigfoot" cropped up in some circles. A charitable interpretation of the latter term might make reference to the figurative shoes she had to fill upon the retirement in 1977 of the most popular state attorney in Dade's history—the formidable Richard Gerstein.

The private Reno was a mid-fortyish spinster who tended to admit frankly—and publicly—that she would "like to be married." So vastly intimidating was the state attorney that it came as little surprise that she was not. Strikingly handsome at times and plain as a burlap sack at others, Janet Reno possessed inner qualities not so readily apparent; there was a quiet kindness, a sharp wit, and a cryptic vulnerability that she allowed few people close enough to discover.

Tough, frank, and as economical with words as she was with the state's money (she stayed in fleabag motels on state business), Reno could unexpectedly retreat into her shell like a beleaguered tortoise when tossed into a purely social setting, a trait that often made people mistake her as aloof or distant. It rarely occurred to anyone that the mighty Reno might be painfully shy. And those who knew her well acknowledged that beneath her giant frame beat the heart of a politician who cared.

It was perhaps politics, possibly concern, or maybe even fate that brought Janet Reno to Apogee this morning in late July. For whatever reason, her visit and the events to follow would mark a period in her private and professional life that the state attorney would not soon forget.

Joe and Laurie Braga ushered Janet Reno into their nest with a sense of cautious anticipation. The state attorney's reputation preceded her, and they knew this audience was to be brief and to the point. The couple figured they had, on the outside, thirty minutes to state their business. They would take what they could get.

Stoutly apolitical, the Bragas were not in the habit of inviting politicians into their world. They couldn't have cared less who ran the city so long as it was someone who cared about kids. But an opportunity had presented itself that they could scarcely ignore.

Just last week, the Bragas had appeared with Barbara Sloan on Channel Six's public affairs show, "Frankly Speaking," to discuss the long-awaited daycare series. During the course of the program, they'd made some rather pointed remarks about the justice system's failure to protect child witnesses, thus circumventing prosecution of crimes against them.

The next morning they received a phone call from a man who identified himself as a Jose Garcia-Pedrosa aide and indicated that the former city attorney was also concerned about this problem and would like them to join forces in making this yet another campaign issue. Unconvinced by this sudden show of "interest" in children's issues, they declined. But it occurred to them that, if Garcia-Pedrosa's people viewed the issue as politically viable, perhaps Reno herself would be willing to hear them out. The state attorney had already established a record as being "pro-kids" during the past legislative session, where she lobbied successfully for a new video-taped testimony law. It had gone into effect just this month.

But Joe and Laurie knew that the new law wasn't worth the paper it was written on if Reno's prosecutors kept treating child witnesses like a lost cause. A phone conversation with Chris Rundle a few weeks before had convinced them that the state could use a little educating about children and their capabilities. Thus Reno's visit.

Though the couple's primary agenda was general, they also had a specific mission to attend to that centered on a phone conversation they had had a few months earlier with yet another prosecutor. "The cases we really work on," he said, "are the ones that get the heat."

If any case ever warranted heat, they believed, Scotty Goldman's did.

Joe and Laurie wanted to talk about the temple.

The state attorney listened attentively to the Bragas' diplomatic attempt to explain that there was something inherently flawed with a system of justice that would allow a twenty-two-year-old man to rape a two-year-old boy and walk away scot-free—only to turn up working for yet another daycare center. As laymen, their sensibilities were shocked by what they considered an egregious abortion of justice. From the outside looking in, it seemed inconceivable that the best the state could offer Scotty Goldman was a shot of penicillin and a wish for better luck the next time around. As it stood now, across the country, it was open season on any child under the age of seven—and the child molesters knew it.

"What would help?" asked Reno.

"A center," they replied. A special place where these victims could enter the system as what they were—children.

Thirty minutes crept into two hours. Reno relaxed, exuding, to the Bragas' amazement, a warmth they hadn't been prepared to expect. But then, Apogee had that kind of effect on people. It was difficult to partition one's thinking in a place without walls; even the impossible seemed within reach.

"This is so exciting," the state attorney kept saying as together they conceived a plan that would allow future child victims access to the justice denied Scotty Goldman. The Bragas offered creative alternatives derived from the science of child development. Reno set the legal parameters. What they proposed was possible, she knew, by stretching old statutes to their logical boundaries—and by getting the legislature to pass some new ones, long overdue. What they proposed was possible, but was she willing to fight a battle that yielded such uncertain results? Children had fallen prey to deviant adults since the beginning of time, and the laws of man had rarely been able to intervene. It had always been the most "unprosecutable" of crimes. What made this pair of idealistic refugees from the sixties think they could remedy a problem for which no one had ever found a solution? And why did she sense that they just might have a point?

Janet Reno left Apogee that day having reached one conclusion about the unusual couple and their equally unusual ideas: these people were anchors, not sails.

These people were for real.

She had no way of knowing that within two weeks that conclusion would prompt her to make either the best decision or the worst mistake in her career.

Or that she would spend the next year wondering which it was.

4

It was just past 7:00 A.M. when Susan Maxwell awoke to the familiar sounds that usually signaled the start of her day. A curious cooing and gurgling was emanating throughout the house over the intercom system. Kyle was awake, and once he finished conversing with the stuffed friends who shared his crib he would demand to be released to greet the new day properly.

Susan rolled out of bed and headed for the stairs to retrieve her son. As she approached his room, the sounds grew more insistent. The toddler was ready to be sprung from his slatted cell. She peeked through the doorway and caught a glimpse of the radiant smile that hailed her arrival every morning. Kyle never faded into the world; he sort of grinned into it.

Susan slung him over one hip and carted him over to the changing table. His diaper was soaked, no doubt, even though she'd changed it during the night. After eighteen months he still slept through the process. She wondered how long she would continue to get away with it.

Kyle lay contentedly tugging at her waist-length hair as she leaned over to fasten his diaper. Each day she marveled that this wondrous creature actually belonged to her. She gazed at the tousled curls and saucer eyes. He was hers all right, a miracle of modern medicine.

She finished dressing him and carefully made her way down the stairs. As soon as she plopped him on the carpet the chubby legs made a beeline for the kitchen, his mother close at his heels. Breakfast was the first order of business.

Susan stopped to latch the wood accordion gate at the landing, one of several strategically installed to ensure Kyle's safety. This particular one prevented him from clambering up to the second floor. The others, located at the entrances to the kitchen, dining, and family rooms, enabled her to cordon off entire sections of the cavernous house.

The Maxwell home was the largest and most expensive in Country Walk, almost four thousand square feet of potential trouble for the curious toddler. The gates provided an expandable maze of safety zones where she could monitor his play.

Susan strapped him into his high chair, served his meal, and began methodically packing his belongings into a large brown duffel bag—four bottles of juice, his blanket, a few toys, and what looked like a week's supply of disposable diapers. She stopped to consider whether to add a couple of bottles of milk, then decided against it. No sense in worrying about Iliana keeping it properly refrigerated; Susan tended to fret about such details.

The bag was beginning to swell. Good thing she hadn't tried to use the diaper bag, she thought. Half of this stuff wouldn't have fit. She took a quick inventory of the contents and stuffed in a banana, a cheese sandwich, and two changes of clothing—just in case. A visitor might have guessed the child was going on a safari, not to a neighbor's house for a few hours.

Susan began to feel a twinge of anxiety about the experiment she was about to conduct. Other than an occasional well-screened teenager (applicants might well have thought they were to guard the progeny of the Prince of Wales; in truth, they were to guard the great-grandson of a former head of state—Kyle's bloodlines were not undistinguished), only relatives and close friends had been entrusted with Kyle's care. Now she was about to leave him with a stranger. It was a move that weighed heavily on her conscience.

A lawyer by degree and a prosecutor by profession, Susan had not returned to work after Kyle was born. That's not the way she had planned it. But then, she hadn't planned on becoming a career mother. Instead of courtrooms and depositions, her days were now filled with outings to the zoo and playschool. Since no one could love Kyle as much as she did, she reasoned, no one else could give him the best possible start on life.

But at age thirty-one, Susan was growing increasingly aware that the longer she stayed home, the less marketable she would be in the work force. It was time to see if Kyle was ready to relinquish her constant companionship. The problem was finding a suitable surrogate. Her husband, Richard, liked the idea of a live-in nanny. Susan had dutifully interviewed several, eliminating each based on what she considered basic flaws in personality, hygiene, or education. Since Kyle would soon be talking, Susan considered diction a high priority. Richard liked to point out that few Harvard graduates would be applying for the job.

The answer to her dilemma had come last week from Debbie Lancaster, a woman she knew from regular encounters at the community pool. Debbie told her about a woman named Iliana Fuster who regularly babysat her four-year-old daughter, April. Iliana was tops, Debbie had said. And the Fuster home was located just a few blocks from Susan's. The arrangement sounded ideal. Kyle would be cared for by a responsible young housewife, who kept only a couple of other kids. That was better than cooping him up at home with a housekeeper and no playmates. She would give it a try; if Kyle adjusted well to a half-day trial run, she could gradually increase his visits and eventually go back to work part-time—maybe three days a week.

Kyle finished his breakfast and was demanding to be let out of his high chair. Susan unstrapped him and scooped up his bulging bag. She headed for the car, her son trailing behind. She led the little boy to her Chrysler New Yorker (the "family" car she had traded her compact for when she found out she was pregnant with Kyle) and methodically fastened him in his car seat.

Her friends teased her about being overprotective. She considered herself "precautious."

When Susan arrived at the Fuster residence, April Lancaster and Iliana's six-year-old stepson, Jaime, were playing in the toy room, a half-finished space partitioned off from the family room. Kyle immediately toddled in to join them. The ever-resilient toddler didn't object when his mother left without him. To Kyle, the world was a wonderful place filled with caring people. No experience in his short life had taught him otherwise.

Reassured by Kyle's casual acceptance of the situation, Susan drove on to the Country Center for a morning of tennis. It was the first time in over a year that she had had a day to call her own. It felt good.

Around noon she called the Fuster home to check on her son. No answer. She quelled the urge to rush over to the house. No, she thought. She wouldn't play the role of hysterical mother. Maybe Iliana was feeding the children lunch outside and couldn't hear the phone.

About twenty minutes later, she tried again. This time Iliana answered. Kyle was doing fine, the sitter assured her. Susan hung up the phone feeling a little foolish for being so overprotective. Iliana came highly recommended, she told herself. And she had seemed quite pleasant and capable when she interviewed her. She was just being paranoid.

Bolstered by this self-administered pep talk, Susan decided to leave things as planned and go to lunch before she picked him up.

About two hours later, when she returned to the Fuster home, Kyle rushed into her arms. She noticed he looked a little dazed. Iliana explained that he'd just awoken from his nap. She also mentioned that she'd put some cream on a rash on his bottom. Susan was puzzled. Kyle didn't have a rash when she dropped him off. In fact, he'd had diaper rash only once in his life, several months ago.

On the drive home, Kyle sat listlessly in his car seat, the perpetual smile wiped from his face. Susan was perplexed. Her son didn't wake up like that.

"Doesn't he look odd to you?" she kept asking her tennis partner, who rode in the passenger seat.

Her friend smiled tolerantly. Susan was so hypersensitive to every nuance of her son's behavior. Of course, he was such a darned consistent kid that any deviation seemed to stand out. Maybe he was a little disoriented from the change in his routine, she suggested.

Susan pulled up to their home and carried him inside. Maybe her friend was right. There was probably a logical explanation for her son's seeming a little "off." Kyle plopped down in the middle of the family room and picked up one of his wooden blocks. Susan was at first amused and then concerned as he idly banged his head with it, harder and harder. If it hurt, and Susan thought it surely must, Kyle wasn't showing it. Alarm set in as she watched him stand up, walk into the sliding glass door, and slump to the ground, his eyes fixed in a vacant stare. Susan started feeling sick.

Oh, my God, he's drugged.

She didn't know what to do. She couldn't exactly call the police and say, "Hey, I think my kid's been drugged." She frantically tried to reach Richard at the office. He wasn't in. She tried her pediatrician and got his answering service. Finally, she settled into a couch to watch her son. And wait.

When the doctor returned her call, Kyle was back to his old chipper self again. It had been about two-and-a-half hours since she had picked him up from Iliana's. She explained her concerns to the pediatrician and asked if she could bring Kyle in for a blood test. If he'd been drugged, she wanted to know. The doctor asked a few questions and determined that it was the toddler's first time away from home. She sensed his skepticism. Finally, he told her that if the child had been drugged, which he considered unlikely, too much time had passed to leave any traces in his system. Dejected, she hung up the phone. She knew he thought she was being irrational. But she also knew her son. She'd spent just about every waking hour of his life with him. Something was terribly wrong.

The rest of the night became a muddle of phone calls as she set out to track down anyone who knew anything about Iliana Fuster. Each call compounded her fears. There were rumors, she was told, that something wasn't quite right with the babysitting service. Several parents had quietly discontinued sending their children there. And a few had complained to Joanne Menoher, Country Walk's activities director. Joanne told Susan that a woman named Jeannie Pierson might be able to give her more specific information.

Susan spent the next two days trying to track down Mrs. Pierson, to no avail. She had reached a dead end. Late afternoon on the third day, Joanne called from the Country Center to ask if Susan could fill in for some tennis doubles. She agreed, welcoming the distraction. Richard was home watching Kyle.

Halfway through the match she discovered that one of her opponents, a woman named Jean, was none other than the elusive Mrs. Pierson. Susan could hardly contain herself.

After the final point was played, Susan took Jeannie aside and questioned her about the rumors. The woman was evasive. She said there were rumors of sexual abuse but she didn't believe them. Susan asked if she was still sending her kids there. No, said Jeannie. She took them out "just to be on the safe side." Her daughter had been there only a few times, anyway. Susan pressed on, asking if there had been anything strange about her son's behavior while he was going there. No, Jeannie said. Andy was just fine. Susan pushed again; she wasn't getting the whole story. Jeannie thought for a moment. Well, Andy had become overtly modest. It seemed like he couldn't get his clothes on fast enough after his bath—that is, when she managed to get him into the bath. He was a bit phobic about it of late. She supposed that did seem a little odd for an agreeable two-year-old.

Susan felt like someone had just stabbed her with a knife. It was a visceral reaction. She hadn't even entertained the possibility of sexual abuse—just drugs, possibly neglect. Not sex abuse. She was beginning to feel sick again. One last time she appealed to the woman to share what she knew. Reluctantly, Jeannie gave in. She had a friend whose three-year-old son had asked his mother to kiss his private parts. The child told his mother that Iliana did that "to all the babies."

That child, Susan would later discover, was Steven Vickers, son of a high-ranking Arvida employee.

Susan sped home and got back on the phone. She'd been trying to get ahold of Debbie Lancaster since that first frantic night. Tonight, she reached her.

Susan filled her in on the events of the past few days and warned her that the rumors about Iliana were beginning to sound like reality. Perhaps she should consider removing April from her care until the situation could be checked out.

Debbie was incredulous. No, she said. April had been going there almost every day for the past six months. The Fusters sometimes even took her to the beach with them on weekends—without charge. They said she was like their own daughter; April was "family." Debbie would know if something like that was going on. She was a good judge of character. Besides, she and April had a "special" relationship.

Her daughter told her everything.

Susan asked if Debbie had ever noticed anything unusual, anything April might have said or done. Well, April did come home one day and say she'd seen Jaime Fuster's "pee-pee," she told Susan. But that was just a "kid thing."

Susan asked if she'd spoken to Iliana about it. Debbie said no; she figured Jaime had already gotten into enough trouble without her rubbing it in. Look, this is crazy, the mother continued.

Nothing has happened to April. Everything is just fine.

Susan hung up the phone, still clinging to the hope that what had transpired over the past few days was the result of some bizarre misunderstanding. But she couldn't shake the feeling that it wasn't. She had to know for sure if something had happened to Kyle while he was there. And there were the other children who were still going there to consider.

She didn't know where to turn next. Calling the police was out of the question. What would strangers think of her story when her own pediatrician hadn't taken her seriously?

• • •

On the morning of Friday, August 3, the assignments editor was ensconced in her favorite chair at the kitchen table, digesting the contents of the *Miami Herald*. Two cups of coffee later, she planned to catch half an hour of CNN headlines, followed by the local midday news.

Radio reports in the car would keep her up to date until she arrived at the station, where two more newspapers would await her perusal. Sometimes it seemed like she spent a third of her day on the job and two-thirds preparing for it. But she wasn't complaining. It came with the territory.

So did frustration. It had been two weeks since Barbara Sloan's series on daycare centers had aired, and the revelations about serious problems with the system hadn't created even a ripple in the community. She was disappointed but hardly surprised. Who would *want* to acknowledge that what the series proposed might be within the realm of possibility?

Anyway, after almost three months of dealing with the subject, she'd been relieved to put it behind her and move on to other things. Today it looked like the always-entertaining antics at City Hall might be newsworthy . . .

The phone rang, breaking her train of thought. Irritated by the interruption, she picked it up. It was Susan Maxwell. Her irritation dissipated when she heard the tone of her friend's voice. Susan was clearly upset. After fifteen years, she was in a position to know.

The two had known each other since high school and had formed a friendship based as much on their differences as on their similarities in temperament. Both could be a bit overbearing and sometimes cynical to a fault. She just hid it better. Tact wasn't a prominent element of Susan's social repertoire; her brain seemed to lack the editing function that might otherwise blunt her thoughts before they reached her vocal cords. Susan had little patience for inaccuracy or hyperbole, and a first-time acquaintance more often than not could be left with the distinct impression that the former prosecutor had cross-examined him or her as thoroughly as a witness for the defense. Susan, of course, meant no disrespect in dissecting some innocuous anecdote as though it were being offered into evidence.

Together, they had edited the largest high school newspaper in the county. Susan might well have pursued a career in journalism had the study of law not beckoned her to seek not only truth but justice as well.

Graduation sent them on their separate ways. But as their paths crisscrossed the state over the next decade, they'd managed to keep tabs on one another. Neither time nor distance had broken their bonds, and when they both turned up in Miami again last year, the relationship had resumed. In fact, it was Susan who had introduced her to Country Walk. After a thirteen-year separation, they were now neighbors, their homes facing each other across one of the development's grassy parks.

So a phone call from Susan wasn't unusual. But her emotional state this morning was. It took something major to rattle Susan.

It must be Kyle.

She listened to her friend's account of what had transpired over the past three days. She knew that Susan wasn't given to flights of fancy. Still, she did tend to be a little overprotective with Kyle. Maybe she just wasn't ready to trust anyone . . .

But as Susan rattled off the information she had extracted from the other mothers, the pieces of the puzzle began to fall into place. The circumstances certainly invited inspection. The assignments editor knew from her lengthy venture into the world of child sexual abuse that just about anything was possible. That was why Susan had called her. Susan knew about the daycare series and hoped her friend might have some idea of how to proceed under the circumstances. The matter was further complicated by the fact that someone had registered an anonymous complaint with HRS last May. A caseworker had run a spot check and deemed the complaint unfounded.

Susan's friend stifled her contempt. An "investigation" by HRS held all the credence of a visit from the tooth fairy. The caseworker probably took one look at the Fuster's $150,000 home, checked the refrigerator for maggots, and called it a day. These kinds of things didn't happen in "nice" neighborhoods.

Maybe they didn't. But Susan wanted it checked out, partly hoping to be proven wrong, mostly fearing she might not be. The assignments editor told Susan she would give it some thought. She would get back to her a little later.

There was one more thing, said Susan. It seemed that Iliana's husband had some kind of flexible job—construction, she thought. Anyway, several mothers had mentioned that he was always in and out of the house throughout the day. In fact, he was more often there than not. His name was Frank.

As the editor hung up the phone she pulled off her reading glasses and rubbed her eyes. This was one problem she didn't need this morning. Or any other, for that matter. She stared out the window, wondering what peculiar twist of fate kept dropping this issue into her lap. She thought she'd put it behind her a couple of weeks ago.

But she couldn't ignore the situation, wishing it to disappear. Her days of blissful ignorance had ended the day she discovered the ordeal of a little boy named Scotty Goldman. Justice still eluded

Scotty. If the children of Country Walk shared a similar fate, would justice elude them, too?

She considered her options. She knew a way to guarantee a proper investigation. But she sure hated to play that card. Reluctantly, she picked up the phone and dialed the state attorney's office.

Chris Rundle, forewarned by his secretary that Channel Six's resident barracuda was on the line, took her call with his usual polite but wary demeanor. This wasn't his favorite way to start the day. She made him nervous, always poking about, asking questions for which he had no satisfactory answers. Rundle was mildly surprised to hear from her since this "childcare thing" she'd been working on had already aired. Maybe she'd come up with some new, improved method to make his life miserable.

"How might I help you?" he ventured.

She didn't quite know where to begin. She stalled, explaining that she was calling on personal business, not news.

Rundle seemed bewildered.

She took a deep breath and launched into Susan's account of her experience with Kyle's babysitter. When she paused, Rundle broke in. "Is that it? The children are possibly being drugged?" Narcotics, after all, wasn't his territory.

No, she said. There was more. She proceeded to relate the scraps of information Susan had gotten from the other mothers. She could almost see Rundle's spine straighten. "We'd better take a look then, hadn't we?"

The circumstances invited inspection.

As casual as he sounded, she knew he would be thorough. She'd been looking over his shoulder all summer, and he had no reason to believe she wouldn't continue to breathe down his neck. She felt a little awkward placing herself in this position. Even though she was sincere in approaching him as a private citizen, she knew he couldn't exactly ignore her access to the airwaves. She thanked him for his time and started to hang up.

Rundle stopped her and gingerly broached the subject. "You know it will hurt our efforts if this shows up on the news before we've completed the investigation?"

"Where've I heard that before?"

Breaking a story on the investigation right now would be premature at best. She would monitor the situation to see if anything concrete turned up—like an arrest warrant.

She hung up the phone and headed into the bedroom to get ready
for work. She had a long day—and night—ahead of her. As she
stepped out of the shower, the phone was ringing again. It was one
of her police sources. It seemed that a *Miami Herald* reporter was
sniffing around about the temple case. Swell, she thought. When it
rains, it pours.

Just as she was about to leave the house, Rundle called. A detective
from Metro would be out to Country Walk that afternoon, he said.
Whom should they contact? She gave him Susan's number, then
asked if the *Miami Herald* had contacted him about the Goldman
case. "Yes, they're planning to break the story next week, I think."

"Monday?" Her mind was working a mile a minute. She could
have the story on the air by tonight.

"I'm not sure." Rundle hesitated, almost afraid to ask. "What are
you going to do?"

She started thinking aloud: "I'll have to talk it over with the news
director. It's his call. We've waited this long, and the status hasn't
changed. The case is still open. The only reason to run it now would
be to beat the *Herald* on the story, and I'm not sure that's a good
enough reason. I will tell you this: if the *Herald* breaks it, I'll let
loose with everything I've got. Nobody's got what I've got on that
one—not even the *Herald*."

Rundle understood. Once the story broke, there was no way she
could ignore it. That she would consider sitting back and letting the
Herald beat her on it was the only puzzlement.

Once again she hung up the phone. She was getting a massive
headache. She decided she'd better call Susan and warn her that the
cavalry was on the way. She wondered if her friend might get cold
feet at the prospect of police showing up on her doorstep. She didn't
think so. Susan had pursued it this far. She wasn't likely to back off
at this stage of the game.

She was right. Susan said she couldn't rest until she knew the
truth.

She wouldn't rest afterward, either.

• • •

Metropolitan Dade County's Justice Building is situated west of
downtown, a brisk walk from the county jail that intermittently
houses many of its visitors. Nine stories tall, the innocuous building
contains the offices of the state attorney, the public defender, and all
the peripheral machinery that complements the courts of the

Eleventh Judicial Circuit of the state of Florida.

The lobby is dominated by two escalators that ascend to a maze of courtrooms on the second through fifth floors.

The assignments editor breezed past the escalators to the rear of the lobby and boarded an elevator. As always, it was stuffy and crammed with attorneys, police officers, and the odd assortment of characters who find themselves caught in the revolving doors of the criminal justice network.

If the building itself is innocuous, its occupants are not. Many of them (including some of the lawyers) looked like they'd slithered out from under the nearest rock. She clutched her purse a little tighter. She was relieved when the doors parted at her seventh-floor destination—the court clerk's office.

She had done a little checking on the Fusters. It seemed that the family also went by the surname Escalona and that the business operated as the Country Walk Babysitting Service, an appellation that apparently displeased Arvida Corporation no end. Just last week Arvida's attorney had sent the Fusters a letter ordering them to cease using the development's name and logo in their advertising. Possibly prompted by the rumors that had been circulating about the place since May, Arvida was currently appealing to the zoning board to shut the service down on the premise that the business couldn't operate in a residential community. So far, no action had been taken.

Joanne Menoher, Country Walk's activities director, had seemed pleased (and not at all surprised) when she stopped by the Country Center to inform her of the pending investigation. Joanne confirmed that she had filed the anonymous complaint with HRS in June based on information she had been given by one of the homeowners in the community. Joanne said she knew Frank Fuster.

And that she was afraid of him.

The assignments editor decided to stop by the Justice Building in case the court clerk's files contained any further revelations. She didn't really expect to find anything, but it wouldn't hurt to look. She hung a left as she entered the office and went to the wooden table that supported the massive directories to criminal case files. She paged through one looking for "Fuster."

No entry.

She tried "Escalona."

No Iliana.

She almost closed the book before she realized what she'd just passed over. She looked at the entry again, this time in disbelief: "Escalona, Francisco Fuster."

She was stunned.

She couldn't be sure until she got a positive ID on the birth date, but if her instincts were on target, this was the "Frank" with the "flexible job" that Susan had told her about.

And if it was, Iliana's husband was a convicted child molester.

5

The husky little red-haired boy knelt on the floor of Deputy Chief State Attorney Abe Laeser's office, seemingly absorbed in dismantling a large toy truck. His eyes remained downcast, his expression inscrutable, as he concentrated on the task, paying little attention to the kindly man with the silver ponytail who was sprawled before him on the blue-green carpet. The child's studied indifference extended to the other grown-up in the room, a pleasant woman with calf-length chestnut hair swept atop her head, who sat beside him cross-legged, demurely trying to maintain some semblance of modesty with the hem of her dress.

Jason Harrison frankly had never met any grown-ups quite like these two. He covertly sized them up as he plotted how to evade questions about The Subject, should it come up.

He was sure it would.

Large for his five years—and very bright—Jason had a pretty good idea why he was here today. What he didn't know was that he was about to become the State's star witness.

Neither did Doctors Joseph and Laurie Braga. Summoned that morning by Chris Rundle, they knew only that they were to interview some children who attended a babysitting service run by a couple named Frank and Iliana Fuster. They had entered the Justice Building a few hours ago, never suspecting that the cold, colorless structure was to be their second home for the next two years.

As they stepped into the elevator, the couple received more than a perfunctory glance from the other passengers. The spritely man with the startling ice-blue eyes wore a three-piece suit, his hair neatly clasped at the nape of his neck with a coated elastic band. Instead of a briefcase, he carried a colorful satchel bearing the likeness of the comic strip character Snoopy.

His willowy wife, wearing a powder-blue minidress that revealed a good portion of her unshaven legs, carried a paper sack filled with peanut butter sandwiches. These, and each other, would sustain them through the long day and night ahead.

As the elevator doors parted at the sixth floor, the lettering on a transparent glass panel informed them that they had reached the offices of Dade State Attorney Janet Reno. But it was Rundle who appeared to escort them through the electronic doors that shielded the machinations of law and order from the outside world. It was to be a new and intriguing perspective.

As they followed the prosecutor down a narrow corridor, they could hear the sound of children in the distance—a dissonant chorus amid the other sounds more appropriate to the business of justice. The source of the anomaly was located at the end of the hall, where the Bragas came face to face with the kind of organized chaos only the State could create on such short notice.

In one office, seven distraught parents and five of their offspring, ranging from two to five years old, waited anxiously as assistant state attorneys, detectives, and assorted office workers milled around the cramped quarters. In an adjacent room, Abe Laeser was hurriedly clearing out his office, which had been commandeered for the occasion. Near his doorway, two technicians frantically tried to make sense of the video equipment they had just snatched from the training department.

Chris Rundle stationed himself nearby, eyeing the camera with no small degree of apprehension. The Bragas had insisted that their interviews with the children be videotaped, citing the new, still untested state law that had gone into effect the month before.

Rundle considered the taping a risky business. What if Country Walk developed into a rock-solid case, only to be trounced in court by any perceived inconsistencies in a child's testimony now recorded for posterity? But the Bragas were adamant. The tapes not only could spare the children the trauma of subsequent reinterviews, as the law intended; they would also document their encounters, leaving no room for what they had read was becoming a common defense argument in similar cases across the country—that the children had been coached in their testimony.

Impervious to the bedlam surrounding them, Joe and Laurie went to work unpacking the contents of the Snoopy suitcase. With the notable exception of four anatomically detailed dolls, the puppets, trucks, and blocks looked like a random assortment of children's toys. But for the Bragas, they were carefully selected tools that would help them gauge a child's particular level of language and thinking ability. Their significance would become increasingly evident to prosecutors as the case progressed.

The Bragas knew how to interview children. But this would be the first time they would apply their skills for possible court purposes. Intuition and the principles of child development would be their only beacons. Matters of law would have to take a backseat to their own self-imposed mandate to "first do no harm." Their gentle probing was to be structured to inflict no damage where none existed. If it turned out that the child had been victimized, the encounter was to be positive and constructive, allowing the psychological healing process to begin. And if a situation arose where there was a conflict between the prosecution's needs and the children's, the children would prevail.

The ground rules laid, the Bragas turned their attention to the task at hand. As they studied the guileless child before them, it was difficult to conceive that his five-year-old mind might hold secrets beyond normal human comprehension. But Rundle, having spent last night at Country Walk talking to the child, had determined that the possibility existed. He had also determined that the key to unlocking those secrets lay beyond his expertise in matters of law.

It was Janet Reno who had offered an unorthodox solution to the problem. She knew of a couple who could "speak children." Why not give them a call?

Thus, the Bragas found themselves closeted in Laeser's office, facing this apprehensive preschooler. So "speak children" they did. Ever so gradually, Jason began to warm up to his new playmates. Ten minutes passed. Then twenty, thirty. Amid small talk about movies and birthdays, Jason labored over the toy truck, his co-conspirators in the project occasionally throwing out hints to help him figure it out.

All the while, Joe and Laurie carefully noted his levels of development: his motor skills, his ability to express himself, his ability to understand them—how his mind worked. They adjusted their approach accordingly. It was more than a matter of vocabulary—and much more than establishing a physical balance between them by joining him on the floor. They were establishing a level of communication that few adults are privileged to share with a child.

They were entering his world.

The phenomenon was not lost on Jason. The little boy had been doing some evaluating of his own, trying to get a sense of what these unusual grown-ups were all about. Not only did they use words he could understand, structuring them in a form similar to his own; they actually seemed to *think* like he did. It began to dawn on him that this child-man and child-woman might be trusted. But he'd better be careful; the stakes were too high.

The truck was now completely dismantled, and the small talk drew to a close. The Bragas were about to tread into what the child considered to be very frightening territory. Armed with the barest knowledge of what they might be looking for, the Bragas embarked on what was to become a convoluted journey through the mind of a troubled little boy. As Joe would later describe it, "It was like swimming through Jell-O."

"Do you know why you came here today?" Laurie ventured.

The little boy didn't look up from the truck. "Yeah." He knew they were about to broach the same subject that Rundle had the night before.

"Would you be willing to talk to us about the same stuff?" Her tone conveyed a genuine request, letting him know from the start that this was not to be an interrogation.

"Yeah." Jason started putting the truck back together, his eyes still concealed by a veil of lowered lashes. He hesitated, then added, "My dad had his birthday in July."

Laurie was puzzled. "Is that one of the things Chris asked you?"

"Yeah." Jason gave her a measured glance. How long would they be satisfied with monosyllabic responses?

Laurie plodded on. "And did he ask you about the place where you went to the babysitter's?"

Again, the child averted his eyes. "Uh, we're just having trouble." Clearly uncomfortable with the subject, he renewed his efforts with the truck.

"Does it make you sad to talk about it?" asked Joe.

"No, it's just that, um, we discussed about it yesterday, and, uh, I don't want to talk about it again." Jason stole a glance to gauge their reaction. Grown-ups didn't like it when you didn't answer their questions. The way he figured it, now was the time for the requests to end and the demands to begin.

"I can understand that," said Joe.

"It's kind of a hard thing to talk about," Laurie chimed in reassuringly.

For the next few minutes the Bragas tried a couple of different approaches, never pushing him further than he was willing to go.

He clearly knew something, but they would let him decide when he was comfortable enough to tell. They did note that he seemed receptive to the idea that they needed him to help them understand how to talk to his two-year-old brother, Joshua, about the same matter.

The conversation shifted to small talk as they let his attention wander back to the truck for a while. Not until it was completely reassembled did they get back to the business of the babysitting service.

This time, Joe pulled out the dolls. Jason jumped to his feet, fascinated. He noticed immediately, even though they were fully clothed, that these were unusual dolls. For the first time, Joe and Laurie had his undivided attention.

"Let's pretend for a minute that this is you," Joe began cheerfully, pointing to one of the dolls. "Wanna sit down for a minute?"

Jason sat down. His curiosity was getting the best of him.

"Now, you don't have a moustache yet, do you?" Joe continued, pointing to the fuzzy yarn attached to the doll's upper lip. "And he doesn't have red hair, all right? But let's pretend this is you over here, all right? And I want you—this is you, OK?—to ask your brother questions about what happened at Frank and Iliana's so I can understand how I'm going to be able to ask him. So you show me, and maybe I can do it better. Would you try?"

Jason nodded. "Uh-huh." This was a whole new ball game. These people weren't asking about what happened to him. They wanted to know about Joshua. He could use the dolls to tell them a little about that.

Hesitantly, he picked up one of the dolls and began to relate what had happened to his little brother. "Iliana's changing his diaper and, uh, playing with his, uh, penis. And it's not very good. He would like, hit her or something."

"So, he didn't like it?" asked Laurie.

"No." Jason tried to read their response. They didn't seem the least nonplussed at this embarrassing piece of information.

"Did she hurt him?" asked Joe.

"No. She just, um, played games with his penis and all that." Jason hesitated. "And it's not very nice."

Count one: lewd and lascivious assault.

"Do you think she did it more than once?" Joe wondered.

"Yeah, she did it more than once." The little boy wasn't about to volunteer any more than he was asked. The less he told, he figured, the less likely he was going to find himself in hot water.

"Was Frank around when she did it?"

"No, he's at work most of the time." Jason wondered if they could tell he was lying.

"Is he ever around much?" Joe sounded casual.

"Yeah, he's around. But he's outside." Then wavering, he added quickly, "But sometimes he comes inside."

"He did come inside sometimes?" Joe's tone remained excruciatingly casual.

"Yeah."

"And what happened?" Joe wondered.

"No, when Iliana changes my brother, um, he's not inside." Jason clearly wasn't ready to deal with the subject of Frank.

Joe got the message and took a different tack. "Were you there when Iliana changed his diaper ever?"

"Yeah." Jason was relieved. They stopped asking about Frank.

"So, did you see her do it?" asked Joe.

"Yeah, I always see her." Jason was absently pulling the clothing off the doll.

Joe noticed that the child was easing into a demonstration. "What does she do?"

"She like, uh, does this." Jason continued stripping the doll.

"Oh, you mean to change his diaper?"

"Yeah." Jason was on a roll. "She does this. And then takes this off and goes . . ." The little boy was fondling the doll's penis. "This is what she does."

"And you saw her do that?" asked Joe.

"Yeah."

Laurie entered the conversation. "What did Joshua do when she did that?"

"Umm . . ."

"Did he cry?"

"No, um, he just, um, hit her."

"He hit her?"

"Yeah." Jason was distracted, wondering if he dared retract a certain untruth that was nagging at him.

"Then she would stop?" Laurie was still exploring the particulars of the incident.

"Oh, yeah." Jason took a deep breath and blurted out, "Um, Frank knew." He could hold it in no longer.

"How did he know?" Laurie's voice was calm, unconcerned.

"Because he, um, he's home half of the time. And um, Frank, um, he once saw her do it." Jason was ready to start edging toward the truth.

"What did he say?"

"Um, he didn't really like it."

"How do you know he didn't like it?" asked Joe.

"Because I saw them do it."

Joe picked up on the plural pronoun. "You saw Frank *and* Iliana do it?"

"Yeah."

"So, did Frank play with your brother's penis, too?" Joe figured he'd better get crystal clarification on this one.

Count two: lewd and lascivious assault.

"Yeah." Jason knew he'd reached the point of no return. They were going to ask a lot more questions about Frank. But somehow he didn't feel quite as frightened at the prospect as he had before. The grown-ups were reacting to all this like he was telling them about his latest trip to Disney World. And they weren't being pushy about it.

"So how did he do it? Can you show me with either of the dolls?" Joe requested.

"Um, OK. He first, um, takes his shirt off." Jason demonstrated with the doll. "Then he does this. And then . . ."

"And Iliana was there at the same time?" Joe asked.

"Yeah."

"Did they talk to each other when he was doing it?" Laurie was trying to get a better handle on exactly what was taking place.

"Yeah," Joe chimed in. "What did Frank and Iliana say to each other when they were doing it?"

"Nothing." Jason's voice was flat, expressionless.

"Nothing?"

"But they were arguing a little. See, um, they were arguing about not doing it. They don't want to do it. But they just keep doing it." Jason's five-year-old mind had apparently been working overtime in search of a reasonable explanation for his caretakers' bizarre proclivities.

Joe found it an intriguing bit of insight for a child of such tender years. "Why do you think that?"

Jason didn't answer. He had something else on his mind. "And they don't know *we're* doing it."

Joe was puzzled. "They don't know we're doing *what?*"

"We're, um, we're talking about this," Jason looked worried.

"Did they tell you not to talk about it?" asked Laurie.

"Yeah."

"What did they say?" she asked.

"They said don't tell your mom or dad because, um . . ." Jason searched his memory for the most benign threat he could offer. To verbalize the others would force him to confront a terror that ran so deep within him he couldn't begin to describe it. "They're not gonna, um, they're not gonna babysit here anymore."

"If you told, they wouldn't let you go back, right?"

"Yeah."

"Did you want to go back?"

Jason noticed that Laurie was speaking in past tense. "Yeah, but we're still going."

She wasn't sure what he meant by that. Maybe he was under the impression that someday he and his brother would be going there again. But surely he hadn't been there since the investigation began last week. The enormity of Jason's act of faith and courage in giving them this information would have struck her like a bolt from the blue had she even suspected that the brothers had been left in the Fusters' care as recently as forty-eight hours ago. But no one had told her.

"So you liked it there?" she continued.

"Yeah."

"You just didn't like what they were doing?"

"Right."

Joe was wondering what the little boy was holding back. "So they told you . . . they said keep a secret?"

"Yeah. They said keep a very *good* secret."

"How did they tell you that?" Joe asked. "Do you remember what words they used?"

Jason looked perplexed. "They, um, they don't use any bad words . . ."

"No, but *any* words. No, I wasn't looking for you to say any bad words," Joe assured him. "I was just wondering what words they used to say it. Like did they say, uh, 'Don't tell the secret 'cause it's our secret'? Or did they say, 'Don't tell the secret 'cause something will happen'?"

"Yeah. They said, um, 'Don't tell the secret 'cause something will happen.' "

"Like what?"

"Like, um, I won't come there ever again. But . . ." Jason considered how far he should stick his neck out, then opted for the safer route. "Another thing—my mom'll be mad at them."

"Did they say anything bad would happen to you or your brother if you told anybody? Your mom or dad or anybody?" Joe sensed there was more that Jason wasn't telling. He just didn't know how much.

"I told my mom and dad," Jason volunteered.

"I know," Joe said buoyantly. "And it's a good thing you did, 'cause they should know. 'Cause you should never keep secrets from Mom and Dad. But did they say anything bad would happen to you or your brother if . . ."

"They never did it to me." Jason wanted to make sure his new friends didn't think that he had participated in these shameful activities.

"They never did it to you." Joe suspected otherwise, but he also knew that it was important for Jason to distance himself from that reality for the time being. Instead, for the third time, he asked the question that Jason had thus far evaded. "Did they ever threaten you if you talked? Something would happen to you or your brother . . ."

"That you would get hurt?" Laurie finished the sentence. She was as anxious as Joe for the answer to this crucial question. If they could isolate his fear and defuse it, then Jason would be free of the secrets that festered inside him like an open wound.

"No, they wouldn't be mad," Jason mumbled. The little boy's body spoke louder than his words. He had positioned himself with his back toward Joe, sideways from Laurie. Jason was clearly distressed by this line of questioning.

Laurie wasn't sure she had heard right. "They *wouldn't* be mad? Or they *would* be?"

"They *wouldn't* be mad." Jason was adamant. "Because, uh, because, uh, because my, um, mom and dad like them. But we don't like them when they do that. That's what I mean."

Joe nodded. "I see."

Laurie interjected soothingly, "You just wish they wouldn't do that."

"Yeah."

"Because it makes you feel uncomfortable when they do that, I'm sure, right?" added Joe.

"Yeah. Uh, they never do it to me," he reminded them.

"Did they try?" asked Laurie.

"No. They never did." Jason was concentrating on the floor.

Joe offered him an out. "Did they ever talk about doing it but you said no?"

"Yeah, they talked about it." Jason's eyes remained averted.

"And what did you say when they talked about it?" asked Joe.

"I said I would tell my mom and dad, and they said, '*No.*' " Jason had saved face. They mustn't know that he hadn't the courage to refuse the advances. His fear and shame welled so deep that he wasn't quite sure where he had found the courage to tell as much as he had already. All he knew was that he was beginning to feel better having done so. The fear and pain inside him was beginning to subside. It was a great comfort to him that the grown-ups weren't shocked or angry. And they weren't making him do things their way. They gave him full reign; he, Jason, was in control. And that was gradually making him feel secure enough to discuss a situation in which all control had been wrested from him. He was too young to identify the experience as the return of his self-respect.

"So they said they wouldn't do it if you didn't tell?" Laurie knew it was important to go along with Jason on this one.

"Yeah, but I told my mom when they didn't know," he said.

"So it became like a secret for you and your mom," said Joe.

"Yeah."

"Yeah, well, I understand that," Joe responded.

Laurie was beginning to suspect there was more here than met the eye. She and Joe had taken Jason's talk about telling his parents as a reference to last night's meeting with Rundle. She wasn't to find out until much later that the little boy had dropped hints to his parents long before the babysitting service came under investigation. They had somehow missed the cues. "What happened when you told your mom?" she asked.

"Um, nothing. 'Cause they didn't know."

"So Frank and Iliana never knew that you told your mom?" Joe was beginning to get the picture.

"Right."

Laurie decided it was time to break new ground. "Did they do something to other kids besides Joshua?"

"Yeah."

"Can you tell us about that?"

"Um, yeah. They were, um, playing with their penises a lot and all that." Jason wondered how much he dared tell.

"Did they, like, take any of the boys or girls into a room alone, or did they do it with everybody around?" asked Joe.

"They took 'em into another room." Jason was studying the floor.

"What room?"

"The bathroom, the dining room . . ." Jason began ticking off rooms.

"The kitchen? Or not the kitchen?" Joe wanted to know if he was getting the real story or if the child was naming rooms at random.

"The kitchen, the bedroom, their room . . ." Jason continued.

The grown-ups would later come to find that the child wasn't just rambling. Virtually every room of the house was employed for the activities that occurred.

"What about little girls?" Joe was groping in the dark. He'd been told so little about the case that he wasn't even sure if there *were* any girls. So far Jason had talked only about boys and penises. But surely some little girls must have been left with the Fusters. He had seen one outside in the waiting room when he arrived.

"Um, they would, um, take 'em into the bedroom."

"By themselves? With one little girl or one boy, or would they take . . ." Joe was searching for the best way to phrase the question so Jason would clearly understand. "How many children would they take into their room at one time?"

"Um, three."

"Three at a time? All the time?"

"Yeah."

"Did you ever see what they did?"

"N-no." Jason knew he was on shaky ground again. These grown-ups obviously didn't shock easily. But what he had given them so far was pretty tame stuff compared to the reality of the situation.

"So they just took them into the room, so you don't know what happened when they went in the room? Or did they leave the door open?" Joe was making a concerted effort to draw Jason out.

"They left the door open. But I didn't see because I saw them do it to my brother."

Laurie knew what he was trying to say. "So you thought it was just the same thing as what they did to your brother?"

"Yeah." Jason was grateful that they weren't pushing the issue. He really wished he could tell them, but . . .

Laurie sensed he was wavering. She decided to give it one more shot. "But you didn't see them do anything to any of the other boys and girls except for your brother? Or did you see other boys and girls that they did it to?"

The little boy's head hung down. "Yeah. I saw it once." Maybe if he told them a little . . . "A girl."

"What did they do to the little girl?" Laurie's voice was soft, encouraging.

"Um, I don't know. 'Cause I just peeked." He really felt bad about not leveling with these nice people. But he felt better when he realized they still weren't angry with him for not. In fact, Joe was chuckling.

"Oh, yeah? How'd you peek?" Joe was genuinely amused at Jason's choice of words.

"I just went by the door, and they didn't see me." He suppressed a little grin.

"Aha! Private eye detective, right?" Joe was kidding him into telling more.

Jason was pleased with himself. He felt a small surge of confidence as the words came tumbling out. "They didn't know what I was doing. They saw me, but, uh, they, uh, they tried to shut the door, but I slammed the door open."

"And then what happened?"

"And then, um, I don't remember." He was getting nervous again. Maybe he'd said too much.

"You don't remember?"

"Because I, uh, ran into the TV room."

" 'Cause you didn't want to see or you were afraid they'd get mad?" Joe wondered where all this was leading to.

"No, um, because I broke the door down," said Jason, looking a little sheepish.

Joe was skeptical. "How'd you break the door down? What's it made out of?"

"I once broke *my* door down." It was both a boast and a confession. He figured they should know that he certainly was capable of breaking down doors.

Joe, once again, was amused. "Did you? How'd that happen?"

The little boy smiled and mumbled something unintelligible.

Joe tried again. "When you say 'broke open,' you mean the door opened? The door didn't fall to pieces?"

"Yeah, it does," Jason replied matter-of-factly.

"Did it really?" Laurie was beginning to think he was serious.

Joe searched for a logical explanation for something that appeared so patently illogical. "What kind . . . was the door made of glass?"

Jason cut him off before he finished the question. "Yeah."

"Or wood?" Joe finished.

"Wood," said Jason.

"Wood?" Joe was still skeptical. "And it fell to pieces?"

"Yeah."

"Ah, you're putting me on," said Joe.

"No." Jason wondered why he sounded so incredulous.

"A whole door? A door like that?" asked Joe, pointing to the one in Laeser's office.

"Yeah." Jason wondered if maybe he wasn't explaining it right.

"How many pieces?" Laurie was humoring him.

"Um, um, two."

Joe was having a hard time believing this. But the child seemed sincere. "Two pieces?"

"Two splinters," said Jason.

"Oh, two *splinters.*" Joe was beginning to get the picture.

So was Laurie. "A lot of *little* pieces." They would later confirm from Jason's parents that the child's story was accurate. The Fusters had informed them that their son had broken an accordion gate that enclosed the family room. "Was that at your house?"

"No. At Iliana's."

"What did they say?" Joe was having a hard time figuring this one out.

"Nothing. They just, um, did it." Jason was ready to get back to the original subject.

So was Joe. "When you peeked into the room, was it their bedroom?"

"Yeah."

"Or the TV room?" Joe was trying hard not to lead the child's statement.

"The bedroom."

"The bedroom," repeated Joe. "And they were in there? And this was a little girl?"

Jason nodded silently. He seemed to be having trouble talking about the little girls.

Joe handed him a girl doll. "Can you pretend that's the girl and tell me what they did to the girl? 'Cause . . ."

Jason cut him off abruptly. "*No.* Boys were in there."

"Not girls?" Joe wondered about this sudden about-face. "I thought you said you saw them do something to a little girl?" His tone was unchallenging.

"But, um, they didn't do it. They *tried* to do it." Jason was getting uncomfortable.

"They tried," Joe repeated. "What did they try?"

"They, um, I don't know. But I saw 'em try. . . ." Jason's voice trailed off. He really didn't want to talk about this.

Laurie prodded gently. "What did they try to do?"

"Um, I don't know." He didn't even know where to begin.

Joe could see he was having a problem with the subject. "Can you show me what they were doing if you don't know how to explain what it was?"

"I don't know what they were doing." The little boy's tone was sharp, adamant.

Laurie got the message but thought she'd better make sure she was reading it correctly. "You don't want to talk about it? Or you really just don't know?"

"No, I really just don't know." Jason insisted.

"You didn't see anything?" Joe asked.

"I didn't see anything." As far as Jason was concerned, the sooner they got off this track, the better.

Joe felt the child's discomfort. "Can I ask you a couple more questions?"

"Yeah."

" 'Cause I don't want you to get uncomfortable." Joe meant it. The boy had been through enough already.

"I'm not uncomf'terble," said Jason, looking uncomfortable. Jason knew he could end the interview right now if he wanted. The grown-ups had clearly demonstrated they would respect his feelings. But he wasn't quite ready to let go of this opportunity to unburden himself. It was frightening, yet somehow comforting at the same time.

"Good," said Joe. He could sense the child's mixed emotions. As long as Jason was willing to talk, he would continue to ask. One particular item came to mind. It would prove to be the $64,000 question. "Uh, did they play games with you?"

"Not with me." Jason still needed to keep himself out of this business. "They played . . ."

"With the other children?"

"Yeah. They played games with Chad. The boy, you know, the boy who has problems with his speech?"

Joe nodded. "Uh-huh." He didn't have any idea who Chad was, but he would certainly find out.

"That's who they played with," said Jason. He wondered if he was getting Chad in trouble by telling.

"And what did they do?" Joe asked gently.

"Um, I don't know." He was getting cold feet again.

"Did they have a name for the game?" asked Laurie. She wasn't sure whether he didn't want to talk about it or he just couldn't find the words to describe it.

"No, but I knew they were playing a game. I don't know the name." The little boy was worried again. He'd opened his big mouth. And why was he even considering telling them about the most frightening game of all?

"How could you tell it was a game?" asked Laurie.

"Because I saw them play the game."

Joe knew they were onto something. "Can you tell me what you saw? Because it really would be helpful if you could tell us what you saw. It would be very helpful."

Jason wavered a little. "They were, um, just, they were trying to get each other."

"They were trying to get each other?" Joe wondered what "get" meant.

"So, they were like chasing each other?" asked Laurie.

"Yeah." Jason hoped that would satisfy them enough to drop the subject.

Joe wasn't ready to do that yet. "Can you tell me about that? Or could you pretend with the dolls what they were doing?"

"They were just, um, chasing each other. That's all." He was really sorry he'd brought the whole thing up.

Joe was determined to see this one through. For the first time since the interview started, he persisted even though the child clearly wanted to drop the subject. "You mean, like, hide-and-go-seek? Or tag? Were they playing tag?"

"No. They were playing a dumb game, but I don't know what it is." Jason refused to look at them.

Suddenly, Laurie recognized the body language. Embarrassment. She knew what question to ask. "Did they have clothes on?"

"Off." He wondered how she'd figured that out.

"Was Frank there, too?" asked Joe.

"Uh, yeah. And he had his clothes on."

"So . . . the children had their clothes off."

"Right."

"And Iliana and Frank had their clothes on."

"Right."

"And did . . . Iliana and Frank chase the kids?" Laurie was trying to piece the game together.

"Yeah."

"And what happened if they caught somebody? What would they do?"

"Um, they would just catch 'em and chop their head off." Jason's tone was very matter-of-fact.

"Chop their heads off?" Laurie was amused.

"Yeah."

"What did they . . . what did they actually do?" Laurie was having a hard time figuring this one out. The kid meant what he was saying.

"They really chopped their head off," he said sheepishly.

Laurie really wanted to suspend judgment on the veracity of Jason's statements, but this one was stretching her imagination beyond all reasonable bounds. "You really want me to believe that, huh?" She was smiling.

"Yes. They played 'Who loses the head?' " Jason couldn't quite grasp why this information should seem any more bizarre to them than the other things he'd already told them.

Laurie shot Joe a look. Why would the child suddenly start doing a number on them? She decided to play along. "And what would they do once the head was off—lie it on the ground?"

"No. They would eat it for dinner." Well, she asked, he thought.

"Eat it for dinner," said Laurie, nodding her head. She was being had by a five-year-old. "That sounds like a good story."

"Sounds like a good movie," Joe interjected.

Jason knew it was neither, but he didn't know what else to say. "Well, it's true. I mean they would really chop their head off."

Joe and Laurie looked quite amused. Jason was grateful for that. It lessened the terror he felt about what he'd just told them. In his discomfort in talking about it, he had left out one small detail that would have made them understand what he was trying to say. The heads that were cut off weren't the children's.

They were the birds'.

• • •

Jason sat on a chair in the office next to Laeser's, alone with his thoughts for the first time in two hours. His little brother, along with his mother, were in there now being interviewed by the two grown-ups. He wondered if Joshua would tell them more than he had. And if he did, would they be mad at him for holding back so much?

He didn't think so. No one had gotten mad at him yet. In fact, Joe and Laurie had told his parents—right in front of him—that they should be proud of him for being so brave.

But he didn't know about the other conversation. The one that had taken place behind closed doors.

Joe had been left with the onerous task of breaking the news to Jason's parents that their worst fears had been confirmed. Their son, he told them, had given them information that led them to believe that he had been molested, that he had observed sexual activity, and that he wasn't comfortable enough yet to really talk about his participation. It was very evident to him and Laurie, both verbally and nonverbally, that Jason had participated, Joe continued. But that was fine. That was Jason's way of dealing with it. And it was a constructive way for him to deal with it. Joe offered the Harrisons some advice:

"You'll have to do the best acting job of your lives. And it's going to be one of the hardest things you've ever had to do, but it's essential for Jason's well-being. I know right now you're probably in a state of shock. Next comes anger. That's normal and to be expected. But it's crucial that Jason feels he can talk to you about this and that he doesn't interpret your anger as being directed at him. He needs to know that, no matter what he tells you, you won't be upset and he won't get in trouble.

"Most important, he needs to know that he's done nothing wrong, that whatever happened to him wasn't his fault."

Joe had no idea that this would be a message he would personally deliver to scores of parents over the next few months. They would find his prediction accurate. It would be one of the hardest things they'd ever been asked to do.

As Jason sat in the waiting room beside his father, he tried to sort out his feelings about the day's events. He'd shared part of his secret, and, contrary to what Frank and Iliana had told him, he had survived. And he wasn't in trouble. In fact, his parents told him how brave he was and how glad they were that he had told. And they assured him that nothing bad would happen to him, that he and Joshua had done nothing wrong. The terrible fear within him wasn't quite so monstrous. He felt better than he had in a long, long time. He wondered if Joshua would feel the same relief.

But Joshua wasn't talking. The Bragas' interview with the two-year-old cherub was more notable for what he didn't say. Joshua had spent the better part of an hour comfortably nestled in Joe's lap, playing with blocks, when Laurie asked cheerfully, "Could you tell us about what happened at Frank and Iliana's?"

The little boy promptly jumped to his feet, crawled into his mother's lap, stuck his thumb in his mouth, and covered his head with a blanket.

End of interview.

• • •

It was a new Jason who marched back into Laeser's office later that afternoon. Bolstered by the calm reaction to his lurid tale, and relieved finally to have shared at least part of his nightmare, the little boy was willing, if not eager, to tell more. He felt good about himself, good enough to square his shoulders and meet Joe and Laurie's questions with a direct gaze. If eyes are the windows of the soul, then Jason's was clearly being reborn.

So the three of them—the sturdy little child and the two child-adults—gathered once more on the floor of this office of law, the video camera in the corner still recording every moment of their encounter. There would be no warming up this time, no mincing of words. All three were ready to get down to business.

It was decided that Joe would direct most of the questions since he and Jason had established a quick and special bond during their earlier encounter. Joe had some specific questions in mind. He had suspicions about what the group activities Jason had obliquely hinted at might entail.

His opening question was an educated shot in the dark.

"Can you tell us anything about any masks or anything, or any games that Frank and Iliana played?"

Jason shot him a wide-eyed look. How could Joe know these things? With only a split second's hesitation, the words came tumbling out. "Yeah, they played ring-around-the-rosy and the pee-pee game and, um, the masks—Jason's Lucky Day, Gremlins, and, um, Werewolf."

"Werewolf. What was the Werewolf game?"

"What?" Jason looked confused.

"How did they play Werewolf?"

"No, those were all masks." Jason realized that he'd run the list of games and masks together.

"They were masks," said Joe. "They would put on masks . . ."

"Yeah. They just put 'em on and scared us."

"What did they say to you when they scared you? Did they just say 'Boo'?" Joe was trying hard to find out exactly what terror had buried the secrets so deeply within this child. If he could just find out what it was, then they could confront the fear and diminish it. But it wasn't to be.

"No, they were growling and, um, and, talking like . . ." Jason summoned a guttural sound. ". . . like that and scaring us."

"Why do you think they were scaring you?"

"I don't know."

"Did they tell you at any time that anything would happen to you if you told the secret? About what was going on?" Joe saw that Jason continued to balk at the question. "You see, if you tell us, then it will go away and you won't have to be scared anymore."

"I know, um . . ." Jason wasn't convinced.

Joe tried again to explain. "We can make it go away if you just tell us anything that they told you would scare us. By telling us, it will never be anything to worry about anymore."

"Um, um, uh, they would . . . let me think . . ." Jason carefully considered spilling it, then decided to lead the conversation away from this unpleasant topic. "Uh, they would play ring-around-the-rosy," he offered.

"How do you play . . ." Joe began, then thought better of the wording. "How do *they* play ring-around-the-rosy?"

"Um, they play it dumb. They'd dress up naked and play it." Jason paused to consider whether this was clear enough, then added, "They would take their clothes off and play it."

"Who would take off their clothes?" Joe's voice was soft, curious.

"Um, all the girls and boys."

"What about Frank?" Joe felt they were making headway. The child wasn't nearly as reticent to talk about the sex as he was the threats.

"Frank and Iliana—he, uh, they would undress."

"They would undress?" Joe repeated, hoping to draw him out a little more without further prompting. But Jason wasn't taking the bait.

"Yeah."

"And what would they then do?" Joe caught himself slipping into adult vernacular and quickly rephrased the question. "What would happen then?"

"Then they would play ring-around-the-rosy."

"Can you show me with the dolls, ring-around-the-rosy?" Joe feigned ignorance. " 'Cause I don't know how to play ring-around-the-rosy." With Jason's approving nod, Joe reached for the dolls. "How many? Will four be enough?"

"No. There were just two." Jason wasn't willing to drag too many of his friends into this mess.

"There were two? Who would the two be?" Joe was being very deliberate and very casual. So far, Jason had been willing to name only one child other than his brother.

"Uh, Chad was playing, and, um, let me think . . ." Jason considered his answer carefully. "April was playing."

"April, too?" Joe made a mental note.

"Yeah."

"So, Chad and April, and who else would play with them?" Joe hoped he would volunteer names of who else was involved so he wouldn't have to lead him with a direct question.

"Uh, no one else. Oh, yeah, and, um, Iliana would just, um, undress. On the couch."

"She would . . . she would . . ." Joe was grasping for a better understanding of the dynamics operating here. "Show me."

"She would, um . . ." Jason looked at the pile of dolls on the floor in front of him. He wasn't quite sure where to start.

Joe stepped in to help him. "Let's say that this—give me that— let's make this Iliana. And you show me what happened."

Jason awkwardly disrobed the doll. He was astonished to find that it had breasts. He'd never seen a doll like this before. He looked a little closer. It had orifices. Three of them. Oh, what he could show them with a doll like this.

Joe plodded on with the questions. "So would she take off all her clothes? Did she have underpants, too?"

"No. She just took off all her clothes, and um, everybody else took 'em off." He paused to consider whether to offer another piece of information, then relented. "Frank was in the game, too." Jason reached for the adult male doll and began undressing it.

"Frank was in the game?"

"Right." He was beginning to feel a new surge of confidence.

"OK, so we'll make that Frank and this Iliana, OK?" Joe pointed to the dolls in Jason's lap.

"Yeah."

"And you said Chad?" Joe said as he selected another doll.

"Yeah."

"So we'll make this Chad. Did Chad have any clothes on?"

"No. Off."

"Well, can I take the clothes off? Then this will be Chad?" Joe undressed the doll with Jason's nod. "All righty," said Joe, not unlike a coach sending his team onto the field for a kickoff. "OK, here's Chad, that's Frank, that's Iliana. Tell us what happened."

Jason hesitated. Joe had forgotten someone. He reached for a little girl doll. "And, um, this is April."

"OK, this will be April." Mustn't forget April, thought Joe.

"She had her clothes off, too," Jason reminded him.

"She did?" Joe's tone implied, Excuse me for my ignorance.

"Yeah." Jason pulled the clothes off the doll. "OK, now . . ." Jason mused over the logistics of his demonstration.

"All right, now," Joe prodded gently. "Let's see what happened."

"Let me see now, what I need . . ." Jason was studying the dolls, making sure he kept straight just who was who.

Suddenly Joe had an idea. "Now you notice this doll . . ." he said, like a used-car salesman pointing out a particularly impressive feature. "This doll has, has like, fur here."

"Yeah." Jason had noticed it before. These dolls really came fully equipped.

"Would this look like Iliana? Or would that look like . . ." Joe rephrased the question. "Which one would look more like Iliana?" He held up both female dolls for the boy to choose from. Jason pointed to the adult doll. "How come?" asked Joe.

Jason wasn't sure what he was driving at. "Because, um, I mean this one." He switched to the little girl doll. "I don't . . ." Jason was confused. Neither one really looked like Iliana. "I mean this really would because her hair is always back like this."

"I see." Joe understood the reason for his confusion. He got more specific. "OK, what about the rest of her body? When she had her clothes off? Which would look more like Iliana?"

Now Jason understood. "This one, because she has hair there."

"Iliana has hair there?" Joe's tone implied that this was news to him. "So you saw Iliana's hair, here, between her legs?"

"Right." Despite Joe's apparent ignorance of female anatomy, Jason was quite positive about his own observations.

"How could you see that?" Joe continued innocently. " 'Cause she had her clothes on? Or off?" Joe was establishing the child's veracity beyond any reasonable doubt.

"No clothes on."

"OK, what about Frank?" Joe continued. "Now let's say this is . . ." Joe selected both of the male dolls. "Which one of these two dolls would look more like Frank? This one? Or this one?"

"This one."

"How come?"

"Because, um, Frank has hair right here." Jason was quite sure about this, too.

"I see, OK. And he's bigger, too. He's much bigger." Joe was ready to shift gears. "All right, here are our dolls. This is Iliana, this is Frank, and this is . . ."

"Chad. That's Chad."

"That's Chad, and that's April," Joe continued. "Can you show us what happened?"

"OK, um . . ." Jason had something in mind. "How 'bout if you make it—this is, um, Chad," he said, selecting the adult male doll.

"OK."

"And this is Frank," said Jason, designating the little boy doll.

"OK."

"OK, now . . ." Jason was ready to begin.

But Joe suddenly wondered if there was a particular reason—one he should know about—for Jason to switch the doll's identities. "How come? Chad doesn't have hair there, does he? Does Chad have hair there, too?"

"No, but, um, we could just pretend."

"OK."

"OK, now . . . what do I need . . ." Jason was still figuring logistics. "Iliana joined in, too. So you'll have to do that," he said, tossing the "Iliana" doll to Joe. "And you'll have to do that," he directed Laurie, handing over "April." "They were holding hands."

"Everybody?" It was the first time Laurie had spoken since the interview began.

"Yeah. Everybody."

"OK, let's do it this way," Joe suggested. "I'll hold this hand and this hand and this hand." Joe proceeded to arrange the dolls in a circle as Jason had directed. "And nobody had any clothes on?"

"No. And they're just going around. And then they would go . . ." Jason crumpled his doll to the floor, making a crashing sound. "Everybody would fall down."

"Everybody would fall down," repeated Joe.

"Yeah. And then they'd get up and try to get each other."

There was that word again. "Get." Joe was certain that the key to unlocking the secret somehow involved getting Jason to spell out what it meant.

"How would they 'get' each other?"

"Um, they would just go . . ." Jason crashed two dolls together face to face, accompanied again by the crashing sound. ". . . and they'd fight."

"They would fight?"

"Yeah."

"They would hurt each other? Or they would just play-fight?"

"They would just play-fight."

"And when they would play-fight, would they touch each other?" Joe was sitting on a gold mine. It was just a matter of navigating the tunnels to the mother lode.

"Oh, yeah!"

"Tell me how they would touch each other." Joe was negotiating the tunnel carefully.

"They would, uh, go, like this . . ." Jason repeated the doll-crashing scenario. "And then that was all. They would just tackle each other." He hoped they wouldn't ask for more. Joe and Laurie had taken this naked version of ring-around-the-rosy in stride. But he wasn't sure they would be quite so serene about the other things.

Joe sensed the problem. "OK, and what . . . would they touch anybody anytime when they were like . . . if . . ."

Jason knew what he was getting at. He was beginning to realize that his big "secret" wasn't such a secret to Joe.

"Yeah. They would touch here," he said, pointing to the penis on the "Frank" doll. "And . . ."

"How would they touch there?" Joe broke in gently.

"They would go . . ." Jason took the hand of the "Frank" doll and rubbed it on "Chad's" penis.

"Like that, OK." Joe's voice carried the nonchalance of someone who's just been told that his dinner is served. "Would they touch each other here, at their bottoms?"

"Yeah." The little boy wondered how he could possibly know.

"Tell me about that."

"OK, they would do this," he replied, taking "Frank's" hand and placing it on "Chad's" anus.

"With their hands?" Joe suspected there was more.

"Yeah." Jason was wrestling with a dilemma. How much should he tell? How much *could* he tell?

"What if . . ." Joe began.

But Jason cut him off. He had decided. "They would stick it inside."

"What would they stick where?" Joe pleaded ignorance.

"Um, they would stick their finger inside their butt."

"Who would do it? Frank would do it to himself?"

Jason wondered how someone so smart could be so *dumb* sometimes. "No, Frank would do it to *him*," he explained, placing "Frank's" hand on "Chad's" bottom.

Jason gazed expectantly at his interviewer.

"Didn't it . . ." Joe paused to consider which doll was which. "Now who's this? This is Chad? Didn't it hurt Chad?"

Jason considered the dolls' identities and remembered he had designated a switch earlier. "No. *This* is Chad," he corrected, indicating the adult doll.

"OK," said Joe. "And this is Frank?"

"Right."

"So, OK, what did Frank do?" Joe decided to start from square one to clarify who did what to whom.

"He would go . . ." Jason carefully inserted "Frank's" hand into the hole in "Chad's" bottom.

"Didn't it hurt Chad?"

Jason shook his head vigorously. "*No.* It wouldn't."

"How come?" Joe sounded mildly curious.

"Because, um, uh, I don't know why but it doesn't . . . it *wouldn't* hurt Chad," he insisted.

"Did Chad mind?" Joe suspected Jason was answering for himself, not Chad.

"No."

"He didn't mind?"

"He *minded* but not a lot," Jason was thinking about things he minded more.

"How come?" Joe wondered aloud.

"They would go . . ." Jason demonstrated once again with the dolls as though another reenactment might clear up the matter.

"Like that," said Joe.

"Yeah."

"OK, uh, did Frank, like, ever kiss Chad's eyes, or kiss Chad's hands, or kiss Chad anywhere?" Joe was exercising a great deal of caution not to lead the child's statement.

"Um, he would do this to him," said the little boy as he stuffed one doll's penis into the other's mouth. "He would go . . ." He worked to make sure it was all the way in. "He once kissed his penis." Jason figured he would qualify it with "once" to soften the impact on the grown-ups. "Once" didn't seem as serious as twice—or a hundred.

"Who kissed whose penis?" Joe's tone remained even, unconcerned.

"Um, Frank kissed Chad's penis." Jason noted with relief that this, too, the grown-ups were taking in stride.

"Oh. Did Chad mind?" Joe wondered.

"Yeah." Jason was embarrassed.

"Did Frank ever . . . what did Chad say? Can you remember?"

"Uh, nothing. He didn't say anything."

"Did Frank ever ask anybody to kiss *his* penis?" Joe wondered.

"Um . . . no." Jason couldn't bring himself to talk about that part. Not yet.

"No," Joe repeated. "How about Iliana? Did Iliana ever kiss anybody? Chad or anybody's penis?"

"Um, she would, um, do this . . ." Jason placed Iliana's hand on the other doll's penis.

"To who?"

"To, um, Chad."

"Chad," repeated Joe. "How about Frank?"

"No." No sense opening up that territory. Not now.

"OK," said Joe.

"Just to Chad," Jason insisted.

Joe opted to cut bait and switch streams. "How about the 'get me' game. You said . . ."

"But in *this* game . . ." Laurie interrupted. She didn't want to leave ring-around-the-rosy without exploring April's role.

But Jason had eagerly seized on Joe's question. "The 'get me' game . . . they would do this . . ." he told them as he pressed the dolls together and carefully inserted the penis of one doll into another's mouth. "And then they would bite their penis."

"I see." They now knew what "get" meant. "Who would do it to who?"

"Um, Frank would do it to Chad."

Laurie entered the conversation again. "And what about . . . what would happen to April?" she said softly.

"April?" Oh, yeah, he'd forgotten about April. "Uh, which one is . . ." Jason searched the pile of dolls to find "April." "Oh, right here," he said, extracting "April" from the pile. "Um, they would do . . ." He placed "Frank's" mouth on "April's" vagina. ". . . right there. And, um, right here," he added, turning "April" over and placing "Frank's" hand in her rectum.

Up to this point, both the Bragas had maintained a cheerful facade for the child. The task was more easily accomplished by Joe, who was more preoccupied with negotiating the complex maze in the boy's head than with the grim reality that was unfolding before them. Although Laurie was doing more listening than talking, she, too, was occupied with the mechanics of the interview and thus was able to maintain an emotional distance from the subject matter. But suddenly, the full impact of what Jason was saying hit her like a ton of bricks. A wave of nausea took hold as she absorbed on a gut level just what the children had been subjected to. Quietly, she placed her hand along the side of her face, shielding it from the camera and the little red-haired boy who so trustingly shared his secrets.

For a fleeting second she thought she might have to leave the room. But she managed to collect her feelings and lock them away to be dealt with later. Jason was never to know of that moment of anguish. It passed too quickly, too quietly, to attract his attention.

"With his hands?" Laurie returned to earth to the sound of Joe's calm, reassuring responsive listening.

"Yeah. With his hands. And Iliana would do this." Jason placed "Iliana's" mouth on the doll's penis.

"To?" Laurie reentered the conversation.

"To, um, Chad. Let me see . . ." Jason was busily stuffing the penis all the way into the mouth. "Like that."

Laurie's hand went to her face again. She was still feeling a little queasy.

"Did this only happen one time?" asked Joe.

"Yeah. Once." Once was better than more than once, he reasoned.

"One game? Or one day? Or . . ."

"Just one time," the little boy assured Joe.

"And what other games did they play like that?" Joe resolutely kept swimming through the Jell-O.

"Just, uh . . ." Jason considered his options. "They played other games." He'd told them this much. Why not more? "OK, it's a kind of ring-around-the-rosy game. But first we have to hold each other's hand again."

"OK," Joe and Laurie obediently chimed in unison as they reached for their assigned dolls.

"I'll be Chad; here's April," the child directed, handing Joe another doll.

"All right!" Joe's voice rang with enthusiasm as though they were about to embark on an exciting adventure.

"Now, would April stand next to Iliana or next to Chad or who?" Laurie was keenly interested in the little girl's fate, which Jason seemed to ignore pointedly.

"Next to Frank," shot back Jason without hesitation.

"Next to Frank. OK."

"So that makes her here," said Jason, moving the doll to the appropriate position in the circle.

"This is another time they played this game?" Joe had lost count of the violations Jason had recounted thus far. But he sensed that it would be useful to the prosecutors later to separate each incident whenever possible.

"Yeah. And then they would go . . ." Jason danced the dolls around the circle. "This is how they would do it. And then they would go . . . they would do this," he said as he stuffed a doll's penis into another's mouth.

"Um, hmm," said Joe. "What did they call this game? Do you remember? Would they call it anything?"

"No, they would just do it. They would do this." Jason continued his demonstration of oral copulation.

"Now this is Iliana and Chad?"

"Yeah." Jason was immersed in the mouth-stuffing task. "They would bite it. They would stick his penis inside his mouth, OK. And April would [Laurie handed him "April"] do this. The same thing. The same thing with Frank."

"So April would kiss Frank's penis?"

"No. They would bite each other's."

"Jason, let me ask you a question," Joe ventured.

"What?" The little boy was mildly exasperated. What's one more? He'd already asked about a thousand.

Joe trudged on. "Um, at any time, in any of the games, did Frank ever take his penis and put it in anybody's bottom?"

Jason eagerly scooped up two dolls. "Now, pretend this is Frank."

"This is Frank," Joe nodded.

"Yeah."

"OK, and that's Iliana?" Joe recognized that Jason had selected the adult female doll.

"Yeah." Jason was holding the dolls in the air with "Frank's" penis penetrating Iliana from the rear. The little boy pushed harder to make it fit.

"OK," said Joe, noting that the angle of the bodies could be achieved only by a contortionist. "Can you show me *exactly* the way they were?"

Jason pushed the penis farther into the doll's bottom. "They would do this."

Joe tried to explain. "Well, Frank—now if Frank was like this, he would've been hurtin' 'cause he can't stand like that. So pretend *just* like they *actually were*. What you remember seeing."

"OK." Now Jason understood. "They would do this," he explained, placing "Iliana" on the floor, bending over, with "Frank" behind. "OK, and they would take it like this and stick it in here," he continued, placing the penis in "Iliana's" rectum. "And, um, they would do this." He turned the dolls around and put the penis in "Iliana's" mouth.

"Now . . ." Joe began.

But Jason wasn't finished. ". . . and do this," he continued as he rubbed the penis on the doll's breasts. "Stick it on her boobies."

"She would stick it on her boobies," Joe mused. "Would she be standing up? Lying down? Kneeling?" His penchant for detail was part of an ongoing test of the child's credibility. No judge, no jury— no one—would be able to deny that the little boy's intimate knowledge of sexual activity was the result of anything other than firsthand experience.

Jason was quick to oblige. "Um, like this." His words came tumbling out as he deftly repeated the demonstration. "Then he would do like this. Like this. And like this."

"Now, where were the children when they were doing this?"

"Well, they were still naked." Jason was getting very comfortable talking about these things. The grown-ups weren't batting an eye. "Um, they were like this," he added, piling three dolls on top of one another, face down. "Then, uh, pretend this is Chad . . . I mean Jaime." Jason could barely contain his newfound courage.

"Jaime?" Joe almost whispered the name, wondering if the child would realize what he'd let slip. Jason had just written a new character into the script. And it wasn't just any character. It was Francisco Fuster Escalona's own son.

Oblivious to its significance, Jason plunged into his story. "Yeah. OK, Jaime would do this." He demonstrated another act of fellatio.

"To who?" Joe's tone carried a quiet urgency. He sensed they were on the verge of a major breakthrough.

"To, um, Ch . . . to Chad . . . to, uh, Frank. I mean Chad." To everybody, Jason thought grimly. Everybody to everybody.

"So they had the children . . ." Laurie paused to consider her wording. ". . . do it together?"

"Yeah. They had the children do it together." The statement was stark, emotionless.

"What about boys and girls together?" Laurie noticed that he was still neglecting to mention little girls.

"Girls?" He didn't like to talk about the girls. "See, the boys . . . the boys were right over here," he said, tossing the boy dolls to one side. "See, um, where are the . . ." Jason's eyes were scanning the floor, looking for the dolls' clothing. Laurie gathered a pile and handed it to him. "I just need . . ." He began sorting through them. "Let's see, I need men . . ." He continued searching through the clothing. "I don't need this," he decided, tossing a dress aside. "I need men's clothing."

"The men's clothes?" Laurie joined him in the search, sorting through and pulling out a couple of garments. "I think what we have here is a pair of underpants for Chad and a pair of underpants for, uh . . ."

Jason cut her off. "No. Frank didn't dress."

"Frank didn't dress?"

"Right. Just Jaime. Just Jaime dressed. See, Frank wasn't in there."

"He wasn't there that time?"

"Yeah."

"This was another day?"

"Yeah. This was another day."

"So, only Iliana was there?"

"Right."

Joe had an idea. Ever so casually he asked, "Were there any other adults that ever came over?

"Yeah." Jason felt his face redden. "There was a booby girl who showed her boobies."

Sensing his embarrassment, Joe made light of this newest piece of information. "A *booby* girl? What's a booby girl?" he chuckled.

"She showed her boobies and . . ." Jason smiled shyly.

"Why did she do that?"

"I don't know." Your guess is as good as mine, his tone implied. Why any of this?

"Did she take off all her clothes?"

"No, she just . . ." Jason hesitated, ". . . showed her boobies."

"Did everybody think she was silly?"

"Yeah." Jason had nothing more to say about the mysterious "booby girl."

"Let me ask you a question." Joe had a theory germinating in the back of his mind. Now was the time to test it. "You know what a camera is?"

"Yeah."

Joe mustered his most laid-back manner. "Did anybody ever take any pictures?"

"Yeah."

"Did they?" Joe was the picture of innocence. "Who took pictures?"

"Um, Frank."

"Did he?" Joe was walking on eggshells. It wouldn't do for the child to clam up suddenly. Not when they were so close to the truth. "Did he have a camera?"

"Yes." Jason didn't bat an eye.

"How big?" Joe wondered.

"Um, about as big as that one over there," said Jason, for the first time acknowledging the existence of the video equipment in the corner of the office.

Joe formed his hands as if to take a snapshot. "Was it a camera like this?"

"No." Jason's response was firm as he rose to his feet. "A camera like that one." His finger pointed steadily at the piece of equipment that had silently recorded his entire testimony.

• • •

It was approaching midnight when Joe and Laurie wearily made their way out of the Justice Building that steamy August night. Physically and mentally exhausted, emotionally drained, they had completed interviewing the last child just two hours before. Five children in all. Tomorrow there would be more—and many, many more in the days, weeks, and months to come.

But the Bragas didn't know that. And it was just as well. For tonight, they were drawing on the last of their reserves just to make it home. The events of the day had caught up with them and were finally taking their toll.

Conducting the interviews, in itself, was a grueling task. Eight hours on Laeser's floor had left their muscles cramped and Joe's arthritis flaring. Between children, they had squirreled away bites of peanut butter to sustain their bodies. And they stole a few moments afterward to sustain their spirits with a silent embrace, the Braga method of recharging batteries. These were the only times when they didn't have to be "on" for someone—quieting the pain of the shell-shocked parents and reassuring the terrified children who grasped at the lifeline they'd just been thrown. Even the horrified prosecutors sought their emotional support as they watched one of the most offensive crimes they had ever encountered unfold before them: a tale told by children barely out of diapers. A crime involving infants who were still in them.

When the last family left, the Bragas, the prosecutors, and a detective huddled in Laeser's office, reviewing the tapes of the children's interviews. Some of what Jason told them was corroborated by other children. But none were as forthcoming as the plucky little redhead. Jason's testimony had virtually blossomed during the last part of the second interview. It was as though the finger plugging the dike could hold no more, and information came flooding out faster than he could spill it. They would have to suspend judgment on much of what he said until they could exact further corroboration, especially of what he had to say about a peculiar use of excrement in the household.

But as Laurie viewed the tape, a spectator for the first time, she had the frightening realization that the child's story—all of it—rang true. Her hands began to tremble, and soon her whole body was shaking uncontrollably—just like Scotty Goldman's on the night he woke from a nightmare only to discover that it was reality.

It didn't occur to her at the time that they had only stumbled onto the tip of the iceberg. In unlocking Jason's secret, Doctors Joseph and Laurie Braga had just opened Pandora's box.

Part II

A BURDEN SHARED

"I'm so ashamed."   —Jason Harrison, age five

6

The nightmare was now reality, though it had commenced officially the previous Friday, when Detective Donna Meznarich passed through Country Walk's tree-canopied portal into a world she assumed different from her own.

The people who lived here were what the policewoman and her friends might call "rich" people. The kind who paid "other" people to clean their pools and mind their kids while they "had it all" for reasons less concerned with survival than with success.

"I should have their problems," she said.

Meznarich wheeled into the Country Center parking lot and began to scratch out the notes that would eventually be shaped into a sixty-nine-page police report, her badge of enlightenment as to the frailty of all assumptions:

At 4:00 P.M., on 03 August 1984, this investigator responded to 14601 S.W. 144 Street and spoke with Joanne Menoher. Miss Menoher advised she works in coordinating the recreational activities at the Country Walk Country Center and, therefore, was acquainted with a lot of residents of Country Walk.

Miss Menoher stated sometime prior to 22 June 1984, Jeannie Pierson, a Country Walk resident, had told her, in confidence, that she had taken her child, Andy, out of the babysitting service at Frank and Iliana Fuster's due to a conversation she had had with another Country Walk resident, Jill Vickers. Jill Vickers had told Mrs. Pierson that one day her son, Steven Vickers, had come out of the shower naked and stated, "Mommy, kiss my body." As Steven Vickers refers to his penis as his "body," his mother asked him who had kissed his "body," and he replied, "Iliana."

Miss Menoher advised she had become concerned about the situation, and shortly after the conversation with Mrs. Pierson had made an anonymous report to HRS. Miss Menoher could not recall the date that she made the report but advised she thought it was the first week of June 1984. The HRS workers, in fact, responded to the Country Walk Babysitting Service because Miss Menoher says two black females, who identified themselves as HRS investigators, stopped at the Country Center and asked her for directions to the Fuster residence. When the Fusters continued to operate the babysitting service, a letter, dated 17 July 1984 and signed by the director of property management, Steven J. Vickers, Sr., was sent to "Mr. and Mrs. Fuster." The letter stated the Fusters "may be running a formal babysitting service under the apparent business name of 'Country Walk Babysitting Service' " and "may have distributed business cards imprinted with the name 'Country Walk Babysitting Service' " and "may have represented" (i) that you have received Arvida's approval to use 'Country Walk' in your name; (ii) that you are zoned as a commercial enterprise; and (iii) that you have licensing from the Department of Health and Rehabilitative Services to care for a maximum of fifteen children in your home."

The letter goes on to say that "Country Walk" is a service mark and trade name registered in both the State of Florida and Dade County, and Arvida "never gave permission to any homeowners allowing them to use the 'Country Walk' trademark or name."

Additionally, they were advised that the "Homeowner's Association documents for Country Walk prohibit operation of a commercial establishment in a residential unit." Reference was made to the fact that "neither the Building and Zoning Department nor the Department of Health and Rehabilitative Services can confirm that you are zoned for a commercial enterprise or licensed as a childcare facility."

The letter advises the Fusters to "refrain from either operating a babysitting service out of your home or using the 'Country Walk' name." See a copy of the letter, which has been made a part of this case file, for further information.

Miss Menoher advised an advertisement for the Country Walk Babysitting Service had been placed in the May 1984 issue of the *Country Times*. The *Country Times* is a newsletter that she puts out each month to the residents of Country Walk, which contains news and some advertisements. After talking with Mrs. Pierson, Miss Menoher says she did not let the advertisement for the Country Walk Babysitting Service appear in the *Country Times* again.

Regarding Frank and Iliana Fuster, Miss Menoher stated Frank Fuster had resided in the patio homes for a period of time; then, after he married Iliana Fuster in September of 1983, he had moved to the estate home at [address]. He had operated the Kendall Decorators Warehouse, at 14145 S.W. 142 Avenue, but had closed that business and opened the Mobile Showroom at his residence.

Miss Menoher went on to say Mr. Fuster had had his wedding reception at the Country Center on 24 September 1983. When using the center, Mr. Fuster had given Miss Menoher the name "Escalona" and stated he used that name also. Miss Menoher advised that she thought Frank Fuster was approximately 48 to 49 years old and that Iliana Fuster was approximately twenty-one years old. She went on to say during one conversation with Mr. Fuster, he told her he had known and dated Iliana for only three weeks prior to their marriage. Mr. Fuster had a seven-year-old son, Jaime Fuster, from a prior marriage.

Miss Menoher advised that she knew of approximately eight families that used the Fuster babysitting service but thought that perhaps as many as twenty families used it. . . .

Meznarich went to work tracking them down. Her orders conveyed implicit urgency: there was reason to believe that an unknown number of children were currently in Iliana's care, at unknown risk. The state attorney's office wanted answers—quickly.

For three days the detective knocked on doors and waded into a sea of maternal apprehension.

"Hi, I'm Detective Donna Meznarich, Sexual Battery Unit, Metro PD. And I'd like to ask you a few questions about your babysitter?"

She collected an odd assortment of anecdotes that collectively, she decided, didn't add up to diddly-squat:

KYLE MAXWELL, age nineteen months. Came home from his first and only visit to the Country Walk Babysitting Service glassy-eyed, apparently drugged. Also had rash on buttocks, which mother says is now gone. No information from child. Doesn't talk yet.
Referred to Iliana by Debbie Lancaster.

ANDY PIERSON, age two. One of the first children to attend Country Walk Babysitting Service, from December 1983 until May 1984, when his mother was advised of the Vickers boy's statement.
Mr. Fuster's son, Jaime, is in her daughter Amy's second grade class. Mrs. Pierson once noticed marks on Jaime's face and asked if someone had hit him. Amy had problems with Jaime at school. She

complained that he would chase and try to kiss her. Amy's older brother once told Mrs. Pierson that "a boy on the bus" told him that Amy "has a nice pussy." She has since discovered that the "boy on the bus" was Jaime Fuster.

Mrs. Pierson advises that her youngest son, Andy, went to the Fusters' Monday through Friday, from 8:00 A.M. to 4:30 P.M. Her daughter went there three times on school holidays. She says Andy would cry when dropped off, but that Mrs. Fuster assured her that he always stopped as soon as she left.

When she dropped Andy off in the mornings and picked him up in the afternoons, Frank Fuster would be there. On one occasion, Mrs. Pierson looked through an open blind near the front door and saw a young girl, about three years old, lying on a couch watching television, wearing only a shirt. After Mrs. Fuster let her in, she quickly grabbed a towel and wrapped it around the girl. Mrs. Fuster told her that the girl's mother had not brought any diapers for her. Mrs. Pierson later learned that the little girl was April Lancaster and that the child doesn't wear diapers.

It often took Mrs. Fuster from three to five minutes to answer the door. Mrs. Pierson once observed Mrs. Fuster wearing sunglasses inside her residence. Mrs. Fuster said she had an eye infection. Later in the day, however, Mrs. Pierson saw her without the glasses and noted her eyes appeared swollen below and that it didn't appear to be an eye infection.

Was referred to Iliana by an ad in the *Country Times*.

KRISTEN COLLIER, age fifteen months. Stayed at Fusters' two or three times a week from March 1984 through 4 August 1984, when Jeannie Pierson advised her mother of the current investigation. Mrs. Collier reports her daughter never fussed before or after being left with Iliana. Says the Fusters made a "big deal" over Kristen, saying she was so cute and pretty. Mrs. Fuster, on several occasions, told Mrs. Collier they had taken photographs of Kristen and even showed her some. In all of the photographs her daughter was clothed, and she thought nothing of it other than it seemed strange to waste money taking pictures of someone else's child. Mrs. Collier says that Iliana once told her that she couldn't have children of her own.

Once, when Mrs. Collier picked her daughter up, she was told that Iliana and Frank had been in bed with Kristen. She had taken it to mean that they had been playing. The only thing Mrs. Collier found unusual was the fact that it would sometimes take four to five minutes for Iliana to answer the door.

Was referred by an ad in the *Country Times*.

KEVIN CARTWRIGHT, age eighteen months. Mrs. Cartwright would not speak to the investigator until she consulted with her husband. However, Jeannie Pierson advises that Mrs. Cartwright once told her that she used the Fusters' babysitting service often and would sometimes leave her son there overnight. A few times, her son returned home "groggy" and "glassy-eyed." Mrs. Cartwright told Mrs. Pierson she once saw Iliana with a black eye.

CHIP LEVY, age two. Mrs. Levy reports that several times she would ring the doorbell and knock for approximately five minutes before anyone answered it. On two occasions, when she turned the doorknob, she discovered that the door was unlocked and went inside. The first time, Iliana came out of the master bedroom and closed the door behind her. As Mrs. Levy was speaking with Mrs. Fuster, she could hear a child on the other side of the door saying, "I want out. I want out." Mrs. Fuster responded, "I'll be there in a minute, Andy," and explained that she was trying to get the boy to take a nap.

On the second occasion, Iliana again emerged from the master bedroom and closed the door behind her. This time, a little blond boy opened the bedroom door and stood there totally naked. Iliana said, "Andy, go back in," and the child did so. When Mrs. Levy inquired about what she saw, Iliana told her that she was in the process of changing the child's diaper. Mrs. Levy said she didn't see Mr. Fuster there either time.

On a few other occasions when she picked her son up, Mrs. Levy saw Mr. Fuster sitting at his desk in the bedroom, which had been converted into an office.

Meznarich was unimpressed. A few worried mothers dredging up fragmented memories of "unusual" occurrences did not a case make. A naked child, an eye infection, a long wait at the door—all could be explained away in most plausible terms.

Possibly the woman wasn't the world's best babysitter. Was she supposed to arrest her for it? The only child who had even hinted at impropriety was the Vickers boy, and he was out of town with his parents on vacation.

The detective called it a day.

On Tuesday, 07 August 1984, at 8:00 A.M., this investigator responded to the MDPD Records Section and requested a victim/subject check to be made for the names Frank and Iliana Fuster, from 1980 to 1984.

The electronic keeper of records awoke with a sputtering start and spit into the detective's somewhat dumbfounded hands an extraordinary amount of paper bearing a computerized version of four years in the life of the husband of a local childcare operator.

On 15 December 1980, Frank Fuster reported that persons unknown had broken into his van and removed $3,114.98 worth of property and money. The case is open-pending.

On 18 December 1980, Frank Fuster reported that he was the victim of an aggravated battery. According to the report, Mr. Fuster opened the door of his office, Tiles and Decorating, at 7890 W. Flagler Street, to allow a white male to enter. The subject pointed a gun at Mr. Fuster and ordered him back inside the store. The subject shot Mr. Fuster one time in the right ear, then fled from the store. The case is open-pending.

On 23 September 1981, Mr. Fuster reported that he was the victim of criminal mischief in that someone came to his residence, identified himself as a police officer, and requested to see him. Mr. Fuster was not at home, and his wife and maid spoke only Spanish and, therefore, were unable to communicate with the subject. The subject then walked to where Mr. Fuster's van was parked and broke the window. Mr. Fuster advised that the subject was possibly a Metro-Dade police officer. Internal review was contacted and photographs of the entire Station Five/GIU Section were shown, but no identification was made. The case is open-pending.

The same day, a woman reported that her nine-year-old daughter had been fondled by Frank Fuster. The investigation indicates that, while the victim was riding in his van, Mr. Fuster fondled her breast and genital areas. Mr. Fuster denied touching the victim. Mr. Fuster stated that he had a previous conviction in New York State for homicide and had served four years before being paroled and has since had his rights restored. Mr. Fuster had psychiatric care in New York.

Mr. Fuster also indicated he had been a suspect in an alleged rape of a girl he had picked up at a shopping center and subsequently had intercourse with. Mr. Fuster said the matter was unfounded, and he was never arrested.

Following a six-day investigation, Mr. Fuster was charged with lewd and lascivious assault on the nine-year-old and was subsequently found guilty by a six-member jury. The judge placed him on a two-year probation, which expires November of this year [1984].

One of the child victim's relatives is said to be a Metro police officer.

On 16 November 1981, Frank Fuster was reported as the subject in a landlord-tenant dispute. According to the report, Mr. Fuster and his sister-in-law went to the office of the apartment complex where she lives. Once there, Mr. Fuster and the apartment manager became involved in an argument in which it is reported that Mr. Fuster verbally threatened the manager. The case was Exceptionally Cleared.

On 27 February 1982, Mr. Fuster reported that he was the victim of a battery. The report indicates that Mr. Fuster was jogging when a white female threw several eggs from her vehicle, which struck him. The case is open-pending.

On 20 April 1983, Mr. Fuster reported that someone had removed business papers, a Bressler's, a calculator, and a tape recorder from his business, KDW Enterprises, Inc. The case is open-pending.

On 12 November 1983, Mr. Fuster was reported as the subject of an aggravated assault. Mr. Israel Mendosa stated that he and Mr. Fuster were involved in a domestic argument when Mr. Fuster pulled out a handgun and threatened to kill him. The case was Exceptionally Cleared when Mr. Mendosa declined to prosecute.

Donna Meznarich proceeded to the Metro Justice Building to advise Christopher Rundle that the man whose wife ran the Country Walk Babysitting Service was no stranger to the local police.

7

Maggie Fletcher made an unlikely victim, having garnered privileged insight into the human condition through ten educational
years in the Miami Police Department. A decade crawling along
society's underbelly scraped from her whatever gullibility she might
at one time have worn.

Sergeant Maggie Fletcher took nothing for granted.

Criminals looked like everyone else. Ordinary folks, who just
happened to deal drugs, rob banks, and murder people on the side.

Such was life in the big city.

Maggie wore her suspicion more openly than her husband, who,
with two years to every one of hers on the force, had reason to
navigate even more cautiously through life. Lieutenant Peyton
Fletcher trod his road more quietly than Maggie, and thus more
indiscernibly.

They were a complementary pair of opposites, though the couple
sometimes failed to grasp the symmetry of their union.

Soft-spoken (when spoken at all), Peyton was a curious package,
a man whose biceps swelled from the sleeves of his starched white
patrol shirt like veined balloons as he cradled his daughter on his
massive chest. Conan the Pussycat.

The lieutenant never said much—unless he had some specific
business to attend to. But the words were there when he needed
them. He delivered brief but thoughtful opinions when anyone
bothered to ask. But mostly Peyton listened, residing on the fringe of
conversations like a silent shadow. At times, his eyes spanned a great
distance, and it would become apparent that Peyton's thoughts had
just departed for parts unknown.

Maggie rarely noticed her husband's occasional "vacations" from
the here and now, being the one to whom Peyton (and everyone else
in the room) was most likely listening. Maggie had numerous
opinions and wasn't stingy in the least about sharing them. The

92

lady sergeant could be downright pushy, though her natural (but not fully developed) political instincts tended to temper any inclinations that might impede her career progress.

In less than a decade, she'd managed to pull herself up from "hooker" patrol (where she wandered Biscayne Boulevard in search of men who wanted to rent her body, so she could arrest them) to her current administrative assignment, where she managed a multimillion-dollar police expansion budget. The position was not without visibility.

Nor was the lady police sergeant without ambition.

Maggie was a mover and a joiner. She was secretary of this, chairman of that, and currently president of the women police officer's association. The public didn't know her, but the boys at City Hall did. And that would play more than a minor role in events that were about to unfold.

Sandwiched between a mother who spoke mainly to groups and organizations and a father who spoke mainly to himself was a honey-haired imp by the name of Crystal Marie, whose tiny, foot-stamping petulance no doubt was spawned from maternal genes.

Crystal was an exuberant child who cheerfully accepted the unusual parenting arrangement shared by two cops and a kindly housekeeper who had mothered her since she could walk. Consuelo was the stabilizing force around which the household revolved. And it was Consuelo's departure that set into motion the events that Sgt. Maggie Fletcher, bathed in the glaring certainty of twenty-twenty hindsight, now realized must have occurred during nine days in May.

Nine days that she now viewed from a new—and horrifying—perspective.

She was a cop.

She should have known.

But the trap had been so carefully laid . . .

Maggie stayed home from work the first two weeks while she scouted out a babysitter. Two recommendations—one from neighbor Debbie Lancaster, the other from the Country Center—brought Maggie and Peyton to the Fuster residence for a look-see.

Both Fusters being present at the appointed time, Lieutenant and Sergeant Fletcher proceeded to interrogate the couple politely for the better part of an hour.

Mr. Fuster supplied most of the answers, Maggie the questions.
How many children did Iliana babysit?

"Three or four. My wife is just taking in a few children to help out with the money." (You know how it is these days.)

What would Crystal be doing? Would she be able to play outside? Would she watch television?

"No, no, no." (Iliana keeps them busy. She has the day all planned out—time for meals, outside activities, games, and so forth.)

Were they licensed?

"Of course." Frank produced a binder. He showed them an occupational license. He produced HRS forms. He handed Maggie a medical form and told her to have Crystal's pediatrician supply proof of vaccination.

What did Mr. Fuster do for a living?

"I install rugs, put up blinds . . ." (A little interior decorating, home improvement.)

Would he be around during the day?

No, my wife will be the only one here to watch the children. "But Iliana is very efficient."

How old was Iliana?

"Twenty-one," she replied.

The next afternoon, Maggie picked up Crystal and asked about her first day at the Country Walk Babysitting Service.

"The big boy scared me with a masket."

A mask? "What did he do?"

"He put it on and chased me around and went 'ooh, ooh.' "

"Did you cry?"

"I was scared."

Maggie shrugged. The Fusters' son must have been horsing around.

Later, when she opened Crystal's lunchbox, she noticed the untouched Sip-Up. The nightmares began.

On Tuesday, the Sip-Up came home again. That night, another nightmare.

On day three, Maggie couldn't continue to ignore the still untouched Sip-Up, which by now had made six journeys to and from the Fuster home.

"Why aren't you drinking your Sip-Ups?"

"I don't want them."

"What do you drink all day?"

"Water."

Maggie shrugged. That night she put ointment on an inflammation on her daughter's vagina. Heat rash, she thought.

On Thursday, Crystal offered her finger for her mother's inspection. "Iliana's bird bit me."

Maggie's inquiry brought an explanation from Iliana that Crystal had gotten pecked sticking her finger in the parakeet's cage. Funny, Maggie hadn't noticed they had a bird.

Crystal now resided nightly in her parents' bed. There were monsters, she said, in her own. The nightmares continued.

Though patience was not among Maggie's most promising virtues, she humored Crystal, marveling at the impact the loss of Consuelo had had on the little girl. In less than a week, her exuberant daughter had become uncooperative, sullen, and angry. She wouldn't eat. She broke her toys. Sometimes she tried to shove them up her rectum.

Iliana never crossed Maggie's mind. And only vaguely did Frank—on Crystal's eighth visit to the Country Walk Babysitting Service.

Maggie pounded and knocked for the several minutes generally required to gain entry to the Fuster home. Iliana always had a good excuse when she finally made it to the door. On the phone. Changing diapers. Kids were loud, couldn't hear the knock. But today it was Frank who appeared in the doorway.

Carrying Crystal in his arms.

Maggie flinched. Just a week ago Frank had assured her that he wouldn't be involved with the children.

But his presence didn't disturb her nearly as much as the proprietary way he held her little girl. Maggie couldn't quite put her finger on it, but something looked wrong with this picture.

Something told her she needed to find a new babysitter.

Maggie took two more days off from work to care for Crystal while she made new arrangements. And that would have been the end of her association with the Fusters had Saturday night not brought a crisis.

She and Peyton had a social commitment—an important one—and Maggie's mother canceled out on babysitting at the last minute. She thought of Iliana. Crystal was bathed and ready for bed, Maggie reasoned. The little girl would be asleep for the few hours she had to leave her there.

Just a few hours. One last time.

It was close to midnight when Frank Fuster met Lt. Peyton

Fletcher at the door and led him to the bedroom where his daughter slept so deeply she couldn't be roused. As he carried her to the car, Peyton noticed that Crystal's long, honeyed hair was drenched from roots to tips.

Like it had just been washed.

Two days later Consuelo returned, and life at the Fletchers' resumed as before, though the housekeeper noted that her beloved Crystal had developed some rather peculiar habits during her three-week absence.

Gradually, the nightmares and the temper tantrums diminished. The "phase" seemed to be passing. The nine days in May were all but forgotten until two months later, when a late-night phone call from a worried mother brought Maggie news of the investigation.

The senseless now made perfect sense.

But that didn't blunt the impact of the blow that came a few days later when Dr. Laurie Braga emerged from the interview room and said quietly, "I'm so very sorry."

Sgt. Maggie Fletcher went into shock.

The tears would come later.

• • •

Although the Fletchers and the Herschels lived half a Country Walk mile from each other, they would never have established more than a nodding acquaintance had they not suddenly found so much in common.

The two couples, each in their third decade of life and their first of marriage, shared little more than geographic location, though this, in itself, qualified them for membership in much the same club. The zip code was nothing to sneeze at.

Still, the families roamed in different circles.

Had they the occasion to meet (as the two women infrequently had, during chance encounters at the Country Center), no divining instinct would have caused them to form even a casual friendship.

The Fletchers and the Herschels would not have considered their priorities conducive to intimate acquaintance.

Thomas Herschel's family owned, among other things, a few select pieces of New York City. The land baron's son would never want for meat on the table and shoes without holes.

Young Tom teetered his way through a troubled yet privileged adolescence, then drifted into young adulthood without specific aim until he met Shari Herschel (née Mason)—a former Miss Teenage America who caught his eye, family legend has it, in a South Florida hot tub.

The issue of their eventual union turned out to be two extraordinarily photogenic children who delighted in seeing themselves in magazines and catalogues.

The Herschel kids were child models.

Missy, a veteran at age four, was a sweet, passive child who possessed a maturity as startling as her appearance.

Missy was a vision.

Platinum curls waved down her back and fringed around her sculpted cheekbones. A dimple appeared on each side of her flawless mouth, as though someone had pressed in two thumbs before the child masterpiece had set. Her wide blue eyes spoke to the camera.

Missy needed little direction when a lens zoomed her way.

Brother Chad was less experienced, though no less enthusiastically photogenic.

So Tom Herschel, errant rich kid, former sixties dropout, grew to raise a family in hot pursuit of the American Dream. A BMW. A Mercedes. Split-level suburban home. A once-titled wife. Two extraordinarily handsome and precocious kids. And a live-in housekeeper.

The lifestyle suited him.

Lt. Peyton Fletcher had an extraordinarily beautiful and precocious child—daughter Crystal, not quite four. And he had everything else Tom Herschel did. Nice cars. A nice house, though a somewhat more modest version than the Herschels' spacious estate model. A pretty wife. And a live-in housekeeper.

But Peyton Fletcher had spent twenty years—since high school—driving around Miami in a police cruiser to earn his ticket to the side of the tracks that Tom Herschel casually occupied by birthright. It seemed unlikely that the quiet cop and the decidedly verbal son of a millionaire would someday form even the most tenuous bond.

But that was before the man and woman who raped their children welcomed them into their nightmare.

• • •

"Mommy, there's monsters in Country Walk."

Chad had spoken the words with conviction, if not clarity, so many times that Shari Herschel had truly lost count. They held no special meaning for her at the time. And now she dared not even contemplate what they meant, though each day she grew more sure of their truth.

Because it now seemed so logical.

There were monsters in Country Walk.

Chad had seemed so sure of that. And no matter how many hours she spent trying to convince him otherwise, her two-year-old son had stood his ground.

There were definitely monsters in Country Walk, he continued to inform her.

It became a bedtime ritual in the Herschel home. Shari would take Chad by the hand, and together they would search the closet and look under the bed.

"See? No monsters," she told him.

Then they would tour the house, and Shari would let him inspect the doors and windows to see that they were locked. Chad's father presently tired of the charade and told her to stop letting their son so blatantly manipulate her. It seemed to him that Chad had stumbled on an effective diversion that served to delay bedtime anywhere from fifteen minutes to an hour. Every night.

Shari disagreed.

No matter how irrational Chad's fear appeared to them, she could see in her son's eyes that it was very real to him. She couldn't bring herself to closet him in his bedroom to face the night alone. Shari remembered what it was like to be small and frightened. She couldn't pull the rug out from under him just to make a point.

So when the monsters closed in on Chad at bedtime, and when he woke screaming in the night, Shari continued to assure him that Mommy and Daddy would protect him.

She told him he was safe.

It never even occurred to her that he was not.

Chad told her about the monsters in other ways, though the clues were too subtle, their content too vague to set off any alarms in her unsuspecting mind. He gradually developed little quirks and phobias that surfaced with erratic frequency and duration.

He became aggressive and fearful. Monsters occupied his thoughts by day as well as by night, although from a different perspective. Morning brought a cup of courage that allowed him to assume their identity and, therefore, power, if only briefly. Chad liked to pretend that he was a monster.

Shari blamed too much TV.

His potty training started to slide, Chad having developed an irrational fear of bathrooms and everything in them—the toilet, the tub.

Chad would urinate in the tub if Shari bathed him alone. Or he would pee on his sister's head if she happened to be on hand. Shari wondered if he did it just to get a rise out of Missy, who was quite vocal in her disgust about the whole situation.

He would defecate in the yard. Shari would remind herself that he was, after all, only two and that bowel control was a relatively recent addition to his repertoire.

He walked around the house pulling on his penis as if it were a game. Shari didn't want to make a big deal of it. This, too, would pass, she was sure.

But none of it did. And Shari found herself running out of excuses for her son's recently acquired peculiarities. She consulted her childcare books. The phrase *terrible twos* caught her eye. The text assured her that her son was going through a "phase." Shari breathed a sigh of relief, then sought a second opinion. Just in case.

Chad's speech pathologist concurred that he might be traversing a developmental stage and suggested that Chad's speech impediment might be amplifying the problem. Perhaps he had reached a temporary plateau in his communicative skills and was "striking out" in frustration.

It seemed reasonable.

Shari resigned herself to wait Chad out.

It seemed even more reasonable when Chad's odd behavior began to taper off. She didn't correlate the passing of the "phase" with her discontinued use of the Country Walk Babysitting Service. There had been no logical connection between her son's irrational fears and his irregular visits to the babysitter a few times a month.

Not until yesterday, when Joanne Menoher told her that a police officer was wondering whether any parents might have noticed anything unusual about the children who attended the babysitting service in Country Walk.

Shari almost threw up.

• • •

A great ceramic leopard guarded the foyer in the Fuster home. Judy Prince remembered it distinctly.

She first noticed it the day of Corey's picnic—May 14, 1984. The day she left his brother Brendon with Iliana. Five hours borrowed from one son to give to another. It should have been a fair trade.

It wasn't.

Judy didn't have much use for babysitters, having taken great pains to work her household schedule around two sons, one visiting stepson, and a kind but absent husband who allowed himself precisely one-half day per week away from the family-owned auto parts business.

But two-year-old Brendon wasn't welcome at his brother's school picnic. And none of her friends or relatives was available to keep him for a few hours. So she decided to leave him, just this one time, with the woman who did babysitting in Country Walk. Iliana Fuster.

Her next-door neighbor.

Judy was running a little behind schedule that morning. She dropped Brendon off at 11:00 A.M. with a quick word to Iliana not to put him down for a nap. Then she flew off to run a few errands for her husband before joining Corey at school.

A little more than five hours passed before she returned to pick up her youngest son. When she was admitted to the Fuster home, Brendon stood near the front door, hugging his pillow. Crying.

Iliana stood to one side of him; Frank to the other. Judy didn't see any other children.

"What's the matter, honey?" she asked, bending over to give him a hug.

Brendon kept crying.

"Oh, he's just afraid of that big leopard," said Iliana.

Judy looked at the leopard. Well, OK, she thought. It's big, he hasn't had a nap . . . OK.

She gathered up Brendon and took his brother's hand. "Come on, guys. Let's take a quick nap."

She hadn't given it a thought since.

The first few days after she found out that the people next door might be perverts, Judy chain-smoked her way from room to room, paralyzed from the neck up. She couldn't remember how to make a bed. She would forget whether she'd strapped Brendon into the car seat. So she would pull over to the side of the road to check it. Five minutes later, she would pull over again. She functioned on autopilot, or she didn't function at all.

They were her neighbors.

That meant something to Judy Prince. She wasn't exactly the neighborhood Welcome Wagon, but she liked to know the people who lived around her just the same.

Judy's social acquaintance with Frank and Iliana extended little further than a passing "Hi, how ya doin'?" She didn't even know their last name. They were just "Frank and Iliana," the couple next door that ran a licensed babysitting service. At least that's what Frank told her.

He also told her that the babysitting was Iliana's little project. He, himself, was far too involved with his decorating business, "winning the bread," to bother with his wife's two-dollar-an-hour venture. Then he showed up on her doorstep, handing out business cards imprinted in thick black ink:

"Country Walk Babysitting Service."

The space below was occupied by the prophetic boast:

"We may not be the best but people do talk."

One day Judy had found Frank's son Jaime and a little red-haired boy in her backyard, breaking the branches off her tree. When Judy confronted them, Frank had appeared.

"No one's supervising these kids," she said.

"I'm watching them," he replied.

Sometimes Frank brought Judy avocados, which she didn't eat, and once a cake, which (inexplicably) she tossed into the garbage can untouched.

He was friendly, but not too. And just a bit odd, she thought. But then, who wasn't in one way or another?

Judy didn't see much of Iliana, though she recalled one memorable encounter where she stepped outside to find Frank's wife perched on a stepladder, scrubbing the outside of the house with a soapy sponge.

"Iliana, what in the world are you doing?"

"Oh, I am washing the house," Iliana had replied in heavily accented English. "It is white and gets very dirty. I have finish three sides. This is the last."

"Well, when you're finished there you can come on over and do mine," said Judy as she walked back inside, shaking her head. These people were so *odd*, she thought.

But child molesters?

She didn't know what to think.

Judy thought about Brendon. Thank God she'd left him there only once. He seemed fine, and she wouldn't allow herself to consider that he might not be. She tried not to dig too deeply into memories that might offer revelations that she was not now emotionally equipped to handle.

But some of the memories snuck past her first line of defense in picture form. Her mind's eye saw the great ceramic leopard. And Brendon, standing in the foyer, hugging his pillow—the ragged friend he had brought from home to comfort him from scary thoughts about being left with strangers.

Judy had warned him about "strangers." But these weren't really strangers, as he understood it. There were "good" strangers and "bad" strangers. The "bad" ones had not earned his mother's seal of approval. Her label of trust.

And there he stood, wrapped around his pillow, crying as though his heart would break. Judy kept shoving the persistent picture aside, grasping instead at the straws that bound the last of her sanity. It was only five hours. If something bad had happened, wouldn't her son have told her? Brendon wasn't old enough to know the meaning of the word *secret*, much less keep one.

She was counting on that.

Because even a false hope was better than no hope at all.

• • •

Brendon Prince toddled across the lawn and came to an abrupt halt at the grass line that marked the end of his property.

He had something on his mind.

At thirty-one months, Brendon was entering the age of person-hood; he was beginning to tell grown-ups who he was for the first time. His ability to communicate knowledge was about to catch up with his skill at gathering it.

He was learning how to speak his mind.

The only trouble was that adults still tended to treat him like a piece of furniture when it came to conversing about things they would have talked about in private had they even suspected his keen interest in their dialogue.

So Brendon knew what was going on.

He'd seen all the men and women carrying notepads and cameras. He knew about cameras like that, though the last one he'd seen had been in The House next door, not out on his front lawn.

All these people kept knocking on his door, asking Mommy about The House. They held microphones in her face and asked her questions about the man and the lady who lived next door. Mommy looked upset. Very upset.

The people asked her if he had ever stayed with Frank and Iliana. She said yes. Once.

They asked her if she thought anything bad had happened to him there. She said no.

Brendon wanted to tell her. But he was afraid of what might happen. And he wasn't quite sure that Mommy was ready to know. He could sense it.

Someday he would tell her about The House and the man and woman who lived in it with the blinds drawn. He would tell her what they did to little boys who were left there.

Even the little boys who were left there for only five hours.

But for now, Brendon could only stand at the spot where a lawnmower had drawn the line between his innocence and the loss of it and stare at The House next door.

Someday he would make her know how clearly a two-year-old boy understands the meaning of the words:

"If you tell, your mommy will die."

This was a man who could make things die.

Brendon would eventually tell his mother how the bird went "cheep cheep" as Frank cut off first its wing and then its tail. There was blood all over.

He would tell her about the tall camera with the gun on top.

And as Judy quietly slipped out of his room to retch in the toilet, she knew that nothing else that might confront her in life could possibly be worse than this.

And then Brendon told her what it was like to have a woman's finger and a man's penis pressing into his anus.

They were her neighbors. And they had raped her little boy.

8

Christopher Rundle was possessed of a most problematic circumstance. A man who apparently liked children too much in the wrong way was having them delivered to his home by an as-yet-to-be-determined number of unsuspecting parents. That alone was enough to furrow The Brit's brow without the added complication of having to conduct his investigation in secrecy.

The parents—the ones Meznarich had been able to locate—were edging toward hysteria. With a police detective tromping about Country Walk, news of the investigation lumbered through the development with glacial collision. It was only a matter of time before it reached the Fusters, who would then be in a position to destroy whatever evidence might exist.

And physical evidence, he knew, would be critical to a case where his only witnesses were children of tender years.

With each new scrap of information the sexual battery detective laid on his desk, Rundle grew more anxious to identify and remove—as quickly as possible—any children who remained in Iliana's care.

True, the data suggested little more than a woman who might not win any awards for childcare, whose husband happened to be on probation for molestation.

Legally, Rundle had no grounds for probable cause.

That did little to appease his mounting anxiety about children being delivered to Frank Fuster like pizzas.

The Brit conceived a plan.

He would bring the state's regulatory agencies in on the case and allow bureaucracy to take its natural course. Red tape and technicalities could buy him some time.

HRS could slap an injunction on the babysitting service for operating without benefit of a license, as Arvida had so conveniently determined. And Rundle was quite confident that Frank's parole officer would be most interested to learn that his child molester/client's wife was engaged in a business that put him in close and constant contact with young children—a condition that logically must violate the terms of Fuster's probation.

Thus the children would be out of the house. And Frank would be tucked away behind bars, freeing Rundle from time's race to gather evidence.

But the prosecutor overlooked the fatal flaw in his premise.

He assumed bureaucracy to be logical.

• • •

Tuesday, 7 August, 1984

This investigator responded to 14601 S.W. 144 Street, the Country Center, and spoke with Joanne Menoher. Miss Menoher provided this investigator with a list of other persons who she thought had used the service. . . .

Meznarich went back to gathering bits and pieces of collective weirdness, though conclusive evidence of impropriety continued to elude her. Her notepad runneth over:

CHAD and MISSY HERSCHEL, ages two and four. Attended the Country Walk Babysitting Service from February through May 1984. Mrs. Herschel advises that when she took Chad there he would cry, but Mrs. Fuster told her that her son would be fine five minutes after she left. Mrs. Fuster always made a fuss over the children and seemed to care about each of them. On one occasion, Mrs. Herschel observed Iliana wearing sunglasses and was told it was an irritation.

Mrs. Herschel says the blinds of the residence were always closed, making it dark inside, and that it always took five to ten minutes before someone answered the door. Sometimes she telephoned the Fuster residence and got no answer. Mrs. Fuster had explained that she did not answer the telephone during the time she was feeding the children.

One day Mrs. Fuster came out of the master bedroom with a child in her arms, which had only a towel wrapped around it. Mrs. Fuster said the child had had an accident in its pants.

On another occasion, Mrs. Fuster came out of the master bedroom with a dust cloth in her hand and told Mrs. Herschel she was cleaning. A child suddenly walked out of the same bedroom, and Mrs. Fuster stated, "Andy, go back in there." The child was clothed.

On two or three other occasions, Mrs. Herschel noticed that there were children in the master bedroom.

Mrs. Herschel said that her daughter, Missy, went to the Fusters' on one occasion in April 1984 for approximately five hours. She said that her daughter told her that she had watched *Conan the Barbarian* with Frank in the den.

A month shy of her fifth birthday, Missy Herschel was the oldest child the detective had encountered in Country Walk and the first that she would interview.

Miss Herschel stated she went to Frank and Iliana Fusters' twice. The first time, she played with her brother, Chad, until he went to take a nap. She then went into the den, where she sat in a chair and watched television. Miss Herschel advised Mr. Fuster was also in the room, but he was sitting behind his desk doing paperwork and, at times, watching the movie. Miss Herschel stated that at no time did Mr. Fuster touch her. This investigator asked Miss Herschel if her school had ever shown any movies or the teachers had told them about "good touching" or "bad touching." Miss Herschel advised they had. This investigator asked Miss Herschel if Frank or Iliana had ever touched her in a "bad" way or somewhere they shouldn't have and she stated, "No." This investigator asked Miss Herschel if she had ever taken any of her clothes off while at Frank and Iliana's, and she again stated, "No." Miss Herschel advised she could not remember what she had done during her second visit to the Fusters' but still thought she had been there twice.

Missy's memory, as it turned out, was less fallible than her mother's.
She *had* been there twice.

This investigator then interviewed Chad Herschel. Due to his age and the fact that he has a speech impediment, his mother was present. This investigator attempted to ask Chad Herschel questions; however, he ran about the room ignoring them. Mrs. Herschel also attempted to ask her son questions but was ignored. Mrs. Herschel asked her son if Frank had ever hurt him, and he stated, "Yes." When she asked, "How?" he slapped his nose with his hand, then hit the front lower part of his shorts with his hand; and according to Mrs. Herschel, said "Hit." Mrs. Herschel asked, "Did Frank hit your pee-

pee?'' and her son said "Yes.'' Mrs. Herschel asked her son, "Did Iliana ever hurt you?'' and Chad Herschel took his right hand and hit the right side of his buttocks. According to Mrs. Herschel, he stated, "Tush.'' The interview was then concluded.

APRIL LANCASTER, age four. Attended from February to August 1984. Mother says her daughter once told her that Jaime Fuster had shown his penis to her.

Mrs. Lancaster said that it always took a long time for someone to answer the door, and as April was then "ready to go,'' she rarely went into the residence. One time, April opened the door and let her in. From the door, she observed Iliana lying in bed (perhaps watching television) and heard children at the other end of the residence.

The mother said she had already asked April if anything had happened at the Fusters' and had been told, "No.'' When she asked if anyone had got a spanking, April told her, "Jaime.'' When she asked where, April replied, "His face.''

This investigator attempted to interview April Lancaster; however, she first hid behind the sofa, then behind her mother. Despite the fact that her mother urged her to sit in the chair, she refused to. April then ran into the kitchen, saying she wanted some ice cream. Mrs. Lancaster said she would get it and for April to return to the living room. April returned with two kittens, which she showed to this investigator. When asked if she would talk with this investigator, Miss Lancaster picked up the two kittens and left. When Miss Lancaster returned to the kitchen area where her mother was, this investigator went to that area; however, April immediately left and went into the living room.

At that time Maggie Fletcher [whom the investigator had spoken to earlier] arrived at the Lancaster residence. Mrs. Fletcher stated that she had also remembered that while Crystal Fletcher had been going to the Fusters', she suddenly developed the habit of "French-kissing.'' Mrs. Fletcher described that her daughter would place her hands on either side of the person's head, turn the head sideways, then kiss the person with the mouth open and her tongue out. Mrs. Fletcher went on to say that when she had mentioned this to Mrs. Lancaster earlier in the day, Mrs. Lancaster told her that April had also started kissing in the same manner. Mrs. Lancaster confirmed the fact. . . .

This investigator responded to Mrs. Fletcher's residence and spoke with Crystal Marie Fletcher, three-year-old W/F. At the time of the conversation, Miss Fletcher was in the kitchen sitting at the table. Miss Fletcher advised she remembered going to Frank and Iliana's. When asked if she had ever taken her clothes off there, she stated, "No." Miss Fletcher was asked if Frank or Iliana had ever scared her, and she stated, "Yes." When asked "How?" she replied, "Mask." When asked, "What color was the mask?" she stated, "White." This investigator asked Miss Fletcher where she learned to kiss, and she shrugged her shoulders. When asked, "How do you kiss?" she put her lips together and stuck them out. When asked, "Where does Frank kiss you?" she placed her finger on her lips. When asked where Iliana kisses her, she again put her finger to her lips. This investigator asked Miss Fletcher, "Where do you kiss Frank?" and she again placed her finger on her lips. In response to "Where else?" she shook her head "No." When asked "Where do you kiss Iliana?" Miss Fletcher again placed her finger on her lips.

During the conversation with Miss Fletcher, Mrs. Lancaster arrived at the Fletcher residence, accompanied by April Lancaster, who had apparently indicated that as long as Crystal was talking with this investigator, then she, too, would talk. Miss Lancaster was also brought into the kitchen and sat at the table. April Lancaster immediately began a conversation with Miss Fletcher about the Disney World figures on the plates they were eating from. This investigator attempted several times to talk about the Fusters; however, Miss Lancaster would ignore the questions. This investigator asked Crystal Fletcher to describe the mask, and when she replied, "It was white," Miss Lancaster stated, "No, it was green." Both Crystal and April then began a conversation as to whether the mask was white or green, then decided there were two masks. Both, when asked, "Who was wearing the mask?" agreed on Frank. During the conversation, this investigator asked Miss Lancaster if she knew the difference between telling the truth and telling a lie, and she stated that she did. When asked what happened to you if you told a lie, Miss Lancaster replied, "Your mommy sends you to your bedroom and washes your mouth out with soap." After talking about the masks, neither child again spoke about the Fusters. Miss Lancaster, when asked about them, merely got up from her chair and walked to another part of the kitchen to examine something. The interview was then concluded.

Donna Meznarich was growing weary of this ongoing exercise in futility. She had better things to do with her time than conduct "interviews" with the coddled offspring of people who were "letting their imaginations run wild."

These weren't abused kids, she decided.

Abused kids were supposed to look abused. These were spoiled brats, who didn't have the manners to sit still for a minute and answer a few questions. They giggled when they talked about things that supposedly scared them.

The detective had seen enough sexual batteries in seven of her eleven years on the force to think she ought to know a victim when she saw one.

If it were up to her she'd close the case.

But she had the state attorney's office breathing down her neck.

• • •

Rational thought was a vanishing commodity in the early days of August during the Country Walk investigation as the parents of the children became enmeshed in the chain of events that would propel them onto a fifteen-month roller coaster ride from which they could not disembark.

They became unwilling students of life, the media their first relentless instructor.

Their television sets suddenly became transmitters of persistent and unsettling information that, for them, had come too late—the telltale symptoms that, read correctly, might have told them what their children apparently could not. Nightmares. Excessive modesty. Seemingly irrational fears. Peculiar comments that might have been the children's way of saying, "Ask me the right questions the right way, and I'll tell you more."

"Iliana kisses all the babies' bodies."

"I saw Jaime's pee-pee."

"The big boy scared me with a masket."

Looking back, many of the parents would realize how many conversation openers had been aborted with a shrug.

Guilt became a constant companion. Not only had they somehow failed to protect their children by leaving them with Iliana in the first place, they had failed even to realize after the fact that it had happened. And it seemed the children hadn't trusted them enough to tell them. They were so sure they knew their kids. They were so sure their children told them everything. Where had they gone wrong?

Worst of all were the "what ifs" with which they flagellated themselves to various degrees and with varying regularity over a period of months. "What if" they had listened more closely to what their children had to say? "What if" they had questioned odd circumstances more closely? "What if" one of them had only found out sooner and brought the children's nightmare to an end that much more quickly?

But that would have hastened the onset of their own bad dreams.

Nightmare and *bad dream* are the terms they would use most frequently when trying to explain what their lives had become as their eyes gradually opened to what had been done to their children.

And what it meant.

And even when their eyes opened, they still couldn't wake up.

Not even their most diaphanous vision had conceived a couple who could set up shop in their neighborhood and charge them $2 for every hour they abused their children.

It was not possible.

Then the sea of possibilities opened. Reported cases of sex abuse in daycare centers were springing like mushrooms from points all over the map—a threatening reminder that their predicament wasn't unique. Or uncommon. California. New York. New Jersey. Georgia. The plague drifted south like a determined pathogen.

The parents took to opening their morning newspaper with the care and uncertainty accorded to a potential letter bomb, the opener braced for a headline to lunge accusingly from atop yet another story reminding them that times had changed. The overcoated stranger bearing candy and promises had become the man next door and the grandmotherly daycare operator. The message the parents received was clear: these things happened. A lot.

Perhaps they always had.

On Day Four of the investigation, as speculation about police checking into the Fusters raced through Country Walk on an electric current, the parents of the children who attended the Country Walk Babysitting Service spilled their morning coffee over the prominent headline:

"Boy, 2, believed attacked at temple."

Little Scotty Goldman had surfaced just in time to rock the sinking ship. This message was wrenching in its clarity: two-year-old boys could get gonorrhea of the throat at a preschool. No one had ever told them that before. These things not only happened. They happened here.

This one hit too close to home.

So did the words the reporter chose to quote from Christopher Rundle, the man who was in the process of determining their own uncertain fate: "You would be horrified if I told you about the sexual abuse of children that goes on in this town—thousands of cases. . . ."

To the parents of Country Walk, "horrified" seemed a most appropriate choice of words.

• • •

Chris Rundle was beginning to believe the whole bloody world had gone mad. He had a child molester babysitting kids, and HRS was diddling about trying to decide whether the Country Walk Babysitting Service (a) was licensed, (b) was not licensed, or (c) didn't need to be. The HRS caseworker who ran the spot check in June had noted a document on the wall but hadn't recognized that it was a county occupational license, not a state daycare permit. This was the same caseworker who had been so impressed with the fact that Iliana had picked up a child and kissed it in her presence that the observation was officially noted in the investigative report, which she mentally stamped "unfounded" before the Fuster door closed behind her on the way out.

"This is abuse?" read the notation. The question dangled suggestively as though no further explanation was required.

But if HRS seemed inept, the Department of Parole and Probation was a viable candidate for "Ripley's Believe It or Not." Fuster's probation officer was neither surprised nor ignorant of the little business operating out of his client's home. As he understood it, he told Rundle, Fuster's wife was doing the babysitting. He couldn't find fault with that. Of course, if Frank was the one actually operating the babysitting service, then that was an entirely different matter.

Rundle hadn't yet determined Frank Fuster's official role in the childcare operation. What difference did it make? Wasn't it enough to know that the man clearly had access to the children?

Rundle was fit to be tied. Could it possibly be this complicated to put a child molester out of the babysitting business—if only temporarily? Five days had already slipped through his fingers; time's race passed him by.

Because Frank Fuster now knew that someone was peeling back the layers of his life and had found the rot beneath the veneer of respectability he had polished to a fine luster.

He had some explaining to do.

If he hadn't figured it out by Day Four of the investigation, when a neighbor suggested that he and Iliana "get out of town" by sundown, it must have sunk in by Day Five when the police hauled Bobby Dean away in handcuffs. Dean, father of a thirteen-month-old girl who had spent a third of her life at the Fusters', was arrested in front of Frank's house with a loaded gun tucked in his waistband.

He looked ready to use it.

Temperance wasn't Bobby Dean's strongest suit under the best of circumstances. The Vietnam vet was known to have a short and volatile fuse.

So on the night of his thirty-fourth birthday, when his wife informed him that the police were looking into the possibility that their babysitter might have been messing with his only daughter, Bobby went off like a Roman candle.

Bobby Dean didn't doubt it for a minute. He'd had his suspicions before. Months ago, the day his baby girl had looked so groggy on the way home from the Fusters' that he had told his wife, "I think they're drugging her."

No, his wife assured him. It was probably the antibiotics the baby was taking for a bacterial infection.

Bobby shrugged. He just mixed cement for a living. His wife was better equipped to judge the baby's health.

She was a nurse.

But tonight a lot of things fell into place for Bobby right away. He grabbed two guns, donned a fake beard, and jumped into his truck. Meanwhile, Connie Dean wandered over to the house next door and announced flatly, "Stop him. He's got a gun." Dazed, she struggled with the single vision that kept popping into her head. Small pieces of plastic.

The electrical outlet covers.

She remembered the day she had brought Iliana a handful of them to install in the Fuster home.

So her baby would be safe.

Right after the police hauled Bobby Dean away (frothing at the mouth like an angry dog), Frank started calling on parents, Iliana in tow, and explained that his wife would no longer be doing any babysitting. People were saying terrible things about her, he said. Someone at the Country Center was spreading rumors about her abusing the children because Iliana was taking business away from their half-day preschool and summer camp programs. These were all terrible lies, Iliana's husband explained.

His wife loved the children. She paid special attention to them. Ask them yourself. They will not lie to you.

Sgt. Maggie Fletcher didn't exactly roll out the welcome mat when the couple appeared in her yard. In fact, she was sorely tempted to greet the Fusters with the gun that resided permanently beside the hairbrush in her purse. But she was a cop. And she couldn't allow herself to cross the line to finish the job Bobby Dean apparently had intended to do.

No matter how much she wanted to. And she wanted to a lot.

Instead, she informed him curtly that some of the children indeed had a few things to say about the matter, though she didn't say what.

"Then they are liars," he replied.

And the nine-year-old he was convicted of molesting back in 1982, was she a liar, too? Maggie inquired.

"She was a liar, too," he said. "The children are liars. All liars."

Maggie trembled as she watched them walk away.

She thought about her gun.

• • •

Wednesday, 8 August, 1984 [Day Five]

. . . this investigator responded to [address] and met with Iliana Fuster. Mrs. Fuster stated her husband was in the shower and would be right out. Several minutes later, Mr. Fuster appeared, and both he and Mrs. Fuster were advised that an investigation was being conducted due to the fact that some allegations had been made by the parents of the children his wife was babysitting. Mr. Fuster immediately denied that he had done anything to the children. This investigator advised Mr. Fuster that, prior to his being asked any questions, he had to be advised of his rights per Miranda. This investigator presented Mr. Fuster with the "Advice of Constitutional Rights Before Interview" form. Mr. Fuster glanced at the form and stated he would not sign anything until he spoke with his attorney, whom he identified as Jeff Samek. This investigator asked Mr. Fuster if he wished to call Mr. Samek, and Mr. Fuster stated he would the following day. Mr. Fuster went on to say Mr. Samek was handling his appeal from when he was found guilty of "touching the other girl." Mr. Fuster was advised that this investigator was aware of the case and the fact that he was on probation. Mr. Fuster stated that the other girl had lied, and even the judge had known it because he put him on probation rather than send him to jail and had appointed Mr. Samek to handle his appeal.

Mr. Fuster then stated that his wife did the babysitting, and he was never at home when the children were there. This investigator again advised Mr. Fuster that, before he could be interviewed concerning anything that had happened, he would have to be advised of his rights. Mr. Fuster then stated he would check with his attorney.

This investigator advised Mr. Fuster he could voluntarily take a polygraph examination if he wished to do so. Mr. Fuster stated he would not take a polygraph examination due to the fact that he had taken two during the investigation of the previous case, passed both, and still had to go to court. Mr. Fuster advised this investigator that, if all the parents were contacted, they would state that his wife cared for the children as if they were their own, and the children loved him and his wife. . . .

• • •

Oblivious to the storm quietly brewing to the south, the media's attention focused on the windstorm whipping up over the alleged rape of a two-year-old boy at a temple preschool in Miami Beach.

Every news operation in town turned out on Wednesday, August 8, for a hastily organized showdown between temple officials and almost two hundred agitated parents who demanded to know how a toddler placed in the care of temple teachers came to be raped by a janitor. And why they came to find out about it three months after the fact over breakfast.

Was the temple trying to sweep the incident under the rug?

Embarrassed temple officials assured the angry mob that there was "*no* evidence in any way, shape, or form that is conclusive that the *alleged* incident ever occurred on the premises." And that it "*absolutely* could not have occurred during school hours."

When one of the parents pointed out that "alleged" seemed an inappropriate qualifier in light of the physical evidence—venereal disease and a perforated rectum—a temple spokesman took the opportunity to explain that this particular child's parents were "transient" and had employed "numerous babysitters at the homestead."

There was a brief pause to allow the words to evoke the intended vision of a family of gypsies who slept in alleys and dumped their offspring on all manner of unsavory characters.

"You are besmirching the reputation of the parents of this child," remarked one of the temple mothers.

The Goldmans, having left town shortly after Scotty's assault, were not present to explain that "transient" apparently referred to the fact that Scotty's father held business interests in two states and that the only "babysitter" they had employed "at the homestead" was a fifteen-year-old honor student who lived in their condominium complex.

Had Rachel not been two thousand miles away, she might also have told them what Scotty's teacher said the day she told her about her son's rape and who he said had done it. "Oh, no, that couldn't be," Rachel remembers the teacher telling her. "We're like family here. The maintenance workers love the kids. Sometimes they watch them when the teachers need to take a break."

Rachel wouldn't soon forget that conversation, so close had she come to losing her lunch when she realized that this was how a janitor had been able to lure Scotty away from the classroom. The children not only knew the man; they trusted him. They had been placed in his hands before.

"Our school is safe and secure," the temple official insisted. "I don't know how to say it in any other words."

Many of the parents breathed a sigh of relief as they left the meeting. What the school's directors said made sense. If a child had really been raped in this temple, then surely there would have been an arrest.

But many more went home that evening with the words of a Miami Beach policeman ringing in their ears:

"As you know, anything is possible these days."

In less than three weeks, HRS issued a report on the result of its investigation of the temple school's "level of compliance" with state standards.

The report concluded, among other things, that there was a "lack of direct supervision of the children at all times" and "uncontrolled traffic" in the daycare program's area.

HRS slapped the school with a $1,615 "administrative" fine.

• • •

As the lights of the Miami Beach temple glared into the night, more than a dozen anxious shadows slipped into the Herschel home in Country Walk, strangers drawn together by mutual fears and doubts about the truth. Neighbors by circumstance of geographic accident, they found themselves living an identical nightmare.

Parental purgatory.

Some paced. Others chain-smoked. Tension danced across the Herschel family room like sparks trailing from a firecracker.

Right before it explodes.

Any family who knew about what was happening and didn't run away from it was there. The Maxwells, both former prosecutors. The Fletchers, both police officers. The Princes, a housewife and a merchant. The Piersons, a secretary and an engineer. The Herschels, a part-time model and a real estate broker. And others who would not come to play as pivotal a role in the drama about to unfold, but who bore no less a burden in coming to terms with the death that had come to visit their families.

A death of innocence.

The roster of potential casualties was growing longer by the hour.

Among the last to suspect, and the first to know for sure that childcare wasn't a high priority at the Country Walk Babysitting Service, were Mark and Jackie Harrison, whose five-year-old son had given Chris Rundle some rather startling information earlier that evening, shortly before Bobby Dean headed for the Fuster house with one gun in his waistband and another on the front seat of his pickup.

The Dean family wasn't represented at the meeting, Connie having gone downtown to bail her husband out of jail. Neither was the Levy family, who had decided to take an "emergency" vacation to Marco Island. Had they remained in Country Walk, they would have heard that their two-year-old son's name had come up in Jason Harrison's conversation with the assistant state attorney that evening. The Levys would be among the last of the parents to discover that the truth couldn't be avoided.

Just delayed.

The parents who gathered at the Herschels' felt that perhaps they had delayed long enough. No one was telling them anything. And what they were finding out on their own, as they assembled an elaborate jigsaw puzzle of collective observations, nauseated them. Though too many pieces were missing to define clearly just what they were dealing with, a pattern was swiftly emerging that sent chills skipping down their vertebrae.

Spread on the coffee table was Frank Fuster's impressive rap sheet, courtesy of Sgt. Maggie Fletcher, who ran him through the computer herself, the minute she got wind of the investigation. The parents fairly devoured the word *convicted*, which appeared in the same sentence as *homicide* and *lewd and lascivious assault*.

They compared notes on their children's behavior. The peculiarities grew ominously familiar. Nightmares. Tantrums. Masks. Monsters. Fear of toilets and bathtubs. Sex play. And most puzzling, Sip-Ups that kept coming home in lunchboxes.

That was one piece that didn't seem to fit anywhere.

Most distressing were the latest developments of the day. Crystal Fletcher and Chad Herschel had been taken to the Rape Treatment Center that morning and had demonstrated explicit sexual acts with anatomically correct dolls. Both told a counselor that the activities took place on the floor.

"Always on the floor."

A physical examination of both children had revealed a sore in Chad's rectum and a nonspecific vaginal abnormality in Crystal.

Hours later, Jason Harrison told Chris Rundle that he'd seen Iliana play with his brother's penis.

An explicit statement from an eyewitness.

And still no arrest.

Their eyes widened as they began to realize how difficult it was to arrest someone for molesting a child. For the first time, they understood why the Fusters had done this to their children.

Because they could.

And they would have gotten away with it indefinitely had not a bold stroke of providence brought to the Fusters the one child whose behavior was so consistent that any deviation tended to stand out like a spot on an empty canvas.

Drugging Kyle Maxwell proved to be the babysitters' fatal error.

Ignorance had been the parents'.

They considered themselves good parents. They took their kids to the doctor at the first sneeze of a cold. They used car seats long before they were required by law. And they "baby-proofed" their homes to the extent that it made normal adult habitation difficult.

And when it came to arranging childcare outside their home, they took above-average precautions. They got recommendations from their peers. They checked references. They looked for the trappings of legitimacy. Nice home, nice neighborhood. Official regulatory documents. All seemed to be in order.

When they interviewed Iliana, it didn't occur to them to inquire whether she planned to molest their kids.

Given the realities of living in South Florida, a parent was more apt to scrutinize a babysitter for telltale signs of drug dealing than for child abuse. Kilos of cocaine washed up on the beach or bales of marijuana floating in the bay seemed far more substantial than the scraps of newsprint about a preschool scandal in Manhattan Beach, California. Weird things happened in California all the time.

Florida mostly had a drug problem. That's what the newspapers said. A day didn't pass without a story about the "Vice President's Drug Task Force" coming to town, or the Coast Guard seizing another ship, or some cop stealing drugs from the police property room.

But the news media never told them that a third of all the patients treated at the Rape Treatment Center were young children. Or that the state's "official" seal of approval on anything wasn't worth the ink it took to stamp it.

They were grossly uninformed of the quiet national epidemic that claimed a child every two minutes of every hour of every day. And of the loopholes in the system that made the carnage possible.

In the beginning, they blamed themselves—and to some extent each other—for not having realized what was going on sooner. Had they known that each of them held key pieces to the grotesque puzzle, they might have. But their paths had rarely, if ever, crossed before a detective named Donna Meznarich appeared on their doorsteps.

The price of ignorance, they were soon to find, would cover their admission to six seasons in hell.

Oblivious to the bewildered gathering at the Herschel home, Chris Rundle paced at the Country Center, mulling over his evidence—and his options. The prosecutor was quite certain that the Fusters would be out on bond before the ink was dry on the warrant if he picked them up based on the "demonstrations" of two children who happened to have unusual insight into what adults do behind closed doors.

Rundle had spent five days seeking a witness who was willing and able to make a clear, cogent statement about what, if anything, had taken place at the Country Walk Babysitting Service.

There were doors, he was certain, between what was known and what was not. He needed a door. And someone to open it.

Tonight he had found the little red-haired boy.

Tomorrow, he would find the Bragas.

9

Jason's interview with the Bragas on Day Six finally gave Rundle enough to keep Frank in an indefinite state of pretrial detention while he got to the bottom of this mess. No bond.

Showing that he had violated his probation was the most expedient way to get him off the streets for a while. As long as he was officially under the corrections department's supervision, he was expected to keep his nose squeaky-clean.

Probation violation allowed the State to sidestep—temporarily—the burdensome proof required to establish probable cause in the crime they really sought to charge him with: the sexual battery of children.

Under the circumstances, charging Frank Fuster with violation of probation would have been a routine stopgap measure used to buy Rundle some precious time. But an eight-month rookie probation officer had elevated stupidity to an art form by granting a "self-employed" child molester who worked out of his home permission for his wife to babysit kids there.

Rundle never ceased to be amazed.

Now he had to link Frank to the actual operation of the babysitting service before he could touch him. Once he was able to do that, he could have him picked up on the most minute technicality—the kind of infraction a parole officer might turn his head to if his client seemed otherwise to be keeping his nose clean.

Rundle scratched around until he gathered a handful of "technicals" that seemed superfluous when placed beside the name of Jason Harrison, which appeared on the affidavit violating Frank Fuster's probation.

> . . . due to the fact that Mr. Fuster: (1) changed his employment without first procuring consent of his probation supervisor in that he, on or about 28 March 1984, owned and operated Country Walk Babysitting Service [based on the fact that the County occupational

119

license which the Fusters told the parents was a "licensing permit," was in Frank's name]; (2) failed to make a full and truthful report to his probation supervisor on the form provided for that purpose, and that he failed to fully and truthfully answer the question of where he was employed by omitting that between 28 March 1984 and 29 June 1984 [when, a records search showed, Frank had turned in his occupational license and marked across it "O.O.B.," Out of Business] he owned and operated Country Walk Babysitting Service; (3) by failing to live and remain at liberty without violating any law in that between 28 March 1984 and 29 June 1984 he owned and operated Country Walk Babysitting Service without a state license [HRS had finally determined that he needed one], which is in violation of Florida Statute 402.312; and (4) that between 01 January 1984 and 08 August 1984, he did unlawfully commit a lewd act in the presence of a minor, Jason Harrison, age five years, in violation. . . .

That was enough to let him cool his heels without bond for a while. But he still wasn't formally charged with a crime. And Iliana was still out there. Rundle had enough from Jason to haul her in on a lewd and lascivious and maybe a sexual battery or two. But of the children he'd seen, only Jason Harrison was even remotely capable of giving direct answers to direct questions as might be required in a bond hearing. And a judge would have to decide whether to incarcerate a young woman (who is presumed innocent until proven otherwise) indefinitely, based on the word of a confused and frightened five-year-old boy who still believed in the tooth fairy.

Rundle didn't want to take odds on the outcome of such a hearing.

He didn't doubt Jason's word for a minute. He had replayed the taped interview a dozen times. Backward and forward. There was no mistaking the child's quiet shame.

This had nothing to do with tooth fairies.

But a judge might not see it that way on paper.

What he needed was corroboration.

Careful, clean corroboration, which offered no legal escape routes—now or later. What Rundle really needed now was a smoking gun.

The videotapes.

And for those he needed a search warrant.

• • •

The investigation took six days and on the seventh, August 10,

1984, thirty-six-year-old Francisco Fuster Escalona surrendered himself to a judge in response to a warrant sworn out for his arrest the night before.

> Friday, 10 August, 1984 [Day Seven]
> Mr. Fuster appeared before Judge (Robert E.) Newman and was taken into custody. At that time, Mr. Rundle and Mr. Laeser requested Mr. Fuster's son, Jaime Fuster, be interviewed by the Child Protection Team and HRS to determine if he had been the victim of any sexual abuse and to place him in a temporary shelter if, in fact, anything occurred. Judge Newman ordered that Jaime Fuster could remain in the custody of his stepmother, Iliana Fuster, and a hearing would be held on Monday, 13 August 1984. . . .

Over the State's most vigorous objections, six-year-old Jaime Fuster was sent home with the woman it planned to charge with rape. There was no telling what the weekend might bring for the one child who had seen it all—twenty-four hours a day, possibly since birth.

The State was in jeopardy of losing its most promising witness. The slim chance that the boy might betray his father was reduced to none when Iliana walked out of the courtroom with a free ticket to a weekend with her stepson.

The battle for the boy would be won by the other side before the State fired the first question. No telling what they would do to keep his mouth shut.

Come Monday, the prosecutors would learn that the weekend brought Jaime a visit to the Dade County Jail—so he could fully appreciate the squalor his father now enjoyed. And his father spoke to him.

The visit made quite an impression on Jaime.

So did jail.

• • •

Much had transpired in the twenty-four hours between the time of Jason Harrison's first meeting with Doctors Joseph and Laurie Braga and his second visit to Abe Laeser's office-turned-nursery.

He and his brother had been poked, prodded, and swabbed for traces of venereal disease at the Rape Treatment Center, Frank had been arrested, and his father had punched a fist-sized hole in the living room wall.

It was a long night all the way around.

Jason had a lot on his mind, not the least of which was the apparent fulfillment of his babysitters' prophecies of doom should the secret be told. His family—and his world—were falling apart.

So he wasn't at all unhappy to see the unusual doctors again. Their very presence somehow quieted his mind—and his parents'. Life didn't seem so upside down when he was with Joe and Laurie.

Even when they wanted to ask him questions.

They wanted to know about the tapes.

The ones he had seen Frank make of the children. Jason wasn't all that sure he wanted them to find the tapes, because if they watched them they would know. And Jason wasn't ready for them to know. They might hate him.

Joe and Laurie wanted to know where the tapes were kept and when he had last seen them. It was important.

In order for Rundle to persuade a judge to sign a search warrant, he would need to establish that Jason had seen the tapes sometime within the past thirty days and demonstrate that the child's concept of time was reliable.

No small feat for a very small boy in an acutely confused state of mind.

But he wasn't alone. Joe and Laurie had helped him tell his story all along. Not in the sense that they had interpreted his words, but in that they translated to him the questions that other people wanted to ask. They conceptualized on his level. They knew his brain was only beginning to develop the capacity for abstract thought. The Bragas served to bridge the gap in communications between the boy and the system.

So, instead of asking him to expound on the differences between truth and lies, they reduced the concept to its most basic form.

"If I said your name was Jason, would I be telling the truth or a lie?"

"The truth."

"If I said my name was Laurie, would I be telling the truth or a lie?"

"The truth."

"If I said my name was Mary, would I be telling the truth or a lie?"

"A lie."

"If I said your name was Douglas, would that be the truth or a lie?"

"A lie."

It was in much the same manner that the Bragas addressed the matter of the tapes. The "where?" was the easy part. It was the "when?" that took some work.

The tapes were under the Fusters' couch and inside "books" in the bookcase, Jason told them. And he had seen them last Wednesday.

Rundle got his search warrant.

Jason's apparent composure belied his battle within; thoughts and emotions waged a silent war in his head.

Guilt was starting to get an edge on fear.

Had he betrayed his best friend? Who would take care of Jaime if his stepmother and father were in jail? Was Frank's six-year-old son considered an innocent child, like himself, or a Fuster, like Frank and Iliana?

He was worried about Jaime, he told Joe and Laurie, because, "One day I might want to visit him, and he might be in a bad place."

Jaime is just a little boy, like you, they told him. He'll be in a happier place.

None of the children did anything wrong.

Jason was having some difficulty grasping this concept, though Laurie had explained yesterday, before he went home, that most grown-ups weren't like Iliana and Frank and that they may have been nice in some ways but that in *this* way they had a problem. "They made a mistake. They shouldn't have done it," but the children hadn't done anything wrong.

Even so, Jason couldn't quite distinguish the difference between what the Fusters had done to the children and what the children had been made to do to each other. If what occurred was a crime, wasn't he a partner?

Joe and Laurie said he wasn't. His mom and dad said he wasn't. But they didn't know the whole story.

No one did.

Laurie wondered if Jason might be able to offer some insight into why April Lancaster wouldn't talk to her and Joe about Frank and Iliana. The four-year-old girl had been a fixture at the Fuster home for the past six months. Six days a week. For the moment, the Bragas were more concerned about April's prognosis than about the rest of the children combined. This child, it was clear from the testimony of the other children, had been the focus of much of the Fusters' perverse attention.

Yet she wouldn't talk about it. Laurie would spend an hour calming her down, only to have her spin out of control at the very mention of Frank and Iliana. She would skip around the room, lighting briefly in one corner and then the next. She climbed on tables and under chairs, all the while chattering and laughing. Perpetual motion—the flag of distress that even a smile couldn't hide.

For a long while, Laurie would remain on the floor where she and April had been playing with blocks and follow the little girl around the room with her eyes, waiting for the child to calm herself. April devised a game in which she would hide somewhere in the room and beckon Laurie to find her.

Laurie found it rather symbolic.

April Lancaster was very much in hiding.

And that's what had Laurie gravely concerned. This was one of the most distressed children she had ever seen. Not hyperactive, as the casual observer might assume.

Distressed.

April was a bright four-year-old who regressed to immature behavior only when certain buttons were pushed. And each of these buttons opened the door to memories locked inside her head. Unless the memories were released, and the fear and guilt defused, the memories would grow out of proportion to their place in her young life. She would grow into an emotionally crippled adult whose self-hatred and fear of intimacy could go on to affect her relationships for the rest of her life.

Laurie was walking a fine line in trying to repair the damage already done to the child without creating new tears in the fragile defenses April had woven around herself. Laurie prodded gently but retreated whenever the child became anxious.

Rundle hovered impatiently outside the interview room. This was one child who could fill in a lot of missing pieces—if only she would. He wished he could just go in there, pull up a chair, and say, "Sit down, little girl, and tell me about this and this." That's what he would do with an adult rape vicitim.

But he couldn't do it with a child. For one thing, if he asked her any direct questions like, "Did he put his penis in your mouth?" he would be accused by the defense of contaminating the child's testimony—something he didn't have to worry about with an adult witness. Children were assumed to be highly suggestible. He could, therefore, only hope that the child would volunteer specific responses to vague questions.

Right now it didn't appear the child was about to volunteer anything. The Bragas had explained to him that withholding information—refusing to talk—was the only means children had of exercising control over adults. April had found herself in a circumstance with her babysitters where all control had been wrested from her. Joe and Laurie didn't find it the least bit inconsistent for her to exercise some of that lost control now. No one could make her talk if she didn't want to.

And no one, the Bragas told him, should try. They had opened the door. Now it was up to April to walk through it. In the meantime, they looked to Jason for guidance. In exploring his fears, they might better understand those of all the children.

Jason said April was probably "a little afraid" to tell about what Frank and Iliana did because "she thinks that the children did something wrong."

Jason hadn't spoken to April since the last time they were at the Fusters' together, but he was pretty sure she felt about the same way he did.

Were there any other things he would like to talk about while he was here? asked Laurie.

Jason looked thoughtfully into the distance.

"The masks are giving me nightmares," he said.

Those should be going away now, Joe told him. "Now that you've told the big secret to us all, you know the masks can't hurt you anymore . . . never, ever, ever will they be able to hurt you."

"But sometimes when you're asleep—even though you know that when you're awake—when you're asleep, it might scare you a little, right?" added Laurie.

"No," said Jason. "But I dream things."

"Like what?"

"Like, um . . . Vikings and all that."

"And does that scare you when you dream about those things?"

"Yeah. Um, it's . . . um, um, it's not scaring me, but I just wake up at night because I, um, see it."

"In your dream?" said Joe. "But isn't it good to wake up and know that it was just a dream? Because in the real world, it's nothing like that."

Jason looked at his feet.

The real world he knew about was a lot like that.

"Is there anything you'd like us to tell your mom and dad that you think might be helpful to you?" asked Laurie.

A wide range of emotions played across Jason's face. This was one question he hadn't anticipated. There were lots of things . . . "Um, let me think.

"I'd like you to tell 'em that, um . . . let me think . . ." Jason didn't know quite how to come right out and say it.

He took the indirect approach. "The reason is . . . I think April is scared because she's been talking about this too much and she doesn't know what you're doing. That's what I think's wrong."

"You're probably right," said Joe.

"And she feels like everybody wants her to tell something," added Laurie.

"And she'd just as soon not talk about it, right?" said Joe.

Jason nodded.

"Well, if you don't feel like talking about it anymore to anybody, you don't have to," Joe told him. "But you know that your mommy and daddy want you to anytime you *want* to talk about it to talk to them. 'Cause they care and love you very much. And they're not worried at all, and they think everything is fine."

"But if you *don't* want to talk about it, you just tell them, all right?" said Laurie.

That night, Jason screwed up the courage to tell his mother what she had heard before only from Joe and Laurie. About Josh and Chad and April and Jaime. And if she handled that all right, he might someday tell her the rest.

"And then what happened?" Jackie had responded as Joe Braga instructed. She didn't have to hide her emotions from her son. She didn't think she had any left.

Not since the haze descended over her in the waiting room outside the office where her son told strangers what he hadn't been able to tell her. So fogged was her thinking that she was surprised the message from the man with the silver ponytail had penetrated.

Don't question the boy.

But if he wants to talk about it on his own, be willing to listen.

Don't let him know how upset you are. Make him feel comfortable about getting it out of his system. And then he'll begin to heal.

Because a burden shared was no longer a burden.

If you don't remember anything else I'm telling you, Joe had said, please remember that.

Jackie felt trapped in some kind of surrealistic nightmare. She heard herself say to him, "Tell me we're all dreaming."

And if she lived to be a hundred, Jackie Harrison would never forget the pain in Joe Braga's ice-blue eyes when he assured her that they were not.

Driving home that evening, Jason's father clenched the steering wheel until his knuckles turned white and said quietly (too quietly) to his wife, "You know they raped Joshua, don't you?"

Jason looked out the window.

So had he.

10

The media windstorm that had kicked up with the temple story, then fanned to furious intensity with the arrest of Frank Fuster, was proving as much a hindrance as a help to Donna Meznarich in her quest for additional victims.

Frantic parents were calling *her* now, having seen a couple they thought they knew well prominently displayed on their television screens. Some of them gave her the names of people they knew had used the service.

Meznarich went back to knocking on doors and this time got them slammed in her face.

"Fusters? You must be mistaken. We didn't leave our children with the *Fusters*."

And so it went.

Meznarich plodded on. The few families who would admit acquaintance with the suspect babysitters offered little more information than names, dates, and the observation that, yes, they had seen Frank there at times.

But the detective managed to scrape up a few new tidbits that were worthy of note in the public record:

JAMES and DWIGHT LEE, ages eighteen months and nine years. Dwight was a frequent playmate of Jaime Fuster and on one occasion had gone to the beach with the Fuster family. Dwight stopped associating with the Fuster boy around early summer and would offer his mother no explanation as to why.

Dwight's baby brother had been left with Iliana on two occasions a few months ago. The first time, he returned with a throat infection. He required hospitalization. A few months later, he was left there for five days in a row. When his mother picked him up, she immediately discovered that he was running a 104-degree temperature. Again, he was hospitalized. Mrs. Lee says that Iliana didn't seemed to notice that he was sick, and she had not brought him back since.

Mrs. Lee had discussed the situation with her husband, and they had decided that they didn't wish to become involved.

They had suffered enough embarrassment.

KEVIN CARTWRIGHT, eighteen months. Mr. Cartwright told the detective that his son had attended Country Walk Babysitting Service for several weeks during the summer, three days weekly. Sometimes, when Mr. Cartwright picked his son up, Mr. Fuster was in his office working. Other times he was playing with the children.

On two occasions Kevin went with Mr. and Mrs. Fuster to his [Frank's] mother's and once they took him out to dinner.

After hearing "rumors" at the pool about the Country Walk investigation, Mr. Cartwright says he took Kevin to be examined by a doctor. Since there were no signs of trauma or abuse, he and his wife were satisfied that nothing had happened to him.

They did not wish to become involved.

So uninvolved did Mr. Cartwright wish to be that he couldn't admit the truth about a pile of canceled checks the State discovered he had written to the Country Walk Babysitting Service, which showed that his son had stayed there more than a few days a week during the summer.

A whole lot more.

• • •

The crime was unspeakable.

And that's what had a lot of parents running for cover in one way or another. Denial was their first line of defense.

Many of the parents could not yet bring themselves to acknowledge that their child was among the casualties.

This couldn't possibly have happened to their kid.

He was there only once.

She would have told me.

He was there at a different time of day than the ones who got molested.

She seems fine.

They told themselves anything that might get them through the night.

The kids picked up on the subtleties of a tentatively broached,

"Nothing happened to you at Frank and Iliana's, did it?" They got the message.

Tell me anything. Just don't tell me *that*.

It was not extraordinarily difficult for the Bragas to identify the offspring of a mother and/or father whose need to know the truth had not yet overtaken the desire not to.

These were the children in acute distress.

The two-year-old boy whose eyes glazed over with terror when Laurie inquired cheerfully, "Did you ever play ring-around-the-rosy at Frank and Iliana's?" and then made a beeline for the door.

The four-year-old girl whose father grew impatient with the Bragas' gentle probing and demanded that she sit herself down, answer the questions, and get the whole thing over with.

The more he demanded, the more hyper she became.

And then there was the classic. The six-year-old boy who took the Frank and Iliana dolls and tried methodically to destroy them as he parroted the phrase his mother taught him as she careened down the interstate on the way to his interview.

"Nothing bad happened to our family."

She almost lost control of the car.

"Nothing bad happened to our family," said the little boy.

By the time the interview was over, it was grossly apparent—even to the mother, who watched on closed-circuit TV with hands figuratively clamped on both her ears—that something bad had.

She rewarded her son's candor by clenching his arm and dragging him out of the interview room, muttering, "Nothing bad happened to our family."

In her other hand she clutched the frail arm of her three-year-old daughter, who, without uttering a word, had shown Laurie with a finger and a doll what Frank and Iliana had done to her.

Mommy was saying that they must never talk about this again. It might cost Daddy his job.

Laurie and Joe watched, horrified.

With whom were these children supposed to share their burden so that they might heal?

Who would remind them that they had done nothing wrong?

• • •

Only Frank and Iliana Fuster know how many young lives they had touched during their one-year union, but Christopher Rundle was able to identify at least thirty they had not only touched, but apparently ravaged, during three seasons of 1984.

Now all he had to do was prove it.

His youngest known victim was a six-month-old infant whom some of the children referred to as "the little black baby," whom Frank and Iliana would take into their bedroom and "kiss" on the vagina. Among other acts.

She was in no position to comment on the matter.

From the center of his list of victims spread a cluster of predominantly two- to four-year-olds who had demonstrated in varying degrees and through various methods, clear indications of sexual abuse.

Above this assemblage of bewildered preschoolers rose the child oracle, Jason Harrison, age five.

He alone possessed a well-developed memory bank and at least the wavering courage to retrieve information from it. Key elements of Jason's story were checked and cross-checked with the bits and pieces of information the smaller children offered as a minor gesture of confidence in their interviewers. The Bragas had informed Chris Rundle that he could expect more information to be forthcoming from most of the children once they got used to the idea that the world wasn't coming to an end because they told and that no one was freaking out about it.

At least not outwardly.

Laurie likened the children's expected evolution over the next several months to a child running down the beach on a chilly day. He sticks his toe in the water and then retreats. If the temperature appears promising, he might make several more tentative approaches before he decides to take the plunge. And at any point during this process he might have second thoughts and scurry back to his blanket.

Many of the children were just now sticking their toes in to test the waters: If I tell you this, how are you going to react? How about if I tell you this?

The children's growing willingness to talk about what happened was dependent on their parents' willingness to listen—attentively, reassuringly, and dispassionately. And that was something that went against every normal and natural inclination in their bodies, minds, and souls.

They wanted to explode. Some of them did.

But the ones touched by the Bragas made a Herculean, if not always successful, effort, not to let the children see them fall apart. They were beginning to see the world through their children's eyes.

And it looked very scary.

The Bragas began to drift into separate but overlapping roles. Laurie had refined the swimming-through-Jell-O process to such a degree that Joe began to spend less time in the interview room and more on the other side of the door, consoling and guiding the parents. He told them they might expect to see a radical change in the children's behavior now that someone had come scratching at the door to the compartment where they had locked the secret. There would be new nightmares. Insecurities. They might start to "act out" some of the things that were done at the Fusters'.

The child who had always "seemed fine" suddenly might not. The turmoil he had kept hidden all this time would rise to the surface.

The parents wondered if they should seek immediate therapy for their children.

Joe said no. Not right away. Right now the parents could provide the kind of therapy that money couldn't buy. Support. If at any point the parents felt they might need help in coping with the child's problems, then perhaps they should seek a competent therapist.

Joe saw no need for a child to be subjected to a weekly session, where on the appointed day at the appointed time he was supposed to get things off his chest. Not if there was an understanding ear at home he could turn to whenever he felt the need.

If he could help the parents cope, then the children would be OK. But if the parents collapsed, then so would the children's whole world.

And they might grow up to wonder what might have been if only they hadn't told the secret.

Jason Harrison, having survived the toe-dipping stage, was now in a tentative approach pattern. His courage visited on a more regular basis as he offered pieces of the puzzle with ebbing hesitation. But he was still holding back, of that Joe and Laurie were sure.

Give him time, the Bragas told his parents. Let him do this on his terms. He'll tell more when he's ready. He's just not entirely sure about what happens next.

He was confused and frightened.

He was also the State's star witness.

Rundle had little else.

He had statements from children that grew more bizarre with each passing day. This wasn't turning out to be his usual adult-gets-kicks-fondling-kids case.

There was more here than met the eye.

Rundle was having a great deal of trouble making sense of "pee-pee" and "ca-ca" games that, according to the children, entailed not only the handling, but the eating of excrement. Urine was apparently the main component of a "magic punch" they drank from paper cups. (This revelation caused more than one mother to gag as she remembered the returned Sip-Ups.) There were numerous perversions of traditional nursery school games—Old MacDonald, Simon Says, and duck-duck goose. Ring-around-the-rosy, as demonstrated by some of the children, appeared to be an almost hypnotic rite that worked its way to a frenzied sexual climax.

And then there were the pictures.

Jason Harrison wasn't the only child to mention that a video camera was present to record the activities—whether for posterity or profit, or both, Rundle couldn't be sure.

He *was* sure, however, that he faced a cunning opponent. Frank Fuster hadn't been sloppy about what he was doing. None of the children had sustained physical trauma, though a few examined at the Rape Treatment Center presented some physical irregularities. Nothing conclusive.

It hardly surprised him. There were publications floating around these days—little underground pamphlets that were once circulated hand to hand and were now turning up in legitimate bookstores here and there around the country—that taught adults how to have sex with children without leaving "injury" (read evidence).

Without physical evidence, any case against Frank and Iliana would amount to the word of two adults against that of very young children, whom the court might not allow to take the stand even if their parents would let them.

Frank knew the score.

The nine-year-old back in '82 had testified against him, but these little ones were fair game.

Even if they told, who would believe them? Especially if the only marks left were ones that couldn't be seen. And those didn't count in a court of law.

Frank had become an attentive student of the system. In fact, he seemed to relish the challenge of trying to beat it.

So far, he was holding his own, having discovered that the taking of a man's life would cost him but four years of his liberty—and the taking of a child's innocence would cost him nothing.

This time, there would be no witnesses. Frank was certain, his son would later tell the Bragas, that the children would never talk. And he had taken proper precautions in the unlikely event that one of them did.

Considering what the children said had been done to them, Rundle considered it a minor miracle that they were talking at all. But a jury might not see it that way.

A jury might not be able to conceive that almost three dozen children could be sexually abused over a period of nine months without one of them telling a soul.

Six men and women might find it difficult to put themselves in the shoes of a very small child who has become intimately acquainted with the concept of death in the home of a trusted friend of the family.

And there was no physical evidence.

No injury. No smoking gun. And no tapes.

Meznarich had come up virtually empty-handed when she executed the search warrant on August 10, the night of Frank's arrest.

The house was, for all intents and purposes, abandoned when she arrived, Iliana and Jaime having checked into a local motel. She and the crime lab technicians seized only a handful of "family" photos, several rolls of undeveloped film, a few magazines, a small bag of marijuana, and—most notable in retrospect—one leather thumb cuff and a wooden crucifix under the mattress in the master bedroom.

Not exactly what the prosecutor might call ironclad proof of anything.

He suspected that what he was looking for had already been removed from the premises—the day before Frank surrendered, when Judy Prince reported seeing several bulging cardboard boxes being loaded into a white van.

Judy had called Maggie Fletcher, who immediately notified Detective Meznarich that the evidence might be walking out the Fusters' front door.

When the detective failed to follow up, Judy could only watch as the van drove off with its mysterious cargo. Shortly thereafter, the Fusters hurried away carting suitcases and totebags.

So all Rundle had to take into court with him right now was a bunch of little kids who came close to wetting their pants at the mention of their babysitters' names, who had absolutely no frame of reference for what was done to them. If Rundle couldn't comprehend the crime, how could he expect them to?

How could he make a jury understand that there were people walking around this city who, for reasons not universally understood, enjoyed doing unspeakable things to children?

And that Frank and Iliana Fuster were two of them?

• • •

A group of parents met for six straight days, following the first memorable gathering at the Herschel home on the eve of Frank's arrest.

These were the ones who, because of their children's words or their own conscience, could no longer deny the reality of the nightmare that someone else had created for them. Denial having been snatched away as a source of comfort, they had progressed to a state of cold fury. They were angry with the Fusters and with the system that had failed to protect their children from them. They were angry with themselves for not knowing. And some of them harbored a simmering hostility toward their children for not telling sooner.

One father even asked his four-year-old daughter why she didn't just say no. As if she didn't already have enough guilt on her shoulders.

The father was too blinded by his own pain to see hers.

All the parents were trying to cope as well as they could. They tried to function throughout the day until the children were in bed. And then they would gather at a designated home to try to make sense of the situation and sort it all out.

New children were pouring into the state attorney's office for interviews every day, their parents having reached the conclusion that knowing the truth couldn't possibly surpass the agony of not knowing.

Most had been processed through the Rape Treatment Center for evidence of physical injury or venereal disease. This, in itself, had proved a mind-expanding experience for the parents who came to refer to the facility as "a chamber of horrors." The children were slapped unceremoniously down on tables, their legs spread, and instruments inserted into various orifices as two—and sometimes three—people held them down while they screamed.

Their mothers stood by helplessly and watched their children being raped again—this time by the system.

All of this took place in a makeshift trailer outside Jackson

Hospital's emergency room, while battered adult rape victims wandered in and out. In one cubicle, the hysterical mother of an incest victim screamed as HRS seized temporary custody of her toddler.

"Please don't take my baby!"

The words bounced off the walls.

The children must have thought they'd just passed through the gates of hell. Their parents were sure of it.

That's what it felt like. Strolling through hell blindfolded. A cop shows up on their doorstep, wondering if their babysitter had sex with their kids. They were asked to allow their children to be interviewed by two unusual-looking strangers. And they did. They were told to have the children examined for injury and venereal disease. And they did.

They did everything they were told—numbly, without question. But now that the initial shock was wearing off, and their senses gradually were being restored, they had numerous questions, the foremost in their minds being "What now?"

Frank was in jail.

Iliana was tucked away in some hotel.

Formal charges on both were pending further investigation.

Jaime had been placed in the custody of his natural mother, Frank's second wife.

There would be a trial in which their children would be the expected centerpiece.

Without them Frank and Iliana Fuster would be free to slip into another unsuspecting community and go through another thirty or forty kids a year for the rest of their natural lives. They apparently lacked neither the incentive nor the unmitigated gall to do so.

So the decisions facing the families who would come to be known as the "Country Walk parents" required a distant vision that was just now coming into focus.

They had no intention of offering their children to the State as sacrificial lambs of the justice system. Yet if they failed to cooperate in the prosecution, they would share responsibility for perpetuating the nightmare.

If they turned their backs on the situation and tried to return to business as usual, they could only pretend that it was over—or try to forget that it had happened at all. And then the public would never know what they now knew.

That their children were in jeopardy.

Because the system designed to protect them didn't work.

The media would come to play a prominent role in the lives of both the children and their parents. A TV camera in the living room would attract little more notice than a visiting relative. And the telephone would ring in spurts and fits with reporters seeking comment on the latest developments. What did they think? How did they feel?

"How do you *think* we feel?" they would ask. But not aloud.

Instead, they began transmitting their own message, a lesson in reality they expected would be paid no more heed than the ones they had previously ignored:

If it happened here, it could happen anywhere. Of that they were certain.

Within three days of the story breaking, the "involved" parents no longer needed to call the local paper and explain to a distracted editor that he-or-she-was-a-parent-of-a-child-who-attended-the-Country-Walk-Babysitting-Service,-which-had-been-shut-down-because-of-allegations-of-sexual-abuse-against-its-operator,-a-convicted-child-molester. By then, the salutation "Hello, I'm a Country Walk parent" was sufficient to send a reporter scrambling for the nearest notepad.

Before long, this group of ordinary people who had come to share an extraordinary problem became a major force in the community.

The media couldn't easily ignore a case in which the victims were as fascinating as the crime.

These were the children of Middle America.

And their parents were loaded for bear.

The parents began to grant interviews to the reporters who lingered around the Country Center in the days following Frank's arrest, eagerly seeking comment from a flesh-and-blood "victim." In exchange for their thoughts, they required anonymity. Newspapers withheld their names to protect the children's identities. Television interviews were taped in silhouette.

But the parents began to consider that they were hiding their identity not so much to protect their children as to shield themselves from humiliation.

They shared their children's shame.

Then they began to absorb the message the Bragas had delivered from the very beginning:

They had done nothing wrong.

Their children had done nothing wrong.

Why should they be ashamed?

In less than a week, they decided collectively that they were not.

They looked at the reporters who prowled their streets looking for the next twist in the case and decided to give them something to do.

• • •

On the evening of Thursday, August 16, six days after Frank Fuster's arrest, state and county officials appeared before a packed crowd at the Country Center to answer for the sins of bureaucracy.

An explanation that had become more polished in a week of telling.

Governmental agencies had reacted within hours of Frank Fuster's arrest. The sun had not set before embarrassed bureaucrats announced that they would launch an "immediate" review of regulatory procedures and close any gaps that threatened to allow the circumstance that had occurred at Country Walk to happen again.

Assuming that it hadn't already.

Fuster had skated through the system so effortlessly that it was difficult to conceive that others had not. Literally hundreds of home daycare centers throughout the county were operating without even the thin veil of legitimacy so carefully cultivated by Frank and Iliana. They operated illegally and anonymously, mostly suburban housewives taking in a few kids to help buy groceries. They had no occupational license because (theoretically) applying for one might draw attention from the zoning department, which, more than likely, would not allow the business to operate in a residential neighborhood. And they didn't apply for HRS licensing because the state would demand that minimum requirements for safety, health, and documentation be met as well.

Frank Fuster had stumbled on a convenient "Catch-22" in the system. He had applied for an occupational license for the Country Walk Babysitting Service in the same manner as he had for his various home improvement enterprises.

The occupational license functioned as "proof" that the county business tax had been paid and that the business agreed not to violate zoning laws. That neither the zoning department nor HRS had been notified that Fuster had been granted an occupational permit was explained as possible "human error" or, even more likely, that Frank told them that his wife would be caring for fewer than five children, in which case he needed neither a zoning permit nor state regulation.

In either case, he was able to open up shop bearing documents that appeared to the parents to carry an official seal of approval, though many might have assumed such red tape unrequired of a nice neighbor woman who kept a few kids. The license provided Frank with just a few more drops of honey with which to bait his trap.

The scary part was the ease with which he accomplished it.

HRS had beeen doing its share of squirming in the spotlight. The fact that its "investigation" into Joanne Menoher's original anonymous complaint consisted of a caseworker dropping in on Iliana and asking her whether she was abusing any kids proved only slightly less embarrassing than the fact that the state employee failed to recognize that the license displayed on the Fusters' wall was not one issued by her own agency.

Even more sobering was the certain knowledge that, had Frank been so bold as to apply for HRS licensing in Iliana's name, the agency in all likelihood would have issued it without a second thought. Background checks were run on only the operator, not family or staff. Frank's name never would have been entered into the computer, nor his past revealed. Nor would the computers offer pertinent information about his wife. In fact, it would offer no information of any kind.

Because Iliana Fuster was an illegal alien.

For all practical purposes, she didn't exist.

Parole and Probation was taking its share of licks in the matter, having to answer for the actions of a probation officer who, they admitted, was just a tad wet behind the ears. A more experienced officer, they said, would have found it a little out of the ordinary for a child molester to ask if his wife could babysit some kids in their home.

The problem was, the bureaucrats pointed out, they were overworked, understaffed, undertrained, and barely paid.

Realistic funding was the answer.

And so it went inside the Country Center, six days after Frank Fuster's arrest.

Outside, in the parking lot, electronic masts towered from television news vans that would beam the fiery confrontation ("live at eleven") to homes in three counties.

The networks would save their footage for viewers of the morning news magazines.

The local papers and radio stations were on hand for the event, as were the national wire services.

The guest list was impressive, to say the least.

State Attorney Janet Reno. Assorted civic leaders. Representatives from the governor's office. A handful of state lawmakers.

And Doctors Joseph and Laurie Braga, who received a standing ovation from the parents, which brought the rest of the room to its feet.

Three hundred–odd citizens from all over the county turned out to support the affected families, who demanded a grand jury investigation into HRS's and Parole and Probation's role in the matter and issued a formal complaint about the handling of the initial investigation by one Donna Meznarich—the skeptic who arrived at their doorstep wearing what the parents called an attitude "a mile wide." They also demanded the resignation of the judge who allowed a nine-year-old girl to suffer the ordeal of a trial, then turned the freshly convicted child molester/murderer loose on probation. Hizzoner not only didn't resign. He was reelected.

Sparks flew as it became increasingly apparent that every single check and balance in the system had failed to protect their children.

During lulls in the action at the podium, TV cameras scanned the audience for the haggard, shell-shocked faces that almost certainly identified parents of the alleged victims. They weren't hard to spot.

Tonight, they would officially shed their cloak of anonymity. But none shed it so abruptly as the little blond cop who emerged as their leader.

Sgt. Maggie Fletcher took the podium and in a clear but wavering voice told the auspicious gathering, "My husband and I are both police officers. We never thought that anything like this could happen to us. But it did.

"And we just want you to know that it really, really hurts."

The television cameras silently recorded and froze in still-frame a single tear as it rolled down Maggie's cheek. And from that moment, the parents of Country Walk would never speak from the shadows again.

Twenty-four hours later, the parents were notified that one of the children's lab results had come back positive.

Jaime Fuster had gonorrhea of the throat.

All of the children were ordered back to the Rape Treatment Center to be reswabbed and recultured.

On Saturday morning they lined up once again outside the chamber of horrors.

It was then that they realized that the nightmare had only just begun.

11

Mark and Jackie Harrison aspired to no material summit, having placed their destiny in the hands of the Almighty some years ago. What they sought was a rock on which to plant themselves where they might raise their sons and pursue a pious version of the American Dream.

That's where the house in Sausalito, a nearby subdivision, entered the picture.

They had prayed for that house. Or rather, they had prayed for the stability it represented.

Mark's work as a mechanical engineer had taken the couple to seven states in the first two years of their marriage. The next eight proved only slightly less nomadic. A decade of packing, shipping, and renting had left them with an incessant yearning for roots. A permanent home with a big yard and a swing set for the boys. Maybe even the proverbial white picket fence.

When the Harrisons leased the tiny patio home in Country Walk, it was agreed that the next place they lived in would be their own.

Then they found the house in Sausalito.

At eighteen months, Joshua was too small to comprehend the particulars, but four-year-old Jason understood clearly that Jesus had found them a house of their own. And that his mother would have to work very hard for one year—and one year only—to earn enough for the down payment. Neither boy was enamored of the idea of Jackie's taking a full-time job, but the Harrison family was not unfamiliar with the concept of sacrifice, though Mark and Jackie tried to minimize the boys' share.

A registered nurse, Jackie signed on for the second shift at a Miami hospital, which meant that she would see little of Mark during the week but would require her sons to be in daycare for only a few hours before Mark could pick them up on his way home from work. Their father could care for them the rest of the evening, until Jackie took over at 6:00 A.M. It wasn't their idea of the ideal lifestyle, but it was only for a year.

And the house loomed on the horizon like a magnet.

Fortune seemed to multiply when Jackie located the perfect circumstance in which to fill the three-and-a-half-hour gap in parental responsibilities. The Country Walk Babysitting Service.

Five days a week, Jackie dropped them off, Mark picked them up, and the household ran as smoothly as could be expected under the circumstances. Each weekend, the family piled into the car and drove to the site of their cherished soon-to-be-home. Block by block, they watched it being built, and as Jason saw it rise from the rubble of a vacant lot, the little boy noted that Jesus had indeed provided for them a very fine home.

And when Josh and Jason would plead with her to stay home and not go to work, Jackie would remind them of the house and promise that within a few months the year would be up and she would be home with them again.

And at night, when they said their prayers, they thanked Jesus for the house.

The memory made her physically ill.

Had Jason kept his mouth shut and stuck it out because he knew his ticket to hell was stamped with a fixed expiration? Had he been willing to pay this temporary price for the house that Jesus had found for them?

Jackie wondered what must have been going through his head as he watched his glorious new home being built, his parents unaware of its true cost.

The family would never live in the house in Sausalito.

Jackie was six paychecks short of the closing costs they were expected to produce by the end of September. She couldn't possibly return to work under the circumstances. The kids needed her full and immediate attention.

It boiled down to a choice between the kids and the house. And suddenly the house didn't seem so important anymore.

Don't worry, they told Jason. Jesus will find us another house. Right now, He would prefer that Mommy be here for you.

• • •

August 10, 1984

"They would beat me if I told. They said I would be in big trouble."

"How often did these things happen?"

"Always."

"What do you mean always? Once a month? Once a week?"

"Every day."

"Did Jaime ever tell you about what they did when April was there alone without any other kids?"

"They would play ring-around-the-rosy without clothes on and have to eat penises. They would eat Jaime's, too. Iliana and Jaime hit Joshua in the face with a belt . . ."

"Why did you have nightmares about the bathroom?"

"Because I'd hear screams and cries from the bathroom."

The notes began the evening of Frank Fuster's arrest, when Jason initiated his first conversation with his mother about his babysitters.

It would be a week before he found the courage to look his father in the eye, much less confront him with reality. Jason was less sure of his reaction than he was of his mother's. Mark was so utterly devastated.

So, in the beginning, the task fell to Jackie to record Jason's spontaneous statements as instructed by Chris Rundle. For what purpose she wasn't entirely sure. But she was told to take notes, and dutifully she did.

So did one of her friends. The very next day.

August 11, 1984, 10:45 A.M.

Jason is over playing with my four-and-a-half-year-old son. They have been friends since May 1983. Jason asked me if I saw the 11 o'clock news last night. I said, "Yes." He said, "Did you see Iliana and Frank?" I said, "Yes."

Then he opened up and told me many things Frank and Iliana had done and said. Our conversation flowed for about fifteen minutes with Jason very anxious to talk. I didn't need to ask questions.

He told me of playing tag in the nude. And of being fondled once himself. He said Iliana would change his brother's diaper, and she would play with Joshua's penis. He said Iliana and Frank did sex acts with children. He said Iliana and Frank told him he would get into a lot of trouble if he told anything to his parents. At that point Jason said, "I wasn't bad. They were."

He said Iliana and Frank would put masks on. (Green and white. Frankenstein with bolts on his head and Dracula with a point on his forehead and teeth with blood.) Jason said that scared the little children. They would scream. But he wouldn't. He and Jaime would punch and hit Iliana and Frank. He said Iliana and Frank liked that.

Jason said Iliana and Jaime hit Joshua with a belt in the face. He said Jaime would hit Joshua without getting permission from Iliana first. Iliana also hit Jason with a belt. Frank would hit Iliana with a belt in the face and eyes. Jason said Frank took pictures of the other children and they watched scary movies. He seemed to indicate Frank might have filmed the children nude.

Jason said Iliana would give him pills and he would put them in the trash can. Jason would come over at 6:15 at night after being at Iliana and Frank's. He would be very hyper and aggressive at play, running and yelling, "Kill, kill, kill, kill." He would talk about sexy girls and guys. One time he was playing Simon Says with my boys and had his pants down. I reprimanded him and sent him home immediately. I called Mark. He also reprimanded him and punished him.

Jason must have been so confused.

I wish I had recognized the signs before this, but they happened gradually over about a six-month period.

It's now 1:45. The boys turned on a Debbie Reynolds movie. Some people were dancing. Jason said, "That's sexy." I said, "Do you know what that means, Jason?" He said, "Well, no, but we all have sex in our pants."

He seemed to want to talk about himself again. He said, "Chris, has Ricky ever been touched like I have?"

My heart broke for him. . . .

Jason had begun walking through the door the Bragas left ajar, but he still seemed to hover at the threshold.

Following his confession to his playmate's mother, which was the first time he came to admit that he, too, had been "touched," Jason became strangely quiet on the subject of the babysitters as his family numbly went through the motions of normalcy.

Food was consumed as a necessary measure of survival, not because it was desired. Mark went to the office each morning, not even pretending to function. Jackie's sister came on weekends to straighten out the house. Emotional paralysis prevented Jackie from performing even the simplest task, as she drifted from room to room in a daze.

Then it happened.

Iliana's arrest on August 24 broke Jason's fortnight of silence.

With both Fusters now safely behind bars, the little boy suddenly
loosed a stream of consciousness that began that night and carried
into the next several days.

The Harrisons couldn't believe what was coming out of the
mouth of their five-year-old son:

August 24, 1984

Jason wants to talk about Iliana's "hypnotizer."

"Iliana would swing it back and forth and then put it on your toe,
and it would stay on because it was 'energy.' She wore it on her neck
and would swing it back and forth. It has energy from Blackbeard. It
causes Blackbeard's people to come up and get you, and 'pee' devils
and 'ca-ca' devils and dragons will come out of the toilet to get you.

"Iliana says you will always be hypnotized. I told Frank that Iliana
hypnotized all the children, and he beat her up.

"Iliana says I have three people in me: God, Jesus, and the Holy
Ghost. Also demons."

Talked about the mask with white eyes.

"The hypnotizer has energy from Blackbeard, and slimy things are
on it. Brown-black slimy things. The mouth opens, and they put it on
every child, and it bites them. It's golden with three sharp teeth and
nine spikes. It bites on hands, feet, 'ginas, penises, butts—everywhere.
Jaime says he killed a cat with it. When it bites, cold slime goes into
you and stays until you get your temperature checked."

They would do to Jason:

Hynotize him, make him drink slime (described as Gatorade with
water). He would go to sleep and awake. He describes walking with
his arms outstretched very stiff because he was asleep.

J. says, "My body would turn to slime. I looked in the mirror and
I was slime. Iliana stuck my penis in her mouth. I was asleep when
I was full of slime, and I drank the slime when this happened.

"They made me do bad things when I was full of slime. I played
with Chad's penis. They made me kiss April's 'gina. They made me
stick my finger in the hole in April's 'gina and play with her butt.

"Frank sticks April's 'gina in his mouth. Heather gets a bath when
she's covered with slime.

"Iliana checked my penis and poured cold slime on my penis with
icky blood, then she'd say a magic word.

"I had to kiss Iliana's butt. I had to play with Frank's penis a lot.
I'd bite on it. He'd pee in my mouth, and it didn't taste good, and
everybody had to watch—Jaime, April, Chad, Josh.

"Frank hated me.

"They'd pee in something, put slime in it, put punch in, mix it up, put ca-ca and turtle skins in, and everybody would drink it."

Jason demonstrated "connecting minds." "Iliana says you can connect minds like this": He put his hand on my forehead and his head together.

Jason describes a game called "Who's gonna lose their head?" Frank played it with a knife.

Jason said, "I don't want to die. I'm only five years old, and dying is bad . . ."

August 26, 1984

Driving the car to the theater when we went to see *Jungle Book*.

Jason: "I want to connect to that tree and talk to it with my mind."

"Jason, you can't talk to a tree. It doesn't have a brain."

After *Jungle Book* I asked, "What did you like best about the movie?" and he said the snake. And I asked him, "Why?" and he said, "Because it hypnotized."

August 27, 1984

Near the car at McDonald's.

Jason stood by Josh and said, "We're going to play the whipping game." Started tapping him in the face with taps getting harder until Josh started getting upset.

I said, "Jason, I didn't teach you that game. Who did?"

He laughed.

It was another three weeks before Jason told her about the sodomy.

Jackie slumped at the dining room table, responding mechanically, "And then what happened?"

Jason demonstrated how Frank made him kneel on all fours, while he pushed his penis in from behind.

"How do you know it was his penis, not his finger?" she asked.

"Because I turned around and looked."

"How did it feel?"

"Like a snake squeezing a giraffe's neck."

Frank would lean over, he added, and place the blade of a knife against his gums. "He said he would cut me if I cried."

Then he drew a picture.

Jackie wanted to die.

The next day, she told him, "Jason, I'm gonna have to tell Dr. Joe what happened to you."

"It didn't happen to me, it happened to Josh," he said.

"Jason, I know it happened to you because you told me."

"But I'm ashamed."

"You have nothing to be ashamed of," said Jackie.

"But I'm guilty."

"No. You're not guilty. Frank is."

"Is Jaime going to jail, too?" asked Jason.

"No. He's a child like you are."

"But he did it, too."

Jackie tried to control her rage over how these people had messed with her son's mind.

"Children do what their parents tell them to do," she said.

"Why did Frank do it?" he asked.

How could she possibly explain to a child something that she herself couldn't fathom?

Haltingly, she tried. "Sometimes people like to do things, and they're selfish . . . and they like it so much that they don't care how other people think or feel."

"But I'm scared to talk to Dr. Joe," he said.

"They like you a lot, Jason. They were never mad at you no matter what you told them because they knew it wasn't your fault," said Jackie.

"Well . . . I'm a little bit afraid, but I'll tell them."

"You let me know when you're ready, OK?"

"Do you love me, Mommy?"

"Yes, Jason. I love you bigger than the universe."

• • •

On the evening of Mark Harrison's thirty-sixth birthday, Jason told his father that he would like to do some drawing.

In the five weeks since Frank's arrest, the Harrisons had grown accustomed to their eldest son's unpredictable urges to draw or talk about things that happened at the Fusters'. Mark and Jackie had even taken to carrying a paper and pencil wherever they went should the child oracle wish to purge more memories.

On this night, Jason drew two figures, which he explained to his father, represented Iliana sticking a knife into a bird's mouth. Suddenly, he blurted out a string of words that sounded to his astonished father very much like the cadence of a prayer.

Mark scribbled furiously, asking Jason to go back and repeat the passages he'd missed. Jason knew it backward, forward, and sideways. He'd obviously heard it more than once.

Jason said Iliana would say the words every time she killed a bird.

His father stared at the piece of paper on which he had written the words dictated by his five-year-old son and knew with stark clarity that in his hands he held the one piece of the puzzle that, for him, connected all the rest.

>Devil, I love you.
>Please take this bird with you
>and take all the children up to hell with you.
>You gave me the grateful gifts.
>God of Ghosts, please hate Jesus and kill Jesus because
>He is the baddest, damnedest person in the whole world.
>   Amen.
>We don't love children because they are a gift of God.
>We want the children to be hurt.
>   Signed, Iliana and Frank
>   Amen.

The Harrisons and several other families of victims quietly arranged to have their homes blessed by a priest.

Part III

TRIBULATIONS

"The last time I had a four-year-old on the stand, it took me less than forty-five minutes to break her down."
—Michael Von Zamft, Frank Fuster's attorney

12

Only a hurricane converging on the South Florida coast could have commanded as rapt public attention as the disaster that occurred at Country Walk during the summer of 1984. Few local denizens failed to feast on the news that a convicted child molester had boldly infiltrated not only one of the county's most "secure" family havens, but one of its most sanctified institutions—childcare.

The implications staggered the community's collective mind.

Parents stirred visibly, thus confronted with a disquieting array of possibilities—the most unnerving of which was the stark realization that nothing stood between their offspring and possible harm but their own good judgment. And their confidence in that, of late, had wavered, as a contingent of well-spoken, educated, moderately affluent men and women stepped into the white-hot glare of television lights to sound a tearful yet strikingly rational alarm.

Your children, the Country Walk parents informed anyone who would listen, are not necessarily in safe hands.

Government officials from West Palm Beach to Key West reacted swiftly to close the gaps in the system that had allowed what no one thought possible to occur. Task forces were assembled overnight to "study" the problem and promulgate emergency measures to head off an impending childcare crisis. Lawmakers from almost every district publicly pondered solutions.

More money. More training. Better laws.

With an uneasy eye cast toward November, on whose first Tuesday rested the making or breaking of political futures, public officials and ranking civil servants rushed for a platform on which to denounce the molesting of children, a plank with which few registered voters would be inclined to disagree.

Though many would give the matter scant attention once the polls closed, retreating instead to tally whether their short-lived efforts on behalf of "young future leaders" had yielded any measurable returns, there would emerge one lawmaker whose intense and personal interest would grow with each passing day.

State Senator Roberta Fox quietly began to assemble the most sweeping child protection and judicial reform laws to be proposed since the signing of the Constitution, a document in which people who raped children, she was coming to learn, too often wrapped their darkest deeds.

The media fanned the fire that ignited spontaneously following the side-by-side disclosures of a child sodomized in a temple and a truckload of prodigious sons and daughters defiled behind the respectable but vulnerable facade of a red-doored estate home in the heart of Country Walk.

Child sex abuse was *the* lead story in the weeks that followed—a sustained wave of news coverage that rivaled the intensity of attention paid to a presidential assassination. Newspaper and television editors began to tandem daily updates on the inching progress of the investigations, with one and sometimes two or three "sidebar" stories that examined the childcare/child abuse issue from every possible angle. Whole "blocks" of television newscasts, from commercial to commercial, and whole pages of newspapers were committed to exploring the newly exposed nerve that began to grow raw from repeated disclosure.

"Tonight, a closer look at childhood venereal disease."

"We'll show you how to be sure which daycare center is *right* for you."

"We'll tell you how to spot the signs."

And most disturbingly repetitious of the daily headlines, "Tonight, another suspected child molester behind bars."

It wore all the trappings of a bona fide epidemic.

Within fourteen days of Frank Fuster's surrender, police had executed as many arrests—all separate cases, some involving multiple children.

The South Miami Police Department's 1983 "Officer of the Year" was suspended from the force while internal affairs—and the State—reinvestigated a three-month-old complaint that the policeman had placed his penis in the mouth of a three-year-old boy who was left in his wife's care, one of dozens of children who had attended her neighborhood babysitting service over a period of more than a decade.

The case of Officer Harold "Grant" Snowden would become the most prominent uncovered in the wake of Country Walk.

And perhaps the most significant in retrospect.

But at the time, its importance was diminished by the sheer volume of cases that poured into the state attorney's office within a few short weeks:

- A fifteen-year-old employee of a city-run daycare center, hired as part of a summer jobs program, was charged with a lewd assault on a six-year-old girl.
- A twenty-year-old man, a summer worker at another city-funded daycare facility, was charged with fondling a four-year-old boy in a bathroom. He was found to have a previous record of child molestation.

  Both would confess. Neither would be brought to trial.

- Twenty-six-year-old twin brothers were charged with raping a four-year-old girl and her six-year-old brother, who had been left in their care by the children's mother.

  Both would plead guilty to a reduced charge.

- A thirty-four-year-old Hebrew teacher was charged with fondling one of his eleven-year-old students over a period of a year. He pleaded guilty to a reduced charge of simple aggravated assault.
- A thirty-nine-year-old convicted child pornographer was arrested when police investigating a stolen-property ring stumbled on hundreds of photographs of him and other adults engaged in sex with young boys. The house in which he lived, where the pictures were seized, was located across the street from an elementary school. Two days following his release on bond, he checked into a Miami motel, put a gun in his mouth, and pulled the trigger.
- A fifty-year-old man was arrested for the rape of an eight-year-old girl. A longtime friend of the family, he was found to be in possession of hundreds of photographs documenting his assaults upon her from the age of four.
- A seventy-four-year-old once-prominent research chemist who "treated" his neighbors' children to dinner was arrested for "treating" them to kiddie porn and fondling as well. He was, at the time, on probation for molesting another child.
- An eighty-year-old man was charged with sexually assaulting a four-year-old girl his wife was babysitting. So shocked was he by the arrest that police were obliged to transport him to

Jackson Memorial Hospital's coronary care unit instead of to jail.

He pleaded guilty.

A parade of handcuffed prisoners continued to march across home television screens. People from every walk of life, of every conceivable age, were being accused of molesting children—an invisible crime of illogical motive.

And all of the suspects had been residing comfortably and anonymously in Dade County.

For years.

Parental comfort twitched at the suggestion that seemingly normal people might secretly engage in such distressingly abnormal pursuits. The sorting out of friends and enemies suddenly loomed as a complex task.

Parents began to panic.

Switchboards and hot lines were jammed with calls for more information on abuse identification and prevention. HRS was deluged with requests to verify whether any complaints had ever been lodged against their child's daycare center or to report that the one they were using wasn't licensed.

HRS moved to shut down some forty illegal childcare facilities in a matter of weeks, ranging from small home daycare operations to large, elaborate (and very visible) centers.

All doing business without benefit of regulation.

Mothers of the children who attended the enjoined daycare centers scrambled to find alternate childcare.

The local daycare industry was launched into chaos. Owners and operators were put on the defensive as parents began making unprecedented (and often suspicious) inquiry into their hiring practices and credentials. Mothers and fathers began showing up at odd hours of the day, conducting spot checks—a function for which they had previously assumed the government was responsible.

Some stayed home from work altogether to contemplate the things that can happen to children when their parents are away.

Country Walk became two words to which South Floridians reacted with instant, if not flattering, recognition. The community became known not for its "blueberry skies and butterflies," but for the "pervert" who babysat kids there. Residents who gave out their address in order to have furniture delivered or pests controlled could expect to be greeted by pregnant pause and raised eyebrow.

"*The* Country Walk?"

As though the address-giver had just admitted to living among a colony of lepers on Jupiter.

The merits of the case came to be examined and debated openly on the street, on the bus, in offices and grocery lines all over Miami, a circumstance to which Frank and Iliana's defense counsel would point when asking a judge to move the trial—and an unspecified number of child witnesses—out of Dade County.

"There is *no way* our clients can get a fair trial in this jurisdiction," they announced loudly and repeatedly over the course of the next year as the discomfiting topic of child-adult sex, once barely whispered, came to be bandied about over produce at Publix and donuts on coffee breaks.

Some of the exchanges were marked by a peculiar ambivalence.

"What about this thing at Country Walk?"

"I think the kids are lyin'."

"Why would they lie about something like that?"

"I dunno, but somethin' isn't right here. How could somebody do somethin' to three dozen kids and not one of 'em tell? I could almost understand if maybe they just got 'touched.' But puttin' it in their mouth? Somethin' just isn't right here.

"And how 'bout these parents? You mean to tell me that out of fifty or so parents, none of 'em could tell just by lookin' at their kid that somethin' been done to 'em?

"Something's not right here."

Something wasn't, indeed.

• • •

Among those held captive by the drama being played out by the media in intricate detail for all to see was a young woman by the name of Christy Casey, a school psychologist who was in the process of searching out an amenable situation in which to place her infant daughter when she returned to work the following month—a schedule that conformed to the overall plan she had arranged to accommodate both career and recent motherhood.

Daughter Patricia would be six months old in September, a circumstance that coincided happily with the start of the new school year. Christy faced the date with a mood of apprehensive anticipation, the act of relinquishing her daughter to the will and whim of strangers becoming a more imposing task than she had envisioned before the lump in her belly became a living, breathing child. Unexpected maternal instincts were engaged.

So it was with due caution that Christy Casey swept the county for an appropriate situation in which to place Patricia while she was counseling other people's children.

She looked into private daycare homes and found none to her liking. Too unsanitary. Too unstructured. Too dull.

She looked into daycare centers. Too impersonal.

One place told her to pack a lunch that six-month-old Patricia could feed to herself, as the staff could not be of assistance during the mass feeding that occurred each day at noon.

Another center director explained to her that no child was permitted to sleep without shoes. Imagine how disruptive it would be, she smiled, if the staff were to have to remove and replace all of that footwear before and after every nap.

A third daycare center saw no problem if Christy wanted her daughter to sleep unshod, the enforced three-hour nap period allowing the staff ample opportunity to summon their energies.

Christy was incredulous. How could they possibly schedule fifty kids to lie motionless for three straight hours? Nonetheless, on a subsequent late-afternoon visit, she arrived at the center to find neat rows of cots lining the walls, a toddler bedded on each. A few drowsed, but most stared at the ceiling, unable to sleep or rise. Marking time.

Disillusionment paid Christy a brief visit during which she evaluated her predicament. Reality had intruded discourteously on the perception her mind's eye had initially drawn. Her fantasy surrogate didn't exist.

Thus cleansed of idealistic fervor to find a clone of herself, Christy renewed her search with a baleful eye toward compromise. Matters of intellectual and emotional stimulation were the ones she carried foremost in her thoughts.

Matters of a sexual nature never crossed her mind. That is, until she turned on the evening news and found a babysitter and her husband—with remarkable nonchalance—stand charged with committing grotesque atrocities on babies smaller than her own Patricia.

Christy Casey, child psychologist, mother, and wife of a state prosecutor (who had anguished over four child sex abuse cases in his brief but brilliant career), didn't doubt for a millisecond that Frank and Iliana Fuster had done everything the children said they had.

And probably more.

But she did not even suspect that the drama she now watched unfold on her television screen would soon enter her own home.

She did not know that her husband would be one of two prosecutors whom Janet Reno would select for the task of convincing a jury that pedophiles weren't obviously degenerate strangers who preyed on someone else's child.

That they were, in this case, the people next door.

• • •

Sgt. Maggie Fletcher nervously fingered her speech as she stepped to the podium that faced, among other pillars of power, the governor of the state of Florida, two state legislators, and a judge. Silently she cursed the chain of events that had brought her here today, six weeks after paradise went awry, to address the Governor's Constituency on Children.

Behind her, clustered in the first few rows of the packed auditorium-sized county commission chambers, sat roughly a dozen men and women whose hands locked in stoic solidarity. Eyes dry for lack of tears, and swollen from those already shed, they glanced warily at the bank of television cameras that would sweep in to capture their mood throughout the hearing. Some visibly winced. None relished the thought of having their raw pain paraded before the world in living color.

The Fletchers. The Princes. The Harrisons. The Herschels. The Maxwells. And Jeannie Pierson, freshly shed of a husband, who sat uncoupled. These would remain key players in the yearlong drama about to unfold. These were the "core" of the Country Walk parents. There were others who would put in a cameo appearance today and on future occasions, and still more who would reside on the fringes of the stage, not quite certain of their place. Regardless of their destined roles, all who gathered here today shared the certain knowledge of what had occurred at the Country Walk Babysitting Service—a circumstance with which they were just now beginning to cope. They found solace from each other, which eluded them in the presence of relatives and friends.

"I'm sorry, I know how you must feel," rang hollow in their ears. Though appreciative of the well-intended gestures of sympathy, the parents of the Fusters' victims (both possible and known) were thrust into emotional isolation.

Horrified outsiders could not envision the depths of their grief and despair. The parents could explain that no more effectively than they could describe colors to a blind man.

Among themselves, no explanation needed to be spoken.

Thus attached, the Country Walk parents directed their collective energies to confront more distant valleys. It was beginning to dawn on them that the child victims were also witnesses, and they were just now learning what that meant. None among them were willing to offer their child for rape once again—this time by the court system, which offered a five-year-old victim less legal protection than his thirty-six-year-old assailant.

Yet none failed to realize the consequences if Frank and Iliana Fuster were not brought to trial.

Though publicly they announced unwavering intent to see the case through to conviction, the Country Walk parents acknowledged privately to the State that they would not hesitate to withdraw their cooperation should it not extend every effort to minimize trauma to their children. The State's representatives shuffled uncomfortably and explained the realities of how the law worked.

Then the law is wrong, they decided, as were a number of other aspects of the justice and the regulatory system they wished to see changed.

They mobilized immediately to create a nonprofit organization that carried in its name their express intent—Justice for Sexually Abused Children, or J-SAC, as it came to be known. Joining their ranks were more than two hundred interested citizens, most residents of Country Walk, who, for their own reasons, had been touched by the parents' plight. Many had walked in their shoes before, sexual abuse having visited their own lives in days or years past.

One man, a distinguished Cuban life insurance salesman, retained temporary custody, along with his wife, of a seven-year-old granddaughter who, a court had determined, was repeatedly raped by his drug-addicted daughter's boyfriend. But Alfonso Ruíz spoke little of his anguish over his own predicament, which now entailed a protracted court battle in which he beseeched a judge not to return his terrified granddaughter to the home where her rapist lay in wait, the courts and her mother having forgiven his deeds. Alfonso instead immersed himself in the cause of the parents of Country Walk, a cause for which he had previously battled alone as he waded through the system, crying out for justice to be done. A single voice that no one heard. But now there were many voices he could help to be heard. He would speak very little himself, but to secure justice for sexually abused children, Alfonso Ruíz would do the work of ten men.

More consumed by her own personal plight was a woman by the

name of Carol Parker who told a story that, in light of the Country
Walk parents' increasingly educated perspective, rang with a certain
measure of credibility. The mother of a son and a daughter, ages
four and six, Carol described to them a nightmare that surpassed
their own. Each Friday, she explained, she delivered to her ex-
husband custody of both children. Each Sunday evening she would
listen to their frantic pleas not to return them to their father's
intrusive hands. The children told a judge the details of their weekly
visitation, but the court was unmoved. Carol was ordered either to
deliver her offspring to their father or to relinquish their custody
entirely. She went through half a dozen lawyers. Nothing, they told
her, could be done.

Carol was a basket case. She sometimes thought of disappearing
with the children, starting a new life in a place where weekends
didn't loom as assigned days of torture, an act that might cause her
children's pictures to be affixed to milk cartons throughout the
land, the word *missing* stamped below their chins. Should they be
"found," the children would be "reunited" with their father—full-
time. The risk was too great. So on weekdays Carol harangued
attorneys with increasingly desperate pleas, and on weekends she
delivered her babies into the hands they told her were unsafe.

Anita York, a tall, redheaded Texan with a Phyllis George smile,
was in the process of exacting her own justice (from the teenaged
neighbor who defiled her two young daughters), when J-SAC's call
for membership reached her ears. Anita would eventually extract a
pound of flesh, though the cost to her family could be neither
weighed nor measured.

The York girls had been obliged to recount for a judge the places
the neighbor-boy had touched them—and with what. The hours of
humiliating testimony bought the boy-molester and his family a
one-way ticket back to South America from whence they had come.

At one point during the initial investigation, police had asked the
boy why he did it.

"Because they were little," he replied.

His father, he told them, had been supervising his sexual "orien-
tation" since he was but three. Thus, he explained, he was only
doing unto others what had been done for many years unto him.

Anita was only marginally grateful that he and his family would
be "doing it" back in Venezuela, not in Country Walk.

For her efforts in removing a child molester from the immediate
vicinity, Anita and her family were rewarded with ostracism, her

neighbors having been offended by the fervor with which the tall Texan pursued such a "benign" circumstance. They did not wish to consider that the York girls might not have been the only children the alien teenager had "sampled" on the block. Most bewildering, Anita found, was the Arctic blast she received from her next-door neighbors, a psychiatrist and his wife whose own small daughter had been lured into a van by a visiting carpenter, where he molested her within three slim yards of her front door. The psychiatrist and his wife wanted to know why Anita didn't just put the matter behind her, as they had. Seal it over. Forget it.

When she persisted in her "persecution" of the "nice young man" who had made her daughters wise beyond their years, Anita saw the neighborhood welcome mats withdrawn from beneath her little girls' feet as they knocked expectantly on doors through which they were no longer admitted. Every child on the block was forbidden to associate with the "allegedly" molested York girls whose parents refused to forgive and forget their neighbor's possible trespasses.

Carol saw no recourse short of a change of residence.

The York home was placed on the market at an attractive price— a prime piece of real estate offered at an impressive value. But even exceptional properties weren't flocked with bids in the fall of 1984 if they happened to be situated in Country Walk, former home of the infamous babysitters. The Fusters, whom she had never met, inadvertently cut off her escape from neighborly exile. It seemed a poetic justice that Anita York would come to share a fragile union with their victims.

Sgt. Maggie Fletcher was expressly suited to have assumed the role of official spokesperson for the parents of Country Walk. Petite (barely five feet tall), blond (courtesy of a regular dose of peroxide administered by husband Peyton), and pretty enough for a police recruiting poster, Maggie possessed an agreeable chemistry of quiet grief and righteous indignation that played well on the six o'clock news. The little blond cop was properly pissed, and she didn't care who knew it.

But on this fifteenth day of September, thirty-six days after Frank's arrest, the gash was still fresh, and Maggie would bleed, not rant, as she stood before the governor and his panel, her face an open wound.

The policewoman drew a breath and read from the paper she gripped in her hands.

"My name is Maggie Fletcher," she began.

"I'm the mother of a little girl who was sexually abused by Francisco Fuster Escalona and Iliana Fuster at the Country Walk Babysitting Service."

Maggie's voice quavered. She forced back the tears that threatened to abort her message. Behind her, tears began to stream down the faces of the parents for whom she spoke.

Maggie continued.

"The most difficult thing I have ever had to do was to stand out publicly and say this has happened to my daughter. I come here before you, and I do this without shame, because I don't feel that it was my daughter's fault."

Maggie swiped at the tears that flagrantly disobeyed her command not to flow. She summoned composure.

"I'm also here as the acting chairperson of an organization, Justice for Sexually Abused Children. I'm a police sergeant. My husband is a police lieutenant. Two of the parents I speak for today are former state prosecutors, and one is a former chief assistant state attorney in another circuit.

"We live in a beautiful community with twenty-four-hour security, in a relatively crime-free area. I bring this out to show that anyone's children are a target for sexual abuse, including yours, and that it happens everywhere, regardless of race, sex, or social status.

"I want to give you some facts in our particular case as this will make many of you realize that some parents will never know if their children are sexually abused, due to the failure of our present system.

"Francisco Fuster Escalona was a convicted murderer in New York. He was later convicted by a jury in Dade County of sexually abusing a nine-year-old girl. A judge placed him on probation and returned him to society because the judge felt, as he has indicated to the media, that sexual abuse of young children is not a violent crime, but a crime against our social standards.

"Francisco Fuster had all intentions of continuing to sexually abuse children. So, therefore, he opened the Country Walk Babysitting Service. Francisco Fuster applied and received an occupational license from Dade County to run the babysitting service.

"Numerous parents used this service, and as many as twenty-five children, many under the age of two, were sexually abused.

"We have the Department of Parole and Probation in charge of supervising Francisco Fuster from his sexual abuse conviction. A probation officer visiting the home of Francisco Fuster sees numerous children, but shows no concern, regardless of his conviction.

"Then we have Dade County issuing an occupational license for a childcare center in a residential area, without requiring that he obtain a license from the Department of Health and Rehabilitative Services.

"In early May of 1984 [actually it was June], the Department of Health and Rehabilitative Services received a complaint of sexual child abuse at the Fusters'. They visited his home, never asked to see his HRS license, and totally disregarded the complaint because the facility was clean.

"This HRS employee states that she made a note to check if her agency had licensed the facility, but failed to do so because she apparently didn't think it was important enough.

"This case is a classic example of everything that is wrong with the present system; that it relates to the low priority that our governmental system places on the welfare of our children.

"The law provides a sentence of life imprisonment for sexually abusing a child under the age of eleven. I cannot think of any other crime that carries a life sentence and receives less attention.

"An adult witness is competent unless proven incompetent. A child is incompetent unless proven competent.

"Young children do not make up these stories about sexual abuse. We must believe them, and the law must provide an avenue to allow them to testify without harassment. The present law protects the criminal.

"Who protects our children?

"We provide better facilities for the criminal, the criminally insane, the juvenile offender than for the children who are victims of sexual abuse.

"In our case, we brought the children to be examined and interviewed in a facility in Dade County that was not geared for young children. We found that no centralized or permanent facility existed to examine the victims of the over four hundred cases of child sexual abuse processed in the Dade County Rape Treatment Center alone last year. . . .

"In the juvenile system we found no one trained in interviewing children. The one salvation the parents had was Joseph and Laurie Braga. Their expertise and care and attitude toward the children helped the parents deal with the trauma.

"I cannot express the pain, the anger, and the frustration that we are going through. The realization that my daughter was sexually abused is more than any parent can bear, and it's even more frustrating when we find out our system *failed*.

"If there is anything . . . good that comes out of our tragedy, it is that people are more likely to follow through in reporting sexual problems and discussing their problem without shame.

"Because of the media and the parents of the victims who decided to come up publicly, this tragic incident could not be buried under the carpet by any bureaucracy. Those of you here who have the power to change our system and make the difference for our children, do it—if not for anything else, but for your own children and grandchildren.

"Thank you."

The gallery of parents behind Maggie rose as one in thunderous approval. Tears flowed freely. By the end of the hearing, even the reporters who covered it as part of a day's work would bite their lips to discourage the moisture that welled in their eyes.

Senator Roberta Fox, seated to the left of the governor, made notes.

The next morning, a three-column photograph dominated the front page of local news in the five-pound Sunday edition of the *Miami Herald*. It was not the tear-stained face of Maggie Fletcher, as might have been expected, but the sharply focused profile of a man, whose silver ponytail was blocked from the camera's view by the image of a dark-haired woman whose hand he clasped. For it was the words of Dr. Joseph Braga that had been received most soberly by the photographer who framed the stunning portrait—and anyone else who attended the governor's hearing.

He spoke, as was his custom, for the children.

Allow these young victims to testify as what they are, he implored—children. Shield them from intimidation and harassment. Let them be heard, not further harmed.

Dr. Braga dipped his brush into his palette and with bold strokes laid down an image that was beheld by some as an act of legal heresy.

He envisioned a cheerful room, he said, in which would be placed child-sized furniture and toys. In the room with the child would be an expert trained in the area of children's language and development, who would wear an earpiece into which attorneys for the State and the defense could issue each question they wished asked of the child. The child development expert would then put the question to the child, in words and syntax he understood, a court reporter recording both versions should a question of interpretation arise at any point along the way. Opposing counsel and the judge could view the entire proceeding through a one-way mirror on one side of the room. On the other, a video camera would record the testimony through a similar unintrusive arrangement.

The defendant, he continued, could be seated in another room, monitoring the proceeding on a television screen, linked to his attorney by an earpiece. The image of the accused would be displayed on a second television monitor, located in the interview room in full view of the child.

Through this procedure, Dr. Braga continued, both the spirit and the letter of the law would be met, and the child victim could be allowed a measure of protection not currently offered by the courts. The scales of justice cried out for balance, he said. And this system achieved it.

The child could tell his story in an environment that offered warmth and security, instead of perched on a king-sized chair in a sizable barn with mile-high ceilings. Courtrooms were designed to intimidate. The interview room he proposed was designed to comfort—the very least the justice system was obliged to offer a child who found himself thrust into the bowels of the justice system through no fault of his own, he suggested.

At the same time, there being a person knowledgeable in child development with whom he interacts, the child could enjoy his right to understand the questions being asked of him. For this was the only way the truth could be achieved, he pointed out. And wasn't the aim of justice to seek truth, not subvert it?

The court would not expect to arrive at the truth by questioning an English-speaking adult in Portuguese. How could it expect to question a child accurately in a language he has not yet learned— the language of adults and law school graduates?

This isolation of the child witness would in no way infringe on the rituals of jurisprudence, assured Dr. Braga. Cross-examination would be conducted as it would through any language interpreter. And motions, rulings, and objections could be argued in the same manner they would in a traditional courtroom—but outside the child's confused and unknowledgeable perception.

Most important, the two-way video monitor setup would satisfy constitutional requirements that the accused be allowed to "confront" his accuser. The Founding Fathers did not etch in granite that the "confrontation" should necessarily enclose a victim in the same room with his attacker.

We have the resources and the technology to do this, he said. It should—and must—be done.

"They have suffered *enough* at the hands of these people," said Joe Braga, his vocal pitch preparing to rise from indignation to outrage. "They do not need to have them glaring at them, baring their teeth, giving them dirty looks, and attempting to intimidate them. Because in many cases the perpetrators of these crimes have told these children, '*If you talk,* terrible things will happen to you. *If you talk,* your mothers and fathers will die.'

"There are instances in which perpetrators of these crimes have taken live animals and killed them in front of the children and said, 'If you tell what has happened, the same thing will happen to you.' We *can't* put the children in the same room as these people when they're trying to give their testimony.

"It would be cruel and *inhumane.*"

13

It appeared to some people (among those who knew him well or not at all), that Michael Von Zamft harbored a perfect fear that the day might come when he would stand accused of being—deep down inside—a really nice guy.

"There are sleazy people like me out there," he once said. "We all have our own styles. There are people I can't emulate. No matter what I do, I'm never going to be able to do that. There are people who speak softly. I cannot emulate people who speak softly. There are people who come off friendly. I cannot emulate someone who comes off friendly. There are people who are gracious.

"I've never been gracious in my life."

His peers, though not universally pleased with his manner and methods, regarded him as both a choice ally and a formidable foe. Von Zamft was considered a master player of the justice game, so it mattered very little that he made no visible effort to contain his enthusiasm for himself. He was smart. He was combative. And he was not averse to turning law libraries and witnesses upside down to prove a point.

Especially witnesses. Von Zamft looked forward to cross-examination the way a frog lies in ambush of a fly. It was his favorite way to spend an afternoon—in one-on-one combat with the human center-pieces of the State's case. Von Zamft, it was said, could turn a priest before the jury's eyes into a nearsighted, untrustworthy alcoholic, a task in which, alas, he frequently found little to challenge his intellect. Nothing got the brash attorney's adrenaline pumping like a good fight. And nothing ticked him off more than getting pinned to the mat. But Michael Von Zamft, more often than not, came out on top.

So it happened that at the age of thirty-eight the attorney's star was still spiraling upward, his position as chairman of the criminal justice arm of the Florida Bar Association earning him professional merit, and his four-year-old law practice earning him an increasingly comfortable living—one to which he felt entitled following nine zealous (and monetarily unfruitful) years spent as a public defender.

Von Zamft enjoyed career-long repute as a staunch defender of the underdog, a protector of individual rights. A firm and outspoken believer in the adversarial legal system, he perceived his role to be the noblest balance in the scales of justice—an advocate for the accused, who were, by law, innocent until proven guilty.

So strongly aligned with this particular cog in the justice machinery was Von Zamft as a law student that one of his professors encouraged him vigorously to serve his internship with the state attorney's office. Von Zamft had not the slightest interest in quarter-backing for the home team. He liked to fight, and he liked to win. But this was clearly not his game.

And though his cause was noble and his conviction firm, he was never mistaken for an idealist. The attorney viewed the world not with widened eyes of unguarded anticipation, but through a narrowed squint of cynicism. Everybody had an angle, the attorney believed. It was just a matter of time before he flushed it out.

Michael Von Zamft followed no rainbows.

And he reserved a special dislike for people who did.

Despite his fractious disposition, Von Zamft could count among his colleagues a healthy ration of friends and admirers. Jeffrey Samek was among those who considered himself a member of both clubs, he being possessed of a similar (though less abrasive) temperament and an uncommonly zealous pursuit of his advocacy role—a duty about which the two lawyers spoke often. With conviction.

Though Samek didn't enjoy the same measure of reverence paid Von Zamft's cunning courtroom maneuvering, he was, nonetheless, deemed a capable counselor of laudable professional comportment. Jeffrey Samek, it was said, handled himself like a gentleman, though, like Von Zamft, he could draw blood with his tongue if he chose. He just didn't go out of his way to do so. Thus, Samek was generally perceived the "nicer" of the pair.

But in the summer of 1984, Frank and Iliana Fuster didn't need a "nice" attorney. They needed one who could get them out of jail.

Frank turned to Jeffrey Samek, who had handled the (unsuccessful) appeal of his previous child molesting conviction.

Samek called in his friend Von Zamft.

". . . Jeffrey showed up and surrendered Frank, at which point I realized when the courtroom was packed with . . . the press and others that I found out—probably much later—were parents. . . .

"I am walking in when this happened. 'Say, what's going on? Why is this so big?' Being a semibright person, I realized that this is more than just a simple surrender of a guy on probation and caught on fast.

"I then got angry, which is my wont. I tend to get angry a lot. I used to be called the 'Last Angry Man.'

"I thought, 'Here's a guy who's shown that he has come in. He has surrendered. He is not running away. He is not hiding. Why can't we get him bond?'

"And they go through this whole thing, 'Well, he's a danger to his child.' And I said, 'Well, tell you what, judge, I'll bring the child in Monday, surrender him, let them examine the child. Let's get all that done and then, when they say there is nothing wrong with the child, get bond.' . . . That's what I essentially agreed to do that Monday. . . .

"I'll bring in Jaime, show that he was OK—because as far as I knew, everything was fine—and then, once we showed everything was all right, then there would be no reason to deny a bond because he's not a danger to somebody.

"I may be a little naive, but I didn't know what was going on in the case. I didn't know that we had half of a development called Country Walk upset. I didn't even know there was a Country Walk.

"It's not my kind of housing area. I wouldn't live out there.

"Frank got surrendered and was taken in. Jeff and I, we probably talked about it for a while, at which point he and I agreed we were going to handle the probation violation. . . .

"What we knew at the time was the guy had a house and his family was going to try to help. We knew that he had a business. So, we said, 'What the hell—probation violation. How bad can it be?' . . ."

Samek and Von Zamft waltzed smugly through the first few weeks; their clients were innocent, their crimes alleged. Then Jaime Fuster tested positive for gonorrhea of the throat, a circumstance that threw a dangerous curve into the smooth road they had envisioned before them. The State now demanded that the court order the Fusters tested in the same manner as the children had been.

Samek objected vigorously.

Von Zamft fairly roared. "That's going to require the taking of a swab and/or a catheter," he said, pacing furiously before the judicial backdrop, "and *placing* it inside the *head* of the penis of Mr. Fuster.

"There is *no way* that Mr. Laeser can tell this court that that's not intrusive into his body."

Judge Robert Newman offered a compromise, as he would through the course of the case, suggesting that a blood test would perhaps remedy both the State's quest for evidence and the defendants' bodily rights. The State agreed, ignorant of the fact that the disease it hoped to find residing in the Fusters could not be detected in the bloodstream. They were obliged to convene for a second time to refight the "battle of the swabs." The State's subsequent victory would visit briefly, then evaporate when the test results returned bearing an unwelcome proclamation: Frank and Iliana would test free of venereal disease.

Some of the parents attending the hearings bristled in mouth-gaping disbelief that the defense could speak of "intrusion" after what their children had been subjected to, a sentiment they conveyed to a sea of reporters outside the courtroom. Von Zamft spat back his reply, which was duly reported on the evening news.

"The *alleged* victims did it by choice," he pointed out. "We're talking about being forced to do it. I don't know about you, sir, but if I were going to have it done to me, I'd want to at least have a choice.

"If somebody's gonna hold me down and bend me over and stick their finger up my rectum, I want to have a choice about it. You may enjoy that.

"I don't."

The parents listened, speechless. They did not expect to grow fond of this man.

Jeffrey Samek and Michael Von Zamft had limited avenues available to them that the counsel of an accused child molester might tread should his client wish to take the matter to trial.

As the Fusters most assuredly would.

For Frank and Iliana remained resolute in their protests of innocence—he, the outraged (and persecuted) Cuban "businessman," and she, his devoted (and seemingly bewildered) wife.

Neither claimed to imagine what circumstance might have inspired the children to say "these terrible things" about them. It appeared increasingly improbable that either would become willing to strike a bargain for a plea of guilty, should the State become so inclined.

Frank's most-favored phrase, "I am *one hundred percent* innocent-of-these-charges," came with growing frequency and conviction. His wife was no less possessed of an apparently clear conscience.

"I could never hurt a child," she said sweetly. And often.

It was generally considered by the State that Frank was likely to wear his mantle of innocence well into the hereafter—a belief bolstered by the profile they began to construct from the pieces of his past.

Iliana, on the other hand, was eyed covetously as a possible trump card that might someday salvage a losing hand—or enhance the odds on a good one. It was not inconceivable that a few months of enforced severance from her husband—spent in the privacy of her cell at the Women's Detention Center—might prove inspirational to Iliana's memory of events the children said had occurred.

She just might sing.

This, of course, promised an expedient resolution to what might otherwise become an unwieldly emotional, legal, and political process—a major child sex abuse trial.

Something both sides eventually aspired to avoid.

But neither the State nor the defense knew enough of Iliana to predict her future whims.

They knew only that the self-possessed young woman who announced her age to the parents as twenty-one, twenty-three, and twenty-five, and to the court as twenty-two, was, in fact, seventeen.

A circumstance that sent Von Zamft and Samek scurrying before a judge into whose hands they triumphantly deposited a Honduran birth certificate that announced in Spanish that the girl-child Iliana Flores had arrived on the 28th day of November, 1966. That made her, by their calculations, three-and-a-half months too young to have been charged with a capital felony.

The State has made a grievous error, they told the court. Dismiss the counts of capital sexual battery against her and transfer the remaining lewd and lascivious violations to the juvenile system for appropriate dispensation.

This, however, did not coincide with the State's plans for Iliana, it being somewhat reluctant to relinquish the minimum mandatory twenty-five-year sentence attached to each life count. Nor was it at all enamored of the idea that the felonious babysitter would be incarcerated with the wayward shoplifters and runaways of Youth Hall—a child molester among children.

If it please the court, Christopher Rundle interjected into the proceedings, the young lady in question—on more than one occasion—had sworn before this court that she was twenty-two years of age. Let the capital felonies stand.

Judge Robert Newman did.

It no doubt occurred to Frank Fuster that his seventeen-year-old illegal-alien bride might not share his supreme confidence in the foibles of the American justice system, which, he felt sure, would soon release them both with apology for having inconvenienced them in this way. Iliana, he decided, must be kept continuously apprised of this eventuality, lest she mistake the State's elaborate charade for a serious intent to take this matter to trial.

Frank launched an impressive letter campaign to woo his wife's continued faith and allegiance. His pen caressed each page with unrestrained terms of endearment, which reminisced of "the bond" they shared for eternity. So great was his husbandly worship that the letters attesting to it grew to a volume measurable in pounds, not pages.

"God," Frank wrote to Iliana, "would prove" them innocent. For only "God" knew the "purity" of their union.

His child bride responded with no less effusive a display of boundless affection, the gist of her fervent replies centering on the recurring theme, "I adore you, I need you, I love you, I want you. Forever."

Iliana wrote her beloved spouse four to five letters daily, beginning the first as she rose from bed ("I wake up thinking of you . . .") and closing the last before retiring with a similar sentiment.

On the 24th day of September, 1984, Iliana Fuster dispatched to her husband's cell—a distance of a block and two buildings from her own—warmest wishes on this, the first anniversary of their wedding.

Four weeks in jail had apparently not caused Iliana to reevaluate the "purity" of their union, nor had it dampened her apparent enthusiasm for her spouse.

"For My Husband," read the salutation on the front of a card that pictured, on its cover, a pair of candlelit champagne glasses.

Inside, a printed message announced:

Here's to
the most beautiful moments
in my life . . .
the moments
I spend with you!
Happy Anniversary
with Love

Unconvinced that the card company's hired poet had conveyed the depths of her affections, Iliana penned, in her own cursive hand, a series of messages designated by Roman numeral to be read in a fixed sequence.

Not to escape the attention of prosecutors at a later date was the curious fact that this (and the majority of communications between the couple) was written in English—a most unexpected choice of language for two people who would later request a Spanish translator to aid them in a pretrial hearing.

Nonetheless, it was in laborious, fractured English that Iliana came to sing the praises of her love:

Happy Anniversary, Alma de mi vida [love of my life].

I. Now is not me who's written this words, but my heart that is also your heart.

II. Thank you honey!! for made me your wife! I love you . . . very much. God love both of us . . . and he'll united us again and this time forever. . . .

III. You are everything in my life, because:
    you're good
    "   "   sincere
    "   "   love me
    "   "   wonderful
    "   "   the best husband in the planet
    "   "   the best father
    "   "   "   "   human being and God knows it . . . honey,
    that's enough for us to be happy and live with him, in
    him, for the rest of our life.

IV. GOD BLESS YOU!
    Your wife with love,
    Iliana Fuster.

Only time would tell if Iliana's ardor could withstand her equally strident survival instincts, which were—according to psychiatrists who examined her for mental defect—remarkably well developed. One of the men who explored Iliana's mind affixed to her a label that grew more meaningful in the months ahead.

Iliana Fuster, he decided, was a "chameleon."

Each of the letters that passed between the Fusters during their incarceration eventually found its way into the State's grateful hands.

Samek and Von Zamft issued increasingly distressed directives to their clients to cease and desist in their written communications, warning that their words could (and would) be used against them at a later time and place—a prophecy that, for one of the Fusters, would someday be fulfilled.

Still, the letters continued.

The couple's bond was no less rigorously maintained during occasional "contact" visits, in which Frank showered his child bride with tender attentions, which she eagerly reciprocated in a glass booth under the watchful eye of a guard.

During their frequent court appearances, seated in the jury box (according to pretrial custom) where a panel of six men and women would someday sit in judgment of their alleged crime, the couple exchanged affectionate glances and an occasional note.

The bond appeared not the least bit frayed. Both continued to maintain their own—and each other's—absolute innocence, even as the State continued to assemble the evidence with which it hoped to prove, beyond any reasonable doubt, that they were not.

• • •

Samek and Von Zamft could march down one of two mutually exclusive roads to acquittal. One acknowledged the crime, and the other did not.

But both strategies relied on the defense's ability to discredit the only witnesses to the crime, the oldest of whom had not yet seen his sixth birthday.

Counsel for the defense could offer one of two explanations to the jury as to how their clients came to be charged with this "most unfortunate" kind of crime:

1. Misidentification of the suspects (the children may have been

abused by someone, but not the Fusters), or

2. It didn't happen (the alleged sex acts were the figment of the children's—or someone else's—imagination).

Under ideal circumstances, from a defense standpoint (absence of physical evidence and the presence of a single child witness), either strategy afforded fertile ground in which to plant the seeds of reasonable doubt—the only burden the defense was expected to bear. But in the case of Country Walk, Jaime Fuster's gonorrhea and the sheer number of eyewitnesses to the crime (young as they might have been) tended to obstruct at least partially either escape hatch open to Frank and Iliana's zealous defenders.

The Fusters' son was unlikely to have become infected if the crime had not occurred, nor would more than a dozen small fingers have been likely to point collectively to the wrong man and woman if, in fact, it had.

The first defied common logic, the latter common sense.

Still, the incongruity between the evidence and the Fusters' staunch denials was not, in itself, an insurmountable gap to bridge, should the jury's attention be drawn successfully from contemplating too seriously these irreconcilable circumstances.

The obvious remedy was trial by diversion.

The facts of the case did not necessarily have to get in the way of a well-orchestrated and strategic smoke screen, the most viable and historically successful being "It didn't happen."

But if Samek and Von Zamft were to suggest to a jury that the rapes "didn't happen," they were obliged to offer a reasonable explanation as to how numerous otherwise unrelated children came to say that it did.

They appeared not the least concerned.

• • •

The office from which Janet Reno labored to dispense with assaults on the peace and dignity of the people of the state of Florida was a cavernous den—a space as cold as it was austere.

The floor was uncarpeted, adding an even colder, more vast dimension to the sparsely dressed work space that she had furnished in a style best described as "Early Functional."

A massive desk, behind which the state attorney conducted her business, occupied the center of the room. The desk's polished surface bore only items of essential faculty, maintained in meticulous order. Not a paperclip strayed from its assigned berth.

Two chairs stood at attention before the desk, a matched pair of sufficient discomfort to discourage any visitor who might otherwise be inclined to take up too much of Janet Reno's carefully allotted time.

Behind the desk, within the state attorney's lanky range, a credenza displayed a treasured collection of trophies and awards. Accolades she accepted, more times than not, with head slightly bowed to conceal a sheepish grin. Reno didn't like to flaunt her thrill of victory.

A dark blue cap, emblazoned "Reno's Raiders," dangled from a silver trophy awarded to the office softball team. This, and a few malnourished shrubs, lent the room not even a modest air of warmth. For the only warmth in Janet Reno's office came from the photographs displayed on her desk—pictures of nieces and nephews to whom their spinster aunt was deeply attached.

Janet Reno liked children, though she was destined never to have any of her own. And it was with particular disregard that she held anyone who caused them harm.

So it was not entirely unexpected that she might expend considerable energies to place Frank and Iliana Fuster behind bars, though there were other factors that may have heightened her resolve.

An election loomed ominously on the horizon, and though the state attorney preferred to run a subdued campaign, Country Walk had thrust her office into the limelight, in microscopic view of the registered voters.

It was a case tailored to make or break elections.

And Janet Reno liked being state attorney.

Reno was appointed to (and made her presence felt in) every task force and panel that had been created to caulk the cracks through which the Fusters had slipped into the daycare system, most notably the county task force that tried to hammer together an emergency ordinance that would require fingerprinting of all daycare workers. Some task force members called the proposed background checks "overkill." Reno called it inadequate, pointing out that the measure didn't provide for checks on crimes outside the state of Florida.

"This ordinance will not reveal if that person has three priors for DUI and he's been driving the kids around. It will not reveal that he has a sexual battery past in the state of New York. It will not reveal a number of things.

"And for the person who has no priors—or has had his record expunged for some reason or other—it won't reveal *that*."

At each of these meetings, Reno was dogged relentlessly by a bank of outstretched media microphones into which she was persistently invited to spit the progress of her star case.

A circumstance in which the state attorney would fix the would-be interviewers with a stony, bespectacled stare, set her angular jaw, and offer the concise rejoinder, "I will do everything humanly possible to see that justice is done."

Janet Reno could promise no more. Because she had come to find in her prosecutorial career that "everything humanly possible" had not been enough, in too many instances, to secure justice on behalf of the victims of an illogical crime that, by nature, produced little unspoken evidence. And the only ones who could speak what they knew had recently worn diapers.

It was an almost-perfect crime.

No more encouraging was the state of the investigation itself. Neither the police nor the prosecutors had ever been confronted with a crime of such sweeping magnitude in which a period of covert surveillance to gather evidence had been ruled out of the question. The urgency to remove the children at risk overshadowed evidentiary imperative.

So the State was running a little heavier on victims than it was on physical evidence. The tapes, among other possible "smoking guns," had apparently departed among the boxes Judy Prince had watched (and reported) being loaded into the mysterious white van the day before Frank's arrest. But the search warrant had produced a few seemingly innocuous items that the Fusters might someday regret having overlooked in their hastily assembled search-and-destroy mission—among them, a nauseating recent photograph of Jaime Fuster sitting on a toilet, the floor surrounding him smeared thickly and thoroughly with excrement. Jaime's expression was pained.

His father took the picture, Jaime would later tell the Doctors Braga. For what purpose, he said, he didn't know.

There were other pictures from the Fusters' "family" photo album to which a jury's attention would be drawn. None were individually damning, though their collective content was expected to serve as a reminder to six randomly selected citizens of Dade County that the defendants' thought processes were in no way similar to their own.

These, and the laboratory culture in which mucus from Jaime

Fuster's throat had caused to grow a venereal disease, represented the most potentially damaging imperfections in the almost-perfect crime.

The children's scars, which might have proved the most resounding indictment, couldn't be erased like the incriminating tapes. But neither were they readily visible.

So it came to be grasped quickly by both the prosecution and the defense that it was the words of the children that would beat at the heart of the case—their word against Frank and Iliana's. And there were those who intended that the children's words not be heard.

Janet Reno began digging foxholes, preparing for what was shaping into one of the least promising legal dogfights of her career.

• • •

The media staked out the Metro Justice Building, coveting any scrap of information that might waft out of the mysterious suite of offices that had suddenly appeared on the ninth floor, future site of the soon-to-be-relocated sexual battery unit. For it was from this suite that arrest warrants for the sexual abuse of children were being issued at an historically significant rate.

The suite was composed of four functional units. An outer, plant-draped reception area led to an elongated waiting room, roughly the shape and depth of two bowling lanes, side by side. From there, a choice of two doors could lead to a private office equipped with a one-way-mirrored view of the adjacent interview room to which the remaining door directly led. On the far side of this most noteworthy cubicle had been built another, more impressive, one-way mirror, which concealed from the room's visitors a control room occupied by a small electronic arsenal and one video technician.

The room wore its purpose.

Warm pastels glowed from the walls, while primary colors leapt from the pictures and posters that hung from them like dazzling accessories. A stuffed fabric macaw paused in mid-flight on a perch that hung from the ceiling. Across the room, a life-sized toucan swung above a child-sized table and four tiny chairs.

And there were rainbows everywhere.

No doubt, the Bragas were in residence.

On a wall down the corridor from this unprecedented addition to the drab halls of justice was placed a black plastic marker on which was inscribed "State Attorney's Center for Children," an ambitious designation for the hastily assembled nursery/interview facility, but a promising one nonetheless.

For the seeds planted at Apogee one morning in late July (could it have been only five weeks ago?) had taken root at the very top of the Metro Justice Building, where they were beginning to sprout under the watchful eye of Joe and Laurie Braga, the happy farmers.

It was the foundation for the annex through which child victims could enter the justice system without fear of further harm. It was a facility that told the children they were important enough to warrant a special place in which to talk about being small and afraid and confused about the world. It told them that other children had been there before them.

That they weren't alone.

The children needed such a place, the Bragas had told the state attorney. And Janet Reno had agreed. But then it was a pipe dream. Now it was a necessity. The State found itself ill-equipped to deal with the bundle of child victims that had been dumped unceremoniously in its lap.

Give us the space, said Joe and Laurie. And our foundation will donate to the State the necessary equipment.

The State could not accept gifts, Reno replied. But it could accept the equipment on loan until the funding was secured to replace it.

Agreed, said the Bragas. Consider it on permanent loan.

Reno waved her imposing wand, and within twenty-four hours of her request the last brush of paint was laid and the last piece of electronics installed.

When Janet Reno wanted something done, it was. And the state attorney wanted an interview facility for children.

The magnificent suite was a far cry from Abe Laeser's floor, which had absorbed so many spilled Cokes and potato chip crumbs over the course of the first few days that the Bragas had declared it a public health hazard and demanded either the carpet be cleaned or a new area located.

The interviews were moved up to the ninth-floor investigations unit, where the Doctors Braga took up temporary residence on the floor of the conference-room-sized office of George "Ray" Havens, chief of investigations for the Dade state attorney's office. The Chief, as most everyone in the building felt compelled to call him, was away on vacation at the time, so he was not apprised of the startling new developments at his place of work.

The morning he returned to find a couple of [what looked to him like] "hippies" presiding over his office space, he decided that Janet Reno had taken leave of her sanity in his brief absence.

There were kids everywhere and a man with a ponytail holding hands with a woman whose hair cascaded all the way down the back of her unshaven legs.

The Chief shook his head in disbelief. Now he'd seen everything.

Then he saw them talk to the children.

14

By September, the Bragas had become the talk of the Eleventh Judicial Circuit.

In the beginning, the quiet whisperings in the corridors and noisy speculation in the break rooms centered on numerous perceived eccentricities of the small, ponytailed man who strode purposefully through the building as though he held its deed and the quiet woman constantly at his side who radiated calm.

But it was their appearance, not manner, that sparked most of the initial Braga controversy. Joe and Laurie's hair was a topic of intense interest and debate among the building's inhabitants, the latter's shaggy legs generating even more discussion than the five-foot mane she generally roped and pinned into a bun atop her head.

Their wardrobe ran a close second as the most popular subject of scrutiny, Joe's conservative but dated three-piece suits, Mickey Mouse ties, and Snoopy briefcase commanding less vigorous attention than Laurie's vintage sixties pastel minidresses and thick, brown leather sandals from which her bare toes protruded quite visibly.

The Bragas, not oblivious to the stirrings and buzzings about them, became both amused and bewildered that anyone would devote such energetic interest to their existence. Having spent much of the past decade conducting their daily lives either in the Coconut Grove melting pot (where extraterrestrials were unlikely to warrant more than a passing glance) or in daycare centers (where the children were more likely to relate to their warmth than to their attire), Joe and Laurie had come to wear their "difference" so comfortably that it tended to startle them on the rare occasions when people from outside their world visibly regarded them as "otherworldly."

They just couldn't see what all the fuss was about.

Christina Royo wasn't one to stick her neck out for strangers, though her job required that she lay her life on the line for the faceless people of the state of Florida each and every day.

Christina was a cop. More precisely, she was an investigator for the Dade state attorney's office, reporting to Chief George "Ray" Havens—a distinction for which she had turned in her municipal police uniform two years past.

Though outwardly conservative, the twenty-eight-year-old detective harbored a quiet tolerance for the packages in which people came wrapped, her own being somewhat "different." She was, she liked to remind people, a "triple minority," being a Hispanic female of olive skin and short curly hair that could be coaxed—should the occasion warrant—into cornrows.

Christina had prowled along the edges of the Country Walk investigation almost from the outset, her ear having captured the murmurings in the hall outside her door, which spoke of children and deviant babysitters—and something called "the Bragas," whatever that was. Her curiosity sufficiently piqued, Investigator Royo engaged her antennae and set off to find further facts. She paid casual visits to the areas not far from her office door, where interviews were being conducted and tapes reviewed. She was awed, if such an expression could be applied to someone who displayed openly so limited an emotional range. Christina played life like poker, with a regulation deck and a suspicious eye on the other players. Just because she played by the rules didn't mean she expected anyone else would. She played her own cards close to her chest—as a matter of personal choice and professional demeanor.

That was about to change. Inwardly, at least.

Christina searched out further facts. She listened with deceptive disinterest and mounting irritation to lunchtime banter about the goings-on in the sexual battery unit, around which the entire office had come to revolve. Restless waves of speculation rippled from floor to floor. The mysterious suite of offices and its enigmatic occupants marked a dramatic departure from the comfortably routine procedures under which the system had functioned for eternity. "Outsiders" had been given a parking space and the well-guarded combination of numbers that opened the electronic doors—the ones that shielded the machinations of justice from the rest of the world.

Never before had Christina seen Janet Reno's kingdom so rife with impassioned controversy. Who were these people? Where did they come from?

Surely the state attorney had gone mad, suggested some.

"They look weird."

"They dress weird."

"They act weird."

"They hold *hands*," noted several in a tone that suggested the commission of a second-degree felony. And they addressed each other as "beloved," not "honey" or "dear."

They waltzed past protocols with maddening guileless grace. When the mood (and pertinent business) arose, they gave not a thought to dropping in on the state attorney's sixth-floor suite to inquire of her secretary, "Can the boss spare a minute?" For the Doctors Braga, she usually could.

The rumor mill churned out conflicting reports that "the visitors" must be either very important or very rude. Or perhaps they had not noticed that only Reno's circlet of chief assistants dared intrude on the master suite without benefit of appointment or invitation.

Christina, herself, had not in two years found occasion to cross the threshold into Janet Reno's cold and tidy den.

The investigator was intrigued, though not as mystified as some of her co-workers, because she had glimpsed beyond the hair and eccentricities and was beginning to sense what this highly irregular circumstance was all about. Still, she, too, was curious about the couple. Why didn't Laurie shave her legs? Why didn't Joe cut his hair? Not being one to beat about the bush at any length, Christina finally posed her questions point-blank.

Laurie didn't shave her legs because she had better things to do with her time and energies, she replied. And Joe didn't cut his hair because Laurie held her own for ransom. Neither was enamored of wearing the hair, Joe explained, but each had committed it to the other.

Reasonably satisfied that the couple's packaging posed no clear or inherent threat, Christina found herself, for some inexplicable reason, defending the strangers. "What difference does it make if they're green with purple polka dots? Come see what they're doing with the children."

And they did.

Word spread. Police, prosecutors, and investigators trickled in increasing numbers to the suite of offices in which the couple who "talked to the children" were getting answers in explicit and irrefutable detail.

"What did he do then?"

"He peed in my mouth."

"Did it taste bad or good?"

"Tasted *yuk!* I spit it out."

"Was his penis hard or soft?"

"Hard."

The visitors would leave shaking their heads. Their horror over what these "babies" had been subjected to was exceeded only by their certain and professional knowledge that the people who did this stood an even chance of walking out of a courtroom hand in hand, free to seek out another place where men and women were in need of safe and convenient childcare.

These children could not withstand systematic dissection on the stand with Frank and Iliana Fuster staring a hole into them from a distance of five yards, of that the visitors were sure. Equally certain were they that a jury would never see the tapes of the Bragas' interviews, which had captured the children's poignant moments of first disclosure. The tapes were compelling. Even haunting at times.

But the law wouldn't allow a jury to see them. The tapes were considered hearsay—statements made outside a courtroom, un-riddled by the rituals of jurisprudence. A defendant could not be improperly prejudiced.

Even by the truth.

Still, some of those who visited the State Attorney's Center for Children began to note the prosecutorial possibilities opening before them. They began routing their smallest victims to the ninth floor instead of out the door.

It was during the first frenzied days of Country Walk that an earnest young assistant state attorney approached the good doctors with an apologetic request. He wondered if they might find the time to interview a brother and sister who had, according to the physical evidence and the boy's statements, apparently been raped by a friend of the family.

James and Katie Evans had been left for three days in the care of neighbors, when their mother checked into a local hospital to give birth to her third illegitimate child. The babysitters—corpulent twin brothers—frequently volunteered their services to grateful mothers who inhabited the poverty-stricken Anglo-Hispanic South Miami Beach neighborhood where welfare checks paid the rent on rat-infested rooms with hot plates.

The Scribner brothers did not charge for their services, money not being as gratifying to them as the small and tempting bundles delivered to their care. They were always glad, they said, to help out a neighbor.

Upon her release from the hospital, the mother discovered from her son that the children's stay with the Scribner brothers had amounted to one continuous sexual assault.

They were brought to Chief Havens's office, where Laurie joined them on the floor. A week of hearing Country Walk children tell tales of the Fusters was not sufficiently numbing to blunt the impact of the Evans/Scribner odyssey. These children knew no polite words for what had been done to them, Laurie would remember, even in future years, with a blush.

Four-year-old Katie, who peered at the world through lenses as thick as the bottom of a soft-drink bottle, was borderline mentally retarded, but her words were crisp and clear as she described how one of the men tried to make James "suck his dick."

"I told him, 'Leave my brother alone,' " she said. " 'I'll do it for him.' "

And she did.

But that bought her six-year-old brother only a temporary reprieve, as became apparent when he described being sodomized at knifepoint several times by both brothers, who encouraged a thirteen-year-old neighbor boy to do the same.

They held the knife to his throat and threatened to slit it if he told.

"Did he put anything on his penis before he put it in?" asked Laurie.

"Yes."

"What?"

"Vaseline."

A subsequent investigation revealed the existence of a South Beach child sex ring in which "chicken hawks" like the Scribners preyed on unattended neighborhood children, often bartering candy bars, drugs, and motorcycle rides in exchange for sexual favors. Kids were swapped and traded among them. This circumstance, being not uncommon in poverty pockets throughout the community, and being incidental to the investigation of the Scribner/Evans affair, was determined not worthy of the resources it would require to clean up the neighborhood. Keeping the twin hippopotami out of circulation for a while would be an accomplishment in itself. Preferably without the expense and uncertainty of a trial.

Twenty-six-year-old William Scribner, charged with five counts of sexual battery and one of lewd and lascivious assault, eventually pled guilty to one count and was sentenced to life in prison, with a minimum mandatory twenty-five years to be served.

His twin brother, Edgar, charged with two counts of sexual battery and one of lewd and lascivious assault, pled guilty to the lesser charge, punishable by a maximum of five years in prison.

For the repeated rape of James and Katie Evans, he would, in all likelihood, serve less than two.

• • •

"Utter chaos" would most kindly describe the state of Chris Rundle's world in the days following the arrests of Frank and Iliana Fuster.

Every phone line to the sexual battery unit stayed permanently lit. The patch of paper shingles next to his desk, which flagged his "priority" case files, fanned out in an ever-widening circle, threatening to engulf the wall. Reporters lay in wait to ambush him on the way to the soft-drink machine. His clothing rumpled from workdays that ran through the night, Rundle had little appetite for the Betacams that followed him through the corridors.

He felt grubby and worn. His brow furrowed over reddened eyes, which had been robbed of their mischievous glint, either by fatigue or by the nightcaps that had helped him find sleep the night before. Country Walk was an albatross tied firmly to his neck in a hangman's noose.

The case was a nightmare. Two defendants—a sociopathic pervert and a bride, who might or might not be of legal age; two "kid shrinks," who presented a curious appearance, but who otherwise seemed to know what they were doing; fifty-odd stunned and angry parents, who might or might not continue to cooperate with him once they regained their senses; and three dozen children, some of them now residing in other states, most of them too young to set foot in a courtroom, anyway.

And then the floodgates opened.

Sex abuse cases began pouring into the State Attorney's Center for Children at an astonishing rate, spawned in part by the reopening of HRS case files that had as much as six months earlier been declared clinically dead. In an effort to salvage the state's credibility in the wake of its agencies' incredulous role in the debacle of Country Walk, the governor ordered a special team to sweep through Florida, reinvestigating every child sex abuse complaint that had been deemed unfounded in the year 1984.

There commenced a rattling of Pandora's box.

The lid, like the HRS case files, became unsealed. A growing number of "unfounded" cases were discovered, upon closer inspection, to be very founded indeed.

If the children happened to reside in Dade County, they were brought to the Bragas, who now juggled fifteen-hour days between new cases and the incoming wounded that continued to arrive via interstate from a place called Country Walk. There would be more than one hundred before the year was done.

Janet Reno eyed the human carnage washed so conspicuously up on her shore and declared child sexual abuse cases the number one priority in her domain. Rundle issued a distress call. He needed more bodies. More help.

The state attorney siphoned prosecutors out of other divisions into the sexual battery unit—on temporary loan. Chris Rundle received additional clerical help. The Bragas were given a receptionist and a full-time video technician who doubled as nursemaid for the children while the doctors conferred with parents and prosecutors.

If he needed anything else, The Boss told her sexual battery chief, he had only to ask.

Rundle was little consoled, having flown by the seat of his pants since August ninth on blind and tenuous faith. He hoped The Boss and the Bragas knew what they were doing. Because if they didn't, Frank and Iliana Fuster would stroll off into the sunset—a vision too paralyzing for him to contemplate.

The Bragas didn't appear to share the prosecutor's dark and doubtful perspective. They realized the problems that lay ahead, they told Rundle, but frontiers weren't blazed without effort.

Rundle hinted at ominous clouds on the horizon. "You two don't know how the law works," he pronounced with disturbing conviction.

Then teach us, they replied. Teach us about the law, and we'll teach you about children.

It was agreed.

• • •

Though Christopher Rundle found little time to take advantage of the proffered crash course in child development, Deputy Chief Abe Laeser drank deeply from the well of knowledge the Bragas brought each day, returning to refill his cup often, a man consumed by unquenchable thirst. He devoured every word they had ever written—books, articles, voluminous vitae. He picked their brains into the night.

Rundle's boss began to perceive the bridge the Bragas were attempting to construct between the children and the law. And though they knew little of the law, he saw they had intuitively grasped its processes.

The defense, they suggested to Laeser, will build its case around us. We will be the targets, because we are the only common denominator between the children other than the Fusters. That is the posture being taken in the mass abuse cases all over the country. The attorneys for the abusers are crucifying the people who talk to the children. That's what's happening right now in California and Minnesota and Nevada and New York and West Point. That's what's happening in the big cases all over the country.

"Jurors are uncomfortable with the whole idea of children being raped," said Joe. "They would rather believe that it didn't happen, so anybody that gives them an excuse—they'll accept that."

"Because people's initial reaction," interjected Laurie, "when all the publicity started coming out about the amount of sexual abuse that existed in the country, people's reaction was, 'It can't possibly be that widespread.' Especially when the accused can't be picked out of a crowd.

"If the accused is a policeman or a banker or a teacher, that's very upsetting, because that puts them in the uncomfortable position of not knowing who to trust."

Amid that kind of inner conflict, they pointed out, reasonable doubt is not difficult to cultivate. A jury would rather believe that the five-year-old witness tripped over the living room sofa and impaled herself on a toy than that the nice-looking family man seated at the defense table raped her, as she had testified.

Traditionally, the defense used to trot out "experts" who would testify that, "of course, everyone knows that children are inherently untrustworthy fantasizers." Bolstering this argument, they would invoke Freud and speak of "seductive" behavior and oedipal urges, claiming that the children's accounts arose from their fantasies of having sex with their parents.

Juries weren't as quick to buy that anymore. And now that cases were surfacing involving multiple victims, it was necessary for the defense to sell the idea that the interviewers had caused the children to deliver these unwanted messages.

It was the only way to explain to a jury how numerous children might have come to tell the same graphic "lie."

That was one of the reasons, the Bragas continued, that they had insisted that their interviews be videotaped. That was also the reason they never spoke to a child without the camera to record it.

Each time they reviewed a tape with Laeser, they explained the methodology behind the interview process. It was then that Abe Laeser began to perceive the scientific method behind the Bragas' madness.

15

"Mommy, are you supposed to eat shit?"

Maggie froze in her tracks, braced for the revelation sure to follow her four-year-old daughter's unusual query. "No, you're not," she said evenly, trying to still the tremor that rose in her throat.

"Well, Frank and Iliana made me eat shit," Crystal informed her, as though the item consumed were a least favorite breakfast cereal, not human waste.

Maggie was no longer astonished by her daughter's disclosures about life in the Fuster home. Just nauseated. Crystal's spontaneous recollections, though infrequent, sketched a portrait of terror and degradation Maggie couldn't begin to comprehend.

"They would poo-poo and rub the ca-ca in their hands and face," continued Crystal. "Then we had to eat it."

This Maggie noted for dispatch to the State, another piece to be added to the grotesque puzzle of the Fusters. She now knew from her daughter that Frank would put groups of children in the bathtub and "pee" on them. He would chase Crystal wearing horror masks, brandishing a knife "this big," Crystal had said, extending her hands two feet apart—a description that matched an instrument that some of the other children had called a "sword" or a "saw." When he caught her, he would hold the knife to her neck and ask if she wanted to die, if she would be the first to lose her head. Then he would threaten to cut off her nose. Once, said Crystal, Frank pushed his finger up her rectum while Iliana and another man (whom she identified as one of Frank's relatives) stuck their fingers inside her vagina. Three adults and one small and frightened child. On the floor. "Always on the floor," said Crystal.

Maggie trained herself not to visualize the pictures her daughter painted. The visuals, she knew, could push her over the edge.

189

The Orange Bowl blazed in the night sky with the radiance of a hundred million candles, from the distance a glowing monolith ascended by a multitude of ants who clamored to behold the man who wore a single glittered glove.

"Michael! Michael! Michael!" the faithful chanted as one.

Maggie and Peyton Fletcher hurried from their car toward the arena, each firmly gripping one of four-year-old Crystal's hands as the child bounced excitedly between them.

The concert was about to begin.

"Michael! Michael! Michael!" The decibels rose to a hazardous din as the Fletchers passed through the stadium gates. Suddenly, the night fell black and the crowd silent. Michael Jackson rose with the stage, the first strains from "Thriller" heralding his entrance.

Crystal screamed and tore herself loose from her parents' hands before Maggie and Peyton could react. Their daughter ran from the stadium into the night. Her sturdy legs, pumping frantically, carried her nearly a block before her astounded father closed in and plucked her off the ground.

Crystal was hysterical.

Lt. Peyton Fletcher looked into his daughter's eyes and beheld the most consummate terror he'd ever witnessed. He would see it many times more, whenever his daughter encountered a clown or anything else that wore a mask. Hours passed before Crystal's sobs were stilled and she fell into a fitful and exhausted sleep.

What had frightened her? they asked. The noise? The crowd? The darkness?

The music, she replied. That was the music Frank and Iliana played when they put on the "maskets."

• • •

Chad Herschel bustled about the playroom, preparing a feast in Missy's toy kitchen. He held a small plastic dish on which he had placed one of his stuffed animals, which he told his sister was "the little bird" they would have for dinner.

"First we do this to the bird," he instructed, pretending to cut the "bird" with a plastic knife. "Then we put it in the oven and bake it."

Chad placed the dish that held the "bird" into the oven. "Then," he continued, "we put the bird in the freezer, and then we freeze it."

His mother watched silently from the doorway as Chad replayed the ritual he had told her he saw performed in the Fuster home. The killing of the animals was among her three-year-old son's most vivid recollections—the snake laid across the kitchen counter and pulverized with a screwdriver, the birds maimed by a knife, blood and life flowing from their bodies as they writhed in a dance with death.

No experience in Shari's life had prepared her to deal with the events of the past few months. The Herschels were in crisis.

For the first few days, Shari closeted herself in her bedroom in sedated isolation. But even chemical comfort eluded her. She felt like something very precious had been taken from her son: his sense of trust, his sense of self. It was like a part of him (and her) had died. She couldn't begin to speculate on what the future held for a little boy so touched by the dark side of humanity.

Her thoughts often turned to Missy, who continued to deny that anything out of the ordinary had occurred during her two visits of approximately five hours each to the Fuster home. She watched *Conan the Barbarian* with Frank in the den, the little girl had told the detective. Days later, she told the Bragas much the same, adding that Frank had pinched her thigh. She would say no more.

Shari remembered the night Iliana had called and urged her to bring her daughter, then four, more often. Missy was such a wonderful little girl, so well behaved, so helpful, Iliana told her. In fact, Iliana continued, she would be happy to care for Missy without charge.

Please, God, not my daughter, too.

Shari shoved the emotions deeper and deeper inside, fearing the breakdown that might occur if she allowed them to surface. But the compartment to which she willed them began to fill, until they had no place else to go. Within days, Shari began to hemorrhage. She was hospitalized. Finding no physical cause for his patient's internal disorder, her doctor dispatched a psychiatrist to her bedside, who proceeded to tell her to get her rear end home and take care of her family. When Shari sputtered an explanation about what was going on in her life, the doctor told her he wasn't interested in hearing her problems and delivered a lecture about pulling oneself up by one's bootstraps.

Fury having replaced despair, Shari packed her bags and checked out of the hospital.

Chad went into a two-month tailspin. The old fears and nightmares revisited, mingled intermittently with a rage no longer bottled. He would talk of Frank and Iliana with increasing agitation until he spun completely out of control, pounding pillows and throwing toys as his mother and father tried desperately to calm him.

The Herschel home became a battlefield. Tension assumed a physical presence as Shari and Tom, nerves drawn and torn, fought and snapped over matters of little consequence. Missy hovered near the sidelines, a silent and terrified witness to her family's disintegration. Some secrets, she decided, were best not told.

In the beginning, Shari and Tom had only a vague sense of what the babysitters had done to their son, Chad having offered only that Frank and Iliana had "hurt" his bottom and private parts. Gradually, he disclosed additional bits and pieces of information. One day, he deposited a bowel movement on the floor, informing Shari that this was the expected method of defecation in the Fuster home. Another time, he told Shari about a "duckie" that Iliana tried to push into his rectum as she gave him a bath.

The Herschels requested that the Bragas conduct a second interview with their son.

Chad ignored Laurie's questions as he raced around the room in perpetual motion. Laurie produced the dolls.

Chad said they were "monsters" and proceeded to take them, one by one, and place them in the hallway outside the door. Tom and Shari remained in the room, urging him to tell Laurie what he had told them—about the "duckie." But Laurie shook her head as she watched him. Chad was being very precise as he removed the "monsters" and lined them up against the wall outside. His actions were telling her more than his parents realized.

Presently, the little boy asked Laurie to come outside the door to see where he had put all the "bad" people. He told her they needed to be spanked. Chad took the two adult dolls and spanked them. But when he reached for the child dolls, Laurie intervened. "Oh, no," she said. "Not the children. The children weren't bad. We need to comfort the children." And she picked up a doll and held it on her shoulder, patting it. Chad eyed her curiously as he picked up the other child doll, and together they "comforted the children."

Suddenly Chad understood. He began to talk about Frank and Iliana.

Shari and Tom froze, silent and ashen, as their son stripped to his Mickey Mouse briefs, pulled them down, and described in vivid detail what Frank and Iliana had done to his private parts. The Herschels—having expected only a retelling of the "duckie" incident—were devastated.

But even his latest revelations didn't prepare Shari for the day she would walk into her bathroom and find her son trying to have intercourse with his sister.

The roller coaster never stopped.

● ● ●

Jeannie Pierson was among the meekest of the mothers and perhaps the one who carried the heaviest burden of guilt. Jeannie had agonized over what to do about the Country Walk Babysitting Service from the day in May when her friend Jill Vickers swore her to secrecy about her son's statement that Iliana kissed all the babies' "bodies." Jill told her that she wasn't convinced of its truth and that they would both be liable for slander if they told anyone about it.

Jeannie had gone home and asked Andy, then two, if Iliana had ever kissed him there and he said, "Yes." Her son must have realized that he'd just knocked the wind out of his mother, for when she asked him if it was really true, he quickly retracted the statement.

Jeannie didn't know what to think.

She wrestled with her dilemma for a few weeks after she stopped sending Andy to the Fusters, and finally decided to tell Joanne Menoher. When HRS didn't move to shut the place down, she was relieved though plagued by a nagging doubt. Then Susan Maxwell showed up with a lot of questions.

And suddenly the impossible wasn't.

A child now three, Andy Pierson was the third progeny of a recently failed marriage. Fair and bright, he radiated an almost beatific aura, an effect enhanced by striking clear blue eyes that matched his mother's. The youngest of the Pierson children, he was also perhaps the boldest.

The plucky little boy sat on his mother's lap on the floor of Chief Havens's office, facing Laurie. He began to rock back and forth. This, he told them, was the "rock-a-bye" game that Frank had played with him. Andy continued to rock rhythmically from side to side. Frank didn't have any clothes on during this game, said Andy. And neither did he.

Jeannie wrapped her arms around her son as he continued to rock, and calmly responded, "And then what happened?" Laurie noted with no small measure of admiration the mother's remarkable self-control. Jeannie's eyes welled with tears, but her voice continued to smile. Andy, snuggled in her arms, his back to her chest, was unaware that his words had almost caused his mother's heart to stop beating.

From that moment, Jeannie was haunted by a recurring vision. She saw herself holding Andy on the Fusters' doorstep, arms outstretched, as she gratefully placed him in the hands of monsters.

And she thought about the mothers who might not have done the same had she not been bound by a promise to a friend.

• • •

"I want to talk about Frank and Iliana."

Judy Prince thought she would completely lose her mind if Brendon closed one more day with those words.

For months, she had listened to her son's steady stream of bedtime purging, which had begun with his first disclosure to Laurie Braga. Ever since, Brendon seemed hell-bent on replaying his five hours at the Fusters'. Both Judy and her husband, Roger, understood what the Bragas told them about Brendon needing to get it out of his system, but the horror never lessened with repetition. It was becoming increasingly difficult for them to cope with their son's seeming obsession.

Sometimes he woke in the middle of the night screaming. Judy frequently rose in the morning to find him sleeping in the hall outside their room or on the floor pressed up against her bed. Brendon would wake during the night and quietly burrow out a spot as close to her as possible.

He suddenly wanted nothing to do with his father. Roger couldn't even hand him a glass of water. His son wouldn't come near him. Each night at bedtime Roger would lean down for a kiss good night, only to have Brendon push him away. Roger would bite his lip, smile, and say softly, "That's OK; save me a kiss for tomorrow, OK?" Tomorrow didn't come for eight months.

Sometimes his son would say, "I want you to leave. You hurt me." Roger was cut to the quick.

One day Brendon didn't make it to the bathroom on time. Judy found him crying in the family room.

"I wet my pants," he wailed.

Judy couldn't imagine why he had become so upset. "That's all right," she said. "We'll just put on some new pants."

"But I got it on the rug," he sobbed.

"That's OK. That won't hurt the rug. The rug is fine," soothed his bewildered mother.

Judy fetched a clean pair of shorts and began to remove the soiled ones.

Brendon became hysterical. "Don't touch me. You'll hurt me like you did before!" he screamed.

Judy couldn't imagine what was wrong. "I've never hurt you, honey. We're just gonna change your pants."

Her son's eyes glazed in terror. "Yes, you did! You stuck your finger in my butt."

Then she knew.

"Honey, I never did that. I'm your mom."

"No, you're not. You're Iliana."

Judy tried desperately to calm him. It was no use; he kept backing away from her until he had backed himself into a corner. "I want my daddy! I want my daddy!" he screamed.

Judy was left with no choice but to summon Roger home from work. Brendon cowered in the corner for nearly an hour while his father fought his way through traffic to rescue his son from his memories.

Judy made an appointment with a child therapist.

Brendon's "worry doctor" had a large swivel chair on rollers into which the boy, not quite three, would climb each week. He would position himself in such a way that his toes could touch the floor. Brendon would push the chair in circles and talk about Frank and Iliana, continuously revolving as the words tumbled out. The bird. The blood. The babysitters. Round and round.

Like a blond ball of yarn unraveling.

• • •

The parents thought they were going crazy.

Once the blessed, numbing shock wore off, they discovered that only a few fragile threads held what was left of their sanity together. Each time they leveled off emotionally, a new twist of circumstance sent them on a precarious plunge from which they could only hope to recover their equilibrium. The roller coaster ride careened in an unending circle in the weeks and months following the Fusters' arrest.

The late-night phone call that brought them news that one of the children had tested positive for gonorrhea proved to be one of the most debilitating blows. There was no denying how the disease found its way into Jaime Fuster's throat. Even sleep couldn't erase the visual images that began to haunt them. Their ability to deal with their children's molestation as an abstract concept was replaced by the raw horror of reality.

The horror took on a new dimension as the children's stories began to unfold through spontaneous disclosures. Blood sacrifice. Excrement ritual.

The State called in an expert on Santería to review the children's statements. She concluded that although it was apparent that the children had been subjected to some type of "belief system," the rites they described were not characteristic of the Afro-Cuban religion that flourished in South Florida.

This offered little comfort to the parents left to grope for remedy to their offspring's incomprehensible fears and fetishes. The children required constant reassurance that the Fusters were still in jail and could not escape. One little girl drew her mother a picture that showed Iliana doing just that. Many became preoccupied with the subject of death. And feces.

Even less unusual behaviors were cause for parental worries. The line between normal and abnormal became blurred. Were tantrums and obstinacy and regressions directly a result of their experiences, or were the children going through an expected developmental stage? The distinction was especially difficult for the parents who were rearing their first and only child, thus unfamiliar with what might be "typical" for a three-year-old going on four.

The Bragas' phone rang incessantly. By day, they would pause between interviews long enough to return the parents' calls. Late at night, upon returning to Apogee, they would be greeted by the phone as they walked through the door. The early morning hours brought more calls. A distraught mother needing immediate counsel regarding a son's nightmare. A grieving father unable to sleep. The Bragas, often wakened from an already meager sleep, took every call. Some nights the sky outside Apogee's glass walls would turn from black to grey to blue before the phone was returned to its cradle. Then they would dress and return to the Justice Building.

The parents beseeched the Bragas to meet with them as a group. To tell them whether they were going crazy. The State balked at the idea. If Joe and Laurie were to meet with the parents, the defense might attempt to formulate a "conspiracy" theory—that the parents and the Bragas were in collusion to frame the Fusters. The parents were incredulous. They hadn't even known each other, much less the Bragas before all of this. They were going crazy, and some lawyer was going to try to get the babysitters off the hook by pointing the finger at *them*? The whole world must be crazy.

The parents persisted. They wanted a meeting with the Bragas. Joe and Laurie went to Abe Laeser. "They need us," they told him. "If we help the parents, we're helping the children."

The State reluctantly agreed, warning them to steer clear of discussion about either the Fusters or the impending trial.

Vehicles lined both sides of the street in front of the Prince home where the parents gathered in a semicircle around the long-haired couple seated in front of the fireplace.

Joe opened the meeting with an answer to the question each had asked him over past weeks. "No," he said. "You're not going crazy."

Joe and Laurie explained the transitions they could expect to pass through as they worked out their grief. They related it to their previous work with parents whose children had died. Denial. Anger. Bargaining. Acceptance. The stages would be the same for all of them. Only the speed and method of transit would vary.

Some of the parents talked about their own inability to function sexually anymore. Other couples in the room glanced at each other and shifted uncomfortably, surprised to find that apparently no one in the room had enjoyed conjugal relations since the first week in August.

That, too, said the Bragas, would eventually pass.

They met into the night, the Bragas dispensing coping mechanisms, the parents assimilating them. This evening would remain with them through the months ahead, a point of reference to which they would return each time the emotional roller coaster the Bragas described seemed to career out of control. If Joe and Laurie told them there was light at the end of the tunnel, then it must be so.

"Dignify what has been done to your children," the Bragas told them, "by making things better for all children.

"Channel your grief."

As the parents drifted outside to their cars, each cast a furtive glance at The House next door, which loomed dark and vacant in the night.

• • •

The tall, red-haired man with the neatly trimmed beard sat quietly in the visitor's gallery of Courtroom 4-2, a solitary Lincoln-esque profile of erect and quiet dignity. Mark Harrison looked neither right nor left, his pale blue eyes focused in intense concentration on the proceedings before the judge's bench over which hung an enormous wooden plaque gilded with the words "We Who Labor Here Seek Only Truth."

Truth, Mark was beginning to perceive, had very little to do with the justice system as he was coming to know it. And he was coming to know it well, this being but one of an endless series of Fuster hearings he would attend.

The father of the State's star witness was a permanent fixture in Judge Robert Newman's court, the one parent who would monitor every pretrial maneuver with the intensity of a first-year law student. For what occurred in this courtroom in the course of the next year would profoundly affect his family's future.

Mark understood little of the legal terms that assaulted his ears in judicial shorthand. It was like watching a foreign film without subtitles. *En Limine. En Camera.* He was a mechanical engineer, not a Latin major. Sometimes he had to stop a prosecutor in the hall outside the courtroom to learn the end result of the motioning and objecting he had witnessed for the past hour. What is the bottom line? What happens next?

But most of his time was spent studying the judge, whose thoughts on the issues at hand were of monumental interest to the star witness's father. Judge Robert Newman, Mark decided, was the kind of man he would have hoped to find presiding over his son's fate in a court of law. He was a solemn man, slightly rotund, with thinning white hair and a neat beard—a distinguished, though unmerry, Kris Kringle. His face was an unreadable map, his mouth immobile, his eyes, distant, dispassionate, yet possessed of a perceptible passion. Mark read a conscience behind Judge Newman's eyes, and a conscience was all he asked of a man who would decide to what extent the law would allow him to protect a five-year-old boy.

At times Mark's eyes would drift to the jury box where sat the creators of his nightmare. Frank, six feet tall, with a rapidly receding hairline and dark eyes—almost black—piercing even under his gold-rimmed spectacles. Iliana, small and wan, became younger every day, her long nutmeg hair loosed from the severe bun she had always worn, her flawless skin no longer concealed beneath a thick layer of cosmetics. She looked not a day older than her seventeen-year-old Honduran certificate of birth.

This was not the couple Mark had known. This was not the same couple with whom he had celebrated the July Fourth just past, a circumstance precipitated when Jason had begged his father to invite his friend Jaime on their holiday boating excursion. Mark assented, extending the invitation to include his son's friend's parents as well. Mark had spent the entire day on a boat with the people who were satanically raping his sons. And he had not had a clue.

He thought about that day a lot.

"Daddy, do you hate Frank and Iliana?" Jason asked him one day.

"Jesus tells us to love our enemies," Mark had replied, though he was having trouble reconciling this particular concept himself of late. Mark Harrison was the gentlest of men, who came to be regarded as the strongest voice of reason among the parents. A devout man of God who lived by scripture, he nonetheless required from others no enforced dedication to his beliefs, though he shifted uncomfortably in the presence of those who would take his Lord's name in vain.

God had given Mark as his cross to bear an unsuitable intolerance for spirits, which stripped him of his gentleness and reason. Mark was a recovering alcoholic whose battle with the bottle seemed all but won by the summer of 1984. And then the roof fell in.

Why had God done this to him? He searched the scriptures for an answer—some clue as to how this profane obscenity fit into His plan. Mark struggled to forgive as the Bible instructed, an emotion in conflict with the frightening magnitude of the rage that simmered within him. God instructed that he forgive a man whom he could gladly strangle with his bare hands. Sometimes he sought a bottle to dull the pain inflicted by his war within, an act that unleashed unspeakable fury. Mark's tumbles from the wagon, though infrequent, were terrifying to behold, yet the other parents stood firmly behind him, certain that their voice of reason would soon return. As it always did.

Mark would eventually carve out a fragile peace within himself, though the cease-fire was hard-won. In the meantime, he struggled to comprehend the hand that fate had dealt him. Many of the answers he sought were revealed to him in Courtroom 4-2, where the defilers of his children calmly regarded him from across the room.

Mark began to see the source of their content as he came to understand the nature of the law. The tapes, his son's disclosures to him and Jackie, testimony from a group of very small and frightened children, and Frank's prior record—all added up to one large pile marked "inadmissible evidence." Jason Harrison appeared the only child old enough and durable enough to speak for the other children.

From where Mark sat, it looked as though the burden of prosecuting the Fusters rested squarely on the small shoulders of his red-haired son—a responsibility that he was not yet convinced he would accept for either himself or Jason. Mark's thoughts often turned to the words of the Fusters' attorney, Michael Von Zamft, which had come to him via the evening news.

The scene took place in the hall outside the courtroom as reporters flocked around the defense lawyers clamoring for their reaction to additional charges that had been filed against their clients. Von Zamft's intentions were clear as he informed the cameras, "The last time I had a four-year-old on the stand, it took me less than forty-five minutes to break her down."

Over his dead body would Mark allow anyone to break his already broken son. He would watch the Fusters walk free before that would happen. Or he would go to jail. His son was not a pawn to be sacrificed by lawyers who played at justice like a game. His son had suffered enough.

16

If all that is verifiably known about the first two decades of Frank Fuster's life was laid in a row, the data wouldn't fill a single sheet of paper.

Double-spaced.

For this reason, the account of Frank Fuster's early years is largely his own, as told to law enforcement and mental health professionals over a period of sixteen years.

It is difficult to offer insight into a man whose masks were so many, his truths so few, that only a handful of people ever came to know that over a period of thirty-six years the human being born Francisco Fuster Escalona ceased to exist, his humanity gradually replaced by a hollow darkness that functioned according to two primitive and unbridled instincts.

Self-gratification and survival.

These appeared to have become the sum total of his existence.

Precisely when this monstrous evolution began, and how, may remain the missing factors in an equation for which the correct but unfortunate solution is already known. Because the only ones close enough to suspect the true nature and origins of the workings of Frank Fuster's mind either helped contribute to the birth of the beast or are too fearful to acknowledge publicly its creation.

So all that is known about Frank Fuster is largely what Frank Fuster wanted to be known, resulting in a kaleidoscopic self-portrait, which he colored in accordance with the audience for which he found himself on view at any given time.

Hard worker. Model prisoner. Religious family man. Victim.

All were elements he built into the carefully constructed face of respectability he wore for public consumption. Only his deeds and his victims bore witness to the man who lived behind the mask, though the mask itself offered certain clues.

Though Frank's autobiography varies in texture and detail, each version suggests an unsettled yet unextraordinary childhood.

The first of two sons born to Angela Escalona and Francisco Fuster, on December 10, 1948, Frank described himself as an "example kid," raised in a "very strict" household where the conservative rules were to be obeyed without question.

His father's "persistent philandering" led to his parents' divorce when he was either seven, five, or three-and-a-half. Some three years later, his mother remarried "a good man" to whom he became closer than to his biological father.

At the age of twelve or thirteen, Frank and his younger brother emigrated from Cuba to the United States, where they lived in New York under the legal guardianship of a maternal uncle. It would be four years before the mother and a younger half-brother would escape from Cuba. The stepfather never would.

Fuster was enrolled in a public school program for Spanish-speaking students, which he said he found "difficult" because the other students spoke English better than he. Although school records label him a "persistent truant" of "unsatisfactory" scholarship, he admits only to being "disciplined" for "talking in class." At the age of nineteen, he was discharged from high school—without a diploma.

It is possible that his extracurricular activities throughout this period may not have been conducive to academic achievement.

At the age of fourteen, Frank established a common-law relationship with a woman named Martha, approximately five years his senior, who bore a child that bears his name, though not (until the Country Walk trial) his acknowledged paternity. The relationship lasted a matter of months.

A second Martha, also several years older than he, made him a father for the second time. The couple married when their daughter was five months old. Frank was seventeen.

It was in the third year of this union that Frank Fuster first came to the attention of the law.

• • •

On the evening of January 16, 1969, twenty-year-old Francisco Fuster Escalona leveled a gun at Jacob Isenbek's heart and pulled the trigger. Twice. The twenty-nine-year-old Bronx man died instantly, the victim of a violent settlement of a traffic dispute.

The victim of a murderous rage.

The off-duty New York City policeman who witnessed the incident and stared for a few brief but prayerful seconds up the barrel of a .22-caliber rifle as Frank Fuster engaged the chamber with another shell, didn't pull the trigger of the service revolver he held cocked in his hand.

Frank was indignant over his arrest for what he described as an "accident" that occurred while he was trying to effect a "citizen's arrest" of an unruly motorist who was not only "high," but armed and dangerous. His proffered versions of the circumstance sustained amendment over the years, until a decade later, when he came to tell acquaintances that he had been involved in a "traffic homicide," leaving the recipient of this prized disclosure to envision the weapon of death to be an out-of-control vehicle, not a carefully aimed carbine.

In any case, Frank called the version represented on the police report "a lie" and Patrolman Doyle "a liar."

A New York grand jury called it murder.

In the first degree.

Advised by his attorney that an off-duty police officer would be difficult to impeach as an eyewitness, and that his victim was unarmed (no weapon other than Fuster's .22 caliber Mossberg rifle, with nine rounds of live ammunition and two spent shells, had been recovered from the Willis Avenue Bridge, scene of the crime), young Frank began to realize that the state of New York was unwavering in its intent to relieve society of his presence—permanently.

So he copped a plea, later explaining that his life had become forever tarnished for lack of competent legal counsel. He pleaded guilty, he said, only because his family had engaged a lawyer who had no experience with "crimes similar to" his, that she received her "$2,000 fee" before she ever appeared in court with him, and that the only alternative she recommended to him was to "cop out."

Fuster said he was told that he could get "at least seven years" just for carrying the loaded rifle in his car.

Frank allowed that he wasn't entirely innocent of killing the man, anyway, as he should never have pointed the weapon at him. Besides, he hated being held at Riker's Island, and his lawyer offered a "25 percent" chance that he might get off on probation.

Frank Fuster (it would later become apparent) liked to deal in percentages.

He pleaded guilty to a reduced charge of manslaughter and on

Halloween, 1969, was sentenced to ten years in prison.

For the murder of Jacob Isenbek, he served not quite four.

Fuster was a model prisoner.

His institutional adjustment log, a record kept for purposes of parole, reported in 1972 that:

Fuster has adjusted well during his period of confinement and has received no disciplinary reports. According to his cellblock officer, he is a polite, cooperative individual who gets along well with others and is rated as being a good inmate. He performed well on the one industrial assignment he had at this institution before he was assigned to a vocational program. In the academic phase of his training he appears to be an average student, but he has been in school too short a time for a complete evaluation. According to the subject, he, in addition to taking radio/TV vocational training, is taking a cell study course in electronics. The subject was a Catholic but stated that he has now given up his religion and is currently attending Pentecostal services in the institution. . . .

Recreational: According to the subject, he has very little time for recreation as he keeps busy with his schooling work and studying. . . .

Associates: Claims no close associates. . . .

Psychiatric: In a report of 1/15/70 from the Reception Center the diagnosis was "Inadequate personality with dyssocial trends—marijuana user." With a guarded prognosis and a recommendation for group counseling. . . .

Psychological: In a report from the Reception Center of 12/29/69 the subject's IQ was reported on three levels because of wide discrepancies in testing. . . . He was found to be functioning at the very upper limit of the average range of intelligence in Spanish verbal area but attained only the midpoint of a dull normal range of intelligence on the English test. In the nonverbal area his scores were in the low end of the average range with evidence that he was capable of higher functioning.

Unbeknownst to the author of his parole assessment, the young Cuban prisoner was amused that a battery of "stupid tests" would label him "average."

Francisco Fuster Escalona was a superior specimen.

Of that he was certain.

EVALUATION FOR PAROLE

The Board of Parole may wish to consider referring this inmate under the Special Psychiatric Procedure (Homicide). . . .

Fuster is a tall, well-built young man who is almost a compulsive talker. He goes into great details about everything that he discusses and much of the information that he provides differs from that available in the Probation Report. It does not appear that he accepts full responsibility for killing the victim of the instant crime. . . . It does not appear that he has a great deal of remorse over the fact that he killed a man. He has adjusted well in the institution and is taking advantage of training programs available to him here.

On October 18, 1972, almost three years to the day of his sentencing, Francisco Fuster Escalona was released on parole from the Wallkill Correctional Facility.

Two years later, he was accepted for supervision in the state of Florida, where parole reports indicate that he was "extremely cooperative" and had made "very satisfactory" progress. In June of 1977, Fuster was arrested for shoplifting. The charges were later dismissed. A year later, the state of New York approved Frank Fuster's final discharge from parole.

He was on his own.

In the decade following his release from prison, Fuster attended real estate school, opened his own interior decorating business, married for a second time, and fathered for a third. Martha number two, Fuster's first legal wife, was replaced in 1975 by Martha number three, who bore him a son, Jaime. It was during the sixth year of this union that Francisco Fuster Escalona found himself on the wrong side of the law once again, this time for lewd and lascivious conduct with a nine-year-old girl.

Hilda Gonzalez told police that she was riding as a passenger in a van driven by Fuster when he asked her to sit with him in the driver's seat and offered to teach her how to drive. When she did so, he put his arm around her and began rubbing her breast and genital areas. Fuster asked her several questions, including her age and address. She told him her correct age but gave him an incorrect address.

Fuster admitted having been in the van with the victim, but denied having touched her.

A six-member jury believed the girl.

Prior to the trial, Frank was subjected to a psychiatric examination in which he related how fate and the system had once again dealt him a bad hand.

He offered a somewhat modified version of his family history, expounded on "the injustice" of his imprisonment for the unfortunate "traffic accident," and expressed his bitterness that the "false" charges against him for shoplifting couldn't be expunged from his records because he was an ex-convict, a circumstance in which he had been wrongly placed by a policeman who "lied" and an attorney who was "incompetent."

Of the latest charges against him, Frank "spoke at great length, and in great detail," about what he saw as completely unwarranted persecution by the victim's family, including her "grandfather, who is a police detective, and his colleagues."

He explained that he, the alleged victim, and a number of other family members and friends were at a party, at which he had several drinks. However, he insisted, he was not drunk and never had been in his life. He was a social drinker, and he used no other intoxicating substances. He didn't even like to take medication.

As a result of a rather complicated transportation situation, he and the alleged victim ended up together—alone—in his van. He said he was quite sleepy and concerned that he might fall asleep while driving, so he asked the girl to sit next to him and make sure that he didn't close his eyes.

Fuster insisted that, if he did touch her at all, it was not with any sexual intent because such an act would be "sick and evil."

"Fondling a baby is a sick and disgusting act. The law protects the mind of the child. The child's mind could be greatly affected. It could cause trauma. . . ."

Of his sexual history, Frank said he had no formal sex education. He admitted to masturbating briefly in his early teenage years but was careful to note that he didn't continue the practice into adulthood. He went on to say that he was opposed to pornography and cited an instance when he and his wife mistakenly walked into an X-rated film and immediately walked out.

He denied that he had ever been sexually molested as a child (although a relative, years later, would disclose her own knowledge that Francisco Fuster Escalona had been sexually abused—repeatedly and systematically—by a male member of his extended family, beginning at the age of thirteen).

Frank told a drastically different version of his "first" sexual experience, describing it as his "seduction" at the age of thirteen by an "older woman" in the rest room of a restaurant for which he worked at the time.

It is possible that young Frank grew to find it less painful to remember his introduction to sexuality as a romantic encounter, the concept of "seduction" replacing the reality of betrayal, the fantasy of an "older woman," replacing the humiliating actuality that "she" was an older man.

Frank went on to estimate that he had approximately twenty-five sexual partners since, and admitted no difficulties in sexual function. He said he had never contracted a venereal disease.

He indicated that he and his wife (Martha number three) had a mutually satisfying sexual relationship (although Martha herself stood uncomfortably mute when confronted with any questions of a sexual nature) and that three years ago he had had a vasectomy, which removed worry about unwanted pregnancy.

Frank was "Joe Normal."

Wasn't suicidal, wasn't deluded, wasn't violent. Didn't hallucinate, didn't fantasize (although throughout the interview he appeared preoccupied with mentally constructing a just revenge, which took the form of his charging various people with perjury).

He had no abnormal thoughts or impulses, though most everyone else he knew of suffered some mental defect.

The policeman who sent him to prison for the first time was "a liar." The people who had brought the current charges against him (his relatives and former friends) were "very low" people—"animals, marijuana users, dealers, and winos."

The world, it seemed, was out to get him.

Once, about four years ago, he said, a very beautiful but "demented" young woman had tried to get him arrested for rape. During his wife's ninth month of pregnancy, he "foolishly" arranged to take the luscious stranger to dinner. He being a devoted husband and father-to-be, but "a man" nonetheless, and she being a most willing seductress, one thing led to another, he explained. The next thing he knew, her mother had reported to the police that her daughter had been raped.

No charges were ever brought, he said, because the young woman was "found to be demented."

Fuster was administered the Minnesota Multiphasic Personality Inventory (MMPI). The resulting profile suggested, according to the psychiatrist, that Fuster

. . . has a very strong need to see himself, and be seen by others, as an extremely virtuous individual. He presents himself in an unrealistically favorable light with regard to self-control, morality, and a lack of common human frailties.

He appears to be an inflexible and very defensive person who demonstrates poor insight and a tendency toward psychological denial. It is hypothesized that his rigidity and demanding perfectionism are ways of compensating for underlying feelings of inadequacy.

He is hypersensitive and susceptible to social and vocational stresses. He tends to be suspicious and to harbor a brooding distrust and resentment of others.

When things in his life do not turn out the way he would like, he projects the blame on others.

He is somewhat restless and has a relatively high energy level; poor behavioral controls lead to impulsive actions and minor transgressions of social limits. . . . His rigidity and intolerance can lead to sudden flare-ups of anger.

The psychiatrist concluded:

Mr. Fuster is a man of above-average intelligence who has over the years developed a lifestyle and world view characterized by compulsive and paranoid features. In the past year he has undergone a number of major life stresses, including being critically wounded in a robbery, the death of two close family members, and his arrest on the present charges. These events have led to an exacerbation of his typical coping strategies to the point that his contact with reality is becoming impaired.

There are elements in his personality profile which are certainly similar to those found in many offenders who commit these crimes against children, but these are characteristics which are also found in many other people as well. There are, on the other hand, a number of other features which are frequently found in these offenders which Mr. Escalona does not appear to have. He does not show, for example, the typical ineffectual, nonassertive behavior, and lack of social skills most often associated with this type of individual.

In sum, although I cannot absolutely rule out the possibility that he committed this offense as alleged, there is not sufficient psychological information to brand him as having a "typical child molester personality."

Eight months later, following his conviction for performing a lewd and lascivious act with the nine-year-old girl (who, by the time of trial, had turned eleven), Frank Fuster was evaluated by another psychiatrist as part of his presentence investigation.

During this examination, Frank spoke angrily and at length about this latest miscarriage of justice in his life, stating that he had "lost faith in humanity" over the way he had been treated by the system.

In the opinion of this particular psychiatrist:

> . . . this defendant does not suffer from a major mental disorder, although he is apparently an emotionally unstable individual who could benefit from receiving psychiatric care to assist him in a better level of functioning in life. This recommendation is limited to outpatient psychiatric treatment since at the time of this evaluation clinically there are no reasons to refer the defendant for further evaluation and/or psychiatric treatment as an inpatient.
>
> On the basis of the description offered by the defendant as to his frame of mind at the time of the alleged offense, it is considered that he was sane.

The Florida Department of Corrections then recommended:

> Based on all available information and considering the subject's background, this investigator feels that society and the subject would best benefit by the subject's being placed on a period of probation. Although the crime committed is indeed of a very serious nature, the subject's lack of any record of a similar related offense, as well as his present role in the community as a businessman and a family man, would make sentencing to any period of incarceration inappropriate. Therefore, it is this investigator's recommendation that the subject be placed on probation for a period of five (5) years with special condition of psychiatric treatment in a program for sex offenders, if such treatment is determined necessary by a psychological evaluation.

Prior to sentencing, Frank Fuster addressed the court:

"Your Honor: Since this case has started, since I was accused of this crime, I have defended myself in every possible way, according to the resources.

"However, I don't think that in this crime that the district attorney has seemed to care about searching for the truth. I think he is more interested in convicting me.

"I never touched Hilda Gonzalez.

"And, Your Honor, I have learned a lot in this case.

"I have seen a police officer take the stand and, under oath, lie to help the district attorney get a conviction, which I didn't think, in the United States, I would ever see that.

"Me, my family, we have all been through a very, very horrible experience for over one year and a half.

"Hilda's—a nine-year-old—family made an allegation. Due to that allegation, I was arrested, which there are no clues.

"I submitted myself to a lie detector test.

"I submitted myself to this for five hours, sitting in a chair, and was given tests, and I passed them both.

"I submitted myself to Dr. Krieger's psychiatric evaluation, which lasted over five or six hours, and I passed it.

"However, I don't see that Ms. Hilda Gonzalez has been appropriately interrogated. I don't see that she has been taken to a lie detector test or a psychiatric evaluation.

"Just based on this, the allegation of this girl, she has moved the entire court system against me, and I believe that the district attorney knows that I am innocent.

"I think he is pretty convinced by now.

"I don't understand much of the procedure. I wish I had a chance to testify in court. I wish I had a chance to talk to the jury and be able to express myself to them as I am doing now.

"Excuse me, I am trying to put myself together.

"I have learned, Your Honor, not to take any minors in my car ever again. My only mistake was to make a favor that I should never have done, and I repeat, I know how the parents must feel, and I have placed myself in their position.

"I don't know to what extent Hilda Gonzalez is lying.

"Sometimes I think she has been coached by adults to lie the way she did in the courtroom, in that chair.

"I never touched Hilda Gonzalez.

"That's all I have to say."

Judge Steven Robinson apparently found the jury's verdict and the corrections department's recommendation of five years' probation to be too harsh for a local businessman convicted on the word of a child.

On November 29, 1982, he sentenced Frank Fuster to two years' probation and appointed him a private attorney, Jeffrey Samek, to appeal his conviction.

For that, the parents of Country Walk would later demand Hizzoner's head on a silver platter.

• • •

Frank said he divorced Martha number two because of conflicts with his mother-in-law and because he resented that she didn't cook or "care for the house," even though he was going to school and working all night.

That for the last portion of his marriage he was dating sixteen-year-old Martha number three apparently was not a consideration.

Martha number three was born in Peru, the oldest of five sisters. At the age of thirteen, her family moved to New York where, three years later, she met Frank Fuster, whom she saw as her knight in shining armor come to rescue her from a family in which she felt unloved.

The fact that her knight was another woman's husband who had recently been imprisoned for having killed a man apparently was irrelevant.

Martha's family was vehemently opposed to the match, begging, and at times bribing, her to end her association with him.

She refused.

When her father excluded Fuster from a family Christmas dinner, Martha made her final choice. She moved in with Frank and married him two years later.

She bore him a son.

Although Martha would come to describe her marriage to parole officials (for purposes of getting her husband sentenced to probation on the child-molesting conviction) as "very happy," she would come to tell a different story in later years.

In a word, the marriage was "tough."

According to Martha, she and Frank "fought constantly" and had broken up on numerous occasions. Each time, she said, Frank would coax her back, saying she was his "guardian angel," without whom he would "go berserk."

Frank "liked [being in] control," said Martha. He chose her clothes, discarded her friends, deposited her paychecks, and forbade her to drive a car.

Still, she loved him.

Although Martha acknowledged that her husband "had a bad temper" and that she was afraid of him because he slapped and cursed her, she insisted that her punishment was deserved, the beatings most frequently coming when traffic or co-workers delayed her evening homecoming.

She was the one, after all, who insisted on holding down a job even though her husband wanted her home.

"He was macho—a big man. No one could get near him. In prison, he used to have to prove himself 'a man' all the time."

He used to pick fights with strangers, she said. And brawl in the streets.

But, she added, "he was never out to hurt anyone or kill people deliberately."

In late 1982 (also for purposes of establishing the depth of his character for the judge who would sentence him for molesting Hilda Gonzalez), Frank described his marriage as "happy" and his wife as something of a saint who "never hurt anyone."

Martha, he said, was "wonderful, beautiful, and smart." He spoke with apparent pride about her successful career as a credit manager. His only complaint was that his wife tended to eat too much and sometimes slept later than he would like on her days off.

Their relationship, he said, was "very deep."

Throughout the trial and the years following it, Martha steadfastly maintained her belief that her husband was innocent of molesting nine-year-old Hilda Gonzalez.

Nonetheless, she left him less than three months after the judge granted his wish that he be placed on probation and returned to his happy home. Frank had grown "paranoid," she said, and had started accusing her of having "set him up" on the molestation charges.

Although numerous (and conflicting) stories would come to be offered in explanation of the couple's final breakup, they did not preclude the possibility that Martha number three was also beginning to outgrow her knight in shining armor, perhaps from her point of view, but most likely from his.

When we met, I was a child, she said.

"And he liked that."

• • •

Frank Fuster came to place a great deal of significance on an event that occurred in his life in late 1980, almost a full year before he was arrested for the sexual assault of nine-year-old Hilda Gonzalez.

On the morning of December 18, Frank Fuster responded to a knock on the door of his business and was greeted by a silent intruder who shot him point-blank in the side of the head. Fuster reported it to authorities as "an attempted robbery," although the assailant took neither money nor merchandise with him when he fled the scene. Police quietly speculated that the incident more closely resembled an attempted "execution" than robbery, though they could discover no motive for anyone to mark Frank Fuster for death. The parents of Country Walk came to formulate their own ideas as to why, in 1980, someone might have wanted to see Frank dead.

In any event, the bullet he claimed to still carry in his skull is said to have rendered him unconscious for ten minutes, shattered his jaw, severed nerves on the right side of his face, affected his memory, and left him with (what he alternately described as) a buzzing, whistling, or ringing in his ears, which at times, he said, would "drive me nuts."

According to Frank, in the six months that followed, he was hospitalized, twice underwent surgery, and became depressed.

According to Martha, he became very paranoid, didn't trust anyone, and bought guns.

As a condition of his probation, Frank received court-ordered psychiatric treatment from the beginning of 1983 until August of that year, when he announced to his therapist that he no longer required her services, a circumstance apparently not pursued by his probation officer.

The social worker who conducted his prescribed weekly twenty-dollar-per-hour mental health visits set out to treat what she had labeled his "antisocial character disorder," by "dealing with" his rage about life, "working through" his feelings about his divorce, and "reeducating" him about parenting.

There seemed little point in addressing his sexual problems in view of the fact that he staunchly refused to acknowledge that he had any. Through the course of his therapy, Fuster became annoyed (and sometimes angered) when pushed to discuss issues of a sexual nature.

Nor would he allow the subject of the convictions against him to be brought up. He would discuss neither manslaughter nor molestation beyond an unwavering proclamation of his innocence on both counts.

He chose to concentrate, instead, on matters in which he could explore, in great detail, his role as victim. The 1980 shooting was a favorite topic: Frank the hapless shopkeeper gunned down in broad daylight, left to suffer the long-term (and possibly lifelong) effects of periodic memory loss and "blackouts."

When Frank wasn't talking about "blackouts," he dwelled at length on Martha's most recent (and apparently most serious) departure from his life and on the confusion he felt over his role with his wife (whose "custody" he lost) and son (whose custody he retained).

A veil of mystery came to surround the circumstances under which Martha Fuster came to relinquish guardianship of her six-year-old son to his father. Martha said Frank had threatened to kill her if she tried to take Jaime, an act that she was inclined to believe he would carry out—without hesitation. Later, it would be suggested by Frank's third wife, Iliana, that Frank Fuster "bought" his son from his ex-wife for $5,000 down and a series of monthly installments. Martha countered that the checks she received from her former husband were payments to settle an "arrangement" she and Frank had made with regard to the house in Country Walk, which they had purchased jointly prior to their divorce.

In any case, Jaime lived with Frank and Martha didn't.

Frank agonized with his therapist over his failed marriage and his "concern" for his son's well-being. So much so that he sometimes brought his son and/or estranged wife to participate in his therapy sessions, where he underwent "reeducation" about parenting.

Frank Fuster's effusive interest in his son's welfare would appear particularly gruesome in future light, when came to be revealed the fate of a child born of a monster that looked like an ordinary man.

• • •

In April of 1982, six months after his arrest for molesting nine-year-old Hilda Gonzalez, and five months before his conviction for same, Frank Fuster and Martha number three bought the house in Country Walk.

A month prior, he had established a corporation by the name of KDW Enterprises, Inc., an "interior decorating" business that "specialized in window treatments," apparently Frank's somewhat hyperbolic way of saying he installed verticals and miniblinds.

Despite few apparent financial resources, the fledgling entrepreneur/ex-convict and his clerically employed wife had no apparent problem coughing up the 10 percent down payment for the house or keeping up with the monthly mortgage of $1,161.

The Fusters' finances would always remain something of an enigma.

Frank had opened six bank accounts in Florida over a ten-year period, four of which were still active at the time of his arrest for the Country Walk assaults. Money flowed through them in erratic fits and starts. Lump sums ranging from ten to twenty thousand dollars were deposited, the source attributed to unsecured "loans" signed over to him by "former clients" who considered him "a good risk." Contacted during the investigation, Frank's benefactors confirmed that he had seemed an honest, hardworking businessman to whom they would write checks for large sums of money without a second thought.

The bank accounts also reflected Frank's habit of writing checks to himself for four or five thousand dollars at a time.

Although the sums of money that passed through Frank Fuster's various bank accounts weren't sufficient to indicate illegal dealings of any size or scope (by Miami standards), the amount was sufficiently large and mysterious to spawn speculation among authorities that perhaps he at one time had been gearing up to launch a project unrelated to decorating homes. Perhaps drugs. Perhaps pornography.

The children's testimony of their assaults having been photographed, along with an unsolicited disclosure by a relative that Frank had approached an adolescent niece about appearing in a "naked movie," lends credence to the latter hypothesis.

It was even speculated that Frank may have been in the business of producing "custom" home videos, tailored to a client's particular perversion—a circumstance that might help bewildered lawyers and investigators make sense of some of the more bizarre behaviors the children recounted. The five-billion-dollar-a-year worldwide kiddie porn industry would no doubt welcome the fresh new faces and bodies of the predominantly blond-haired, blue-eyed sons and daughters of Country Walk.

But no tapes could be found.

And if he was making money on them, the transactions had to have been cash. Because there came a time when the Fuster bank account took a definitive turn for the worse. The lump sum transactions ceased, and the money that flowed into the account was precisely sufficient to pay the household bills.

Right about the time his ex-wife Martha moved out and a Honduran teenager by the name of Iliana moved in.

The State would have liked to explore further the financial mysteries of the self-employed miniblind installer and his affluent lifestyle. Especially when the Fusters' attorneys moved successfully to have their clients declared indigent for the purpose of obtaining court-appointed legal services.

Chris Rundle was incensed that taxpayers should pick up the tab for a man who lived in a house worth $150,000 and drove a 280Z, but there was little he could do to prevent it.

Unraveling the mysteries of Frank Fuster's finances would have required more time and manpower than the State was willing to commit with so many other aspects of the case requiring investigative attention.

• • •

Martha and Iliana Fuster had more in common than a husband, though Martha was perhaps more attuned to their "sisterhood," having ten years more insight into the path she trod than the young and single-minded Iliana.

Both had immigrated to the United States from underdeveloped countries—Martha from Peru, Iliana from Honduras. And both had met, at the age of sixteen, the man who would permanently alter the course of their lives.

Although a decade separated their births, both women were reared in traditional Latin households, where virtue was honored and obedience expected, an attitude that clashed culturally with the ways of their American peers.

It was possibly this culture shock, or perhaps a surge of adolescent independence, that steered Martha and Iliana into conflict with their families. Martha, the oldest of five daughters, felt pressured by her parents into setting an example for her siblings. She perceived their love as conditional upon her ability to get good grades and to do as she was told without question. Iliana, whose mother left her to be reared by her father in Honduras while she pursued the American Dream, claimed to be devastated when she later joined her mother in Miami to find her mother living with another man.

Iliana had lived for fifteen years not knowing that her mother and the man who had reared her for the past nine had never bothered to marry. And now her mother was married to someone else.

Iliana despised the man who had replaced her father.

So it came that by the time each girl had reached her sixteenth birthday the stage was set for the entrance of the knight in shining armor who would take them away from their troubled families and on to a new life.

Frank Fuster, it is said, could be most charming when there was a purpose to be served by the effort.

But he apparently wasted none of it on his sweethearts' families, who voiced vigorous objection to their daughters' consuming interest in the tall, dark, bad-tempered stranger.

Through either their own underestimated sense of determination or the strength of Frank's influence, Martha and Iliana chose the knight over their families, in which they came to enjoy the status of "black sheep."

Although both women would come to be described by mental health professionals as "naive, immature, dependent, and fearful," there were indications that, though submissive, the Fuster wives could also be manipulative, a subtlety that apparently escaped Frank's attention.

Martha continued to work outside the home, to her husband's apparent violent displeasure. But she still turned her paychecks over to him. And she eventually divorced him, though the degree to which Frank resisted the idea remains unclear. What is known is that, following the divorce, Martha continued to live with Frank and their son on weekends up until the time Iliana entered the picture.

According to one account offered by Martha following Frank's arrest in the Country Walk case, she returned from a visit with relatives in New York, during the summer of 1983, to her ex-husband's announcement that he planned to marry a young Honduran girl he had met at a flea market. He told her to pack her bags.

Dependence being one of her stronger suits, Martha is said to have begged Frank to let her continue to live with him and his new child bride.

The child bride is said to have stamped her foot loudly at the prospect of spending her honeymoon—and her marriage—with Frank's discarded spouse.

There appeared no love lost in the relationship between Martha and Iliana Fuster.

Frank's ex-wife and his new one had little contact with each other following the latter's September wedding in 1983, Martha's occasional visitations with Jaime being the only cause for their paths to cross. Martha said that on the occasions she would visit Country Walk, Iliana was "all over Frank" in a proprietary display of affection. She said that when she would call to talk to her son on the phone, Iliana always listened on the extension.

On one occasion, said Martha, Iliana smugly informed her that Frank wasn't "beating up" on little Jaime anymore because, as she put it, she knew "how to handle Frank."

• • •

On the afternoon of Friday, August 10, 1984, Martha Fuster received a frantic phone call from Iliana informing her that Frank had been arrested "for the same thing as last time." A man who identified himself as "Frank's attorney" took the phone from the distraught Iliana and informed Martha that, unless she came to Miami "right away" for a guardianship hearing, the State was about to seize custody of her son, Jaime.

Martha came running.

On Monday, Jaime's natural mother was granted temporary guardianship of her son, and a date was set for a hearing for permanent custody following an investigation into her fitness for the task.

At the time, Martha did not appear incredulous at the possibility that Frank Fuster may have abused their son. In fact, she remained strangely quiet on the subject. Following Iliana's arrest, Martha developed a keen interest in her former rival, repeatedly offering empathetic inquiry as to her well-being.

When asked why she seemed to identify so closely with the woman who had apparently committed no less a crime than her husband, Martha replied with a meaningful nod of her head.

"You don't know Frank," she said, as though that said it all.

Yet she began, after a time, to claim disbelief that anything out of the ordinary had occurred between her son and his father.

"I never noticed anything unusual between Frank and Jaime. Looked like an ideal father-son relationship to me."

When confronted with the fact that the father-son relationship appeared less than "ideal" to numerous observers who had seen Frank publicly respond to his son's more minor transgressions—like interrupting a conversation he was having—with a backhand to the mouth, Martha conceded that Frank often struck Jaime, but only "because he loved him" and wanted to teach him right from wrong.

The fact that Jaime had to be treated for gonorrhea and had said to her, "Mom, do you know that all the other kids saw my daddy put his penis in my mouth?" did not sway Martha's profession of her ex-husband's innocence.

She would point out that Frank had always expressed extreme attitudes about child molesters, advocating execution for the perpetrators. How could he possibly commit an act he so vehemently abhorred?

It is possible that Martha Fuster's denial of what was emerging as so clear a reality might have resulted from her inability to reconcile her continued (and admitted) attachment to her ex-husband. It is equally possible that she looked toward the women's detention center where Iliana resided in an isolation cell and considered that "but for the grace of God," there sat she.

Martha knew what it meant to be the wife of Frank Fuster.

• • •

Doctors Joseph and Laurie Braga met Jaime Fuster for the first time on Monday, August 13, 1984, the day on which a juvenile court judge was scheduled to determine in whose hands he would place for safekeeping the six-year-old son of a child molester, arrested three days previously.

The child was in an acute state of confusion.

Within the past five days, Jaime Fuster had resided in a household in crisis. The tension began building last Tuesday morning when a neighbor informed Iliana that "there was talk" of what she and her husband had been doing with children at their babysitting service and that they'd best "get out of town." Jaime saw things being packed in boxes. Video equipment. Guns. That night, a man carrying a gun was wrestled to the ground by police in his front yard, handcuffed, and led away. It was the father of a little baby girl about whom the boy knew many things.

All of them disturbing.

That night and into the next morning, the packing of items continued in earnest. That afternoon, after the many boxes had been spirited away in a white van, his family fled from the home in Country Walk and checked into a hotel. The next morning, his father surrendered. Over the weekend his stepmother took the boy to visit Frank in jail.

Only Frank, Iliana, and Jaime Fuster know the specifics of the conversations that took place among them over this frantic five-day period during which their collective as well as individual worlds began to crumble. One can only speculate on the nature of the discussions conducted by a man faced with the desperate need to ensure his wife and son's silence.

So it was in the wake of these events that Jaime Fuster came to see

Joe and Laurie at the Metro Justice Building, three days after his father's arrest. Though the day was not half over, the little boy had already undergone a head-to-toe physical (including the obligatory poking, prodding, and swabbing for venereal disease) and attended a court hearing in which he was legally separated from the stepmother with whom he had lived for the past year.

Whether he was to be placed in foster care by the state or sent to another city to live with his natural mother and aunt rested on the decision of the Bragas, who had been appointed by the court to determine which would be in the child's best interest.

Joe and Laurie faced the six-year-old boy before them with the certain knowledge of the horror of his existence and the turmoil in which he had lived the past several days.

Jaime Fuster's world was in the process of being shattered. And no matter how macabre that world might have been, it was the only one he knew.

The Bragas saw Jaime Fuster on three consecutive days, during which they continued to interview additional children who had attended the babysitting service at Country Walk.

But the initial interview of Jaime Fuster was markedly different from that of the other children, both in purpose and in content. For the Bragas sought no information from the one child who, by virtue of his age and relations, could best enlighten them about life in the Fuster household. Instead, they sought to determine how well he was coping with the immediate distress of his world turned upside down and the best way to help him through it.

Jaime first entered the interview room in a state of cheerful agitation. Hyper, outgoing, talkative, the little boy gravitated directly to the toys and flitted from one to the other, his thoughts disorganized, his attention brief.

Perpetual motion. The very behavior that had caused teachers and school counselors to label him "learning disabled" and "a problem."

Joe and Laurie recognized him as a child in distress. A bright boy whose energies and intellect had been singularly channeled into helping him fend for himself emotionally in the face of a father and stepmother who did things to him that he didn't understand.

Laurie asked if he had anything he might like to talk about, any worries he might have.

He wasn't worried about anything, he told her.

Then he spotted some paper and crayons and asked if he could draw. For the next half hour, he drew a series of pictures, offering a running narrative of the stories that went with them.

He first drew a picture of himself, a five-armed Jaime who carried signs on which he carefully printed the words, "Stop, Help, No, Red Light, and Don't Go."

On the second sheet of paper, he drew "Super-Jaime," explaining to the Bragas, "Here's me and I'm real big. I'm eleven. Here I am flying up into the sky."

"Super-Jaime" could do things that little Jaime couldn't. Like protect himself. "Super-Jaime" showed up in most of the other pictures he drew, as did rocketships that took him "to the moon."

"How about drawing a picture of your father?" Laurie suggested.

"In jail?" he asked.

"No, not necessarily," said Joe. "However you see him."

"I will see him happy," said Jaime.

He drew a picture of his father jumping rope, "with muscles here and muscles here, and here and here." His father was "very strong," said Jaime. "Muscles on his legs . . . his legs are strong, his nose, his eyes.

"Everything about him is strong."

Iliana he drew with "glasses," apparently the dark ones she wore frequently, which covered her blackened eyes. He drew a necklace on her. ("She always wears this.") And beside her, he drew little Jaime and a "little ghost," which he said was his "make-believe" brother.

"And there's my father," he said, "up on a ladder. Watching."

It was on Jaime's second visit with the Bragas that he had his first opportunity to deliver the script his father and stepmother had written for him.

Following a discussion initiated by Jaime about his hope that his father would be out of jail in time for his birthday, Joe, for the first time, broached the subject of life in the Fuster household with him.

Frank's son had no way of knowing that his friend Jason Harrison had already been in to see the Bragas and had laid it all out, including Jaime's own role in the nightmare.

"Before, when you were living with Frank and Iliana, tell us what happened."

"There were babies that were always crying, too much."

"You had children at your house? All the times? Weekdays? Weekends?"

"The weekends were vacation time."

"When the children were there, what games did they play? Ring-around-the-rosy?"

"Yes, we would hold hands up and go around in a circle."

"Did Iliana play with the children?"

"Yes. Iliana played with the children."

"Exactly how did they play the games, and did they play 'catch me, catch me'?"

"Yes. Hide-and-go-seek."

"What happened when they got caught? Did everyone have their clothes off?"

"Just the babies had their clothes off. You know how little babies are . . . always playing and watching TV."

"Did Frank and Iliana wear masks?"

"Yes, they wore masks sometimes . . . not to scare me—playing. Yes, it did startle me, made me jump. They would wear masks and say, 'boo, boo!' "

"Did you see videocassettes?"

"No."

"Did anybody ever take any movies of you?"

"No." Suddenly Jaime blurted out, "I am doing this just to get out of here. I don't like to come here every day. I want to go fishing, to the beach. I don't want to be bothered with this thing."

"What things are bothering you?"

"When I was reading and trying to write numbers, the children were saying, 'ca-ca pee-pee, ca-ca pee-pee, ca-ca pee-pee,' over and over, yelling and screaming, and the baby says, 'shit, shit, shit, shit.' This boy, Jason, and then some babies were fighting. . . ."

"I know it is scary seeing your father in jail, and I know you worry about your father. Do you know that children do not get sent to jail?"

"Ca-ca pee-pee, ca-ca pee-pee," laughed Jaime. "They say, 'shit, shit, shit.' You know that word motherfucker? A bad word, and the babies are saying that loud, loud. I couldn't control my mind."

"What other child?"

"None. Babies."

"Can you tell me some more things that have been worrying you?"

"No. I miss my dad. I am praying for God . . . telling everybody I love him."

"Did your dad ever hit you?"

"Only when I am bad."

"Would he hit you very hard?"

"Yes. I am being better at school. I will be an angel someday."

"You haven't done bad, but if you think you have done bad, talk about it and you will feel better. Your mom, Iliana, told you to tell everybody that your dad is good?"

"I love my dad—bad and good. Iliana said I could save my dad."

"It is not up to you to save him. It's not your fault."

"Somebody put the lie on him, my mom said."

And so it went, Jaime delivering the message he had been issued in order to "save his father," and Joe and Laurie allowing him to deliver it, knowing that it was unfinished business to which he must attend in order to reconcile the conflict within him—his love for his father and his fear of Frank Fuster.

They would not try to force him into betrayal.

On the third day, it was Jaime who requested that he be allowed to speak to the Bragas. He strode into the room and, before he sat down, informed them that he had two "questions" that he wished to discuss.

"I'm worried and I miss my dad."

"You miss your dad? I understand that," said Joe.

"And I'm worried."

"Tell me what you're worried about."

"About my *dad*."

"You worried about something happening to him? Now, when you went to see him, didn't he look OK?"

"Yeah, he looked OK."

"Did he look sick?"

"Sick? No. The only thing I'm worried because he was crying when I saw him."

"Well, he's crying because you and he are separated. And he's not sure whether or not he's gonna see you anymore. I think that's what he's worried about because, you know, he's in the jail."

Jaime settled onto the floor, cross-legged, with his elbows on his knees, his chin resting comfortably in his hands in rapt attention, a marked contrast from the child who, two days before, had entered the same room in perpetual motion.

Joe took the opportunity to plant the seeds he hoped might grow with the child as he became a man.

"Look," said Joe. "This might be a little hard to understand, Jaime, but try, OK?

"When you're a father—and you will be a father, probably, someday—the most important thing to you is that your children are

OK. That becomes very important. More important than even yourself.

"When that happens, and you're separated from your children, like has happened to your father, you worry 'what's gonna happen to my child? Is he gonna be OK? Because I can't go to him if he has some need. If he's in trouble, if he's unhappy, I can't go to him.'

"That is why your father was crying. Not 'cause he was unhappy about himself. Because he's a grown-up. He can take care of himself. Remember how you said how strong your father is?"

"Yes."

"Your dad can take care of himself. Whatever happens, he's an adult. And he's gonna take care of himself. But he's worried, 'What's gonna happen to my little boy?'

"And that's why he cried. And you're now with your mother, who loves you very much. There *is* someone who can take care of you. And your father is going to know that.

"See, when you saw him in jail this past weekend, you didn't know—and he didn't know—that you were going to be able to be with your mother. And that she was gonna be able to take care of you.

"So he was worried, and he was scared, and he cried, 'What's gonna happen to my little boy?' Even if he didn't say those words, that's what his tears meant . . .

"And if he doesn't know now, he'll know soon, that things are gonna be fine because you're with your mother. That's actually good for him. Let me tell you *why* that'll be good for him.

"It's good for him because if he knows you're in good hands, with your mother, then he doesn't have to worry about you anymore, and he can start putting all his energy—and all his concern—on worrying about himself and what he's going to do in this situation for himself. And for Iliana.

"So the very best thing—the *very* best thing—that you can do for your father, and for Iliana, and for Jaime, is to try with your mother to learn with her to be happy . . .

"You have a chance for a brand-new start. No matter what happened. No matter *what* happened," said Joe.

"Everything that comes after is good?" Jaime was assimilating every word.

"*Yes*. Because you have a new chance to start over fresh. All new. And you have that with your mother."

Laurie broke in with a few thoughts of her own. She told Jaime, "What happens to your father . . . I know that you *wish* that you can make things better for your father. And I know that you said Iliana told you that only *you* could save your father. But that wasn't fair of her to tell you that, because it isn't up to you to save your father, OK?

"Your father is a man. And your father and the people who are helping him, it's up to *them* what happens, not up to you, OK?

"So no matter what anybody *told* you—that something bad might happen to you if you said something or that if you *didn't* say something that you could make it all better—you're just a little boy. And you're a very special little boy."

Joe reentered the conversation by alluding to the subject that had remained unspoken during all the hours the three had spent together. "You have already *said* what you had to say," Joe told him.

"Now you've done it. And now your responsibility—now—is over. You've done what has to be done. Now you get on with the rest of your life. And let your father and Iliana take care of *their* business."

"All right." Jaime nodded solemnly. Now he realized that they hadn't bought a word of the "I can't imagine why my father's in jail" smoke screen. They knew all along what he couldn't tell—and why.

"You *did* what had to be done, yourself," Joe continued. "You did what they asked you to do. You don't have any more—do you understand what the word *responsibility* means?"

"Responsibility?" Jaime thought for a moment. "It means that, um—my rights."

". . . Let me put it in different words, then. If, um—if I have a little boy, a son, and when he's growing up, *he's* my responsibility. *He's* who I have to take care of because I'm his daddy. Until he grows up, I am responsible for him.

"It is my *duty* to take care of him . . . *You* have done your *duty* for your father. You have done your responsibility. You did what they told you you should do. And therefore you did your job.

"You don't have to keep doing your job. Now your job is to begin to enjoy your life with your mother. And become like—remember the drawing? Super-Jaime at eleven?

"That's your job now. To become happy. . . ."

"See," added Laurie, "no matter what anyone said to you, you did nothing wrong, OK?"

"OK," said Jaime.

"You're a good boy," she continued. "And everything's gonna be OK. And sometimes if you feel unhappy, or sometimes if you feel like maybe you didn't do the right thing, talk to your mother. And no matter what anybody said to you—even your father and Iliana— no matter what they said to you, because they're a little scared right now, they want the best for you, too. They want you to be happy, too. And they wouldn't *really* want to do anything to make you unhappy.

"So, if there's anything they said that maybe makes you feel a little scared, that maybe you're not doing the right thing, or you're not doing what they think you should do, don't *worry* about that. Because what they *really* want—deep in their heart—is for you to be happy.

"So you make yourself happy. And you take care of *Jaime* first. Because you're a little boy. You have your whole life in front of you. And your job—first—is to you. It's not your job to take care of your father. He's the father. You're the little boy."

Jaime understood. "So, it's my job to protect me, it's my dad's job to protect him, and my mom's job to protect her."

"Yes," said Joe. "And it is your mother—Martha's—job to take care of you. That's her responsibility now, and she wants to do it.

"And you can help her do it. You can help her to help you be happy . . . you can help her to know what the things are that worry you.

"You should learn to talk openly to your mother about your feelings. And about *anything* that's on your mind—good things and troubling things. That's the best thing that you can do for your mother, and that's the best thing you can do for Jaime.

"And that's the best thing you can do for your father, because your father wants you to have a good life. . . ."

When Joe finished, Jaime Fuster looked as though a great weight had been lifted from his small shoulders. He had done his duty, yet had still had his cry for help heard.

Joe asked him if he would like to make a "good-bye" drawing for him and Laurie.

Jaime drew them a series of "happy" pictures. And the happiest of all was a calendar for the month of August on which he circled the fifteenth day, telling them, "I want you to keep this so you will remember this day."

It is unlikely that Doctors Joseph and Laurie Braga would ever forget how they spent their sixteenth wedding anniversary or the present the son of Frank Fuster unwittingly gave them.

On a smooth, clean sheet of manila paper, he drew a picture of the couple standing side by side. Smiling. And under them he printed the words "Thank You for . . ."

"How do you spell *everything*?" asked Jaime.

Part IV

JUSTICE
FOR SOME

"Men occasionally stumble over the truth, but most of them pick themselves up and hurry off as if nothing had happened."
—Winston Churchill

17

No one had ever gotten a conviction on a case like Country Walk. But then, no one had been quite as determined as Janet Reno, who was fully aware of the sobering contents of the children's taped interviews. It was indeed an invisible crime of illogical motive. But it had—without question—occurred.

In the fall of 1984, weeks prior to the November election, the Dade state attorney vowed unwavering commitment to the service of justice in the case called Country Walk. And as she mentally assessed the resources that would be required to make good her promise, her eyes fell upon John Hogan, a prosecutor of noted conviction rate and quiet ambition, who had, nonetheless, never prosecuted a case of child molestation.

John Hogan's star was rising rapidly in the fall of 1984, he being at the time one of the ablest trial lawyers in Janet Reno's stable of assistants and, not incidentally, her frequent companion on campaign excursions to evening debates and preelection ventures through the heart of Miami's ghettos, where a state attorney—even an imposing one—was best advised to wander at risk.

The job of campaign escort (bodyguard) suited the pleasant (and large) John Hogan, who fully appreciated how firmly his star was hitched to the outcome of next month's election. Dependent on the whims of Dade County's ethnically polarized registered voters, the thirty-five-year-old career prosecutor had what some election-watchers were calling "an even shot" at occupying either the throne to Her Majesty's left or an unemployment line.

Reno's loyal and trusted lieutenant could not expect a warm welcome from a new regime, despite his well-documented legal talents. In the politics of power (and few things are more powerful than the authority to indict), it would matter little that John Hogan hadn't lost a case since 1980—and never a major felony.

231

Should Reno lose this election, his aspirations might require some adjustment.

A new regime, it was noted, also might not share Janet Reno's keen interest in keeping the Fusters off the streets.

An untested administration would find it far more expedient (and politically sound) to "examine" the evidence more "closely" and deem the charges too hastily filed by its unworthy and unseated opponent than to take a well-publicized child sex abuse case to trial and lose—a prospect of historic probability. For no district attorney in the nation had ever succeeded in convincing a jury that large numbers of very small children had been systematically raped and terrorized in a trusted childcare environment.

Hogan knew little of Country Walk, having winced at the headlines and offered brief prayers of gratitude that someone other than himself was dealing with this depressing situation. The prosecutor's aversion to sex crimes was legend among his colleagues, who marveled at his willingness to barter away one rape for two of their murders. Hogan would rather face a battalion of bereaved relatives than a single weeping woman who was about to be assaulted again, this time by the system of which he was a part. At least with a homicide the victim didn't also become a victim of a trial.

He couldn't imagine going through that with a child.

Much less dozens of them.

By late October, the Country Walk parents were coming to grasp the fleetness with which public interest would visit and depart from their cause. The media storm that had whipped with such unexpected fury just weeks before had disintegrated to a distant rumbling—the calm before the next of many storms.

But the parents didn't perceive it quite that way.

They felt abandoned.

The media's suspended interest in no way granted a moratorium to their own blinding pain—a condition that, nonetheless, unleashed a vision of remarkable focus:

They were not victims of a freakish twist of fate. Rather, they were coming to realize, they rode the crown of an uncharted iceberg.

As a united front, the Country Walk parents set out to chart it for themselves. They began clipping articles and taping news specials and talk shows dealing with child sex abuse, especially that which occurred with ritualistic overtones in mass-access environments—

daycare centers, Boy Scout troops, karate classes, choirs. They found disturbing similarities in the stories being told by very small children behind closed doors all over the country—painfully detailed accounts of sex and Satan and death and terror and cameras.

And excrement and drugs.

Were the Fusters copycats? Had they extracted the most novel aspects of the case in California, or the one in Jordan, Minnesota, and woven the most bizarre into their own activities?

Or were these practices and their meaning dispensed through informal networking, like the "newsletters" put out by a handful of organizations dedicated to securing the "free, uninhibited, and Constitutionally protected right" to pursue their sexual preference for children?

Either circumstance spoke of possibilities. For the details of Country Walk's well-publicized predecessors in other parts of the country were as accessible as the addresses of organizations that catered to the mutual interests of people consumed with children the way a dieter is consumed with thoughts of chocolate mousse. The link to kindred spirits resided in any public library, where large and official directories sprinkled their names (and post office boxes) above and below the listings for the Lions and Jaycees.

This was, after all, America.

Society's last sexual outcasts were forming (and legally incorporating) their own clubs. Thus released from secretive sexual isolation, they found reassurance in their numbers and the appearance of normalcy that led them to the collective conclusion that they weren't sick—society was. For society was imposing "unnatural" inhibitions on their "natural" sexual bent. Why should they be denied broccoli simply because the "ruling mentality" liked carrots?

The literature they circulated among themselves was direct and to the point: the child-adult sex advocates, as they liked to call themselves, had every intention of becoming "a productive force in the world," much in the spirit of the movements for feminism and gay liberation—events to which pedophile organizations referred with tones of historic destiny. At least one "child-lovers'" society decried in print the "cowardice" of sexual liberation pioneers who drew the line at children. One pedophile wrote to his comrades:

> These movements have, by and large, retreated to reform and reaction, and they now disown connections to pedophilia (and incest) and deny their possibilities as the basis for personal and social

liberation. The historic similarities of present pedophile movements are still in process, and for the first time seem to be surfacing in explicitly political and collective ways.

In this context, codified and moral "how to" manuals appear at a slightly later phase than when a *movement* begins to *spread* [ed. italics]. Much of the instruction and knowledge of pedophilia (as well as several other sexual interests) have appeared historically in forms that are initially designated as "pornography" by the ruling mentalities. Written and visual representations of these interests are based on possibilities: they are wishes and desires, and—fully recognized by and frightening to the administrators—they can be taken as intents: promises to try it if the chance ever occurs. This is the essence of all wants that are subversive to an established order.

The editors of these "handbooks" for the "child liberation" movement did not confine themselves to intellectual discussion of developments on the revolutionary front. There was additional information of vast interest and import to their diverse and burgeoning readership.

There were advertisements that brazenly offered to buy photos of "Girls, 7-14. . . . Swimsuits, panties, sleepwear. . . ." or to sell a confidential mailing address to which materials "of interest" might be sent.

There were movie reviews, which focused on entertainment value that tilted slightly askew of center. To a critic for one publication, a mediocre box office sitcom held promise of a titillating evening:

> *Author, Author*—Al Pacino stars as a playwright whose life is in chaos on the eve of his big Broadway opening. . . . Near the beginning of the movie his wife and the two girls (Elva Leff as Bonnie and Ari Meyers as Debbie) wish him Happy Birthday by smashing a cake in his face. The two girls are both equal to Brooke Shields in *Pretty Baby*. They are about eleven years old with long silky hair and just as spunky as Brooke was. The most heart-throbbing scene occurs thirty-five minutes after the start of the film: One of the girls comes out of the bedroom wearing a sensuous white baby-doll top with lace trim and little yellow panties that barely cover her gorgeous fanny. . . .

The review continued for several more inches to extol similar points of interest to be noted in this film, none of which included an assessment of Pacino's acting abilities.

The parents also secured, from the Florida Department of Law Enforcement, copies of a variety of semiprofessional-looking publications the agency had stumbled on in the course of routine investigations—publications whose covers featured photographs of children in poses that did not resemble a visit to Santa's knee. There was, however, a rear view of a naked boy mounting a motorcycle, which was stapled to ten pages of "affirmative" information about the membership's much-maligned "interests"; an article in which "A Woman Talks [in most refined and eloquent terms] About [her advocacy for] Pedophilia"; and a datelined story hailing news from the revolutionary front:

> MINNEAPOLIS—The issue of man-boy love is now being widely discussed in the Twin Cities of Minneapolis and St. Paul, Minnesota. A forum on the issue June 21 drew a turnout of 200 despite its being moved twice, the second time that morning as a result of bomb threats. . . .
>
> The forum heard presentations by David Thornstad, who summarized [the organization's] views on consensual sexuality, [and] Carl Chrisman, a consciousness-raising teacher. . . .
>
> Chrisman talked about John Wayne Gacy and how straight society turned him into a mass murderer. He said Gacy was given electroshock and sexual aversion therapy to cure his attraction toward boys. "The object of his desire became the object of his scorn," Chrisman said.
>
> All the major Twin Cities news outlets covered the forum. At least one TV channel gave live coverage from outside the hall.
>
> The coverage was considered fair. . . .

Not only were child molesters holding conventions—they were apparently pleased with the nature of the media coverage.

Included among the literature the parents continued to gather from law enforcement agencies was a publication that reprinted for its interested readers a "marriage manual" style guide that explained "How to Have Sex with Children." It was a document worthy of lengthy introduction by a Mr. David Sonenschein of an entity called "Austin Pedophile Study Group II," who could be reached, it was mentioned, through a post office box in Austin Texas. He wrote:

> The paper that follows was produced initially I am told about 1980,

revised and enlarged in 1981; it is the latter version that appears here, very slightly edited. As a somewhat academic exercise, I would like to introduce this into the growing archives of the pedophile and children's liberation movements as a gesture of public education.

It clearly has connections with other political and cultural currents, and as an artifact and act, it needs to be preserved. . . .

As an artifact, the leaflet emerged because of the very wide-spread existence of pedophilia, and because there is no *Joy of Sex with Children* in the bookstores of America celebrating it as part of our culture's knowledge and aspiration. Sex between adults and children ["children" being variously defined] is illegal, although that is certainly no index to its ethical and productive merit; if anything, it is a recommendation, given the corrupt system of "justice" under which we now have to live. . . .

The article that warranted this thoughtful articulation was then published in its entirety with a disclaimer from the editors that ". . . the questions of power differences between adults and children, especially between adult men and female children, are more real and serious than the leaflet seems to indicate."

The leaflet, in fact, scoffed at the notion that ". . . a sixty-pound child pinned under a 270-pound man who is forcing his penis down her throat . . ." was having anything other than "fun."

And there were ways, the leaflet noted, to enhance and expedite the experience. There were, for instance, a variety of ways a creative individual might meet new sexual partners. Occupations and hobbies promised fertile hunting ground if well selected. And, if all else failed, there was always the old standby:

> Get to know parents.
> Sometimes [the author prattled cheerfully], you can take babysitting tasks or you can just take the kids places when they know you and know that the kids like being with you.
> Sometimes parents can introduce you to other kids, too.

Once an interesting sexual partner is secured, the article continued, there were ways to effect a timely and "welcomed" seduction. This could get a little tricky, it was noted.

> Sex is play, not work. Sometimes it is best when beginning sex with someone to do it as part of a game. . . . For adult males, it might be

a good idea not to show an erect penis to a partner right off, especially
for kids who have not had sex before. . . .

In general, it's been our experience that kids enjoy nonpenetrating
sex the best—sex that involves body-rubbing, friction and movement
of any kind, and especially oral sex. Almost anything goes in
nonpenetrating sex and experimentation is the key—try it all! There
are only a few cautions that need to be mentioned.

If a kid has trouble with taking the entire head of a penis in their
mouth, or doesn't want to (ever swallow a baseball?), show them how
just sucking and licking the underneath, just below the head, is just
as good. Another note is: *never* blow air into the vagina. This is
extremely dangerous and can be fatal, some medical experts say. . . .
Another is not to fool around with the vagina after fooling around
with the anus. Bacteria that live in the rectum where they help the
body can cause bad infections in the vagina. . . .

Now as for penetrating sex, we don't mean that it's bad for kids or
that kids don't enjoy it. Many do and many want it. Just about
everything that adults can do together, an adult and kid can do
together—but of course you have to be sensitive to size differences.
Most very young or small kids cannot and should not be penetrated by
an adult penis or dildo. Sometimes a finger is OK, but with a finger,
lubrication is recommended. And watch those fingernails! Even small
cuts can become infected. Some people say use only K-Y jelly . . .
others, Vaseline! Saliva is always available and usually the best
lubricant; it's fun to try different oils, too.

Having chewed for a spell on this mordant feast of rationalized
aberration, the parents of Country Walk sought additional paths of
enlightenment on their informative quest, and they found—more
iceberg.

The scattered forces of the pedophilic underground appeared—
from the official (and obscure) reports they were able to obtain—to
be growing more organized and gathering more force, like a tropical
storm banding around what was emerging as the eye of the
hurricane.

Kid porn.

A three-*billion*-dollar—per year—U.S. industry that grossed
twice that worldwide.

It was bigger than Disney.

Much bigger.

Either 30,000 Americans were spending $100,000 apiece each year to purchase pictures of children being raped, or a hundred times more were willing to allot $1,000 of their annual budgets to support their recreational viewing habits.

Kid porn provided them with the vital link through which they found each other and commiserated on the "unfairness of an intolerant society" and the "normalcy" of their deeds. Kid porn gave them the means by which they could dedicate many of their waking hours to pursuing their pleasures. For what better circumstance than to travel in circles where great monetary worth is placed on such pleasurably obtained documentation of achievement?

Kid porn sanctified their desires, even as it lined their pockets with gold plucked from sweaty, eager palms. There were many "collectors," as they called themselves, who traded pictures of kids like baseball cards—one "golden shower" (a child being urinated on) for two fellatios. Each separate act was assigned specific value in "circles of friends" who generally shared a common fetish—bondage, excretion, ritual. And each "documentation" was snatched up for a sizable price before the negatives dried, by men and women who harbored uncontrollable urges and secret desires of confused or unknown origin.

And then there was Frank Fuster.

A molested child grown twisted by a particularly grotesque burden he had borne through adolescence and adulthood? Or a "bad seed" planted by fate to fertilize a union dedicated to evil? A union that embraced a religion compatible with its combined world view of mistrust and fear and hate.

A religion in which children became the ultimate sacrament in the worship of power.

Frank Fuster was obsessed with power.

And compelled by control.

He controlled his women. He controlled his child. And he controlled himself, to the point of compulsion. Frank was a gesturer, a paper-folder, and an aligner of objects, whose hands, when not busy, were in the process of being washed. He also took a lot of baths. And he had his wife wash the outside of his "temple" with a ladder, a sponge, and a pail of water.

He collected literature that covered various routes of access to power beyond his castle in Country Walk. On the night Detective Meznarich served a belated search warrant on the abandoned Fuster residence, Frank's library boasted an assortment of reading materials of curious interest to an ex-convict who had earned his high school diploma at the age of twenty-one—in jail.

There was a selection of biographies on leaders of the Black Power movement and blueprints that traced paths of global scope drawn by the architects of world policy—the negotiators of treaties. And there were textbooks on human behavior, Pavlov being Frank's apparent mentor in this intriguing field of interest.

The control of human behavior.

The master key to power.

Missing from the house that night, along with numerous other items (some known and some not) that left the day before in the mysterious white van, was a book called *I Am*, a book that Frank read aloud to Jaime and Iliana each and every night. Roughly translated, *I Am* holds that God is within each man and that therefore Man is God.

There was every reason to believe that he embraced the concept quite literally. In fact, there was early speculation that Frank Fuster might have been a Reverend Jim Jones in the making—an aborted replica of the man whose pious wife helped him poison nearly a thousand men, women, and (mostly) children in the jungles of Guyana in November of 1978.

Drugs and psychological warfare administered by her ordained husband persuaded Jones's once gentle wife to believe that she occupied a seat at the right hand of God, who instructed her to lace Kool Aid with cyanide and syringes with the same. Mrs. Jones, herself, administered injections to children who refused to drink the fatal brew. Children, survivors reported, who as "punishment" for minor infractions, had been routinely required to perform fellatio on the Reverend Jones before an audience of fellow residents of Jonestown.

Had Iliana—through similar tactics—similarly succumbed to her husband's unusual appetites? If so, did it excuse her actions?

It was a question the parents pondered frequently as they pursued knowledge not only of *what* had happened in the Fuster home, but of *why*.

Always, the answer was the same.

Because it could.

The reports and articles they waded through grew deeper and more ominously brazen. Some of the "how to" manuals were heralding daycare centers as the "happy hunting grounds" of a new and exciting age. Pedophiles weren't just stumbling into the Fusters' line of work; they were being directed to it by underground newspapers and over-the-counter booklets that could be purchased at some of the same stores that sold *Bambi*.

They came across an article published by the Federal Bureau of Investigation, dated January 1984 and written by Kenneth V. Lanning, a special agent considered to be the Justice Department's inhouse expert on child sex abuse. Lanning outlined the methods of child sex rings known by the FBI to be operating around the country. He presented a case study of forty convicted child pornographers and sex ring operators, noting, ". . . almost half of the offenders used their occupation as the major access route to the child victims. The adult had a legitimate role as an authority figure in the lives of the children selected for the ring and was able to survey vulnerable children through access to some type of family records or history. . . ."

Special Agent Lanning would someday be consulted by the state regarding the Fuster case about which he made a most unusual inquiry: Did the authorities find in the Fuster home nonsexual pictures of the children?

Hundreds, came the reply.

Typical, said Lanning.

A legal memorial to hundreds of illegal acts.

• • •

As a steady stream of victims continued to flow through the State Attorney's Center for Children, the crimes against them went largely unreported by the media. What was once "news" was now considered commonplace—no more worthy of mention than a burglary in Miami Beach.

So, unknown to the public, which perceived the sex abuse furor to be over with and (quite frankly) overdone, children bearing rectal scars and torn hymens and an assortment of sexually transmitted diseases continued to tell their stories to the Bragas. These were the ones who had fallen prey to "amateurs," for those who regarded their sexual preference as a "profession" would have never left behind such sloppy and revealing markers of proof.

While the flow of victims was steady, the issuance of arrest warrants was not, the state attorney apparently having regained her insight into the futility of taking the perpetrators to trial.

There would be no arrest of the principal of a local Christian academy who, among other acts mentioned by his three-year-old victim, liked to eat grapes off her belly.

No arrest of the therapist of a learning-disabled seven-year-old, who had named him as the source of infected semen that had been ejaculated into his body.

No arrest of the preschool cook who was named by twin sisters as the source of their own disease.

The public did not know of the teachers and janitors and bus drivers named by the children, who were nonetheless allowed to pursue their pleasure unchecked. For the public still did not perceive that a single small witness could not a case make—regardless of the certain knowledge that the crime had occurred. Unless the children were of sufficient maturity to function as adults in court, their cases would not be pursued—no matter how willing the parents were to see them through to conviction.

Little had changed in the wake of Country Walk.

Except that words like *witch hunt* and *hysteria* had begun creeping into print, peppering the quotes of the accused and their representatives. An enormous propaganda machine began dispensing clouds of fog that pandered to the public's inherent need not to know of these unpleasantries.

"It didn't happen," had such a nice ring to it.

It was imperative at this stage of the "revolution," noted some of the "child liberationists," that public outrage not be allowed to drench their embers before they finished building the bonfire. This was not the time in which to emerge so boldly from the closet.

They needed to ignite a backfire to assuage the public's discontent, which threatened to focus official attention more intently on their activities—an act that could abort the "movement" in midgestation.

This apparently was what led them to discover the ideal dispenser of their smoke screen—defense attorneys.

Defense attorneys were always receptive to new and creative strategies, especially successful ones. So popular was the "It didn't happen" defense that it was routinely invoked in even the most egregious circumstances.

Denials of their clients' guilt and charges of "child abuse hysteria" poured from their lips, even as their hands gripped Polaroid snapshots of their clients engaged in sex with toddlers, or medical reports that bore the word *positive* next to *gonorrhea.*

Words like *witch hunt* would be remembered. The pleas of guilty that followed, ignored.

The parents of Country Walk viewed this dark and doubtful backlash with a growing sense of frustration and outrage as Samek, and especially Von Zamft, labeled as patently absurd the secrets that their children had harbored under penalty of death—and the memories that still caused them to wake screaming in the night.

Lest the public fail to grasp the comfort of "it didn't happen," there was a supplement of sufficient personal interest that preyed effectively on adult logic: "It could happpen to you."

"Child abuse hysteria" and "witch hunts" raged so rampant, cried the increasingly organized rumor mills, that no law-abiding mother, father, or daycare operator was immune to swift arrest, financial ruin, and disrepute based solely on the words of a child.

Daycare workers, ignorant of the difficulty with which even a convicted murderer/child molester was being brought to trial, were "warned" to keep their hands carefully clear of their potentially dangerous clients, who might mistake an affectionate hug or a diaper change for a sexual advance. They did not stop to consider that their small charges were not apt to confuse a diaper wipe with a penis, the concept of "molest" being touted by even confessed molesters as a misplaced pat on the behind.

It didn't seem to occur to the panicked public that a child was as able as any human being to sense an adult's telegraphed "interest"—a phenomenon no less subtle than the "messages" encountered in a single's bar on a Saturday night. "Witch hunt" had replaced the faculties of logic that might have led them to understand that a child, though not schooled in the chemistry of sexuality, nonetheless was capable of recognizing the difference between a bath and a sexual assault.

The parents were left to raise the human wreckage left by the Fusters, while their attorneys showered salt into their wounds. They wondered among themselves whether Jeffrey Samek would be inclined to leave his own eighteen-month-old daughter and four-year-old son in the same building with the Fusters, much less in their depraved hands.

They thought not.

• • •

The trial became the sun around which the parents' lives revolved—the light at the end of the tunnel through which they must pass in the processing of their grief. A process through which many would continue to evolve in the years to come.

Denial, anger, acceptance, denial again—a continuum that recycled their emotions like so much hazardous waste. For all of them the process was the same, though in varying degrees of transition and evolution.

There occurred among the thirty-some affected families a decisive split within hours of the news of Frank Fuster's arrest. The core group of parents who had bonded on that first horrifying night of collective discovery at the Herschel home—two nights before Samek and Von Zamft surrendered the murderer/child molester to a judge—became and remained cautiously committed to following the path that led to a courtroom.

Their numbers were few compared to the ones who closed their doors to Donna Meznarich in the beginning and now only cracked them occasionally in order to shoo off any additional inquiries from the law. Most didn't want to get "involved."

Some continued to deny, even to themselves, that they were.

A few announced intent to help "clear the Fusters' name," a resolution that began to fade as their children's "peculiarities" became too pronounced to ignore in this new and revealing context. Nightmares. Masks. Monsters. Excessive masturbation. French kissing. Inserting toys into rectums. Irrational fear of the bathroom. Unusual toilet and bathing habits. Regression. It was the mosaic blueprint of a Fuster victim.

Yet still some parents denied. Even those who knew without question what had happened to some of the children—would not accept that it had happened to their own.

Chip Levy's parents straddled the line (but failed to cross it) between the group of parents who chose to be "involved" and those who did not. Barry Levy was a private practitioner of civil and criminal law—a cynical man who was nonetheless pleasant, if not gregarious. His wife, Sara, was a nurse who worked part-time, and who had on a dozen or so of these occasions left her son Chip—then not quite two—in the care of Iliana Fuster.

Sara had, after a time, grown "uncomfortable" with her babysitting arrangements—enough so that she abruptly ceased her patronage of the Country Walk Babysitting Service, having twice wandered into the Fuster house, uninvited, when her pounding at the front door failed to elicit response from within. Twice she heard her son's playmate, Andy Pierson, plead to be released from the master suite, from which Iliana had emerged, locking the door behind her.

"He doesn't want to take his nap," Iliana had shrugged on the first occasion, with apparent nonchalance. But the second—and last—time that this occurred, Iliana's appearance was disheveled, her manner nervous.

The little boy who called from the other side of the door, "I want out! I want out!" managed to work the lock free and toddled into Sara's stunned view through the master bedroom door.

Andy Pierson was stark naked.

"Not a stitch, not a sock," Sara would later testify in Courtroom 4-2 as tears welled in her angry eyes.

"She said she was changing his diaper.

"I felt very, very—uncomfortable."

It took the Levys a number of weeks to acknowledge that Chip had stayed with the Fusters more than "a few" times and considerably longer for them to realize that even a single visit, in some cases, had been more than enough.

Then there was the interview.

The exceptionally verbal Chip had grown uncharacteristically silent during his one and only encounter with Laurie Braga—right about the time she dropped the names Frank and Iliana into the conversation. Laurie would not soon forget the look of clear and penetrating panic in Chip Levy's eyes when she offhandedly inquired, "Did you ever play ring-around-the-rosy?"

Chip began tugging his mother toward the door, which promised escape from this terrifying line of questioning. Sara Levy wavered at this threshold of discovery, but was no less inclined to flight.

Laurie didn't protest the abrupt conclusion to the interview. Chip, she believed, must be allowed to protect his mother from the words he sensed she wasn't prepared to hear. The choice must be his to tell her in his own way in his own time. Or not at all.

And the choice must be his mother's whether to listen.

Laurie told Sara Levy that she had no clear indication that Chip had been abused by the Fusters, but that, given his visible reaction to mention of a certain childhood game, he may have "seen" something in the Fuster home that had "frightened" him.

Without hearing it from Chip's own mouth, Laurie would not speculate as to the possibilities of his fate, which ranged from his having "seen something" to his having experienced—repeatedly—a terror for which he could not (or would not) find words. Or something in between.

But Laurie had her suspicions, based on other pieces of the puzzle she continued to assemble. If one were to give credence to the grotesque stories being offered by children who could not otherwise know so intimately the details of events that lay beyond their full comprehension—a telling often accompanied by deftly accurate demonstrations with anatomically correct proxies—it would seem that the Fusters had ravaged most any child they managed to entice over their threshold.

Even the little boy who passed a brief five hours in their home. The one who lived right next door.

There were, however, two sisters who, the Bragas believed, might have been spared the Fusters' special brand of childcare, having offered no visible confirmation, in word or behavior, that indicated that they were either distressed in general or specifically reactive to memories of time spent with the Fusters. Laurie got the distinct impression that these two, unlike the rest, had nothing out of the ordinary to tell. As she puzzled over this newest wrinkle in the Fuster tale, Laurie looked for a key factor that set these children apart from all the ones the Fusters chose as victims. True, the sisters were infrequent guests in the Fuster home.

But so were many of the others.

There seemed no extenuating circumstance that might have caused the babysitters to pass up sampling these two new additions to their pantry—save one.

Laurie winced at the implication, but the truth of the matter was that the only apparent difference between the sisters and the Fuster victims was their physical appearance. The Fuster victims were children of exceptional (and radiant) beauty—prime (and photo-genic) specimens that would command a premium in the world "chicken" photo market. Conversely, the apparently unmolested sisters were uncommonly homely—a genetic blessing in disguise, which may have exercised profound influence on their destiny.

Chip Levy was not so fortunately unendowed.

And then there was the eyewitness account.

Jason Harrison's first disclosure to Detective Meznarich and Christopher Rundle, the night before the Bragas were asked to interview him, described an act committed on Chip.

But the Levys shied from this distressing train of thought and placed themselves in a fragile state of limbo, where false hopes kept them afloat in their sea of despair. Sara retreated to her home to incubate, in solitude, the new fears and dreads she felt for the baby she carried in her belly—the baby conceived in more innocent times, just weeks before the Fusters turned in their masks. Some days she phoned the "involved" mothers in search of recent developments in the case. How were the "other" children doing, the ones who got molested? Other days she preferred not to know. Mostly, she was very angry.

Her husband, Barry, on the other hand, was mostly very busy. If he was "busy," he didn't have to think about Chip. What might have happened to Chip? What would happen to him now? If Barry was "busy," Sara couldn't bring up the fact that Chip had locked himself in his room to masturbate with his pillow all afternoon for the fifteenth day in a row. Nor would he have time to contemplate the implications of his small son's compulsions.

But he did have time for J-SAC, where he carved himself a niche along the perimeter of the most active circle of parents. He attended meetings, argued strategies, and volunteered to draw up the organization's incorporation papers. Barry was an active voice and a very interested party. But he drew the line at being categorized as an "affected" one.

Chip, he would explain to anyone who inquired, didn't go there "all that much," and he was there at a time of day when a lot of kids were coming and going—too much traffic, wrong time of day. He may have "seen something," but he would forget it in time, if in fact he remembered anything at all—he was, of course, only twenty-one months old at the time of his last visit.

Chip told his secrets only to his pillow.

• • •

Once "due process" firmly wedged all matters pertaining to the State's case against the babysitters into the machinery of the judicial system, the "involved" parents grew restive for news of progress along Janet Reno's celebrated road to prosecution.

Nothing seemed to be happening.

Their early visits to the Justice Building, which were now a blurred memory of confused and frightening emotions, had given them a link to the case and to each other. They were *doing* something back then—putting the pieces together, assembling the puzzle of truth.

By mid-October there was little left for them to do, truth having revealed itself most convincingly over the past several weeks. Now what? they wondered.

The case of Country Walk was, they were told, a matter for

lawyers, not victims. We'll let you know if we need you for anything. Go on home and put your lives back together.

Sure, they thought.

The children—especially the older, more articulate ones—continued to inquire as to the whereabouts of the Fusters and as to whether their current residence came equipped with locks and bars.

"Will they be there forever? Could they ever get out? Like maybe could they dig a tunnel or sneak a saw inside a cake?"

How could they explain to a five-year-old child that just because the Fusters drugged, tortured, and raped them and put knives to their throats didn't mean they would need to stage an elaborate "jailbreak" in order to walk among children again?

Not when there were so many attractive legal alternatives.

This led to a delicate bit of maneuvering on the parts of the individual families, none of which had the foggiest notion as to the "correct" response to these kinds of questions—"correctness" ideally being measured in terms of its contribution to the child's emotional well-being.

Sometimes they just whistled in the dark.

Two-year-olds—especially "uninvolved" ones who had, nonetheless, expressed uncharacteristic interest in the babysitters' whereabouts—were generally told in tones of finality that Frank and Iliana were in jail, they would never be able to hurt children again, and now we'll all forget about it and live happily ever after. This particular form of parent–child exchange would someday be painted by the Fusters' defense as a not-so-distant relative to "brainwashing."

Surely you can see, the jury would be told, how the parents' acknowledgment that the Fusters were in jail implanted in the minds of these "impressionable" young children the "unproven" idea that the Fusters were "bad" people—a circumstance that naturally caused them to spew forth hours of lurid testimony to two strange-looking individuals who called themselves child development specialists.

Funny, thought the parents. All along they had thought what they were doing was answering the kinds of questions that kids who'd been raped and terrorized might ask.

The older children were more probative in their inquiries, their concerns expressed in terms of the future as well as the here and now. These called for decidedly more complex and realistic answers, to all of which the defense would later attribute insidious implication. These kinds of exchanges would be "revealed" (in questionable context) to the jury by the Fuster defense as "proof" that the parents were "participants" (possibly inadvertent) in the "fabrication" and/or "reinforcement" of the "lies" being told by children against the defendants.

"Mom, will Frank and Iliana *stay* in jail?"

"I don't know; it depends on the judge."

"When will we know for sure?"

"After the trial."

"What will happen at the trial?"

"Well, there'll be Frank and Iliana and a judge and a jury, and the jury will decide if they did it."

"But they *did* do it."

"Yes, and you might be asked to tell the jury about it."

"In front of everybody? Will Frank and Iliana have handcuffs? Will there be police?"

"They can't come near you. The judge will make sure."

"But I'm scared."

"Maybe you'll feel more ready when it's time for the trial. You think about it. It's up to you."

"If you and Daddy die, who will I live with?"

"Mommy and Daddy are not going to die. Whether you tell what happened or not."

"Frank and Iliana said. . . ."

"I know what they said, and they lied. No matter what they told you might happen, it was a lie.

"Frank and Iliana will never, ever hurt you again."

The case be damned, thought the "involved" parents, if the defense intended to pervert their sometimes-blundering attempts to comfort their children into some kind of subliminal current that induced mass hysteria—the condition that, as the defense sought to imply, caused them to believe this fantastic tale.

The case be damned, if quieting their children's fears would be displayed as an act of contamination, not love. No one was going to stop them from assuring their children that the Fusters would never hurt them again.

It was the one thing they could promise.

Because it was the one thing they could control.

• • •

Abe Laeser perched on the edge of Jeannie Pierson's sofa,

occasionally rising to his feet and extending his hand in greeting to the dozen parents who had gathered here at the appointed time— 6:30 sharp, a week before Halloween.

It was to be the first Halloween their children would celebrate since their introduction to the Fusters' house of horrors, where masked monsters visited darkened bathrooms and invoked evil spirits that lurked down the hole in the toilet. The house in which toddlers were fed a steady diet of horror films—*Friday the 13th, Poltergeist, The Shining,* and an unnamed masterpiece in which a woman was butchered in a bathtub and heartily consumed by two men, a scene some of the children found as memorable as the dramas played out in the Fuster kitchen, where animals were slaughtered in worshipful irreverence to life.

Always in the kitchen—where the blood could be sponged from the floor with a squirt of disinfectant, the aroma of which was frequently noticeable upon entering Frank and Iliana's enviably immaculate home.

Every day was Halloween at the Fusters'.

Laeser chatted amiably about nothing in particular until the last expected guest had arrived—an achievement of no small measure for Janet Reno's towering, lantern-jawed deputy chief whose somber manner and funereal taste in attire earned him the whispered nickname "Darth Vader."

A designation that the prosecutor viewed with sternly concealed humor.

It was Deputy Chief Abe Laeser who had steadied the reins in Chris Rundle's wavering hands during the first frantic days of the Country Walk investigation and who had stood at the sexual battery unit chief's side during initial court appearances lest the presiding judge fail to perceive the seriousness with which the State viewed this particular case.

Laeser didn't tread into courtrooms on trivial matters.

But this was one matter he passionately hoped to see through to its conclusion. He didn't yet know that this plum was about to be plucked from his teeth and bestowed on the lanky man with the broad Irish face who occupied the other end of Jeannie Pierson's couch, his lips smiling tightly as his eyes scanned from the elaborate buffet spread along the kitchen counter to the men and women who clustered in groups of two and three, picking at cold-cut-laden plates.

As John Hogan studied the strangers with whom he would spend the next year of his life, he marveled at the equanimity with which they discussed the rape of their children—a subject over which he himself remained squeamish. As Janet Reno's division chief for major crimes, his days revolved around the most hideous Dade County had to offer. And though he took the parade of murders, tortures, and mutilations in efficient stride, he was unable to build a shell thick enough to completely dull the pain he felt inside.

He was not unlike Abe Laeser in this respect.

Neither felt comfortable murmuring words of consolation.

But their eyes clearly said, "I'm sorry."

It was not the State's custom to tutor the relatives of victims on the finer points of case law.

But Country Walk was no customary case.

And these were most uncustomary victims.

It had come to the State's attention that the parents who chose to involve themselves in the prosecution were not content to await further instruction by subpoena. They showered Chris Rundle with phone calls in which questions poured from their lips with increasing urgency. Would the case go to trial on January seventh, as scheduled? Were the children expected to testify? How? Which ones? Why?

Questions to which Rundle generally sputtered a lengthy response that made cryptic reference to "the complexities" of the case. Some days he reduced his answer to its purist form with a curt "I don't know."

Tonight Rundle occupied the third cushion of the Pierson couch, displaying little more comfort about participating in this highly irregular house call than the men who flanked him on either side— to his left the dark, brooding Laeser and to his right the fair Hogan, who was the only one among the three who soaked in the entire scene with the intensity of a soon-to-be-appointed chief of felonies who was about to try the most complex case he had ever taken into a courtroom.

Or most likely ever would.

Tonight John Hogan would not stir in his seat as Abe Laeser laid out a map of the Country Walk case on which he pinpointed an expected course of events that might or might not occur between now and the conclusion of the *State of Florida* v. *Francisco Fuster Escalona and Iliana Fuster*.

The course thus laid, Laeser described the roadblocks most likely to appear in their path—prophecies of gradient probabilities at which he arrived by tempering cautious optimism with a healthy dose of legal reality.

This was to be a "model" case in which they planned to stretch the law to boundaries that no one had yet dared test. The State was gambling, at this point, said Laeser, that they could protect the children as they were fed through the system, without risk of a reversible conviction.

The threat of reversible error would sustain great weight in any decisions that carried with them controversial issues that an appeals court might judge too liberally resolved. And though the State was willing to take these issues to the United States Supreme Court, if necessary, it planned to break the new ground with the utmost caution. At what price would they have won the children's protection if the conviction were overturned on appeal, forcing the victims either to endure another trial or to watch the Fusters walk free— leaving them to choose between quicksand and a pit of vipers?

It was all very complicated, said Laeser.

But he would try to explain.

First of all, he did not expect this matter to come to trial until late summer or early fall of the following year.

An audible groan filled the room.

The parents had been warned to expect delays, but nothing of this magnitude. Each day the trial loomed like a final obstacle over which they must leap before they could attempt to live "normal" lives. Mark Harrison would fix the engine on his aged but sea- worthy boat, which gathered cobwebs in his garage, "after the trial." Maggie Fletcher would pay more attention to her family "after the trial." The Herschels would move to Colorado "after the trial." Judy Prince would be able to pull into her driveway without averting her eyes and swallowing bile when the Fuster house came into her line of vision "after the trial."

Everything was supposed to be better "after the trial."

And though they recognized, to some extent, the magical think- ing that guided these plans, the end of the trial was at least a definable point from which to start reassembling and making decisions about their lives.

Now Laeser was telling them that the carrot upon which they expected to pounce within ten weeks might be kicked around the court docket for as much as a calendar year.

Until then, their lives were effectively placed on hold. Laeser met their cries of "foul" with patient explanation. There were certain problems inherent in this case, he told them, because of the publicity surrounding it and the sheer scope of the charges. While the State was bound by speedy trial rules, which required it to be prepared to prosecute within 180 days of the arrests, the defense was bound by no similar constraints. And since there were almost two hundred witnesses to be deposed by both sides, he fully expected the defense to ask for a continuance.

In fact, he said, Samek and Von Zamft would most likely try to delay the trial indefinitely in the hope that the children's memories would grow appreciably dim with time.

No witnesses, no crime.

The parents shifted uncomfortably at this double-bladed dagger that Abe Laeser had just unsheathed. As much as they wished to see the Fusters caged for life, they wished even more fervently than the defense team that their children's memories of the Fusters would grow dim—as quickly as possible.

Would the children forget?

Laeser smiled faintly, as though reflecting on the folly of his very good friend Michael Von Zamft who, he predicted, would probably base most—if not all—of his defense strategy on his own misconceptions about children.

The prosecutor waved his hand toward the long-haired couple seated quietly among the group that gathered around the sofa. Ask the memory lady, he said.

Neuropsychology—the study of brain function and development—happened to be one of Dr. Laurie Braga's areas of concentrated knowledge. The news she delivered was not what they wished to hear.

"They won't ever forget this," she said. "They'll simply grow more articulate in explaining it." Any child over the age of two—and some as young as twenty months—had sufficient brain function to retrieve information seared so indelibly into their memory banks.

The children would remember, Joe chimed in. But hopefully they would become comfortable discussing it with their parents so that the incident could assume appropriate proportion in the context of the rest of their lives. "This is probably the worst thing that will ever happen to them," said Joe. "But they need to know from *you* that it's uphill from here."

"You know as adults how difficult it is to have a problem that can't be shared with a spouse or a best friend. It's no easier for a child. Don't close your ears or change the subject if they come to you with a question or a concern.

"Let them put it behind them when *they're* ready.

"Not when you are."

But the defense, Laeser broke in, wouldn't delay the trial nearly as much as the impending court battles with the media. Their "three-hundred-dollar-an-hour lawyers," as he called them, were already gearing up to lay claim to videotapes, pictures, depositions, and other evidence that both defense and prosecution would just as soon keep confidential.

Numerous side issues not related to the trial itself would have to be dealt with in hearings on a case-by-case basis, delaying the trial indefinitely, said Laeser.

The biggest issue, he predicted, would be access to the trial itself.

The media, Abe Laeser told the parents, would color in many ways the course and direction this case might take before it came to trial. There would be gross invasions of their privacy. Pretrial publicity might even prompt a judge to order a change of venue. And, while the State wasn't anxious to take its show on the road, said Laeser, he believed that moving the trial to another locale would pose no special threat to the State's case. "We've moved big trials out of town before."

He did not at the time consider the possible ramifications of uprooting small children—the centerpieces of the case—and putting them through a trial in a strange courtroom in a strange city where they lived in a strange motel.

The defense, on the other hand, was expected to move heaven and earth to have the case tried outside of Dade County where the public hue and cry welled with little empathy for its cause.

Alternatives, from Samek and Von Zamft's point of view, were limited. They needed a large metropolitan area, not some small "cracker" town near the Georgia border, where residents might be more inclined to lynch their clients before they checked into the county jail. That narrowed the possibilities considerably.

An accented Cuban with dark-tinted glasses married to his second sixteen-year-old wife would be difficult for even the citizens of Jacksonville or Orlando to relate with.

That left only Tampa, with its large pool of Hispanic voters from which to draw a desirable jury pool. The citizens of Tampa, "uncontaminated" by Miami's media-spawned "hysteria," just might be persuaded to buy the defense party line.

But securing an appropriate change of venue was an "iffy" proposition. Von Zamft would quickly turn his energies toward slanting the local press coverage to his advantage. "There are times when you can turn the press your way, and there are times when you can't. . . . I have done it before. I have turned the press to my advantage. It helped in a case or two. . . .

"But I came to the realization fairly quickly that it wouldn't matter if I had the pope come down and stand there and say, 'I believe Frank Fuster.'

"The press was never going to turn. Public opinion wasn't going to turn. . . ."

Michael Von Zamft never came to realize that he, himself, devised his own media Waterloo.

The day he attempted to "kill" Joe Braga in Courtroom 4-2.

Laeser's concern over the impending media wars was not entirely unfounded. Unless the State and the defense could convince a judge to seal the case files, the evidence—by law—would become public record as soon as the defense requested it during the "discovery" process.

That meant it was fair game for the media.

Florida was one of only two states in the union whose rules of procedure required reciprocal discovery. There were no Perry Mason twists in a Florida courtroom. No surprises.

With certain exceptions, both the prosecution and the defense were required to provide the other side with their evidence. Intended witnesses were to be announced and posted with enough advance notice that the opposition could interrogate them—for hours, and sometimes days, on end. The witness was required to answer queries by attorneys about anything considered relevant (and at times not so relevant) to the case.

Should the witness refuse to answer the question, it was then "certified" and referred to a judge, who would rule on whether the witness would be required to reply under pain of contempt.

These sworn proceedings, at which each side sizes up and prepares to demolish the other one's case, are politely referred to as "depositions."

Numerous other kinds of evidence must be similarly shared.

In the case of Country Walk, there would be not only hundreds of depositions, but also drawings the children made, the parents' notes and logs, the State's seizures, results of medical examinations. Just about anything the State had, the defense was entitled to.

For these reasons, Laeser and Von Zamft came to enter a gentlemen's agreement in which co-counsel for the defense would hold off on petitioning the prosecution's evidence against the Fusters—a privilege to which they were entitled by law—until the State could move to have it sealed from public inspection.

From the very beginning, the most crucial piece of evidence Samek and Von Zamft lusted for was the Braga tapes.

They had absolutely no idea what might be on them. If fortune were smiling on co-counsel for the defense, the tapes would show little more than some kid being browbeaten into admitting that Fuster's hand had brushed across the front of his pants—a reasonable foundation from which to construct reasonable doubt.

Such an "inadvertent" act could certainly have been mistaken for a sexual overture by a four-year-old with a healthy imagination, don't you think, ladies and gentlemen of the jury?

Much as Samek and Von Zamft needed to discover the contents of the tapes to formulate their defense strategy, they did not wish to have them displayed on the evening news before they could determine whether it would be advantageous to do so. Neither was the State anxious to have the case tried in the press or the families' privacy intruded on. The children had shared a secret with two trusted interviewers, unaware that the video camera on the other side of the mirror had made it possible for their private moment of disclosure to be broadcast coast to coast.

And, much as the parents wanted the public to know—in no uncertain terms—what these "animals" had done to their children, they, too, feared the repercussions of their release. What if the children's friends saw them and humiliated them? What if Jason, or Missy, or Chad, or any of the other children were to turn on the television ten or twenty years from now and see themselves describing gross sexual aberrations as part of file footage in some future documentary?

They blanched at the thought.

Thus, the State and the defense found mutual interest in fighting the tapes' release. This, of course, was expected to bring dozens of media attorneys scurrying out of the woodwork shrilling First

Amendment epithets, proclaiming the public's right to know.

Of more immediate concern to the worried parents was not whether the public would be allowed to view the tapes, but whether a jury would.

They clung to the hope that the tapes could spare their children the long walk to the witness stand from which they would be expected to engage in an adversarial interrogation before a court-room of strangers, under the penetrating gaze of Frank and Iliana Fuster.

The people who made things die and who hurt them because, as they were told, "children are the gift of God."

Laeser had little of comfort to offer them on this point. The Braga tapes were inadmissible. Those, he explained, had been made for purposes of investigation only. They were in no way admissible in a court of law—not by the State, anyway.

The defense could get them admitted, he continued, though Laeser, having seen the tapes firsthand, was certain that Samek and Von Zamft would no more want a jury to see those tapes than they would want to see their clients offering a full confession on the stand.

Words could not adequately describe the compelling nature of what the tapes contained. The children's expressions and body language were as damning as their words.

What about the new law? the parents wanted to know. The one that took effect last July?

Laeser explained that the videotape testimony law, which had not yet been tested in any case in the state, referred to the children's actual testimony—which still must be given in accordance with constitutional requirements affording the accused and their counsel the right to "confront" the accusers.

The State hoped to offer compelling arguments that this should not be interpreted as a "face-to-face" encounter. Rather, the State planned to suggest a creative twentieth-century alternative that would conform to the letter as well as what he perceived to be the spirit of the Sixth Amendment. Thus far, he added, the State's legal department had been able to find only one precedent to support their strategy—a lower-court case in New Jersey where dual video monitors were used for just this purpose.

But this was just a lower-court case, he warned, and judges were never quick to embrace case law that had not yet been affirmed on appeal. The jury, so to speak, was still out on that one.

"Don't expect miracles," said Laeser. "We'll do the best we can to make this as easy for the children as possible, but you must know that the children will have to be questioned by Fuster's lawyers both prior to and during the trial. We'll try to at least keep them from having to sit across a table from the people who did this to them."

Realistically, Laeser continued, he saw no way to completely avoid putting children on the stand. Even if they could get future taped testimony admitted using the new law, he believed strongly that live testimony from a few of the older children would be more effective from a jury's standpoint than a two-dimensional image on a TV monitor. For that reason, said Laeser, he would be approaching some of the parents in the future and asking them to allow their children to testify in court.

The parents remained silent.

Chris Rundle, who had sat silently at Laeser's side during his boss's lengthy discourse, sensed that this was a good moment to change the subject. He cleared his throat conspicuously and tiptoed into uncharted terrain.

The lawsuits.

Three families, within six weeks of Frank's arrest, had filed lawsuits seeking millions of dollars in damages from the state agencies involved, the Fusters and, most notably, Arvida Corporation and its employee, Steven Vickers, Sr., whose son first told his mother in May that "Iliana kisses all the babies' bodies," a circumstance, attorneys for the parents claimed, that had been ignored and/or concealed by employees of the developer.

The Vickers family gave wide berth to the militant parents, many of whom they wouldn't recognize if they lounged next to them at the pool. Their shared tragedy remained unacknowledged.

More suits would follow.

"I don't want to influence any of you in regard to your pursuit of civil recourse in this matter," Rundle began delicately, "but I should caution you about certain—ahhh—complications—which might arise as a result of the lawsuits many of you have filed."

Rundle shifted uncomfortably. The State was not allowed to interfere in any manner with the parents' civil matters. The prosecutor didn't begrudge the victims their compensation. He just wished they had not taken legal action of their own before the trial was resolved. The civil suits not only gave the defense a major opportunity to help themselves to the fruits of the labors of the attorneys defending the civil suits, but it also now gave them a reason to suggest that any testimony the parents themselves might offer was tainted by greed.

"Depositions taken from you in the civil cases will become public record, and Samek and Von Zamft will be able to get ahold of them. Numerous statements and depositions is a free opportunity for the defense to be prepared to poke holes in your testimony later on and allows for contradictions to surface as well as evidence that might not have ordinarily," said Rundle.

"I'm not telling you to drop your suits, just to be careful and be consistent with what you say in the depositions for them."

Laeser foresaw a different kind of wrinkle creased into the fabric of the case by the filing of the families' lawsuits. "We want you parents to remain cohesive," he said. "You can't do that if you run around suing each other and slapping each other with subpoenas.

"Any family conflict could cause trauma for the kids, and that's the last thing they need right now. I'm not trying to influence what you do.

"I just don't want to meet with you again and find three of you in one corner," he said, his arm sweeping to the left, "two of you over there, and one over here, with a lawyer at your side. . . ."

Laeser was interrupted by the chime of the doorbell. When Jeannie Pierson responded, a burly stranger thrust a subpoena in her hand.

The Fletchers' attorney cordially required her presence for deposition.

The first of the evening's prophecies to become fulfilled.

18

Iliana was the wild card in each and every hand dealt out in the game of judicial poker being played within and without Courtroom 4-2.

To Jeffrey Samek, she was a useful ornament to place at the defense table beside her husband—the sweet and bewildered wife who could attest that the industrious Frank had neither desire nor opportunity to commit such unfathomable acts. And what jury could be made to believe that this doe-eyed little "Catholic" girl could have witnessed, much less participated in, what the children said? And if the children could not be believed about their telling of Iliana's role in this obvious fantasy, then how could anything they said be believed?

Double acquittal.

Frank was of much the same mind.

He knew the score.

And he most assuredly had educated his wife as to these general legal concepts.

Iliana no doubt was well indoctrinated as to her "rights" by a husband who enjoyed immense appreciation of the American system of justice—a system that had to prove and prove and prove, beyond any reasonable doubt, that one had committed a crime or that even, indeed, a crime had been committed.

He had, after all, been caught at killing one man—before the eyes of a policeman—and emerged in four years with a high school diploma and an associate's degree in computer programming.

Child molestation reaped even more bountiful rewards.

There is no way of knowing how many children had come to be placed in the hands of Frank Fuster since he became a father at the age of fourteen—the age at which the Cuban adolescent first began to emit signals that hinted of the path he would someday choose. It is known only that his activities were not first detected until he had reached the age of thirty-three. And when they were detected, he was released with a quasi-apology from a judge and the state's permission to open up a babysitting service.

Iliana knew of these things.

She knew of other things, too, regarding her own involvement. Yet it is difficult to determine the nature or the extent of her early concerns.

A week following her husband's arrest, Iliana Fuster began to pen in eloquent (though punctuationally deficient) Spanish a "diary" of her thoughts as she faced the greatest crisis she could expect to face in her lifetime. Yet it remains unclear as to whether at that particular point in time the chameleonlike Honduran teenager grasped the gravity of the situation into which fate and a drugged toddler had deposited her. Her "diary," written during the fourteen days between Frank's arrest and her own, reveals, only in retrospect, that her single certainty was that her husband would not remain in jail.

It is now 11:30 P.M. August 16, 1984. Half an hour ago I finished talking with my husband from prison. We are living the most sad and painful moments and very full of loneliness that a person has ever suffered, we are victims of the dirty and malicious society in which we develop. But I know that this is a very big and hard test to which life has exposed me and I know it, and due to the great and immense love that I feel for my son Jaime and my husband Frank is why I continue and will continue with the strength to the end giving up to the last drop of energy which I have left, because my God I'm ready for anything as long as I can once again obtain my happiness next to my family. I suffer so much at night seeing myself alone without my son to give me a good night kiss and without my husband to caress me at night and to pray together and talk about everything we want to talk about, it is something incredible what I'm feeling at this moment, but the "fact" that my son, wherever he is, is thinking about me gives me consolation, and my husband adores me and even though we are not physically together our hearts are together "now, before and forever." What's happening to us now is the worst injustice that could happen to anyone but my dear (Frankie) we will be together again because life and God knows we are innocent. All of this has happened so fast and weird that it looks suspicious to me and I have no doubt that someone is behind all this that is happening now.

It is now Friday . . . I just finished reading the news in the *Miami*

Herald where they speak about the meeting which took place at the Country Center, where all these people who have destroyed our family life were present and who are supposedly the victims before the country's public; they keep on bringing out my husband's past who has only been a victim of the judicial system of the U.S.A.

These people don't realize that with their false allegations have destroyed the financial and "moral" life of a decent family who has never since we formed it nor before has done harm to anyone.

8/22/84   Until today my husband continues to be detained I feel sad, ruined, alone and very desperate not having Frankie and my son with me; I stopped writing since the 16 because I was with Frank's mother and I didn't have the book [*I Am*] with me.

Publicity has been so great and full of lies that has destroyed our name at this moment I don't even know what's going to happen to our lives, I hope and I trust that we will be together very soon and no one will ever separate us, because after this crime they are committing against us I have learned a lot from life and from human beings, before I used to trust everybody I lived blindly among society but I was always wrong, how sad that I've come to this realization in this painful way. Now the only thing I want is for life and God to return my husband and son to me.

On this date I ask of you God of my life I trust that you will hear me because you are the only person who can help me and that also knows we are "innocent." Now the attorney went to see Frank told him that maybe by the 29 he might get out on bond, I trust it will be that way.

Two days later, on August 24, Iliana Fuster was arrested and charged with capital sexual battery on a child.

• • •

Michael Von Zamft, unlike Frank, from very early on, began to perceive that he had signed on with a "loser" no matter which way the case was sliced. And as the new year rolled around, the defense attorney had pretty much taken stock of the situation, which he then reduced to two basic points of conclusion.

Point 1: He and Samek hadn't gotten the Fusters "off" yet, as he liked to put it. They couldn't even get them bond.

Point 2: They never would.

Interestingly, Von Zamft's sense of futility was not piqued by the difficulty with which he could expect to represent such a brazenly guilty client who did not seem likely to plead. Rather, Von Zamft was convinced that the Fusters weren't going to get a "fair" trial in Dade County, under any circumstances, the attorney's attempts at putting the media on to the trail of "It didn't happen" having failed to divert their attention from prior convictions, medical reports, and some sixty hours of interviews in which the children most convincingly said it did, the tapes having been released to the media.

Nor did he foresee likelier prospects beyond the county line. "Sure," he reasoned, "we will take a Cuban with an accent who looks like Frank Fuster, charged with molesting white, middle-class children from a nice, upper-middle-class . . . residential neighborhood, who has priorly been convicted of child molesting, and we will let him go to trial in Orange County, Florida, which is Orlando."

A few miles from Disney World.

Theoretically, Frank's prior convictions were inadmissible, but, as Von Zamft asked himself often, "Who knows what a judge might do?"

And Iliana, he reasoned, would be the kiss of death. What was a thirty-six-year-old man doing with a seventeen-year-old girl who happened to be his second child bride?

Yes, decided Von Zamft, this case had "loser" written all over it. But Von Zamfts didn't throw in towels—at least not without a fight. "Sometimes you're gonna lose," his big brother once told him. "But if you see you're gonna lose, at least make sure the other side doesn't enjoy winning."

Words Michael Von Zamft lived by.

The attorney began to construct mentally an escape route still open to him—a plan that would prove as diametrically opposed to the interests of one of his clients as it would to those of his friend, Jeff Samek, who got him into this mess in the first place.

The State, no doubt, would be much obliged if at some time in the future, prior to the trial, one of the co-counsels for the defense was able to produce an adult witness to bolster its case, should Iliana suddenly cease to sing the praises of her love for Frank Fuster.

Iliana was the weak link.

At the age of seventeen, she faced multiple life counts, each of which carried a minimum mandatory twenty-five years served without eligibility for parole. Perhaps the strange bond she shared with this child molester might fray as she began to realize that she stood a chance of dying in jail for him.

Von Zamft liked to keep his bases covered. From every angle. Juggling co-defendants happened to be one of his specialties. And if he couldn't somehow squeeze a win out of this one, he would at least have a helluva good time trying.

Or so he thought at the time.

The parents knew that the State was amenable to shifting Iliana from the defense table to the witness stand, the matter having been discussed at the October meeting where Abe Laeser had mapped out the game plan. The State might indeed at some point offer to shave a century or so off Iliana's sentence should she wish to come forward and spare the children the agony of testifying at a trial. The State very much wished to hear Iliana speak, but no one would will her to speak so fervently as the parents of the victims of Country Walk, who silently beseeched the young woman to tell what she knew so that they might know the full content of the nightmares that continued to wake their children in the night. They wanted to know.

Almost as much as they didn't.

During their first nine months of incarceration, the Fusters continued to shower each other with passionate prayers of deliverance from their shared and unjust plight. They yearned, in poetic prose of almost identical style, for the day when God would reunite them. Iliana took to making court appearances dressed in ruffled pinafores. Her hair, loosed from the severe bun with which she had checked into jail, cascaded halfway down her back, clasped neatly from her face by a pair of tiny barrettes.

Joan Crawford playing Dorothy in *The Wizard of Oz*.

Iliana gradually began to look like fifteen going on twelve.

Some of the jailers took pity on the wayward waif who occupied a solitary cell—albeit for only a few hours a day. Others noted that the accused child molester could get "bitchy" at times. Especially when the infirmary ran behind schedule in dispensing her drugs—prescription painkillers for which Iliana might or might not have been in need.

One guard got into the habit of removing the scrawny teenager's handcuffs when escorting her to and from court appearances—a practice he quickly abandoned the day she tore from his side to reach her husband, whom she spied in the corridor ahead of her.

It took two guards to pry Iliana from Frank Fuster's body.

A curious prelude to circumstances still to come.

• • •

Michael Von Zamft's greatest ambition in the spring of 1985 was to be anywhere but Courtroom 4-2 when the Fusters came to trial. The celebrated case was not paying the rich dividends that had beckoned with such promise but two seasons before, when he had agreed to assist Jeffrey Samek in handling a well-publicized parole violation.

Every time he turned around, someone was raining on his parade.

His clients now faced trial on twenty-eight counts of sexual abuse of the children in their care. The deed to the red-doored estate home in Country Walk, which he had expected would finance his services, was now locked in a bank vault—repossessed when Frank Fuster failed to make payments from his jail cell. Fuster's business, KDW Enterprises, Inc., existed only on paper, none of which was green or gilded in gold. The Country Walk Babysitting Service had no visible assets. And Frank's four checking accounts yielded a combined sum of $75.

The Fusters were broke, and Von Zamft was stuck. For fate had dealt him yet another bad hand. Crystal Fletcher, one of the victims, was the niece of a public defender, a familial tie that created an instant conflict of interest. The "indigent" Fusters would have to be represented by court-appointed counsel outside the public defender's office, and Judge Robert Newman thought it only logical to tap the two attorneys who had rushed to their side from the beginning.

Samek and Von Zamft, at that point in time, did not appear entirely displeased. Lawyers adept enough to get these two off could expect bountiful admiration and referrals from their peers. Monied clients seeking to purchase justice would be inclined to be more impressed with the attorneys' success than put off by their prior clientele.

The cause, after all, was a noble one.

The problem was, it didn't work out that way. Both lawyers began to lose referrals, the prospective clients declining to be associated with the men who appeared responsible for continuously reducing Sgt. Maggie Fletcher to frustrated tears on the six o'clock news.

Samek couldn't even get cable TV, the technician having beaten a surly departure in mid-installation upon realizing that the familiar face that greeted him at the door was the one he'd seen on television defending Frank and Iliana Fusters' "rights."

Even their peers, who fully appreciated the complexities of the adversary system and would have been inclined under ordinary circumstances to offer sympathy and support, privately tsk-tsked at some of their methods—most notably Von Zamft's legendary forays before the television cameras. His zeal knew no bounds and frequently strayed—in the eyes of more than a few legal minds—perilously close to the edge of professional canons.

The parents, who could not have been expected in any case to grow affectionate toward the defense team, took an instant dislike to the men who so arrogantly dismissed their horrors—past and present—as the "lies" and "fantasies" of brainwashed brats.

Where was Michael Von Zamft on the nights they spent extricating two- and three- and four-year-old siblings from attempts at copulation? Where was Jeffrey Samek?

The parents were rarely reluctant to share these views with the enraptured public that gathered around department store televisions so as not to miss the latest scheduled episode of the Maggie Fletcher/ Michael Von Zamft show, taped live at noon, five-thirty, and six from the corridor outside Courtroom 4-2.

"You know," Von Zamft would later reflect, "that's the most fatal mistake I made. . . . I misjudged how bad the press was going to be . . . the public outcry . . . and the tenor of the strength, through the press and others, of the people in Country Walk.

"I misjudged that completely."

Otherwise, he said, "I might not have tried to toy with the press the way I did and just started early on with, 'Sorry, nothing to say.' I can do that, you know."

Fortunately, from the parents' vantage, Michael Von Zamft had very much to say. Otherwise, they would not have come to realize so early on that the defense team would "get the Fusters off" at any cost—including the destruction of any child who might get in their way.

Of less fortune was their failure to realize—until it was too late— that it would be the quiet and courteous Jeffrey Samek, not Michael Von Zamft, who would justify their fears.

• • •

Within three months the case of Country Walk had snowballed to proportions that greatly surpassed both Samek and Von Zamft's most distant vision. One "routine" parole violation had blossomed into two counts of capital sexual battery, which had multiplied into twenty-six additional counts.

The children were talking.

Still, a few dozen child witnesses, one with venereal disease pumped down his throat, and sixteen boxes of circumstantial evidence did not an unshakable case make. In California, the McMartin defense team was doing quite nicely against odds far greater—more than a hundred child witnesses as old as eleven and a truckload of medical reports bearing documentation of scarred genitals and anuses. Even as Samek and Von Zamft were getting their bearings in Miami, a pretrial hearing was in process in a Los Angeles courtroom, where seven defense attorneys were attempting to "break down" children who squirmed on the witness seat for lengths of time that stretched to sixteen days.

This seemed to Samek and Von Zamft an expedient resolution to their own troublesome case. They would simply demand that the judge hold a similar hearing in which the children could be "persuaded" to admit that their recollections of sex and violence at the Fusters' were as reliable as their belief in the Easter Bunny. If they were turning ten-year-olds into pretzels in California, these toddlers could be dispensed with in a matter of hours.

End of case.

At the very least, such a hearing would provide the parents of the children a mind-expanding preview of what they could expect should they choose to continue on this road to justice. That in itself could reasonably be expected to urge even the most committed to withdraw their children from further involvement.

End of case.

But when a judge declined to allow them to parade the child victims before the bench for systematic and repeated interrogation— a close judicial call that was monitored with great interest by a courtroom filled with parents and reporters, the defense lost its first major round.

It was beginning to look as though the case might see a jury.

Undaunted, co-counsel for the defense began to explore other possible chinks in the State's armor. And their eyes came to rest on the parents and, of course, the Bragas. The taxpayers hired for the Fusters an investigator whose primary appointed task was to sweep for skeletons in each and every closet associated with the case— especially the closet of the people who had "made" the children say "these terrible things." The Bragas were the single link to the children.

A link that must be broken if the Fusters were to walk.

There commenced conspicuous study—by those paid to represent the Fusters—of the Bragas and their lives; an exercise of monumental frustration. For the couple's "lives," the Braga-watchers began to perceive, were intertwined into one. And because of the "peculiarities" of the style in which they lived that life, the answers sought by the defense were contained in no computer.

If Samek and Von Zamft expected to learn exactly who the Bragas were, they would be obliged to comb the closets in which the immense leather-bound volumes of "Our Story" grew daily.

The Bragas were prolific pack rats who collected their histories as industriously as they plucked discarded pieces of Americana from garage sales and flea markets. Their life, like the treasures they extracted from piles of junk, they believed, had not been without worth. "Our Story" was their private acknowledgment of that belief.

They also believed in paying cash for everything they bought, leaving the defense no trail of mortgages, bank cards, and loans to follow in their pursuit of knowledge about the State's experts.

The extraordinary unit at Apogee had been purchased outright in 1975. Likewise their twelve-year-old Volkswagen. The Bragas' Apogee tree house was less a residence or office than it was a museum.

A very expensive museum of obscure endowment.

The Bragas' finances were of intense and primary concern to the defense, money being the root from which motive or discredit might be coaxed to sprout. But the psychologists' refusal to be paid by the State had eliminated the routine remedy of brushing them off to a jury as the prosecution's "whores"—a term bandied about corridors outside America's courtrooms ever since *insanity* and *diminished capacity* began to appear in books of law. The marketing of psychological conclusions was a healthy and visible industry in judicial circles. For every "expert" produced by the defense, the prosecution could shop for (and purchase) its own to neutralize the other side. And vice versa. Usually, an "expert" whose primary income was derived through performances on the witness stand would tend to work predominantly, and even exclusively, for either the defense or the prosecution, a point that, no doubt, would be brought to the jury's attention.

How much are you being paid and by whom?

"Nothing" and "no one" was not the response Von Zamft and Samek desired to hear. The jurors would, no doubt, attribute a healthy measure of credibility to two people who had no vested interest in speaking for the children. They appeared from "nowhere" and accepted no fee. We work for the children, they said. Not their parents. Not the State. Not the defense.

If we work for the children, we can't be employed by anyone else. The children have as much right to be represented as Frank Fuster.

Michael Von Zamft didn't buy it. The Doctors Pollyanna had to have an angle. All he had to do was find it.

What did these people do for a living, if they did their work for free—these long-haired relics of the sixties whose wardrobe predated the fall of Saigon? He had to know who these people were.

But the Bragas—both their finances and their lives—remained an enigma. Blocked from conventional routes of inquiry by the couple's unconventional lifestyle, the Fusters' court-appointed, county-paid investigator presumably stepped off the beaten path and explored a few alternate trails—all of which led to dead ends. The Bragas began to receive long-distance phone calls from puzzled voices of their past. Chicago. Boston. Someone, it seemed, had been inquiring of Joe's former students and colleagues as to whether there was any dirt to be scraped from the professor's squeaky-clean hide. Did he sleep with students, dodge the draft, or hang out with Abbie Hoffman and Bobby Seale?

These questions reportedly having been met by the couple's former acquaintants with peals of merry laughter, the investigator reportedly followed dirt to its most obvious source and began furtive inspections of the Braga garbage—an intrusion to which the doctors took philosophic offense. The way they saw it, Frank and Iliana had opened up a babysitting service and raped a couple of dozen kids, the kids had told the Doctors Braga, and then suddenly a grossly overweight private eye had begun making trench coat moves on their trash cans.

This guy was sifting through peanut butter, tofu, carrots, and lo mein noodles as if therein lay the key to Frank Fuster's jail cell. It angered Joe and Laurie to see the system so blatantly abused. But nothing (Janet Reno kept telling them) could be done.

Fine, shrugged the Bragas. Let him paw all he wanted. They could even throw out with the trash a few false but amusing leads—perhaps the phone number to the State Department scratched out on a napkin. Perhaps the Pentagon. They could give him lots of garbage to inspect. All he wanted.

And even then he would fail to discover the legacy of Louis Pizitz, whose great-granddaughter had filled with magic a spent and practical life.

• • •

The defense investigator wasn't the only one attempting to unravel the mystery of the Bragas. Chief George "Ray" Havens was not at all comforted to discover that The Boss had placed all of her eggs in a basket about which he—and she—knew very little.

The Chief launched an immediate, covert, full-scale inquiry into the strange creatures who greeted him from his office floor on the day he returned from vacation.

Within days, the doctors' curious Apogee neighbors advised them that a detective had come to call—armed with a fistful of loaded questions.

The Fuster defense, no doubt, was the Bragas' first guess.

No. It was a law enforcement agency.

The Bragas did a slow burn that began to flame as they marched on the master suite. Thank you, Ms. Reno, they fumed. If the State wants to know who we are, why not ask us instead of sneaking around behind our backs? Have we not been straightforward? Have we not provided comprehensive vitae to Chris Rundle, unasked? Have you not pronounced our work "outstanding"?

We don't mind if you check us out. Just be up front about it. You want our tax returns? You want our bank accounts? You want our diplomas? Just ask. We'll be happy to supply The Chief with anything and everything he needs. We have nothing to hide.

Our life is an open book.

You're welcome to open it.

The state attorney was stunned by the gentle doctors turned rabid. The Bragas, she discovered, could bite.

She meant them no offense, Janet Reno told them. Perhaps they should sit down with The Chief.

They'd been interviewing children for more than two months when the meeting took place. Joe and Laurie arrived lugging a grocery bag full of documents. Chief Havens faced them across his desk, his manner not unfriendly. Almost apologetic. What he planned to do, he told them, was to interrogate them much like the defense attorneys would when they took their deposition. Samek and Von Zamft, said Chief Havens, would be looking for any little crack in their lives that might be used to divert the jury's attention from the issues at hand.

What was important, he continued, was that the State be aware of what they were so that there would be no surprises at the time of trial.

"Don't worry," he said. "Everybody's got skeletons."

"We don't," said Joe.

Sure, said The Chief. But not aloud.

He questioned them for two days. Their credentials. Their experience. Their references. Their books. Their lives. He bullied and cajoled. No one could be this squeaky-clean.

"What about your motives?" he asked. You won't take money. Or are you in this for more long-term rewards?

Did they expect to emerge with a long client list with which to practice triple-digit therapy?

"We don't do individual therapy," said the Bragas. "We're researchers and educators. An hour spent with a single child would rob many more of the help we can offer through the work we do in the community."

"But you could do therapy if you wanted to?"

"Certainly. As academic faculty members we, in fact, trained graduate psychology and psychiatry students to do clinical therapy. As such, we're exempt from state licensing laws. It is assumed that if an accredited institution—such as Boston University or the University of Miami's Medical School—deems one competent to teach therapy, then one must be competent to do it."

What if they decided to open a private practice?

"Then we would need a license. We have never—nor will we ever—hang a shingle.

That's not—our—job.

We told Janet Reno a month ago that, if she felt it prudent for us to get a state occupational license for what we're doing here, we'll simply mail a check to Tallahassee and get one.

Ms. Reno said that wouldn't be necessary.

"We're already legal.

"We personally believe it would have been counterproductive, anyway. Our role here is defined as investigative interviewers. The other people around the country who've interviewed children in these kinds of cases have been vulnerable to attacks by the defense who portray clinical therapy as a form of 'brainwashing.'

"Our role is to enable a child to make a truthful, cogent statement, and while we consider the by-product of that to be beneficial to the child, it is not considered—in the traditional sense—to be therapy."

"So if you don't plan to make a killing on therapy after all this is over, what is it you expect to gain? A book, perhaps?"

"We have no intention of writing a book about this case."

Then what's the angle? Why are you doing this for free?

"Our services have always been free of charge. For the past twenty years we've worked through governmental agencies to enhance children's poverty programs in one way or another. Why should we start charging now?

"If we accepted money, we'd be working for the people who pay us, not the children. And the people who paid us might not necessarily have the children's best interests in mind.

"We never want to be in a position where we can't fold our tent and bow out of a situation in which the children's interests aren't being served."

"Then how do you make a living?"

"We have independent means."

"And just exactly what does that mean?"

Would it be sufficient—for purposes of the public record—if they were to cite book royalties, lecture fees, and family investments? they asked The Chief.

"Yes, it would," he replied. But if they did not seek to become rich from this celebrated case, then was it possible that they sought recognition?

"We already *are* recognized," they replied. "Perhaps not so much on a local level, because one tends to happen upon few clinical therapists in the ghetto, which is where we do most of our work. If you attended a Dade County Psychological Association meeting and asked around, 'Who are the Bragas?' you'll probably get a blank stare. But if you go into Liberty City or Overtown, knock on a few doors, and ask the same question, they'll most likely say, 'Oh, yeah. They're the people that help the kids.'

"We're better known in psychological circles outside the state of Florida than in it. We've done definitive research in the area of child development over the past two decades.

"We haven't just read the books.

"We wrote some of them.

"Besides, we didn't seek this case. The state attorney sought us."

The Chief chewed on this for a few moments. These two talked a good game, but there still had to be an angle. "What, then, are your plans?" he asked.

"The state attorney has invited us to stay for an indefinite period of time. We'd like to stay for as long as we feel we can make a significant contribution. We'd like to see this case through to its conclusion. And we'd like to get the new assessment center rolling."

"What assessment center?"

"The State Attorney's Center for Children.

"We have the temporary facility in place. Ms. Reno is in the process of seeking funding and approval for a permanent children's facility where child victims can be brought to a central location which houses all the agencies that become involved in these kinds of cases—representatives of the police sexual battery units, HRS, and a permanent prosecutor to be specially trained in handling child sex abuse cases. Investigators—perhaps attached to your unit—can be trained in child interviewing techniques, child language, and child development.

"You don't need a psychology degree to interview children. You need a caring heart, common sense, and a trainable mind.

"The way it works now, the child is questioned first by the police, then by the Rape Treatment Center, then possibly by the Child Protection Team and/or an HRS caseworker, and then repeatedly by prosecutors.

"That is, until we opened up shop here.

"We'd like that to continue—on a more systematic basis—when we leave. The children could give one thorough, taped interview, and everybody can review their statements without having to trot them in every other day to tell yet another stranger, 'He put it in my mouth. I told the other lady, I don't remember what color his shirt was.'

"We'd like to stay long enough to assemble the center and train the interviewers.

"And then we'll fold our tent and move on.

"That's our payoff.

"We'll have set something in motion that hopefully will continue to help children long after the weeds have covered our graves."

The Chief looked at them in utter exasperation, his eyes fixed beneath the lenses of his gold-framed glasses. "You know, I love that woman down there to death," he said, thrusting his chin toward the master suite. "But if she thinks that she's gonna make things any different than they've always been—and always will be—then she's more full of pie-in-the-sky than you two."

The Chief's gaze softened.

"That's just the way things are."

• • •

In January, fate delivered to Michael Von Zamft a belated but nonetheless generous holiday gift, presented (not surprisingly) by the corpulent private eye, who placed in his hands a document that made them tremble and begin to rub in jubilant anticipation.

He had just latched on to the Bragas' angle.

Von Zamft's ticket to paradise came inscribed with the solemn, crested letterhead of Boston University. He reread the second paragraph several times over before he allowed the excitement that had crept over him upon the first read to take hold.

January 29, 1985

Dear [Investigator]:

The information you seek regarding Dr. Joseph L. Braga, I consider personal and confidential, and the type of information that is protected by the Family Educational and Rights to Privacy Act of 1974, more familiarly known as the Buckley Amendment. Therefore, unless I had a release from Dr. Joseph L. Braga, I could not answer the questions you have posed in your letter of January 8, 1985.

By the way, according to our records, Dr. Joseph L. Braga is a decedent and therefore, any permission that you would have to obtain must come from the executors of his estate.

Most cordially,
Jon V. Haywood
University Registrar

By the way . . . Obviously Jon V. Haywood did not grasp the momentousness of the information that followed this inglorious introduction.

By the way, Michael, you've just won the lottery.

Headlines, no doubt, began to dance deliciously through Von Zamft's head.

State Experts Revealed as Frauds!

Man Who Interviewed Children Dead!

Fuster Lawyers Expose Child Brainwashers!

The publicity would be astonishing. The State would retreat in mortal humiliation. And, best of all, the Doctors Pollyanna would be exposed as con artists bearing rainbows—which, in the world according to Von Zamft, undoubtedly they must be.

Already the attorney could taste exquisite victory.

• • •

Assistant State Attorney John Hogan strolled into Courtroom 4-2, an unsuspecting lamb being led to public slaughter. He noted in passing a television camera stationed in the gallery and a single newspaper reporter lounging outside in the hall. And though he was growing accustomed to the microscopic scrutiny under which each step of the case had been followed, he entertained a fleeting curiosity as to why reporters would roll out of bed at this early hour to witness some "routine motions," which Michael Von Zamft had casually mentioned just yesterday afternoon he intended to file this morning with Judge Newman.

Hogan didn't anticipate the Spanish Inquisition.

Still blissfully ignorant of the glint in Von Zamft's eye, Hogan plucked his copies of the aforementioned motions from the clerk's hands and, without glancing at them, asked the court to recess the hearing until he had an opportunity to study them and prepare his arguments—a reasonable request, he pointed out, given the haste in which he had been advised of their existence.

Two hours should be sufficient, said Judge Newman.

Hogan strolled back out of the courtroom and was met at the door by a reporter who held the motions in her hand—motions that had just that moment been filed before the bench and that were not, theoretically, available yet to the media.

"Mr. Hogan, what is your response to these allegations?" she asked.

Hogan looked at her blankly, noting with mounting unease that she and the TV reporter who hovered nearby were the only media present and the only ones who had, for some time, conspicuously shadowed Von Zamft about the Metro Justice Building, gathering the pebbles he "dropped" in his wake, a circumstance reflected vividly in their stories.

"I don't know. I haven't read them yet," the prosecutor replied, brushing past her toward the elevator, where he began to shuffle through the documents, his brow growing furrowed, his eyes wide.

The Defendants, through undersigned counsel, move this Court to appoint a special State Attorney to investigate the true background of the persons claiming to be Joseph and Laurie Braga and as well the relationship between these alleged experts and the office of the State Attorney and additionally, any personal or professional relationship between the alleged Joseph and Laurie Braga and Janet Reno, State Attorney, and any of her assistants, and as grounds therefore, the defense would state the following:

1. In her deposition, the person claiming to be Laurie Braga, stated that they were brought to the attention of the State Attorney's office (Assistant State Attorney Chris Rundle) through Janet Reno, the State Attorney.

2. That they were utilized, and their services retained by the office of the State Attorney at the specific direction of Janet Reno, State Attorney, and Christopher Rundle, Assistant State Attorney.

3. Our information leads us to believe that Joseph L. Braga is deceased and the person in Dade County claiming to be Joseph Braga is a fraud.

4. A special State Attorney is needed to investigate the relationship of these persons claiming to be Joseph and Laurie Braga to the office of the State Attorney, individually and collectively.

5. The special prosecutor should be required to investigate who the persons claiming to be Joseph and Laurie Braga really are. . . .

Two additional motions demanded that the State supply Samek and Von Zamft with every conceivable scrap of documentation on *both* the Bragas—everything that by law of personal privacy the defense investigator had been unable to obtain:

> income tax returns
> FBI and police checks
> fingerprints.
> copies of degrees and diplomas
> military records
> birth certificates
> biographies
> their marriage certificate

But it was the fourth and last motion that lunged maliciously for the throat, for it sought an injunction against the Bragas' interviewing any more children—a document that contained the skillfully worded phrase ". . . we cannot know that this person calling himself Joseph L. Braga is not himself a child molester."

Hogan's heart skipped fewer than ten beats before the fleeting doubt was rapidly displaced by a simmering anger.

This was not the variety of pool he expected to see played by the president of the criminal justice arm of the state bar.

Von Zamft had given him virtually no notice about some "routine motions," then proceeded to rush the judicial bench, hurling slurs at the people who stood between him and a win, without investigating further the validity of the strange annotation in Boston University's computer. He hadn't even produced a death certificate, though the precisely worded motions never actually declared Joe legally "dead."

Just a possible fraud and potential child molester.

• • •

Chief George "Ray" Havens might have squirmed momentarily over these unsettling new developments had he not personally conducted, four months before, an investigation into the Bragas' background that was worthy of their induction into the CIA.

These people had the cleanest closets he had ever inspected. Not a box out of place. Not a shoe unaligned. Not a spot. Not a mark. Not even a parking ticket.

And their credentials were impeccable.

Chief Havens wasn't alarmed. Just puzzled.

How had Joe Braga's alleged 1972 "death" come to be placed so recently in Boston University's computer? It wasn't there on either of the two occasions he had checked during the fall.

The phantom death notice intrigued Janet Reno's chief investigator.

Joe and Laurie bustled into Havens's office bearing grocery bags filled with the hastily assembled pieces of their lives, all bound, of course, within the volumes of "Our Story" that preceded 1972, the year Joseph L. Braga allegedly died.

The Bragas' good humor appeared not visibly dampened by this latest assault launched on behalf of the Fusters. They had, as usual, located the silver lining in this unexpected cloud. How promising a circumstance, Joe and Laurie smiled, that the defense could find no more workable method to dismiss the rape of children than to declare Joe dead.

Von Zamft and Samek, they concluded, must be desperate.

But mixed with their amusement was a welling apprehension, and an almost resigned knowledge, that this episode would not only blemish their flawless history, but leave a nasty scar as well. They knew that not everyone who read today's sensational headlines would turn to the back page tomorrow to discover that it was all a mistake. A decade from now, there still might be people who associated the name *Braga* with the words *child molester* and *fraud*.

Joe summed up his feelings in five words: "I'm not dead. Just assaulted."

Within the allotted two hours, the hearing over Von Zamft's "routine motions" reconvened before a packed and electrically charged courtroom. The two reporters who held ringside seats at the early-morning dropping of Von Zamft's bomb were now wedged in the media room amid an electronic obstacle course composed chiefly of wires, cords, and microphones. Tape decks from networks and the local affiliates lay in wait between the legs of breathless reporters who had rushed to witness the blood about to be let. The mystery of the "dead" and "fraudulent" child interviewers promised days, if not weeks, of suspenseful investigation—the latest twist of certifiable weirdness in the tale of Country Walk.

A contingent of parents occupied one wing of the gallery—the regulars, along with a handful of not-so-regulars, all of whom appeared in striking good humor given the circumstance that one hour ago each had been abruptly notified (as the State had dutifully promised they would) that the fur was about to fly in Courtroom 4-2. And though this late-breaking development sent their adrenaline gushing as they raced to find their car keys, they were calmed by Abe Laeser's words of last October:

"The Bragas will be the defense's target. That takes the heat off you and the kids."

Quite frankly, the "involved" parents didn't care if the Bragas were veterinarians—they were *there* at three in the morning at times when it felt as though the world was coming to an end. They were *there* at four-thirty to reassure them that it wasn't.

Serenely they watched Samek and Von Zamft lounge near the defense table, looking for all the world like a pair of cats with yellow tail feathers protruding from their mouths. Clearly co-counsel for the defense perceived they had caught the mighty Ms. Reno with her pants down. How unwise for the state attorney to install "experts" in her office whose credentials she had not bothered to verify. How sloppy of the fastidious Reno to have accepted at face value the cornerstones of one of the biggest cases to be tried in Dade County.

But the attorneys' smiles became tight and drawn as Chief Havens, at John Hogan's invitation, stepped before the bench and launched into a monologue of great length and detail about his previous inquiry into the people the State had summoned to talk to the children.

In addition to his previous investigation, which was, he pointed out, exhaustive, he had this morning secured additional proof that the Joseph Braga seated in the courtroom today was not, and never had been, dead. Just two hours ago, Chief Havens told the court, he had asked Dr. Braga to supply him with the names of two individuals who had known him both prior to and following his alleged death in 1972. The Bragas had also supplied him with a passport dated 1968 and an ancient Massachusetts driver's license, both of which displayed a photograph of a younger, less abundantly tressed version of the man with the silver ponytail. "The same man," said The Chief, "who is sitting there in a brown suit, with a red tie, and a blue and white striped shirt to whom I am pointing at this time."

Von Zamft, who by now had grown ashen, stepped briskly to The Chief's side and requested that the pieces of laminated plastic be placed in his hand. He paced slowly, examining them as Chief Havens continued pulling evidence from the State's hat with military precision.

"Your Honor, I telephoned Boston University myself," he continued. "For the third or fourth time. I spoke with Mr. Jon Haywood, who is the person who authored the letter . . . and he says (and he cannot explain to me why) that there is an annotation in their file (and he doesn't know when it was put in there) indicating that in November of 1972 Joseph L. Braga died and is subsequently deceased.

"He has no idea *how* it was put in there, *who* put it in there, or any other information. . . . He said he was in the process of personally reviewing all of the information, gathering all the microfilm information, and he had no idea who put it in there. Or the validity of that information."

Samek and Von Zamft grasped wildly at the victory that was quickly slipping through their fingers. Just how reliable was The Chief's information? So what if the prints taken from the fingers of the "alleged" child development experts were free of criminal record? Had Chief Havens obtained fingerprints prior to 1972 with which the current ones could be compared? Had he verified the authenticity of the passports and driver's license? Passports could be altered, Von Zamft pointed out.

The Chief regarded the attorney with mild exasperation.

Judge Newman looked bemused at this further muddying of the river. "I'm sure Dr. Braga would not like this cloud hanging over him. I know I wouldn't. . . ."

With that, he appointed Chief Havens an officer of the court and dispatched him to Boston with orders to return posthaste with the irrefutable proof that Dr. Joseph Braga, a former Boston University student and instructor, on this, the eve of his forty-fourth birthday, was in fact the same man who had been swearing out affidavits all over the Eleventh Judicial Circuit seeking protective intervention from the court on behalf of scores of children.

There were child sex abuse cases sprinkled all over the docket that would instantly disintegrate should the Bragas' signatures become tainted by controversy unresolved. In the months and even years to come, Joe Braga's "death" could be dusted off and dropped into pending cases by zealots who chose to practice defense by diversion: "Yes, Dr. Braga, but did the court ever say you *proved* your innocence of these grave allegations?"

Von Zamft leaned against the railing near the jury box, hands in pockets, staring across the room at the ponytailed sprite whose eyes sparkled with a maddening twinkle.

A year from now, Michael Von Zamft would recall having had "a lot of fun" sprinkling ashes all over the Doctors Pollyanna and their little white hats. But at this particular moment he looked more like a punctured—and furious—balloon.

Von Zamft did not attend the "Resurrection Hearing," as it came to be called, in which his prized motions would be flushed down the judicial toilet as Chief Havens presented his latest findings to the court. Von Zamft well knew the game was lost, an embarrassed and bewildered Boston University official having publicly acknowledged the phantom death notice to be a mystifying "error" even before The Chief had finished packing his bags for Boston.

Nonetheless, The Chief had kept his date with a blizzard, for two days beating a snowy path across the university's campus, clutching an expired Massachusetts driver's license in his gloved hand.

Havens aimed to close this chapter once and for all.

Back in Miami, the Bragas' fingers were dipped again into an ink pad and rolled onto cards so that their prints could be fed through nationwide law enforcement computers a second time. Joe's foot soon followed, so that his heels and toes and instep could be compared with the impression made by a baby born Joseph Lynde

Braga forty-four years before—baby footprints being one of the items Joe Braga could locate without great difficulty in the precisely ordered archives of his life.

Not only was he a pack rat; he was an organized one.

Comparative analysis was also conducted on his handwriting, Dr. Braga having produced for the State canceled checks predating 1972. Laurie was similarly processed.

Escorting them from place to place in which they deposited samples of their flesh pattern and signatures was Christina Royo, the only member of the current prosecution team who had worked the case from its inception, Laeser and Rundle having been officially replaced by John Hogan before the champagne served at Reno's victory party (following her landslide election win) had gone flat.

A search was then conducted throughout Janet Reno's kingdom for a prince who could ride into the courtroom at John Hogan's side. A list was made and the names narrowed down to two. Then one:

Daniel Casey, chief of Janet Reno's robbery division.

And should anyone mistake the state attorney's degree of determination to keep Frank Fuster caged, she added to the Country Walk prosecution roster the name of Richard Shiffrin, head of her legal department.

She had virtually redistributed caseloads in three major divisions and plucked from them their chiefs in one clean sweep. Janet Reno was going for broke on this one.

But Janet Reno chose not to attend the "Resurrection Hearing," a point not noted in news coverage of the event. Considering the infrequency with which the state attorney set foot in any courtroom, her presence was far more worthy of mention than her absence.

The entire prosecution team, however, had assembled for the auspicious occasion. And even a handful of Havens's investigators, who had nothing to do with this case, had selected seats in the gallery to witness The Chief's most unusual courtroom appearance.

Christina Royo found herself a seat next to the beaming Bragas and placed on her lap a pile of further "evidence" gleaned from the doctors' family archives. She stared at the defense table with no hint of a smile, though her eyes said, "Make my day."

Chief Havens strode before the bench, grasped the sides of his pulpit, and drawled out a not unamusing account of his cold and wet journey through Joe Braga's past. Jeffrey Samek stood alone to face the music Von Zamft had selected, as The Chief cheerfully rambled on, depositing documents in an absurdly large pile, finally concluding with a broad sweep of his arm in the direction of the man with the silver ponytail, who sat in the gallery with a tape recorder in his lap, collecting for posterity this latest chapter in "Our Story."

"Your Honor," boomed The Chief, "I don't know in today's society whether there's anything that's 100 percent certain . . .

"But Your Honor, I am 99.99 percent certain that that man right over there is Joseph Lynde Braga, white male, date of birth February 7, 1941. And he is not now, nor has he ever been, any other person.

"And unless I'm wrong, Your Honor, I don't think he's dead."

Judge Newman nodded solemnly, his eyes crinkling at the corners.

"I'd like to think this matter has been put to rest."

19

The building in which Florida's laws are made is a complex maze of tiled corridors that fan out like the fingers of a web spun by a demented spider. A newcomer could become lost for weeks within the capitol's bowels, unable to locate either his destination or an exit.

A piece of legislation could get lost forever in much the same way.

By the spring of 1985, Sgt. Maggie Fletcher had come to know her way around this building, having two prior visits and an able sense of direction to her credit. So it was with sure, hurried strides that she led a very small, but determined-looking contingent through a back entrance, across a vast stretch of lobbies and down corridors to the elevator that would take the parents of Country Walk to the offices of Senator Roberta Fox, who was soon to be anointed by the media as ringleader of the "Mom Mafia"—a reporter's designation for the key engineers of a legislative dogfight not soon to be forgotten in the corridors of the state capitol.

The elevators were located along a vast, circular walkway that jutted into the hollow core of space that rises through the center of the capitol from its floor to its dome. A sturdy, not-quite-four-foot wall was all that stood in the way of a multiple-story plunge to the rotunda below, where, on this crisp April morning, an assemblage of high-school-age students followed their impassioned conductor in a glorious rendition of "We Are the World."

Maggie Fletcher, Jeannie Pierson, and Tom Herschel paused in their journey to peer at the spectacle below and smiled. How unfortunate that the Lancasters wouldn't be arriving in time to behold the governor's unintentional welcome of them to Tallahassee.

It was a fleeting but memorable moment, after which they paced back to the elevator and resolutely pushed the button that would take them to the ultimate battle they chose to fight.

The battle of the law.

Maggie had spent the better part of two seasons pulling every string she had in her grasp to shake down the whole damned system that had let her daughter get raped.

She was not without connections. Much of the young sergeant's decade with the Miami Police Department had brought her administrative assignments attached to City Hall. Miami was not an unnotable place in which to have close acquaintance with the people who run it. Not that she enjoyed unanimous support.

Nothing enjoyed unanimous support in the city of Miami.

Amid this turbulent atmosphere, where ranking civil servants and police officers contemplated their futures with fingers crossed, Sgt. Maggie Fletcher occupied a snug berth. Affirmative action being a major component of the most recent turmoils at her place of work, Maggie was, at the time, assured smooth passage up the ranks. The City Hall–connected Peruvian-born daughter of an American airline pilot/executive qualified as a double minority: Hispanic female. It didn't matter that she looked and sounded like she hailed from Ft. Lauderdale, no trace of accent belying the fact that Maggie spoke fluent Spanish—yet another small circumstance that would come to play a major role in events still to unfold.

Frank and Iliana Fuster couldn't have made a more unfortunate choice of victims than the daughter of Sgt. Maggie Fletcher. Few police officers on the force possessed the influence of the little blond cop.

And not one had her unmitigated gall.

When the Country Walk case broke, Maggie went off like a cocked rifle, scattering birdshot in all directions.

As the other parents weighed carefully their decisions as to whether to speak to reporters through a cracked front door, Maggie sat in her living-room-turned-television-studio with Peyton at her side. Impulsive, stubborn, headstrong Maggie rarely weighed anything she did—especially when provoked.

And this situation made her as mad as hell.

Maggie's emergence as the leading light for the organization Justice for Sexually Abused Children followed a bloodless coup during J-SAC's infancy, when the Country Walk parents ejected from leadership a couple who claimed not to have been involved with the Fusters and whose philosophical bent conflicted with that of the victims' in terms of priority.

The "unaffected" couple placed high on the list of J-SAC's goals the securing of victim's "compensation" from the state. Richard

Maxwell, father of Kyle, and the most politically experienced of the group, went through the roof.

"No money," he said. "You attach money to your goals and you'll get ignored. You've got to ask the legislature for something that won't cost them one red cent—something they can't kill in a budget subcommittee."

How very well for Richard Maxwell, the "unaffected" couple sniffed. What about the victims all over the state who did not enjoy the apparent financial security of the residents of Country Walk?

Some of the parents shifted uncomfortably. They did not yet know each other well enough to admit that their lifestyles didn't necessarily reflect the size of their bank accounts. Or that some months their bills and loans and mortgages got paid by narrow margin. Many of the families had been plunged into a sea of financial difficulty as a direct result of the Fusters' actions. The mothers who could not get an extended leave of absence to tend to their emotionally needy offspring had quit their jobs cold—the much-needed paychecks notwithstanding. And even as their income shrank, their expenses multiplied. Changing laws and restoring the families' psychological health was not an inexpensive proposition.

So the proposed demand for victims' compensation was not altogether unwarranted or unappealing. But they readily agreed that Richard Maxwell had a valid point.

It would be a mistake to attach a price tag to justice.

There came, within a week, a parting of ways between J-SAC's self-appointed leadership and the families of the victims whose coattails the former had seized from the moment that a covey of reporters trampled through the flower beds of paradise gone awry.

The "unaffected" couple was out. Maggie was in—a logical and not unagreeable choice of leader among the parents. Who better symbolized the boldness of this crime than a cop upon whose daughter a child molester had knowingly preyed? A cop whose husband wore the uniform of a Miami police lieutenant when he called at the Fusters' door to retrieve his daughter at the end of the day.

Maggie was the one the parents initially thrust (not entirely against her will) before the very interested eyes of the public. She spoke for the organization. But the reporters kept a handy list of alternates to be contacted for comment on the latest of the bizarre twists this already twisted case would take, should Maggie not be located in time to meet inflexible deadlines.

Tom Herschel topped the list of alternates, being the most agreeable of the flock to welcome the media into his home at any hour of the day or night. The father of Chad and Missy seemed to some of the other parents, at times, to be too agreeable. They expressed among themselves a concern that his sometimes unrestrained streams of consciousness might in some way jeopardize the case or flavor them as members of the lunatic fringe.

But though his performance fell short of flawless, Tom Herschel's public impact was not necessarily as counterproductive as some of the parents perceived. In essence, he grabbed the public by the lapels and with serious intent seemed to plead, "Don't you see what is happening here? Don't you understand the implications of all of this?"

Maggie Fletcher did much the same. It was just that her positions had been more or less agreed upon by committee.

Other parents could be coaxed before the cameras from time to time. The Princes. The Lancasters (briefly, before they moved to a place they picked randomly off the Florida map—a place that was anywhere but Country Walk). Jeannie Pierson. Richard Maxwell. Even quiet Peyton Fletcher popped up now and then.

Interestingly, the Harrisons, upon whose son rested the weight of a trial, would remain for some time the most invisible from the public eye, though at every hearing the TV camera in the courtroom would sweep into the visitor's gallery to capture the bearded, red-haired man with the pale blue eyes that closely studied the face of the judge.

Often, a composed Jackie sat quietly by his side, casting an expressionless glance toward the Fusters, who calmly regarded the parents from across the room when their interest in the day's proceedings momentarily flickered. On the first occasion, within weeks of the babysitters' arrest, Jackie's eyes locked briefly with Iliana's.

And in that instant, Jason and Joshua's mother knew the dizzying nausea of absolute confirmation. Her heart now knew what her mind had already accepted. For the rest of the morning, Jackie's attention kept being drawn, as if by invisible force, to the remarkably unconcerned ex-convict who masqueraded as a respectable businessman. Even her tears failed to blur the vision that imprinted in her mind—the thick, cruel lips of Frank Fuster on the bodies of her sons.

Jackie was very angry with God for quite a while.

The Harrisons were a fixture at any meeting that concerned the parents of Country Walk, be it in a courtroom or a family room in one of a half dozen homes in which strategies were planned. And while they on occasion acquiesced to the pleas of reporters and offered brief comment, they preferred to blend into the scenery surrounding the stage that had been set for Maggie Fletcher. They were private people who had little desire to invite strangers into their nightmare. For the parents of the child oracle knew better than anyone the magnitude of what had occurred within the Fuster home. Which is why, when it became necessary, the Harrisons came to step from the shadows to speak for their frightened sons.

And even then they didn't know the worst of it.

The parents were not without diverse and helpful talents, among them three lawyers who offered infinite hours of advice and counsel—a decided asset in terms of the legal mountains they sought to move. Two were former prosecutors. All now practiced criminal law, defenders of the rights of the accused now forced to view the system through the eyes of the victim.

The lawyers laid a steadying hand on the legislative ship J-SAC sought to launch, three voices to remind them of Frank and Iliana's constitutional rights, something in which each of the children's parents apparently believed—witness the fact that the Fusters remained alive to stand trial.

There were, of course, other reasons why one of the parents didn't nail Frank Fuster before he came under the protection of the court system—none of which included lack of motivation.

As one gentle mother put it, "Death was too quick, too easy a payment for what he did. He needs to die in prison. He needs to suffer like we've suffered and our kids will suffer for the rest of their lives."

But revenge was not the driving force behind their activities during the spring of 1985, as they labored to weave a legislative blanket of protection for the children who faced the prospect of being raked apart on the stand under the Fusters' penetrating stare—an experience that no doubt would remind them of the babysitters' prophecy of "bad things" that happen to children who tell secrets they're not supposed to.

The parents' blanket was woven of rational thread and the fibers of good fortune. For what the parents of Country Walk were able to accomplish in the next months was the result of an extraordinary chain of events, which rivaled in its symmetry the pieces of the puzzle that had brought them together in the first place.

The difference was that they were now in a position to control the events, not be controlled by them.

Riding the crest of a momentous wave of public outrage beneath which welled a backlash of scorn, the parents' journey to the state capitol was swift, if not direct. Unfamiliar with the terrain, they picked their way carefully along the road to Tallahassee.

One step at a time.

Within weeks of Frank Fuster's arrest, Maggie Fletcher and her band of not-so-merry men and women had constructed a hasty vehicle fueled solely on public interest. They created J-SAC and testified before the Dade County Grand Jury, the county commission, and the governor. Maggie got herself appointed to the county's task force on childcare/child abuse—right next to Janet Reno.

The parents demanded an investigation of the state's agencies. They demanded that the governor call a special session of the legislature to offer immediate remedy to the childcare system's regulatory deficits. They demanded an emergency county ordinance that would have required the people working with small children to pass police inspection for a lascivious or violent past.

Shortly after Christmas in 1984, the parents got their county ordinance—or rather, they got a watered-down, three-months-in-the-making, token gesture of appeasement that even Janet Reno, who labored on the committee to construct it, declared impotent.

The "emergency" ordinance, which was stamped by the commission to self-destruct in September of 1985, allowed the names of childcare workers to be run through county police computers, but did not mandate that they be fingerprinted or checked for a criminal past that extended beyond the county line. The ordinance also failed to prohibit a daycare operator from hiring anyone convicted of child abuse or violent crimes, the rationale being, according to one commissioner, "I can't believe an employer would hire someone with a record."

A handful of Country Walk parents, under whose watchful eyes the county commission debated the merits of the measure, rose indignantly from their seats.

"If you have a Frank Fuster. . . ."

The commission held firm. This ordinance, they said, would have to suffice until the legislature addressed the issue in the spring.

Without a new state law, their hands were tied. Only the legislature could grant access to FBI computers, which might or might not tell them whether a preschool's bus driver was wanted for murdering three children in Vermont.

So the parents set their sites on Tallahassee; they wanted a law, and they wanted it yesterday. The children of the state of Florida should not remain for another moment in hands that remained unchecked, unregulated, and in too many cases recently discovered unsafe.

They continued to clamor for a special session of the legislature. Noting that two additional cities within his domain—Tampa and Jacksonville—were embroiled in their own daycare molestation scandals, the governor obliged, declaring the state's childcare system to be in "a state of emergency" and summoning legislators from points all over the peninsula to Tallahassee for a two-day pre-Christmas powwow.

In advance of the well-publicized occasion, Governor Bob Graham announced his intention to present to the lawmakers a ten-million-dollar-plus emergency child protection plan that called for more and better-paid state investigators, fingerprinting and background checks of daycare employees, subsidized daycare for nearly four thousand poor children, and free training for public- and private-sector childcare workers.

The legislators were not amused.

There commenced a nasty little presession hissing match in the media in which it was suggested that Governor Graham's zeal might be tied in with his not-so-secret ambition to occupy a congressional seat—specifically the one currently occupied by U.S. Senator Paula Hawkins, who was in the process of putting together a child protection package of her own in Washington.

The governor declared children to be the "top priority" in Florida's future and made a grand sweep of the state, hoping to impel constituents to slap their representatives in his direction. But there seemed precious few points of compromise between the governor's uncharacteristically hard line and the lawmakers who resented being wedged so indelicately between this rock and wall.

Senator Roberta Fox stepped into the fray and concocted a deal between the House and the Senate that would give the governor half his loaf in terms of money, with an extra slice of legislation thrown in to sweeten the pot. The legislature agreed to give him $5 million and authorize *voluntary* fingerprinting and criminal checks for the estimated eighty thousand childcare workers in the state. The rest of his package would have to wait until spring, when they could more thoroughly examine the need for more drastic recourse.

Take it or leave it.

Bob Graham took it, but with little enthusiasm. He had flexed his gubernatorial muscles to their maximum capacity and had not turned the tide. This was not a battle in which he could claim victory. He did, however, emerge with the promise of things to come: a joint commission of legislative leaders and the governor's office was to draft a comprehensive childcare reform package to be presented at the regular spring session.

It was said to be a commitment on the part of the legislature to the children of Florida.

Maggie Fletcher, who stalked relentlessly through the capitol throughout the two-day session, emanating silent but well-read storm warnings, had every intention that the promise would be kept.

• • •

Senator Roberta Fox was a mountainous woman both in height and breadth—her beauty of earlier and slimmer years not entirely diminished by the surplus pounds of flesh she now carried into the spring of her fourth decade. Eight years in Tallahassee (six in the House and the most recent two in the Senate) had earned her both the respect of the legislative leadership and the scorn of some of her peers, who claimed to have paid more dues than this pushy but lovable Earth Mother who happened to be a lawyer.

Fox was of the "pay now or pay later" school of thought. Train displaced women now so they won't be on welfare later. Protect children now so we won't have to be protected *from* them later. The senator enjoyed a reputation of some length as a friend of women's and children's issues. But never had she so passionately embraced a cause as she did the issues arising from Country Walk.

It may have been the vocal rabble being roused in the state's most populous district, or it may have been her own internal sense of alarm that first tweaked the senator's ear. But as time wore on, the parents of Country Walk came to believe that Senator Roberta Fox not only listened, she heard.

Some forty legislative bills dealing with child welfare would be submitted during the 1985 session of the Florida legislature, of which two were of intense and focused interest to the parents of

Country Walk. Senator Fox was fully aware of which those two might be, Maggie Fletcher, in her frequent communications with the senator, having dwelled at length on two issues of immediate concern.

First and foremost, they wanted a judicial proceedings bill for children—one that recognized and addressed the special needs of child witnesses, something their own offspring were soon to become.

Second, they wanted a fingerprinting bill—one that required that people who worked with young children be not only screened but also free of a record that indicated they might be dangerous to a child.

The fingerprinting was so compellingly logical to Senator Fox that she expected its passage to be smooth and unobstructed. It was the judicial proceedings bill that might ride a rocky road to the floor of the House and Senate. But here, too, she expected that logic would ultimately prevail.

Though logic has little in common with the making of laws.

• • •

The first whiff of trouble came during the first week of April, when the childcare control bill (of which the dominant element was the fingerprinting proposal) slammed to a grinding halt as soon as it hit the table of the Senate HRS committee of which Roberta Fox was chair, the committee through which (as recently as the day before) she had expected it to sail. The senator had not counted on the strange and powerful alliance that had been struck by lobbyists who didn't generally walk hand in hand.

Tallahassee's longtime child advocates had joined with a coalition of daycare operators and civil libertarians to strike the fingerprinting provisions from Fox's pet bill.

The fingerprinting, argued the child advocates, would do little to weed out child molestors, the majority of whom went about their business unmarked by criminal record. It was, they said, a waste of the state's money, which could be better spent on training childcare personnel.

It was, added the daycare lobby, a waste not only of the state's money, but of their own, the bill having provided that a portion of the costs be picked up either by the applicant or the employer.

It was also, argued some, a gross violation of civil liberties.

In fact, there was but a single piece of testimony spoken in favor of the fingerprinting bill on its first reading. And that was given by a feisty lady horse-breeder who commuted three hours each day to and from the state capitol, where she knocked on legislative doors and testified before committees on behalf of the fingerprinting bill.

Dorothy Sullivan knew little of Country Walk.

But she knew much about daycare operators with child molestation convictions. Her son-in-law was one.

And her granddaughter—his eight-year-old stepdaughter—was his victim.

An emergency call was placed to Miami.

The Country Walk parents were summoned to commence the battle of the law.

• • •

Maggie exited the elevator and marched her band of parents to the office of Senator Fox, who offered warm but hurried greetings to the contingent from Miami, then raced off to tend to another one of her troubled bills. They could use her office as a base for the work they were about to do, she offered.

Maggie paused for a consultation with the senator's aide to determine just what that work might be. What are the problems? *Who* are the problems? She compiled a list of lawmakers who seemed to be seeing things in a less than enlightened perspective, chose the toughest nut for her own cracking, and split the rest among the other parents, who had not the foggiest notion what they were supposed to do. What were a secretary, a bookkeeper, a real estate broker, and a restaurant manager expected to know about the making of laws?

"Just go talk to 'em," said Maggie, willing them out into the corridor. "Tell 'em what you think. Better yet, tell 'em what you *know*. Educate 'em."

And with that, her heels click-clicked up the hallway, propelling five feet of blond determination. Behind her, two television photographers hoisted cameras to their shoulders and trailed the cop/ mother to her appointed destination. For the next several weeks, cameras followed them from one end of the peninsula to the other, as the parents nudged and shoved from committee to floor a bill they refused to let die.

The problem was money, said the bewildered lawmakers (who were unaccustomed to being lobbied by mothers and fathers who came equipped with television cameras).

There were only so many ways to slice the pie. You've got to set your priorities. You just can't come in here and have it all.

Training or fingerprinting.

Take your pick.

It was readily apparent to Maggie and Senator Fox, that its members were swaying toward the HRS training lobby, which vigorously endeavored to lay claim to more funds with which to fuel the state agency's notoriously mismanaged bureaucratic nightmare.

Training or fingerprinting. Take your pick.

It appeared that some committee members were about to make what Maggie believed to be the wrong choice.

There was no doubt, she argued, that childcare workers would benefit from professional training. But didn't it seem appropriate to discover the characters of the people being hired to take charge of our children, before we teach them how to instruct our sons and daughters in making turtles out of paper plates? Do you think that parents think it's OK if the guy who sweeps the bathrooms has three convictions for assault or murder or rape? You think it's OK with parents that they don't *know* that the sweet spinster who seems so "devoted" to the children had been arrested for poisoning cats, setting fires, and painting swastikas on public buildings? Or that the husband of the neighbor-lady who babysits kids is a convicted child molestor? Don't you think that's the kind of information we have a right to *know*, if we're handing our kids over to them?

If the parents of the state of Florida wanted to leave their children in the hands of felons, she reasoned, they would simply drop them off at the county jail on the way to work. The parents of this state will not tolerate it if you choose to train felons—instead of getting rid of them.

To which one lawmaker responded, "What about the rehabilitated ones? It would be unfair to discriminate against a guy who's paid his debt to society."

Frank Fuster was "rehabilitated," replied Maggie. "Twice."

There are better environments in which to place a "rehabilitated" violent or deviant personality than in the midst of the smallest and most vulnerable of children. We screen our high school teachers better than we screen the people floating around the daycare system. That's just plain nuts, she said to the increasingly restless senator who wished for speedy deliverance from this assault on his sensibilities.

I don't know, we'll see, said the senator, as he nudged the mother/cop toward the door.

Maggie, as usual, got in the last word.

"You don't pass this fingerprinting law, and you may as well string a banner across the state line:

'WELCOME CHILD MOLESTERS.

Have we got a job for you.' "

With that, she turned and disappeared down the hall.

In search of her next senator.

The day following their initial frontal assault on the offices of key senators, the parents testified before the Senate HRS Committee in which the fingerprinting bill had stalled—the first of many hurdles over which it must pass before becoming law. Roberta Fox's latest vote count showed them going in with a shaky majority whose votes were contingent on their satisfaction with the amended product. If a last-minute defection didn't kill the bill, death by amendment just might.

Because Senator Roberta Fox preferred a dead bill to an impotent one.

Maggie Fletcher delivered to the committee a brief version of her "Let me tell you the facts of my case" speech, stopping intermittently to swipe tears from her cheek. She got pissed off all over again every time she talked about the absurdities of the Fuster case. And when Maggie got mad, she cried.

Tom Herschel had more of a quiet kind of mad. The kind that bubbled beneath his temples. He now knew not only Chad, but his daughter Missy, too, had fallen victim to Frank and Iliana Fuster. They had defiled his lovely and perfect little girl.

The one who still—even now—believed in Santa Claus.

Tom Herschel may have been upset beyond words, but that didn't stop him from talking.

"Where does all this business about civil liberties enter the picture?" he wanted to know. "My occupation requires me to be fingerprinted. I'm a real estate broker. This state requires fingerprinting on dozens of occupations, none of which involve working with children. Even the grooms at the racetrack have to be fingerprinted. I would think that our children deserve at least as much protection as we've already given land-buyers and thoroughbreds.

"I've been fingerprinted. I didn't mind."

A not-so-timid Jeannie Pierson took her turn at the podium, churning stomach notwithstanding, and spoke of feelings, none of which she seemed able to touch in the stoic panel of senators before her. None, save Roberta Fox, whose eyes smiled encouragement.

It was when the Lancasters stepped to the microphone that a hush fell over the packed committee chambers. For in her arms Debbie Lancaster carried a beautiful little girl wrapped in purple velvet, with lavender tights and lavender ribbons streaming among the waves of her long nutmeg hair.

Maggie and Tom and Jeannie shifted uncomfortably in their front-row seats, a wide range of emotions playing across each face. They looked at each other, their mouths slightly ajar at the Lancasters' unannounced decision to put their child on display before two hundred strangers and a multitude of media.

There was courage, and there was *courage*, but this brand seemed to them a little off center. They understood what the Lancasters were trying to do—forcing the makers of laws to see a living, breathing child, a point they might wish to consider while they tossed her life around on paper. The parents understood, because a part of them wished very much to do much the same thing. To bring the kids in, one at a time, sit them on the distinguished panel's cold oak desk, and say, "Look at this little girl and tell me she deserved to have this done to her. Look at this little boy who was tortured and raped and made to eat excrement. Repeatedly. And note, if you will, how normal they appear on the outside despite their scars within. We know for a *fact* what was done to these children, and yet none of us— not you or me—could pick them out of a crowd.

"Doesn't that scare you a little? Doesn't it make you a little uncomfortable to wonder just how many more of them are out there? Emotionally maimed children who carry within them a mantle of guilt, shame, and anger that, instead of evaporating with time, congeals and grows out of proportion to its place in their lives—like a wound tightly bandaged, when it desperately needs to be uncovered and allowed to heal properly.

"Don't you wonder how many have carried that wound into adulthood, improperly healed to the point where it rends the very fabric of their lives? Don't you wonder if perhaps this is why your spouse gets undressed in the closet or your grown son has problems establishing trust and intimacy, a circumstance that led him into two failed marriages and a string of unsatisfying relationships? Don't you perhaps wonder if this might be why there are so many sexually confused people walking this planet—people whose introduction to sexuality happened to be perverse and premature?"

Like five-year-old Jason Harrison, who inquired of his mother whether Frank and Iliana shared the same cell. When advised that this was not the case, Jason looked relieved. "Good," he said. " 'Cause if they put them together, they might do those bad things to each other."

How well would he be able to reconcile as he passed through puberty that "those bad things" could be considered good at the right time and under the right circumstance, one free of elements of fear and shame?

"Don't you wonder how profoundly this affects our entire society? Our future? These kids are going to be running things someday."

This was the statement the parents knew that the Lancasters meant to make by laying April on the legal altar. But at what price to their child? wondered the parents.

April peered at the audience over her mother's shoulder, then laid her cheek down on it, seemingly unconcerned as her parents proceeded to tell the stunned committee that if the laws of the state of Florida had been adequate *this* child, their daughter, would not have been raped.

The committee members could not tear their eyes from the little girl who had lived, six days a week for a period of six months, under the roof of Frank and Iliana Fuster.

The house into which, April once explained to her mother, God could not see.

• • •

Two full months had passed since Joe Braga's February "death," and though countless minidramas had been played out in the interim, most had been conducted in less celebrated fashion. And though every hearing thus far had convened under the watchful eye of a varying number of parents and a contingent of journalists, this one drew an unusually large audience to Courtroom 4-2 on this, the twelfth day of April.

The audience was unusually large, even for what promised an interesting courtroom joust as the defense moved to prohibit the "cruel and unusual" pretrial detention that Samek and Von Zamft claimed the Fusters now endured.

What co-counsel for the defense essentially had to say was that their clients—who, they pointedly reminded the court, remained innocent until proven guilty—were rotting in solitary confinement in so-called "safety cells," cramped, dark closets in which roaches crawled and cold food was served on paper plates. The Fusters were, said their lawyers, denied phone privileges, recreation, televisions, exercise, and adequate hygienic opportunity.

Iliana, according to the defense motion, was allowed out of her cell only to "bathe and to visit with her husband once a month."

As a result of this "cruel and unusual pretrial detention," read the motion, "the defendant's emotional and mental state is rapidly deteriorating. Her condition makes it difficult for counsel to communicate with her at all because of the cruel and unusual conditions under which she is incarcerated."

Iliana indeed looked pale and wan as she sat in the jury box, but not because of any matters having to do with "cruel and inhumane" pretrial detention, as Christina Royo had discovered when she paid a lengthy visit to the jail the day before in order to inspect the Fusters' plight.

A social worker at the Women's Detention Center was astonished when the State's investigator advised her that Iliana was displeased with her living conditions. The social worker explained that she had unofficially adopted Frank's child bride and had strived to make the "poor girl's" stay as comfortable as possible. Iliana, it seemed, had the run of the facility, spending much of her day in the social worker's office or trailing around the building after her like a happy puppy. Iliana used her office phone whenever she wished, draped personal photos and mementos over her desk, and usually retired to her cell only to sleep and eat—a cell that in no way resembled the vermin-infested closet described to the court.

There was, in fact, said the social worker, considerable resentment from other prisoners that Frank's bride enjoyed such favored treatment.

And if Iliana's mental and emotional state was "rapidly deteriorating," she added, it was news to her.

Though Frank had found no one in the men's facility willing to "adopt" him, the resourceful ex-con had made a little home for himself in his large barred cell, where a writing desk had been converted to an altar from which precisely arranged articles proclaimed his worship of his wife. Frank's "bathing" privileges, the inadequacy of which he complained about bitterly, allowed him only one shower per day. And no baths. The phone was brought to his cell for his use but one time a day. He was "denied" recreation, the jail guards informed Christina, because the hours during which the gymnasium was open did not coincide with Mr. Fuster's preference to sleep late. And though the taxpayers of Dade County had provided him with a private color TV and VCR (on which he studied the children's interview tapes over and over and over), Frank uttered frequent and vehement disappointment that he was denied cable pay channels.

As John Hogan presented this information to the court, accompanied by sworn affidavits and a hint of sarcasm, the words *cruel and unusual* were beginning to look a little foolish even to the defense attorneys who spoke them.

Another parade rained out.

Maggie sat in the visitor's gallery half-listening to the verbal duel between the defense and the State over the frequency with which the Fusters' cells were sprayed for pests. Ordinarily, she would have been fighting the urge to stalk out the door and toss over her shoulder, "Who gives a shit where you put 'em? They belong in a septic tank."

She never said it out loud, of course. At least not in the courtroom.

But this morning, Maggie was too preoccupied to give her full attention to the latest act to be played in this theater of the absurd. She studied the speech she had frantically assembled in the hours before dawn, waiting for the hearing to adjourn, so that she might step into the corridor in front of Courtroom 4-2 to hold the first press conference the parents had ever called. And although the media had continuously invited themselves into their lives for the past nine months, Maggie was not at all sure that she could beckon them at will.

What if she gave a press conference and nobody came?

The parents' latest plan was hatched just three days ago, aboard a return flight from Tallahassee, where they had just cleared another legislative path for the amendment-riddled fingerprinting bill, over which Roberta Fox had flung her ample body in determined frustration.

Immediately following the startling appearance of five persuasive parents and one little girl wrapped in purple velvet and lavender tights, the HRS committee, much to its chairwoman's delight, quietly (and unanimously) voted "yes" to an amended version of the fingerprinting proposal. Roberta Fox then beat a frantic path between the House and the Senate, furiously putting out brushfires that ignited spontaneously in every corner of her childcare protection package, the companion of which was being nursed through the House by Representative Elaine Gordon, Fox's co-chair on the Governor's Child Abuse Task Force and speaker pro tempore of the House.

This morning, following a brief (but heated) floor debate, the Senate abruptly (and again unanimously) granted passage to the embattled fingerprinting bill.

The ball was in the House's court.

And unless something politically unusual occurred, Elaine Gordon was expected to guide it through, more or less without incident, the battle for amendments having already been waged in the Senate. There were, however, a few noises of opposition still rumbling around the capitol, which led the parents to conclude that it would take one more trip next week to do unto the House what they had done unto the Senate, before they could turn their full attention to the piece of legislation that for nine months had sustained their will to see justice done: the Judicial Proceedings Act—Senate Bill (SB) 290, which realized the Bragas' vision of a courtroom in which children didn't have to be maimed in order to give testimony.

Even the parents most committed to cooperating in the prosecution of the Fusters would not hesitate to withdraw from the case should they not be satisfied with the conditions under which the children would testify. All had clearly stated that they would open the Fusters' cells themselves before they would allow their sons and daughters to be abused in a courtroom.

Janet Reno wouldn't promise that she could secure any extraordinary measures for the Country Walk children—only that she would try. Reno, herself, journeyed frequently to the capitol during the spring of 1985, sometimes finding herself standing three paces from half a dozen parents when she boarded a plane or exited a Tallahassee restaurant.

Always on these occasions, the state attorney offered a wide smile and a few uncomfortable moments of small talk. Though Maggie cheerfully volunteered a diary of her day, Reno would mumble something about a speech or a meeting or other "business" to which she was attending while the legislature happened to be in session. That business, they would later learn, was often coincidental to their own. In fact, independent of the parents, the framework of what was to become Senate Bill 290 had been constructed on the sixth floor of the Metro Justice Building.

And though the parents perceived that the enigmatic Janet Reno might be silently cheering their efforts, they also had a vague sense that the state attorney might be queasy about the height of their public profile.

On the latter count, they were most correct.

On the former, they underestimated the size and scope of their cheering section, for unbeknownst to the parents, the inhabitants of the state attorney's office (including clericals) monitored closely any news filtering down from Tallahassee, their excitement building each time the parents cleared another hurdle toward their legislative goals.

John Hogan and Dan Casey—the prosecution team that was about to take (what had been narrowed down to) a dozen or so children through a trial—viewed each of their victories in delighted disbelief. They didn't even want to contemplate out loud the possibilities opened to them should the Country Walk parents actually succeed in getting SB 290 voted into law.

The children wouldn't have to face the Fusters. They wouldn't have to be deposed by Samek and Von Zamft. Their interview tapes would become admissible evidence. The things they told their parents could be told to the jury. And the children who testified at the trial could do so on closed-circuit television.

For the first time, they could try a child rape case without reraping the child.

It was all pipe dreaming, of course. Hogan no more expected the legislature (which counted in its ranks a very large number of defense attorneys) to pass a new child witness law than he expected to see the pope marry. And certainly not in time to be of any use in the trial of Country Walk, which had just been rescheduled—this time for early summer. Occasionally, though, he found himself toying with pieces of SB 290 as he mapped out his trial strategy—just in case the "Mom Mafia" (Fox, Gordon, Reno, and Maggie Fletcher) pulled this one off.

Daniel Casey allowed himself to indulge a little more freely in magical thinking, since it was the promise of such legal landmarks that had prompted Janet Reno's robbery chief to accept her majesty's invitation to join the Country Walk team—a carefully deliberated decision that reversed another he had made a couple of years ago when he swore he would never accept another child assault case.

They took too much out of the children.

And that took too much out of Dan.

But when Janet Reno summoned him to the master suite, she

spoke in animated tones of her desire for him to help John Hogan construct a "model case" in which every resource available to the state attorney's office would be at their disposal. They were to make prosecutable the most unprosecutable crime in the nation.

Dan Casey put aside, for a moment, the sense of nausea the words *Country Walk* had induced since the first day his wife Christy, who was in the process of seeking childcare for their six-month-old daughter, had informed him of the contents of the news, the day of Frank Fuster's arrest. Casey panicked. A babysitter and her husband. His daughter—his completely defenseless infant daughter who could neither run from danger nor tell him of it—was not to be left with strangers.

He didn't know whom to trust anymore.

Now he was being invited to step into the middle of a tale that gave him nightmares just watching it on television. If he took this case, it would surely take a piece of him with it.

But Janet Reno's intentions intrigued the twenty-eight-year-old prosecutor, who in four years had tried more than eighty cases and could count his losses on one hand with a finger or two left over. The state attorney, Casey knew, wasn't given to effusive displays of commitment. Nor had she ever before relieved three highly placed assistants of the bulk of their duties to assemble one trial.

If Janet Reno was going to shoot for the moon, Dan Casey couldn't easily pass up an offer to ride shotgun.

He rolled up his sleeves, took his place next to the Bragas, John Hogan, Richard Shiffrin, and Christina Royo and began absorbing the pieces of the case like a thirsty sponge. Casey was awed at the crime's magnitude—its boldness, its complexity. And he was compelled by its ugliness to find a way—some way—for the jury to be allowed to see what really happened at the Country Walk Babysitting Service, instead of a legal smoke screen that made a mockery of the truth.

Casey wanted the jury to see the tapes.

Because the tapes didn't lie.

Being a practical young man, Dan Casey expected no miracles. But that didn't keep him from casting an occasional glance toward Tallahassee in search of a rainbow.

· · ·

Maggie stopped by Roberta Fox's office to thank the battle-fatigued senator for doing everything short of prostrating herself on the Senate floor to get daycare workers fingerprinted. Fox looked grey and worn, but her face was one giant smile as she accepted congratulations from her secretary and her aide, both of whom had willed the child protection package through the Senate as though their lives depended on it.

Maggie's thoughts turned momentarily to the larger work ahead. What about the judicial proceedings bill? she asked.

The senator paused for a moment to sort through the myriad children's laws that danced about her head. "Oh . . ." Roberta Fox looked like someone had just doused her with a pail of cold water. SB 290 was in trouble. Big trouble.

"When I introduced it in committee, they almost turned it into confetti on the spot. They went nuts. I sent it back for a rewrite."

Maggie's jaw dropped.

The parents began to apply war paint during the short flight home. They had little time with which to play the hand they'd just been dealt.

Neither they nor Fox the lawyer/lawmaker had expected SB 290 to be gutted before its first reading in committee. Its enemies were few, but apparently powerful. At this point, the parents weren't quite sure who the enemy was.

Their faith in Roberta Fox remained unshakable. They believed that she would turn the Senate inside out before she would give up on it. On the House side, they expected that Elaine Gordon would do her best, although her priorities weren't as focused as the senator whose district encompassed Country Walk.

The bill's enemies in both the House and Senate were no less visible than its allies, and between these harshly defined polarities lay the majority view—confusion and apathy. It was the majority that they would have to—as Maggie put it—"educate."

So the parents pretty much knew how things lined up in the legislature. It was the governor they wondered about.

Having declared children to be the state's "top priority" one season past, Bob Graham had remained strangely silent on the issue ever since. His keynote address, which kicked off the 1985 spring session, placed "Florida's Growth" (and its related legislation) at the top of his hit parade. And though this might have been an opportunity for him to mention that with growth come families (and children), he did not.

He did, however, assign a full-time aide from his Constituency for

Children to work with Fox and Gordon to get the child protection package signed, sealed, and delivered. It was, in fact, the representative of the governor's office who had summoned Maggie and her troops to testify when the fingerprinting bill first began to flounder.

But she had not advised them of trouble brewing over SB 290, which Roberta Fox now told them was about to self-destruct. The parents quickly secured their first copy of the final draft of the bill, scanned the first paragraphs, and stopped dead in their tracks.

Someone had tacked to the front of their "pure, won't cost anyone a dime" judicial proceedings bill an ancillary provision that "The Department of Health and Rehabilitative Services (HRS) shall develop a model plan for community intervention and treatment of intrafamily sexual abuse. . . ."

Maggie was about ready to blow a fuse.

What the hell was a multimillion-dollar HRS "model plan" for incestuous families doing in their bill?

Oh, that was no problem, said the governor's aide—a much-needed service for sexually abused children, don't you think?

"You *knew* about this?" seethed Maggie.

"Oh, it's just a little attachment. Nothing to be concerned about."

"But it has absolutely *nothing* to do with child witnesses," said Maggie, as though explaining to Crystal the difference between apples and oranges.

"Yes, well, we just had this loose end floating around, and your bill was as good as any to tack it onto."

"Then tack it onto someone else's bill."

"Don't worry about it. That's just the way we do things."

Of course, telling Maggie not to worry was like commanding the sun not to set, so she promptly chewed her nails to the quick and scheduled an emergency J-SAC meeting. If Maggie had learned anything in recent months, she had learned that the surest way to get a bill killed was to attach money to it. She had no idea why someone was trying to attach several million to SB 290, but she wanted it detached immediately.

Attorney Barry Levy, father of Chip and incorporator of J-SAC, was not enamored of the ambitious plan Maggie presented at her hastily assembled war council.

The police sergeant proposed that they launch a massive petition drive to throw some heat on lawmakers whose keen interest in child protection appeared to have been cured by an election. One delegate from Dade County, who had rushed to the parents' side last August, now informed her that Country Walk was "a South Dade County yuppie issue" and that the rest of the state had more far-reaching concerns to address this session—like doctors' malpractice insurance.

Maggie was incensed. How dare they walk away from this as though it hadn't happened—or didn't matter if it had?

She wanted to send them a message.

"And who do you propose is going to collect these signatures?" asked Barry Levy, noting that J-SAC's entire "active" membership these days fit neatly into the Herschels' family room—with room to spare.

"We will," said Maggie, looking around the room.

"And how many do you expect to get?" asked Barry.

"I don't know," said Maggie. "As many as we can get."

Barry Levy shook his head at Maggie's half-baked scheme. "What have you got—a week? So we all go knock ourselves out for a week and come back with what—a thousand signatures if we're lucky? What do they care about a thousand signatures from Dade County?"

"We'll go to shopping malls, ball games, the zoo. We could probably get more than a thousand over the weekend."

Barry shook his read in resignation. "I'll help. But I think you're wasting your time.

"People don't like to sign petitions."

"They'll sign ours," said Maggie.

• • •

As Maggie emerged from the hearing where Frank Fuster importuned the court to understand that a man could not be expected to practice proper hygiene with but one shower a day, she was instantly engulfed by reporters, who separated her from the dozen J-SAC members who had surfaced this day to witness their leader's declaration of war on the state's power structure. She squinted in the glare of lights and flashbulbs from networks and the national wire services who today joined the local entourage that generally trailed the parents' activities.

What if they gave a press conference and *everybody* came?

Bedlam.

Maggie became wedged in a semicircle of notepads and microphones, unable to speak above the deafening din. Judge Newman, sans robe and puffing on a pipe, wandered from his office to investigate the commotion outside Courtroom 4-2.

"What's going on?" he inquired of a bystander.

"The Country Walk parents are holding a press conference."

Judge Newman puffed thoughtfully on his pipe.

His eyes creased in the corners as he listened to the little blond cop read from the statement that had been prepared by committee hours before.

Last fall, sexual child abuse was a red-hot issue in the Florida legislature. During the special session, the people of the state of Florida were promised that protection for the children would be a top priority.

It seems that too many of our politicians have lost the spark of concern they showed months ago, but our flame of commitment to the children has not subsided.

The laws of the state of Florida do not protect our children.

Within a week, the legislature will consider the most comprehensive piece of legislation that has ever been introduced in this country regarding children's rights in the courtroom. The state of Florida has the opportunity to lead the nation in protecting children.

We want to see our legislature show the courage and conviction to do so.

We want a law that gives our children as much protection in court as the child abusers now have. There must be a better balance between a defendant's right to a fair trial and the right of a small sex abuse victim to tell his or her story in a court of law.

The people of the state have entrusted the Florida legislature with the power, the ability, and the duty to protect its children. The present laws subvert the truth and allow the molesters to walk free.

For every child molester who is freed by an unfair system, there will be a hundred more child victims. One of those could be your child or grandchild.

We will not stand for this senseless carnage.

To ensure that the legislature and the governor of Florida get this message, we are launching a statewide petition drive demanding that our lawmakers live up to their promises.

This should not be a controversial issue.

We are not asking for casino gambling.

Or even for money.

We are asking for protection of our children. We find it appalling that any of our state leaders, entrusted with representing the people of our state, could turn their backs on our state's most precious resource.

Our children.

Our children are our future. We expect our leaders to give at least as much consideration to them as they now are giving other issues concerning Florida's future growth. If we can get every parent, grandparent, and other adult who loves a child to sign and support this legislation, we will be on our way to creating a safer place for the children of our state.

This is not a white, black, or Hispanic issue.

It is not a Republican or Democratic issue.

It is an issue that concerns each and every one of us.

Our children are what binds us together, whatever other differences we may have. . . . We want to mobilize each and every citizen who cares about children to demand action now.

We want Justice for Sexually Abused Children.

We expect our governor and our legislators to make good on their earlier promises to us.

The message was delivered, the gauntlet dropped.
But its recipients appeared more annoyed than intimidated.

• • •

The petition was by necessity specific and direct, there being four provisions the parents sought to satisfy the children's most urgent needs. They reduced SB 290 to its simplest terms:

PETITION TO PROTECT CHILD VICTIMS OF SEXUAL ABUSE

To: Robert Graham, Governor of Florida
Harry A. Johnston II, President of the Florida Senate
James Harold Thompson, Speaker, House of Representatives

We, the undersigned citizens of the state of Florida, demand that the legislature keep the promise that was made during the 1984 Special Session to make the protection of children its priority in the 1985 legislative session.

We further support the enactment of safeguards for child victims to assure that their right to be free from emotional harm and trauma is protected by authorizing the court to issue certain protective orders in child sexual abuse cases, including:

1. providing procedures to protect the child during confrontation with the accused molester in court proceedings.

2. authorizing the court to qualify persons to act as interpreters to assist the child in understanding questions asked during court proceedings as well as to aid in interpreting the language used by the children in relating their acts of abuse.

3. providing for admissibility of certain out-of-court statements made by the child relating to the abuse.

4. providing procedures for videotaping testimony of certain children in sexual abuse cases.

Within seventy-two hours of hearing of SB 290's uncertain future, the parents had agreed on a game plan, prepared a statement, drafted a petition, run off several hundred copies of it at Barry Levy's law office, held a major news conference, and reconvened to figure out what to do next.

No one knew how Maggie expected to pull this one off (including Maggie), but if she was game, so were they. Saturday morning the parents fanned out in teams to work the crowds at public events that promised to draw large numbers of registered voters with children in tow—a Disney ice show at the Miami Beach Convention Center, a football game at Tamiami Park. Flea markets. Shopping centers.

A handful of J-SAC volunteers joined them, including Anita York, the redheaded Texan who had assaulted the peace and dignity of her neighborhood by ridding it, legally, of a child molester, and Alfonso Ruíz, the gentle Cuban insurance salesman who asked God each day how his only child had grown into a drug-addicted woman who allowed men to have sex with her little girl.

Holding down the makeshift fort was a woman by the name of Virginia French, a neighbor of the Harrisons, who had volunteered countless hours and days in J-SAC's service. Throughout the petition drive, her phone was the designated command post for relaying messages between the teams in the field, who breathlessly assaulted her with jubilant news that the petitions were being consumed by signatures and more blank copies must be produced immediately— a wish instantly granted by a J-SAC member who owned a print shop and opened her doors to the parents' needs at any time of the day or night, free of charge.

By Saturday evening, twelve hours into their frenetic collecting of signatures, Virginia French was telegraphing to the troops the wondrous news that Susan Maxwell, nine months pregnant, had whiled away the early stages of her labor canvassing a stadium parking lot and had collected several hundred signatures before checking into a hospital, where she was currently calling in for updates on the petition count between pains that were now coming two minutes apart.

Having a baby could not distract Susan Maxwell from the other events of this important day, on which she had labored for many children other than the one she was about to deliver.

The former prosecutor knew better than any of the parents what the children faced in the courtroom should they not win them legal protection. It was for them that Susan labored, for Kyle was not to be part of the trial. The sunny toddler was eighteen months old on the day of his only visit to the Fusters' and had neither the memory nor the communication skills to offer any information about his stay. As the other children began telling their stories, Susan grew increasingly frantic to know if Kyle would be "all right." Apologetically, she begged an hour of the Bragas' time, asking that they "interview" her son—which they did, assessing his nonverbal behavior.

Joe and Laurie told Susan that she had raised "a wonderful little boy" who demonstrated no fear, distrust, or anxiety toward the world. If anything had happened to him at the Fusters', the Bragas told her, it was apparently not traumatic to him.

They had drugged Kyle, Susan knew.

But for what purpose she would never know.

The parents petitioned through the weekend, combing crowds by day, consuming pizzas by night as they gathered to plan the next day's strategy.

By Monday morning they had almost fifteen thousand signatures.

They did it in two days, with twelve bodies.

News of the Country Walk parents' assault on Tallahassee had reached large segments of the population who needed little explanation when confronted by a determined mother or father who thrust into their hands the much-talked-about petition. People were actually forming lines, at times, to sign it. Radio and television stations received calls seeking information as to where the petitioners might be located. Occasionally, they ran into a surly skeptic who announced that "this whole business" was a product of the children's imagination or that it wasn't such "a big deal" for them to testify.

"If they can't go in and do it like everybody else, they don't belong in a courtroom."

Salvaging their sanity at moments like this were others of special note. Like the man who studied the petition thoughtfully and took the pen he was offered, remarking as he signed, "You know, as a criminal lawyer, I should have my head examined for signing this. But as a father, I can't morally refuse."

Swept up in a tide of public support that surpassed their wildest dreams, the parents regrouped to determine how best to manage this runaway train. They needed a more efficient system of distribution in order to get the petitions to the hands that reached to sign it.

"You know all those people who told you last August that if there was anything they could do just ask?" said Maggie. "Start asking."

The parents called on friends and relatives to man petition stations. Maggie mobilized members of the Hispanic and women's police organizations. Professional women's groups offered volunteers. An administrator of the Martin Luther King Foundation spent hours sweeping housing projects and street corners in Liberty City.

And radio suddenly emerged as a key medium.

The parents swept the talk show circuit, leaving behind petitions that listeners could pick up and distribute. Radio offered them a forum in which they could explain in great detail what SB 290 was and why it was so desperately needed.

There was also a cultural peculiarity unique to South Florida that contributed to radio's indispensable role in the tale of the parents' legislative crusade.

Radio was the single most effective way to reach the Hispanics, who cherished *los niños* as much as they did their right to vote. Miami's Cuban-American citizens took most seriously their civic duties. And a large percentage of them kept their radios tuned each day to WQBA—a Spanish-language AM station that topped the Arbitrons in South Florida.

The day Maggie debuted on WQBA and explained in fluent Spanish that some of the people in Tallahassee seemed to think that only "South Dade yuppies" cared about kids, nearly one thousand listeners descended on the radio station, paid two dollars to park their cars, and demanded to know where they might place their signatures.

Then they went home and rang up their local legislative representatives. Bewildered House and Senate aides fielded tirades for days. Unfortunately, the fury Maggie had unleashed did not discern between friend and foe, and the fallout rained indiscriminately on their own "team."

Maggie learned of this unhappy circumstance when she was approached by a very angry Rodolfo Garcia, Jr., who at the age of twenty-one had just become the youngest man to have been elected to Florida's House of Representatives. Rudy had come home for the weekend to visit his family and been greeted by a rabid gathering that promised to impeach him if he didn't pass the judicial proceedings bill.

Maggie was mortified. Representative Garcia was one of their strongest allies—and had been from the beginning. The tidal wave welled with unexpected force, which remained to be channeled.

If they had had more time, and if events had not progressed so rapidly, the Country Walk parents might have been able to gather all of the acorns that fell at their feet.

They lacked neither ingenuity nor motivation to do so.

But they had less than two weeks—no time in which to plan an efficient mechanism through which to mobilize the entire state. There was no time to get the PTA and law enforcement networks activated. There was, in fact, no time to do anything except shove petitions and pens in any set of hands encountered. Newspapers remained in their wrappers. Mail was unopened. Bills weren't paid. Meals weren't cooked. Pantries were empty. And sleep was taken four hours at a time.

For ten days the parents lived and breathed SB 290. For the first time since August, they had become consumed by something other than guilt and anger. Life had kicked them in the teeth, and they were just now beginning to feel empowered to fight back.

At night the parents would meet at Maggie's to count petitions and map the next day's course. Comparative pain relief was a popular subject of discussion during these sessions, the merits of Tylenol versus Datril being a lively topic of debate.

So was money.

Once SB 290 was reintroduced by Fox in Senate committee, they would need to shepherd it through several layers of both the House and Senate. And that meant more trips to Tallahassee, which, despite their celebrated image, they could ill afford.

Maggie was the only one among them whose expenses were covered, the city of Miami footing the bill for the cop it had appointed to its legislative task force—a circumstance that also allowed her a great deal of flexibility in work schedule, without which she couldn't have functioned.

J-SAC had survived for nine months on donated services and a few cash contributions. It had no funds to speak of.

The president of a commuter airline offered the parents a handful of round-trip tickets to Tallahassee. He wished, he said, that he could do more.

Maggie Fletcher and her band of renegade parents boarded the plane lugging cargo too precious to ride in baggage.

Fifty thousand signatures and the will to win a law.

They came home with two.

In the spring of 1985, both the fingerprinting bill and the Children's Judicial Proceedings Act were adopted by the House and Senate.

Unanimously.

20

The first time Christina Royo drove down the Fusters' street, she half-expected a tumbleweed to blow across her path. The State's investigator thought it looked much like the main drag through a desert ghost town—one large stretch being occupied by a row of half-constructed homesteads for which plans of completion had apparently been suspended. Even the occupied dwellings of the Fuster block had a sealed look about them—like well-landscaped mausoleums.

The red-doored scene of the crimes itself was locked tight as a drum, a "For Sale" sign planted in the front lawn. The bank that now owned it would find no takers for several more months, despite a price tag that some residents called a "giveaway" by Country Walk standards.

The whole place gave Christina the creeps; a feeling that grew so ripe with time that she came to dread turning into the tree-canopied portal. She despised the tranquil veneer that masked this place of shattered illusions, but she kept the feeling to herself.

She did, after all, have an image to maintain.

Christina was always on duty.

She was a born collector of information—and a suspicious one at that.

The long, lean detective with the Clint Eastwood walk could drop in on an acquaintance for a five-minute chat and leave with a lifestyle summary that included what the subject ate, how he lived, and the name of the dentist with whom he had an appointment next Tuesday, Christina's ability to read notes taped to a refrigerator from a distance of five yards exceeded only by her uncanny knack for deciphering correspondence upside down.

Should the detective linger for a cup of coffee, she could instinctively compile enough material to produce a minidocumentary on her host or hostess's life.

Christina had never worked a child molestation case before. Nor, after Country Walk, did she think she would want to ever again.

She lived it twenty-four hours a day.

And it burned her—inside and out.

During office hours, Christina tracked down leads and potential witnesses in divergent and simultaneous directions—the Fusters' financial documents, their associates, their relatives.

She collected the children's medical records, which documented that many of them had suffered chronic infections during and immediately following the period during which they had stayed with the Fusters—the majority of the complaints being upper respiratory or throat infections, which had been treated by the children's pediatricians with repeated doses of penicillin.

Some of the children had been cultured for strep infections, the results of which came back negative. But not one physician had entertained the notion of culturing for gonorrhea, although that may have been what they inadvertently cured with the liberally administered doses of antibiotic. The State had reason to believe that this phenomenon might explain why the only child who had the disease at the time of his father's arrest was Jaime Fuster.

Another circumstance of viable possibility was that Frank may have "lent" his son to someone else who had the disease. It was disclosed by three of the children that there were at least two adults aside from the babysitters who sometimes partook of the wares in Frank's candy store. The State even knew who one of them was.

To prosecute him would require a separate trial, for he was not a part of the "group" activities that had allowed the state to charge the Fusters as co-defendants.

But neither the State nor the parents were eager to plunge from Country Walk I into Country Walk II. The children couldn't be put through a second trial, even if it meant that a man who shared Frank Fuster's interests remained free to live with his three small sons in another nice suburban neighborhood, fifteen minutes from Country Walk.

His wife had once run a babysitting service.

Several times a week—at all hours of the day and night—Christina would cruise by Frank's relatives' homes, noting vehicles, jotting down license plates, searching for the van in which the videotapes had apparently vanished the day before Frank Fuster surrendered himself in Courtroom 4-2.

She had a pretty good idea who had spirited away the tapes and equipment that had produced them. But they could be just about anywhere now. Sold. In storage. In a safety deposit box. In a relative's home. There was no way of knowing, and even if there were, a search warrant would be hard to come by.

The tapes might have even been destroyed, though this seemed their least likely fate, given the fair market value of the contraband in question—in terms of both dollars and Frank's anticipated future pleasure.

Christina thought of the tapes constantly, though she largely pursued them while off duty, there being matters of urgent substance to which she deferred during office hours—matters directed to her attention in a stream of memos from the prosecutors, which stacked into a growing pile of urgent priorities.

To: Chris Royo
From: Dan Casey
   When you get a chance please contact each of the pivotal parents and get from each copies of any notes and drawings they may have collected from their children.
   Please make arrangements for color slide pictures to be taken of the drawings we got from the Bragas yesterday.
   Thanks.

To: Chris Royo
From: Dan Casey
   Please contact the Doctors Braga at your earliest convenience and obtain a copy of all of the television sequences they have videotaped regarding the Country Walk case.

To: Chris Royo
From: John M. Hogan
   Please do your best to arrange for us to get a sketch of the Fuster residence. . . .

To: Chris Royo
From: John M. Hogan
Please look into the following matters:
1) Was Jason Harrison's rectum checked when he went to the Rape Treatment Center? . . .
2) . . . We need to get copies of lab reports on all of the children checked for gonorrhea. . . .
3) Please review each and every videotape done in the Country Walk

case and list the investigator or person who put the tape in the machine and the person who took the tape out of the machine and anyone else who was involved in the chain of custody for each individual tape that you know of.
4) Get a readable copy of every property receipt whether from our office or from Sexual Battery. . . .

By late spring, the memos came daily and the tasks in multiples. Christina spread herself all over the county—and at times further— in hot pursuit of the loose ends that must be tied in order to bring the Fusters to trial. She had little time to pursue "smoking guns" that, if they still existed, might have already found their way halfway around the globe.

Still, she couldn't help thinking how differently this case might have evolved had the Fuster home been searched before the white van disappeared with its priceless cargo.

If the Bragas were the emotional bridge between the parents and the State, Christina Royo was the information pipeline. She spoke to many of them daily, eliciting details, alerting them to court hearings, keeping them abreast of each twist and turn in the case.

These Christina found at first to be awkward encounters in which the parents, still tasting the skepticism of the first policewoman who had knocked on their doors on an otherwise sunny August day— regarded her with caution, if not outright suspicion.

Dispassionately, they answered her questions and relayed the latest developments on the homefront, offering no hint of the emotional carnage wreaked on the families by their growing knowledge of what had occurred in the Fuster home and the legacy it had left them.

Likewise, Christina maintained her characteristically detached and professional demeanor, collecting the pieces of the puzzle the State continued to assemble. But the parents gradually came to appreciate that the diligence with which she pursued even the most fragile threads of information exceeded her frequent assertions that she was "just doing her job." There came a time when their strained and distant exchange of information evolved into communication, and the parents began to tell the State's investigator not only what had occurred, but also how they felt about it.

"I'm going crazy."

"I can't take it."

"What's going to happen to them?"

It was a "real stressful" period for Christina.

"I was dealing with a lot of things myself," she would later reflect, "because I was trying to really know what these people were going through . . . trying to put myself in their shoes, and dealing with the system, and dealing with my own feelings, saying to myself, 'I would never put myself through this . . . I'd put up the money to bond that son-of-a-bitch out, and I'd wait for him.'

"But because of what I believe in regard to my job, I kept saying, 'This is going to work.'

"Sure, don't worry, it's OK for your kid to sit in the chair and spill his guts out about what they did to his private parts. . . .

"But there was no other way.

". . . I have to carry with me all these kids' names the rest of my life and know what happened. I'd sure hate to meet Jason Harrison when he's sixteen and playing ball and know that he knows who I am and that I know about his life . . .

"That he would know who I am and that I know about it.

"That bothered me.

"I think that's a private thing. . . .

"You know, you grow up and have certain beliefs, and you're taught certain things—and I work in the system every day. And I see how it doesn't work every day. . . .

"So many things happened to these people's lives because of this guy, and he can walk.

"I tried to convince myself that it was going to work, and yet I had so many fears that it wasn't going to."

But that didn't keep Christina Royo from trying.

Even though she had an image to maintain.

• • •

March 12, 1985

To: Richard Shiffrin (Chief of Legal Division)
From: Dan Casey

Please give consideration to the following possibility:

1. We offer a plea to Iliana Fuster which involves her testimony and cooperation.

2. Samek and Von Zamft both jointly represent Frank and Iliana.

3. Samek and Von Zamft have told Hogan that they have had no privileged communications with Frank or Iliana except denials by both.

4. When we offer our plea, a conflict exists in the joint representation of Frank and Iliana.

5. Given that possibility, Samek and Von Zamft want to represent Frank.

6. Is there a conflict with their representation of Frank, they having had a privileged communication with Iliana?

April 26, 1985

Dear Jeffrey & Michael:

It is my intention to make a plea offer to Iliana Fuster which would include testimony against her husband and codefendant, Francisco Fuster. I need to know to whom I should make the offer. Please let me know as soon as possible your opinion and thoughts on the matter.

Very truly yours,
JANET RENO
State Attorney
By: John Hogan

The State had no reason to believe that Iliana Fuster would be amenable to a plea of any kind since she had not once in the past nine months budged from her bewildered denials.

Hogan was just playing by the numbers, opening the door through which she might walk anytime she chose between now and the seating of a jury.

The question was who might lead her through it.

It was the State's erroneous opinion that, should the Fuster defense be legally separated to facilitate a plea offer to Iliana, Michael Von Zamft, the reputedly tenacious champion of the underdog, would no doubt claim Frank for himself—his penchant for challenge being legend among his peers.

But the State misjudged the depth of the defense attorney's disenchantment with the case in general, and Frank Fuster in particular, though Von Zamft made no secret of his desire to have as little contact with his client as possible.

Even from the beginning, he would later say, the feeling was clearly mutual. "Frank would say, 'You believe me, you believe me,' and I would say, 'It doesn't matter whether I believe you; I am your attorney, and I will represent you either way.'

"And then he would say, 'Well, I couldn't have done those things.' And I would say, 'I don't care if you did them; that's not my job. My job is to represent you. I don't care whether you did them or not; just tell me the truth so I know what to deal with, but I don't care.'

" 'But you've *got* to care,' he'd say. 'It's important that you believe

me.' [And I'd tell him] 'It doesn't matter. It doesn't matter whether
I believe you. I am honestly telling you I don't care.' "

But it was not Von Zamft's disaffection for his infamous client, or
even his eventual belief in his guilt, that caused him to tell Jeffrey
Samek, "You had him first; you keep him."

There were matters of more practical consideration.

He wasn't making any money.

He wasn't getting any clients.

And he wasn't going to win.

But Von Zamfts did not throw in towels, or so the legend went, and
the State naturally assumed that Michael's rained-out parades had
only served to strengthen his resolve to "get the Fusters off"—or die
trying. In the beginning, they had.

Even Joe Braga's humiliating "resurrection" hadn't stilled his
sharp tongue and single-minded intent. The Doctors Pollyanna
were to be disposed of one way or another, and with them the case.

"Just wait," Von Zamft was reported to have announced to
anyone who cared to listen, "until I get Joe Braga in depo.

"He'll know he's been deposed."

Joe Braga, of course, was advised of the attorney's rather serious-
sounding intent to blacken his twinkling eyes. And his twinkle
dissolved momentarily into an ice-blue gaze of distant focus.

Michael Von Zamft, Janet Reno would later say, seriously underestimated the man who conducted his business out of a "Snoopy"
suitcase.

The deposition was a marathon, lasting a total of two days,
twenty-four hours, and almost eight hundred pages of transcript,
throughout most of which Dr. Joseph Braga drove Michael Von
Zamft up a wall.

Q. What is the National Foundation for Children?
A. "It is a public foundation."
Q. When was it formed?
A. "When was it formed—was that the question?"
Q. That was the question.
A. "Can you help me by what you mean, 'formed'? I don't
understand your question 'formed.' "

Joe cheerfully dissected Von Zamft's questions, answering those
he was able to reduce to precise meaning and consistently refusing

to answer any of a personal nature, including whether or not he resided with Laurie.

"You'll have to ask my wife. . . . I will answer no questions of a personal nature. . . . I see no relevance of that question to the matter at hand."

"Certify the question! Certify the question! Certify the question!" Von Zamft spat at the court reporter at each of Joe's refusals to respond unless Judge Newman ordered that the identity of his wife's gynecologist and the location of the bed in which the State's child development experts slept were relevant to the matter of Frank and Iliana Fuster's raping children.

Seated comfortably behind John Hogan's desk, a seat he had deliberately arrived early enough to claim, the good doctor was not the least bit reluctant to expound at length on matters professional, all the while filling the room with clouds of smoke (a long-discarded habit that he and Laurie had resumed under the stress of juggling an endless stream of child victims), which he blew in the direction of his nonsmoking interrogators. Samek and Von Zamft began to wilt visibly toward the end of the first day, as did the prosecutors who attended their key witness's testimony in shifts. Even after they'd worn out their third court reporter, Joe still looked like he'd just stepped out of a shower. Apprised of Von Zamft's intent to wear him down, Dr. Braga had primed himself to go twenty hours if necessary and was somewhat surprised when the Fuster defense suspended the first session in less than twelve.

It was, as John Hogan would say afterward, "a battle of nerves. And I think Joe won."

At times, Von Zamft grew short-tempered with the semantic acrobatics involved in eliciting answers from the maddening man with the ponytail.

At one point, Dan Casey got caught in the cross fire.

"Stay out of it!" Von Zamft snapped.

"Excuse me?" said the speechless prosecutor.

"Stay out of it! I'll keep talking to him. If you have an objection, then make your objection."

"I'm making an objection," said Casey, "and I would like to put on the record the exact tone of the question."

"You can put down any tone you want. He has a tape recorder," said Von Zamft, waving at the silver Sony Joe had propped, over the defense attorney's objections, on the table before him.

There were moments, however—albeit few—when conversation in

the deposition room became less guarded and more philosophical. Samek and Von Zamft bantered about their shared obsession with football and their shared childhood experience with anti-Semitism—a circumstance that, they said, persuaded them to identify strongly with "the underdog."

During one of these relaxed moments, Von Zamft engaged Joe Braga in not-so-idle conversation.

"So, you have no problems, then," said Von Zamft, "doing an interview and allowing a child to have toys to play with or manipulate during that interview?"

"No," said Joe.

"No doubt, from what you're saying," Von Zamft continued, "you feel it assists you."

"Their availability assists, yes." Joe refused to be drawn out further. As far as he was concerned, any conversation with Von Zamft was a deposition—whether the court reporter was on break or not.

"And their use of them there does, too?" prodded Von Zamft.

Joe shrugged. Even today, not two weeks after Von Zamft had attached the words *deceased, fraud,* and *child molester* to motions bearing his name, Joe Braga continued to entertain the notion that Von Zamft could be "reached"—at least to the extent that he might not so enthusiastically "bloody" the children with his "words and intellect" as was his acknowledged custom with any adversary, including the four-year-old he had dispensed with "in less than forty-five minutes."

Professor Braga launched his lecture and didn't come up for air. "It becomes an alternative," said Joe of the tools of his trade. ". . . And also a comforting factor to the child.

"And let me say this to you—as a person who obviously is engaged in this kind of case. . . .

"A room or situation that is child-oriented is much more potentially helpful, no matter *what* side of the legal interview you are going to be on. In a room that is not child-oriented . . . for example—let's suppose that you were going to interview a child in *this* room, and you sit the child at *that* desk. This is an adult environment that tells the child something just by its physical appearance. Whereas, if this were like the room on the ninth floor, with child-sized furniture and children's toys available, that . . . is a very comforting kind of situation. It says, 'This room is inviting. This should be comfortable for you.'

"There's a statement made.

"And I think what I'm trying to say," Joe continued, "both in answering your question, but also in telling you something that I think is very important—because I know as an attorney you want to arrive at the truth.

"In interviewing young children in situations like this, children who are in an environment that is child-centered are more comfortable. And if they're more comfortable, then they're much more likely to be able to be forthcoming about information in sexual abuse cases—one way or the other, because this removes the factor of 'Here you are, the center of attention—the focus of attention—in an adult environment that is controlled by adults.'

"I know I gave you more information than you asked for. But I'd like to think that maybe that information might be of help to you professionally in cases like this."

Von Zamft was amused.

"Well, you just had one wrong assumption in your—in your premise—and John knows what that wrong assumption was," smiled Von Zamft.

John Hogan, whose turn it was to monitor the Braga/Von Zamft/Samek proceeding, burst forth with a rare and knowing laugh, and Joe found himself residing on the fringes of an apparently well-known inside joke. "I did catch *one*," said John.

"And you know exactly what that wrong assumption was," Von Zamft said.

Hogan laughed again.

Von Zamft turned back to Joe, still smiling. "Because that's not my job."

"No," John Hogan interjected. "The truth's not his. That's *mine*."

To which Von Zamft replied, "But at least I'm candid about it. We all know I know my role."

Von Zamft paused, and his humor vanished like early mist.

"The truth means *nothing* to me.

"The *outcome* is what matters.

"That's—my—job."

Words that would return to haunt Michael Von Zamft.

It was noted by the prosecution that Joseph Braga's deposition was the point at which Von Zamft lost some of the swagger in his step and the taunt in his voice. Word around the Justice Building had it that Von Zamft had seriously overestimated the ease with which he could flatten what he would continue to refer to in his motions as the State's "alleged child experts."

Michael, it was noted once again, never knew when to quit.

And so it happened that the State was caught somewhat off guard when, four days after John Hogan offered to talk "deal" with Iliana, it was Von Zamft who positioned himself to intercept the pass.

They never thought he would throw in the towel.

Neither did he.

On May 3, 1985, Judge Robert Newman, in a lengthy public hearing, legally separated the defense of Frank and Iliana Fuster. The court sequestered the defendants and questioned them thoroughly and separately (through the interpreter the Fusters demanded) regarding their understanding of the rights they were waiving to any future claim of conflict of interest.

T's were crossed and I's dotted at every turn.

"Frank Fuster," said Judge Newman, "I wonder if you could tell me what you understand conflict of interest to be."

Fuster stood before the bench, docile, cooperative, even humble, speaking softly through his interpreter. "I understand that if at any time I have said anything that can be used against my wife, or if my wife has said anything that has been or that can be used against me, that information will not—cannot—be used and those are the rights that I am giving up."

"Can you at this time, Mr. Fuster, think of any possible conflicts of interest in this case that exist as of this moment?"

"None," said Frank.

Iliana had been similarly acquiescent in the waiving of her rights, there being nothing she had told either attorney that deviated from the Fuster script.

Von Zamft wanted to be crystal-clear. "It may occur that you become a witness either on your own behalf or on behalf of the State. Do you understand that you have the right *not* to have your former lawyer, Mr. Samek, cross-examine you . . . if you choose not to let that occur?"

"Well, of course," said Iliana sweetly, "I would feel good if either one would ask me anything.

"Because I would say the truth at all times."

June 21, 1985

Dear Mr. Hogan:

A specific polygraph detection of deception examination was administered to Iliana Fuster on this date relative to allegations of her involvement in child molesting at the Country Walk Babysitting Service.

The following relevant questions were asked during the administering of the examination:

1. Did you ever put your mouth on the penis of those children? (Answer—No)

2. Did you take the penis of any of the children into your mouth? (Answer—No)

3. Did you ever put your mouth on the vaginal area of any of the children at your home? (Answer—No)

4. Did any of the children put their mouth on your vagina? (Answer—No)

5. Did you ever play games with any of those children where they would take off their clothes? (Answer—No)

EXAMINER'S REMARKS

The subject's responses while attached to the polygraph instrument were indicative of truthfulness in her answering to questions one, two, three and four. Her responses were indicative of deception in her answering of question five . . .

A second examination was administered to Iliana Fuster during which the following relevant questions were asked:

6. Did you ever see Frank Fuster expose his penis to any of those children? (Answer—No)

7. Did you ever see Frank Fuster with his penis in the mouth of any of those children? (Answer—No)

8. Did you ever see Frank place his mouth on the vagina of any of those children? (Answer—No)

9. Did you and Frank ever have sex together where any of the children could see you? (Answer—No)

The subject's responses while attached to the polygraph instrument were indicative of deception in her answering to questions six, seven, and eight. Her responses were ambiguous and inconclusive to question nine.

During the post-test discussion she stated she had doubts about these activities as far as Frank was concerned but denied ever seeing such activities or having actual knowledge he had participated in such activities. Her responses remained consistently deceptive throughout subsequent testing. . . .

• • •

In the weeks following his wife's polygraph, Frank Fuster grew progressively alarmed that the bonds that cemented their "pure and everlasting union" were beginning to unravel.

He launched his most compelling letter campaign.

July 4, 1985

Dear Iliana:

Only God knows how much we really suffer in this life. I am glad that we are not alone to carry our burden and pain. Up to a point, I felt your pain. I want you to know that we are not guilty for the harm that is done to us. Also, we cannot carry any feelings of resentments through our life. Any negative feeling will do much more harm in time than the original harm that was done to us. My heart is open to you at any time that you feel the need to talk about it again. I am always willing, able and ready to get closer to you and share your experiences, doubts and fears. I enjoy to counsel you and to share "EVERYTHING" with you. I am not your husband to see through you, . . . but to see you through. I am sincerely interested in your happiness and will "NEVER" do anything to hurt you or our love, under no circumstance. "A house that fights against itself . . . It will surely fall."

The "Key" to be able to go through life with "Real Courage" . . . is the word of God . . . "The Bible." The word of God give us "hope," and with hope there is always a Tomorrow! The word of God give us faith, and faith is the root of the Tree of knowledget. Read The Bible daily. Read it slowly, knowing that it is the all powerful word of God. Remember it! Use it to fight all your fears, doubts and "any type of evil." Use it to guide you, to build your character and to make "all" your decisions, no matter how small. This is my advise to you . . . As a Christian and as your husband. Do not ever loose sight of yourself, you are a beautiful goodhearted human being . . . Always willing to show your goodness. God Love you, and so do I.

Frank

July 5, 1985

Dear Wife:

As I go through life I realize how important is for a human being to have the Love and guideness of a mother and a father . . .

In dealing with this trauma of your life, tell yourself that it was not your fault that things did not work out between your parents. As per the sacret Laws of God, you are "One Flesh" only with your husband and your marriage with him is the only one that you can control and care for. . . .

Frank

July 6, 1985

My dear wife and friend:

Look at me as a good friend. Tell me your secretes, your fantasies and your dreams. Share with me your doubts and your fears, and together we shall overcome them. Let me in . . . Open wide the doors of your heart. Keep nothing from me. . . .

I will advise you, to the best of my ability, and will place my knowledget and expirience of life at your service, so that you may learn from them. Bring me your problems and with an impartial open mind I will guide you. . . .

Frank

July 7, 1985

Hi Love!

No one will ever be able to love you as I do. . . .
You are a gift from God. . . .

Frank

The tide suddenly began to turn.
But not in the desired direction, from Frank's point of view.

July 9, 1985

Dear Wife:

Ever since you told me that you accused me of abusing you physically, I have tryed to forget it, but I cannot, because I am very, very hurt. I realized that I have been betrayed by you and I cannot just forget about it. . . . I must deal with it now, and the object of this letter is to do just that. . . . To excuse yourself and to make yourself feel better, you are saying that you were forced to said it, and that there is one woman that saw you with a black eye one day. One day is right, because only one time did you came out with a big lip and a black eye. However, you told your attorney that it happened several times. We had a few fights . . . but only one time did you came out hurt like that. In any case, you know very well that I never meaned to hurt you, because as I remember what took place, I wanted to leave the house and you tryed to stop me. You grabbed me and you got hurt as I was trying to get released from you. Another time I hit you, because you had hit me first. And it was a spontaneous action. That day I also hurt your lip, but not your eye, and I did not hit you with a closed fist. . . . But. . . . There is a God! There is always more than one way to say the truth.

If you think that you are helpping yourself by making me look like an abuser, you are wrong. I am not an abuser of any kind. When your attorney uses your accusations in Court, I will admit the TRUTH.

I do not know just how hurt I am by your low action, but time will tell. . . . You make yourself look like a victim and me like the abuser. Thank You! Be proud of it! I know that you want to get out of prison, but I never thought that you will hurt me in order to get out. It is under preasure that one can learn about other persons. Now I know more about you. You told me that you married me to get out of your house. . . . This means that you never loved me. You lied to me and to yourself. . . . Or only to me. You make me, and induced me, to love you, and ask you to marry me, while all you wanted was to get out of your house. I see it very clear now.

Maybe this is the reason why we are going through this experience. . . .

Iliana, since I met you, I have never lied to you. Not once! I gave you all the details of my life. There is nothing about me that I did not told you. I told you how much I had suffered. Why did you married me if you did not love me? And please do not say that you do with your lips, while your actions said otherwise. . . .

When you see me again, if you do not see the same look in my eyes, do not blame me. I am only human. I pray that you get out of prison. You do not belong here. I know that you have not committed any crime. I do not want to keep on dreaming about us. Only God knows now if we will or will not remain married. . . .

Remember that only God can help you. Von Zamft cannot set you free if God does not want to. If you put your faith in a human being, rather than God, you will have "Fears," "Doubts," etc., etc. . . .

Again, I advise you, have faith that you will win your trial. The power of the mind is very big and God is with us. God bless you.

Your husband,
Frank

Frank's letters went unanswered.

MEMORANDUM

FROM: MLVZ [Michael Von Zamft]
TO: ILIANA FUSTER
DATE: July 10, 1985

[Yesterday] I met with Iliana Fuster and Shirley Blando of the Jail Christian Ministries.

Apparently, Iliana Fuster had been speaking to Shirley Blando about things she was afraid to speak to me about.

During the discussion that ensued, Iliana was upset, distraught, crying, tearful, guilty, concerned, the whole gamut and range of emotions that a young girl would have when trying to tell the truth about certain things. . . .

While working one time, she met Jaime Fuster, Jaime being the son of Frank Fuster. Jaime was a little child who came to her and started talking to her and asking her if she was married, did she have a mother, that he, Jaime, did not have a mother and would Iliana like to be his mother, and would she be his friend. This led to her meeting Frank Fuster, which then led to her getting Frank's number. A couple of days later, after telling her mother about this, and her mother saying, "Don't worry about it, there are many children that don't have mothers," Iliana proceeds to call Frank and gets to meet Frank. She calls Frank and then calls Jaime, and Frank suggests they go out so Jaime could go to the park. That first time they ever went out, Jaime went to the park and they all had a very good time. She, Iliana, went out with Frank a couple more times. Then, after knowing Frank about five days, she had a very bad fight at home, was totally upset with everyone, and wanted to leave and get away . . . and called Frank and asked him to pick her up. Frank picked her up. She was crying, she was upset, she was distraught and just wanted to talk about what was going on at home and all the things that bothered her. Frank then took her to his house. While at his house, she was crying and upset, and at some point Frank apparently tried to comfort her and then talk to her and then finally told her that he wanted her to take off her clothes because he wanted to see her naked, and then he told her he was going to have sex with her and proceeded to, without actual physical beating, force her to have sex with him. It was a very upsetting experience for her because it hurt her very much because it was her first time and it was very painful and he was not gentle and caring.

This is important! Iliana had been brought up with the thought that when you had sex for the first time it was with your husband on your honeymoon, and she had been taught in school that the first time would take two or three days so that the husband would be very gentle and caring and there would be no pain and everything would be wonderful and marvelous. This is all she had ever known about what sex should be. She had also been brought up to believe that if you had sex with someone, then that is the person you must be with and marry and stay with for the rest of your life.

Iliana was ashamed of what had happened between her and Frank, but she felt she would now belong to him because of what she had been brought up to believe. From that time on, Frank continued to see her and he would take her to his house and have sex with her a couple of times a week and continue to enforce this feeling upon her. Sometime later Frank saw a picture taken of Iliana with a group of friends, including some male friends, that was taken before she ever met Frank. Frank became incensed and very jealous. They went to a cousin of Iliana's house and while there Iliana in discussing it mentioned that Frank had been upset and jealous. Frank took her outside and beat her up. From that time on, Frank continued, off and on when he would get angry at her, to beat her even before they were married. He continued to force her to have sex with him.

Iliana felt she was nothing. She felt she must take care of Frank and protect Frank, that he owned her, that everything she did was owed to Frank because she had sex with him for the first time. Iliana continued to believe that. So, therefore, even though everyone [she] knew tried to talk her out of marrying Frank, she married him anyway.

During the time they were married, Frank continued to have sex with her, and he continued to beat her to the point that the beatings were escalating and getting more repetitious and getting to the point where Iliana was beginning to fear that Frank would probably kill her.

Also at this time, although they were living at home and Frank's son Jaime was there, Iliana is sure and specifically remembers that Frank would hit and slap and beat up Jaime if something went wrong. Apparently, Frank has an incredibly violent, vicious temper and would unleash it on people that were smaller than he, or that he thought he could take advantage of. . . .

Iliana still to this day feels guilty about having had sex with Frank, feels an obligation to protect Frank, that she owes him, that he owns her, and all of these matters.

Iliana is absolutely emotionally disturbed and will probably need lengthy counseling, but it has become clear that she is showing all of the signs and symptoms of an obviously battered wife, which started when she was all of sixteen years old and Frank was able to take her sexually and continue to be with her.

Sometime during the course of the relationship, Frank forced Iliana to have oral sex with him, an act which she did not wish to participate in.

Iliana Fuster did not at this time, however, make mention of the gun, the crucifix, the power drill—or the children.

• • •

The State, of course, was not holding its collective breath for Iliana to "spill her guts" and turn State's evidence, recent developments notwithstanding.

For ten solid months she had maintained the "pure" and "everlasting" bond between herself and her beloved "Frankie." And only now, with a little help from Von Zamft, was it beginning to fray.

When he discovered that the jail pharmacy was liberal in dispensing remedies for its residents' pain—both real and imagined—Von Zamft quickly surmised why his client resided in the "Twilight Zone" throughout much of his acquaintance with her.

Iliana had, since the day she checked into the Women's Detention Center, complained of excruciating back pain—the result, she said, of injury sustained on the evening of her surrender following the issue of a warrant for her arrest, when she was knocked to the floor in front of the elevators outside Courtroom 4-2, surrounded by a swirling mass of reporters and photographers. Though the terrified young woman may well have sustained injury, Von Zamft came to realize that the prescribed "treatment"—chemical relief on demand—was doing little to enhance his relationship with his client. Von Zamft did not yet know that Frank's wife had come to enjoy chemical relief long before the jail pharmacy filled her self-administered prescriptions—a circumstance patently evident in a photograph that crime scene technicians seized from the Fuster "family album."

A photograph showing a nude Iliana sitting cross-legged on an unmade bed, her face fixed in a dazed and grotesque smile.

Iliana was subsequently relieved of her open prescription and allowed the drug Motrin, which she took to alleviate "menstrual cramps" that seemed to appear with substantial and uncyclic frequency.

Thus, easing his client into a less altered state, Von Zamft set out to isolate her from Frank's influence, which seeped from the men's to the women's annex via telephone, letter, or the mouth of his mother, who had vowed not to rest until her son's "good name" was cleared. These communications continued to be enthusiastically returned in kind, despite Von Zamft's increasingly terse and clearly futile directives that Iliana cease producing suitcases full of written "evidence" that could (and would) come back to haunt her.

For nearly a month following the rearrangement of the Fuster defense team, Von Zamft found Iliana's shield of denial no more penetrable than on the day he met her. But by June, he began to detect measurable progress, her letter-writing marathons apparently having ceased entirely and her phone conversations curtailed. But Frank's mother continued to pay frequent visits to her daughter-in-law, bearing her son's urgent admonitions not to speak to her "untrustworthy" lawyer.

By July, she was speaking to just about everyone but Frank, a circumstance over which her husband was becoming increasingly anxious.

July 24, 1985

Dear Wife of my Life:

. . . Iliana, this is the most difficult letter that I ever written to you. It is a very painful letter as I am very hurt. . . . My feelings are motivated by your actions, your words and your own feelings toward me, but mostly by your inexplicable silence. . . .

The day we got marry in the presence of God and in the house of God; we took an oath. You have profaned your sacred oath, with your words; actions and feelings.

While you have been telling me that you love me . . . you have been lying to me. . . . While you have been telling me that you do not want to hurt me . . . you are making very damaging false declarations and twisting the true, as when you accused me of beating Jaime and beating you. . . . You gave me a black eye once, do you remember? Did you do it intentionally? You know very well that you have a very bad temper and that you used to grab me when I wanted to leave the house and even hit me. Have you told this to your attorney? No you haven't! Why are you lying? Do you have any guilt to hide that I do not know about? . . .

I believed in your big pure love and your love for my son Jaime. . . . And today you are saying that all you wanted was to get out of your house and that "The Only Reason" you married me, was because I forced myself into you after having dated me seven or nine times. Doesn't all of this come to your mind when you pray to God? . . . As far as our incarcelation is concerned . . . it is not my fault that some parents accused you of sexually abusing their children. I believe that you are innocent, but lately you have been acting as if you are hiding something. . . . I did not do anything to bring us to prison. . . . You have always care about yourself only. And that is what you are doing today. You are an egotistical human being, Iliana Flores. My son Jaime introduce me to your "outside." Now God is presenting you as you really are "inside." . . .

On July 7, 1985 was the last day that you called me. Why did you stoped calling me? Do not you know that I need you? Do not you know that I love you with all my being? Do not you know that I do not want to go on living without you? Why are you hurting me so cruelly? . . . I will never love again. . . . No one can love you as I do. . . .

Last week I told Samek that I was going to divorce you because I am so hurt. But it is not true. I love you to much to divorce you. I being like crasy. I am losing my mind. I cannot live without you, Mi Niña. I honestly love you forever.

Before our incarceration, I used to love you like a man. But today I have the spirit of Jesus with me, and I love you as a Christian man. I pray to God to forgive you, but I must also urge you not to do or say anything that may affect your relationship with God. Make sure that all your actions, words, thoughts and feeling are to glorify God and not Satan. Please be full aware that Satan is real and that he is our enemy. Right now he is doing all that he can to brake our beautiful and pure marriage. . . .

Do not allow yourself to be manipulated by anyone. . . . Ask for a contact visit with me. . . . Come back to my Love where you will always belong. Your husband forever,

Frank Fuster

It was done.

Frank had pushed every button within reach.

Time would tell if one of them would launch a missile powerful enough to penetrate the wall Von Zamft was erecting around his client.

• • •

On the evening of Frank Fuster's latest plea to his wife, four-and-a-half-year-old Bonnie Martinez threw a conversation stopper into the family's evening meal.

"Know what Mommy? Iliana and Frank locked me and Jeremy in the closet."

Her mother almost choked. Linda Martinez had lived for the past year with little direct knowledge of what had been done to her children in the Fuster home. Although Bonnie had awakened screaming every single night since May of 1984, while she was still attending the Country Walk Babysitting Service, it wasn't until after Frank Fuster's arrest that her daughter told her that the night terrors occurred because "Iliana and monsters were dancing on the roof."

Still, when Linda brought her daughter to be interviewed by the Bragas, Bonnie had whirled into perpetual motion and refused to talk about the Fusters.

As had her three-year-old brother, who was in the habit of spreading his sister's legs, putting his mouth on her vagina, and attempting to get her to reciprocate.

But in January, Bonnie came to Linda and told her about the masks that Frank and Iliana used to frighten the children. Then she drew them. She said she had some things she wanted to tell Laurie Braga.

And Bonnie did.

But around the house the children spoke little of the Fusters. And though her daughter had occasionally approached her with tentative bits and pieces of information, Bonnie's comment over the dinner table was as unexpected as it was matter-of-fact.

Linda chose not to close the door just opened.

"Did they lock anyone else in the closet?" she asked as evenly as possible.

"Yes—Crystal and Jason and Joshua."

"Did you play any games?"

"No, we just played 'cut their heads off.' That was the only game."

"How did you play that?"

"We got in a circle, and we took turns being in the middle. Then they pretended to cut our heads off. I cried one time 'cause I thought it was gonna be with a real knife. I didn't like that game."

"Bonnie, did they take your clothes off?"

The little girl's mouth began to quiver. "Yes. She was lying. I thought she was really gonna kill you guys.

"I don't want you to be killed because I love you.

"They locked me in the closet naked, and Jeremy was naked too. Iliana and Frank took their clothes off, too.

"Frank layed on top of Iliana."

Bonnie Martinez had finally walked through the door.

The State had another witness.

• • •

July 10, 1985

TO: JANET RENO
    State Attorney
FROM: John M. Hogan, Chief
      Assistant State Attorney

On July 11, 1985, Iliana Fuster was seen by Dr. Charles Mutter. The interview was conducted in Dr. Mutter's office and videotaped. The purpose of the interview was to see if Dr. Mutter could elicit information from Iliana that would facilitate pending plea negotiations.

On Friday, July 12, 1985, Dr. Mutter called me. We set up a three-way call where Dr. Mutter, Michael Von Zamft, and I could all speak. In that conversation Dr. Mutter summarized his conclusions. Dr. Mutter was of the opinion that Iliana is extremely immature for her age. According to Dr. Mutter she is "like a six-year-old" when it deals with maturity. Although Dr. Mutter indicated he doesn't know if she's telling the truth or not, she clearly does not have any sort of amnesia or memory disturbance. According to Dr. Mutter, she either doesn't know of any misconduct on behalf of her husband or she is simply trying to protect him.

Dr. Mutter went on to characterize her as frightened and immature. Dr. Mutter also was of the opinion that Iliana was not a sex offender. He indicated that she was very masochistic and that from everything he learned she fit well with Frank, who is a sadist.

Dr. Mutter also indicated that Iliana fit the profile of a battered individual. He indicated that she was extremely passive and extremely dependent. He indicated that it was unlikely that she was involved in molesting children since she was having enough trouble dealing with her own sexuality.

Dr. Mutter suggested that if Mr. Von Zamft were to attempt to talk to her he should not point out or stress the fact that if she doesn't cooperate she'll go to jail. According to Dr. Mutter, Iliana has an unconscious need for punishment, which fits in with her masochistic personality. Dr. Mutter also pointed out that in his opinion Iliana was emotionally retarded. He did, however, say that she was clearly competent to stand trial and was sane at the time the alleged crimes occurred.

Dr. Mutter indicated that if Iliana did in fact involve in sexual activity with children, she did not do it out of her own wishes. He indicated the only way he could conceive of her involved in such contact is if she did it out of fear of Frank.

Dr. Mutter also told John Hogan that if Jason Harrison said otherwise, he was "a liar and confabulator."

• • •

Judge Robert Newman was, by reputation, an even-tempered magistrate of thoughtful and deliberate opinion who was not fond of appellate disagreement, so he rarely inched out toward the end of limbs elastic enough to snap back at him with a reversal.

His rulings were conservative and his profile low.

Judge Newman was known not as a legal scholar, but as "The Great Compromiser." He aspired, as one attorney put it, to "keep everyone happy."

Judge Newman also aspired, as was widely known about the Metro Justice Building, to preside over matters more civilized than those involving assaults on the peace and dignity of the people of the state of Florida.

And so it happened that he stood on the threshold of a requested transfer to the county's civil division when a cruel twist of fate placed the name *Fuster* on his calendar.

As luck of the docket would have it, Judge Robert Newman's criminal swan song came to be Country Walk.

It was a judge's worst nightmare.

Country Walk was a case of legal complexity that rivaled that of any ever tried in the Eleventh Judicial Circuit—or anywhere else, for that matter.

It was a trilateral balancing act among the rights of the victims, the defendants, and—of equal, but less considered, importance—the public's right to know.

The vast majority of the very first and last issues to be litigated hotly in Courtroom 4-2 revolved around the media's access to the evidence and at times to the proceedings themselves.

Protective orders routinely blanketed the bench, issued by the

State in an attempt to protect the victims' privacy and by the defense to protect their clients from prejudice. Media attorneys routinely lined up to fire First Amendment missiles at Judge Newman. As one outraged media representative fumed at the distinguished, white-bearded magistrate, "The fact of the matter is, I and my colleagues have been down here for these proceedings more than in any other[s] . . . in the last ten years . . . to deal with restrictions on access and steps [taken] to close off to the public what goes on in this courtroom. . . ."

Judge Newman was, as he put it, "taken aback" by the tirade, having exercised an open-door policy to reporters throughout the year-long ordeal. But he had, in fact, on select occasions, stepped uncharacteristically close (if not onto) an appellate limb, when the combined interests of the State and the defense overshadowed, in his opinion, the interests of the representatives of "the public's right to know."

The media attorneys papered the Eleventh Judicial Circuit and later the Third District Court of Appeals with motions crying constitutional "foul," there being more at stake than access to a most interesting case.

They would, they assured Judge Newman, "as always," demonstrate their ability to conform with the spirit of fairness, responsibility, and restraint in keeping with the delicacy of the issues at hand. And they would take whatever measures necessary to make their presence as unobtrusive as humanly possible, for the sake of the children. But they would not concede in any manner that their right to access be abridged. To do so would create dangerous precedents that threatened to erode the very foundation of its nobly appointed role as protector of the public's right to know.

But intent, Judge Newman knew, did not erase the potential for abuse in any doctrine, however noble—including the mass media. And it was the potential for abuse that Judge Robert Newman attempted to minimize in his three-front war.

Judge Newman was determined to hammer out some kind of balance in his own mind, having abandoned any notion of "keeping everyone happy" in the case of Country Walk.

He would do, as he came to preface most of his decisions, "what I think is right."

The peace in Judge Newman's traditionally sedate courtroom was punctured with increasing frequency as July 15—the third and "final" date he had set for the trial—drew near.

On June 7, Von Zamft and Samek appeared to request yet another delay—a motion to which Janet Reno, herself, objected most vigorously, the first and only time in anyone's memory that the state attorney had personally appeared in a courtroom to argue a pretrial motion.

The towering Reno rose from her seat and expressed the State's view in no uncertain terms.

"These children are victims of a *horrible* crime, and they have certain *rights* here," she fairly seethed through clenched teeth.

"This crime—for the children and their families—has been a *night*mare, and to continue . . . to drag them through it after this court has told them that they were going to trial, to leave this trial hanging over the heads of *these* children into the school year . . . is simply not fair to them."

John Hogan expressed similar sentiments, wondering into the court record what Mr. Von Zamft and Mr. Samek had been doing with themselves for the past year—an observation that launched Von Zamft into a furious colloquy before the bench.

"If you want to give me a full salary, I will *close* down my office; I will get rid of *every* case I've got, and work . . . on this and get it done.

"If *they* [the State] want to do that, that's fine. If *they* want to pay me what *he's* getting . . ." raved Von Zamft, waving his arm toward John Hogan.

"But they *cannot*," he continued. "Because the statute doesn't permit it."

By this point, Von Zamft's tone had wound to a whine.

"So I needed to try to earn some *money* during February, March, and April. I know that's something that *nobody* in this courtroom seems to understand except Mr. Samek and I. . . ."

Janet Reno offered few condolences.

Von Zamft, she hinted, had made his own bed. And now, because the coach was beginning to look like a pumpkin, he didn't want to lie in it.

And that, as far as the State was concerned, was basically "too bad."

"I would be perfectly willing," Von Zamft told Judge Newman, "not to be involved with this case. This case has done nothing but injure my reputation, injure my personal life, injure my practice. . . ."

Judge Newman also offered few condolences.

"I have no intention of releasing either attorney from their appointment in this matter. I don't think I could find better attorneys to represent the interests of the defendants.

"We have to keep in mind not only the defendants' interest before us, but that of the victims as well. . . .

"I am going to grant the motion [for continuance] because I feel I have to. . . . I am not doing it with any great amount of feelings, but I think I have to."

Von Zamft had requested six weeks. The State wanted none.

As was his custom, Judge Newman split the difference.

The case, he said, *would* go to trial on August 5.

"My body will be here . . ." said Von Zamft. *"Ready?* No." Nobody won that round.

• • •

Jason Harrison fidgeted in the car on the way to the Metro Justice Building, where his parents had been ordered by subpoena to deliver him for deposition by the Fuster defense. At least, his mother thought, with a twinge of gratitude, it was to be Jeffrey Samek, father of two, and not Von Zamft who would question her very nervous son.

"What am I supposed to do?" Jason asked.

"Just tell him the truth," said Jackie. "That's all he wants to know is the truth. It's his job to represent Frank, and he might try to trick you or confuse you, but that's his job, just like it's John's job to be *your* lawyer.

"Just listen to the questions carefully and don't be afraid to ask him to say them again if you don't understand. Don't be afraid to ask over and over again, until you're sure you understand what he wants to know."

Confident now of the ground rules, Jason seemed to relax.

Slightly.

Mark and Jackie tried to mask their apprehension.

• • •

The Country Walk parents appeared stricken as they poured into the hallway outside Courtroom 4-2 the day they lost the battle of the subpoenas that Judge Newman had just refused to quash.

Tom Herschel looked ready to eat the microphones that beckoned his comment on the ruling, which allowed Samek and Von Zamft to interrogate the child witnesses prior to their appearance at trial. He thought about Chad and Missy, two months shy of four and six years old, closeted in a room with two strange men who would smirk skeptically, as they did on television, at the things that had been done to them. Didn't anyone understand that the children couldn't be switched on and off anytime someone decided to rehash the gory details? Couldn't they see by the tapes how difficult it was for the children to talk about it? Wouldn't anyone consider that it had taken the children literally a year—at their own pace, on their own terms—to disclose, in increments, the horrors they'd lived?

Missy would be mortified.

One of her most vivid memories was of Frank and Iliana spreading her legs as she lay on the floor, surrounded by the other children, as the couple, one on each side of her, pulled open the lips of her vagina and laughed and joked about her "ugly" private parts.

His daughter understood that she would have to tell her story to a jury, something she was willing to do only if it would, she told her mother, "keep them [Frank and Iliana] from hurting more children."

Tom wasn't entirely sure whether she could hold up at trial, but he was certain that she wasn't prepared for a pretrial interrogation by two strange men—not when she couldn't even bring herself to discuss it with her father. It was, she told her mother, a "ladies" subject.

Then he thought about Chad.

"Do you think it's going to be easy for a three-year-old child or a four-year-old child to go through a deposition?" he spat at the reporters. "I don't think so. It's very traumatic. And it's very trying. . . . They've been through *enough*. And they're going to have to go through more."

Shari Herschel stood beside her husband and lifted her tear-streaked face from a handkerchief long enough to blurt, "They've still got the *trial!*"

"What do you think the harm is going to be?" asked another reporter, at whom Shari gaped in disbelief. "What do you *mean*, 'What do I think the harm is going to be?' I think it's *vicious* . . ." she sobbed. "It's *vicious*."

Tom could barely contain himself. "Do you know how traumatic it is to be deposed as an *adult*, let alone as a *child*? Have you ever been deposed? It's very traumatic. It's very nerve-wracking. It was hard for *us* to go through depositions."

Joe Braga was no less incensed over the day's ominous developments: ". . . we continue to expect these young children to again and again and again have to tell the details of their *rape* to people.

"I think this is *wrong*," he continued, his words spurting with the velocity of an automatic weapon. "I think that it's an *outrage*. These children have suffered *enough*.

"The videotaped interviews that were done are sufficient information for people to know what these children have said about the situation. . . ."

This, of course, was the position argued by the State, which had hoped to legally block an adversarial showdown between members of the Florida bar and a boy who had just graduated from kindergarten, upon whose red head rested much of the case's credibility.

Though there were now as many as a dozen children, as young as three-and-a-half, whom the State was considering calling to testify, it was Jason Harrison who held the many pieces of the puzzle that independently corroborated the other children's accounts.

And though it was likely to be Jason who was in for the roughest ride, none of the children could be expected to emerge from enforced questioning without acute distress.

"An adversarial deposition could possibly make the prosecution of this case impossible," John Hogan reminded the court. ". . . the kids will simply not want to go through it again.

"This isn't the average case, Judge. . . .

"We've never had a case quite like this before, where we had the abuse going on over a long period of time and in such an organized fashion. And because of that, and because of the way the crime impacts on the children involved, it makes it special."

The Braga interviews, John Hogan argued, supplemented by the information available in depositions given by the parents, the police investigators, and the children's private therapists, already provided the defense with anything they might wish to "discover" through further and unnecessary interrogation.

The Bragas, said Von Zamft, who would continue to beat this dead horse indefinitely, had influenced everything the children had to say.

He intended to get at "the truth."

You could, as one reporter put it, almost hear a pin drop when Judge Newman set down one of the most crucial rulings in the case, for of all the possible wounds the system could have inflicted on the children, it was deposition that threatened to leave the most profound and lasting scars.

Attorneys would not—and could not—do in open court what they could do behind closed doors.

There was no jury to witness the taking of a deposition.

And in the case of the children, few witnesses at all.

The depositions would be taken, ordered Judge Newman.

And the media was to be barred.

Maggie Fletcher left the courtroom and in the hallway aired her most definite views.

"I am not going to put my daughter in the same room with Mr. Von Zamft or Mr. Samek. I'd rather be jailed for contempt."

And then she politely crashed the judge's chambers, followed by notepads and cameras poised to capture what promised to be a most interesting afternoon.

Judge Newman, who had seen more media in the last year than in the past quarter-century he'd spent in courtrooms, looked momentarily taken aback by this impromptu stampede on his sanctuary. Samek and Von Zamft, who had hoped to hammer out the particulars of the deposition procedure in the privacy of the judge's chambers, looked more than taken aback. Hogan and Casey smiled faintly and shook their heads.

It made them very nervous when the parents took matters into their own hands. But who were they to argue with success? These people had won a law.

Now all they had to do was get a judge to use it.

"Don't tell me I *can't*, because I *can*," said Maggie, as she rallied the troops once again. "We've beat 'em on every count so far. Why stop now?"

The parents needed little encouragement.

Protective orders were drawn for the seven children Jeffrey Samek had subpoenaed—seven of the fifteen who appeared in the charges—this time by civil attorneys who represented the children, the State having no recourse short of a higher court.

The parents returned to radio, carefully trying to avoid outright alienation of any affection Judge Newman might harbor. It was the ruling, not the judge, they offered politely but firmly, with which they took exception. Senator Roberta Fox, also taking to the airwaves that night, was less tactful.

". . . I have a sense of rage because we won a legislative battle to ease the burden for children in judicial proceedings and now the courts are ignoring that. And I have a great sense of frustration because this is being called model legislation for the nation.

"Other states are calling us to find out what we've done in Florida to protect children. And yet we find that the courts won't enforce the law that we passed. And I feel a great sense of sadness for the parents and the children because this is going to do more harm to the children, and they've suffered enough."

"Senator Fox, do you think that this ruling is going to make your child abuse legislation a bit worthless?"

"Well, I don't think it's precedent-setting because it's only one trial judge saying that, but I would say that, if judges that sit on our trial benches cannot follow the mandate of the legislature to safeguard children's rights when children have been victimized, then the judges should resign from the bench."

Roberta Fox was not known to mince words.

But though she disagreed vehemently with the judge's ruling, she understood his reluctance to clamber out on this particular limb. The law had taken effect just two weeks before, signed and sealed by the governor in May and affixed with a request that the state supreme court promulgate "emergency" procedures for its implementation—without which the law could not be used. The Supreme Court had referred it to the criminal procedures rules committee of the Florida bar for review, whose chairman indicated at the June committee meeting that the matter could be more conveniently addressed in September.

No hurry.

The chairman of that committee was Michael Von Zamft.

Still, the State had not argued on behalf of the new law, but an old one that allowed the court "to enter appropriate, but unspecified protective orders upon showing good cause." This, Hogan had argued, was "consistent with the actions and intent" of the legislature in "recently enacting" the Judicial Proceedings Act, which specifically provided for the prohibition of taking depositions of a child.

On July 29, 1985, eleven attorneys took a number in Courtroom 4-2 for a chance to address the bench, as two of the attorneys, representing five of the subpoenaed children, made one last stand to bar the depositions.

They failed.

The children would be deposed.

And the media were to be barred.

But the depositions would proceed with special provisions, Newman ruled. They would be taken in the ninth-floor children's room and videotaped through the one-way mirror. The Fuster attorneys would question the children directly, but Frank Fuster would not be present.

One parent and one Braga could be in the room with the child for moral support, but neither might utter a word.

And only children whom the State actually planned to call as witnesses, and/or for whom the defense could show good cause to interrogate, could be deposed, not the twenty-seven Samek planned to eventually blanket by subpoena—some of whom were six months old at the time of the assault, who had recently mastered walking but not bowel control, and whose communicative repertoire consisted of a ten-word vocabulary.

This clearly, argued the State, was an abuse of the deposition process, which, he had reminded the court on numerous occasions before, was currently practiced in only two states in the union.

Judge Newman apparently agreed.

The defense was not pleased with this unorthodox arrangement, which imposed "numerous" restrictions on their zealous search for "truth" on behalf of their clients—whose rights they were charged to protect. Von Zamft and Samek systematically argued every point. The Bragas and the parents were the ones who had "influenced" the children's stories in the first place, for reasons unknown but loudly speculated. ("There are, let's not forget, millions of dollars in civil damages at stake here.")

And how do we know that we can't produce two children who say nothing happened at the Fusters' for every one the State produced who said it did, unless we separately question each child outside the "influences" that planted these strange ideas in their young minds in the first place?

But they "most vehemently" and "most strongly" objected to the memorializing of the deposition on videotape, presumably for one of the same reasons they fought so diligently (and successfully) to conduct their questioning without benefit of an audience.

". . . it's very difficult to tell the court whether the presence of the press would be inhibiting. Certainly it may well be in the case of at least *one of the defense attorneys*," said Von Zamft, his voice beginning to rise in pitch, "the one who *seems* to be under *the most public scrutiny*, the one who *seems* to have *his future* the most at stake.

"Certainly *that* attorney's questioning may well be *inhibited* by the actions taken by the press or the public in terms of the depositions taken."

Michael Von Zamft was speaking for himself, of course.

He'd just come off what he would later recall as "the worst week" of his life.

Having won entrance to "confront" the children, a victory that almost made up for past rained-out parades, and having just completed what he termed a "brilliant" interview with the governor for an appointment to head a brand-spanking-new state program with a multimillion-dollar budget, Von Zamft was in better spirits than he'd felt in quite a while.

Things were looking up for Michael. His luck, he believed, was about to turn. A coveted state appointment loomed on the horizon, and the case—from a defense standpoint—was beginning to look salvageable.

The parents were finally making noises about pulling out, their precious law having been snatched out from under them.

Country Walk might not even make it to trial.

And if it did, Von Zamft still had his ace-in-the-hole—Iliana, who had grown increasingly forthcoming in recent weeks, pouring most startling revelations into the unselective ears of one of her therapists. This presented for the career court-appointed psychiatrist a circumstance in which his opinions swayed whichever way Iliana was blowing on any given day.

But she was coming along. Coming along nicely.

His star once more on the rise, Von Zamft slipped out of state to try another molestation case, in which he and the expert whom he and Samek had engaged to explain to the Fuster jury that the story the children told was the product of a marriage between brainwashing and fantasy, would stage a scaled-down Country Walk dress rehearsal in a Georgia courtroom.

The state where a month previous (unknown to Von Zamft), Dr. Joseph Braga had introduced into testimony for the first time in its history the Child Sexual Abuse Accommodation Syndrome, which was to become the vortex of the "model" case being assembled in Miami.

Von Zamft sensed storm warnings as he approached the Georgia courthouse—located in the town of Eatonton, population two thousand—and spotted an immense statue erected to Br'er Rabbit residing on the front lawn. This was the heart of Uncle Remus land, he quickly assessed—no place for a brash Jewish attorney from

In what psychiatrists would later term "a transient hysterical episode," Frank Fuster attended his pretrial hearing in an apparently catatonic trance.

THE CALM BEFORE THE STORM: Iliana Fuster (right) stoically planted herself at her husband's side as Frank Fuster surrendered himself in a Miami courtroom. A week following his arrest, and a week prior to her own, she wrote in her diary, "We will be together again because life and God knows we are innocent. All of this has happened so fast and weird that it looks suspicious to me. . . ."

THE FACES OF ILIANA FUSTER: 1) Frank Fuster's wife is taken into custody as attorney Jeffrey Samek (rear left) looks on.

PHOTO: THE *MIAMI HERALD*

2) In the course of the year, Iliana gradually began to appear age fifteen going on twelve. "I am innocent of all these charges," she said. "I have never seen such a case in my life before."

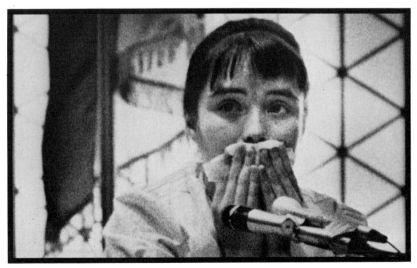

PHOTO: THE *MIAMI HERALD*

3) According to one psychiatrist, Iliana Fuster's survival instincts were remarkably well-developed. She was, he decided, "a chameleon."

February 21/'85

My Dearest Love,

     I'm thinking about you always, with the most beautiful thoughs my mind can gather. When I close my eyes I can see your beautiful, masculine body before me, the tenderness of your skin, the warmth of your lips your gentile caress. When you put your arms around me you make me melt. I start to tingle from my head to my toes. I can feel your sweet gentle lips pressings against mine; with all the pleasure that flows through your body. I can feel your transfer your warmth right to me. When I look into your eyes I can see the gentle yet strong love you hold for me. Such special glow flows from hands into my body as we hold one another. I love you very much sweet — heart.

MY HEART BLEADS FOR YOU.

I look forward to when our greatest dream can become reality.
Darling we're one for ever in God's name, may the love of our savior be with you always,

                   your wife,

I love you !!...

                   Iliana
                   Fuster...

TERMS OF ENDEARMENT: Iliana illustrated her letters to Frank with commercial-quality drawings, but for her therapists she would draw only stick figures.

The Mobile Showroom, Inc.
Prime Source of Interior Construction And Home Improvements

COUNTRY WALK BABYSITTING SERVICE
"CHILDREN'S RECREATION PROGRAM."

AGREEMENT FOR BABYSITTING   DATE_____
The Children's Recreation Program provide Child Day Care Service, indoors and outdoors. The undersigned hereby assume all the risks, and hereby hold the Operator harmless from any and all liability in conection with the Children's Recreation Program. The terms here of shall serve as release and assumption of risks for the members of the family of the child: "Operator" , as used herein, shall include the Operator, Program Director, Owner, Country Walk Babysitting Service, The Mobile Showroom, Inc. and assistants in the program. And the "undersigned", shall include the father and/or mother, or the guardian The undersigned shall assure that the child is provided with a mid-morning and mid-afternoon snack, in addition to the number of meals necessary to meet the child's nutritional needs. All meals, snacks and formulas must be provided by the undersigned everyday. All the children will be individually fed, or supervised at feeding. All children will be encorage to take a daily nap. The undersigned MUST fill out the Recreation Program Registration, Consent and release form and the health form (H.R.S. 3040), no later than 30 days.

"MONTHLY, WEEKLY, DAILY AND PER HOUR RATES FOR NON-PAMPERS"

Monthly Rates: (Every four weeks)
Full Day Hours are   8:00am to 6:00pm   Monday to Friday $175.00
After School Hours are 2:00pm to 6:00pm   Monday to Friday $096.00

WEEKLY RATES:
Full Day Hours $045.00
After School Hours $025.00

DAILY RATES: * 8:00am to 6:00 pm   Monday to Friday $015.00

HOURLY RATES:
Full Day Hours   (Two hours minimum)   . $002.00
Any other time   ($1.00 per 20 minutes or part of it)_____ $003.00

INFANTS using Pampers will be charged $1.00 extra per day.
Second child of the family has a 10% cash discount.
For special days and time, please call the Director.

1)_____   2)_____
Parent or Guardian's Signature   Date

Address   Zip

Child's Name   Nick Name   Date Of Birth   Age

Home Phone   Mother's Employment Phone and Name   Of the father

Other persons to be notify in case of illness or accident

BAIT FOR THE TRAP: The "Agreement for Babysitting," which was presented by the Fusters to parents for their signatures (and which appeared on Frank Fuster's own business stationery), stated that the Fusters would not be held responsible for any liability in connection with their babysitting service. The number of parents who innocently signed the agreement remains unknown.

PHOTO: PETE CROSS, THE *MIAMI HERALD*

DOCTORS JOSEPH & LAURIE BRAGA: At times over the past two decades, their voices resembled the proverbial cry in the wilderness. Little did they suspect the price they would eventually pay to be heard.

Miami Beach to be defending an accused child molester. Nor did the little Georgia courtroom seem a likely stage for an Orson Wellesian minister-turned-Ph.D. who made his living explaining to juries throughout the land that children were, by nature, deceitful and "out of touch" with reality. Dr. Ralph Underwager was also wont to explain that whoever interviewed *this* particular child—police officer, social worker, therapist, psychologist (fill in the blank)—had used methods that (as he explained on the Phil Donahue show) conformed "precisely, exactly, and in detail" to the methods used by the Chinese Communists, the North Vietnamese, "and all tyrants who've sought to control and to dominate people throughout the centuries."

But the Georgia jury would not hear of the oppressive and abusive tactics of child interviewers, there being a more interesting wrinkle Von Zamft chose to pursue. The defendant, said Underwager, was impotent and therefore could not have committed the assault. And besides, the Minnesota Multiphasic Personality Inventory (MMPI, the same one administered to Frank Fuster in 1982) showed that the accused did not fit the "profile" of a child molester.

The jury was less impressed with the defendant's inability to produce an erection with his various wives than with the child's testimony that he most certainly didn't have any problem producing one with her.

The trial, raged Von Zamft, was a travesty of justice, the judge having slapped down his vigorous objections to everything from the certification of the "so-called" expert the prosecution had engaged, to the introduction of the "so-called" Child Sexual Abuse Accommodation Syndrome.

The jury returned a swift and sure verdict of "guilty," and the judge sentenced his client on the spot—an event that caused the elderly defendant to collapse before the bench. The judge, to Von Zamft's utter astonishment, lifted his robes to step *over* the prostrate child molester, whom paramedics were in the process of trying to revive, and drawled "good luck" as he swept out of the courtroom. His Honor appeared not overly concerned about the health of this particular gentleman, having listened for three days to what he had done to a little girl.

His frustration threshold rapidly falling, Von Zamft was bombarded with news of even more distressing developments in Miami, where the parents waged full-scale war on the deposition ruling.

And Senator Roberta Fox waged war on *him.*

As Michael Von Zamft waded through the quicksand in the Georgia courtroom, the senator was back in Miami, noting most publicly that she considered him to be in need of an ethical attitude adjustment.

She saw, she told reporters, "a definite, direct conflict of interest" between Michael Von Zamft's role as chairman of the Florida bar committee that stood between the State and its use of the Judicial Proceedings Act and his defense of Iliana Fuster, whose interests remained diametrically opposed to the children's—recent developments notwithstanding.

"It would be as though tomorrow Von Zamft were to replace Judge Newman and sit in judgment on this case."

Von Zamft testily allowed that the good senator certainly overestimated his influence over the criminal procedures rules committee. Besides, the only reason he had asked the supreme court for a delay in the matter, he said, was because a number of committee members were going on vacation.

There was, he insisted, *no* conflict of interest.

"But then," he added, "I'm being objective about it."

Maggie Fletcher had her own views, which she expressed in a tired monotone, exhaustion having become more or less her permanent state in recent weeks. "The defense attorneys," she said, "are hoping that the parents will pull out of the case and the Fusters will be released."

The following day Senator Fox launched her second—and most devastating—missile, which landed on the front page of the local section of the newspaper, in sweeping black type:

"Fox seeks to block Fuster lawyer from post."

The senator, it seemed, had learned that Michael Von Zamft was being considered by the governor to head a new state program that provided appeal lawyers for death row inmates. The article quoted Fox as calling Von Zamft too "insensitive" to head a state program.

"Michael has a reputation for being a brilliant lawyer in the courtroom, but he's just wild, aggressive, crazy. . . . You have to have somebody in a program like that who is sensitive to how his words or feelings are perceived by the public. Otherwise, it could kill the program."

Von Zamft's response was reported to have been: "I have become the target of a campaign by Senator Roberta Fox to prevent me from getting a position which I believe is a very important one, a position I am willing to change my life to take."

The problem, the senator explained, went deeper than that.

In a deposition, she said, "Michael indicated he wasn't concerned with finding the truth, but getting his clients off." Fox also mentioned the attorney's reference in open court to the effect that he didn't particularly care about kids, his concern being only for his client.

Von Zamft, the article went on to say, "does not recall making either of the statements. . . .

"I don't run from fights," he said. "I can only hope the governor would take into consideration the totality of what's going on and disregard the hysteria of Roberta Fox."

It was into this windstorm that Von Zamft flew at the end of the week, with his "child brainwashing expert" at his side. Dr. Ralph Underwager had allotted a long weekend in the midst of his cross-country tour of witness stands, upon which he fervently doused the flames of "child abuse hysteria" for a minimum fee of $1,000 per day—plus expenses.

Underwager was the high priest of the "It didn't happen" defense, having given the time- and credibility-worn "seductive child/Oedipal fantasy" tap dance the added dimension and intrigue of conspiracy, resurrecting seventeenth-century Salem as a fitting parable to how large groups of children can come to tell the same terrible "lies."

Underwager attended the birth of an organization by the name of VOCAL (Victims of Child Abuse Laws), whose membership, as the name might indicate, was composed largely of accused and/or convicted child molesters.

Founded in October of 1984, VOCAL produced its first newsletter the following spring, to which the following cover sheet was attached and mass-mailed to defense attorneys:

Protect Your Clients From The
WITCH HUNT
For Child Abusers

- Access top experts—nationwide—In Child Psychology, Sexual Abuse, etc.
- Tap into an extensive nationwide source of data concerning tactics and background of expert witnesses used by the prosecution.
- Keep updated on research destroying the myths that:
  Children do not lie.
  Anatomically correct dolls are valid investigative tools.

Social Service workers are trained in their area of responsibility.
* Access of Hotline for immediate aid for you and your client, including reference to support groups.
* Follow the trends and decisions—the news media and the public's mind.

VOCAL is now offering a bi-monthly newsletter which is targeted for use both by victims of false allegations and by professionals involved in child abuse or marriage dissolution custody cases.

60 chapters nationwide give VOCAL the national data-collection capacity that could make the difference between a hopeless case and winning the potential for civil action against the same agencies bringing the abuse charges.

Have you been FALSELY accused of:
  Neglect?
  Physical Abuse?
  Sexual Abuse?
Is nobody listening to you?
Have you been presumed guilty?
  Right from the start?
  With no objective investigation?
You are not alone!

What VOCAL seeks to resist and change—abuse of government power to foster witch hunts and violence to innocent people has been a part of human history for thousands of years. . . .

Now, as then, those who attempt to resist the dominant culturally imposed hysteria will pay a price.

VOCAL is paying a price.

The suspicion that VOCAL is a refuge for guilty child abusers remains active in the media and in the minds of reporters. You can expect that any actions VOCAL engages in to support others or to tell the story of being abused by the laws will be interpreted negatively wherever and whenever possible.

VOCAL was the answer to Frank's prayers.

The State had wished for some time to engage Dr. Underwager in deposition, no other prosecutors in the country having had the opportunity to explore in any depth the minister/psychologist/entrepreneur's philosophies and/or credentials.

Underwager had never before testified in Florida, so he had not experienced the rigors of the state's "reciprocal discovery" provisions. At all other points on the map, he had arrived with the blusterous fanfare of an "out-of-town expert," who would light on the witness stand long enough to pontificate on the striking similarities between people who interviewed children about sexual abuse and the Red Chinese. Then he would beat a regal retreat from the courtroom before the prosecutors knew what hit them.

But Underwager would have to be deposed if he intended to set foot in Courtroom 4-2. And with less than two weeks left to trial, John Hogan grew increasingly irritated that the professional expert's schedule could not seem to accommodate him, though the prosecutor had offered to fly to Minnesota at Underwager's convenience. John suspected that the doctor might become "available" only for brief inquiry just prior to his testimony.

That would limit considerably the many avenues that Hogan wished to explore regarding Dr. Underwager's conclusions and his qualifications to draw them.

Von Zamft did not plan to mention to the State that the defense's star witness happened to be returning to Miami with him from Georgia. He had, in fact, said little about his out-of-state business other than to leave a number where John Hogan could contact him if it became necessary, plus his dates of departure and anticipated return.

So the attorney did not expect the icing that would frost this most memorable week as he disembarked his flight from Georgia justice and watched the long, lean detective with the Clint Eastwood walk stride up to his immense and bearded companion.

"Dr. Underwager?"

"Why, yes," he beamed.

"My name is Christina Royo," smiled the investigator. "My apologies for welcoming you to our fair city in this manner, but State Attorney Janet Reno most cordially invites you to be deposed on Monday."

Then she slapped the Fusters' expert with a subpoena.

Flattened by the events of the past week, Von Zamft sank like a rock to an all-time low.

The next day, Abe Laeser, wracked from the emotional wounds of another close friend's recent suicide, placed a call to Von Zamft's wife and warned her that Michael had threatened to do the same if he didn't receive the state appointment to head the death row appeals program.

Maggie Fletcher, Von Zamft believed, was the direct source of all his problems. Maggie Fletcher and the Doctors Pollyanna were at the root of it all. The Bragas, he fumed, "have infiltrated" the system. He planned, he said, "to sell tickets" to Joe Braga's cross-examination.

He was convinced, he announced, that the State was tapping his phones.

How else, he asked, could Christina Royo know that Dr. Underwager would accompany him on this flight? How, in fact, did she know which plane to meet?

Von Zamft didn't know that the State had inadvertently come into possession of his itinerary when a Georgia district attorney placed a call to John Hogan and wondered what the lead prosecutor on the Country Walk case might know about a Dr. Ralph Underwager, who was about to take the stand.

And neither was it Maggie Fletcher or the Bragas who had brought to Senator Fox's attention matters of conflict of interest and disregard for truth, as Von Zamft had surmised.

It was one of the fathers.

Von Zamft, it was whispered in the corridors of the Justice Building, was "losing it," having hit rock bottom in his year-long plunge. But the weekend brought substantially brightening news from Dr. Charles Mutter, who had suddenly come to the conclusion that Iliana Fuster was incompetent to stand trial.

It was the best news he'd heard all week.

• • •

Jason Harrison was already seated in the children's interview room when Jeffrey Samek bustled in to take his deposition.

"Jason, my name is Jeff," he said briskly, seating himself directly opposite the state's star witness.

"I know," said Jason.

"You know? How do you know?" asked Samek.

"My mother told me," said Jason.

"Your mother told you?" Samek leaned forward and stared at the little boy, his eyes like cold slits. "You've been saying a lot of things about Frank and Iliana, haven't you?"

Joe Braga, who was seated a foot away from both of them, grew uncomfortable with the attorney's abrupt change in tone. Several children had already been deposed more or less without incident, though little was actually "discovered" from them.

Interviewing children—especially three-year-olds—was not as

simple as the Bragas made it look, Samek found, each time he dropped Frank and Iliana's names into the conversation.

Jeremy Martinez had crawled into the Sesame Street bus and pulled the top up over his head.

Brendon Prince had hidden under a table.

Just moments ago, Jason's little brother, Joshua, had responded with a flat "Forget it" when asked about what he did at the Fuster home.

Clearly the children found the enforced questioning distressing, there being no subtlety to their attempts at escape from it. Samek had dealt with each of them courteously, though at times his patience seemed to wear thin.

But he hadn't gone out of his way to inflict additional harm.

"*You've been saying a lot of things about Frank and Iliana, haven't you?*"

"Yes." The single syllable trembled. Jason, too, had snapped alert to the edge that was creeping into Jeffrey Samek's voice.

"You've been talking to Daddy—I'm Frank's friend, and I want to help Frank, and I think you're lying," said Samek, the edge growing sharper, accusatory. "I think you're lying."

"No," Jason whispered, stunned to find that the man he was told was just going to do his job was—by his own introduction—Frank Fuster's "friend."

Samek didn't miss a beat as he lit into Jason, firing a barrage of questions and accusations at the pudgy little boy who was scheduled in two months to enter first grade.

"I don't think any of the things that you've been saying about Frank are true. Do you know what a lie is?"

"Yeah."

"What's a lie?" Samek's cold slits bored through Jason.

"When you—" Jason faltered and looked away. "I don't know."

"No, look at me," ordered Samek. "You know what a lie is. What's a lie?"

"When you do something—when you say something that's not true."

"OK, that's right. That's *exactly* what a lie is. I think you've been lying to me about Frank and Iliana, I don't think Frank and Iliana ever did anything to you, I don't think Frank ever did anything to you, Frank didn't do anything to you, did he?"

"Yes, he did," said Jason, who looked very much like he wanted to crawl under the table.

"Frank never put his mouth on your penis, *did he?*"

"Yes, he did," Jason whispered.

"When did he do it?"

"Partially." The word barely came out.

"Huh?

"Partially." Jason was on the verge of tears.

"Jason, *look* at me when you answer—"

Joe Braga, whose head had for the past three minutes bobbed from face to face as if he were watching a ping-pong match, could stand it no more. He rose to his feet and said quietly but determinedly, "I think we should take a break now."

John Hogan, who had reached a similar conclusion seconds behind Joe, nodded quickly.

Samek shrugged. Fine. "Stop the tape and let the judge come up and see the tape."

The judge would see that he was just doing his job.

Jason Harrison's civil attorney was the first to address Judge Newman in the hastily assembled court proceeding that took place in a prosecutor's office, across the hall from the viewing room where His Honor screened a replay of Jason Harrison's three-minute deposition.

The tape had captured what a transcript could not.

"Judge, what we just saw there in that tape is exactly what the rules were designed to prevent. . . . Let's get one thing understood over here. We're trying to find what the truth is. . . . What he was trying to do right now is intimidate that child. Trying to harass him, intimidate him. Tell him, 'You're a liar, a liar, a liar. . . .'

"He's not taking a deposition to find out what the facts are or the truth in this case. He's taking a deposition because *that* child is the most vocal child of all. He has repeatedly told what has happened in that house. And he knows he can stop that child. . . ."

John Hogan, who had formed a special affection for the red-haired boy, was as visibly furious as he had ever gotten.

"I think this is outrageous for an attorney to first come in and start ordering a child—I've *never in my life* heard an attorney order a witness that they had to look at him.

"I know of no power he has to do that. Maybe he's doing that because he wants to break him, or maybe he enjoys yelling at six-year-olds.

"Whatever the reason, I think it's outrageous and embarrassing to the profession of law. . . . I think it's a travesty. In fact, at this point, before we continue, regardless of what the court's ruling is, I think we ought to talk about whether we renew the motion for protective order.''

Dan Casey was no less livid. ''. . . You saw him squirm, you saw him fidget. Not because he wasn't telling the truth, Judge, but because someone was sitting across the table from him, staring him in the eye, telling him, 'You're a liar.' Telling him, 'I'm Frank's'— that's how he introduced himself! 'I'm Jeff. I'm Frank's friend. I'm looking to help Frank.'

''The man who had *terrorized* this child.

''Judge, it's an atrocity what happened to that child. I've never seen it done to an adult in that way before, let alone a child who just turned six, who understands what went on in Country Walk.''

Jeffrey Samek was courteous and calm amid the three irrational musketeers who had obviously, from his point of view, let their emotions distort the reasonableness of his interview with the child.

''Judge, fortunately you have the tape. And you can see exactly what happened . . . and you can, I hope, agree with me that counsel are very much overstating what occurred—are very much dramatizing what occurred.

''And I really don't think I need to answer for my conduct at all. I'm not finished [with the deposition].''

Judge Newman commenced to slap Jeff Samek's wrist in a fatherly ''now Jeff'' fashion.

''Let me just say that . . . when I denied the State's motion for protective order, I think I indicated at that time that we're dealing with children, and the deposition of a child is different from the deposition of an adult. . . .

''My grandchildren . . . they don't look up at me, Jeff. They do what they're doing, and they answer questions as best they can.''

''I find the contrary to be true, Judge,'' insisted Samek. ''I've found that when somebody is telling the truth, they look you in the eye.

''I also think, Judge, that this child, in particular, having been interrogated so many times, by so many people, has been so brainwashed, and so coerced, that the only tactic—that just about the only way to have any possibility whatsoever of *breaking* the *spell* that has been cast on this child—''

Samek's explanation for the necessity of such extraordinarily ''rigorous'' discovery ceased abruptly as he turned to confront Jason Harrison's civil attorney (who happened to be the uncle of another Fuster victim). Stewart Williams was emitting silent editorial comment that stopped just short of thrusting his finger down his throat.

"Mr. Williams," bristled Samek, "I was courteous enough not to make faces and not squirm around in that manner when you were making *your* comments—"

"Don't talk to me," Stewart hissed. "Just talk to the judge."

Whereupon Samek resumed his argument to the court.

"The only tactic that I can possibly take is to confront this kid and tell him that I don't think he's telling me the truth."

"Maybe you could slap him around," suggested Hogan.

"I feel the depositions should be taken," said Judge Newman. "I'm not going to go through my ruling on that. But if I think the children are being—I don't like to use this word, 'harassed,' for lack of a better word.

"And I'm not using it, saying it is being done, you know . . ."

John Hogan couldn't believe his ears. "But Judge, it *has* happened." The prosecutor had seen Jason's face when he emerged from the interview room into his parents' arms.

"I thought he wanted the truth," said Jason.

Hogan could not believe that Judge Newman was contemplating ordering Jason back for more. Samek had made his intentions clear.

"This kid has been traumatized by this. I'm almost in a position that if we had to . . . let Frank Fuster walk out on the streets tomorrow, Judge . . . I don't think I can in good faith say, 'Mr. and Mrs. Harrison, send Jason back in here.' Because I don't want to have to think of Jason Harrison like that the rest of my life.

"They don't *pay* me enough for that."

Jeffrey Samek was unmoved.

"Judge, they're really satisfied with it when the deposition results in nothing. When the kid sits around and plays with my ties and climbs all over me and chats about lions and alligators and won't say a word about anything else.

"They're really *happy* with *those* conditions.

"But when the condition starts *turning* a little bit . . . maybe it's that the child we're deposing now may actually tell the *truth* for the first time since he was interrogated by the Bragas, then they start getting squirmy. . . .

"I'm real happy there is a tape here. Because they're making me look like Attila the Hun.

"And I'm quite comfortable with the way I have conducted myself."

The Harrisons, however, were not.

The Harrisons had endured death threats by phone, obscenities by mail, dead chickens on their doorstep, delays, legal harassment, financial ruin, derision, and endless hours of waiting in lobbies and courtrooms of the Metro Justice Building.

As had any parent who cooperated in the prosecution.

"Anything it takes," they told John Hogan.

As long as Jason was protected.

And now he was not.

Judge Newman refused to bar further interrogation of the State's star witness, though he suspended it for the day.

And the media would not be there to "inhibit" what would continue to proceed behind closed doors.

Even John Hogan's last-ditch compromise hadn't flown.

"I'd ask that Dr. Braga be allowed to address the court," he said.

Joe stepped forward to offer his thoughts on the matter.

"I have asked Mr. Samek to assist him in any way, as far as getting the children to talk about things, sexual or otherwise. In the depositions I have seen so far, the children have not said anything because—unfortunately—Mr. Samek is not familiar enough with that age child. . . .

"It's really a matter of the child understanding what they're being asked, so that they can come forth and make statements.

"As I stated to Mr. Samek, when I said, 'Let's take a break,' I did so because in observing the child, I did feel that we were getting extremely close to the edge of damage to that child.

"This is emotionally charged information for a child to talk about at that age, and the child was becoming distressed.

"I would again proffer that I would be more than willing to assist in any way—for the court. I am not an employee of the state attorney's office. I'm not paid or . . . vested in any way other than as a professional in an objective manner. And I would be more than willing to assist him in an attempt to get the children to be willing to talk to him about the subjects that they want, if that were the court's desire."

Jeffrey Samek was not interested.

Mark and Jackie took their sons directly to the beach following the aborted deposition. Jason was subdued and withdrawn.

"Maybe," he said to his mother, "you should have checked 'em out better."

"Who?" asked Jackie.

"Frank and Iliana."

Jackie winced. She thought she had.

Her son made one other comment of note, following the three minutes in which "Frank's friend" called him a liar.

"Maybe God will punish him," he said.

"Maybe he'll have a car accident on his way home."

It was then that Mark and Jackie knew that there was *no way* Jason was going back into deposition—court order notwith-standing.

The defense no longer need speculate as to the Harrisons' threshold for abuse. They knew they had reached it when their gentle son wished a man dead.

And meant it with all his heart.

• • •

Michael Von Zamft was most happy to leave the children's depositions in the competent hands of his good friend Jeffrey Samek, though he would later make a special point to depose Crystal Fletcher—an uneventful episode in which Maggie's daugh-ter stacked blocks on a table to separate herself from the man who questioned to no avail. "Being a fairly bright person," Von Zamft had recognized that the "atmosphere" in which he was required to conduct his "confrontation" would "inhibit" his successful im-peachment of the child witnesses. And discrediting the children's testimony was one of the few mutual interests shared by the now-separated Fuster advocates.

In fact, an entangled dual-strategy was emerging as Von Zamft concocted a creative supplement to the "It didn't happen" defense. While Samek laid out to the jury that the only witnesses to the "alleged crime" had been "mesmerized" by the Bragas into making the "false" accusations, Von Zamft would tack on an addendum: it didn't happen, but if it did, it was because his client was "mesmer-ized" by Mr. Samek's client. And if the children's account differed from Iliana's, it was because, as Mr. Samek explained, the children had been "mesmerized" by the Bragas.

Von Zamft was collecting many baskets in which to place his eggs, and thus he found more pressing tasks to keep him from joining Jeffrey Samek's "discovery" of the "truth."

On Friday, August 2, three days before the trial was scheduled to commence, two court reporters were assigned to record the most recent developments to unfold in Courtroom 4-2: Iliana Fuster's competency hearing.

Mrs. Fuster, Von Zamft had offered in a motion filed at the beginning of the week, was not competent to assist in her defense, based on the findings of Dr. Charles Mutter, who had conducted some fifteen hours of interviews and found her to be an eighteen-year-old woman who functioned emotionally on the level of a six-year-old child and lived under "the total mental subjugation" of her co-defendant husband.

Along with Dr. Mutter's latest considered opinions, Von Zamft filed a most unusual affidavit in which Iliana's attorney personally swore:

> The only valid defense that counsel perceives in this case requires that this defendant be prepared to give testimony against the co-defendant. . . .
>
> This defendant is so immature and unable to comprehend the nature of the proceedings and unable to separate her own judgment from that of her co-defendant that she would be "like a masochist" and allow herself to be injured rather than do anything to injure Francisco Fuster Escalona.
>
> Counsel is aware of conversations wherein Francisco Fuster Escalona has told and conveyed through family and friends to Iliana Fuster that her attorney is trying to hurt her and hurt him, and therefore she should not communicate with that attorney. . . .

Iliana, said Von Zamft, was "a child." Iliana could not fairly be expected to defend herself should she be required to stand trial in the shadow of her husband.

It was, said Von Zamft, "the most *unique* competency question which a South Florida court has ever confronted."

Thus, in the space of one week, the State had been confronted with another turn of events that threatened to abort Country Walk before it came to trial. For if the State lost this one, there would be two separate trials.

And the charges against Iliana Fuster would be dropped, because the children couldn't be asked to do it twice.

It wasn't even a consideration.

• • •

Iliana was not present for the day-long dissection of her psyche in the ever-packed Courtroom 4-2, where two court-appointed psychologists and one psychiatrist presented their overlapping yet conflicting views, none of which agreed wholeheartedly with Dr. Mutter's assessment.

Doctor number one offered that in his opinion, with two reservations, Iliana Fuster was competent to stand trial. Her ability to do so, he added, might be "influenced" by Frank Fuster's presence, but "not sufficiently so to say she would be incompetent."

She was, he said, naive, immature, easily led and misled.

She was also, he said, "fearful and intimidated" by the ever-present television cameras that pointed her way.

Doctor number two agreed that the presence of Frank and television cameras might "impinge" upon "her abilities," but not to the extent that it rendered her incompetent to stand trial.

According to this doctor, she did, however, perceive her husband "as a dominant, dominating, aggressive person"—an evaluation he said was supported by the results of "psychological response pattern testing" that, he concluded, "indicated strongly" that Frank's wife was "an extremely immature, subservient young girl . . . involved in role-playing as a mature adult."

He produced a drawing of a house she had made for him and deemed it "similar" to the art of "young children." The house had no windows, he pointed out, which was a clear indication that Iliana was an "emotionally closeted" individual. The trees and flowers indicated "affective needs." And the elongated necks on the human figures indicated "intellectualizing," he added.

This, coupled with her responses to inkblots ("the turmoil involving the father-figure symbols emphasized the submissiveness . . .") and on sentence completion forms ("MY MIND: is sometimes tired of thinking"; "I HAVE A FEELING: that I will see my father again"; "MOST BOSSES: are very bossy persons"), led him to conclude in his written report to the court that "the emotional immaturity is enormous, and this defendant would not be capable of withstanding pressure for obedient behavior from her husband."

Assistant State Attorney Daniel Casey, who had listened to the doctor's "psychological response pattern testing" testimony with the attentiveness of a Boy Scout learning to tie new knots, rose from the prosecution table to cross-examine on this clearly muddled issue.

Was she or was she not competent to stand trial?

She was.

Doctor number three allowed that Iliana indeed appeared "quite anxious and fearful" about having Frank in the courtroom with her and that she expressed an intense desire for her intimate relationship with Frank not to be aired on the six o'clock news.

But she was, he said, quite competent to stand trial.

"She is *not* helpless. She has considerable adaptive abilities."

She was, said doctor number three, "manipulative."

Feeling the first sprinkles of yet another rained-out parade, Von Zamft argued that Dr. Mutter's evaluation was more reliable than the three additional (and unnecessary) ones solicited by the court, because Dr. Mutter had spent fifteen hours with her, not one or two, and had thus sufficiently "gained her trust."

Von Zamft entered into evidence a videotape of Iliana's first interview with Dr. Mutter in which she explained—as she had the previous day to her attorney—the details of her "courtship" with Frank Fuster, the only deviation from her original account being that her first sexual encounter with her husband was not, after all, a forceful seduction on their fifth date, but a rape on their first, adding the new dimension of pinches and slaps.

Still, she insisted, she was not aware of any improprieties as far as the children were concerned. Frank was very gentle and very loving to them.

She couldn't imagine *anyone* molesting children.

The State called to the stand Lt. Peyton Fletcher, who, in full uniform, testified that he was not in the habit of leaving his daughter in the hands of individuals who exhibited an emotional age of six. Iliana, he said, had seemed quite competent to him in May of 1984, and he had had no reason to believe that she was one day younger than the twenty-one years claimed.

"Did you run a police check on her?" asked Von Zamft.

"No," said Peyton.

"No? Then just how particular are you about the people you leave your child with, if you don't even run a police check on them?"

He was not, said Peyton evenly, in the habit of abusing his position by running his neighbors through computers.

Richard Shiffrin closed the State's arguments with the admission that certainly he could understand that Iliana might "prefer" not to face her husband in the courtroom, but that this was not at all an unusual occurrence among co-defendants in a trial. Three court-appointed mental health examiners had found her competent, he pointed out. And only the doctor hired by the defense to "assist" plea negotiations had concluded differently. The court could minimize her trauma by erecting a distance, and perhaps even a barrier, between the defense tables.

But if Iliana didn't want to lie in the bed she'd made, that was "basically too bad."

"Amen," breathed the parents who had listened for hours from the gallery to their former babysitter's plight.

No one had found it worthy of mention that their children were going to be required to face him *and* her.

Judge Newman ruled Iliana Fuster competent to stand trial.

He would, he said, order that appropriate measures be taken as to the physical courtroom setup so that Iliana wouldn't have to see her husband.

Von Zamft was now faced not only with going to trial (Iliana had rejected a seventeen-year plea offered by the State, although she accepted, her attorney said, "in principle," the idea of testifying against her husband, should Janet Reno wish to consider making it worth her while) but also with doing so next week with a client who steadfastly maintained that "it didn't happen" when even *he* knew that it had.

At least as far as Frank was concerned.

But Iliana faced fourteen separate counts of independent sexual assaults, and that was going to take some explaining. She could have done it only under "duress," Dr. Mutter had concluded, if indeed she had done it at all.

But "duress" carried a high standard of proof of imminent danger—like a gun being held to the head. That would require, the State presumed, that Von Zamft build into his strategy the admission of "battered wife" testimony designed to demonstrate a condition in the Fuster home of constant danger as imminent as a cocked Magnum.

The State was not of a mind to allow side issues to further confuse the issues at hand; namely, that a number of young witnesses were prepared to testify that Iliana had assaulted them both in Frank's presence and, most notably, in his absence as well.

"Duress" wouldn't wash, Richard Shiffrin had concluded following his most recent rendezvous with his computer. Iliana's continued refusal to do anything that might "hurt Frank" (the State having refused to up the ante) placed Von Zamft in the position of offering a curious combination of two mutually exclusive defenses. It didn't happen, but if it did, Frank made her do it.

Besides, said Shiffrin, no case he knew of had ever entertained a defense of justifiable child rape by reason of "duress."

Von Zamft was not amused when the State prepared to quash any notions he might have of using his one and only viable defense.

To: File   Date: August 5, 1985
From: Dan Casey
          Assistant State Attorney   Subject: Country Walk

In discussions with Michael Von Zamft today, Michael mentioned that the basis that he anticipates we will use in striking his duress defense would not wash.

He mentioned that he anticipates the State will object to his duress defense because of the inability of Iliana Fuster to admit the underlying charges.

Michael questioned our ability to do so if he proffered that Iliana had told him in confidence that she would be able to admit the facts.

Michael then went on and stated that he would so proffer, regardless of the truthfulness of that proffer.

When questioned as to his desire to so proffer untruthfully, regardless of the truthfulness, Michael stated that if it got Iliana off he would do it.

This conversation took place in the presence of Christina Royo, investigator for the state attorney's office.

Michael wasn't the only attorney with problems.

21

The Third District Court of Appeals resides on a scrubby tract of land outside Miami's city limits, a mile or so off the nearest beaten track.

It is as different from the Metro Justice Building as the sun is from the moon, though neither is possessed of remarkable exterior aesthetics.

Two sets of polished plate glass doors admit the few and select visitors who find business in the state's higher court, depositing them in a vast lobby laid with carpeting padded to the texture of a putting green. To one side stands a single, somberly business-suited bailiff/butler/bouncer who shushes whispers that grow too loud and bellows at anyone who lights a match to a cigarette, lest an ash drift onto the spotless cushion below.

Anyone who ventured to the far side of the expanse, where were situated the "rest" rooms, risked instant and vocal challenge from the receptionist/sentry who received all visitors from the other side of a transparent (presumably bulletproof) shield. Where are you going, please? Yes, sir, you in the brown suit and green tie. Where are you going? Oh. OK, fine.

Everyone was very cordial.

Very civilized.

The violet backdrop of the Third DCA's judicial amphitheater stretches the length of the rear wall, along which curves a massive platformed hardwood bench.

The nine judges in the circuit take turns occupying three overstuffed thrones placed on this impressive stage—a stern and robed admissions committee at heaven's gate.

Even Von Zamft was subdued.

The parents—the regulars—clustered in one section of the gymnasium-sized gallery.

Mark and Jackie Harrison, as fit the occasion, since they were the ones who had summoned the court to session to consider the matter of protecting their son from further interrogation by Jeffrey Samek, sat apart from the others.

It was their final shot.

If the appeals court refused to block the continuance of Jason's deposition, the Harrisons were pulling out.

So might the rest of the families.

The Harrisons' other civil attorney (they had two) presented to the panel of jurists, who sat in unsmiling judgment on this day, a writ of *certiorari* that sought appellate relief for six-year-old Jason, whose deposition Judge Robert Newman had suspended until further order of the court.

As it stood right now, attorney Steven Hunter argued, Jason Harrison lived under the shadow of imminent resubpoena, and from Judge Newman's remarks, following his viewing of the deposition videotape, it appeared that he was not inclined to quash it when it arrived.

The child's parents were asking, Hunter explained, that the higher court intervene and preclude the defense from further pretrial questioning of this particular child, who had, according to an affidavit sworn by Dr. Joseph Braga, already suffered considerable trauma during his three minutes spent with Mr. Samek. As an alternative, the petitioners would ask that all proposed questions be propounded in writing to, and approved by, the trial court and/or that further depositions be conducted in the presence of the trial judge.

He would like, he said, to offer into evidence the videotape of Jason Harrison's deposition and let the court decide for itself whether the discovery process had been abused.

The three magistrates who languished in apparent boredom throughout Steven Hunter's presentation came suddenly to life, hurling piercing interrogatories at Jason's attorney as to the appropriateness of addressing on the appellate level an issue on which the trial judge had not entered a clear and final ruling.

Come back if and when he actually orders the child back into deposition.

That, argued Hunter, would be too late.

The judge who occupied the center throne was a pleasant-looking fiftyish gentleman with dark, thinning hair, a boyish round face and eyes as penetrating as a cobra's.

Chief Judge Alan R. Schwartz, Harvard graduate, was one of the most respected legal minds in the Third District Court of Appeals. And he appeared most interested to see what was going on behind the closed doors of the children's interview room, Judge Newman having barred the press to avert additional pretrial publicity—a ruling the Third DCA had upheld on appeal.

The chief judge said he would like to see the tape.

A video monitor was placed before the distinguished panel, where the three judges lounged with chins propped in hands—a languorously regal triumvirate of unreadable sentiment.

The tape was played.

Jackie viewed a second monitor that faced the immaculate gallery. Tears rolled down her cheeks.

> I think you've been lying to me about Frank and Iliana, I don't think Frank and Iliana ever did anything to you, I don't think Frank ever did anything to you, Frank didn't do anything to you, *did he?*

For the next three nights her son had not slept.
She wondered if Mr. Samek had.

• • •

Richard Shiffrin, the third and least visible member of the Country Walk prosecution team, was a strict constitutionalist with a conservative bent when it came to interpreting the forefathers' words—a circumstance that left him disinclined to embrace the state attorney's intent to "rebalance" the Sixth Amendment, which guaranteed the Fusters' right to confront their accusers.

There was no way, Shiffrin advised Janet Reno, to legally temper the realities of the adversary system. If the children couldn't withstand the rigors of traditional court procedure—including at least two face-to-face encounters with both the Fusters and their lawyers, one pretrial and the other during the trial—then they didn't belong in a courtroom.

Janet Reno had suggested that he find a way.

Shiffrin spent the better part of a year behind his computer trying to do just that, searching case and common law as old as the British empire and as new as the electronic age to find where were written— by law, not custom—the conditions under which the children must be "confronted" by their abusers.

But it wasn't written, in so many words, "confront" being a concept of imprecise meaning and elastic intent. Of only one thing was Richard Shiffrin certain, and that was that the founding fathers had not intended that the adversarial system arm defendants with "two-by-fours" with which to assault six-year-olds.

"I would suggest to the court," said Shiffrin, when he rose to join Steve Hunter's motion, "that if this tape showed Mr. Samek hitting this child over the head with a two-by-four, the court wouldn't be entertaining questions of evidentiary hearing.

"I would further suggest that what Mr. Samek *did* do is the equivalent of hitting the child with a two-by-four. . . .

"I'm rather concerned that unless you offer *broad* relief [to all children still under subpoena], another child will be hit with a two-by-four."

Michael Von Zamft had by now reached his customary level of agitation, having endured yet another lashing with his own mis-spoken words when Steven Hunter tossed into the appellate record his celebrated comment on the subject of "breaking" four-year-olds.

Von Zamft announced that he was growing tired of his deeds being twisted to unflattering shapes. "The kid was lying. What was I supposed to do—sit there and let her lie?"

That out of his system, he argued that the only "evidence" that Mr. Samek's questioning was of detriment to the child was an affidavit sworn by Joseph Braga, who was "not a competent expert" and who, along with his wife, was responsible for "brainwashing" the children in the first place.

This was, he continued, the precise reason for Mr. Samek's zealous pursuit of statements that could later be used to properly impeach the child witness.

Chief Judge Alan Schwartz cut Von Zamft off in mid-rant, his voice low but echoing like the report of a rifle—an abrupt reminder to Iliana's attorney that today's performance was not taking place in Courtroom 4-2.

"What *basis* is there in the rules which says that a deposition may be taken for the purpose of developing a prior inconsistent statement?"

Von Zamft's turn at bat slid steadily downhill from there, the garrulous and testy magistrates bloodying the incredulous Von Zamft with a shower of thinly veiled contempt.

Still, he missed the message and continued with the game.

"It's not just this case . . . there are *hundreds* of cases this could affect beyond Jason Harrison. It would *emasculate* the rules of discovery in future cases!"

If Jeffrey Samek had, when it came his turn, offered his apologies to the court and explained that he had experienced a momentary lapse of judgment in his zeal to advocate for his client, things might have turned out differently, Richard Shiffrin would later say.

But Jeffrey Samek did not apologize for his conduct.

And he offered no assurances that he wouldn't do it again, given the chance.

Perhaps he had been inattentive to the undercurrents that had tugged at Von Zamft just moments before. Or perhaps he hadn't seen the perceptible narrowing of Judge Schwartz's penetrating eyes, which left the screen on which Jason's deposition was replayed long enough only to dart one time in Jeffrey Samek's direction.

Perhaps he failed to notice how they now smoldered at him.

There were compelling reasons, Jeffrey Samek explained when he took his turn at the podium, for the nature of the questioning of this child.

"I believe that the repeated interrogation of this boy by the State investigators has put him under a *spell*," said Samek, pausing to allow the court to digest this startling revelation. Chief Judge Schwartz's face was flushed, his eyes two lumps of glowing anthracite, as he leaned forward for further clarification. "And you're trying to *break* the *spell* by *breaking* the *child*?"

"That's right," said Samek, pleased that the court understood.

The judge's eyes glinted dangerously.

"I'm not trying to break the *child*. Please, Your Honor, I implore you, . . ." pleaded Samek, who explained that the expert who had been hired to assist the Fuster defense advised him that the Bragas had systematically "brainwashed" the children into believing that this "fantasy" had actually occurred. The Bragas had woven "a spell" around the children, which Dr. Ralph Underwager advised him must be forcefully broken.

He hoped only to discover "the truth" by breaking the spell, not the boy.

The judge oozed contempt.

"I find *that*," he said, motioning toward the now-dark television monitor that had captured what a transcript could not, "is about as *disingenuous* as anything I've ever *seen*. I am *personally* going to supply a transcript of this deposition to the Florida bar."

Samek, now nervous, but no more inclined to see any error in his ways, explained that he simply wanted to discover how the child would "react" to certain kinds of questioning.

"You want to discover how he will react when he is called a liar?" inquired the chief judge, his eyebrows raised to what used to be his hairline. "And you believe that is the *purpose* of a discovery deposition?"

The judge right of center entered a question that dashed any hopes Samek might have entertained that the chief judge was airing a renegade opinion. "You wouldn't be permitted to call him a liar in court, would you?" he asked the wilting Samek, who continued to sputter noble intent.

Judge Schwartz leaned forward again, his voice no less soft, his eyes no less daggered than they had been upon viewing the videotape. "You," he said to Samek, "want to conduct yourself in such a manner that he won't be able to testify against your client *at all*."

"I want the boy to tell the truth," pleaded Frank's attorney.

The magistrate leaned intently over the bench and hissed quietly, "But you already know what the truth *is*, don't you, Mr. Samek?"

• • •

Jeffrey Samek did not require the additional complication of possible disbarment at this particular point in his life, the events of the previous year—and indeed the previous day—having sapped his tolerance for high drama.

For the client for whom he advocated before the Third District Court of Appeals had just yesterday dropped a bomb that placed higher on the evening's local newscasts than the stories commemorating the fortieth anniversary of Hiroshima.

Frank Fuster had called a press conference.

Jeffrey Samek had called an emergency hearing.

And the local press corps hovered between the jail and the Justice

Building, watching the battle lines being drawn. Today's episode in the continuing saga of Country Walk was already being colloquially slugged "Frank Freaks Out."

This time the players assembled in Courtroom 4-1, the matter of Iliana's proximity to Frank's influence having been resolved to the judge's satisfaction (if not Von Zamft's) by moving the proceedings to the cavernous arena across the hall, where, at the time of trial, a physical barrier was to be erected between Frank and his child bride.

But Iliana was not present on this occasion.

"Mr. Samek, I understand you have a matter of emergency to bring before the court."

"Yes, sir, I do, Judge. I want to thank the court for making itself available so quickly. I want the record to please reflect Mr. Fuster is here. I also would like the record to reflect, immediately before this hearing began—not more than fifteen seconds ago, I went over to Mr. Fuster to try to speak with him and he did not acknowledge hearing me.

"Frankly, he looks very disturbed to me. I said to him . . . 'Frank, if you can hear me and just don't want to respond, please at least tell me that you can hear me. . . .'

"I just want the record to reflect he did not. He sat exactly the way he's sitting now, without moving a muscle, looking right down at the floor, and not at all making any indication that he could hear me. . . ."

John Hogan, ambushed by this unlikely turn of events, tried to buy time to regroup. "At this point," he said, "I would be asking that the court order emergency evaluations of the defendant prior to proceeding. . . ."

"Let me hear what he has to say," said Judge Newman.

Jeffrey Samek, for the first time in a year, assumed center stage and injected a most unusual narrative into the court record.

"I am moving to withdraw as counsel for Mr. Fuster, Judge. . . .

"From the time that I became counsel for Mr. Fuster in this matter, this has been a very *unusual* case and . . . my name has been in the paper. I was misquoted even when I made comments that weren't substantive.

"I was willing to accept that.

"I was subject to incessant personal harassment such as 'How can you defend Mr. Fuster? Your client is such a . . .'—you can fill in any number of verbs, adjectives.

" 'How can you look at your own children after you are defending Mr. Fuster?'

"And I was willing to accept that.

"My family has been harassed. . . .

"My home was harassed. . . .

"I was the subject last week of a story . . . suggesting—not suggesting, *concluding*—that Your Honor has reprimanded me. . . . My actions in this case have been called in court pleadings 'the most abusive, offensive, insulting verbal attack the writer has ever witnessed. . . .'

"And I was willing to accept all these things because I have . . . and I have sought . . . an ethical obligation to defend Mr. Fuster and defend the unpopular cause.

". . . I advised Mr. Fuster not to write any more letters to his wife because they would end up on the front page of the *Miami Herald* and lo and behold . . . the letters ended up . . . on the front page of the local section. . . .

"So he didn't take my advice then.

"I spoke with him this afternoon. I advised him of recent developments—that being the court's decision to permit the State to proceed with the probation violation hearing."

Samek paused to glance at his client, who appeared in a catatonic trance, a white terrycloth washrag clamped to his face with both hands, tears oozing from the corners of his eyes.

"Please let the record reflect," noted Samek, in passing, "Mr. Fuster's demeanor has not changed in the slightest in any of the time that I've been talking.

"I advised him that the government would be proceeding on the probation violation hearing, and I gave him—with all due candor— my understanding of what that would involve and what that result might be.

"I told him that he would, of course, have an opportunity to be heard at that hearing. . . .

"He advised me he wanted to talk to the press. I told him that I don't think it would be helpful. I instructed him that I did not want him to talk to the press, and he responded by saying, 'You want my blood, you'll get it. *You're* part of the system.'

"I was very angry.

"I was angry because I have taken abuse from everybody in town to fight with every ounce of strength that I have for this man, and he turned around and tells me that I'm not fighting for him. . . .

"We had further discussion and Mr. Fuster said, 'OK, I understand how you feel. . . . Forgive me. . . . I didn't really mean it's you. . . . I'm under a lot of pressure.'

"I said 'OK, Frank.'

"I went back to my office. . . .

"I received a call . . . from Mr. Fuster that—contrary to my suggestion—he had already contacted every one of the media he could contact. And that he was having a press conference at four o'clock whether I liked it or not. . . .

"I responded as patiently as I could, Judge. And I said, 'Frank, please don't do this' . . . and finally I said, 'If you have a press conference, I'm going to move to withdraw, because I cannot represent you if you will not listen' . . . and he again said, 'You want my blood, you'll get it. I'm having a conference at four whether you like it or not.'

"I'm not willing to take the abuse from Mr. Fuster. . . .

"He is operating contrary to my advice.

"He is operating behind my back.

"He is entitled to counsel, or he is entitled to represent himself. . . . If he wants me to represent him under my terms, he can't do that anymore. He's already written letters contrary to my advice that have damaged his defense no end. . . .

"I'm asking that I be permitted to withdraw."

Judge Newman attempted to capture the attention of the man with the white jail-issued terrycloth pressed to his face.

"Mr. Fuster. Mr. Fuster. You don't have to respond to me, but I know that you heard the comment of your attorney. Is there anything you'd like to tell the court at this time?"

"Judge," Samek said quickly. "Before Mr. Fuster says anything . . . someone has to tell him that anything he says . . . will be taken down by this court reporter and written down as quickly as Mr. Casey can move his pen."

Samek approached and whispered to his apparently catatonic client, then turned back to the court.

"Judge, I asked Mr. Fuster if there was someone else he wished to speak to. The court can see . . . that he continues to hold the towel to his head and sounds to me as if he's crying—sobbing, actually. . . . He seems to be shaking."

John Hogan took this latest development in pleasant, tight-lipped stride. The prosecutor was, however, clearly irked, a reaction not

entirely masked by his easygoing courtroom delivery, which—
though constant in volume and tone—was punctuated by variable
speeds ranging from a stammer to a race.

On this day, Hogan raced.

"I think our first question is whether or not the defendant is
competent. I have my own personal opinion about it.

"Obviously we need to have doctors look at him; he is acting in an
unusual manner.

"Whether . . . it's a great act or whether he has some sort of other
problem is obviously something that doctors have to address. . . ."

Hogan's smoldering monotone threatened to ignite.

"I have very strong opinions about this," he said, struggling to
keep the volume from rising in his throat. "Again, don't let my
voice mask my strength—that *this* man not be allowed to dictate
when he faces the music for what he's done.

"I can understand he may want to sit here and cry now, but he has
no right to dictate when he goes to trial. He's had eleven months to
prepare. The fact that the day after the case is set for trial, he
suddenly wants to act irrationally—misbehave toward his attorney—to postpone this, simply is something this court cannot
allow."

Three doctors were summoned to make immediate examination of
Frank Fuster's already much-examined mind.

The next morning, the front page of the *Miami Herald* was
dominated by a striking photograph of the hearing's unexpected
finale, when Frank's mother, who had leapt over the railing behind
which her son sat immobile, took his face in her hands and screamed
a stream of rapid-fire Spanish: "Be *strong*, Frank. Be *strong* like
your mother. Be *strong* against the enemy."

Her son failed to respond.

• • •

The scheduled trial date of August 5 slipped by as the court
labored to resolve the issue of the defendant's competency.

August 7, 1985

Dear Judge Neuman [sic]:

In response to your Rush Order to examine this defendant, I was
able to see him this morning at the County Jail. I found him to be

pleasant and cooperative, fully capable of understanding all of the proceedings, and quite loquacious in a detailed, explanatory manner. . . .

He told me he was receiving psychotropic medication that had been started two weeks ago, and the medications had been changed last night because they weren't helping sufficiently. He told me he didn't remember much of what had occurred in court the day before, but he apparently had suffered a rather severe emotional episode in response to the magnitude of the threats of his circumstances, and had been rendered incapable of responding to the proceedings or being fully aware of his surroundings as he was wracked by a prolonged period of crying and emotional involvement. This has never happened to him before, and he was unable to explain it or understand it himself. . . .

The defendant was well oriented, his fund of information certainly seemed to be adequate, and mental faculties were generally adequate. There was a certain amount of depressive difficulty that he felt was greatly due to his present circumstances, particularly the difficulties between him and his wife, which had been rather shocking and unexpected. . . .

This most recent episode of disturbance seems to have been a transient emotional reaction in response to the tremendous pressures and threats of his present circumstances. . . .

He spoke well of the relationship between him and his attorney as being his only real support opportunity. He did state that the attorney had quite frankly and coldly outlined to him the various probable results of a trial, and the patient said that he had been demoralized by the probable outcome of the litigation process. . . .

There will be opportunity for additional emotional response at times, in view of the probable traumatic courtroom proceedings, but with the judicious use of psychotropic medications and the support of his attorney and others, he should be able to maintain sufficient composure to be present and involved in the trial process.

Two additional psychiatrists were of much the same mind: Frank Fuster exhibited no major mental disorders. He was clearly competent to stand trial.

Not good news for Jeffrey Samek, who yesterday had been brutally thrashed by the chief judge of the Third District Court of Appeals— an event that inspired headlines no less spectacular than Frank's "transient hysterical episode" the day before that.

Samek was up to his ears in limelight.

He wanted out.

"There has always been a significant question," Samek told the court, "as to whether or not Mr. Fuster could get a fair trial on the merits of this case. I think the most recent developments yesterday at the Third District Court of Appeals . . . [the story] is the largest headline on the [newspaper's] local section—'Judge Seeks Bar Probe of Fuster Lawyer'—makes it impossible for Mr. Fuster to get a fair trial with me as his attorney. . . .

"I do not feel that I can zealously represent him as I have tried thus far. I certainly cannot give him my undivided attention.

"Unquestionably my cross-examination of many of the witnesses in this case will be affected by the chill that I feel based on the chief judge . . . as to how he viewed my questioning of one of the children and his intention to take it further."

The State, announced Dan Casey, would be registering the most "strenuous objection to Mr. Samek's withdrawing at this time from this case.

"The people of our community have been waiting for this case to be resolved, and our victims and their families have been waiting for this case to be resolved. . . .

"The victims and witnesses who lived through this case need an opportunity to get this behind them, Judge, and that's only going to come with the completion of this trial.

"We've been waiting a year. . . .

"I do not believe that any member of the public, or any member of the appellate courts, or the other members of us in our profession will now hold Mr. Samek to any greater responsibilities than that which has already been placed on him by our canons of ethics. . . .

"If Mr. Samek—as zealously as he can—conducts himself in trial within those canons, no one can hold him to fault."

Judge Newman did not seize this opportunity to mention that he himself might wish to be excused from this case with a fervor possibly exceeding that of Samek and Von Zamft combined.

He'd spent precisely one year inching his way along a narrow ledge, and the trial hadn't even begun. His opinions—previously rendered in the cloak of anonymity granted judges whose dockets boasted few matters of elevated profile—were now subject to conspicuous public consumption and appellate dissection.

Even his most amiably hammered-out compromises sent one party or another kicking and screaming from the bench. If it wasn't the defense, it was the State. And if it wasn't the State, it was the media.

Last week, it was the parents.

Yesterday, it was the Third District Court of Appeals.

And although the Third DCA's two-to-one *per curiam* opinion dismissed the Harrisons' plea for appellate relief as "premature," it left the door open for future appeal "if and when the trial court enters some further order requiring that the child be deposed."

But Chief Judge Alan Schwartz, the dissenter of the three, attached to the appellate court's opinion a scathing addendum, lest Judge Newman miss the subtlety of the *per curiam*'s invitation for the Harrisons to return "if and when" their red-haired son was ordered to report for further interrogation.

In resolving the discovery issue before us, we must balance the cognizable, permissible interests legitimately to be served by taking this child's deposition—which, as opposed to the impermissible, indeed reprehensible ones it actually promotes, I believe to be utterly nonexistent—with the potential harm to the child which would be obviated by precluding it.

Judge Schwartz cited three appellate cases dealing with this issue.

On that basis, I think it clear that the trial court abused its discretion and departed from the essential requirements of the law in denying the motion for a protective order that no deposition whatever be taken.

Hence, I would quash the order under review outright.

The chief judge's message was clear.

Judge Newman should never have allowed the children to be deposed in the first place.

Thus, having just been summarily slapped by the chief judge of the Third District Court of Appeals, Judge Newman could certainly empathize with Jeffrey Samek's wish to be relieved of Country Walk.

But not enough to let Frank's attorney off the hook.

"I don't know of anyone," Judge Newman told him, "who could have done any more for your client in this type of situation—assuring him of his full due process of law—than you have.

"And I think he has been, up to this point, very well
represented. . . . The court has to balance the due process due the
defendant, and also due process due other people. Victims, if you
will. Witnesses, families, et cetera.

"Sometimes that's a very difficult balance for this court.

"Knowing you, I'm convinced you can continue to do what is
right for your client. . . ."

Motion to withdraw denied.

Frank Fuster leapt to his feet.

"Your Honor, I believe that before you had granted or denied the
motion of Mr. Samek, you would have liked to hear what I have to
say."

"Go ahead," said the ever agreeable Judge Newman.

"During the separation of the cases—"

Whereupon Samek abruptly cut his client off and asked, for the
second time in three days, that Judge Newman advise Frank Fuster
of the consequences of opening his mouth.

"Another example," fumed Samek, who did not customarily rant
or rave, "of Mr. Fuster's unwillingness to proceed with the defense
along the course I wish to proceed. I can't muzzle him, Judge."

"Neither can I nor would I," said the court.

Frank Fuster chose to speak.

"I am in a very hard and in a very difficult position to prove to
this court—and to the nation—that I am innocent of all the charges
that have been present against me and my wife. . . .

"These people have done an excellent job," he continued, strolling over to pace along the railing behind which the children's
parents sat, "the media has done an excellent job to make me look
guilty in front of everyone.

"Monster.

"The child molester.

"The *worst crime* a human being can commit. . . .

"I think that Mr. Samek has done everything within his power up
to this point to prove my innocence, but . . . he has also anticipated
me very bad news. He hasn't given me a fifty-fifty chance. He hasn't
tell me, 'You got fifty-fifty chance.' No, he has already tell me in
advance that I will be found guilty when I am not guilty. . . .

"I couldn't believe it.

"I went to my cell, and I built myself up with my Christian
counselor. I built myself up again, and I'm going to fight this
matter. And I'm going to do everything within my power to prove

to Your Honor and to this court, and to everyone that is listening to me throughout the nation, that Frank Fuster Escalona is not a child molester, doesn't have any *desires* to become one, and I am very sorry that there are some human beings walking on the earth with that kind of sickness in their head."

Frank turned on the parents who would sit in mouth-gaping wonder as the man who raped their children stabbed the air in front of their faces with an accusatory finger.

"Every one of these parents sitting there—you, you, you, *you* and *you* and *you*—used to love my wife and used to care for my wife. And we loved you too.

"And not *one* of your child ever suffer *anything* in my house."

Frank turned back to the judge.

"They put multimillion-million-dollars suits. Now, they have their own interests to protect and defend. Now they cannot back up.

"The child have already been *brain*washed. So now it's very hard for me to get a fair trial here or any other county.

"For now, Your Honor, this is all that I will say. Please reconsider your motion, and whatever your decision is, I will respect it and go along with it. Thank you, sir."

Frank Fuster took his seat.

Steam began to billow from Jeffrey Samek's ears, as the grace with which he had accepted the court's refusal to release him from defending the articulate murderer/child molester began to evaporate. Still, he neither ranted nor raved. Rather, he sputtered incredulously at the unsubtlety with which his client had just raped the court record.

"First," said Samek, "I would renew my motion. It is obvious . . . Mr. Fuster will not follow my advice not to talk to the court outside of testifying.

"Mr. Fuster said that he had retained Mr. Von Zamft and I to represent he and his wife. So there are no *misstatements* on the record, Mr. Fuster retained myself and Mr. Von Zamft to represent him in the probation violation—and the court appointed both Mr. Von Zamft and I to represent both Mr. Fuster and Mrs. Fuster in the substantive case.

"I have on numerous occasions, as Mr. Fuster says, advised that he follow our advice—and my advice—or he would have to follow someone else's advice. And all of those issues related to his wanting to make public expressions regarding the trial or that he not write his wife any further, or that he not speak.

"What he says is true, but I think it needed some amplification.

"I do *not* assess numerical probabilities as to the outcome of a particular trial, and if Mr. Fuster recalls my saying that he had any percentage chance of winning or losing in this trial, his recollection is inaccurate.

"With all due respect, I did tell him what I believed based on the evidence and the tenor of the community and all the other variables that you can try to put into the equation of a trial or hearing—what I believe, would be the likely result. . . .

"When Your Honor expressed your ruling, I said, 'Very well.' I intend to go back to my office and continue with the last-minute preparations involved.

"As I said, I'm ready. . . .

"The file is ready. The case is ready.

"But I think there really are other variables that have to be considered. . . ."

Motion to withdraw respectfully denied.

Frank Fuster looked not at all displeased, having commanded for forty-five minutes the rapt attention of the television camera in the corner of the courtroom that would, no doubt, "prove to the nation" that he, Francisco Fuster Escalona, was not a child molester, had no desire of ever becoming one, and was "very sorry that there are some human beings walking on the earth with that kind of sickness in their head."

Frank had had his press conference.

The first of many.

Whether Samek liked it or not.

22

Assistant State Attorney Daniel Casey was a tall, broad-shouldered young man, with eyes that grinned and a smile as wide as the Florida Panhandle—a good-natured, bespectacled cross between John Denver and Clark Kent.

The twenty-eight-year-old prosecutor seemed, upon first meeting, more boy than man, his boundless enthusiasm for his work—and indeed his life—evoking images of a half-grown pup turned loose in a field of butterflies.

But Casey could as easily leash his energies as set them free, his reputation for meticulous case preparation being exceeded only by his exuberance for presenting it at trial.

For the courtroom was Dan Casey's natural habitat.

He was most comfortable in this intimidating place of law, a quality reflected in his style. Casey would amble, not stride, before the jury box, his left hand carelessly shoved into his pocket, his right jabbing the air with a pen, head cocked thoughtfully as he chatted with the jurors, who could not help taking an immediate shine to this warm, bright young man.

Indeed, Casey's performances drew visitors from all corners of the Justice Building—colleagues and even clericals stealing a few moments to slip into a Casey trial to observe the young prosecutor saunter about the judicial stage chewing on the tip of his pen, a favorite nephew delivering an enthralling lecture to a cluster of doting aunts and uncles.

Defense witnesses tended to become similarly lulled by Casey's ambling, "gee whiz" cross-examinations, only to be jerked abruptly back to earth by one of the prosecutor's select—and well-aimed— slam dunks.

Unlike John Hogan, who eroded witnesses like an incoming tide relentlessly dismantling a sandcastle, Casey's questioning was more like a tidal wave erupting from a calm sea at unexpected intervals.

A highly disciplined—and polite—tidal wave.

So it was without reservation that John Hogan delegated to Dan Casey the cross-examination of Frank Fuster at his probation violation hearing—an event billed by the media as a "sneak preview" of the Country Walk Trial.

There was no question in anyone's mind that Frank Fuster would most definitely take the stand in his own defense. The convicted murderer/child molester seemed genuinely convinced he had "lost" his 1982 trial because his lawyer "did not provide an opportunity" for him to take the stand and "express myself to the jury so they can see for themselves I am telling the truth."

Frank would no doubt testify whether Samek thought it was in his best interest or not.

And Dan Casey was very much looking forward to it.

• • •

The matter of probation violation—the instrument through which Chris Rundle had sworn out the original warrant for Frank Fuster's arrest—came before Judge Robert Newman on August 9, 1985—the day after His Honor adjudged him competent to stand trial.

A date that coincided with the first anniversary of the opening of Pandora's box on Deputy Chief Abe Laeser's floor.

Frank Fuster, as one psychiatrist put it, understood "all too well" that he was facing some serious time even if a jury acquitted him. Jeffrey Samek had recently explained the differences between violating probation on an old crime and being convicted on a new one, a subtlety that had apparently escaped his client.

The State had already proven in 1982—beyond any reasonable doubt—that Frank Fuster had molested nine-year-old Hilda Gonzalez.

Now it need only demonstrate to Judge Newman a "preponderance of evidence" that the convicted child molester had violated his conditional freedom and should be required to serve his time.

Fuster's probation violation was a separate matter from the substantive case against him, and one that seemed almost incidental in the shadow of the fourteen counts of sexual assault on which he would stand trial.

Still, the probation violation hearing was a three-day event—a "minitrial" of major import that was expected to guarantee Frank

Fuster fifteen years under lock and key—even if a jury were to acquit him at the main event that was scheduled to commence next week.

The State was confident it could persuade Judge Newman to revoke Frank Fuster's probation, having compiled a substantial chain of paperwork linking Iliana's husband directly to the operation of the babysitting service, including a county occupational license taken out in his name—not his wife's.

But in order to persuade Judge Newman to step beyond state guidelines in imposing sentence, the State would have to show a gross violation, not a technical one.

And it planned to do it without placing a single child on the stand.

Jeffrey Samek was not unaware that Judge Robert Newman, when confronted with the State's evidence, was not about to buy the defense he was about to offer. But that didn't induce Frank Fuster's attorney to present it any less vigorously—a point that even the parents appreciated as somewhat remarkable in light of the battering he'd taken over the past week.

The parents did not, however, appreciate his strategy.

Timid Jeannie Pierson, who nonetheless had demonstrated an intense and quiet strength throughout the past year, was the first to get a taste of what the victims and their families could expect at the "real" trial.

Does your son tell you things that are true?
"With regard to what?"
Just in general. Does your son tell you things that are true?
"I imagine he does."
Does he tell you things that are false, that he believes are true? Let me give you an example. . . . He might lose a tooth in the future and leave the tooth under the pillow and wake up the next morning with a dollar bill, say, "Mom, the tooth fairy came and left me a dollar." He might really believe that's true. You, of course, know that it's not. That's the kind of thing I'm asking. . . .
"He's told me Santa Claus has come. . . ."
You believe at that time he believes that there is a Santa Claus?
"Yes."
So then is it fair for me to say, at least on one occasion he has told you something that was false that he believed was true?
"Yes."

Jeannie, though frustrated, resisted the urge to dignify Jeffrey Samek's convoluted impeachment of her son by arguing apples and oranges.

Mark Harrison was no less constrained.
Are you aware . . . your son Jason told Detective Meznarich that nothing had happened to him at the Fusters'?
"That was not what he told me on August 8. . . ."
Are you aware that's what he told the Bragas on more than one occasion during one of the several interviews that they had with him?
"Yes, sir, I am."
What category would you put that statement into?
"A kid that was scared to death that he would die or his mommy or daddy would be killed."

And Maggie, of course, was—Maggie.
Your daughter's never slept for ten hours?
"No, not like that. Not when I picked her up and have taken her home. She always wakes up. She's a very light sleeper."
Did you call your pediatrician because of your concern about that behavior?
"No, because at the time I didn't think anything was going on."
And now the Bragas have told you your child told them something was going on and your daughter subsequently told you, you now believe that something was going on and so you assume they must have done something to her that made her sleep so long?
"No, Mr. Samek. My daughter talked prior to going to the Bragas."
When did your daughter tell you that? When did your daughter tell you that Frank put his finger in her vagina?
"At the Rape Treatment Center. . . . She pointed where he did it. Then she used dolls, undressed the dolls, and put the dolls one on top of the other and the hand where it goes. That was prior to the Bragas' ever meeting my daughter."
Did your daughter ever tell you that she had been the victim . . . before she went to see any mental health professionals or psychologists or "psychology imitators"? (This was one of Samek's favorite pseudonyms for the Bragas, and he injected it into the court record as frequently as possible.)
"The night Detective Meznarich was at my house, she told me

about the masks. She told me how Frank taught her how to French-kiss, how he picked her up and held her up . . . with nothing on—with April Lancaster at the same time."

• • •

Mr. Fuster, why don't you adjust the microphone. I would like you to speak nice and clearly to pick up what you're saying.

State your name please, said Jeffrey Samek, as his client settled in for his long-awaited day in court.

"Francisco Fuster Escalona."

You also use the name Frank Fuster?

"For business purposes."

Where do you live, Mr. Fuster?

". . . in Country Walk."

Do you still own that house, or do you reside someplace else?

"No, I been residing in the Dade County jail for a little over a year now. I do not own the house any longer."

Mr. Fuster, have you ever put your penis into the mouth of Jason Harrison?

"I have never done that."

Mr. Fuster, have you ever committed any sexual battery, any sexual act whatsoever on your son, Jaime Fuster?

"Never in my life."

Have you ever placed your penis into or in union with the vagina of April Lancaster?

"Never in my life."

Frank Fuster breathed a dozen flat denials into the microphone, his lips caressing it, as he responded to his attorney's questions in a heavily accented stage whisper that resembled a vampire in a low-budget horror film.

Nay-verrr.

Nay-verrr.

Nay-verrr.

On occasion, if there were . . . children in the house, and your wife was occupied with some of them, inquired Samek, *would you perhaps keep an eye on some of the children, or pick one of them up and bring them to the door, or bring them to the kitchen to eat, or something like that? Would you have—or did you have—no participation whatsoever?*

"Not that I remember," said Frank. "However, April went with us to the beach. Jason Harrison went with us to the beach. April used to go out with us almost every weekend to the movie, to the beach, to the zoo, to eat in restaurant, to go shopping.

"April became like a member of the family, and perhaps I at one time I may have carried Joshua to help Mr. Harrison with his bags. I may carry Joshua to Mr. Harrison's car after six o'clock. Sometimes he came to pick up, I was already home.

"Usually [I do] my work until after six. But when I don't have a contract, I do a lot of telephone calls, and I was doing those phone calls from my house. . . . "

Did you have a bird in 1984? asked Samek.

"No. One day I found a bird outside my house, and I tried to feed him but he died in my hand while I was trying to give him water. That's the only time I remember having a bird in my hand. . . . "

Do you know if any of the children would have had an opportunity to see the bird?

"No. I never own a bird. I never own a parakeet or bird, or any pet for that matter, except for my cats."

Did you have a two-foot-long knife?

"No."

Have you ever put a knife to your son's throat?

"No."

Have you ever chased Crystal Fletcher around the house threatening to cut off her head if you caught her?

"I have never talked to the Fletcher kid."

Have you ever urinated or defecated on any children?

"Never in my life."

Do you have any idea how—do you believe your son ever had gonorrhea?

"No, I'm sure that my son has never had gonorrhea. As a father, if my son would ever be sexually abused, I will know. . . ."

You had an opportunity to read the transcript of the interview with Dr. Miranda and your son. Do you have any idea why your son would say you had abused him?

"The testimony of Dr. Miranda," shot back Frank, as he prepared to launch into precisely the disjointed soliloquy his attorney hoped to avoid, "only proved to me that the field of psychology can only go as far as helping an individual that is—"

Please answer the question, Samek said more abruptly than he probably would have liked. *Please answer the question.*

"Yes, sir," said Frank, bowing his head in apology.

You know any reason why Jaime would have said those things—said he was abused?

"The only reason I could think of is he was conditioned by the severe interview by the doctors or the same Mr. and Mrs. Braga, and some other people under the office of the district attorney."

No further questions.

Daniel Casey rose from the prosecution table and stood, for the first time, within a foot of the man who had done things to children that still turned his insides out.

Good afternoon, Mr. Fuster, he said pleasantly. *It's important that you understand my questions completely. Should you not understand any questions I ask you, you'll let me know, all right?*

"I sure will, sir," Frank beamed.

Did you ever report the existence of the Country Walk Babysitting Service to your probation officer?

"No, sir, because the Country Walk Babysitting Service really doesn't exist."

Casey paused and chewed thoughtfully on his pen. *The Country Walk Babysitting Service doesn't exist?*

"No, sir. It never did."

Did you ever call a babysitting service in your house the Country Walk Babysitting Service?

"Not me. My wife wanted to name her service—the fact that she was babysitting two or three kids in the house—by that name. . . . It was a name that just came up. . . ."

Casey turned from the witness stand and strolled the six feet back to his podium on which were stacked his notes, various documents naming Frank Fuster the operator of the Country Walk Babysitting Service, and an assortment of photographs—mostly of children posed around the Fuster home, sometimes adorned with adult clothing—oversized sunglasses, earrings, and floppy hats.

A handful were infants under the age of twelve months.

But most of the photographs were ordinary snapshots of children placed in front of the camera—fully clothed, though few wore smiles. And the ones that did wore them without enthusiasm, as if on command.

Regardless of which way the children's lips turned, their eyes all reflected a deep and disturbing melancholy. They were not the eyes of children captured in play.

Casey pushed the photographs aside for the moment and extracted from the pile the Country Walk Babysitting Service business card that Frank Fuster had distributed to a number of parents—"We may not be the best, but people do talk."

Did you ever have cards printed up, Mr. Fuster? inquired Casey.

"My wife had one time some cards printed up. I just still have 997 cards. . . ."

Let me ask you about how the babysitting service got started. When was it that your wife, Iliana Fuster, first babysat for a child in your home?

". . . I believe during the month of November 1983. A family came to my house, and they asked my wife if she could babysit. This family was sent by Joanne Menoher. When I came home, I found my wife babysitting a little boy and a little girl. I questioned who they were. My wife told me she was doing a favor for this family, that they needed to go out, and they needed a babysitter in an emergency. Since Joanne knew my wife did not work outside the house . . . she sent them over."

Is that when the idea of babysitting in your house—is that when the idea really came from?

"No, the idea came from Joanne Menoher, when she saw us on the swimming pool. . . . She told my wife, 'You do not work; perhaps you could, you know, do some babysitting.' "

How many people were involved in running and managing the babysitting service?

"Only my wife. It's not—you keep on saying babysitting service, only because my wife babysitted two or three kids on a part-time basis. That wasn't a business. You keep—you want to make it look like a business for the purpose of this hearing. That was not business. Many mothers babysit throughout the nation."

Dan Casey stopped in his tracks, and the pleasantness flickered from his face. *Is* that *what this was—a mother babysitting "like mothers babysit throughout the nation"?*

"Right. My wife was babysitting three or four kids. That's all. . . ."

Did you have any problems with any of the families who sent their children there?

". . . I only knew some of them. . . ."

Let me ask you about one kid in particular, one child in particular—April Lancaster. You knew her especially well, correct?

"I knew her. . . ."

Would you characterize her—would you have called her your favorite of all the kids that were there?

"No. . . ."

Who was your favorite, Mr. Fuster?

"My son."

Except for Jaime. Except for Jaime, who was your favorite?

"I don't have no favorite with the other kids."

Would you have told April Lancaster's mother, Debbie, that April, in fact, was your favorite? You loved when she came over?

"I have never said that. . . ."

Before many of the parents entrusted their children into your care, or the care of the babysitting service at your house, they came over and had what they characterize as "interviews"; is that correct?

"They never talked to me. . . ."

You heard Maggie Fletcher testify a moment ago that, before she sent her only daughter to your place, she came and had an interview at your house where you and Iliana Fuster both were present; is that untrue?

"Very untrue. . . ."

What about any of the other parents? Did any of the other parents ever meet you and Iliana before they sent their children to your place?

"No, sir."

Never?

"Never."

Absolutely sure of that?

"Absolutely sure. . . ."

Did you ever tell any of the parents that the babysitting service run out of your house—we'll call it that—was licensed by HRS?

"No."

You're sure of that, too?

"Hundred percent. I would have been lying. Throughout the entire situation, I haven't lied yet, and I don't intend to. . . ."

Let me ask you about a few individual children, said Casey, who cut bait and switched streams every time he hooked Frank, without ever pulling him in—one of his favored methods, which left tantalizing threads to be wrapped up in the lawyer's celebrated closing arguments.

Most of today's threads he would let dangle until the trial.

Do you recognize the child depicted within State's Exhibit No. 14?

Frank cast a perfunctory glance at the snapshot Dan Casey placed on the stand and said with a world-weary shake of his head, "I saw that picture when you show it before to Mrs. Fletcher and you asked her. That's the first time I see that girl. That's the first time I see this picture other than the day I saw her asleep. I didn't see her face."

Who's that a picture of?

"That's Mrs. Fletcher's daughter."

What was her name?

"I cannot remember now."

If I told you Crystal Fletcher?

"Crystal, right."

You only saw Crystal Fletcher one time; that's when she was asleep. Is that what you're telling us?

"Right. Her father came to the door to pick her up, and he was, it was like 1:00 A.M., and I supervised with my wife when he pick her up and gave her to him."

You supervised when who went in?

"I supervise. By supervise, I mean, you know, at that time of the night, a man that comes in obviously have a couple of drinks in him, I'm not going to allow my wife to do by herself. I stood by the door, and I saw with my wife, gave him his daughter. . . ."

Are you telling us that Mr. Fletcher came to your house with a few drinks in him?

"Well, they went to a party."

Just is it yes or no? Then you can explain.

"It appears to me that way, sir."

That would be a yes, I would imagine, said Casey dryly. *Is that what you're saying?*

"I cannot honestly answer 'yes' that question. I will have to say I don't know."

When a man comes to the door with a few drinks, you're just talking generally . . . ?

"Right. I knew they had gone out to a party. I mean, due to the time. Let's assume he didn't have no drinks. If a man comes to my house at one o'clock in the morning . . . I'm not going to allow my wife to answer the door by herself."

You're telling us that it was Iliana who went over and picked up Crystal and took her to the door? Casey was trying to picture the frail Iliana struggling to lift the slumbering, sturdy little Crystal from a bed and cart her to the front door to hand to Maggie as the six-foot, two-hundred pound Frank and the muscle-bound Peyton stood by with hands in pockets.

"That's what I'm saying."

You heard Maggie Fletcher testify . . .

"There's not a word of truth in anything that Mrs. Maggie Fletcher said up to this point."

Not even a word *of truth . . . ?*

Casey returned to the podium and selected another photograph, one of some three dozen he planned to produce for Frank Fuster's perusal.

The prosecutor plucked from his pile the photograph of a lovely, sad-eyed toddler by the name of Kevin Cartwright, the then-two-year-old boy whose father had informed Detective Donna Meznarich at first knock that he had personally inquired of Kevin whether anything unusual had occurred at the Fusters', and was satisfied not only that Kevin was definitely not molested, but that he would be most happy to work to clear the Fusters' good name.

No, Mr. Cartwright had informed Donna Meznarich. He did not want Kevin interviewed by the Bragas or anyone else. He did not want the subject brought up ever again. Consequently, Kevin's picture resided in Dan Casey's stack by sole virtue of the fact that his photograph was among the hundreds seized from the Fuster "family album."

There was a little boy named Kevin Cartwright, said Casey, who was momentarily interrupted by Jeff Samek's vigorous objection to the State's parading of his client's entire stable of children before the judge.

Do you remember, Casey continued, *a little child by the name of Kevin Cartwright, a little blond boy . . . still in diapers?* The prosecutor placed the photograph before Frank Fuster, who picked it up and said softly, "That's Kevin, all right," a smile spreading across his face.

Casey paused in mid-amble, stunned by the frank pleasure with which Frank Fuster regarded the little boy who had not betrayed him. *Was he one of your* favorites? asked the startled Casey.

Frank couldn't tear his eyes from the photo in his hands. "Kevin is a cute boy. Don't you think so?" he said, now grinning from ear to ear.

The young prosecutor involuntarily stepped away from the witness stand as though suddenly discovering its occupant carried a communicable disease. But astonishment planted Casey's feet to the floor once again, and he turned back to quizzically study the all-but-drooling defendant. A number of responses came to mind.

He voiced none of them.

I happen to think so, said Casey, looking Frank in the eye. *Yes, sir.*

Frank Fuster's memory of Kevin Cartwright, however, was far more vivid than that of the children who were named in the charges. He had, he said firmly, never seen Chad and Missy Herschel in his life, prior to his screening of the Braga tapes.

"I know *Mr.* Herschel," said Frank, flashing the judge a smile. "He's suing me for eleven million dollars."

As for Brendon Prince, his next-door neighbor, "I seen [him] in his house playing around, never in my house. As far as I'm concerned, my wife have never babysat that child."

What about thirteen-month-old Angie Dean? inquired Casey. Did Frank remember her?

"Yes, *and* her *father*." Frank leaned forward expectantly.

Let me show you what's previously been marked for identification as State's Exhibit 1Y and ask you if you recognize that as a picture of Angie Dean?

"Yes."

Where was that picture taken?

"In the Florida room of my house."

Who took the picture?

Frank had thus far been evasive in answering any questions as to who had taken the pictures of the children. But this time he answered immediately. "I did."

So you were there at least that time to see Angie Dean?

Frank leapt on the question enthusiastically. "Sure, yeah, I was there. You know what time they used to pick up Angie? Sometimes 10, sometimes 11 P.M. I used to take Angie to her father's car because he came so drunk that he couldn't do it."

So you picked up Angie and carried her to the car?

"Yes. . . ."

What about a little boy by the name of Steven Vickers? Do you remember him coming to your house?

"No. . . ."

Do you remember a young child by the name of Chip Levy?

"No."

Do you remember two little children by the name of Bonnie Martinez and Jeremy Martinez?

"I don't remember the children, but I remember the one time I went to his house—or their house—with my wife. . . . A check . . . bounced, so my wife went there to collect a check."

Do you remember seeing Bonnie Martinez at your house?
"No."
Did you ever remember her being at your house when you were there?
"No." Frank, noting the gleam in Casey's eye, edged away from "Hundred percent."
"I don't remember."
What about Jeremy Martinez?
"No, I don't remember."
Do you remember regularly babysitting the Martinezes?
"No. The Martinezes were in my house only like three days, four days the most."
Do you recognize the child in diapers portrayed in State's Exhibit 2 double A?
"I don't."
What about the little girl in the back of the child that Iliana is holding in the picture contained within State's Exhibit 2B?
"Let me see," said Frank, concentrating intently. "This is a little girl there, but I don't recognize her."
Who would have taken that picture, sir?
"I did—of Jeremy and my wife. I don't know the little child."
Jeremy, sir? snapped Casey, quick to seize this slip.
Frank grew faintly flustered for the first time. "What is the name? Kevin? I'm confused so many times. Kevin."
In that particular picture, Casey continued, *a picture of Iliana with Kevin and a little girl in the background, do you recognize her as Bonnie Martinez, the person you don't remember having ever been in the same house as you?*
"No!" exclaimed Frank in apparent astonishment. "The Martinez kid? How do you know?"
Dan Casey wasted no time marveling at the glibness with which Frank Fuster lived his lies. *Do you remember this little girl having been there at your house?*
"No. Obviously she's at my house."
Obviously you were there 'cause you took the picture?
"Right, but I don't know the kid."
For hours, Casey plucked pictures from his pile.
For hours, Frank continued with his fog machine.
Do you recognize where that picture was taken? inquired Casey, producing yet another child photographed in the Fuster living room.

"Yeah," said Frank proudly. "You got a picture of me when I was in the U.S. Marines here."

Casey never ceased to be amazed. No branch of the armed services had ever heard of Francisco Fuster Escalona.

Christina Royo had already checked.

Well, said Casey pleasantly, not at all unwilling to take advantage of this "free" pretrial deposition, Frank having most eagerly waived his right to remain silent by taking the stand. As Samek well knew, Dan Casey was collecting volumes of impeachable statements that he would save for the main event.

When were you in the U.S. Marines? Casey seemed much impressed that Frank Fuster liked to count himself among the "few good men."

"Marines cadet," corrected Frank.

You were never in the Marines, of course? said Casey, nodding his head. *You were a Marine cadet?*

"No. Marines cadet. . . ."

Did you ever see any children doing any sexually explicit acts in your home?

"Of course not," spat Frank imperiously. "I would not have allowed that. . . ."

I believe you said on direct examination testimony that Iliana did all of the babysitting of the children at your home; is that correct?

"Hundred percent."

That you did not assist her in any way in any of the babysitting; is that correct?

"That's correct."

You never participated, even to help her out when she was in another part of the house; you would never go change a baby's diaper or anything like that; is that correct?

"Never. I ever never changed a diaper. Not even my son's."

You have never changed a diaper? Casey's eyebrows crept above his heavy-frame glasses.

"No."

So, am I correct to assume that you never took a bath with any of the children?

"You are hundred percent correct in assuming that. . . ."

Did you ever have a videocassette recorder . . . in your living room?

"Never I own one, touch one."

Sorry? I didn't understand.

"I have never owned one."

Owned one what, sir? inquired Casey.

"A video equipment."

Well, just so you're absolutely sure when I say videocassette recorder, said Casey casting a glance in the direction of the court reporter, *I'm talking about an item commonly known as a VCR.*

"I have one in my cell," said Frank. "I know what it is."

Plays these kind of tapes?

"Right."

Are you telling me you never owned or touched a videocassette recorder?

"That's what I said. . . . Prior to the date that I got one in my cell, and Mr. Swit, the counselor, came and teach me how to use it."

What about the one that was in your house . . . ?

"No, sir, not in my house. . . ."

Since you didn't have a videocassette recorder, did you have any need for a video camera that would go with a VCR?

"No, sir. Never owned one."

Did you ever have one in your house?

"No, sir."

What about a large tripod? When I say "tripod," you know what I mean?

"Yes."

It's a stand?

"I know what it—"

Samek jumped to his feet. "Mr. Fuster is not charged with taking photographs."

Casey fished several more streams before relinquishing this helpful dialogue with Frank Fuster.

Did you ever coerce your wife or beat her in any way to make her have sexual contact with the kids?

"No, sir. Never."

Did you exercise any kind of mind control over your wife in order to get her to have sexual contact?

Frank was aghast. "If I had that *power,* you think I would use it against—? You know, I don't, I have *never.*

"I'm a normal *human being.*"

Do you ever read to your wife from a green book of mind control?

Frank smirked indulgently. "The green book is called *I Am,* which is the name of God, and it's not a mind control book."

Sir, did you ever have venereal disease in the summer of 1984?
"I be more explicit. Never in my life."
Did you ever contact a doctor because you had exhibited symptoms of a venereal disease during the summer of 1984?
"That was not venereal disease, why I contacted the Dr. Lopez."
So what is the answer to your question, sir?
"The answer is no. . . ."
Of course, sir. Do you still feel, as you stated in court last week, that crimes such as those charged against you are the worst crimes a human being can commit and that you're sad and sorry that people are walking this earth who suffer that sickness in their head?
"I'm very sorry that there are some human beings walking our earth sexually abusing our children, and I'm also very sorry that there are some district attorneys using their power to put innocent families in jail. . . ."
I have no further questions of Mr. Fuster. Thank you, sir.
Dan Casey ambled back to the prosecution table, where sat John Hogan and Richard Shiffrin, filling yellow legal pads as fast—as Jeffrey Samek would say—as they could move their pens.

• • •

Throughout the probation violation hearing, John Hogan's thoughts often turned to the trial that would immediately follow. He knew that he could fill the cavernous courtroom with several dozen small fingers pointing in Frank and Iliana Fuster's direction and still risk acquittal, unless he could neutralize whomever the defense had hired to neutralize the truth.

Curiously, the focus of the case had shifted entirely from the only eyewitnesses to the Fuster crimes—Frank, Iliana, and the children— to people who had never before set foot in the state, much less met either the victims or the perpetrators.

The witness lineup for the Country Walk trial was taking on the proportions of a psychological shoot-out at the OK Corral, the Bragas having directed the State toward several leading authorities who offered empirical research in specialties that complemented their own child development and interviewing credentials.

Never had such a depth of child sexual abuse knowledge been assembled for a single trial. Hogan was prepared for any eventuality. Should the defense call some local yokel to spout textbook Freudian theory, Hogan intended to counter with the nationally recognized leaders in highly specialized fields who spent more time studying children than testifying about them.

There were few members of the nation's psychological community—and no respected ones—who would be inclined to sit on a witness stand and tell a jury that regardless of what the most eminent researchers in their respective fields had to say, three-year-olds were not capable of distinguishing fact from fantasy, but nevertheless were adept at memorizing long, sequential, detailed stories and regurgitating them on request, like tiny POWs imprisoned by the interviewer's cunning manipulation.

And there was but one who would conceivably go so far as to view the children's interview tapes and be willing to declare under oath that the Bragas' "technique" was even more sinister than the "witch hunt" he'd uncovered in Jordan, Minnesota, where, he had testified, law enforcement officials and social workers had "brainwashed" dozens of children to tell sordid tales of a sex ring involving some two dozen adults—including some of their own parents.

When a Jordan jury acquitted the first husband and wife to come to trial (largely due to Dr. Ralph Underwager's premiere performance as an expert on Communist-inspired interrogation tactics), District Attorney Kathleen Morris dropped all charges still pending against the other participants named by the children and one adult who turned state's witness—an action that rained blows on the prosecutor from near and afar.

In the sleepy little town of Jordan, the winds of "witch hunt hysteria" began to whip as children, humiliated and ridiculed, began to recant their incredible statements. The psychologists and social workers who interviewed them were condemned as programmers who filled the children's heads with ideas that caused the fantasy to grow larger and more bizarre.

Fondling. Oral copulation. Sodomy.

Excrement fetish. Animal sacrifice.

Ritual murder.

The state attorney general issued a terse report that flogged the lady DA for too zealously and indiscriminately filing charges in the matter of the alleged Jordan, Minnesota, child sex ring.

Kathleen Morris was flirting with impeachment when a tidal wave struck the beleaguered district attorney from another angle—this time from Washington, D.C. The U.S. Attorney, upon concluding its independent investigation of the evidence in the Jordan case, issued its own scathing report suggesting that the district attorney was derelict in her duty by not proceeding with prosecution of the additional adults charged.

There was, concluded the federal agency, ample evidence to convict.

But a jury had found it more reasonable to believe that the children had been, for some undetermined reason, "brainwashed" through methods that "conformed precisely and in exact detail" to the methods employed by the Red Chinese, the North Koreans, and "oppressive tyrants everywhere" than to believe what the children were saying.

The Bragas, Underwager told the Fuster defense team, had done the same thing—only worse.

John Hogan looked forward to meeting Dr. Ralph Underwager in the courtroom (both at the probation violation hearing and the trial), having had the opportunity to question him at length, thanks to Christina Royo's skillfully served subpoena.

And thanks to the Bragas' six-month crash course in child development, memory, and fantasy, Country Walk's lead prosecutor walked into the deposition with a sizable advantage.

Hogan had always been somewhat intimidated in cross-examining experts, who could psycho-babble their way out of any corner, leaving him without the faintest notion of what they were talking about. But now, armed with a considerable depth of information assimilated and stored in his memory banks—and fifty pages of questions prepared by the Professors Braga—he was about to deliver an examination that would measure the depth of the Minnesota entrepreneur's credibility, information he expected would be as useful to him in the probation violation hearing as it would at the main event.

It was a test that John Hogan was fully prepared to pass, but he suspected strongly that Dr. Ralph Underwager was not.

What is the average number of words a three-year-old child would be expected to understand, Dr. Underwager?
"I don't know the average number a three-year-old would be expected to understand."
When I say "three-year-old," I mean a child of the developmental age of three?
"I don't know. . . ."

How about to speak?

"They understand so much more than they can speak, but I don't know how you would assess that."

Do you know of any study that has been done in this area?

"Not offhand."

What is expressive language?

"Expressive? Anything that has to do with the expression of the motion more than description."

What is receptive language?

"I don't know."

Could you explain the changes that take place in cognitive development in children between three years of age and four years of age?

"Not right now."

Could you explain the changes that take place in social development in children between four and five years old?

"Between four and five years of social development?"

Uh-huh.

"Not right now."

Could you explain what changes take place in language development in children between the ages of two and three?

"Not right now."

How about changes in motor development between children two and three?

"Not right now."

Is there a difference in your mind between the age in which a child distinguishes between truth and falsehood and when they begin to realize the impropriety of telling falsehoods?

"Approximately puberty they begin to recognize impropriety. Some may a bit before that. . . ."

Do you feel that children whose tapes you saw in this case have been brainwashed?

"I feel that the children whose tapes I have seen have been influenced to produce statements that were desired by their interrogators."

Would you classify that as being brainwashed?

"I don't like to use the term *brainwashed*. . . ."

Would you compare the techniques used by the Bragas in this case with those used by the Chinese or Red Chinese or North Koreans or North Vietnamese?

"There, certainly a comparison can be made. . . ."

Tell me how the Red Chinese would program someone.
"I can't."
How about the North Koreans? What specific techniques did they use?
"Much the same. And the best report on North Koreans is from Bernette Scheim."
What is your understanding of how they brainwashed or forced people to conform?
"Used a lot of subtle pressure, repeated interviews, repeated interrogations."
What type of subtle pressures? We're talking about the North Koreans.
"Things like that; saying, 'You will help,' 'We need you to tell us these things, and, if you do, things will, you know, get better—improve.' Right now I don't recall anything more specific."
How about the North Vietnamese?
"They use many of the same techniques."
So you would compare anyone that says "Things will get better" to another human being, is similar to the Red Chinese, North Koreans, North Vietnamese . . . ? You compare the techniques used, to "conform precisely and—"
"Right."
The techniques used for the Chinese, Red Chinese, North Koreans, North Vietnamese, and all other tyrants, too? All other tyrants? Is that a correct summary of your statement?
"Yes."
So which techniques of the Red Chinese, North Koreans, North Vietnamese, and other tyrants were used by the Bragas?
"I can't say that right now."
Can you tell me any?
"Not right now."

The Minnesota-based Lutheran minister had, for the past two decades, dabbled in everything from psychology to sex therapy before lighting on this most recent and creative way in which to make a living. So it came as little surprise to John Hogan, five minutes into deposing the bearded, one-man medicine show (who warned viewers of Phil Donahue that they, too, could fall victim to this "witch hunt" for child molesters), that Dr. Underwager knew little more about children than he did about Chinese Communists and military brainwashing techniques.

Still, nothing prevented him from clambering up on witness stands for a minimum $1,000 per day "plus expenses"—each well-paid courtroom appearance "certifying" him as more expert than the last.

Country Walk would be an impressive notch to add to the former minister/fledgling court "expert's" rapidly expanding belt. But Underwager would never return to Miami following his enlightening sworn deposition, which would, for some time to come, remain a document of supreme interest to prosecutors across the country.

John Hogan didn't know why the defense's star witness vanished from the case. Possibly Jeffrey Samek had removed his blinders long enough to realize that he had a highly vulnerable witness on his hands. Or perhaps it was Underwager who chose to extricate himself from Country Walk, having (as Hogan later discovered) retained Jeffrey Samek to defend him against charges of perjury, which he seemed to believe he faced in Dade County.

Perhaps he simply had better things to do.

All Hogan knew was that he would never realize his opportunity to engage the self-anointed "child sex abuse" expert in meaningful dialogue at either the probation violation hearing or the trial. Samek had given him two hours' notice that the defense would not be calling Dr. Ralph Underwager, after all, as noted on the witness list, but rather another "expert" from California—a psychiatrist by the name of Lee Stewart Coleman.

Who had no intention of saying, "It didn't happen."

Only that it was *impossible* to know for sure if it had.

• • •

Jeffrey Samek continued with the defense of Frank Fuster's probation violation.

Doctor, inquired Samek of his new star witness, *in relation to this case,* State of Florida *v.* Francisco Fuster Escalona, *what have you done?*

"I have reviewed police reports of the investigations. I reviewed reports of Dr. Simon Miranda, as well as notes and some psychological test materials, some Dade County school materials of Jaime Fuster. I have reviewed approximately thirty hours of videotapes of the following children: Jason Harrison, Joshua Harrison, Crystal Fletcher, Chad Herschel, April Lancaster, Jaime Fuster, Missy Herschel, Andy Pierson, and Steven Vickers. . . ."

Doctor, as a result of your review of these tapes, have you reached a conclusion whether or not what Steven Vickers says in the tapes is a reliable indicator of what may or may not have occurred to him?

"Yes, I have."

What is your conclusion?

"That it's not a reliable indicator."

Upon what did you base that conclusion?

"Well, I base it on observing the videotapes. That methods that were used lead me to the opinion that the child is being influenced by many, many factors. Plus, the child's level of development is such that I don't think you could conclude that even the child would be able to tell the difference between truth and falsehood. . . ."

What are the methods you take issue with?

"First of all, one of the things that is done is that the child is told, 'Let's pretend. Let's pretend and play a game,' and then the statements by the child are then taken as factually accurate when a child has been invited to pretend. . . .

"The very beginning of the interview on August 14—there was some play which was not particularly specific with regard to the issues in this case. Then the child is introduced to the so-called anatomically correct dolls, and then Laurie Braga says, 'Do you want to play a make-believe game and pretend?' . . .

"I wasn't able to write down exactly the rest of the sentence. Then Steven says, 'That's Daddy.' The child identifies the adult male doll as 'Daddy.' Laurie Braga does not allow him to do that. She says, 'Let's call him Frank.' Immediately then, the child has been manipulated and directed. . . .

"Laurie Braga then goes on to say, 'Let's call him Frank, let's call her Iliana, let's call him Steven.' These are the terms of the ball game, having now been circumscribed by an adult. . . .

"Here's what I did. I went through all the videotapes taking notes. . . . I went back over the notes and wrote down the techniques that, in my opinion, summarized the opinion that I had already formed—that there are children being badly manipulated and basically indoctrinated. So I wrote down what those techniques were, in my opinion. . . .

"The next thing I have note of here is when the child would be asked whether some sexual things had happened, in this case, 'Did you ever play the pee-pee game?' and the child says 'No.' The response, in this case, from Laurie Braga was disbelief. Whereas, if the child said something—that something sexual or some sexual game happened—there would be belief and praise.

"So that in this case, when the child said, 'No, they didn't play the pee-pee game,' a response from Laurie Braga was 'Did somebody tell you not to tell? . . . Did they tell you that maybe you'd get in trouble?'

"Now, this is, in my opinion, a rather outrageous example of implanting into a child's mind certain ideas. The child is essentially being told, 'Somebody told you not to tell. Somebody told you you'd get in trouble,' and she has absolutely no way to know whether that ever happened.

"Of course, a child of this age is totally powerless, if these things are repeated a few times, to be able to keep separate what, in fact, they've been told from what somebody tells them they've been told. Pretty soon it's all a jumble, and they don't know."

What other methods? inquired Jeffrey Samek of Dr. Lee Stewart Coleman.

"Next, on the other side of the coin, besides expressing disbelief if you say nothing happened, is praise and positive responses if you say something did happen, and what she said to him was, 'If you tell the secret, you'll feel better,' and another one which is a consistently recurring theme, 'Mommy will be proud if you tell,' 'You'll feel much better if you talk.' So, after those kind of statements, 'Now let's try again. Let's play ring-around-the-rosy again.' . . .

"The next thing was, again, the child was asked by Laurie Braga, 'Did somebody tell you not to talk to me?' The same comment I made earlier, 'Did somebody tell you not to tell, that you'd get in trouble or that you'd get hurt?'

". . . These children are so young, and they're talking about things which maybe to an adult seems not that long ago, but a few months to a child of this age is a huge percentage of their life; their memory capacity has not—obviously are very immature. If you have a child like this being told by a parent and an interviewer, 'Did somebody tell you that you would get hurt?' . . . the child is relatively helpless pretty soon to decide whether or not they were told that or not. . . ."

Do you think the dolls are an effective truth-finding tool?

". . . In my opinion, use of the dolls to try to reconstruct the truth is very problematical because children, even if they were not invited to pretend, are probably going to bring some of it themselves to the interview because that's what they do with dolls."

They can't distinguish these dolls from Ken, Barbie, He Man, or Masters of the Universe, or any other doll?

"Well, my opinion is that a child of three, four, or five years old is used to thinking of a doll as a play toy, something you make up stories about. . . .

"Something I saw with a lot of other children is telling a child that that child had told the interviewer a certain thing in a previous interview when, in fact, that's not what the child had said . . . therefore distorting the reality of what had been said in the interview, with the child in a relatively powerless position, because the child's memory is not able to go back and remember exactly what they had said. . . .

"I think clearly the example that struck me the most was when Jaime Fuster was told on two subsequent interviews that he had said during the first interview that he was told by Iliana only to say good things about Frank in order to get him off. And that is not what the child said. The child said that he should say the good and the bad, that's the only way to help Frank, or something to that effect. . . .

"I consider that child abuse in itself.

"Another method that was being used was that, if the child, after being invited to pretend . . . and the child then gives a lot of information, and some of the information is obviously impossible—such as cutting heads off. Then the obvious impossibilities are dismissed without influencing the interviewer's apparent credibility of the child being interviewed. So, for example, if the child says ten things, and a couple of them are clearly fantasy and impossible, and you might think that that would raise some questions about the credibility of the eight things that were said.

"But it doesn't seem to happen. The things that were obviously impossible were just tossed out the window, and then the other eight things were taken as fact. . . .

"I didn't find any evidence that the interviewers were at all concerned about the possible influence on the children having talked with people other than the interviewers, investigators, or parents. . . .

"I believe it is evident that the parents themselves have been manipulated, that out of their love and concern for the children they are vulnerable to adopting some of the same techniques that interviewers are using, feeling that they're doing the best thing for the child but, in fact, ending up leading and suggesting things like . . . I'm not sure what child it was—kissed her mother, and I guess what the mother felt was a good, strong kiss [April Lancaster inserted her tongue in her mother's mouth], and she said to the child, 'Is that how Frank kissed you?' Again, sort of leading the child in a certain direction."

You didn't speak to any of the parents, did you?

"No, I haven't spoken to anybody. . . ."

Are you aware, Doctor, of any behavior that you could call a specific factor reaction to child abuse?

"No, there aren't any. There are no specific markers, indicators of child abuse. It would be nice if there were, but what I mean by that, of course, in the sense we would have a foolproof way of investigating and finding out if something happened. Unfortunately, there aren't any.

"There isn't any such thing."

The State had precisely two hours that evening in which to depose Dr. Lee Coleman in preparation for cross-examination the following morning.

It was Daniel Casey's turn to play "quiz the expert."

Have you formed any opinion on whether Frank Fuster is guilty or innocent?

"No, I haven't."

Would it matter if you felt he was guilty or innocent in your testimony?

"No, absolutely not."

Have you been informed of the statements that many of these children made before they even saw the doctors?

"Yes. As I recall, there were some things mentioned in the police reports. I'm not exactly clear in my own mind the timing of when they said it. . . ."

It couldn't be contaminated by the Bragas because the Bragas hadn't conducted their interviews by the time the statements were made; is that correct?

"That's correct."

Are you aware that the statements were made to their parents and the acts displayed before the Bragas were even brought into this case?

"It's my understanding that the allegations were raised before the Bragas even talked to anybody. . . ."

Are you familiar with Frank Fuster's background?

"I know some about it. . . ."

Are you aware that Frank Fuster's wife is also on trial?

"Yes."

*Are you aware that the defense her attorney has chosen to raise
for her is that all of these things happened to the kids—and they
were done just exactly like the kids say—but that Frank forced her
to do it?*

"No, I'm not familiar with what the defense is going to be. . . ."

Nor, apparently, did he care.

The facts of the case weren't relevant to Dr. Coleman's "theories."
He said so—repeatedly and without apology. It was his opinion, for
which he was handsomely paid.

Truth, Dr. Coleman would frequently remind the forgetful prosecutors, was not his job.

Casey soon abandoned his fruitless quest for anything Dr. Coleman might know and trod into territory more familiar to the career
psychiatrist/expert witness—his opinons.

What, asked the ever-pleasant Dan Casey, *is the general impression of the quality of the interviewing technique used by the Bragas
in the tapes you have reviewed?*

Dr. Lee Stewart Coleman sat erect, as though Dan Casey had just
inserted a fresh battery and pulled his string.

"I think it's terrible. I think it amounts to child abuse. I think that
it's totally misleading to outside people; that is, non–mental health
professionals, in the sense that they are going to believe that people
are helping or clarifying or elucidating something. I think that the
Bragas are caught up in all the misconceptions that are currently
plaguing this field of allegations of child sexual abuse. By that I
mean the assumption that something happened, working from that
assumption, leading questions, manipulating the child, and all of
the things that I talked about. . . ."

Casey allowed the doctor to wind down before continuing to
gather the script Lee Coleman could be expected to deliver on cross-
examination in the morning.

*What do you feel about the strengths and positive aspects of the
interviewing by the Bragas?*

"I don't think there are any with regard to what they were asked
to do. I think that's consistently misleading and deceptive. If you're
asking me whether they like kids or not, well, that's fine. I'll let
them speak for themselves on that.

"But as far as the purpose of those interviews is supposedly to
offer expert assistance in determining whether these children are
molested, in my opinion, those interviews do more than anything
else I have seen to make it impossible to find out from the children
anything that is reliable. . . ."

You have seen many of these little children reacting as they did to simple questions before any subject matter was brought up. Do you think that a layperson looking at those tapes can look at those tapes, and even after hearing your testimony about the methods in those tapes, do you think a layperson could look at those tapes, and come away with any conclusion except that these children were molested at the hands of Frank Fuster?

"I certainly do not. In fact, I think just the opposite. My prediction is, if a layperson were to look at those tapes and be able to put out of their mind the kind of prejudice and hysteria that builds up in a community around a case like this, if they are able to look at the tapes and pay attention to the way the children are being interviewed and listen to all the things the children are saying, I think they will come away saying, 'If anything happened, this ain't the way I'm going to decide that it happened.' "

Do you remember the Joshua Harrison tape?

"I do. . . ."

In the beginning of the interview, Josh was clutching to Joe Braga. Eventually, just through play, through no mention at all of any subject matter, Josh eventually went around the room and started playing with toys, took the thumb out of his mouth, and walked around the room playing with little blocks. . . . The only time the subject matter was mentioned was when Dr. Laurie Braga took out . . . the anatomically correct dolls with their clothes on, so they looked like any other doll, and said something to the effect of 'This is Iliana. Do you know somebody named Iliana?' Whereupon Josh stopped doing what he was doing, crawled into his mother's lap, and stuck his thumb in his mouth and covered his head with his blanket. What manipulation was done to that child in that tape?

"Well, you see, implicit in your question is the same oversight that the Bragas make . . . and that is completely ignoring the possible influence on the child before they got to the Bragas.

"I never said that the Bragas were the only ones who could be manipulating the child. The child could have been questioned about these things and doesn't want to talk about it; he is sick of having people ask him questions. He is sick of talking about it."

It could be that Frank Fuster molested and traumatized him for a period of months?

"I never said—"

I was just interested in the failure you had to list that possibility in the examples that you gave. . . .

Who would you consider authoritative in the proper way to conduct an interview of this nature?

"I don't know. All I can tell you is it would not likely be a mental health professional. . . ."

What is your affiliation with a group known as VOCAL?

"Oh, I have had a number of people who were in VOCAL who were involved in a case, who called me up and wanted to talk to me about what was going on in their case. Some of the cases that I have been involved with, these were people who were members of VOCAL. I gave a lecture at a VOCAL meeting in Los Angeles. I anticipate speaking at a national meeting that they are going to have in the fall. I'm not a member or anything like that. . . ."

Do you know a Dr. Ralph Underwager?

"I have talked to him on the phone. . . ."

What is your opinion of Dr. Underwager as a professional in his field?

"From what I know so far, I think highly of his opinions. . . ."

Doctor, your whole premise in going around the country and testifying over the years has been that mental health professionals can't tell the answers to a lot of legal issues such as competency and insanity and, in this case, sexual abuse. Isn't that really just what you are doing here, coming in as a mental health professional and judging the Bragas?

"I have offered no opinion and do not intend to do so about whether any factual charges are correct. . . . I think that I have some expert methods to evaluate the methods of psychiatry because I have been trained in them. . . . That's not the same as saying 'so-and-so knew what he was doing when he committed a crime or he didn't.' . . ."

Are you aware of any empirical evidence that anatomically correct dolls are unduly suggestive?

". . . Well, what I would consider the best evidence that we have is the outcome of some—of a case like in Minnesota, where they had been interviewed in that way. . . . Strong opinions that the children are being molested, and then it is acknowledged by everybody that the people—that it didn't happen."

Is it your understanding of the Minnesota case—is that everybody is acknowledging that it didn't happen?

"No."

That's what you just said.

"Well, what I mean is not—not that everyone is acknowledging that nothing happened, but that everybody is acknowledging that a lot of things that the children said never happened, such as murders, those type of things.

"Some of the extreme things that the children are saying. I don't know that somebody is persisting in believing that those things are true. Certainly a neutral body such as the attorney general's office of Minnesota concluded that there was nothing like that."

Of course, the attorney general's office is now investigating the prosecutor out there because she dropped both the cases they now believe to be guilty?

That was not, said Dr. Coleman, his "reading" of the report.

• • •

The third day of Frank Fuster's probation violation hearing commenced with the State's gathering of the California psychiatrist's "insights" into the Country Walk case, which he had not heard of until two weeks ago.

John Hogan was up at bat once again, armed with the results of Dan Casey's late-night deposition, which would continue following today's proceedings. There was so much the State wished to know of Dr. Coleman's opinions—and his qualifications to offer them.

In your opinion, inquired John Hogan, *no one in this country does interviews of children who are alleged to have been the victims of sex abuse correctly?*

"I have never seen an interview of a child in which the attempt was made to determine whether the child was sexually molested, which I would consider, quote, 'correct' or worthwhile or helpful to a court. . . ."

So, in other words, it's not just the Bragas [who] are the only ones in the country who don't do it right. You see this as a problem throughout the country?

"That's right. I believe it's not a . . . coincidence that it's being done this way. There is a certain set of myths and a certain set of ideas which these interviewers are laboring under and which is causing them to do the things they do. . . ."

As Casey had before him, John Hogan let Coleman's battery run down before abruptly shifting gears.

For the sake of organization, let's start with the first [tape] . . . that you criticized. . . .

Hogan cross-examined, tape by tape, "technique" by "technique," then returned to matters philosophical.

If you were doing one of these interviews, Hogan continued, *and you just had a child indicate to you—hypothetically—as they're talking, they display a great deal of distress and anxiety, and the child says, "I was told if I related what happened to me, my mommy and daddy would die," would you tell that child that he didn't do anything wrong for telling you . . . ?*

"Given the way you have said it, I might do that, but I have to add that, in my opinion, that is a vicious distortion of what is going on here. . . ."

John Hogan's wake had been steadily nipping at the sandcastle, and now the tide began to roll in.

That's obviously for the judge to determine and not you; isn't that correct? . . . If you could just answer my questions. You can give your speech later.

"I'm trying to respond to your question in the truest context that I can."

I'm sure. So, if that did happen hypothetically . . . ?

". . . If that's what the child said, uncoached, then I would certainly try to reassure the child. . . ."

In the last of your enumerated techniques, you talk about training of parents?

"Yes. . . ."

You're saying the Bragas intentionally manipulated or brainwashed anyone?

"No, I am not."

The example you give here, continued Hogan, *is by what you're saying, they inadvertently did that—both to the parents and to the children?*

"No, that's not exactly what I'm saying. I am not going to presume they did intentionally. In fact, I'm going to presume they did unintentionally. That's my working presumption.

"I don't have any doubt that the Bragas sincerely care about children and want to help children, but I don't think that it would be fair to call it inadvertent. . . . It's not an isolated thing, in my opinion, based on what I've seen in other cases, what the Bragas are doing," said Coleman, avoiding the borderline lunatic fringe slogan of "witch hunt" as carefully as he downplayed his ties with VOCAL, something that Dr. Ralph Underwager himself was in the habit of doing—both doctors having some semblance of reputation to maintain.

"The reason why I think it leads to this abuse," continued the psychiatrist, "is because they're working on a set of assumptions

about possible child sexual abuse which is faulty at its very
foundation. . . ."

*So, you're saying the Bragas always believe the children and are
always finding sexual abuse whether it's there or not?*

"Well, I'm only commenting on this case. . . ."

You've only testified for the defense in this type of case?

"That's correct."

*You obviously have no idea whether they have testified as defense
experts in other cases saying sexual abuse did* not *occur?* [They
had.]

"No, I don't know."

But yet you know what their philosophy is on these cases? John
Hogan resheathed his contempt and moved on to other matters.

*In talking about the Bragas manipulating the parents . . . I want
to know if you ever met a woman by the name of Maggie Fletcher.*
Hogan could barely suppress the tugging at the corners of his
mouth.

Behind him, the occupants of one wing of the visitor's gallery bit
back smiles.

The Country Walk parents hadn't missed a minute of Frank
Fuster's probation violation hearing, and Dr. Lee Coleman's two-
day testimony had bombarded them with alternating waves of
anger, frustration, and, at times, amusement, their appreciation of
the absurd having grown finely tuned over the past year. Mark
Harrison, at one point, planted his tongue firmly in his cheek and
inquired of the Doctors Braga why they hadn't put their celebrated
manipulative techniques to more practical use—such as programming Jason to clean his room and brush his teeth.

Now the parents smiled in anticipation of the small slice of reality
John Hogan was about to inject into the proceedings.

Had Dr. Coleman ever met a woman by the name of Maggie
Fletcher?

"No."

*Have you any idea how easy she would be to control or
manipulate?*

"Never met the woman, but—"

You're not saying Frank didn't *abuse all these kids in the
affidavit, are you?*

"I think I made it very clear, not only in this case, I would never
go into court and give an opinion one way or the other about such
questions.

"I base a significant part of my career in trying to convince others we should not give any credibility to those in mental health who do that. I'm not about to turn around, do it myself."

Hogan smiled.

You're simply traveling around the country telling people for $10,000 a week, "No one nowhere knows how to interview kids. . . ."

Is that correct?

But the prosecutor's smile flickered as he returned to his seat. Without *seeing* the tapes the California psychiatrist had so grossly misrepresented, a jury might perceive his opinions as "reasonable."

Dr. Lee Stewart Coleman might well hold the key to Frank Fuster's cell.

• • •

Judge Robert Newman had presided for one year over the legal entanglements of Country Walk, and yet he knew little of the particulars of the case. It seemed that he either had judiciously avoided frenetic pretrial publicity or had come to absorb what was reported to have occurred as a vague abstraction—"molest," as in "to bother or annoy."

As recently as May, when the State offered the then-silent Iliana a seventeen-year term in exchange for her plea of guilty, Judge Newman had apparently been as irritated as Von Zamft with the State's hard line. "What did she do," the judge is reported to have inquired, "touch them or something?"

There was, said John Hogan, a little more to it than that.

Judge Newman, the prosecutor knew, was not insensitive.

Just unenlightened.

For he had not yet seen the children's interviews.

And he did not yet know the kinds of scars that even a "touch" could render.

He had not yet witnessed the videotaped conversation that took place between Dr. Joseph Braga, almost a year ago, and a five-year-old red-haired boy who had not yet reconciled his shame.

Joe understood what was troubling him.

"Let me explain," Joe had said to Jason Harrison on the little boy's fourth visit to the Metro Justice Building.

"I once had a young man here who was very upset when somebody touched him—an older man touched him.

"His penis got hard, and he was very upset about that because he felt he did something wrong, because he didn't understand that if anybody's penis is touched, it gets hard.

"It doesn't matter who it is.

"That's the way the penis acts.

"He thought that because his penis got hard—he was very confused. I explained that at the very end of his penis, when it's touched, it sends a message back to the brain . . .

"It's like when . . . your nose tickles and you sneeze. You can't stop a sneeze if your nose tickles. Well, if you touch someone's penis or someone touches your penis, it gets hard. . . .

"Sometimes you wake up in the morning, your penis is hard for no reason. . . ."

Jason was listening intently.

It happened that Frank Fuster's probation violation hearing offered Judge Newman his first opportunity to examine the evidence that had sustained this year-long judicial nightmare.

And it was possibly his only opportunity to see one of the children's interviews, the likelihood that the State would get them admitted into evidence in a probation violation proceeding remaining significantly higher than that it would get them admitted at trial—the parents' Judicial Proceedings Act notwithstanding.

The State did not intend even to try.

Richard Shiffrin, who laid numerical odds on probable appellate leanings, warned his fellow prosecutors that there was great risk of reversal by a higher court if Judge Newman agreed to admit the tapes under a new exception to the hearsay rule, which had yet to be addressed by either the state supreme court or Michael Von Zamft's Florida bar committee.

Upon Shiffrin's vigorous recommendation, John Hogan abandoned any plans of attempting to get the tapes admitted into evidence at Frank and Iliana's trial. And though they now had more than enough children who could be judged competent to testify, the Bragas' interview tapes were more crucial than ever.

If Dr. Lee Coleman showed up and did his tap dance for the jury—who would not be allowed to view the actual interviews—six men and women might accept the star defense witness's lucrative and error-riddled representations of them.

Fortunately, from the State's standpoint, the rules of evidence were more elastic for the probation violation hearing, and the State need waste little time either justifying the Bragas' methods or discrediting the supercilious psychiatrist who had seen, over the course of twenty years, "five or ten" sexually abused children and whose ignorance of child development, child memory, and child fantasy rivaled that of the Minnesota minister/psychologist/entrepreneur who had preceded him.

Hogan would save both the Bragas' credentials and Coleman's credibility for the jury, which was not expected to see what Judge Newman would see—a tape of a splendid little towheaded boy whose striking blue eyes gazed into Laurie's like two deep pools.

Steven Vickers, not quite four, the first child known to have volunteered the secret, the boy who emerged from the shower three months before Frank Fuster was arrested and told his mother that Iliana "kissed all the babies' bodies."

He volunteered little else ever again.

Because his mother didn't believe him the first time.

Judge Newman watched Laurie swim through Jell-O for almost an hour, rubbing his beard, his face as unreadable as ever as the child haltingly related a series of explicit sexual acts both Fusters had committed on various children.

It wasn't until near the very end that the horror seemed to sink in. Judge Newman's face began to drain of color.

"Steven, let me ask you a question," said Laurie to the little boy. "When Frank made you bite his penis, did anything come out of his penis?"

Steven Vickers nodded solemnly.

"Yes? What happened?"

"Pee-pee," he whispered.

"Pee-pee came out of his penis? Did it taste bad or good?"

"Bad . . . I could feel it in here," he added, pointing to his mouth.

"You could feel it in your mouth? You didn't like it, huh?"

"*All* the way in there," said Steven, pointing again.

He didn't know the word for throat.

But he knew about ejaculation.

One element of Frank Fuster's lengthy testimony stood out in Judge Robert Newman's mind.

As a father, he had said, he would know if his son had been abused.

Frank had not perceived that the logical extension of that assertion might draw the judge's attention to the visitor's gallery, where sat the parents of Country Walk.

"I cannot find a thread," said Judge Newman, "between the

families involved in this situation and the defendant. I have looked hard, 'cause I know we're involved with children.

"Children sometimes say things, which we kind of scratch our head when they say it. I understand that personally, and from life's experience as well. . . . I looked carefully for that.

"I couldn't find it here.

"There's just too many children involved.

"Too many things have been said."

There was, Judge Newman declared, "a preponderance of evidence" that led him to conclude that Frank Fuster had indeed violated his probation.

Sentencing was scheduled for that afternoon.

• • •

Francisco Fuster Escalona had nodded vigorously throughout Dr. Lee Coleman's testimony. Finally, he seemed to be saying, someone was going to explain this whole insidious misunderstanding to the judge—and indeed to the world.

He hung on every word—a sponge that selectively absorbed vital nutrients with which to feed a rationalization process gone awry.

Frank Fuster lived by his own moral code.

"I Am" was the name of his god.

And the truth was whatever God said it was.

Frank Fuster bowed to no laws of Man—though he was adept at using them.

Frank was well studied in incorporating the defense strategy into the party line he'd refined during a year in solitary confinement, storing for later use even minute subtleties — like Samek and Von Zamft's persistence in addressing the Bragas as "Mr." and "Mrs." or "alleged" State experts, carefully detaching the title "Doctor" from their names. And he had quickly adopted the term *brainwashing* and sprinkled it liberally throughout the numerous in-court "press conferences" he would give over the course of the next several weeks.

Frank Fuster was no longer interested in exercising his right to remain silent, as his attorney so vigorously continued to recommend. He had done it Samek's way, and now he was facing fifteen years in prison—with no parole.

Now he would do it *his* way, by "expressing his true self" to the judge, who no doubt had been "forced" through "technicalities" to revoke his probation.

Surely His Honor knew deep in his heart that he could not have done these things.

He would prove it.

He still had a chance to turn fifteen years into probation.

Just like he had in 1982.

"Your Honor, and everyone present in the court, people of the media and society—" Frank leaned on the podium as if it were a pulpit set before the multitudes. He stood erect, his voice clear and resonant. His unintentional impersonation of a whispery, hunched Transylvanian peasant who had breathed "Nay-verr een my li-i-i-fe" at Jeffrey Samek for two hours at the beginning of the week was now a composed and confident articulator of the "truth," about to address "the entire nation."

"You have, Your Honor—based on the information that has been presented to you—have find me in violation of my probation. I'd like to first touch the points on which you find me that I was in violation of my parole.

"You mentioned the business cards that were made. . . ."

Document by document, Frank went through the pile of paperwork that pronounced him—not Iliana—as the operator of the Country Walk Babysitting Service. This was an error. That was a convenience. And everybody from the zoning clerk to his probation officer had perjured themselves.

That cleared up to his satisfaction, Frank moved on to other matters of evidence.

Briskly, he paced around the courtroom, punctuating his bewildered outrage with excited gestures.

"They had no physical *evidence*, nor does this court has any physical evidence, nor does anybody has any physical evidence! No other than false allegations that have been presented against me and against my wife.

"They have no professional methods to work with—*no* methods professional; not . . . any kind to take a child and talk to a child that has been sexually abused—or has not been sexually abused—and come up with conclusions. *No one* can honestly sit there and say, 'I conclude that Francisco Fuster Escalona and his wife, Iliana, are two child molesters.' . . ."

Frank was just getting warmed up.

"And now we come to Mr. and Mrs. Braga," announced Frank, sweeping his arm toward the front row, where sat the much-discussed but silent Bragas, who had told Abe Laeser exactly one year before, "We will be the targets."

Frank walked their way. "Nothing personal," he continued. "I don't have no respect for their work. I have seen those tapes. . . . I couldn't finish seeing the tapes. I couldn't finish. I couldn't handle it. It made me sick.

"I got a nervous breakdown looking at what they doing and the way they operate. I'm not going to accuse them of doing this with bad intentions. I always like to think the best about any situation."

Frank's gestures grew more dramatic, his thoughts more rambling.

"Today I thought you was going to find me innocent. . . .

"In my mind, I was hundred percent sure that you will find me— dismissed the ridiculous charges against me. . . .

"But the Bragas have a lot to do with it. They were involved in there. They preconditioned the children for everyone else. They brainwashed the children with their methods.

"Now, how do they brainwash the children? I think Dr. Coleman did a very good job in explaining. . . . I think that I couldn't put it in better words, because he is fully aware of the problem that is taking place not only with me and my wife. We are not an insulated case.

"This is happening nationwide.

"The responsibility to stop, stop this problem, falls upon your shoulders, Your Honor, and upon the shoulders of all the people in our society has the great responsibility of serving as God up to a point.

"This district attorney, up to a point—nothing personal—serves as a *devil*. I'm sorry. I don't mean that. Nothing personal.

"Yes, just as my attorney serves as protective.

"They created hysteria in the parents. They created panic, fear, anxiety in the parents with their conclusions. . . .

"The biggest crime they have committed is that they have abused every single child that they have talked in my case. I'm not even going to other cases.

"Let's talk with what is hundred percent sure, because I am, Your Honor, a normal human being. . . .

"Who is a kid that gave them the most information? The kid that elaborated on everything they say and he took all the attention on his own. Jason Harrison. . . .

"If one child knows he's lying, it's him.

"I honestly urge Your Honor to have this child receive medical help for the harm that has been done to him and that he's doing to us.

"After they interview a few children, they couldn't back up—the Bragas. They couldn't back up. . . . All the parents are working with them, exchanging ideas. They advising the parents, 'Get notes when you go home, get a pencil ready, anything your child says,' conditioning the parents. . . .

"All of this had a lot to do with the creation of what has come to be one of the biggest cases in our nation. . . .

"What has been committed with me in the eyes of God is a crime. Unless we actually see an adult abusing a child with our eyes—we *see* it—we cannot be hundred percent sure that the child has been sexually or physically abused.

"Now, we could be ninety-nine percent sure if a mother comes to pick up her daughter in my house and her daughter is bleeding. . . . Something is wrong. Take her to the emergency hospital immediately. This girl has been raped.

"None of that took place in my case.

"The entire case against me has been words, words, and words.

"My advice to the Bragas is that if they really want to help—and I mean this from the bottom of my heart—to stay away from children because you do not have the knowledge, you do not have the training to do what you're doing. And you are harming innocent people.

"I am not a child molester.

"Neither is my wife. . . .

"So if something good has come out of this, it's my words to you to change professions. . . . I don't seem to be able to get through to them by the smile on their face. I don't think they care a bit about what I said, Your Honor. I think I wasted a couple of minutes, so I'm going to keep talking to you.

"I'm going leave the Bragas alone. . . .

"I'd like to speak about the office of the district attorney now. Your Honor, the office of the district attorney have lost sight of their duty to our society. And I have learned this from three experiences. . . .

"First, when I was twenty years old, couple of months prior to becoming a New York City police officer [This, like many of Frank Fuster's "experiences," occurred only in his mind.], I'm accused of being a murderer. . . . Something that arise out of a car accident.

And Mr. Jacob Isenbek knows I pray for him every night since January 16, 1969, the day the unfortunate incident took place.

"I am free of guilt.

"The office of the district attorney have lose sight of their objective . . . to find the truth, not to get convictions. They are misusing the power, and they do have great power. . . .

"The office of the district attorney induced perjury. And I cannot say that they do this unintentionally. . . . There is not a single witness that they have presented in here that have said the truth. . . .

"If this nation does not prevent this situation that is taking place, from keep on taking place, more Frank Fusters and more Iliana Fusters will go to prison. . . .

"The state attorney's office has a lot of power. . . . How can a man—a regular citizen—have any defense from the power of the district attorney? Especially a man like myself, is an ex-convict, no money to hire a private attorney. . . . I'm talking about my 1981 case.

"What happened to me in that case is ridiculous. . . ."

Frank retried the Hilda Gonzalez case in its entirety.

"I know that when the district attorney comes here and talk—Mr. Hogan—he talks very fast. When he talks, it's not as Mr. Casey. Mr. Casey is more human. Mr. Hogan is more . . . cold. No offense. . . .

"The law is good, Your Honor.

"I believe in the law.

"It's against the law that you have incarcerated me and my wife.

"I'm going to prison a free man. Free of guilt, and also free of hate. . . .

"In prison I have become a new man. I am newborn Christian, and some of you will never know what I mean. But I am. Jesus Christ is inside me. . . .

"Self God is in every human being. God does exist. We don't come from no monkey. We do come from Adam and Eve. The Bible is a fact. . . .

"I'm ready for you to send me to prison, Your Honor, whenever you are ready. Thank you for listening to me. I'd like to express my thanks to my attorney, Mr. Jeffrey Samek. . . . I hope he understand the great deal of pressure I was, and I don't know why I feel so calm now. I'm about to be sent to jail. I am not nervous. I'm scared. I don't know why, but I feel calm.

"I like to thank you, Your Honor, too, for giving me the opportunity to express myself, and I hope that what I say today doesn't stay within our local newspapers and is forgotten soon.

"I hope that it makes an impact on the lawmakers and prevent this from happening to other human beings.

"Let's love each other a little bit more. And let's improve our system and believe in rehabilitation.

"Thank you very much."

Frank had spoken for exactly two hours.

It took Judge Newman less than two minutes to sentence him to fifteen years in the state penitentiary.

Without parole.

23

The fresh-faced coed/camp counselor perched on the witness stand and studied her feet self-consciously, occasionally sneaking a peek at the two broad Irish faces that beamed at her from the prosecution table and the dark and brooding ones that flanked the defendant.

Frank Fuster sat erect, studiously solemn, pen poised over a legal pad on which, for nine days, he would scribble copious notations on the parade of men and women from which Hogan, Casey, Samek, and Von Zamft would attempt to select a jury of his "peers." Bespectacled, besuited, and clean-shaven, having once again discarded the black moustache he had cultivated and harvested continuously over the past year, Fuster cut a fine figure at the defense table.

He wouldn't have missed *voir dire* for all the tea in China.

Whether Samek thought it in his best interest or not.

Frank's black eyes penetrated the timid young lady, who looked as though she might have missed piano practice in order to be here today. He did not blink, lest she glance up from her shoes and miss his "communication" with her.

"The power of the mind," Frank Fuster once wrote to Iliana, "is very big."

All eyes in the sparsely occupied courtroom were trained on the pedestal where sat the first unsuspecting potential juror.

"All we're trying to do," the kindly, white-bearded magistrate was explaining, "is find a jury who's fair and impartial to hear this case. . . .

"Have you heard of the case of the *State of Florida* versus *Francisco Fuster Escalona* or *Iliana Fuster?*"

"The names are familiar."

"How are they familiar?"

"I've heard the names, but I don't remember in relation to what things." She squirmed uneasily, as if cornered by a pop quiz for which she had not studied.

416

"Does *Country Walk* mean anything to you?" inquired Judge Newman.

The young woman's blank and puzzled eyes suddenly focused on the rows of men and women seated in the gallery opposite her, who studied her like a specimen on a slide.

Maggie Fletcher and company.

And a man with a ponytail.

Recognition crossed her face. Then alarm.

Yes, said the girl. She knew about Country Walk.

Voir dire was off to an unpromising start.

It was going to require considerable effort on the part of the court to find eight men and women—six regulars and two alternates—in Dade County, sufficiently oblivious to the goings-on in Courtroom 4-2 to sit in open judgment of the notorious Country Walk baby-sitters.

Now more so than ever.

Anyone who might have slept for the past year through the conspicuous waves of news coverage that erupted with the regularity of the irregularities in the case was not likely to have escaped the headlines of the past two weeks:

"Fuster lawyers to question children"

"Competency tests set for Iliana Fuster"

"Babysitter competent to stand trial"

"Fuster breaks down at hearing"

"Be strong, Frank! Be strong like your mother!"

"Judge seeks Bar probe of Fuster lawyer"

"Judge finds Fuster competent to stand trial"

"Parents tell horror tales at Fuster hearing"

"Fuster denies abuse charge, says he never babysat"

"Fuster sentenced to 15 years for 1982 assault"

Country Walk once again, as the summer before, consumed large and leading portions of ink and airwaves.

Nonetheless, Judge Newman was disinclined to put the Country Walk show on the road without first conducting a thorough search through the local jury pool for eight men and women who could presume the Fusters innocent until proven guilty.

Eight individuals who had not seen the repeated broadcasts of the children's interview tapes, which masked the children's faces but not their words—or their hands, which deftly caused dolls to copulate with the precision of a marriage manual.

For nearly two weeks, Hogan, Casey, Von Zamft, and Samek waded through a pool of some two hundred unsuspecting citizens of Dade County, each cut like cattle from the herd and placed on the witness stand for inspection by the adversaries.

Most displayed instant recognition of the two magic words.

Many had already formed an ironclad opinion.

A few voiced it in no uncertain terms.

"Well," drawled one sweet young thing who looked Frank Fuster in the eye. "I kinda go along with what my Daddy says.

"I think we should hang him."

But they did find eight upon whom all agreed—eight who knew little enough of the highly publicized but inadmissible evidence in the case to presume Frank Fuster's innocence. Eight not so tainted by the welling backlash of "witch hunt" and "child abuse hysteria" to deny his guilt when presented with an irrational doubt made to sound reasonable. Eight for whom the year-long daycare scandal remained vague headlines that bore too little—or too much—relevance to their lives to cause them to linger over details.

Four men and four women.

Three were under the age of twenty-two.

Three had children. Grown children.

And not one of them knew what they were getting into.

The crime, John Hogan would later tell them, was "beyond imagination."

Even his own.

• • •

August 21, 1985

Dear Mr. Hogan:

A specific polygraph detection of deception examination was administered to Iliana Fuster on this date relative to her knowledge of Frank Fuster being sexually involved with children at the Country Walk Babysitting Service in Miami, Florida.

The following relevant questions were asked during the administering of the examination:

1. Did you see Frank Fuster expose his penis to any of the children at the Country Walk Babysitting Service? (Answer—YES)

2. Did Frank beat you numerous times? (Answer—YES)

3. Did you see Frank Fuster place his mouth on the vagina of any of those children? (Answer—NO)

4. Did Frank Fuster take ahold of you sexually while the children were watching at the Country Walk Babysitting Service? (Answer— YES)

5. Did you ever observe Frank Fuster playing games with those children, during which time they would remove all of their clothing? (Answer—YES)

EXAMINER'S REMARKS

The subject's responses while attached to the polygraph instrument were indicative of truthfulness in her answering to questions one, two, four, and five. Her responses were indicative of deception in her answering to question three.

During the pretest discussion, she stated she had consumed [Motrin] for menstrual pains on the night prior to this examination and again on the morning of this examination. Her responses were somewhat subdued, but appeared to be adequate.

She stated she had observed Frank Fuster sitting on the floor wearing only his undershorts while playing with one or more of the children. She first stated she had only observed him from the backside while he was moving in a manner which appeared that he was sexually touching one of the children. Later, she acknowledged his penis was exposed during this period of time. Her responses were indicative of truthfulness to this statement (question one) during the testing procedure.

She stated that on one occasion she had observed Frank kiss one of the children all over his body, including his penis area.

During the discussion she stated Frank Fuster had beaten her on numerous occasions and her responses were indicative of truthfulness to this statement. She said she was always very frightened of him. Her polygraph responses were indicative of deception to her denial of seeing Frank Fuster placing his mouth on the vagina of any of the children at the Country Walk Babysitting Service.

While discussing question four, she stated Frank had "grabbed her breast" and other intimate parts of her body through her clothes, while some of the children were watching. Her responses were indicative of truthfulness to this statement.

She said that on one occasion Frank had asked her to change the wet diaper of one of the young boys and had then required her to take hold of the boy's penis.

She also stated she had observed Frank Fuster playing games with the children while they would remove all of their clothes. She said he had played the music loud and they would jump and dance around waving their clothes over their head.

Based on the subject's polygraph responses and comments, it is the examiner's opinion she was truthful, with the above exception.

A second examination was administered during which the following questions were asked relative to her personal involvement with the children at the Country Walk Babysitting Service:

6. Do you remember ever placing your mouth on the penis of any of the children at the Country Walk Babysitting Service? (Answer—NO)

7. Did you at any time place your mouth on the penis of any of those children? (Answer—NO)

8. Did you ever place your mouth on the vagina of any of those children? (Answer—NO)

9. Did any of the children at the house ever put their mouth on your vagina? (Answer—NO)

10. Did you sexually play games with any of those children during the time when they would remove all of their clothing? (Answer—NO)

There was no indication of deception in the subject's responses while attached to the polygraph instrument regarding her answering to questions six through ten.

During the discussion, she denied ever placing her mouth on the penis or the vagina of any of the children at the Country Walk Babysitting Service and denied that any of the children had ever placed their mouth on her vagina. There was no indication of deception to these denials.

During the discussion, she stated she had seen Frank Fuster playing games with the children while they removed all of their clothes, but she denied personally involving herself in those games and there was no indication of deception to this denial.

Unless, of course, one counted the testimony of more than a dozen young eyewitnesses.

August 22, 1985

TO: FILE
FROM: Dan Casey
        Assistant State Attorney

Last night in discussions with Michael Von Zamft, possibly in a moment of frustration by Von Zamft, Michael clearly stated to the group present that if he has to go to trial he'll mistry the case in opening argument. Present at the time were Michael Von Zamft, myself, Christina Royo, [polygraph examiner] Dudley Dickson, and maybe John Hogan.

Michael Von Zamft's "moments of frustration" had grown more frequent and more intense since the week he lost the Georgia case, lost the coveted state appointment, and lost his love of criminal law—the week he hit rock bottom.

Just a week ago, during a deposition, Von Zamft had slammed his fist into a file cabinet with such force that Hogan was sure he'd broken every bone in his hand.

Even so, Von Zamft struggled to make the best of a horrendous predicament.

He had a guilty client.

He had, according to the State, no viable defense.

And the State wouldn't budge from its bottom line of seventeen years in exchange for Iliana's full and truthful disclosure.

Iliana had no intention of serving nine years in prison—what was left of a seventeen-year sentence once "good time" and "gain time" were subtracted.

And the State had no intention of tainting her testimony with too attractive an incentive. If Iliana wanted to make a deal, she would have to serve serious time, lest her words be portrayed as a means by which she purchased freedom.

John Hogan and Dan Casey were fully prepared to let the children speak for themselves.

Iliana's testimony would simply frost their already well-baked cake. It would be nice—very nice—to have an adult witness. But not at a cost that would render her an incredible one.

The State, though not anxious, was most willing to seat her right next to Frank.

And time was slipping away from Michael Von Zamft.

Jury selection had commenced on August 14—the day after Judge Newman handed his client's husband the maximum sentence allowed by law for violating his probation. Judge Newman had, for a second time, denied his motion to sever Iliana's trial.

For a week now, Von Zamft had interrogated prospective jurors as ruthlessly as witnesses for the prosecution—in marked contrast to Hogan, Casey, and Samek, who showered them with ingratiating respect.

If Von Zamft was trying to win any points on *voir dire*, it didn't show. Michael didn't need a fair and impartial jury.

What he needed was more time.

Iliana had passed her second polygraph in as many months, more handily than her first, having revised her answer to whether she might have "seen" Frank Fuster do anything improper with the children from "no" to "yes," and the needle giving the nod once again to the "truthfulness" of her assertions that she, herself, had done nothing out of the ordinary with her charges. There were, she admitted, one or two occasions Frank might have touched one of the little boys—never a girl—and she did seem to recall one occasion on which she herself was directed to touch a child while diapering him.

Nothing more.

But the State wanted "full and truthful" disclosure.

Nothing less.

And a jury was to be seated in less than a week.

• • •

"Do you understand that if you went to trial, and if you were convicted, you could be sentenced to as much as life in the state penitentiary? Do you understand that?"

"Yes, Your Honor."

On August 23, the day before the first anniversary of her arrest, and less than twenty-four hours after her second polygraph, Iliana Fuster stood before Judge Robert Newman to enter a plea of guilty to twelve of the fourteen counts of sexually abusing the children who attended the Country Walk Babysitting Service, the State having dropped one count of aggravated assault and one count of sexual battery on Steven Vickers, whose father, along with his father's employer, Arvida Corporation, was the subject of eight of the nine lawsuits filed on behalf of Fuster victims.

The Vickers family did not want four-year-old Steven participating in the prosecution. His mother, however, was to be called as a witness for the defense.

"All right," continued Judge Newman, who was once again dotting I's and crossing T's. "Has anyone forced you or threatened you in any way to enter this plea this morning?"

"No, Your Honor, no." Iliana's voice was soft and childlike, as she stood before the bench, her straight brown hair, unshorn for twelve months, gathered in a simple mid-back ponytail. A fringe of bangs had been added, but she had abandoned the ruffles and pinafores for a pair of slacks, a shirt, and a sweater vest.

Iliana was three months shy of her nineteenth birthday.

On the day of her arrest, she had looked near thirty.

Today, she looked not quite sixteen.

"Has anybody promised you anything . . . to enter this plea this morning?"

"No, they have not promised anything."

"All right, are you now taking or are you under the influence of any drugs, alcohol, medicine, or prescriptions?"

"No. I just took this morning a painkiller. . . ."

"Has that affected you in any way in . . . reference to what you're doing?"

"No."

Michael Von Zamft, who stood before the bench at Iliana's side, patting her shoulder, interjected, "It's for stomach cramps."

"All right," said Judge Newman. "Have you ever been treated by a psychiatrist or psychologist or spent any time in a mental institution . . . ?"

"Yes. . . ."

"Is that affecting you in any way in reference to what you are doing here this morning?"

"No, it's not. They're helping me."

"Do you understand exactly what you are doing here?"

"Yes."

"Do you understand you're entering a plea of guilty to these charges?"

"Yes."

"Do you further understand that there is a possibility that you could be sentenced to as much as life in the state penitentiary for these crimes? Do you understand that?"

"Yes."

"Let me go over with you some of the constitutional rights that you have and that you are giving up by entering this plea. I want to make certain that you understand everything I say. If you do not understand me, please stop me and confer with your attorney, who is standing next to you."

"I will. . . ."

"Do you understand by entering this plea you are giving up all of these constitutional rights?"

"I understand."

"Are you doing this of your own free will and because you feel it's in your best interest to enter this plea of guilty and receive whatever sentence the court gives you?"

"Yes, I am, Your Honor. . . ."

Sentencing was set for the end of November.

Iliana whispered to Von Zamft.

"I think Miss Fuster would like to say something to the court," he said.

"Judge, I would like you to know that I am pleading guilty not because I feel guilty, but because I think—I think it's the best interest. It's the best for my own interest and for the children and for the court and all the people that are working on the case. But I am not pleading guilty because I feel guilty or because I think I have a criminal mind. . . .

"There were circumstances . . ." Iliana stifled a sob. "I was raped at sixteen. I was taken away from my home and my school. My attorney said just that I am an unlucky person, but I just want you to know that I am pleading guilty not because I feel or that I know that I am—that I am guilty.

"I am innocent of all those charges. I wouldn't have done anything to harm any children. I have never done anything in my life.

"I have never seen such a case in my life before.

"I wasn't raised in an environment like it.

"I am innocent.

"I am just doing it—I am pleading guilty to get all of this over, and I think it's the best for the parents and for everyone. . . ."

The Country Walk parents who had assembled in the gallery on short notice of this unexpected turn of events bristled visibly. Iliana might not feel guilty. But their children did.

They had come to hear the whole truth.

Not half of it.

"There have been no promises made to you," said the perplexed Judge Newman. "I can give you as much as life in the state penitentiary or as little as I should so choose at the time of sentencing.

"I want to make sure you understand that."

"Yes, Your Honor, I understand. As I told you before, I am just doing it for my own good. I just wish I would never come back to this courtroom anymore. . . ."

"Thank you, dear lady."

John Hogan was engulfed by reporters as he exited the court-room. Was the prosecutor "surprised" by this unexpected turn of events? they inquired.

Hogan paused briefly in his march to the elevator and regarded the outstretched microphones with his trademark tight smile before offering one of his few public comments.

Very little surprised him about this case anymore, he said, trying to suppress his mouth's overwhelming urge to grin.

• • •

"Judge, I was appointed to represent Mr. Fuster, and it is no secret that he is displeased with me."

Jeffrey Samek was extraordinarily agitated.

"It's a record, and I think it's been broadcast in any media outlet that is available in Miami.

"Equally legend on the record are his repeated failures to follow my advice.

"Last Thursday, about 12:45, I visited Mr. Fuster in ICDC, where he is incarcerated, to tell him his wife has entered a guilty plea.

"I sat in a chair waiting for him to come to the interview room, which I estimate is about three feet by seven feet. He entered the room, slammed the steel door shut behind him, stood over me, glaring at me with his fist clenched, saying he'd get me for what I did.

"He said Von Zamft would also have to face him one day.

"Then he charged that I had conspired with Mr. Von Zamft and Mr. Hogan and Mr. Casey to effect his wife's plea, and he said, referring, I believe, to Mr. Von Zamft and I, 'You two forced her to plead guilty.'

"More or less simultaneously . . . I rose to try to leave. He first blocked my access to the door, then, when I reached for the door, he held it shut so I couldn't open it. . . .

"I started banging on the door to try to alert the attention of the guards, and he stepped away. I was able to open the door.

"Shortly thereafter, some guards did come and the door was opened, and I believe the guards stood adjacent to the door while I spoke to Mr. Fuster, which, you'll find out in a moment, was a very short visit.

"He continued to harangue me, accuse me, and, finally, to add insult to injury . . . he told me again, contrary to my advice, that he had written his wife another letter. . . .

"Friday evening, I went out to get copies of the evening edition of every newspaper that I am aware of that's published in Miami, in preparation of any possible motions for change of venue or to strike a jury panel in the light of the coverage of Mrs. Fuster's plea of guilty. And lo and behold, what did I find in the newspapers but my esteemed client had again acted contrary to my advice . . . and he held a press conference of sorts. . . .

"He didn't even have the courtesy to tell me he wasn't following my advice. . . ."

Jeffrey Samek's tone began to pitch from indignation to outrage. "It's all too obvious, Judge, that he neither trusts me nor respects me.

"He has assaulted me. He has threatened physical harm. I cannot advise him. I will not talk to him. I will not visit him. I will not sit at the same table with him.

"I will not speak to him privately. I will not discuss anything with him, because anything I discuss with him immediately appears . . . under bylines . . . or in Associated Press wire stories, on the television news.

"I am not going to sit close enough to him or whisper or congress in trial, because I am afraid he is going to stick his hands around my neck and strangle me. . . .

"I am now through.

"I have no attorney/client relationship with this man.

"I *cannot* have an attorney/client relationship with this man.

"He tells the court that he wants me, then he treats me like a piece of dirt. . . .

"He is playing this court like a fiddle.

"With all due respect, he is playing all of us like a fiddle. I am tired of being an instrument. . . .

"I absolutely refuse. There is just so much anyone should have to take. I was willing to take way more than anybody should have to take.

"I am not going to take any more."

Judge Newman begged to differ.

"In open court I advised your client not to have any press conferences, not to do anything without speaking with you, not to write any more letters.

"I'm not going to repeat these things again to your client. You have done . . . as much as, if not more than, anyone could possibly do for a client. But many clients will not listen to their attorneys. . . .

"It's a free country. I guess it shows how free it is. Every client can go against his attorney's advice. And that is what he is doing.

"But, no, I am not going to remove you.

"I am going to trial.

"And this man is going to stand trial like any other defendant. He has been given every single courtesy by this court that I can think of, allowing a speech of approximately two hours one day, and other matters. . . ."

Frank popped out of his seat. "Please, Your Honor, the defendant would like to reply."

Judge Newman regarded the defendant with weary annoyance.

"I just made a statement," he said firmly. "I am not going to accept a reply from you. I am ready to proceed. Mr. Samek will do the best he possibly can do under the circumstances."

Frank was not interested in whether Judge Newman would accept a reply from him.

"It's not fair that my attorney makes all these false allegations without giving the defendant a chance to reply."

Seizing the pregnant pause that followed as implicit permission to engage in dialogue with the court, Frank raced on.

"I had just—fifteen minutes ago I had heard the news that my wife pleaded guilty to crimes that she never committed. I was very depressed. I was very down for my wife.

"When he entered the room and told me to close the door, I tried to close the door. I couldn't because the chair was blocking it. . . .

"We talked to around ten more minutes, and I started crying. I got on my knees and on the floor and swore to this man that my wife is innocent. . . .

"Then, after that, I told him I sent a letter to my wife, and he said, 'You sent a letter to your wife?' And he got up and left. . . .

"But the reason why I do not trust Mr. Samek, not because of anything other than the lies he is coming to tell [you].

"If my own attorney says 'This man physically abuses me, verbally abuses me,' I know that is not true.

"How can I trust him? . . .

"But as it is right now, after my wife pleading guilty, you sentencing me to fifteen years in prison, my poor relationship with my attorney, my poor relationship with everyone against me, I do not stand one chance of proving that me and my wife are a hundred percent innocent of all of the false allegations that have been presented against us. . . .

"Mr. Samek wants to leave the case.

"He already collected my money and he wants out. . . .

"They want us to plead guilty. Since I refuse to plead guilty, he wants out of the case. . . . He cannot convince me to plead no contest.

"I want to go to trial because I am innocent.

"So he wants out of the case, and he is lying to you. I cannot be more clear about it.

"I have never threatened my attorney.

"I have never closed my fist at him. . . .

"I was in desperation. . . . That was my worst day in prison. Not one time have I dropped one tear because of myself, but because of my wife. . . . I know that she is innocent."

Jeffrey Samek squared his small shoulders and waded back into jury selection as though nothing had happened.

He would not ask to be removed again.

Today, he would seat a jury.

Next week, he would go to trial. Alone.

• • •

A steady late-summer downpour had left streets in two counties awash with vehicles stalled on main-arteries-turned-lakes, and the still-drizzling skies filled with helicopters bearing radio traffic reporters, who transmitted points of passage to morning rush hour commuters, several dozen of whom, on this day after Labor Day, had an appointment with destiny in Courtroom 4-2.

The trial of the year was about to begin—one year and one month since the day paradise went awry.

It seemed more like ten.

An election had been won, reputations lost. Babies had been born, and Dr. Joseph Braga had "died." Many of the players had changed, but the puzzle had become more complete.

Time had not banished the children's memories. It had simply allowed them to grow more articulate in expressing them—just as Dr. Laurie Braga had predicted.

The Bragas, in fact, were among the first arrivals to the Justice Building on this appropriately wet and dreary day when the heavy wooden doors to Courtroom 4-2 would slam in their faces. They had known all along that this day would come, when they ceased to be—as John Hogan called them—the "conscience" of the case and became, instead, witnesses for the prosecution, subject to exclusion from the visitor's gallery.

That didn't ease the pain of letting go.

And sending the children into the courtroom without them.

For the next five weeks, they would hover in the corridor outside, tending to frazzled parents who awaited their turn on the stand with knots in their stomachs that periodically sent many of them rushing to the rest rooms to vomit.

The children, Laurie noted as she calmed them for interminable hours prior to their testimony, were in better shape than their parents.

John Hogan stood at the prosecution table, assembling notes, papers, and exhibits—his mouth a horizontal crease across his face. The thirty-five-year-old prosecutor was tense and strained, though his face showed little of the enormous toll already taken by the escalating wars the State had waged daily just to bring Frank Fuster to trial.

Each twenty-hour workday brought a new circumstance that threatened to rock the foundation of the chain of evidence the State had intricately woven around the children.

The pressure was, he would remember for some time to come, "indescribable."

Hogan had lived Country Walk for ten months. He knew the children—some of them intimately. He knew their favorite colors, their favorite foods, their favorite toys. He knew what they wanted to be when they grew up.

He and Jason Harrison shared a birthday.

Hogan had come to know the children as a function of his job. But he had also come to know them as people. And even though much of his time spent with them did not include discussion of the Fusters, he couldn't push from his mind the things that had been done to them.

He could only hope and pray that what the system was about to do to them now wouldn't multiply their pain.

Hogan tried not to think about it.

He had a job to do.

Today, everything went on the line.

Daniel Casey stood to Hogan's left, reviewing the opening

statement he would deliver to the eight men and women who would, as of today, enter the nightmare that Frank and Iliana Fuster had created for them all.

Casey was keyed up, ready, and more than a little apprehensive about what he was about to do. In order to convince a jury that Frank Fuster had systematically abused more than a dozen children, he would first have to convince them that it had happened at all. To do that, he would have to force them to live the horror through the children's eyes. He would have to tear them from the comfort of the abstract and hurl them headfirst into the reality of a three-year-old child confronted with a semen-drenched penis in his mouth. It was cruel. But it was fact. Why didn't the children tell? Stop for a moment and walk in their shoes.

For nine months Casey had. It was possibly the most painful nine months of his life. Children. The tiniest of children. Like Hogan, he had grown to know them well—almost as well as his own Patricia, now eighteen months old, who for half her young life had seen little of the daddy who slipped into her room late at night to kiss her head as she slept and who would linger over her crib, silently apologizing for his absence from her life.

He would make it up to her, he promised. But there were other children—children she would never know—who needed him now.

And there was a man who must never be allowed to do this to children again.

Dan Casey approached the men and women who would decide Frank Fuster's fate with a welcome-to-my-home smile and began his legendary amble along the railing that separated him from the jury.

Brick by brick, he began to lay the foundation of the State's case. He told them about "a little community down South," a place called Country Walk.

"A nice little place . . . just like any other development in the United States until something happened when a gentleman by the name of Frank Fuster and his wife, a woman named Iliana Fuster, moved there and decided to open up a babysitting service. . . .

"That's really where this case begins, ladies and gentlemen. It begins back in November or December of 1983."

Casey unfurled the tapestry of his opening statement. Upon it he painted the parents. Nurses, doctors, lawyers, executives, an airline pilot, a stewardess, a cement-mixer, a schoolteacher. Nice folks who went about their daily lives much like anyone else.

And they had children, he said.

Bright, beautiful, full of promise.

Brendon, Crystal, Andy. And more. Many, many more.

"The children started having terrible nightmares about monsters, about being dead," ambled Casey. "Occasionally when the parents went to pick up their children the children would seem dazed. . . . They appeared like they were—the parents would say—like drugged.

"The children evidenced a lot of aggressive behavior. This began all of a sudden when they started going to the Fusters' house. And also, one other characteristic—the children started showing that they had sexual knowledge beyond their years, doing things and knowing things that little two-year-old and three-year-old boys and girls aren't supposed to do.

"From the convergence of all these signs, you and I can sit and talk, and you can pretty well get a darn good picture of what was wrong at the Fuster house. And as Monday morning quarterbacks, you can sit here and you can think, 'Well, darn it, why didn't these parents realize? Why let it go on? Why did they take their child back?'

"And that's a question that the parents have been asking themselves . . . many, many times since this case was disclosed.

"Some of the parents will tell you, 'Yeah, there came a point when it just got too suspicious, and I quit sending my child there.'

"A number of parents did this.

"The other parents, when interviewed, said, 'Well, not all of these signs occurred to every one of the parents at the same time.' You see, all these parents had one thing in common: they all sent their children to the Country Walk Babysitting Service. Aside from that, very few of them even knew each other except just to see each other on the street and see each other at the Country Center. Very few of them socialized with each other, and they really never had a chance to exchange notes. . . ."

Casey told them about the games. Ring-around-the-rosy, Simon says, duck-duck-goose—Fuster style.

"There was another game called the 'rock me, baby,'" he continued. "That's not a regular children's game.

"But it was at the Fusters' house.

"It was played like this: Frank would take off all his clothes—at least the clothes below the waist. And then he would take one of the littler children—say, a two-year-old boy—would take off his clothes and would sit that child in his lap and hug that child tight, and he would . . . sing 'rock-a-bye baby' like we all sing, and he would rock back and forth, rubbing his exposed penis up against the underside of that little boy. . . .

"There were other games," Casey continued. "I'll let the witnesses tell you about them. The other games frequently involved acts of oral sex, acts of masturbation.

"Frank Fuster—*this* Frank Fuster here—being both the recipient and the performer on little boys and little girls.

"There are a couple of more games that I think you need to know about—one game in particular that I want to tell you about for a special reason, because I want to prepare you for it. Because you are going to hear about it. The evidence is going to show up.

"One of them is the 'pee-pee' game and the 'ca-ca' game. During those games, Frank Fuster would urinate or defecate on little children—either in groups or by himself. Sometimes Frank Fuster would urinate or defecate upon Iliana in the presence of children. And this degradation of these little kids was so that Frank Fuster could get his enjoyment.

"Then there is one other game—in a way, possibly the most horrible of them all. And it ties into another theme I want to get into for a moment with you all.

"It was what the children remember as the 'Who loses their head?' game, part of a series of acts . . . to get these children to never, never . . . tell about what happened at the Fuster house.

". . . The 'Who loses their head?' game involved Frank making threats and maybe sometimes using props—some kind of blade or knife . . . or scissors or whatever he used at the time. He told the kids that if this ever got out—these children—they would die.

"The props sometimes involved monster masks for visual effect. . . . Sometimes it involved killing little birds—helpless little birds. Something these two-, three-, four-, and five-year-old children could associate with. . . .

"And above it all, with constant threats to these two-, three-, four-, and five-year-old children, threats that hit home, threats that they will die or even worse.

"Even worse.

"What is worse to a two- or three-year-old child is hearing their parents would be killed. . . .

". . . The children were taken to the Rape Treatment Center. . . .

They were examined by Dr. Dorothy Hicks, who has been the director of the RTC since it began in 1974.

"She examined them physically—and not surprisingly, found nothing was broken and nothing was torn. She will tell us exactly what that means. And she will also tell us exactly what that doesn't mean.

"But they also talked to Dr. Hicks's staff. . . . Many of the children talked to Dr. Hicks's staff about what had gone on at the Fusters'.

"The children were then taken to the state attorney's office. In that way, the prosecutors in the case would get what they needed to know. At the state attorney's office, the children talked to attorneys, or they talked to Dr. Joseph Braga and/or Dr. Laurie Braga.

"Doctors Braga are child development specialists who volunteered their time to help the state attorney's office interview the children.

"Because these children were just—so—small.

"We were trying to talk to two-year-olds, three-year-olds, four-year-olds, and five-year-olds.

"What the doctors did was they talked to the children and made the children comfortable. Then they talked to the two-year-olds at a two-year-old level. They talked to four-year-olds at a four-year-old level—got information from them about what happened at the Fusters'.

"They—the doctors—weren't doing therapy on the children. The doctors were there to do interviews with the children, as the doctors are developmental psychologists. They are not clinical psychologists who are licensed to do therapy. . . .

"That was how the children in this case—I think I referred to them as 'the babysitting customers'—how it . . . came to be known. But remember? There was another child in that house. Frank Fuster's son."

Casey told them about seven-year-old Jaime Fuster and his diseased throat.

Then he told them about "gripping fear."

"I don't use that term loosely, the 'gripping fear' that many of these children are having to this day that they are going to die. And when they wake up in the middle of the night and go into their parents' room and they don't know their mother is in the bathroom and their dad is in the living room reading, but the bed is empty, they scream horrible screams because they know it finally happened—their parents finally died because they told. . . .

"You will hear about those, and you will hear about the little two-and-a-half-year-old boy who is constantly trying to guide his little three-and-a-half-year-old sister onto his penis or constantly trying to spread her legs and lick her vagina.

"You will hear about the little tiny baby—she was a pretoddler, couldn't walk yet, couldn't toddle yet. She crawled up behind her little two-year-old sister after the little sister had sat in the shower and was drying herself off. She went up and started licking her anus.

"All of these behaviors mean something, ladies and gentlemen.

"Maybe any one of these things will cause us to pause. Maybe it's natural; maybe it's something you can't consider one at a time; you have to consider them on the average because, remember I mentioned that the Country Walk children had one thing in common: they went to the Country Walk Babysitting Service. But they also have another thing in common. They are all showing us signs that something very, very, very different had gone on at the Fuster house."

Casey proceeded to read the charging document aloud to the ashen-faced jurors.

By the time of trial, the State had narrowed down Frank Fuster's nine-month carnage to sixteen separate counts.

He was charged with eight sexual batteries and seven lewd and lascivious assaults on Jason and Joshua Harrison, April Lancaster, Steven Vickers (whose charges, as in the case against Iliana, would be dropped), Crystal Fletcher, Andy Pierson, Chad and Missy Herschel, Bonnie Martinez, Brendon Prince, and Jaime Fuster.

The final (and most creatively drafted) count was a charge of aggravated assault that incorporated a variety of acts committed on a total of twenty-one children, charging that Francisco Fuster Escalona, "on numerous occasions," threatened them by wearing masks, displaying weapons and making verbal threats; played games "which consisted of, but were not limited to" dancing naked, fondling sexual organs, defecating and/or urinating in the children's presence; administered drugs; confined them "against their will" in closets and bathrooms; and induced them to engage in coproghagy and/or coprophilia (the consuming of excrement).

By Florida's "Williams Rule," under which the aggravated assault was filed, the State had to prove only one element concerning any one child in order to obtain a conviction.

The curiously worded assault charge listed the children by initials only (as did the other charges), and served as a catchall to circumvent a problem unique to child witnesses of tender years: if a witness offered into evidence any crime not charged, the State would have a mistrial on its hands. And the prosecutors could not be entirely sure which of the hundreds of stored memories the children might recall on their day in court.

Of the twenty-one children named in the charging document, six were infants and toddlers who had been named by the remaining fifteen eyewitnesses. And of the fifteen who had supplied statements during the taped interviews, only eight were willing and able to testify.

Eight who would speak for the more than fifty who, the State had finally determined, had attended the Country Walk Babysitting Service, the majority of whose parents did not wish to be "involved."

• • •

Under the current circumstances—which included certain matters having to do with the Florida Bar Association and certain well-publicized problems with his client, from whom he had three times in as many weeks attempted to disentangle himself—Jeffrey Samek would undoubtedly rather have been just about anywhere on this day after Labor Day than in Courtroom 4-2, seated next to Frank Fuster.

But the jury didn't know that.

And if Jeffrey Samek didn't mean every word of his opening statement, he never let on. Frank Fuster could have found no more zealous an advocate than the little man who squared his shoulders, marched to the jury box, and spoke on his behalf.

"Now, right from the start as we discuss this, I want you to know that I agree with Judge Newman and the government that child abuse crimes are among the most heinous, atrocious, revolting, disgusting crimes anyone could conceive of.

"That's not the issue here.

"We all agree that those crimes are very unpleasant. And I am equally convinced that the evidence will show that no child abuse was committed in this case.

"The incidents did not take place.

"I believe the evidence will show that Mr. Fuster is not guilty of anything. Not anything whatsoever.

"Speaking of Mr. Fuster, I know . . . that you all understand and it is agreed that Mr. Fuster has constitutional and protective rights not to testify in his defense. . . .

"Although he has a right to remain absolutely silent, just to sit there as he is sitting now, from now until his trial is over, he will take the witness stand. He will swear to tell the truth and he will testify. He wants you to get an opportunity to view him, to see him speaking, to see him react to cross-examination, and to hear him tell you that he did not molest any of these children that he is accused of molesting. Frank Fuster has nothing to hide, and he wants you to hear the truth. . . .

"We will point out to you some of the things that, for whatever reason, [Dan Casey] chose not to tell you, that I believe the evidence will show. First of all, I would like you to know just as sort of a background how I can make that kind of prediction; I'm not a psychic. I don't have a crystal ball. I presume the government has no crystal ball.

"The rules of criminal proceedings allow the attorneys in the case to take sworn statements from anyone with information about the case, so it's pretty much of a general rule. I have already spoken, as has the government, with just about everyone who will testify for you from the witness stand.

"Now, unless they, for one reason or another, significantly change their testimony from what they have already said, from what they say in court, we have a pretty good idea of what we can expect them to say.

"Now, the government told you that the children involved in this case were interviewed by Joseph and Laurie Braga. Well, that is correct.

"The children were interviewed by Joe and Laurie Braga repeatedly. Ad nauseam, if you will.

"Just who are Joe and Laurie Braga?

"They are unpaid, full-time workers for the state attorney.

"Joseph Braga is not a psychologist. He has a degree in education. He is not licensed by the state, Miami, Dade County. . . . He is not a member of the American Psychological or American Psychiatric associations."

Samek would later, in closing arguments, apologize for this "error" before the jury.

"Laurie Braga is a psychologist. She also is not licensed in this state. She doesn't even have an occupational license. She has a bachelor's degree in special education, and to get that degree she took no courses in child sexual abuse. She has a master's degree in special education with no specialty in child sexual abuse. She has a

Ph.D. in learning disabilities, but she spent no considerable amount of time getting that degree working with sexual abuse.

"They interrogated these children, as I said, repeatedly. Jason Harrison was interrogated five times in five days, six times in nineteen days. Jaime Fuster was examined at least four times and on one of those occasions for more than five hours in one day. April Lancaster was interrogated at least four times, one time by Jason Harrison. Crystal Fletcher, Steven Vickers, Andy Pierson, and many of the others were interrogated more than five times."

Hogan and Casey bristled silently from the prosecution table, unable either to correct the defense attorney's faulty mathematics or to explain that the vast majority of the children's encounters with the Bragas had occurred at either their request or their parents'.

"Now, Mr. Casey indicated to you that each of these children had previously indicated that they had been abused. Well, every single child alleged to be a victim in this case has also denied it—also denied ever being a victim of Frank Fuster. Jason Harrison has denied he was abused. April Lancaster has denied she was abused. Jaime Fuster has denied being abused. Jaime Fuster denies he was abused and continues to deny he was abused until Joseph Braga accused him of having gonorrhea and accused him of lying and after telling him that he could only get gonorrhea if someone put his penis in his mouth.

"You will hear all of this.

"You'll hear that the Bragas asked these questions of these children to pretend they accepted what the children said. . . . You will hear that the Bragas had missed what appears to me to be obvious fantasies . . . pretending without questioning subsequently the credibility of the reporter who had given them this obvious fantasy.

"You will hear that they named dolls that they work with on numerous occasions, injecting the name Frank Fuster into the conversations before any of the children had mentioned word one about Frank Fuster.

"You will hear that on the occasions that these children were using these dolls, playing with these dolls—because that's what children do with dolls.

"They play with them. They fantasize with them.

"On the occasions that these children had played with the dolls, you will hear that on many of these occasions the Bragas were not satisfied with the names that the children had given them. . . .

"Well, you can determine for yourself whether [these dolls] are really anatomically correct or just some kind of facsimile, if not entirely correct. But what is different about these dolls, and what I think you will see from the evidence, is that these children were called to see what was different about the dolls. . . .

"This was called to their attention. What attracted them about these dolls was that the doll had a penis, an anus, or breasts.

"It's like a marketing strategy with these dolls.

"When a company markets a doll, they don't say, 'This doll is the same as every other doll that has been marketed,' and hope that people will go out and buy it anyway. They had something different about this doll that no other doll has ever had. The doll may wet. The doll may cry. One doll may wave. One doll may even talk. And they hope that you are going to buy it because your child will be attracted to what's new about it.

"Well, I think the evidence will show that what these children were attracted to about these dolls was what was new about them. They had never had a doll before that had a penis.

"You will hear that the Bragas praised these children when they complied with the Bragas, and perhaps worse than that—because certainly these children needed some positive reinforcement—but worse than just giving them positive reinforcement and praising them when they said what they wanted to hear, you will hear them disbelieve and give them negative reinforcement when they didn't give an answer they wanted, in fact. . . ."

Samek continued to list the litany of horrors perpetrated by the dark and dangerous Bragas. Leading questions. Multiple-choice questions. Distortion.

"Now, the government wants you to believe all the allegations these children eventually made about being abused. Now, these are children who also said that they ate heads, sipped ants through straws, saw doody monsters, broke a door into pieces, started playing sex games several years before anyone alleges Frank Fuster even knew any of these children.

"If, in fact, the children really did know him.

"Rode on sharks and whales, had gone to college. These three-, four-, five-, and six-year-olds saw pee-pee and ca-ca devils coming out of the toilet.

"Now, the government wants you to believe the accusations of sex abuse, but you will hear one of these parents—Jill Vickers—tell you that when her son told her that Iliana Fuster had kissed his penis she didn't believe him.

"Not because this was some ridiculous, startling accusation that she didn't want to bring herself to believe. She will tell you that she didn't believe him because he often made up stories. He often fantasized. He often substituted the names of people when he was telling stories, and he often engaged in innocent sex play typical of all children with his siblings.

"She didn't believe him.

"The evidence will show that she didn't believe him because it is not believable. The government wants you to believe the allegations that videotapes, movies, and still photographs were made and shown to these children, as were similar films and tapes of other children.

"You will hear that no video, no camera equipment, was ever found in Mr. Fuster's house, and Mr. Fuster will tell you that he had no movies or tapes of any pornographic nature. . . .

"You will hear that several hundred photographs were confiscated and that undeveloped films were confiscated. None contained any pictures of anything remotely considered child pornography.

"You will hear that this 'den of sin'—the Fusters' house—was visited unannounced by state authorities while Mrs. Fuster was babysitting and Mr. Fuster was attending to his decorating business. . . .

"You will hear that these people found no cameras or nothing unusual.

"You will hear the Fuster home was visited by the Department of Health and Rehabilitative Services (HRS) for the sole purpose of checking on the babysitting service. You will hear that that visit was unannounced.

"Mrs. Fuster had no way of knowing that these people were coming, no way she could prepare for any visit, and you will hear that these HRS workers found nothing unusual.

"You will also hear that, at the State's insistence, Frank Fuster was tested for gonorrhea. And you know what? He didn't have it.

"You will hear, as I said, that most of the interviews with these children were taped, and I hope you get an opportunity to see the tapes. If you do see them, I ask you to please study them closely . . . the techniques that were used, the way the questions were asked. I want you to note the leading questions, the choice of questions, and the answers from the children.

"You will also hear from the defense. Mr. Fuster will tell you that, absolutely without any question whatsoever, he did not commit any of the acts that he is alleged to have committed. . . .

"The testimony of these children has been so tainted by the repeated interviews that what they say is unreliable. We cannot tell you whether or not they are telling the truth, they are telling you what happened, but we can tell that what they are saying is not reliable. It's unreliable because the children themselves have been so confused by the repeated interviews that they don't know what they sound like.

"They are not at fault.

"I am not saying the children are at fault. They are not lying. They may believe that what they are telling is the truth, but they no longer really know. . . .

"Ladies and gentlemen, you promised when you were selected as jurors, you made a pact with the court that no matter how serious the charges, no matter how revolting, disgusting the allegations sounded, you could give Frank Fuster a fair trial. . . .

"You promised that you would base your verdict on the evidence and nothing else. You promised that you would not base your verdict on emotion. You promised that you would require that this government would prove beyond a reasonable doubt.

"You promised that you would not succumb to the pressure of finding Mr. Fuster guilty because he is charged with a heinous crime. . . .

"I assure you I have that promise. I am sure you will give us your undivided attention as you have all morning, and I am sure that when you have heard the evidence you will be convinced Mr. Fuster is innocent.

"Thank you."

With that, Jeffrey Samek returned to his chair beside Frank Fuster, who had nodded approvingly throughout his counsel's lengthy monologue. Occasionally, he would catch a juror's eye and bob his head up and down some more. See, now doesn't that make sense? he seemed to be saying. See how the children were caused to tell these terrible lies against me?

Throughout the trial, Frank courted the jury like a persistent suitor. He made eye contact with each one personally.

He smiled. He shrugged. He rolled his eyes in exasperation.

Sometimes he looked heavenward, seeking mock deliverance from this travesty called American justice.

And each time his son's name was mentioned, he cried.

When he wasn't playing *to* the jury, he played *for* them, ever mindful that the TV camera to his rear was in a position to capture the expressions that played across the right side of his face. The one with the scar.

He sat in rapt attention, solemn, seemingly absorbed in the witnesses' testimony, leaning forward over a yellow legal pad upon which he scribbled steadily, his demeanor implicit that these were revelations of great import that must be brought to Mr. Samek's attention immediately. When he finished a sheet, he would tear it off the pad, flatten it on the desk in front of him, and precisely fold it into halves, then quarters, then eighths, until it was a small and neatly pressed rectangle—a ritual that apparently required his undivided attention. Then he would throw it away.

Most of Frank's copious "notes" were little more than compulsive doodles.

• • •

The State had scratched onto its dance card about two hundred witnesses, of which fewer than forty eventually would be called.

There would be more than one hundred exhibits, including birth certificates and enlarged photographs mounted on foam backing that the prosecutors planned to flash before the jurors each time a witness referred to any child by name—a pointed reminder that the initials M.K.G. on the charging documents belonged to a four-month-old infant named Melissa—the "little brown baby" upon whom the Fusters, the children would tell them, frequently deposited their waste. Or that the precocious nine-month-old who grinned from the displayed photograph was James Lee, who was hospitalized immediately following each of his two visitations to the Fuster home with a raging fever, and who, his mother would tell them, at the age of two-and-a-half, could now speak only one of the four words he had mastered prior to the Fuster visits—"Da-da."

His developmental "arrest" in the area of speech, a string of specialists had informed her following batteries of neurological tests, was the result of severe psychological "trauma" and not physical defect. Vera Lee would never know why her son became hysterical upon viewing the color red, or why his cheerful play sometimes abruptly disintegrated into panicked screams—the same ones that reverberated through her home at three and four o'clock in the morning.

Neither would James Lee.

For even if his wall of silence could be broken, his memories were not retrievable. They would remain inexplicable glimpses of terror of unknown origin.

His experience at nine months of age had placed him in purgatory. He was too young to remember.

But on a primal level, he could not forget.

Additional pictures were to be pulled from the State's hat—circumstantial in nature, but corroborating the children nonetheless. One showed a couple wearing fright masks, playfully kissing while posed on a sofa in the Fusters' living room—a man and woman identified months before by Jaime as his father and his father's child bride. Frank was expected to testify, as he had at his probation violation hearing, that the only mask he owned would be considered "frightening" only "to Republicans."

"It's a mask of Jeemy Carter," he had grinned.

Another curious snapshot was a rear view of a woman at the Fusters' kitchen sink, alongside Jaime. He had been posed lifting the back of her skirt to reveal her panties, which were heavily soiled with what appeared to be either menstruum or feces.

Posteriors, in fact, comprised a large portion of the Fusters' collection, many of them tightly framed by telephoto lens as Frank's unsuspecting "models" paraded past him at the beach. Curiously, the 35mm camera that had produced Frank's "keepsakes" was among the items missing when Donna Meznarich executed the search warrant on the night of his surrender.

Yes, he owned such a camera, he would testify, but it had been "stolen" two days before he was jailed, on the night Bobby Dean showed up with a gun and Frank fetched the camera to "memorialize" the activities on his front lawn, as "the law" loaded the enraged father into a police cruiser.

No photo equipment of any kind was ever recovered from the Fuster home.

There was also a blown-up diagram of the floor plan of the Fuster home, with which the jury would become as familiar as their own. The prosecutors wanted to acquaint them intimately with the scene of the crime, in which the master bedroom from which many parents saw children and Iliana frequently emerge was on the opposite end of the house from the "play area," which, Frank had told parents, he had personally constructed to meet HRS specifications.

Also to be entered into evidence was a leather thumbcuff with metal spikes.

And a small wooden cross.

Choreographing the chains of evidence presented a logistical nightmare in which the pieces of the enormous and complicated puzzle were to be assembled before the jury in a coherent and memorable structure.

Hogan, Casey, and Shiffrin were notoriously meticulous case organizers—the quality that had inspired Janet Reno's eye to fall on them from the beginning. The precise state attorney was as impressed by order as she was by success.

Of the three, Hogan was known as "the worrier," who anticipated twenty problems for each that came to pass.

He prepared for any eventuality.

Should Jeffrey Samek choose to dwell at length on the subject of children's memory or fantasy—a subject about which Dr. Coleman appeared to know as little as Dr. Ralph Underwager did about the Red Chinese—the State would simply summon the leading national expert in each specialty.

None of whom made regular journeys into courtrooms.

But unless Dr. Lee Stewart Coleman's script was appreciably altered from the one he had delivered a fortnight ago at the hearing, Hogan considered himself well-covered in those areas by the Bragas.

In terms of child development, he was already walking in with a loaded deck. Samek still did not comprehend the depth of the credentials he and Von Zamft had for more than a year dismissed, which dated back to the sixties, when the then–Laurie Davis and professor Joseph Braga headed the American team that trained graduate students in child interviewing techniques for international child development research studies.

Hogan anticipated possible defense moves in other areas as well. Should Jeffrey Samek open a door which suggested (as had Frank's 1982 psychiatric report) that his client did not fit the "profile" of a child molester, FBI agent Kenneth Lanning, the U.S. Justice Department's mass child sex abuse expert, was fully prepared to offer evidence which suggested that Frank Fuster most certainly did.

Thirteen mothers would testify, the prosecution having determined that the horror was best reflected in the women's eyes and not the men's. The volatile Bobby Dean was the only father called to the stand, being one of three parents who would testify that they had seen video equipment in the Fuster living room.

The parents were allowed to testify as to the circumstances of their visits to the babysitter's house and to describe various aspects of the children's behavior.

Shari Herschel was one of three who explained how her son— during the time he went to the Fusters'—had asked her to engage in sexual play. ". . . as I was putting his diaper on, he took my hand and put it on his penis and said, 'Mommy, rub my pee-pee.' "

Jeannie Pierson told the jury that Andy came home one day with a fiery red rash on his penis that she (the mother of three) found so unusual that she called her husband into the room to examine it, and then her doctor, who treated the persistent "rash" for weeks before it was cured.

Maggie Fletcher related her daughter's two-week transformation while attending the Fuster babysitting service, describing how one of Crystal's inexplicable tantrums led to the destruction of her most beloved toy, a dollhouse, which she angrily threw out of a second-story window. Maggie was incensed that the rules of evidence would not allow her to relate her daughter's repeated conversations with her about the eating of excrement and was determined that the jury know. When questioned about whether her daughter displayed any "unusual" behaviors, Maggie inserted the skillfully worded response, "Yeah, she doesn't know if it's 'normal' to eat feces."

The private therapists, however, who had been working with four of the children, were excepted from these rules of hearsay and were able to bring to court the statements the children had made in the course of their "diagnosis and/or treatment," as the old statute read.

The rules of evidence *did* allow the parents to relate words the children spoke when they screamed in the night, "excited utterance" being one of the few exceptions to the hearsay rule. Jackie Harrison was allowed to tell about the previous Easter when Jason awoke screaming, "Don't tell! Don't tell! We're all gonna die!"

But Jason's words, spoken by his mother, could not match her face when she finished her testimony with her recollections of the Fourth of July picnic with the Fusters.

"They told us when we went out on the boat that they were thinking about getting out of the babysitting service. That they would make exceptions for us because we were their friends."

Jackie's eyes brimmed with tears; she struggled for composure as she looked directly at the jury and said softly, "And they raped my babies."

• • •

A human screen separated five-year-old Missy Herschel from Frank Fuster as she made her momentous trek from the entrance of Courtroom 4-2 past the defense table on her way to the witness stand, her mother gripped in one hand, a stuffed seal named Sandy in the other.

Missy was a vision in her ruffled pinafore, her platinum mane cascading beyond her shoulders. She was very proud to be the only child who was willing to testify live in this courtroom.

She was also scared to death.

Missy climbed up on the stand and glanced at Judge Newman, the man she knew would protect her from Frank. The little girl liked the kindly judge who had interviewed her in his chambers to determine her competency to testify. He had spoken to her gently. And he had told her not to be afraid.

She wasn't scared, she told Laurie just a few moments ago. It was important, Missy had said, for her to go into the courtroom and tell the truth, because it was important that the jury know what happened at Country Walk. And she knew what to do if she grew frightened or confused, she continued, because she remembered what Laurie had told her.

"I don't think Frank's lawyer will be mean to you," Laurie had said. "But if he is, you should turn to the judge and say, 'Judge, he's being mean to me.' If you don't understand any questions, you should say, 'I don't understand.' And if he tries to ask you a tricky question, just say, 'That's a tricky question. I don't understand.'"

Missy was now empowered. She knew the rules.

John Hogan approached the witness stand, positioning himself to block her view of Frank's eyes, which bored a hole through his back. Hogan couldn't shake the horrible dread that what might occur in this courtroom today could harm this lovely, innocent child.

Frank Fuster edged his chair to the far corner of the defense table and stared intently at the little girl.

Missy's eyes grew wide.

She asked if she could go to the bathroom.

Judge Newman said, sure.

"He keeps moving closer," Missy told her mother. "He keeps moving his chair."

Shari explained about the men in uniforms standing near Frank Fuster—the man who had once held a "saw" to her throat—and explained about their jobs.

When Missy returned to the witness stand, she checked for the reassuring uniforms. They were there. She was ready.

Hogan directed Missy through her testimony, gently probing, at first, for innocuous information, which she answered in crisp concise terms. She was a very composed little girl.

But as he steered toward *the* questions, her voice grew smaller, her eyes downcast.

The second time you went to Frank and Iliana's, did something bad happen?

"Yes."

Did you play games?

"Yes."

Could you tell us about the game?

"Yes."

What was the name of the game?

"Cut your head off."

How do you play "Cut your head off"?

"Frank asks everybody if they want cupcakes."

She sank so low in her seat she half disappeared.

Still, she didn't waver. Occasionally she glanced over her shoulder to make sure her mother was still seated behind her.

Missy, could you speak a little louder please?

"Frank asked everybody if they wanted a cupcake."

Then what?

"And then if you said yes, he'd say—he would put a knife up to your neck."

Then it was Samek's turn.

It was the first time he'd ever come face to face with the little girl, having abruptly lost interest in deposing children following his thrashing by the chief judge at the Third District Court of Appeals.

Frank's attorney approached the witness stand and said quietly, *Missy, do you mind if I sit down while I talk to you? I have been standing all morning.*

"OK."

Samek pulled a chair up to the witness stand and seated himself level with the blue eyes that peeked at him over the top.

My name is Jeff.
"Hi."
When is your brother's birthday?
"September twenty-second."
That's almost very close to yours.
"Right."
How old will he be?
"He is going to be four years old."
You both are going to have parties, or are you going to have a party together?
"We are going to have a party together."
Are you going to have it at home or are you going to go someplace?
"We are going to go someplace, but it is real close to us. It's where I go swimming."
Country Center?
"Yes."
Are you going to have a cake?
"Yes."
Are you going to have characters?
"Yes. We are going to have a clown."
Who is the clown?
"Minny."
Minny the clown. Do you remember when a policewoman came to your house and talked to you?
"Yes."
Do you remember that she sat down with you and she talked to you—just you and her, nobody else was there?
"I don't remember that."
Do you remember that she talked to you?
"Yes."
Do you ever remember telling her—the policewoman—if Frank ever touched you?
"No. I don't remember that."
Do you remember what you did tell the policewoman?
"No."
Do you remember that you told her he had the clothes off? At Iliana's house?
"I can't remember. . . ."
Did you tell her that you didn't take your clothes off?
"No. I didn't tell her that."

At school, did they ever tell you about good touching and bad touching?

"Yes."

Do you know what good touching is and bad touching is?

"Yes."

Do you remember that you told the police officer that Frank never touched you in a bad way?

"He did touch me in a bad way."

Do you remember that you told the policewoman that he didn't?

"No. I don't remember saying that because he did do it."

And so it went. Jeffrey Samek was on his best behavior.

There were trick questions. And confusing questions. But they were posed politely.

And Missy stood her ground. Even when she had to point Frank out in the courtroom and describe what he was wearing.

Hogan was so proud of her he almost burst. And as he led Missy out of the courtroom, John Hogan saw a vision he would never forget. Missy was positively beaming. She was no longer powerless in Frank's presence. She had taken her shot and beaten him.

Outside the courtroom, Missy pulled Hogan aside. "I need to talk to you," she said. "I want to see the judge again."

Hogan wondered at the appropriateness of such a request, from the judge's point of view, but figured there was no harm in asking.

Judge Newman agreed.

Missy insisted on going into his chambers by herself. She climbed up on a chair and faced the judge.

John Hogan peeked in and smiled.

That was how he would always remember Missy Herschel.

A blond and blue-eyed bundle engulfed by a chair, her legs propped straight in front of her. Not long enough to dangle.

Solemnly, she volunteered to accompany her private therapist, who was the next scheduled witness, into the courtroom and sit behind her like her mother had for her.

"So she won't be scared."

Judge Newman kindly advised that this would not be necessary.

John Hogan felt a great weight lift from his shoulders.

Missy had confronted—and conquered—her greatest fear. She had faced Frank Fuster and told everyone what he did.

He now knew that a child could go through the system and emerge better off for having participated in it.

If handled properly, it didn't have to rape them again.

Of the eight children the State would eventually call, Missy Herschel—a week shy of her sixth birthday—would be the only one to give live testimony from the stand, although three children under the age of four would be called to state their name and age for the court record, an arrangement with which Jeffrey Samek took vigorous issue.

"Judge . . . all they really want to do is parade another cute little dressed-up child in front of the jury so that they can see these children."

Daniel Casey replied, "I understand Mr. Samek doesn't like the fact that the victims in this case are children. I don't like the fact that the victims in this case are children, either. But I didn't pick the victims.

"Someone else did."

The little boy sat in his mother's lap, facing the defense table—a bow-tied cherub in a grey flannel Buster Brown suit, who solemnly answered the two questions posed by the State.

His name was Chad Herschel. And he was three years old.

Weeks shy of his fourth birthday, the highly verbal (and now clearly spoken) Chad had been strongly considered by the prosecutors as a candidate for more lengthy testimony. But the Bragas pointed out that, developmentally speaking, Chad had not yet reached the point of being able to apply the kinds of "rules" that had equipped his older sister to fend for herself under cross-examination.

Chad could tell his story, but he would be helpless to use the coping strategies so well assimilated by Missy. Instead of asking for clarification of questions that confused him, predicted the Bragas, he would be more apt to offer his best guess of what they meant. Samek could make him look like a fool.

Chad would be humiliated and his credibility challenged.

So it was decided that Chad Herschel, who had very much to tell, would be limited to this brief courtroom encounter.

Of which he felt very proud.

When Andy Pierson's turn came, he was immediately concerned that the microphone on the witness stand wasn't working. He had been told there was a microphone. He expected it would work. The determined Andy flipped the switch back and forth until it turned on with a screech.

That settled, he turned to face the prosecutor.

What's your name?

"Andy."

And then he saw Frank.

And your other name?

"I'm not gonna tell."

As Jeannie led her impertinent son past the defense table, Frank Fuster looked pityingly at him and then shook his head sadly at the jury.

See what they've done to this poor child?

Next came Brendon Prince, also now three, who was struck dumb at the sight of the man at the defense table whose anticipated presence his mother had failed to announce. She had hoped that maybe he wouldn't notice.

Brendon stared at his lap and said nothing.

The lap he occupied, however, was a reassuring berth. For Brendon's father wrapped his arms around him in warm and grateful embrace.

His son snuggled in.

For Roger Prince, "tomorrow" had finally come.

Not wishing to raise an appellate issue over the competency of the children, Hogan abandoned plans to call Joshua Harrison and Jeremy Martinez, two additional three-year-olds who, the judge had stipulated, could testify as to their names and ages.

The jury would come to know them only through their pictures and the other children's words.

The four remaining children—including Jason Harrison, who did not wish to have a jury staring at him should Jeffrey Samek again bring out his two-by-four—testified via closed-circuit television, another circumstance to which the defense offered strenuous objection, citing Frank Fuster's right to "confront" his accusers face to face, not on dual video monitors.

The age of electronics, for better or for worse, is upon us, ruled Judge Newman.

• • •

Four-year-old Bonnie Martinez gripped Dan Casey's hand as he led her into the cable-strewn judge's chambers that had, in the course of twenty-four hours, been transformed into what looked to Casey like the bridge of the starship *Enterprise*.

Frank Fuster, chaperoned by Jeffrey Samek and a guard, barged in to inspect the room as Bonnie gripped harder Dan's large and tensed hand. The prosecutor moved immediately to shield her until a bailiff hurriedly escorted the defendant from the room.

Bonnie scrunched on the judge's couch, next to Casey, who questioned her casually, his legs crossed, his arm draped behind her. She responded in single syllables, her voice at times falling to a whisper.

Where did Frank touch you?

Bonnie lifted the skirt of her red, white, and blue sailor dress and pointed between her legs.

Throughout her testimony, Frank Fuster pointedly ignored the video monitor upon which the little girl was displayed, and perused a religious pamphlet entitled *New Life*, as though whatever this particular witness had to say was of no interest to him, nor should it be to anyone else.

Jeffrey Samek declined to cross-examine the child.

"Judge, Mr. Fuster has instructed me not to cross-examine this witness because he feels, number one, that within the time that he is to speak with her, as opposed to the time that she had to speak with all the state agents, state attorneys, et cetera, he wouldn't be able to get her to tell the truth.

"Also, he feels—consistent with my defense—that anything they say is unreliable and whatever they were to tell me would also be unreliable.

"Mr. Fuster has instructed me not to cross-examine this witness."

Excused from further testimony, the little girl with the glossy black hair and freckled nose happily bounced out of the judge's chambers and into the hall.

"I wasn't scared," she told Laurie.

Indeed, she, too, looked very proud.

Jeffrey Samek did cross-examine the impudent Crystal Fletcher, now a sturdy five, who peered curiously at her former babysitter, displayed on the screen before her, his head in his hands, obviously weary of hearing more testimony plucked from the State's "truck of lies."

"What's he doing?" Crystal chirped, pointing at the television monitor.

"I don't know," said Samek. "Maybe he's got a headache."

Following her testimony, Crystal was greeted by a still-beaming Missy Herschel, who rushed to embrace her.

"I'm so proud of you!"

Crystal wrinkled her nose and giggled. "I'm proud of me, too!"

April Lancaster had been through no fewer than three therapists in the past year, and still was capable of "discussing" the Fusters predominantly with a pencil and an outline of the human body upon which she marked Xs at the places that Frank particularly liked to touch.

And she would not discuss it with men, her parents warned.

The prosecutors were confident that either of them could establish a comfortable relationship with April—even if it meant flying up to Gainesville for a few weekends to build a rapport with her.

The other kids had grown very fond of the prosecutors—Daniel Casey, who had never stopped viewing the world through the eyes of a child, and John Hogan, who was relearning how. They had no reason to believe that April would be any less accepting once she got to know them.

But April would have nothing to do with either of them.

They had to recruit a female prosecutor, whose only appearance in the trial was for the purpose of directing "Frank's favorite" through her testimony, which was brief and erratic, as the State had fully anticipated.

April Lancaster had not been brought before the jury because the Xs she drew on paper presented compelling evidence.

The State called for April for reasons more compelling than the words she could not speak. As John Hogan would later tell the jury in closing arguments, "I submit to you that what *you* saw from April Lancaster is as clear a scar of a crime as any bullet wound or knife wound. . . .

"What we saw was a *scar* that April was carrying. Because, as her blocking stopped—as it became closer and closer, and she was more able to talk about it—she became more and more deeply disturbed.

"That's a scar.

"That's a scar that didn't come from holding Laurie's hand. Or from looking at a doll. That's a scar that came from one very simple reason.

"Because *she* was Frank Fuster's *favorite*."

• • •

Dr. Joseph Braga climbed up on the witness stand prepared to go to war. For fourteen months he and Laurie had rolled over and played dead while the defense called their methods "spellbinding" and their credentials "alleged." Today he would set the record straight.

Today he would be qualified for the first time in the Eleventh Judicial Circuit as an expert on child development.

John Hogan settled in for a long but crucially important haul.

Could you please tell the ladies and gentlemen of the jury what child development is?

"The field of child development is one of the most unique in all of the areas of behavioral science . . . a field in psychology and education in which—sequentially—we now have well-established information that, across the world, all children develop in the same sequential way. . . .

"In terms of motor development, all children walk before they run.

"In terms of language development, children speak with one-word and two-word phrases before they speak in sentences.

"In terms of thinking—cognitive development—all children are able to understand concrete things that are there—that are very clearly there—before they can begin to understand abstractions like time, distances.

"In terms of social and emotional development, children learn to play by themselves before they are able to play cooperatively. . . .

"There is a sequence, a stage-by-stage set of behaviors that children go through as they develop. . . .

Do all children progress through those stages at the same rate?

"No, at different rates and different times . . . the same sequence at a different speed. Some kids run early. Some kids take a long time to run. Some kids toilet-train early. Some kids take a little longer. . . .

"The steps that you have to go through to develop before you run are the same across the world—are cross-cultural. . . ."

Is there a practical application for this information when it comes to interviewing children?

"Yes . . . if you know normally what three-year-old children can do, then in working with this child, you try and see if they can do things—if they are three years old—that three-year-old children do.

"If you find there are certain things they can't do, then maybe you might try and see if they can do a slightly lower level. . . .

"If he is not there, go to the stage before that. If he is not *there*, go to the stage before that because we know now from research what that sequence is. . . .

"There are certain things that a child may not be able to understand, and if you are asking them questions they don't understand, then you are not going to get information or you may inadvertently, through questioning them, cause them some harm. . . ."

Does child development affect the type of questions you ask children at different ages?

"Yes, it does."

How does it affect?

"Well, take language development. You, for instance, would not say to a two-year-old child, 'Did this happen in your presence?' because it's quite possible that all the two-year-old child knows about 'presents' is Christmas or birthdays. They may not even know Christmas, but they sure know when Mom and Dad or somebody says 'presents.' They start looking around for boxes to open up."

Dr. Braga did not take this opportunity to point out that "Did this occur in your presence?" was not uncommon verbiage used by law school graduates in questioning children and had, on at least one occasion he knew of, resulted in a child's (much older than two) being impeached on deposition. When she answered "No," the charges were dropped.

"Now, it doesn't mean you start out with language," Joe Braga continued. "With some children, you start off by motor development. You find out what their range of motor development is, what they do with their fingers. Find what they do with the large muscles of their body because that's an indication to you of where they might be in other areas. . . ."

Is the child's nonverbal behavior important in interviewing?

"Yes . . . it gives you information in and of itself. It gives corroborating information. It can tell you that the information that you may be getting from the child is emotional and you should back off before you do any harm. It can tell you that maybe the child's discomfort should lead you to ask more questions in a different direction. . . ."

Are there any characteristics which you identify which are shared by [confirmed victims of sexual abuse] despite individual differences?

"There are quite a few, and I might add that a number of characteristics are seen in every child, but they are characteristics that have been identified both in our research . . . and others' that occur with greater frequency among children who have been sexually abused than with children who have not.

"Some examples of them might be an inadvertent display and expression of sexual knowledge beyond a child's age. . . . So, certainly if you have a child who at age three has the knowledge of sexual intercourse, ejaculation, and oral intercourse, that's way beyond the expected experience of a three-year-old child. . . .

"Night terrors is another good example. Extreme modesty. Bed-wetting. That's a good example.

"If I can elaborate for a minute . . . no one is saying that any child who bed-wets is sexually abused, but if, for instance . . . you had a child . . . showing inappropriate sexual knowledge who is having night terrors, who is extremely withdrawn, and is also wetting their bed, you are now beginning to get information that makes this child look more likely to be a child you should explore more in terms of behavior and asking them questions about whether they might have been sexually abused. . . .

"Let's suppose you have five to eight of the characteristics . . . sudden eating disorder . . . a loss of appetite, swallowing problem, soiling of the underwear, regressive behavior . . . secretiveness . . . excessive masturbation, attempts to involve others in sex play, hostility toward adults or places that does not seem to be warranted. . . .

"I don't want anyone to get the impression that I am suggesting here that any one of these characteristics, or even any two or three of these, says, 'This is a child who may have been sexually abused,' but as a group, one taken together, me seeing children who have [sexual] information, sleep disturbances, fear of sleeping, excessive bathing, wanting to take a lot of baths, wanting to take a lot of showers, excessive dressing—putting on more than one pair of clothing, cleaning behavior, fear of separation. . . . Basically any sudden change of behavior . . . in a major area all of a sudden. . . .

"They have difficulty walking or sitting, pain and itching in the genital area . . . vaginal discharges . . . rectal bleeding. . . ."

Are any one of these signs determinative?
"No."

Jeffrey Samek took his turn at bat.
In your interviewing of children for the state attorney's office . . .would you invite them to pretend . . .then accept what the child says as fact?
"No."
. . . Would you dismiss things that obviously could not possibly be true without decreasing the credibility of the person or, for

example, if a child of two or a child of five told you they already have been to college?

"No, I would withhold judgment."

. . . Would you use leading questions?

"Yes. . . .

"There are different degrees of leading questions and quite clearly in a criminal investigation the more open-ended and less leading the question, the better. . . .

" 'Did John put his penis in your mouth?' is a leading question. 'Did John put anything in your mouth?' is a less leading question. 'Did anyone put anything in your mouth?' is even less leading. 'Did anything happen to you?' is even less leading. 'Hi, how are you?' is even less leading.

"I mean, the issue of leading is one of real degree, and quite clearly my answer is 'Yes,' but the less leading, the better. . . .' "

Doctor, you said on direct examination that you felt there was a basis for the interpretation of the drawings of children who had been sexually abused, say, under the age of seven.

"By me personally or by anyone?"

By you personally.

"Not by me personally."

By anyone?

"Yes, and my explanation to answer your question is, if a child were to make drawings, and as they did the drawings they told me what was going on in the drawings, why they were drawing the drawings, and what was in the drawings, then I will accept that as information.

"But if a child draws a drawing, then handed it to me, I would not say, 'Well, he used the color red, and that can be interpreted to mean this, and he put a star in the far right corner.' "

So, you could make your own interpretation of what the drawings represented?

"No, but with one exception I would consider it important information. If a child draws drawings of people without certain appendages or body parts, that would not necessarily prove something to me but might lead me to consider whether or not there might or might not be something to explore further.

"The reason for this is because in other people researching the area of child sexual abuse, it has been widely and repeatedly reported that children are very often leaving off body parts . . . or exaggerate a body part. . . .' "

Jeffrey Samek had no further questions, but John Hogan stepped to the witness stand to ask one more.

You haven't seen the drawing that has been done by Miss Herschel in this court, have you?

"No."

But the jury had.

It was a drawing of a man she called Frank, whose most predominant feature was a huge penis.

• • •

Jason Harrison, the last of the children the State would call, marched into the judge's chambers, his chin resting near his chest. In one hand, he clutched a stuffed turkey he had plucked from the children's interview room; with the other he patted the pocket in which he had deposited the rosary beads he had rooted out of his mother's bureau that morning.

In the car on the way to the Justice Building, Jason asked his mother to recite the "Our Father" with him.

Neither of them could remember the words.

Jason was pensive and quiet for the rest of the ride.

The last time he'd seen Jeffrey Samek, he'd been called a liar.

"Mom?"

"What, Jason?"

"What if they don't believe me?"

"The people who know you believe you. That's all that counts."

Jason did not dwell on the video monitor through which Frank stared at him. He was nervous and apprehensive, but like Missy, he extracted a measure of comfort from knowing the rules.

So when Jeffrey Samek repeatedly interrupted his testimony with objections (on grounds that he never explained), Jason knew what to do.

Did you ever play games when you went there? inquired John Hogan of his star witness.

"Yes."

What were the games like? Can you tell us?

"Objection!"

Jason looked expectantly toward the judge.

"Overruled," said Newman.

Jason turned back to Hogan. "Yes. Bad games . . ."

Was there anything different about these games than the games

you played in school or, you know, anywhere else?
"Objection."
Jason waited again for the judge to make his ruling.
"Overruled."
"They weren't normal games," answered Jason without missing a beat.
Why weren't they normal games?
"Because we would play them in a certain way."
How would you play the games?
"We would suck on penises."
Painstakingly, Hogan directed Jason through his testimony, which bore striking similarities to information the jury had already heard from the other children and their mothers.

The jurors displayed no more measurable reaction to the details of the assaults than they did to the circumstantial corroboration. But they listened intently.

When you were playing these games, did anyone ever come to the door?
"Yes."
What would you do?
"They would run in the room and dress up real fast. . . ."
Did they ever play any music there?
"Yes."
What music would they play?
" 'Thriller.' "
Who does "Thriller"?
"Michael Jackson."
Do you like Michael Jackson?
"No."

Jason, is there anything else that happened there that you think you'd like to tell the judge about? John Hogan knew how painful a chord he was about to strike.

Jason took a breath.
"About the babies," he said.
OK, what about the babies?
"They would, like, go to the bathroom on them and they would make them watch our games."
Anything else about the babies?
"No." Jason clutched the turkey tighter.
Hogan saw the boy's finger inching under its tail.
Did you ever do anything with the babies?

"Yes." Jason's finger pressed into the bird's anal cavity—an orifice that did not exist.
What was that?
Jason's head hung.
"Went to the bathroom on them."

Jason's shame gave way to apprehension as Jeffrey Samek approached for cross-examination. Jason knew the rules. He also knew from experience that "Frank's friend" didn't always follow them.

Samek, however, did not extract his two-by-four, for reasons he would later inject into the court record outside the jury's presence. "I did think in May, June, and July, and I thought in August, and I *do* think now [that what was done on deposition is] the more appropriate and probably more effective method to cross-examine this child. The only reason I did not do that is I consider myself under a restraint from the Third District Court of Appeals to do so."

Nor did John Hogan expect he would, with Chief Judge Alan Schwartz's dressing-down still ringing in his ears. Rather, Hogan wondered if the jury would grasp the significance that the questions posed by Samek were far more "leading" than any the Bragas would ever dream of asking.

And that they in no way "influenced" what the child had to say.

Frank didn't say anything when he wore the masks, did he? He just wore the mask and turned off the light?
"He wore the mask, turned off the lights, and scared people."
What would he do?
"He would tell them that they are going to die. . . ."
What about the pee-pee devil and the ca-ca devil that came out of the toilet?
"They told us about that."
Tell me about that.
"They would say every time they flushed the toilet they would come out."
What about the time they killed the cat?
"They didn't kill the cat."

Jason did not take this opportunity to remind the "forgetful" defense attorney that the cat he had mentioned a year ago was the one Jaime Fuster had boasted to have killed with the "hypnotizer."

• • •

It took Jason less than one hour to apprise the jury of what occurred in the Fuster home in explicit and consistent detail. But what he and the children had to say mattered little if the jury chose not to believe them.

And a jury, the prosecutors knew, would seize any excuse not to.

When it was over, the little red-haired boy who had, for more than a year, borne the weight of speaking for the children who could not, requested some time alone with his friend, Joe Braga.

"What's it been like for you?" asked Joe of the drama Jason had lived.

"It's been like *Stars Wars* and *Return of the Jedi*," said Jason, who had always been amused that grown-ups around the state attorney's office referred to the dark and brooding Abe Laeser as "Darth Vader."

"Who's John?" asked Joe.

"Chewbacca," replied Jason without hesitation. " 'Cause he's like a big teddy bear, and he protects me."

Dan Casey, Jason continued, was Obi-Wan Kenobi. The two video technicians who taped his interviews were R2D2 and C3PO.

Jeffrey Samek was Jabba the Hut.

And Frank was the evil emperor.

"I saw him today," he added. "And I'm not afraid of him."

Laurie was Princess Leia. "And *you*," he said, "are Han Solo 'cause you're Princess Leia's boyfriend. But you're like Yoda, too," he continued. " 'Cause you're smart and you understand things."

Joe's eyes filled with tears. "And who are you, Jason?"

"I'm Luke Skywalker," he grinned.

"You've been very brave," said Joe.

"That's because The Force is with me."

The children had explained what happened.

Now the State would have to explain the children.

• • •

The State, announced John Hogan, calls Dr. Roland Summit. The distinguished child psychiatrist, who had little appetite for courtrooms, made his way to the stand.

The father of the Child Sexual Abuse Accommodation Syndrome had been most willing to study this "textbook case."

Dr. Summit was as familiar with the dynamics of the sexually abused child as he was with the dynamics of a child sexual abuse trial and the role assigned by the defense to the people who interviewed the children—be they police, social workers, or mental health professionals.

So vigorous were the attempts to, as he termed it, "kill the messengers" of the children's disclosures that the already limited ranks of those willing to participate in such investigations were dwindling steadily.

The child interviewers in the Jordan, Minnesota, case were currently the subject of multimillion-dollar lawsuits filed by its former defendants (the architects of the organization known as VOCAL), who claimed that it was the "manipulative" tactics of the people who spoke to the children that had caused them to spin the fantastic tales that led to their "false" arrest.

In California, Kee McFarland and other therapists who interviewed the suspected victims of the McMartin Preschool in Manhattan Beach, which led to a daycare crisis in that community (when the interviewers elicited statements from the children that directly linked the alleged activities to several other local daycare operations), faced similar civil litigation. At least one of these McMartin-linked preschools was prosecuted unsuccessfully in a case featuring Dr. Lee Stewart Coleman. A few others were ordered closed by authorities, though criminal charges remained to be filed.

The rest were still in business.

The California community was wrenched to its feet by the nature and magnitude of the alleged daycare "rings."

Parents clutched their children in mortal fear, until Jordan, Minnesota, blew them a gust of reassuring news.

It didn't happen.

Obviously it didn't happen, because a jury in Minnesota had reviewed the "evidence" and determined that it had not.

And the most compelling and publicized "evidence" was the words of Dr. Ralph Underwager, who explained to them how the same tactics used by the North Koreans, Red Chinese, and "oppressive tyrants everywhere" had caused the children to tell these "fantastic" stories.

It was a "witch hunt," they were reassured. A false alarm. A collective hysteria that was "sweeping the nation" like a determined pathogen, causing innocent families to be accused of illogical and unspeakable acts.

Where, after all, was the evidence? Where, after all, were the scars?

Even physical scars could be dismissed without extraordinary fanfare. Labs, after all, sometimes made mistakes. And pediatric gynecologists could not offer, as Frank Fuster would say, "hundred percent" assurance that a hymen was shredded by a penis and not the monkey bars in the play yard.

And what the children had to say mattered little, because they were young and therefore unreliable. This could easily be demonstrated to a jury in a matter of a few seconds on cross-examination with the question "Did your mommy [or the prosecutor or the therapist] tell you what to say here today?"

The invariably elicited "yes" that cemented the "coaching" and "programming" arguments was not customarily followed by the query "What *words* did she use when she told you what to say?" For it was not desirable to extract, "She told me to say what happened," or "She told me to tell the truth," on cross-examination.

That it took Michael Von Zamft a highly publicized forty-five minutes to gain this prized admission from the oft-mentioned four-year-old was considered by observers of that particular courtroom encounter testament to the will of the child.

But a child *had* no will, whispered the winds of Minnesota that blew into print and airwaves the words *witch hunt* and *hysteria*, offering fresh breaths of air to gasping Californians.

Slogans were affixed to bumpers on Los Angeles roadways:

"Salem 1692—Manhattan Beach 1984"

The "involved" parents splintered into opposing factions.

And the children wet their beds, ate their excrement, and slept in cardboard boxes or their parents' beds at night.

Even as Dr. Roland Summit took the stand in Miami, a McMartin child faced seven defense attorneys in a California courtroom as the longest pretrial hearing in the history of the United States entered its final months.

The McMartin children's pretrial ordeal made Jason Harrison's deposition look like a picnic. For there were no Doctors Braga in California to plead with the system on behalf of the children's emotional well-being. The McMartin interviewers were the pariahs of the case, the district attorney's office having responded to the personal and professional slurs hurled at them through the media by pushing them out the door.

This, Dr. Summit believed, was what set the McMartin case apart from Country Walk. Janet Reno had not rushed to wash her hands of the Bragas, who would—whether she banished them or not—

remain the focus of the defense case. Instead, she made them an integral part of its construction.

Summit saw the writing on the wall in California.

Criminal counts were being dropped en masse as parents, who were witnessing how few lines the court was drawing at the length and nature of the children's interrogations, withdrew their children from the case. They would not subject them to demands that they simulate oral sex with microphones on the witness stand and endure defense attorneys breaking into peals of merry laughter as they described animals being slaughtered.

Though a handful of families was willing to see the case to its conclusion, Dr. Summit anticipated further disintegration of McMartin—a prophecy to be fulfilled in the months ahead, when the Los Angeles district attorney's office would abruptly drop charges against five of the defendants for "lack of evidence," though the judge who had listened to more than a year of pretrial testimony had ruled that the state of California had more than enough to take them to trial.

In widely scattered pockets all over the country, similar cases were in much the same shape. Country Walk was the beacon to which the interviewers in the trenches were drawn—a "model case" in which the science of child development stood at the foundation of the interviewing process, which had been meticulously memorialized on videotape from start to finish, in the hope that a jury might be allowed to determine for themselves whether the children had been *caused* or *enabled* to say these "terrible things."

Summit had studied the Braga interviews and noted the caution with which they had been conducted, with an eye toward detail and verification. The use of "leading" questions, he noted, was "strikingly rare" and "virtually negligible."

He was also impressed with the Bragas' style. Their demeanor was sober, reassuring, and "adult"—an approach that at first gave him cause for pause, until he came to realize that the children regarded the doctors as "idealized parents."

The Bragas did not "bring themselves down" to the child's level, he noted, by giggling and rolling on the floor. He found their "highly communicative" style an unusually effective way of providing the children with respect and establishing a framework for "the most mature kind of communication."

If the defense could convince a jury that the children had been "contaminated" by *these* interviews, he feared there was little hope for any case in the country.

But Dr. Summit took the stand on this day, not to comment on the Bragas or their methods, but to explain to the jury why children cannot speak of unspeakable acts.

Doctor, inquired John Hogan, *could you please tell us if it's unusual for a child who has been the victim of sexual abuse to not report the incident immediately?*

". . . It's expected and predictable that a child would *not* report it."

Will you please explain to the ladies and gentlemen of the jury why that happens?

"I am not sure. We don't always know why it happens. The most important thing to know is it does. . . .

"Most children never tell.

"Among survivors of adult victims, there is a minority that have ever told—that is, a minority that told anyone when they were children. . . .

"Some of the reasons some children give for not telling are that they are afraid they won't be believed. They are afraid they will be punished. They are afraid that their parents can't tolerate it, or they are afraid of the results that have been threatened to them: that they will get into trouble, that they will be hurt . . . or their parents will be hurt. . . .

"Children are trapped into secrecy by being molested in a private place with nobody watching. They develop a sense—even if they don't understand what is happening—that this is something dangerous and bad. . . . The children develop a sense of blame, of self-blame. . . .

"They generally have a vague notion, based on attempts at prevention—'Don't get into cars with strangers,' 'Don't let anybody touch you.'

"What happens [is] they know they have done bad. The last person they can usually approach are their own parents."

Is it unusual for a child who's been the victim of sexual abuse— once they have made the allegations of abuse—to later retract it? Is that unusual?

"No . . . that's also a part of a more or less predictable pattern. . . .

"They don't tell at all for a long time, even if they're asked if it's happening. They will usually say no. During that time, they are locked into secrecy. So, in a way, any acknowledgment of being molested is a retraction of prior denials. . . .

"Sometimes they are being pressured by people that don't want to be involved and don't want the child to be involved. . . ."

Would that retraction, would that matter if the abuser was a member of the family, or does that matter?

"It doesn't matter. The crucial thing is the acceptance. If the child is believed—and the child needs as much love as the child can get after the disclosure—chances are there won't be a retraction."

Can you explain . . . what may be the factors that may cause the child to equivocate or retract allegations of sexual abuse?

". . . If Mommy is upset, the child takes the first opportunity to fix that by reassuring Mommy it really didn't happen. There is an exaggerated amount of guilt, self-guilt. . . .

"One of the ways children survive being molested is to make believe it isn't happening. . . .

"For their own protection and own comfort, they may need to take on denial . . . and convince all the grown-ups there's nothing to worry about. They can act as if nothing happened. . . ."

Are you telling the ladies and gentlemen of the jury that if a child denies that he or she was abused, then we should automatically conclude that they were in fact abused?

". . . Sometimes kids say they were abused when they weren't or distort the proportions of being abused.

"Everyone has to be alert to determine whether they are trustworthy and accurate. You do everything you can to check the information. . . ."

If a child, in making a statement about sexual abuse, says some things that, when you hear it, it doesn't make any sense or seems impossible, do you feel we should necessarily discount everything that the child said?

"If we do that, we would immediately discount most disclosures or complaints of sexual abuse, since most of us . . . aren't well acquainted with the dynamics of child molesters.

"Child molesters do things that we don't want to believe anyone would do.

"Children give in to various things in ways that we don't want to believe children do. We tend not to believe that a child would so readily submit. . . ."

Would that include a child being defecated upon?

"Those are the more outrageous things. Oftentimes people who believe a child is molested, if it fits some familiar pattern, they believe it's typical of molestation, then label as fantasy and outrageous other things that are said involving spilling of . . . feces or blood or rituals involved in humiliating children. . . .

"Those things are used to argue that it couldn't happen; 'Obviously we are looking at someone who wouldn't do that.' We begin 'screening out' by our wish to believe the best."

Why do we want to believe the best?

"Well, there is simply nothing to be gained . . . by believing that a child is molested. It's a sense of outrage that destroys our trust in our own society. . . . We just want to believe the children are safe when we look at someone who appears to be normal. . . .

"If a person that is implicated is a male, and I think he did it and he's 'normal,' I may be afraid that somebody might think I did it, or I might be as capable of that as somebody else. That is outrageous to my sense of comfort.

"If you are a woman . . . especially if you are a mother with a child in your care, you feel you have failed if somebody has molested your child. . . .

"Many of us were victimized in various ways as children.

"We forget it.

"We denied it, and to come face-to-face with this again is something that is internally painful, almost impossible. So, former victims of sexual abuse are often totally incapable of hearing or taking action when a child has been molested, even if you otherwise believe that molestation could occur.

"If you believe in it, it gives you some obligation to take action. . . . You have to challenge somebody you have trusted, someone your child has been trusted with. You have to convict other people. . . .

"You are bound to be blamed by others who are sure that anybody else would have protected a child, and finally, if you did all those things and succeeded in gaining advocacy outside your family, if you go to court, you are likely to feel very much punished and lose your dignity and freedom by being exposed in the process of being a witness and being attacked on cross-examination.

"It's common knowledge that most folks don't go that far. . . ."

Why would intelligent people . . . simply not notice and put the pieces together?

"In addition to things that I have described which are normal for all adults not wanting to deal with the dirty subject . . . we have created for ourselves the mythology. . . .

"We believe that no one would molest a child except someone who is visibly disturbed—the grimy child molester, the dirty old man, the stereotype that makes people safe. . . .

"Where a neighbor may be a molester—that is, somebody who by career has learned to be likable, easygoing, and someone who really loves children. You can see your children gravitating. You are delighted he or she will take them off for the day in the park. It's a paradox beyond our willingness to accept that someone that nice will take our children and molest them under a position of trust, and also it's beyond our ordinary ability to believe that, if that happens, the child wouldn't tell us about it upon coming home.

"Even more, it's hard to believe that of all the people in the world that the child could tell, the mother or father would be the last to know for the fear of destroying the family. . . .

"We need to—unfortunately—we need to have our greatest index of suspicion for [those] whom we trust the most. . . .

"Strangers very rarely molest children.

"In various surveys, seventy to eighty to ninety percent of those individuals who molest children are people known to the child.

"People seem to believe that a psychiatrist or a doctor could detect a molested child or molester. In fact, doctors are as naive as anyone. . . .

"A psychological test or physical test to be done will show normal. Polygraph tests are usually normal. When someone is doing something, their private belief is OK.

"If you have the child checked, the doctor won't find anything. . . . Most child molestations don't involve actions that are scarring.

"To get a physical examination for reassurance is false reassurance. The doctors are trained: if young children have symptoms in genitals, their reasonable explanation for that is little girls get vaginal infections if they wear nylon underpants . . . or play with themselves.

"Children get rectal problems because they're 'constipated.' We have never been taught that molestation could be a problem. We are not taught that young children could be victims.

"In all of the cases I know where children have been molested, parents have taken children to doctors with concern and been reassured by doctors that nothing is wrong, sometimes by doctors that didn't examine the children because they are so sure that nothing could possibly be wrong."

Are there any other commonly held myths as to children that are untrue?

"Most everybody fails to even conceptualize that a child is sexually attractive.

"We build up myths. . . . It would be an older child, someone beginning to develop sexually. And for years, we have looked among teenagers and preteenagers for those children likely to be victimized. . . ."

Are you telling the ladies and gentlemen of the jury, a four-, five-year-old might be found sexually attractive to someone?

"Those people that find children sexually attractive are attracted specifically to the fact that they are *not* sexually developed. . . .

"The most referrals to health agencies are children under five. . . . We are having to look at the very unwelcome news—not only are very young children sexually attractive, but they are vulnerable because they can't speak out, and most people won't recognize the victimization."

Has it been your experience that young children—preschool, three, four, six years old—have difficulty verbalizing what they experienced while they were being molested?

". . . So often the child is trying to find a way to get it across. They will tell us that they told their parents, or told someone, but the same people never heard it because the message wasn't clear.

"It was more or less deliberately coded by the child in hopes of a way to get around the secrecy threat, but there's a problem for very young children of picking words that adults can pick up on.

"We don't teach kids to talk about their genitals, and we don't teach kids what a sexual act is. If we try to present it, we usually say, 'Don't get involved with strangers.' "

Could you tell us if you think there is a pattern of disclosure for children who have been abused repeatedly, over and over again?

"Yes, there is."

Could you please explain to us what that pattern is?

"It's what I've come to call the 'window of disclosure.' . . .

"In a complete way, it's like the window is closed, and we don't have any way of seeing through, until we try to open just a little bit and we get a little peek. If we communicate properly, the child will open that window further. . . .

"The child has to have trust. We have to demonstrate our willingness to believe. We have to show we are not scared or angry with what we see in the first disclosure. . . .

"As soon as things get anxious, or the child gets anxious, for having said something dangerous, the retraction comes back in that order. . . .

"There is an order of disclosure. If we ask the child, they will say nothing happened. 'I like them.' 'They're nice people. . . .'

"Then the child will acknowledge that something happened, but 'it didn't happen to me.' The self-guilt will be protected and the child will describe other children who are [victims]. I am assuming now situations where there was more than one victim. . . .

"Then the child may describe in some detail everything that happened to all the other kids before ever acknowledging that he or she was personally involved. . . . There will be a sequence of disclosure based on how embarrassing and how outrageous the activities are.

"Generally the child will describe being sexually touched before he can describe sexually touching others. He will describe being a passive victim before acknowledging being an active victim. He will describe approaching to the genitals—or if it's a girl, her genital or chest areas—before talking about approaching to the rear or into the anus.

"There is an assaultive quality about being attacked from behind. You can't see what happened, leaving a person feeling more weak and helpless and more ashamed. We will hear again about manual touching before we hear about genital touching.

"We will hear about genital touching before we hear about anal contact. We will again hear about activities carried out [by] . . . a man before those of women. They also pick up disbelief when we can't believe a woman would do that. . . .

"We have circumstances where eventually, when all this comes together, and you hold the child responsible to talk about it, what you hear then is not all that stuff, but again denying all the most embarrassing things, or the child may come to court and be able to talk about vaginal contact and just [start] bawling on rectal contact."

What is the final stage of disclosure in a large group of children that have been abused over time?

"Well, given an ultimate model, where all kinds of atrocities have occurred, the last thing to come out are the areas of greatest cruelty, where animals may have been killed and especially where children have participated in blood, harm on animals, or sexual activities on each other.

"That seems to be the ultimate to talk about.

"If there have been rituals, or things that the child experiences are very strange, and which, as listeners, we immediately react to with skepticism—those things usually don't come out in initial interviews and will emerge only after several months with parents.''

Is it unusual—in cases where numbers of children have been molested over a period of time—to have some sort of rituals to scare or terrorize the children?

"No. Generally that is predictable in most systems of child molestations.''

Is it also unusual in that type of setting for the perpetrator to evolve into defecating or urinating on the children?

"No . . . that kind of deliberate perversity is part of the dynamics of someone who is so regressed to be sexually involved with children, to be confused with what is exciting, what is dirty, what is sexual—all of that.

"The confusion with bathroom issues is often part of the need of the sexually perverted person.

"It's also a way of creating something outrageous which almost builds its own alibi.

"When we hear this happening, we don't believe it. We think that is a fantasy of children. There is an advantage for creating the amount of outrage.''

Advantage to who?

"For the perpetrator. Also, in most systems of child molestations, [there is] not only sexual intent—sexual gratification—but the need for outrageous power. . . .

"Besides raping someone, there is no [better] way to demonstrate power than to force shit in their mouth.''

Is it unusual for women to be involved in this group molestation—the abuse of a number of children over a period of time?

". . . It's common to find women participating over the domination or leadership of a male that's paradoxical to the overall view of child molestation.

"It's more commonly a one-on-one thing where one individual seeks out one child at a time as a sexual partner. That pattern is predominately restricted to males. . . .

"Overall, it's fairly rare for women to be involved. But in group situations—especially those situations where a number of children are impressed into sexual activities over time—it's at least . . . fifty/fifty, if not something of a majority, to find a woman involved.''

How are they usually under the domination of someone else?

"That varies. I say 'usually' they are, but it's not quite accurate to imagine they work only in reluctancy responsibilities.

"Once a person is enslaved and dominated to the point of submission—perhaps just as the children who can learn to get gratification and power out of the aggressive role—a woman that has been punished, ordered, forced into molesting children may become an enthusiastic and powerful and cruel molester of children through that process."

Do you believe there are any behavioral systems that might give us some guidance in determining whether a child has been sexually abused?

"Yes."

Are any more important than others? Do you feel any are more important or that the jury should be more concerned with in evaluating?

"Yes, there are only a few indications that are specific or almost specific to being molested. Most of the others are symptoms of general anxiety, and they are not too useful except as accessories to central ones.

"The central ones that are most reliable are when the child talks about being molested and says, 'Somebody did something to me,' even though it's rare to get that disclosure.

"When it comes, it tends to be pretty reliable. . . .

"The child comes into the bedroom naked and crawls up to Mommy and takes her breasts in her mouth or discusses putting his penis in her mouth. . . .

"So the two indications that are most specific are either hints . . . sometimes displaced, you know, 'What does it mean if somebody puts a child's penis in their mouth?' "

Would that include taking a sister's head, placing it on a child's penis, or attempting for a young boy to place his mouth on his sister's vagina?

"We don't see that in a population of children that haven't been molested."

I have no other questions of you, Doctor.

There was little that Jeffrey Samek could ask of Dr. Roland Summit that would enhance his case.

If the child does say that a molesting occurred and the adult says the molesting did not *occur, is it your belief that most adults would believe the adult?*

"Yes."

So then, it would be fair to say that you believe children won't be believed by adults?

"On the average, the child who is maintaining verbally that he has been molested, with the accused who has a 'reasonable' explanation to assure that that didn't happen, most adults will be more influenced by the adult's alibi, than by the child's complaints."

Do you believe that this is because of some adult-based sympathy for the alleged perpetrator?

"I believe that the adults act in sympathy for one another and for protection for their world which they consider a safe one for the children."

The state rested its case.

• • •

Michael Von Zamft now held the wild card and was about to play his hand. His client was willing to speak, he said, about life in the Fuster home. He couldn't strike a deal, he knew, having pleaded his client "straight up."

As Jeffrey Samek assumed center stage in courtroom 4-2, Iliana Fuster prepared to give her deposition.

Von Zamft was willing to gamble that Iliana Fuster's words would bring her mercy from the judge into whose hands he had placed her fate. And the State, he knew, would be much obliged to have additional pieces of the puzzle to assemble when it presented its rebuttal case.

The State's recommendation at Iliana's sentencing, which loomed two months away, would carry substantial weight with Judge Newman, who was expected to balance the scales of justice for a woman who raped children for reasons not known.

Great care had been taken to arrange the deposition of Iliana Fuster in such a way as to shield her from aural and visual contact with her husband, though she was aware that Francisco Fuster Escalona would be permitted to eavesdrop electronically from an adjacent room on this, the first sworn statement to be made by an adult witness about what went on inside the neat and tidy estate home where three dozen children had been delivered for safe and wholesome care.

The parents *chose* this house because it seemed an answer to their prayers. Iliana was the perfect surrogate—an affectionate and apparently affluent suburban housewife who welcomed "a few" bundles of joy into her home solely, she told them, because she could have none of her own.

The mothers clucked understandingly and noted how tenderly she consoled a screaming infant or toddler who tugged at their conscience with pleas not to leave them.

Separation anxiety, no doubt.

They just weren't ready to leave the nest.

They'd get used to it.

Iliana said so.

Once they got used to the routine of the academic and creative program she planned to offer, the young woman told them, once the playroom had been partitioned off to HRS standards, the children would be too excited to notice they were gone.

Gratefully, the mothers had agreed.

This was exactly the kind of personal attention and concern they did not expect to find in a daycare center—the kind of circumstance for which they had been willing to pay a premium.

This was the next best thing to a private nanny.

Iliana's entourage encircled Frank Fuster's diminutive wife as she marched down the corridor where the former object of her adoration lounged near the doorway of the room from which he would hear— for the first time—how much of the family's beans his wife had spilled.

He was waiting for her.

It was his one opportunity to meet her eyes.

For Judge Newman had barred him from the deposition room.

Samek had objected vigorously to the manner in which his client was to "confront" his latest accuser.

"He cannot *see* what is going on; he cannot be *seen*; he can *hear* what is going on, but I think that at the very least, he should be able to see. I think, also, that he should be able to be *seen*."

That, the court had ruled, would not be necessary.

Frank advised Judge Newman that it was imperative for him to have physical access to his wife when she "tells her truth."

"She cannot *lie* in front of me.

"She's not *intimidated* by me.

"When we see each other eye to eye, she will not *lie*."

That, the court ruled, would not be necessary.

As she approached the door to the deposition room, Iliana spied the other half of her "pure and everlasting union," broke away from her human screen, and walked steadily past the deposition room to where her husband lounged. The startled onlookers paused uncertainly, as Iliana stopped toe-to-toe with her husband and looked him straight in the eye.

Having thus delivered the only message she wished him to receive, Frank's child bride turned and joined Michael Von Zamft, one of her psychologists, John Hogan, Dan Casey, and the state attorney herself for the first of three evenings on which Jeffrey Samek would question the eleventh-hour witness, whom the State was considering calling for its rebuttal case. Iliana had pleaded guilty "straight up" and thrown herself on the mercy of the court.

Had she not been one month shy of eighteen when she committed her crimes, "straight up" would have brought her an automatic twenty-five-year minimum—and mandatory—sentence on each of the four capital counts. But Judge Newman had the option of sentencing her as a juvenile if he so chose, leaving the confessed child molester's possible sentence open to a spectrum ranging from probation to life in prison.

The court, Iliana knew, would look favorably upon any concili-atory gesture she might make—such as sharing with a jury the things she had already shared with her psychologists.

She would tell all, said Von Zamft.

Which gave Jeffrey Samek the opportunity to ask all.

Iliana, is there any reason why you walked by here just before, and you went into the other direction instead of coming over this way? You walked past Mr. Fuster.

"Not any special reason. I just wanted to face him. I just wanted to see him. . . ."

Did you speak to Janet Reno at any time before you pleaded guilty? continued Samek.

"No, I did not speak to her, but I met her."

What were the circumstances under which you met her?

"It was when . . . my attorney decided about pleading, he talked to me, making a statement as to how he was going to do it, and he had to communicate that, and so it was that I met her during that time— when we decided that."

OK, how many times did you meet with Ms. Reno or see Ms. Reno before you pleaded guilty?

"That was the first time."

Could you say specifically how many times you have seen Ms. Reno?

"I have seen her twice, I think."
So she has visited you two times?
"Yes, sir."
Where does she visit you? Was that over at the Women's Detention Center?
"With a doctor."
How long a period of time did she visit with you the first time that she came after you had pleaded guilty?
"Briefly."
Was it five minutes, two minutes, ten minutes, or was it ten hours?
"No, maybe ten minutes. She and my attorney have been trying to put me into school. . . ."
Why don't you tell me about the things that Frank used to do to you?
Iliana's composure swiftly departed for the rest of the evening, as she clung to her psychologist and on occasion accepted Janet Reno's offered hand—a gesture that seemed to fairly astonish Frank Fuster's attorney.
"He used to keep a cross in between the mattresses, and then when he started giving me drugs every night—"
Well, let's talk about the cross. What did he do to you with the cross?
"He always tried to stick it in my rectum."
Did he ever actually do it?
"Yes."
Did he say anything while he was doing it?
"Just if I didn't happen to be bleeding, just to realize bleeding, otherwise I wouldn't satisfy him. But he would stick it in, and I didn't want him to, and I would start to get aggressive with him."
What do you mean, "aggressive"?
"I mean, like reject. Then he would start beating me up because I wouldn't do what he said."
How did he beat you up? What did he do?
"He would grab me, he would slap my face. . . . He threatened to throw the TV at my head, and he would do things like that."
What else did he do . . . ?
"He beat me. He would put my hands like up; he would hold my hands with his one hand, and then he would rape me, and he would rape me in my rectum with his penis; made me bleed. He made me

bleed." Iliana, by now, told her story through a more or less constant stream of sobs.

How were you positioned?

"On my stomach against the mattress. And he used to put pillows on my head. . . . I wanted him to take me to a doctor."

Why?

"Because I was feeling bad inside, and I was feeling that I was so afraid I was going to be sick, and I needed a doctor to certify me, but he never did.

"And he would put instruments into my rectum, suppositories into my rectum at all times . . . every time I would feel bad—and he said that it was helping me."

How many times was he doing that? If you were living with him for about 330 days, how many times?

"About 250 times."

What else did he do?

"He gave me drugs. . . . He made me smoke marijuana. . . . He gave me different little pills. They were like, blue."

And do you know what they were?

"No. I just know that they were for pain, he said."

What did they do to you?

"I would feel dizzy and relaxed, and I was sleepy—very sleepy."

You would go to sleep?

"Yes, I would sleep for hours. I would sleep until the next day."

Were there any other kinds of drugs or any other kind of pills?

"He just used to give me something in a shake—some milk."

Do you know what it was?

"It was a brown color, brown color. . . . He said it was to be violent; that I had to be strong."

You don't remember anything about it once you drank it?

"I don't remember. I would go to sleep, I remember that. It would help me relax and to be strong. That's what he kept saying. . . . Then he would wake me up because the parents were coming."

So what time of day was this?

"This was in the afternoon. It would be like he would be having me drink it twice a week."

What time did you usually go to sleep at night?

"It was late hours. It was like two o'clock in the morning."

How come it would be so late?

"Because every night he would give me drugs . . . and he wanted to have sex with me, and then I would have to get up . . . about six-thirty in the morning. I would have to get up, and I would have to get Jaime up and ready for school. . . .''

What things did he used to do to you?

"He wanted to—ejaculate . . . he wanted to in my mouth; and not only that, he wanted me to swallow it. So I would start vomiting. . . . I would not let it."

He did ejaculate, and you would swallow it?

"No, I wouldn't. I would start throwing up. He did not like that, and he would get upset. He would say that I was stupid and that I didn't know how to do things. . . .

"I am starting to remember." Iliana trembled as her doctor patted her on the back, murmuring, "That's OK. That's OK. You are OK now."

"It's just so horrible, so horrible about it," she sobbed.

How often did he force you to give him oral sex?

"He wanted me to do it every day."

Well, did you do it every day?

"Sometimes; sometimes not, because my rejection would really, he said, turn him off. And then that night he would become violent . . . and he wanted to put his penis in my rectum while I was standing up, and he would hold my hands up against the wall.

"And then I would be taking a shower . . . and then he would start urinating on me. . . . When he was doing this, he would be standing there laughing at me because he said that I was so stupid. . . .''

Did he make you drink urine?

"No."

What else did he do?

"I don't know where to start."

Start anyplace.

"He would threaten that he would stick a drill up my vagina and that he would turn it on."

He did that, or he threatened that he would do it?

"If he would have done it I would be dead now. . . .

"One time Frank took me to the movies, and then when we came home we went into the bedroom and the drill was there. It was there so that I could see it. . . .''

What else did he do?

"One time I was coming into the playroom, and he was there . . . and he had only his underwear, and there was just April, Jaime, and Joshua. . . . He was there in front of them.

"I came in and I was wearing, I was wearing a T-shirt from my

school that a friend had given me. . . . And Frank, when I came into
the room, he was so weird. Some of the kids had their tops on, and
some of the kids had their tops off, and they were standing in there
in the middle in a half-circle. . . ."

How about bottoms. Did they all have their bottoms on?

"No, they had shorts. . . . And he came in, and he got up, and he
told me, what was I doing with that shirt on? . . . So I said OK, and
I tried to go away.

"He said—he said, 'You are going to have to stay here and you are
going to have to stop sneaking behind doors, and now that you be
here, you are going to have to live with me.'

"Then he started ripping, started ripping off my T-shirt. He
ripped it into pieces.

"Then I was only in my bra, and I was crying. I told him to stop
because the kids were there, and the kids were starting to run
around; they were playing around. I was wondering what was going
on, and then Jaime was over in the corner, and he said, he used to
tell me: 'Mommy, Mommy, you are fine?' and I would not answer
because I was only thinking of myself.

"Then Frank took this knife from between his underwear, and he
just took it up, and he commanded me to take my jeans off. . . . I told
him he must be crazy because I saw what was going on. So he took
the knife, and he told me to do it. He just kept saying to me: 'Do it,'
and then he kept sliding the knife against my leg, and he cut my
jeans . . . and he cut my leg, too. . . .

"So I slowly took my jeans off."

You took them off, or he took them off?

"He told me to do it. . . . Then he sat down, and the children were
there, and this was a very small room. . . .

"He sat down, and I was crying, and he had a knife at my side, and
he just wanted to try to see me bleed.

"Then Joshua was in front of him, and he called me, and he
started kissing Joshua, sucking Joshua's penis. . . . Then he called
me, and then he put me right beside him. Then he put the knife in
my back, and he told me to play with his penis—Frank's. He put the
knife in my back and he was serious, and he said that if I don't do
it that we would all regret it. . . ."

OK, what was Joshua doing?

"He was just running, running around holding their toys in his
hands.

"Jaime was over in the corner, and Jaime kept asking me if I was fine, if I was fine; but I was not asking him because I was only concerned about me.

"I was so afraid. I was so afraid. . . ."

What did you do?

"I played with his penis, and he had sat down—he had sat down to my back with the knife, and he had Joshua in front of him. . . . He started to kiss him all over, stomach area, too; and then he started pushing with the knife . . . and he started to compare himself with Joshua."

What did he say?

"He said that Joshua was like him, and he pushed me, and he pushed me. He pushed me to kiss Joshua's penis. . . ."

What did he do after he had pushed the knife in your back?

"OK, sucking Joshua's."

You did or he did?

"He pushed me to do it.

"Then he got up, and I was afraid, and I wanted to stop it; I was bleeding down from my leg, but he didn't care, he didn't care.

"Joshua got up like nothing, and he went in there, and he got some toys, and he played as if nothing had happened.

"Then he took April."

Who took April?

"He . . . Frank put his hand inside April."

He put his whole hand inside April's vagina?

"No, no, inside the shorts. . . .

"And then he started kissing her, and then he started comparing her with myself. He said that I was stupid, that I was not obedient. . . .

"Then he got up, and he took his penis in his hand, and he started whipping. . . ."

Did he actually hit her?

"Yes. He used to do that to me. . . . He used to say that Frankie would spank me."

Frankie?

"That he would get respect. . . ."

Is there any differentiation between Frank and Frankie?

"Yes."

What is Frankie?

"That is what he called his penis. . . . He used to ask me when we got married to call him that, even asked me to call him 'Daddy.' "

He made you call his penis Frankie?

"Yes . . . but I refused. . . .

"Then I asked him to please let me go because I wanted to take care of my leg, and then he grabbed me . . . and he took me to the bedroom, and he started sucking me, he started sucking my blood. . . ."

What else did he do that night, after sucking the blood on you?

"He had sex with me . . . again, he took the cross. . . . And he took it out of my rectum, and he put it on my side, on my side, and he would push it in my side, strong, and he would say to me, 'Be still,' and he told me to take it easy.

"Then he would put his penis in my ears . . . and my eyes, and all over me, and then he started comparing me with April, and that is why Frankie was so upset, Frankie was upset, Frankie was upset."

Well, what were the children doing?

"They were left in their playroom, and while this was happening the doors were open . . . the bedroom door.

"I was so scared and worried about myself, I did not realize nothing. It was like he was doing this and there was nothing I could do about it. What could I do?"

What else did he do that day?

"He had sex with me, and he said that I was stupid. . . .

"I was taking a shower, and he was dressed up, and while I was taking a shower he turned the hot water on me, and he burnt me. Then he got into the shower with all of his clothes on."

Iliana, are you sure that you are not dreaming all of this?

"No, I am sure of that. I am sure of that."

Well, we will get back to this, but just for my last few questions, I would like to ask you about some items that perhaps would be less painful for you. After Frank was arrested and—

"Yes."

And even after you were arrested, you would call me lots of times on the telephone, and you would tell me that Frank is innocent.

John Hogan interrupted the proceedings for the first time. "At this time I am going to object. I think that when counsel was separated, Frank Fuster clearly waived any rights for you to use anything that you may have gained from Iliana in his defense. . . ."

Samek begged to differ, then shrugged and took another tack.

While both you and Frank were in jail, even the whole time you were married, before you were in jail, you wrote him many, many letters telling him how much you loved him, and how he was so important to you, and how he was your savior.

One letter in particular, I remember, that you drew a bunny, and you wished him a happy Easter. I ask you: Why did you do this?

"When we talked . . . he used to tell me that he needed me. He needed to know that I would love him; otherwise it would drive him crazy where he is.

"He didn't want me to be guilty of that, guilty of that should something happen to him. . . .

"In fact, I know that it was stupid, it was stupid of me for doing that. . . .

"He said that it was going to drive him crazy, and I didn't want to be guilty of that. . . ."

This is a letter that Mr. Fuster gave me, and I would like to ask that it be . . . placed on the record. . . .

Iliana, did you write this letter?

"Yes, I did."

And I want you to look and to tell me the date that it says on here.

"May 29th."

OK, and it says, "To Frankie"?

"Yes."

OK, and was May 29th before or after he was arrested?

"It was before."

So when you said before, that you never wrote any letters before he was arrested, you were making a mistake?

"Yes. I don't remember this letter."

Well, is it in your handwriting?

"Yes, it's my handwriting, and I remember this date. This was the day after he gave me like twenty cards saying that he was 'Oh, I'm sorry.' He was sorry because the night before he bit me so bad that my lips were kind of swollen. . . . We were going to have visitors; somebody was going to come and visit us. And he told me to tell a story in case that they should ask me what had happened.

"Then he gave me twenty more cards saying that he was sorry. He brought flowers and everything. He kept promising me, promising me that he would never do that again.

"But it was not true because it would happen over and over and over again."

Why did you write this letter?

"Yes, I wrote it. I wrote it because of the fact that he was feeling so bad. . . ."

All right, Iliana, this letter says: "To Frankie," and then, "Hi

Gordito" ["little fat one"]. That's the nickname that you had for him?

"Yes."

"Now is 4:15 P.M. I was passing by your office from the kitchen to our room, and I saw this pen and paper on your desk. Then I decided to write something to you. I have so many things to do at this time, but nothing will take my time to write to you."

He didn't make you write that, did he?

"No, he did not."

"Honey, I love you." Did he make you write that?

"No, he didn't, but it made me feel bad when he gave me all those cards. . . ."

OK. Now, you said that this man beat you, bruised you, threatened to put a drill in your vagina, put a cross up your rectum, forced you to have sex, forced you to give him oral sex, threw you against the shower, and because he sent you twenty cards and apologized, you wrote in this letter:

"Honey, I miss you every time that you are not home. I am so proud of being your wife, your lover, your little thing. . . .

"You cannot understand what does it feel to be next to you, to know that you love me. . . . I adore you, I need you, I love you, I want you forever.

"Iliana Fuster who will always love you, your wife"?

"Yes."

"Please do not ever stop loving me"?

Tears streamed down her face.

"Yes," she said. "And I remember that day. . . ."

For five-and-a-half hours Frank Fuster listened to his wife's deposition from his wired room, scribbling and folding notes, aligning pencils and papers, grimacing, imploring the heavens, and groaning for his audience of one—Christina Royo, who sat in mute and dispassionate silence.

Frank courted the young woman with engaging smiles and glances, sometimes fixing her with his most piercing and seductive stare, as if to say, How could a man with my obvious appreciation of women be interested in children?

Several times he tried to engage her in conversation.

"I am a police officer," she would say, as soon as he opened his mouth. "Anything you say to me can—and most certainly will—be used against you in a court of law.

"Talk to your lawyer."

"But, please, just this one favor," he would implore.

"I am a police officer. Anything you say to me can—and most definitely will—be used against you in a court of law.

"Talk to your lawyer."

"But, if you could please place this note in my wife's hands for me," he insisted, still not grasping that beneath the state investigator's dispassionate mask smoldered a hatred that Christina Royo, herself, could not comprehend.

Frank persisted. How could he "prove" his "innocence" if she would not help him facilitate a communication with his wife, so that she would stop telling these lies on him?

Christina regarded Frank Fuster coolly.

"I have been assigned to guard you. That's—my—job. I am not required to converse with you, run errands for you, or interact with you in any way. Don't talk to me. Don't look at me. Don't hand me notes.

"Talk to your attorney."

It was all she could do to keep from wrapping her hands around his neck.

But that would be too quick, too painless.

She would rather shoot him in both legs, haul him out to the Everglades, and let the alligators finish the job—while she watched.

On day two of Iliana's deposition, Jeffrey Samek presented his client's request to speak with her.

"I just would like to go on with the depo and get this finished as soon as possible," she told her husband's lawyer.

"He only wants to talk to you for two minutes?"

"I repeat again, I want to go ahead with the depo, please."

Samek shrugged.

Tell me some other things that Frank did.

"Well, at the beginning, when I start becoming suspicious . . . that something was going on in the house wrong because Frank would lock himself with some of the children. It was one time that I was walking into Jaime's room and . . . there was Andy.

"He didn't have clothes. He was laying on Jaime's bed, and Frank was in front of him. He was wearing shorts, that I remember, and he was kissing Andy all over him and . . . I could use the word—sucking—his penis."

You just stood there watching?

"No."

What did you do?

"I tried to walk back because he didn't see me. He was in his back, but Steven—Steven Vickers—was coming behind me, and so he asked me what Frank was doing, and I got very nervous because I, myself, did not know how to understand that, and the child was asking me. So I tried to best I could, and I just telling him that Frank wasn't doing anything. He was just showing affection. I took him with me into the porch in the back of the house."

Iliana's composure again dissolved.

Did that happen before or after the semicircle day, if I can call it that?

"No, that was before."

Was that—was this the first time you ever saw Frank do anything with the children or was there a time before that?

"I was suspicious. . . ."

You didn't want to babysit, right?

"No, I didn't, but I had to."

Well, when [the first customer] called, why didn't you just tell her, "I don't want to babysit"?

"Because, I told you—Frank has already told me I had to babysit so I could give him money. He was making me feel guilty I couldn't support any money. He was having real bad financial problems.

"I could never imagine that Frank would do anything to the children. . . . I could never imagine at that time."

You couldn't babysit if there were no children, could you?

"Yeah, that was true. Then every day Frank would keep talking about his financial problems, would make me feel bad. . . ."

This man who was raping you every day and beating you every day and making you stay up all kinds of hours, that you were tired every day and giving you drugs and giving you marijuana—you felt bad that he was having financial problems?

"I didn't feel bad for him. I feel bad for me, because he was making me feel bad. . . ."

Would he ask you every day when he came home from work how many children were there?

"He knew it. He was there most of the time. . . .

"Sometimes when the children would come just for an hour, he say that he didn't like it because 'why just for an hour?'

"That if it would be that way, to tell them, stop—to tell them . . . not to bring them because it would be just for an hour. . . . He wanted [them] to come to stay more time."

Do you know how much money Frank made during the year or so that you were married and not in jail?

"I don't know much about income tax, things like that. He took care of things like that, but like, he would try to look for big jobs . . . like, he would—if he find one good job a month, he wouldn't work for two weeks. . . ."

Did you tell [Jeannie Pierson] that you were going to take care of her child, or did you tell her that you and Frank would also be taking care of the child?

"No, that I would take care. . . ."

Did you tell her that Frank would be home or would be spending time with the child?

"We didn't touch the subject. . . . Ms. Pierson now would ask a question like that."

You said you got suspicious about the things that might have been going on?

". . . The children were—would start telling me that he—they didn't like Frank or would start asking me not to leave them alone with him or start asking me questions like, 'Why Frank had to be in the house,' and so that was very weird.

"But I never really thought until I could see it with my own eyes. . . ."

You said . . . that you left the children in the house without you because one time or two times you went to Jaime's school?

"Right. . . . As a matter of fact, when I came back there was one of the weird things when I started getting suspicious. . . .

"Frank told me one of the parents had come to pick up one of the children and that he told the mother that I was in the shower, so that in case she asked me ever about that day, to tell her that I was in the shower. . . . He didn't have to say that.

"He didn't have to lie. . . ."

Were there other times that you left the children alone in the house, left them just with him?

"Yeah, well, every day I had to put water in my plants, so Frank was in his office working while I be doing that. I also washed the house—took me around two weeks, and I would go every day to give a couple hours to the outside. Then some afternoons he would ask me—I was so tired, I would take naps. And I would take two-hour naps. He say he would take care of everything, that then he would get me up by the time the parents would come home.

"And then things started getting more and more, because when some of the parents would ring the bell, come in, Frank would hide himself. He didn't want the parents to see him. It was very weird. Like, one time Mr. Vickers came for the first time to . . . drop

[Steven] off in the morning, and Frank did not want him to see him. . . ."

Is that the only time Frank hid when parents came?

"No, there were more times."

All the time?

". . . No, not all the time. Sometimes the parents would come, and he would be there, and he would even talk to them."

Were there particular parents that he hid from all the time?

"Again, I can't remember which parents or things like that."

Toward the end of Iliana's second evening in deposition, which commenced when the jury was sent back to their hotel, Frank Fuster again tried to arrange a meeting with his wife. Jeffrey Samek was again the messenger.

"Frank gave me this note," he said. "And I'll just read it to you . . . 'Please ask my wife again. I am requesting to talk to her only for a few minutes under the following conditions: You don't have to talk if you don't want to. Your doctor can be present.'

"In fact, Frank writes, 'I want him to be. I will not insult her or disrespect her in any way. She can get up and leave any moment she wants. This will probably be to say good-bye forever. I ask her to grant me this last favor in the name of our God Jesus Christ. I will never bother her again.' . . .

"Up to you, Iliana. Nobody can make you do it. You heard Frank's message: doesn't want you to go alone. You can have whatever support you want and leave when you want. You can say no, but make up your own decision or talk with your doctor and make up your own decision. . . ."

Iliana's decision did not require consultation.

"I have nothing to talk with him . . . I'm not his wife anymore. I just don't wish to speak to him and just want to go on with the depo, please."

Samek shrugged again.

You said that one of the things that made you suspicious was that the children said they didn't like Frank. Which child . . . ?

"Andy . . . April . . . Crystal . . . Jason. . . ."

Anybody else?

"The last person that I know . . . was Jaime, when one afternoon he told me that he had a problem and he needed to talk to me. . . .

"He asked me if it was right for his father to touch his penis, and I was kind of shocked. I couldn't answer him. I couldn't do nothing.

And all I did was tell him that that was wrong, and that maybe he was—he was dreaming. . . ."

Was that before or after the time you saw Frank kissing Andy all over and sucking Andy's penis?

"No, that was before, before. . . .

"One night . . . around midnight, he took me out of the house, and we went to this forest . . . in Country Walk, and it was very dark. I was very scared of snakes or anything that could bit me and then he started telling me stories over there.

"There was, I remember, the story he used to tell me about with a long [finger]nail, you could cut a pigeon head off, just like that. . . . He was very strong, and so I got scared, and he start telling me stories about how people can die."

What did he tell you?

"Accidentally. Nobody will ever know.

"After that night was when the circle game happened . . . and that's when he told me I wouldn't sneak no more behind doors."

I want you to tell me all the things, prodded Samek, as Iliana dissolved once again into wracking sobs.

"Well, there was a time when I went into the garage, and I saw Jaime hanging from his—from his ankle—both ankles, and Frank was spinning him. That's when he used to hit his . . . punching bag, and I had tried to stop him, and I got in the middle, and he said I would be next. . . .

"And so I got very hysterical, and I just remember he took the tape in his hands and he took me to the room, and he took telephone cord. He tied me against the chair, and he put the tape in my mouth on my face and like, I would be next. . . .

"He locked the door. He went back outside to the garage. . . .

"So then afterwards he came back and starts smacking my face. He start beating me up again. He told me not to go in between him, that I was stupid and not to ever, ever get in between what he's doing. And he untied me. . . .

"He tried to have sex with me afterward, and he gave me some marijuana. . . . He said that will help me because I was so hysterical. . . ."

There were children in the house?

"Yes."

Which children?

"Jason. Jason was."

Just Jason? Nobody else?

"Joshua and April. They were the only children that were every day there, and I just don't remember any other children. . . .

"I just remember I was so concerned about my own self about what was going on, but I just remember that the door was open, and I think some of the children could come and see."

Did he have sex with you that day?

"Yes."

Oral sex, anal sex, vaginal sex? Did you masturbate? What kind of sex did you have?

"He had in my vagina. Then he started hitting me with his penis. . . ."

What did he do after he had sex with you that day?

"I can't," Iliana sobbed. "Can I have a break? I can't go on. . . ."

Any other time that comes to mind . . . that Frank did things to you?

"Yes. . . . He tried to spread my legs. He was taking me apart because he like to see me suffering."

Is that what he said? He said, "I like to see you suffering"?

"He like to see me suffering," she sobbed.

"You could see it in his face. . . ."

What else did Frank do to you?

"He just so hard, but it was one of the worst days. . . . He hang me from both my hands [in the garage], and I remember he was wearing the green pants like military pants. . . .

"And he had a chain around him, and a real thick chain, and he hang me from both my hands. He put a tape on my face. He put the chain around my . . . waist. . . .

"And he was hurting me. Then I just remember that he was under a table. . . . He was under a table. Nearby. He would look from there. He would look at me . . .

"And then he came. He had a piece of cloth in his—had some feces on it. He started put it on my body."

Where on your body did he put the feces?

"On my legs."

Where else?

"On my legs. . . . The garage door was closed, but the kitchen door was open. And there were children in the other side. They could see it. . . ."

What other things did you see him do to the children?

"There was one of the nights he used to give me those little pills. . . . I was exhausted. And there was the Saturday we have a real bad fight. And he hit me real bad. And that one of my eyes was swollen. . . .

"And I remember after that happened, somebody called. It was one of the parents. . . . Frank answered, and Frank say OK. I tell him who had called. He just told me to get ready because I was going to take care of two children that night, that they were going to sleep over, and so I refused.

"I told him 'no' because of the way I was, and I didn't want them to see me that way. There was no way that he could cover it. . . .

"I stood in my room, and the children came. And I stood in my room all the time. I did not see him. So he say that if I didn't want to take care of them, he would do it. . . .

"So I never saw the children, so after he came back into the room and asked me again . . . to get out of the room because the children were asking for me. I tell him no. . . .

"I just stood there, and he gave me these pills. . . . I was sleepy. . . . He said [they were] going to calm me because of my pain. And like, all I remember that I opened my eyes and again, it was real late, everybody was sleeping except that I heard—I heard something in my bathroom. . . .

"I was still feeling very dizzy. And I came to the door, and I saw Frank and Jaime. Frank had his penis in his mouth.

"And I didn't want to believe it.

"And then Jaime—he just started vomiting real bad. . . ."

• • •

John Hogan's very first undertaking when Janet Reno assigned him the Country Walk case was to view the videotaped interviews the Bragas had conducted with twenty-seven of the now more than fifty children known to have attended the Country Walk Babysitting Service.

He conceived the ambitious plan of spending half of each day at Apogee, where he could study the children's statements undistracted by the comings and goings in his place of work.

But the prosecutor found that half a workday exceeded his tolerance for horror, finding himself, after but forty-five minutes of viewing, staring vacantly at the television screen, his pen frozen on his notepad. He could take no more.

There was no question in his mind—none whatsoever—that any jury that saw these tapes would deliver a swift and sure conviction.

Dan Casey, upon his own initiation to the case, immediately concurred.

So it came as no surprise to the prosecutors when Jeffrey Samek filed a motion to exclude the admission of the videotapes into evidence even before the trial began. What Samek apparently didn't know was that the State had already regretfully advised the parents that it would not "test" the provisions of their hard-won children's Judicial Proceedings Act at risk of appellate reversal.

The parents offered little protest.

Reversible error, they knew, must be avoided at all costs.

They had spilled blood all over the House and Senate to make the tapes admissible, but it somehow seemed less important now that the law would do their children little good than that the law would someday be used by someone.

"We aren't doing this for our own children," Maggie had said repeatedly throughout the Tallahassee campaign. "We're doing it for everybody else's children, because it won't apply to our children."

And though none of the parents abandoned hope that their own children might benefit from the law's provisions, they were not unprepared to find that they would not.

It didn't matter, said Tom Herschel. "We dignified what happened to our families. I don't think I've ever been prouder of anything I've done in my life than passing that law."

Jeffrey Samek may have been mildly surprised to find that the State's strategy did not include an attempt to introduce the children's interviews into evidence, but he had a surprise of his own in store.

He would introduce them himself.

Every last one of them.

Hogan's astonishment was exceeded only by his delight.

What the prosecution had anticipated, and had come armed with a pile of statutes to fight, was Samek's attempt to introduce only bits and pieces of selected tapes out of context, or possibly the one tape that was significantly deviant in style from the rest—the Jaime Fuster interview of November 26, 1984.

His fourth and last.

It had been arranged by Assistant State Attorney Christopher Rundle, who advised the Bragas that unless he had a statement from Frank Fuster's son—the only child infected with venereal disease at the time of his father's arrest—the case was in serious jeopardy.

Joe and Laurie, who had almost four months before allowed the child his confused need to protect his father and indeed assured him of his father's love, were now being asked to make him confront a horror he continued to refuse to acknowledge.

Jaime Fuster spoke only of his anxiousness to see his father released from jail.

"But you have lots of statements from lots of children already," argued the Bragas.

Rundle wanted Jaime's.

"But Jaime isn't going to volunteer *anything*. He loves his father. His father may be Frank Fuster, but he's still his father."

Rundle didn't care. Unless he got a statement from Frank Fuster's son as to the source of his gonorrhea—whether it be his father or some other adult involved with the Fusters—he might not be able to proceed with the case.

"You've got to get him to talk."

"What about leading questions?"

"Whatever it takes."

What it took, the Bragas found, was a day of swimming through Jell-O. Only their belief in a burden shared allowed them to go along with Rundle's plan. Jaime's mother, Martha, was no less interested in seeing her son unload.

"Please, I want you to ask him the 'hard' questions," she pleaded with Joe and Laurie before they joined Jaime in the interview room.

"What do you mean by 'hard' questions?" inquired Joe.

"About the sex and the disease," she said. "I know Frank abused him, and I don't want Jaime to resent me later."

The "hard" questions were the ones too hard for Martha to ask herself.

When Jaime seemed to tire of playing with toys and dispensing voluminous clouds of fog in response to their queries (Jason who? I don't know no Jason. April who? Pictures? What pictures? Pee-pee? I don't know the meaning of that. Penis? I don't remember anyone ever putting one of those in my mouth.), the Bragas would call for a break.

Finally, Joe told Jaime that he was sorry, but he didn't believe he was telling the truth. I saw a medical report, said Joe, that says that you have a disease called gonorrhea. Did anyone ever tell you that you had gonorrhea? It's cured now. That's why they gave you some shots. But the doctors tell me there's only one way that you can get gonorrhea, and that's if someone puts their penis in your mouth. Do you remember someone ever doing that?

"I don't remember, maybe they did, I don't remember. . . .

"Maybe it happened when I was six. I don't remember when I was six. . . . Maybe I was fast asleep. I don't remember. . . ."

"What could we do to try to help you remember?"

"Nothing. I don't want to remember."

"You don't want to remember?"

"I do remember. I don't *want* to remember. . . .

"I just want to forget about it."

But Jaime did remember, and finally he told the Bragas many of the things his father and stepmother would do "when they were sick." Sometimes, he said, they would "get sick in the head" and do things to the children.

Did Jaime think his father should go to jail?

Yes, he said. Then maybe he could get better.

The next day he asked his mother to bring him to see the Bragas so he could say good-bye. Jaime laid his head in Laurie's lap and cried. "I'm so tired of getting on airplanes," he said. "Always flying back and forth, back and forth.

"I live in Miami."

"No," said Laurie. "You live with your mother now.

"And your job is to be happy."

Over her dead body was anyone going to put this child on the stand. He would never be able to testify. And he should never be asked.

Hogan was not greatly distressed with the fourth and final Jaime Fuster interview, though he was annoyed that Christopher Rundle had pressured the Bragas into deviating from their carefully circumspect interview style, which opened doors through which the children could choose to walk—or not.

Select portions of the Jaime Fuster tape were only potentially dangerous to the State's case if Samek was able to introduce them as "representative" of how the children's statements were obtained, without allowing the jury to view the rest of the tapes. Should Frank's attorney attempt to do that (and if Hogan were he, he would), the State was prepared to argue vigorously that, if the judge allowed the defense to admit one tape, they must admit them all.

But John Hogan failed to realize that Samek had become so absorbed in picking the tapes apart for inconsistencies that he failed to recognize that even these formed a pattern of sorts.

The children had little concept of time and limited mathematical skills, leaving the answers to questions of "when" and "how many times" less than informative. But they recalled vividly the memories associated with touch and taste and smell.

The children's statements were as credible as they were incredible, and as detailed as they were vague.

But their sexual knowledge exceeded that of most adults.

And that alone was enough to impel both the Bragas and the State to examine—rather than discard—information that seemed illogical on its face. As the children became bolder and more articulate, the adults were constantly reminded that they were not dealing with the crimes of a logical—or even human—mind. They came to realize that it was indeed possible for the children to have lived in a world where "ca-ca" devils were to be feared and excrement to be eaten.

Even now, pieces of the puzzle, once cast aside, continued to fall into place. The red and green slime with which Jason saw himself covered when he looked in the mirror seemed less fantastic a tale in light of the suspected hallucinogenic contents of Frank's custom-blended "brown" milkshakes—one of the more minor details of Iliana's deposition that corroborated the children's statements.

They knew the children had been drugged. And they knew that both Frank and Iliana had fed them unusual "brown" concoctions. They had even suspected hallucinogens. Now it was more than speculation.

The Fuster home, according to Iliana, was a regular pharmacy.

It was also Iliana who had inadvertently lent credence to one of the most bizarre statements to come from a child's mouth—and one of the few verbal ones that April Lancaster ever offered.

She said that she put "pennies" in Frank's bottom.

And though they had come to expect few limitations to Frank Fuster's perverse pathology, the penny story stretched even the prosecutors' enlightened perception of what was possible and what was not.

That was before Iliana Fuster explained that when her husband used to have her powder his genitals with talc and diaper him with a bedsheet, he required that she give him suppositories.

And they came wrapped in copper-colored foil.

● ● ●

Though their attention remained undivided, the eight men and women chosen to sit in judgment of Frank Fuster displayed no visible reaction to the State's week-long presentation of its case. Even the children's appearances had elicited no measureable response.

So it must have occurred to Jeffrey Samek that he might have underestimated the impact of the children's intimate first moments of disclosure, when, upon viewing the first of thirty-six tapes he planned to show them, one of the jurors dissolved into tears and others looked visibly shaken.

It was the Jason Harrison interview of August ninth—the one in which he opened Pandora's box.

The same interview that Dr. Coleman would soon dismiss on the witness stand as "just playing," its content not worthy of his meticulous dissection.

Judge Newman sent the jury to lunch.

For nearly two weeks, they ate, slept, and watched the Bragas swim through Jell-O on some sixty hours of video, much of it consumed by the building of block towers and seemingly inconsequential chatter as they developed a rapport with the children and casually tested and assessed their levels of comprehension and communication. "How high can you count?" "What color is this?" "Which is bigger?" "Can you put the ball behind the box; inside the box; on top of the box?" "Do you remember what you got last Christmas?"

By the time Jeffrey Samek's daily taped onslaught drew to a close, the jurors seemed numbed by the periods of prolonged boredom punctuated by unexpected assaults on their deadening sensibilities.

Some even dozed.

The jurors were unaware, of course, that at the end of two of the days the tapes were shown, Jeffrey Samek retired to an office on the sixth floor to gather massive volumes of Iliana's words, which tended to cast his client in an unflattering light.

The media, once again denied admission to Jeffrey Samek's "discovery" of the truth (this one conducted in cordial contrast to that of Jason Harrison), panted in the corridors, as the court reporter's fingers flew through another page's worth of transcript to which they immediately laid claim.

One page at a time.

By the second day, anyone in Miami who was unaware of the drill, the crucifix, the pistol with which Frank Fuster played Russian roulette in a most unusual manner, had either died or left the country.

Anyone but the jurors, whose attention alternately drifted from and riveted to the children on the tapes.

Only five of whom Iliana could—or would—recall.

The parents hovered anxiously in their homes in Country Walk, their function as witnesses spent, but not suspended. Except to testify or accompany their children, the parents were bound by the witness rule to steer clear of the courtroom.

And any other sources of information about the trial.

Theoretically their job was done, but the State could not release them from their subpoenas until after the judge charged the jury, should the prosecutors find it necessary to recall any of them to testify in its rebuttal case.

But it was impossible to pull the plug on the news that their greatest hopes—and their worst fears—were being realized.

Their babysitter was talking.

Finally they would come to learn the full content of their children's nightmares. Or so they thought at the time.

Shari Herschel, who was rushed to a hospital by ambulance in the wee hours of a morning not long after her day in court, experienced renewed heart palpitations upon discovering what her children had not only done but *seen* in the Fuster home and placed a frantic call to John Hogan.

"I heard about the little boy Frank hung from his feet like a punching bag," she sobbed. "Was it Chad? Was it Chad?"

No, said Hogan. It was another child whom he was not at liberty to identify. Chad's name had not been mentioned, he continued. But if it was, he would contact her immediately.

By the way, he reminded her, "You're not supposed to be listening to the news."

Hogan, Casey, and Shiffrin monitored the jury's viewing of the tapes in shifts, there being other matters to which the State needed to attend should Jeffrey Samek's case become even more bizarre than his introduction of the children's interviews.

The prosecutors mused over this unexpected game plan as they viewed the evidence that each had believed, upon their own first viewing, would compel sure and swift conviction.

Did Jeffrey Samek actually believe that any human being could dismiss Andy Pierson's hypnotic reenactment of rock-a-bye in his mother's lap as fantasy? Could anyone on this jury not be greatly disturbed by his repeated insistence that his mother insert her finger in his rectum?

The Andy Pierson tape was even more compelling than Jason Harrison's increasingly graphic disclosures. Because Andy Pierson did not seem to be retelling his experiences as much as he seemed to be reliving them.

He seemed transported to another world.

Perhaps Jeffrey Samek had invested so much energy into subverting the truth that he lost sight of what it was and where it could be found.

Or perhaps he was counting on the jurors' senses becoming sufficiently deadened by the sixty-hour taped marathon that they would be more anxious than ever to grasp the straws that Lee Stewart Coleman would offer them, regardless of their frailty.

That, the prosecutors gathered, as they surveyed the worn jurors, was a distinct possibility.

Crisp and confident, Jeffrey Samek presented the rest of his case.

First on the defense's very short list of people who would testify on behalf of Frank Fuster was the HRS caseworker—a seven-year veteran who in June of 1984 had "investigated" her very first "sexual harassment" complaint.

She dropped in on Iliana unannounced, she told Jeffrey Samek, and asked the woman who answered the door whether she had been "sexually harassing" any children.

As the young woman said no, and the house was "immaculate," and there didn't appear to be any "sexual harassing" going on, she believed the complaint to be "unfounded."

Dan Casey had but a few questions for Samek's witness.

Did she speak to any of the children?

"No."

Did she speak to any parents?

"No."

Did she get any *names* of any children or parents?

"No."

Did she try to track down the source of the complaint?

"No."

Did she do anything other than ask the woman who answered the door whether she was "sexually harassing" children?

"No."

Casey returned to the prosecution table scratching his head. Samek was certainly scraping the bottom of the barrel for witnesses.

Undaunted, Samek called his second witness.

Jill Vickers, mother of Steven.

Schoolteacher. Wife of an Arvida executive.

"Judge," requested Frank's attorney, "may we come side bar prior to my beginning questions?"

There commenced a whispered huddle at the bench.

"Judge, I would ask that the court label Ms. Vickers a court witness [in order to direct her testimony with leading questions]. Her son is alleged to be one of the victims. Clearly adverse."

John Hogan fairly choked.

"She's being sued by the other parents personally," Hogan told the court. "Her husband is an executive for Arvida. They have been the paralegals you've seen Mr. Samek with more or less constantly." Hogan gestured toward the left gallery where a small, rotating army of civil attorneys and legal aides monitored every hearing, every deposition, and every moment of the Country Walk trial, most often from the vantage of the back of Frank Fuster's head, their ringside seats frequently located behind the defense table, from which Samek conferred with them from time to time.

"If you go through the depositions in this case," John Hogan continued, "you'll find out that the defense expert, when [he] met with Mr. Samek, also met with Arvida's attorneys.

"Clearly there is no hostility between Mr. Samek and this witness."

Mrs. Vickers, inquired Jeffrey Samek, *did Steven ever say to you that Iliana kissed his body?*

"Yes, he did. . . ."

Did you believe him when he told you?

"When he told me, I felt he was covering for the girls. Steven often would cover for his sisters, often cover for other kids, maybe he thought had done something. He would substitute names. . . . You know, 'Who spilled water all over?' . . . He would put one of his sisters' names in or substitute one of his friends' names when it should have been, you know, one of his sisters' names. . . ."

Did you subsequently take Steven out of Iliana Fuster's care?

"Yes, I did."

Would you tell the ladies and gentlemen of the jury why you did that?

"OK. For a couple months prior to the point that I took Steven out of Iliana's, I had a couple of conversations . . . with Jeannie Pierson, who was the only mother that I knew. . . .

"I wasn't really happy with the babysitting. I felt Steven was never getting outside. They were never going for walks.

"They were kept in the house all the time. . . .

"I had also just about had it with the emotional feeling of being guilty of taking my child and dropping him off, going through those tantrums about not wanting to go. This had occurred all year long from the very first person I took Steven to.

"It was crying every morning. It was holding onto my leg. I had to go to work. And when I came home, it was very disruptive. . . .

"I just wanted to get him out. And so with all the reasons—combination of reasons put together . . . I spoke to my mother that weekend. She took Steven . . . up in Deerfield. . . ."

Let me ask you. Did you tell Jeannie [Pierson] *what Steven had said . . . ?*

Did you tell her you didn't really believe him?

"I told her, 'You know Steven.' She said, 'Yeah, I know Steven,' and . . . I told her Steven's statements about Andy . . . that Iliana kissed Andy's body."

As a result of your conversation with Jeannie Pierson, were you of the belief that Andy also made up stories?

"Yes. . . ."

Did you speak with the Bragas about the role that you could play in regard to their interviewing?

"Yeah."

Did they tell you that you should reinforce Steven that Mr. Fuster was bad?

"Well, they told me if he told me something—if he came out with something—or told me something happened to him at a later point . . . that I should tell him that was good . . . that he was not bad like Frank . . . and that it was a real good thing he was telling me. . . ."

Did you ever tell Steven that Frank was bad?

"Yeah, I told him that; I guess we talked about it. I just said that [the] couple of times he saw the news. . . . We turned it off, but a couple of times he saw Frank on TV. I would tell him that Frank was there because he had done bad things, but Steven hadn't been bad."

Daniel Casey approached Jill Vickers, marveling once again at the barrel from which Samek was obliged to scrape defense witnesses.

You mentioned to us that Steven frequently refused to go when you took him to the Fusters', correct?
"Yes."
You mentioned that he had previously refused to go to some of the other babysitters, too?
"Always."
But isn't it true, ma'am, that Steven's refusals escalated?
"In April it became really bad. . . ."
In fact, ma'am, it got to the point where your husband would have to discipline Steven, would have to spank him in order to take him to the Fusters'?
"On a couple of occasions. . . ."
I believe Steven said to you, "Mommy, kiss my body"?
"Yes."
Was there anything that you had said to him that elicited that?
"No . . . I was just changing his clothes."
Totally spontaneous from him to you?
"Yes."
He was trying to tell you something?
"He said something. He made a statement to me."
I think in your testimony on direct you mentioned that . . . your attitude about this was annoyance? You were really annoyed when he said this?
"Very."
I imagine that showed about your person, in your demeanor?
"I was annoyed. . . ."
When Steven was telling you, "Mommy, kiss my body," any question in your mind [he meant] "Mommy, kiss my penis"?
"No, there wasn't any question. . . . He said, 'Iliana kisses all the babies' bodies.' And at that, I said, 'Does she kiss Andy's body?' and he said, 'Yes.' "
Then there came a time you decided to lay off it for a while?
"I went back and questioned him maybe ten minutes after he said it. . . . 'Steven, what you just said about Iliana, is that true?' He said, no, no—he was kind of laughing, just walking around his room playing with his toys. Then I waited about an hour. Then I went back. I said, 'Steven, remember that statement you told me before . . .

was it really true about Iliana kissing your body?' He said, no, no, no, no, no . . . then ran off. That was it."

Had Steven ever asked you to kiss his penis before?

"No."

You mentioned that there had been some previous kidding going on in your household, kind of a brother/sister thing?

"A lot of real silliness. . . ."

Am I correct if I said your daughters had talked about bodies before, boys' and girls'?

"Yes."

And your daughters talked about people kissing one another before?

"Um-hum. . . ."

But am I also correct, ma'am, in saying that those two very different concepts have never been put together before?

"No, they hadn't. . . ."

You mentioned Steven sometimes would substitute names. "Kathy spilled milk," or that kind of stuff?

"Right."

Am I correct if I said he never involved adults before?

"It would be children's names. . . ."

Never "Iliana spilled milk"?

"No, he had never put an adult."

"Frank threw mud at the house"?

"No."

To the best of your knowledge—outside of the exposure Steven may have gotten at the Fuster house—has Steven ever been exposed to oral sex?

"No."

Don't have cable TV in your house?

"No . . . didn't at the time."

Ma'am, you mentioned that in your testimony, that you didn't believe Steven when he said this?

"No—well, I didn't believe. No, I didn't believe."

Isn't it a fact, ma'am, that your opinion now maybe has changed?

"Yes, absolutely."

You actually now believe that your son was sexually molested at the Fuster house?

"After many conversations, after seeing, speaking to Joe and Laurie, after reading countless articles, and after a comment that was made by my son to me in September of '84 . . . yes, I do. . . ."

Wouldn't you agree that Steven's [first] statement was a factor in deciding never to send him back to the Fuster house?

"I said it was one of the least important factors. . . ."

Could you explain for the ladies and gentlemen of the jury the context [of his second statement]?

"I had taken Steven to see Joe and Laurie Braga . . . and nothing was said except the same statements that he had told me originally. So we went home. Of course, I was real upset about the whole thing . . . and I really started grilling him and trying to find out what had happened.

"I guess I became almost to the point of being obsessive about it. . . . He would deny everything, 'no, no, no, no,' this kind of thing.

"Well, it got so bad, one point my daughter, the oldest one, said, 'Mommy, leave him alone.' . . . I guess the dawn kind of came across my head; I was just badgering him into submissiveness. I should back off of Steven. . . .

"There were a couple of shows on TV that were on. So we sat down one night. We watched one of those . . . *Strong, Brave and Free.* I believe that was the name of it.

"Anyway, it was about child molestation. . . . I sat in the chair with Steven. We watched it together. . . .

"At one point, Steven started sitting in the chair. He started going, 'hands, arms, knees, legs,' 'hands, arms, knees, legs.' All of a sudden, he jumped out of the chair. He ran off to our toy room . . . and he started playing with his toys. He . . . had this little piano . . . started banging on it. I ran into the room with him. I said, 'Steven, what's the matter?' He wouldn't answer me; just kept banging, banging. . . .

"I said, 'Are you upset about something that happened at Iliana and Frank's?' I said, 'Did they tell you to keep a secret, not to tell me?'

"He said—," Jill Vickers began to break down. "He said, 'They hit me, Mommy,' " she sobbed. "He said, 'They hit me and they locked me in the bedroom.' . . .

"It was like, you know, somebody had taken a shovel and just shoveled out my insides."

Judge, the defense calls Simon Miranda.

His first two witnesses having been summarily converted into witnesses for the prosecution, Jeffrey Samek considered turnabout fair play and recalled a psychologist who had already testified for the State.

Doctor, you previously testified in this case?

"Yes, sir. I did. . . . "

Doctor, what day is it that you saw Jaime Fuster?

"I saw Jaime on the 27th of November 1984 [the day after the Bragas' fourth and final interview]."

And during that visit you conducted an interview with him?

"Yes, sir. That's correct."

And you prepared a transcript of that interview?

"Yes, that is right."

And the transcript has been admitted into evidence in this case as far as you know?

"As far as I know, yes."

Doctor, I'd like to call your attention to page 13 of that transcript. . . . That paragraph was in Spanish. Would you tell the ladies and gentlemen of the jury . . . what it is?

"That is a narrative that I dictated on some of the statements Jaime made to me. . . . "

Tell us . . . the translation of what you wrote verbatim, as best you can.

"Jaime also added that his mother, Iliana—he calls her 'mother' also—put her what he calls 'pee-pee' in the other children, and he says that the other children told him. That is, that that information came to him through the other children. He denies that anything was done to him—that is, that Iliana, herself, did anything to him. . . ."

Are you aware that subsequent to your seeing Jaime Fuster, Jaime Fuster has told other psychologists, "They forced me," and "I was too tired and couldn't fight back" in regards to the admission to you and admission to others—that is, he had been abused?

"No sir. I'm not aware. . . .

"As I recall right now, I think that you questioned me as to that point previously, so to that extent . . . I'm aware. . . ."

Did you make any attempt to investigate whether or not Jaime had said it?

"No, I did not because I . . . saw Jaime as quite capable of doing that. That . . . child had a tremendous amount of persistence and I would say he felt guilty about telling what he was telling. . . .

"In my experience, this is a kind of child that is likely to blame someone else for his talking about the abuse and incriminating someone that he actually loves.''

Dan Casey was not at all displeased to see Dr. Miranda on the stand once again, there being one small matter that he now had the opportunity to bring to the jury's attention.

Your testimony previously was, ambled Casey, *you saw Jaime Fuster for the purpose of medical treatment and diagnosis mostly? You're appointed, correct?*

"Correct.''

You were appointed by Judge Ferguson over in Juvenile Court to take a look at Jaime?

"Yes, sir. . . .''

When you talked to Mrs. Martha Fuster, were your discussions with Martha Fuster about anything Jaime might have said to her . . . pertinent to your diagnosis of Jaime Fuster?

"Very definitely, yes. . . .

"She commented, 'Jaime said to me last night . . . "Mom, do you know that all the other kids saw my daddy put his penis in my mouth?'' ' ''

Thank you very much, Doctor.

Casey ambled back to his corner of the ring.

Three defense witnesses down. Two to go.

The only two who were potentially dangerous.

• • •

California psychiatrist Lee Stewart Coleman delivered a half-day narrative on the unholy alliance he perceived between the fields of mental health and the law, mental health professionals and child witnesses in general, and the "outrageous," "manipulative," "abusive"—and indeed "tricky"—tactics used by the Bragas specifically, which, by the way, in his "experience," conformed to the interviewing scourge he saw "sweeping the nation" from coast to coast.

Under Jeffrey Samek's meticulous direction, Dr. Coleman "refreshed" the jury's memory on certain "critical" points of the tapes through which they had waded, sneering haughtily at the "obvious fantasies" that the Bragas chose not to challenge—"ridiculous" things, like eating excrement and cutting off heads and going to college and breaking doors.

But that was just a small part of it. There was an endless array of "manipulative" techniques that rendered the children totally incompetent to provide any sort of reliable information about anything.

The same ones he'd discussed at the probation violation hearing.

Curiously absent from the psychiatrist's list of "fantasies" he accused the Bragas of disregarding was one he had mentioned in deposition.

Laurie Braga, he said, had failed to "express disbelief" when Crystal Fletcher indulged in "obvious fantasizing" about having an eight-year-old brother named Michael.

Perhaps it was because he had, within the past two weeks, "discovered" what Laurie had right after the interview, when she made a point of verifying the information outside the child's presence: Peyton Fletcher had an eight-year-old son by a previous marriage.

And his name was Michael.

John Hogan approached the man who held the key to Frank Fuster's cell and commenced a lengthy inquiry into the California psychiatrist's credibility. He hoped the jurors were paying attention, for herein lay the key to his case.

To not believe the children was to set Frank Fuster free.

Samek's sixty-hour marathon of taped interviews had been a calculated risk. He was not aware of the State's decision not to reintroduce the tapes. And if he allowed Coleman to testify about the tapes in their absence, he had to consider the possibility that the State might introduce them on rebuttal, where a jury might recognize that Dr. Coleman had "refreshed" their memories of events that did not occur. If a jury was to see the children's interviews, individually, within minutes or hours of Coleman's comments that the Bragas had restated to Jaime "distortions" of what he had said in his previous interview (which Coleman called an act of child abuse by the interviewers), the jury would have been in a better position to recall that Jaime had indeed stated in his first interview that Iliana told him that only *he* could "save his father," which was precisely what Laurie Braga had mentioned in passing in the third "your job is to be happy" interview.

There were numerous areas in which the State needed to highlight the "reliability" of the expert who testified on Frank Fuster's behalf, and supply a motive for his "opinions."

John Hogan wasted little time getting to the bottom of Lee Coleman's pockets.

When did Mr. Samek have you fly out from California?
"On Saturday."
When did the clock [start to] run—Saturday morning or Saturday afternoon?
"Starting Saturday morning."
How much is it running from that point?
"Fifteen hundred dollars a day."
Through today. We're talking about—OK, how much does that add up to so far?
"I haven't added it all up."
Could you go ahead and do that for us, sir?
"Well, Saturday, Sunday, Monday, Tuesday—that would be four days. That would be six thousand dollars for those four days."
That's in addition to the forty-five hundred for watching the tapes?
"Correct."
In addition to the ten thousand you billed in the first week of part-time work on this case?
"Yes."
So, we're over twenty thousand dollars so far, the citizens of Dade County are going to pay you for your testimony?
"Yes."
This is the same rate you charged everyone else in the last six or nine months since you've been interested in sex abuse . . . ?
"That is my general rate. . . ."
Now, whether the defendant is guilty of the charges that he faces has nothing to do with your testimony, does it? In other words, [whether] Frank Fuster molested all these kids has nothing to do with or wouldn't change your testimony in any way, would it?
"That's correct. I'm not offering any opinion as to whether he's guilty or not; [I'm] offering opinions as to whether methods used by mental health professionals are going to lead to reliable results."
So, in other words, he could have been seen by 170,000 people in the Orange Bowl doing these acts; you would have said exactly the same thing about these interviews?
"Well, I suppose if I saw the same interviews, I would say the same thing. I think that's taken out of context, because if he had been seen doing these things by all these people, there would have been no need to conduct the interviews; therefore, I would not have been called into the case."
There would have been no need? The police would not have had

*need to interview them or the state attorney's office would not
have?*

"What I'm saying, if—if there were eyewitnesses who would come
in and say, 'I saw this happen,' this was overwhelmingly shown by
eyewitnesses, there certainly would have not been . . . all these
interviews . . . by the Bragas. . . .

"Therefore, no reason for me to be called in."

*That's something you learned in medical school? That's how the
investigation would be conducted?*

*You've never talked to any of the children in this case—any of the
thirty-odd children who were at the Fuster home; is that correct?*

"That's correct."

You've never personally spoken to any of the parents?

"No. . . ."

*Now, you haven't read any of the depositions in this case, other
than Dr. Joseph Braga's; is that correct?*

"That's correct. . . ."

*You understand that Mr. Samek alone has six or seven boxes
there, and there's a lot more . . . ?*

"That's my understanding."

You've not read any of the parents' depositions?

"No."

You haven't read Chris Royo, lead investigator . . . ?

"No. . . ."

*You have no idea in what context children made statements prior
to going to the Bragas; is that correct, other than what is reflected
in the interviews themselves?*

"I have only police reports. . . ."

*I think you indicated that the main problem you found with the
Bragas' interviews was that they began with a bias. That is, they felt
the children had been molested; is that correct?*

"Yes."

*Do you feel you began your project, your task, with any sort of
bias in favor or against mental health professionals or anyone else?*

"Yes . . . the bias that I have formed based on approximately
fourteen years of studying what happens when mental health
professionals take on tasks that the law thinks they can take on, is
that we're really not able to do it.

"In addition to that, I have seen methods used in these kinds of
cases which I have great problems with. So that it's true that when
I first began to look at these methods, I had already had some serious

questions in my mind about the way these children would be interviewed.

"I was, of course, curious to see just what they would be doing. . . ."

What does the acronym VOCAL stand for?

"Victims of Child Abuse Laws, I believe."

That is an organization formed by some of the defendants in the Jordan, Minnesota, case you talked about; is that correct?

". . . My understanding is that it started there because of the case in Minnesota, but whether or not it was started by defendants, I just don't know. . . ."

They have a newsletter?

"Yes, they do."

That newsletter gives advertisements for you indicating you're available to come to the aid of other people charged with sex abuse around the country; isn't that correct?

"I don't know if it says that. I recall that they mention it, that I had told them of my concern. . . ."

It's your opinion that the jury is as able to determine whether or not someone is telling the truth as you are; is that correct?

"Oh, very definitely. I would say that there's nothing about a psychiatrist which allows us to tell . . . any better than a layperson. . . . "

What your concern is [is] that the jurors . . . shouldn't be misled by an expert who comes in and says either X is true or Y is true, that instead, the jurors should just view things with their own common sense?

"Yes. . . ."

You indicated, in total, you've seen ninety hours of videotaped interviews in your experience the last six to nine months?

"Yes."

Sixty came from this case?

"Yes. . . ."

You indicated you'd published some articles; is that correct?

"Yes."

One of them dealt with child sex abuse; is that correct?

"That article is not yet published; written, not yet published. . . ."

Not the article you published in Hustler *magazine?*

"No."

Which was the article you published in Hustler?

"That was called, 'Lithium . . . Psychiatric Assault' . . ."

Could you please name three or four leading people who have done work in the area of child fantasy. . . ?
"I know Elizabeth Loftus has been doing some work. . . ."
Have you read Elizabeth Loftus's work?
"Some of it."
You have read that since you were last here when I asked you about it?
"That's correct."
But you already rendered your opinion that the dolls created fantasies?
"Oh, yes. . . ."
You indicate that the Bragas dismiss fantasy once a child was asked to pretend; is that correct?
"They dismissed fantasy which was not consistent with material about sexual abuse. They dismissed it as, 'Oh, well, it's just pretend,' and accepted material which could easily have been fantasy if it did indicate child sexual abuse."
Can you read their minds?
". . . I was looking at behavior."
From behavior you could tell what was going on in their minds?
"I could tell from their behavior whether they were acting in a leading and manipulative way. . . ."
[One] fantasy was Jason said April Lancaster was in college; is that correct?
"Yes."
That showed we can't believe anything Jason said?
"Well, I think that's mischaracterizing what I said. My comments about Jason were based on many, many different things. . . ."
Do you know if the Lancasters moved [to Gainesville] while this case was pending, while the investigation was pending?
"No, I don't."
Obviously you wouldn't know where they moved to?
"Correct."
Doctor, let's try another one. Do you know where the University of Florida is located?
"I could guess. I couldn't say I know."
Give us your best guess.
"Tallahassee."
Bad guess. Gainesville. . . . Do you know where Jason's parents went to college?
"No."

You don't know whether they went to the University of Florida; therefore, [Jason] relates Gainesville to college?

"No, I don't. Do you?"

You dismissed—you talked about Andy fantasizing because when he pulled his pants down, you understood him to say, "Mommy did it"? Is that what you heard the child say on the tape?

"No, no, if I'm remembering the one you're talking about, I believe it's the time he was asking his mother to put her finger in his behind. . . ."

Also as an element of fantasy, anytime a child speaks about feces you assumed that was fantasy; is that correct?

"No, but again, it's the totality of many different statements and it would be the combination of . . . what was supposedly done with feces. . . ."

It is obviously . . . unusual for people to play with feces; is that correct?

"Yes."

It's easier to believe that a child is fantasizing than there are people in this world who are capable of such acts; isn't that true?

"I don't know what you mean by 'easier.' . . ."

Have you ever reviewed the charging information in this case?

"No."

Do you know how many charges are filed against the defendant?

"No."

Any idea of the nature of those charges?

"Well, only in a general way. . . ."

Any knowledge of whether any of the items that you label as fantasy were reflected in the charging documents?

"No, I don't."

You talked about [how] they ignored the influence of others. That's the Bragas again; is that correct?

"Yes, I can't say they ignored them. What I can say [is they] didn't seem to show any indication they were concerned about possible outside influence."

You feel on the tape they should have shown that concern?

"I don't know about on the tapes, but I think that's a serious concern in deciding whether or not anything has happened."

You never talked to any of the parents to find out what they told the children, did you?

"No."

You don't know if the Bragas did or not?

"Well, yes . . . there were things on the tapes which indicate that the Bragas talked to parents about conversations between the children and the parents. . . ."

You don't know what the Bragas considered, what they ignored, do you?

"Well, if you're asking me specifically . . . no. What I'm talking about is the general methods. . . ."

In some cases you feel the children were unreliable witnesses before they even got to the interview; is that correct?

"Some of the material I read about Jason led me to have questions about reliability based on the fact that anatomically correct dolls were being used, leading questions were being used by the police, but I really don't have a lot of information. . . ."

John Hogan did not at this time advise Dr. Coleman that Detective Meznarich didn't use dolls, nor did the police report reflect the nature of her interview with Jason. He would save it for closing arguments.

Any other child besides Jason that you felt was unreliable prior to . . . beginning . . . the first interview?

"I don't know."

You feel that the parents in this case enjoyed hearing "sexy stuff"; is that correct?

"Mr. Hogan, I think that is a distortion of what I'm saying," spat Coleman. "What I've said is that I believe these parents were victimized as much as the children were by the interviewing methods—that the parents were manipulated into believing that the Bragas could tell, due to their professional expertise, that the children were molested, and therefore what would follow from that, as good parents, you would want to get from the child information about them being molested.

"This would then lead the parents to manipulate and direct the child because of the way they'd been manipulated. Has nothing to do with them enjoying it."

You didn't [say that] in deposition on August 14, page 303, "The evidence on the tape is the parents and the Bragas liked to hear sexy stuff. They had been told repeatedly, 'We're so proud of you when you talk about these things. We wish you would talk about these things.' "

"Well, that's taking a phrase like the 'sexy stuff' out of context . . .

what I was saying is that that's the information that the parents and Bragas seemed to want to hear. . . ."

Did you ever go through the tapes and determine how many times a child said "no" to a leading question?

"No, I didn't."

Did you ever go through the tapes and determine how many times a child gave information about sex that was not contained in a prior leading question?

"No."

Is it ever necessary to lead a child of three or four years old in an interview, in your opinion?

"It may be. . . ."

It would never be appropriate in this context—in a criminal investigation—to ask a question that is in any way leading?

"I guess what I would say, if you ask a small child a leading question in a manipulative environment, you ought to be prepared for an answer which is not very reliable. . . ."

"Hi, how are you, Joey?" Suddenly the child started talking; that would be an ideal [way] to avoid contamination, correct?

"Well, that's a mythical idea. Of course, it is not going to happen. Yes."

Let's assume, hypothetically, you were interviewing a child who was six years old, who had been diagnosed with gonorrhea, and whom you're interviewing [to] determine whether or not the child's father had sexually abused him.

How would you interview that child?

"Well, I think you would try to build up a relationship with the child, try to make the child feel safe. . . ."

If evidence wasn't forthcoming, what would you do?

"Well, I think first of all I would tell outside parties like lawyers and judges and that, 'Hey, I don't really have a way to get at truth in the child, probably not much better than you do.' . . ."

Anything else you would say to the child?

"Well, I might tell the child that the doctors have done certain tests which indicated that there was a problem and . . . we would be interested if you could tell us anything about anything that might have happened. . . ."

If the child wasn't forthcoming at this point, would you ask any . . . focus questions?

"I might."

Tell us what you'd say.

"Well, again, I don't think that I would do it myself because I would say to people, 'Look, I don't have any way to do this better than a lay investigator.' . . .

"If you're asking me to take on that role, I might easily ask the child more specific questions the way the Bragas did, but the difference would be I wouldn't get as heavy-handed about it. . . .

"The telling the child, 'Hey, the doctors have found some things; this tells us that something must have happened.' I don't have any quarrel with that, per se. . . ."

Are you able to tell us, if we took each child individually, when that child became incompetent and became no longer able to render accurate information?

"No, I wouldn't be that specific. . . ."

You don't know if it's in the beginning of the interview, end of the interview, the first interview, the second interview?

"Well, I can say that in my opinion . . . the minute the interviewers start asking the child to pretend and start encouraging fantasy with these dolls and start rewarding the child for saying sexual things and negatively reinforcing them for denying sexual things . . . the process has now contaminated any chance of getting reliable information."

You would discount any information given from that point on?

"In my opinion, all the information that comes out of these tapes should be discounted because of the Bragas' behavior."

You don't believe the kid even knows his name at this point?

"Well, not what I'm talking about."

How about the fact he was at the Fusters'? Should a jury discount that?

"I don't think they need the children's statement for that."

Should they if they had nothing else?

"I don't know."

You talk about the fact that the Bragas distort statements. Your problem is they don't put the entire statements in context; is that correct?

"It's much worse than that."

You give an example, Crystal Fletcher; am I correct? Specifically, I think your example was in the 9/10 interview she was told, "The last time you were here, you said they took their clothes off," and I think your notes indicate that you felt . . . she hadn't said that?

"It wasn't that she hadn't said those words, yes, out of context in that they ignored the way the child ended up saying that. That was the behavior of the interviewers in getting her to say that."

Because of that, you feel the jury should disregard her testimony and acquit the defendant?

Lee Stewart Coleman half rose from the witness stand and pounded it with his fist. "Sir, I never said a *word* about acquittal or anything like that. . . ."

The reason you don't talk about acquittal—you don't know whether Frank Fuster molested Crystal Fletcher or not, do you?

"Of course not. I would never *presume* to offer any opinion about that in this case or any other case."

You indicate the sessions went too long; is that correct?

"I think in some cases they did, yes."

Which interviews were those?

"Well, I wouldn't be able to answer without studying my notes in some detail."

Do you feel there's a set time you shouldn't go beyond in an interview of the child?

"No."

Obviously depends on whether the child is playing; isn't that correct?

"Well, that would be one factor. . . ."

Obviously if an interview went too long, you wouldn't necessarily discount what happened at the beginning?

"No, I wouldn't."

You indicated you felt it was inappropriate to use two children in the same room; is that correct? You talked about April and Jason?

"Certainly in the way it was done I thought it was highly inappropriate."

That was videotaped; isn't that correct?

"That's the only reason I was able to see it."

So, the jury can assess it as well as you can?

"I think they can."

Are you in any better position, because of training, to assess that interview than the jurors are?

". . . I think what I can do—have been trying to do—is give the jury the benefit of my study and experience. . . .

"I guess the other thing I think I can do is give my opinions as to whether the Bragas are doing anything which is truly expert. . . ."

Any other mental health professional would agree with what you said here today concerning these tapes?

"I don't think so, no. . . ."

You have criticized the tapes the Bragas did. Did you find that problem is unique here in Miami?

"Sad to say it is far from unique in Miami. I'm seeing it going on all over this country."

In fact, every case you consulted with, you've never seen an interview you feel was well done?

"That's true. I have not seen any videotape interviews that did not show essentially the same kind of manipulative, leading bias techniques. . . ."

Or, put another way, no one has ever paid you fifteen hundred dollars a day that you didn't conclude that the interviews were not well done?

"I think that's a *vicious* distortion. . . .

"I could form the opposite conclusion and get paid money, too. . . ."

Doctor, you'd have a problem if you did that because there are people who have spent twenty years of work in sex abuse whom you say are "pro-child." Why would someone pick you, with six months' experience in the area of child sex abuse to testify, when all the leaders in the area are on the other side?

"But, you see, Mr. Hogan, that distorts what these people have done. . . . They may be experts in some things, but they are not experts in studying the way the children are being interviewed. . . .

"In fact, I would say that to my knowledge, at this moment, I have done more study of how children are being interviewed in different parts of the country than anybody else even though it has only been nine months."

You said you saw ninety hours of tape in your experience; is that correct?

"Yes."

Sixty of them this case?

"Right."

This jury—eight people—must be numbers two, three, four, five, six, seven, eight, nine in the whole country in experience; [is that] what you're saying?

"That is right. Well ahead of people like Dr. Summit and others. . . ."

These people, said John Hogan, sweeping his arm toward the jury, *when they get done, can go out and get paid fifteen hundred dollars a day to do what you're doing?*

"No . . . they have had an opportunity to see more of the truth how these children are being interviewed than the people who are going to the conferences and teaching police and social workers to turn around, use the same manipulative techniques the Bragas have. . . ."

You mentioned Kee McFarland?

"Yes."

She has done a number of tapes in the Los Angeles McMartin case?

"Correct."

You've looked at those tapes also?

". . . I looked at about twenty hours so far."

You feel that those are the most atrocious of all tapes you have ever seen?

"Worse. Worse than the Bragas even."

So, of the ninety hours you have seen, sixty hours Braga, twenty hours were Los Angeles; what were the other ten?

"Ten are tapes in the variety of cases I've seen, most of them involving custody disputes between parents who hate each other and, you know, trying to use an allegation that comes up. . . ."

Would you agree that a knowledge of child development is helpful to the interviewing of children who have been sexually abused?

"Yes."

Could you please tell us who three or four of the nationally recognized experts in child development are?

"Generally. I don't know I can give you names. . . ."

It would be important to know those things, wouldn't it?

"I don't know how important it is to be able to recite a specific name."

Have you ever had an opportunity to view any interviews that Mr. Samek has done with the children?

"You showed me a brief tape of a deposition yesterday."

Could you please explain to the ladies and gentlemen—describe the deposition?

Jeffrey Samek rose to his feet with a most strenuous objection to the relevance of the jurors being apprised of his own particular "interviewing" style.

"Sustained," said Judge Newman mildly over Hogan's arguments that the jury be allowed to compare the Bragas' "technique"—one of the "worst" and most "manipulative" Frank Fuster's expert had ever seen—with those of another "interviewer."

That, ruled Judge Newman, would not be necessary.

Hogan shrugged.

You don't know how many charges were actually filed here; is that correct?

"No, I don't."

You don't know whether the charges filed here were based on information that came from leading questions or came from anything else; isn't that correct?

"No, I don't because I have nothing to say about those charges."

You have no idea whether or not Frank Fuster committed every single one of those acts, do you?

"I have no opinion on that. . . ."

And John Hogan had no other questions.

Only prayers.

• • •

Throughout his trial, Frank Fuster—to Jeffrey Samek's continued but resigned displeasure—held press conferences, which the State meticulously recorded and transcribed.

The children were brainwashed. Iliana was brainwashed. Iliana was a Judas. He forgave her. He loved her. He would never look at another woman again. All the State witnesses had perjured themselves. It was a conspiracy. Everyone was against him. He was one hundred percent innocent. Maggie Fletcher was paranoid. Child molesters were sick. He was normal. He was innocent.

And God was on his side.

"God," Jeffrey Samek was reported to have advised his client, "isn't on the jury, Frank."

The prosecutors collected volumes of Frank Fuster's words.

He wanted truth serum; he wanted polygraphs, though, he fretted, it would not spare him this injustice. He had always passed his "truth tests" with flying colors, and still he was convicted.

Jeffrey Samek—at his client's persistent behest—asked the court to allot more county funds so that Mr. Fuster might pay to have these tests administered. If Mr. Fuster were not indigent, Frank's lawyer pointed out, he could pay for them himself.

If Mr. Fuster weren't indigent, John Hogan parried, he could hire an astrologer and the results would be no more admissible as evidence.

But the rules of evidence, Frank believed, did not apply to him.

Dan Casey wished to bring that circumstance to Judge Newman's attention before the defendant took the stand.

The morning Frank Fuster was to testify as the fifth and final witness for the defense, Dan Casey brought the matter before the bench. The jury was not present. And Frank Fuster had just arrived, seated at the defense table, straining to hear what the judge, the prosecutor, and his attorney were "conspiring" in unmuted tones.

"Mr. Fuster gave an interview to a Spanish-language reporter—a series of reporters—last week," said Casey, "during which he mentioned to her, and I quote, 'I am going to try to find an opportunity to speak to the jury. Not what I have been asked . . . by my lawyer or the prosecutor, but to speak to the jury and tell the jury, express my truth—the only existing truth that there is—in my own words, in my own way.' "

Casey looked up from the transcript, cocked his head, and deadpanned, "I think that gives me cause to pause, Judge. . . .

"I just ask the court to restrict Mr. Fuster. . . . Specifically . . . not to mention lie detectors or truth serums. . . ."

"I have told him that," said Samek.

Frank stood and leaned over the defense table. "Your Honor, can I know what is going on, please, because I don't know if he's talking about me but I don't—"

Judge Newman's extraordinary patience was wearing thin.

"Your attorney, Mr. Samek, can explain it to you. I was just telling you—I thought you were hearing me—if you should take the stand, you are to answer the questions, and you can explain any of your answers, but you can't go on and add anything to your answer that was not asked of you. . . ."

"What was that he was reading in Spanish?" Frank demanded. "He said he has Spanish notes, something to that effect?"

Dan Casey reread the quote from the transcript.

Frank looked at the judge incredulously. "You are telling me, Your Honor, that I am not allowed to do this?"

The defense calls Frank Fuster.
Frank beamed at the jury as he made his way to the stand and settled in for his first chance to "express his truth" to the jurors, who, having been sequestered in a hotel for three weeks, were about the only inhabitants of Dade County who had not yet heard it.

Mr. Fuster, said Jeffrey Samek, *please speak up nice and loud so the jury can hear you.*

There commenced a more refined and lengthy version of his probation violation testimony, Jeffrey Samek apparently having advised him that a crisp "no, sir" might appear more "normal" to the ladies and gentlemen of the jury than breathing, "Nay-verr een my l-i-i-f-e" into the microphone like an obscene phone caller.

He was a businessman. A family man. A workaholic, who saw little of his wife, much less the "few" children she babysat "to keep her company." He worked from sunup to sundown five days a week, gave himself a half day off on Saturdays, and often allowed himself the pleasure of a full Sunday with his family.

His work took up all of his time.

"I would be going to buy some merchandise. I have to keep on going back and forth to the lumberyard to pick up lumber. I select my own lumber. . . .

"In order for the walls to be straight, the lumber must be straight. To be perfect, the lumber must be perfect.

"I trust no one in choosing my lumber."

And anyone who said he'd touched a kid was "one hundred percent" wrong.

Dan Casey collected his pen and commenced to amble a path between the podium and the witness box, "gee whiz" written in every step.

Whenever Iliana was babysitting children and she had to go off to another part of the house or had to go anywhere, you never helped her out by watching any of the kids, correct?

"Not that I remember. Correct."

You never took a bath or shower with any of the children, correct?

"One hundred percent."

That's the same one hundred percent like 'it's one hundred percent'?

"No doubt, positive."

Yes, same positive and no doubt that Iliana did all the babysitting, right? Same thing? Absolute? No doubt in that testimony . . . ?

"To my definition of babysitting. . . ."

OK. You testified that you carried two . . . children around. You carried Angie Dean to her car, and you carried Joshua Harrison to his dad's car? Is that right?

"That's correct."

Did you ever carry Angie Dean around when it wasn't to her car?

"No."

Did you ever carry any of the other children around to their cars or in or around the house or play or any activity?

"Not that I remember."

Let me ask you about something, sir. Judy Prince came in here and testified—you know who Judy Prince is, right?

"No."

She was your next-door neighbor.

"Oh, Mrs. Prince?"

Your next-door neighbor. She came in and testified that she saw you carrying Angie Dean around, not out to her car; was that correct?

"That was not correct, sir; as a matter of fact, I never seen Mrs. Prince in my house. . . ."

So, Judy Prince was incorrect, right?

What about Nikki Collier? You know, Mrs. Collier, who testified in this case earlier? She came in here and said she saw you carrying her daughter, Kristen Collier, around. Was she incorrect, too?

"I do not remember. Is that the little baby that is sitting next to the stereo?

"I appreciate if while you are asking me these questions, you show me the picture of the kids because I don't know them by names, and perhaps on one occasion I remember I carried in front of the mother a little baby that is sitting in front of the stereo. If you are referring to this kid—"

Certainly, smiled Casey agreeably. *You had testified before that you didn't carry any of the children, but by showing you a picture you can remember some of them that you were one hundred percent sure you didn't do before? That's fine with me.*

This is one picture of her that was taken from your house. And this is another picture. That's Kristen Collier. Do you remember carrying her around like her mother said?

"I do not remember. I use the word 'perhaps.' . . . If I remembered carrying her for whatever reason, I would tell you, but there is no bad action in that, and I would not have any reason to deny it, and I don't."

What about Steven Vickers? Do you remember ever carrying Steven Vickers around in front of Jill Vickers?

"I have—I am one hundred percent sure I have never carried Steven Vickers."

So, if Jill Vickers came in and testified that you carried Steven Vickers out to the car once for her, she would be wrong?

"She would be one hundred percent wrong."

O-k-a-ay, Jill Vickers. What about Mrs. Brighton? She was taking her child up to your place because she was doing volunteer work at the Mailman Center. She used to teach disabled kids. . . .

Do you remember her child, Haley Brighton? Let me show you a picture because you asked me to do that.

Do you remember that child being at your house?

"It looks familiar."

Do you remember carrying her around in the presence of her mother, Nancy Brighton?

"No."

So, once again, if Nancy Brighton came in here and testified that you, in fact, carried her daughter around in her presence and she had seen it, she would be incorrect?

"Is she saying that? You keep on saying that if she were to come in here. Is she saying that?"

She came in here and said—

"She's wrong. She's wrong."

One hundred percent or less than a hundred percent?

"Hundred percent. I do not remember carrying that child ever."

O-k-a-ay, Nancy Brighton.

You also mentioned, sir, that you never changed any diapers. Not only did you not change any of the diapers of the kids that are there, but you, in fact, never changed diapers of Jaime. Is that right?

"I would not include my son. I do not remember whether I changed my son's diaper or not, but I could tell you positively sure that I have never changed a diaper of any other kid. . . ."

Well, sir, that same Nancy Brighton came in here and testified that you had mentioned to her you had just gotten done changing her little daughter Haley's diapers. Was she correct when she said that?

Frank remained unruffled. "No, sir, she was not correct. I have never told that person that."

That's Mrs. Brighton?

"Whoever said that to you, whatever her name is, that's—that's a lie."

O-k-a-ay. Let me give you the whole context of this.

She did not tell it to me; she told it to the jury after being sworn in under oath. She said that she came to pick up her daughter one day and you mentioned that you had just finished changing little Haley's diaper. That's incorrect?

Jeffrey Samek's teeth began to gnash as they did each time Dan Casey slipped the jury reminders that the victims were cute—and small. Very, very small.

It drove Jeff Samek up a wall.

Was it not already a cruel enough circumstance that he wound up with Dracula for a client, without adding the cast of *Annie* for victims?

"That's incorrect," said Frank.

O-k-a-a-y, said Casey, checking Nancy Brighton off his lengthening list of witnesses whom Frank had accused of perjury, including—to Samek's dismay—the ones who had testified on his behalf. There were but two witnesses in his trial, Frank would say, whose word the jury could trust.

Himself.

And Dr. Lee Stewart Coleman.

Frank had a great deal of respect for Dr. Coleman's "abilities" with the truth. Here was a man who made sense.

Casey continued to dismantle Frank.

Do you remember a woman by the name of Shari Herschel? Mrs. Herschel?

"From seeing her in my house? I do not remember."

You do not remember from seeing her in your house? What about from seeing her when she testified in court here?

"I remember her. Besides, I did a job for her once."

So you know Mrs. Herschel?

"Yes."

Do you remember when Mrs. Herschel came in here to testify one day? She came to the house, and you mentioned that her little son, Chad, had just woke up from his nap and you had changed his diapers and there was some confusion—How come you just put the underwear on and didn't put the shorts on; took the diaper off of him, just put the underwear on, and left the shorts off?—remember, she testified about that?

Casey did not mention, for he was sure the jury would remember, that this was Chad Herschel's last visit to the Fuster home. Shari was "uncomfortable" about the man she found caring for her son.

"I don't remember, but if she said that, that's an incorrect statement."

So, Mrs. Shari Herschel, if she said that—and the jury can remember whether she said it or not—that's incorrect?

"That's incorrect. I have never changed anybody's diapers in the house other than my son, and I not even remember changing my son's diaper."

Would that also include a little child named Chad Herschel, who doesn't always wear a diaper? He's kind of potty trained, so he has to wear a diaper when he naps because sometimes he does not have control over everything like when he is completely awake. OK?

And he takes a nap in his diaper, but after his nap, you take the diaper off, you wipe him down, and you put his underwear and shorts back on.

You have never done that either?

"No, Mr. Dan Casey. I have never done that.

"Again, I repeat to you that I have never changed none of those kids' diapers, and I am full aware that those parents came here, sat in this same chair I am sitting down on, and looking at the jury's face, told each one of them that this had happened. That I had abused those kids and a whole bunch of other allegations that are one hundred percent *false*."

O-k-a-a-y, said Casey, unperturbed, as he checked another "perjured" mother off his notepad.

So that's Shari Herschel.

Mr. Fuster, was there ever a time when your wife left you alone with the children? When she had to go out of the house to do something?

"Perhaps, but I do not remember. But perhaps she never left me alone with the children. Perhaps I was working in my office, and she took two minutes—which is what it takes to go and put some water on the plants. Or perhaps she had a couple of kids in the TV room without my knowledge; not that she left me in charge of the children, if that's what you are insinuating.

"She left the kids by themselves, not with me. Does that answer your question?"

Your wife was in the habit of leaving the children alone?

"Right. In the TV room with the garage door opened, and she goes outside the garage to put some water on the plants that are in the planter by the window."

But what about to do something that takes a little bit more time than that? For instance, what about leaving the children alone in your care while she went to the store?

"No. I do not remember that."

What about leaving the children alone in your care while she went to pick up Jaime at the bus stop?

"No. I do not remember that either, sir."

OK. That same Mrs. Brighton, she came in here and testified that when she came to pick up her daughter, Haley, and she didn't see Iliana, and she talked to you, and she said to you, "I came to pick up Haley; what about her stuff?" and you told her that you were in charge of the children and that Iliana had left the house and left you in charge because Iliana had gone to the grocery store. Was Mrs. Brighton correct?

"She was incorrect."

Incorrect again?

"Again."

OK. What about Mrs. Herschel? That same Mrs. Herschel that you have done business with before and who had brought both of her children to your house to be babysat? Mrs. Shari Herschel came in here and testified that she came to pick up her son Chad one time and Iliana was not home, and you answered the door, and you had mentioned to her that Chad had just woke up from his nap, that's why he looked kind of groggy, and that he just had his underwear on and did not have his shorts on.

Mrs. Herschel mentioned that she waited around for Iliana because she had to pay her, probably waited some ten or fifteen minutes with you and her son alone in the house without Iliana.

When she said that, was she truthful?

"No, sir—"

That also is incorrect?

"When you tell me all the things she said, are you saying that to refresh my memory or because you want to impress the jury with her false testimony all over again?"

Casey smiled pleasantly. *I just want to see whether you are going to agree with us. . . .*

Did you hear the testimony of some of the parents who specifically said, most of the time they were there—either to drop off their children or to pick up their children—you were there?

"I heard those testimony, and I also heard the testimony of other parents saying that they rarely saw me there."

Uh-huh?

"Which is true. I cannot possibly be in two places at the same time. . . ."

A lady by the name of . . . Vera Lee—she lives across the street from you. You mentioned to Mr. Samek on direct that you had been over to their house once. You know whom I'm talking about—Mrs. Lee?

"Yes, I do. That's Dwight's mother."

Correct. It's also James's mother. James is the baby brother?

"Right. Little baby."

That's the baby that was at your house to babysit twice?

"That I know of—only one time."

Only one time?

"That's what my wife told me. I never even knew. My wife told me she had babysat for four days. . . ."

You didn't see the baby when it was in your house?

Then it got sick?

"I said no. I didn't. . . ."

So, were there two different sets of occasions? Was there one for one, another time for four days? You didn't see the baby?

"As far as I know, my wife told me the baby was there for one occasion, not two."

Did you see Mrs. Lee when she dropped off her child there?

"No, I didn't."

Never?

"No, I didn't."

She was one of the witnesses who came in here, sir, mentioned she saw you most of the time.

"She was in my house, according to you, only two times. She saw me most of the time? According to you, two times. . . .

"She worked from nine to five she says. I'm in my office all the time. Does that make any sense?

"Let's get serious."

Well, smiled Casey, *we will.*

But first he produced a few more additional statements from witnesses, and he wondered to Frank whether they might be "incorrect," "mistaken" or "untrue."

"Well," said Frank, "you want to be very polite and call most of these untrue statements. I don't want to be polite. I want to call them what they are.

"I call them lies."

Then Casey explored the business records that named Frank Fuster the owner/operator of the Country Walk Babysitting Service.

"There was no daycare center ever in my house. My wife was babysitting four or five kids."

There were some business cards that were printed out in order to have business cards—professional cards—for the Country Walk Babysitting Service under that name, correct?
"Correct, sir."
Who had the cards printed up?
"My wife and I. . . ."
Is it your testimony, sir, though, that no business cards were ever distributed? The only person who got two or three cards was Joanne Menoher?
"From me?"
From you.
"Right. Because I do not know if my wife ever gave somebody a business card. I'm talking for myself."
Well, sir—
"By the way, I have not said that to you during this trial. So, if you want to ask me the questions, because I haven't said that to you in this trial. But you are right. I mean, you haven't asked me if I gave out business cards during this trial, have you?"
No. I am asking you about it now.

Susan Maxwell, seated in the visitor's gallery, grew suddenly anxious. Having already testified as to the events that led her to seek an investigation of the activities at the Fuster home, and having been released from the witness rule, the former prosecutor was the only parent to witness Frank Fuster's extraordinary performance for the jury.

She was also one of the few occupants of the packed courtroom who recognized the danger of the ground Casey was about to break.

Many elements of Frank Fuster's testimony had changed in the few short weeks since his probation violation hearing.

Dan Casey wished to bring this to the attention of the jury, which was—and must legally continue to be—completely ignorant of the murderer/child molester's unsavory past.

As far as the jury knew, Francisco Fuster Escalona was a Cuban businessman, convicted of two previous felonies. They could not be apprised of the nature of his crimes or the price he had or had not paid for them. The defense, of course, did not wish to mention that the defendant had once murdered and once molested before.

And the State would not be allowed to. A defendant cannot be improperly prejudiced.

Even by the truth.

If Casey wished to impeach Fuster with his own words, the jury could only know that the words had been spoken at "a prior proceeding."

Susan Maxwell gripped the arms of her chair, praying that the word *probation* wouldn't slip from the prosecutor's lips.

Casey was tiring, she knew. He'd been pleasantly hammering away at Frank for hours. And though he made it seem effortless, it was no small task for him to keep his voluble witness under control, constantly altering the length of his leash to allow Frank enough with which to hang himself.

Now he had to control both Frank's mouth and his own.

One slip, and he had a mistrial.

One slip, and they had to pick a new jury and do it all again. All of it.

Susan Maxwell felt sick.

I have a little bit more to ask you, Casey continued.

"In other words," said Frank, "you are telling me something I said to you some other time, not during this trial?

"You have to ask me a question first," said Frank Fuster, refusing to abandon his lecture on the rules of evidence.

Casey never ceased to be amazed.

I will ask you a question, sir.

Is it your testimony that, out of the one thousand cards that were printed out, only two or three were ever given to anybody? Because you—

"No."

Because you still have 997 of those cards?

"That is not my testimony."

Have you ever said that before?

"No, sir, not that I can remember. My testimony is that I have given out some cards to a person—Joanne Menoher, but I do not know if my wife has given out some cards to a person or not.

"I do have perhaps a little more than a thousand cards right there on top of my table. There's a box, and if you open it and care to count them, I am sure you will find a thousand cards in there. It is completely full."

Sir, do you remember testifying at a previous proceeding in this matter at which time you were put under oath?

"Yes."

Do you remember being asked the following question and did you ever give the following response?

Question by me: "Did you ever have cards printed up, Mr. Fuster, using the Country Walk Babysitting Service name?"

And your answer: "My wife had one time some cards printed up. I just still have 997 cards."

"Yes, I remember saying that to you."

OK. So, let me ask you two things about that. One, it was your wife who had them printed up or both of you?

"It was my wife's idea. It was my wife's request. I paid for it. Does that answer your question?"

Right.

Of the 1,000 cards, you still have 997 of them?

"I called the printer . . . and I asked her, 'When you buy one thousand cards, do you get one thousand cards?' which is what I assumed when I made the statement.

"My statement was true, according to my honest belief.

"Mrs. Troy told me, 'No, you don't. You may get 1,000. You may get 1,015 or you may get 999, around there.'

"That's what I was told.

"So when I told you that I had 997, I was incorrect.

"But my statement was true to me at the time. Based on what I believed to be true at the time."

Do you remember in that same probation viola—

Casey couldn't believe it. The very words he had summoned his concentration to avoid had slipped out. His mouth slammed shut, as he swallowed the words back down his throat. He wanted to rip his tongue out of his mouth.

—previous proceeding?

Too late.

Susan Maxwell covered her mouth.

Samek shot out of his seat as if propelled by a spring.

"Objection. Side bar."

There commenced a lengthy huddle at the bench, as the bewildered jurors stretched and yawned, wondering what had turned John Hogan and Dan Casey's complexion a mortal shade of grey.

Frank knew exactly what was going on.

The jurors, Casey had argued, already knew of the probation violation from a videotape that Mr. Samek himself had introduced into evidence. The Jaime Fuster tape, in which Joe Braga explained to a six-year-old boy why his father was in jail.

Jeffrey Samek had opened that door himself.

There would be no mistrial.

Presently, the still-pale Casey stepped back to the witness stand to resume questioning of the now bemused witness.

Mr. Fuster, we were talking about business cards. . . .

Daniel Casey placed State's Exhibit No. 34 before Frank Fuster—the leather ring with silver spikes, which the State identified as "thumb cuffs" seized from the Fuster home, and which Frank had testified was a "ring" he had bought for his son at a flea market.

How old was Jaime when you bought this for him? inquired the prosecutor.

"Jaime? Six."

You bought this for your six-year-old son? Casey's brow crept above the frame of his glasses.

"Yes."

And this stayed with Jaime? This was Jaime's?

"Yes, that was Jaime's. It did not stay with him. Iliana didn't like it, and I realized. I told him later we would take it away from him. I stated that he wear it that day and evening time. I took it away and put it someplace.

"I never saw it again."

That's why when the search warrant was executed on the house—that's why it was found in the dresser drawer in the vanity of the bathroom? In the master bedroom?

"That must be why."

Sir, do you have a family friend who owns a pharmacy?

"I have a customer that owns a pharmacy."

What's the name of the pharmacy?

"My Pharmacy."

Is that the name of it, "My Pharmacy"?

"Yes."

Do you also have a family friend who owns a pharmacy known as Castillo Pharmacy?

"Yes."

And that's a friend of your mother's?

"Yes."

And your uncle, correct?

"We buy medicine there."

Sir, during the summer of 1984, did you ever suspect that you had a venereal disease?

"No, sir, never. . . ."

*Did you ever go to a doctor for a checkup to test for venereal
disease?*

"No, sir, I didn't."

*Did you ever go to a doctor in July, I think, of that year to test for
anything?*

"Yes, I did."

Who was the doctor?

"Hugo Lopez. . . ."

*And what are you telling us that you went to Dr. Lopez to check
for?*

"Well, I went for several—for several tests. I went for, in relation
to what probably you are getting at—I had hurt my penis with my
zipper, and I showed it to the doctor, and that's not a venereal disease
or anything close by it. And I showed him what it was, and the
doctor told me, uh, uh, I went there to check my blood for diabetic,
and my doctor told me, 'Are you sure that's the consequence of
hurting yourself?' I told him that's what I believe. He said, 'I am
going to check you for syphilis just in case, since I already have
blood. . . .'"

*This Dr. Hugo Lopez—he is a family doctor, doctor for your
family, doctor for your uncle . . . ?*

"He is a doctor that I have visited, perhaps, three times during my
life and he had been visited by my family as well."

*Well, Mr. Fuster, in fact, he was at least familiar enough with
you that on the day you visited him, you went to him without an
appointment, at the end of the day, and asked him to take a look at
you then?*

"That's not true. I had an appointment, and he charged me pretty
expensive—$125."

*That's the same Dr. Hugo Lopez whose office is next to the
Castillo Pharmacy?*

*Sir, your testimony today is that you never touched any of the
children in a sexual way, is that correct?*

"Very correct."

Missy Herschel came in here and testified as a witness. . . .

Casey's list of "perjured" witnesses continued to expand. Missy.
Chad. Bonnie. Crystal. Every word they said was "a hundred
percent untrue."

What about Brendon Prince. . . . Is that also incorrect?

"Very incorrect. . . ."

April Lancaster?

"Very incorrect."

Well, how about when she told . . . her private therapist the same thing? Was she incorrect then?

"Yes, sir. She was very incorrect and very untrue. . . . She only said that again after she was brainwashed by Doctors Braga and by the rest of her family to say that. That never took place, Mr. Casey. . . ."

Jason Harrison came in here and testified that you touched him and you touched his little brother. . . . Testified before this jury, took an oath, promised to tell the truth, and testified that you touched him and you touched his little brother and you touched most of the little kids that went to the babysitting service out of your house . . . in many, many different sexual ways. Was Jason also incorrect?

"Yes, sir, he was, and I would like to add to that, Mr. Casey, that I have never in my life been a child molester, and I have never in my life touched or assaulted any children sexually. I do not have those desires. I have never had those desires. And all of this information is incorrect."

Your testimony today is that you have never been a child molester in your life?

Let me finish with this stack of photos. . . .

Casey went through the children one by one.

"Incorrect," responded Frank. Untrue. Brainwashed.

Brainwashed?

"Yes, by the people that are guilty of really committing child abuse against all those children there, which are the Doctors Braga and their own parents and fathers, and I feel insulted that I have to sit here and be answering your question by question for your insulting questions.

"No, sir. I am not that kind of human being. . . ."

Sir, had you ever before this case, had you ever met Detective Donna Meznarich? . . .

"Not that I know, sir."

Any reason at all why she would do anything or say anything to you, against you?

"To the best of my knowledge, no."

What about Judy Prince?

"To the best of my knowledge, no. . . ."

What about Jill Vickers?

"Yes, could be."

Why is that, sir?

"Her husband has two positions in Country Walk. One of the positions is in confliction with the other one. I didn't know that my wife was babysitting little Vickers. When I find out that Mr. Steven Vickers was involved with Arvida, and at the same time involved with the Homeowner's Association, I saw a conflict of interest, and I went to Arvida, and I requested that he be fired out of one of the two positions, and either one of them pays about $35,000 a year. . . ."

Maggie Fletcher?

"She's a police officer."

Police officers are biased against you, sir?

"No, but she's a policeman. They have a mentality. They can't help it, especially once they are in the police department for ten years or so, and her husband is a lieutenant, and this runs in the family.

"Prior to the case, I don't see why she has. Not to the best of my knowledge. After the case started, it is obvious.

"Everybody knows that she went as far as Washington and Tallahassee to make laws against me, and she has made the hysteria, and got all the parents together to form today what is the case that you are trying to prove."

Anything other than the case itself that would have her biased against you?

"Not to the best of my knowledge."

Nothing except the fact that you could have molested her daughter?

Sir, I have just named off seventeen witnesses or potential witnesses in this case, all of whom you have said at least once were incorrect in their testimony and will be incorrect in their future testimony.

I have named five mental health professionals whom you have testified were incorrect in their testimony, and there are in excess of fourteen children whom you have testified are incorrect in their testimony—either in court or on the tapes. All these people have either been incorrect or wrong or brainwashed, sir.

Do you have an explanation why all those people are saying those things about you?

"That's a very elastic question. You presented thirty-four witnesses in front of the jurors and these people; some of them are saying one thing, and other ones are saying other ones. They are all saying something against me and my wife. And sir, they are incorrect. Some of them are honestly incorrect. And some of them are not honestly incorrect; they are lying on purpose, and some of them, like the children, they already believe that these incidents, did in fact, took place.

"You already know that millions of dollars are involved in my case, and you know that political people have gained power through my case. You know that the media has make my case compared to Watergate. It could only be compared—the publicity has been nationwide from one corner to another one.

"You have humiliated me and my wife nationwide.

"You have destroyed my family.

"You have destroyed the family of my brothers, of my mother.

"The crime that you have committed with me and my wife, and our people, there is no way on this earth that you could possibly pay for it, and you still continue on, and I could only speculate as to more reasons.

"But I think the ones that I have given are good enough.

"As far as you are concerned, and your office, and Janet Reno—you want a conviction, and nothing will stop you to get that conviction that you want."

So, your explanation, sir, is that all of these people, some thirty or more—

"Thirty-four."

—Are either wrong, incorrect, or—

"Or lying."

Or lying.

And that you are the one telling the truth?

"I am."

Sir, what about the other possibility that they are, in fact, the ones telling you and telling this jury what actually happened to them, and someone else is not telling the truth?

"I have done everything within my power to prove that I am innocent. I have offered myself for any kind of test that you wish to give me.

"I have maintained my innocence from day one.

"I am innocent of these charges, and you have not been able to prove otherwise."

• • •

Jeffrey Samek was ready to rest his case.

Over Frank's dead body.

"Judge, I do not intend to call any further witnesses in the defense. . . .

"There are several witnesses who I have considered calling and am not going to call at this time. But two of those—Martha Fuster and Jaime Fuster—I met with, spoke with, in addition to reviewing many statements that both of them have made over the course of many years, and I have decided not to call either of them.

"Mr. Fuster has on several occasions—I am going to use the word *insist*, rather than labor for a more appropriate word—but he has insisted that I call them, and I advised him yesterday that the only witness he could compel me to call is him. And that's what I did.

"I called him as a witness.

"And that he could not compel me to call either his ex-wife or the son. I don't think it is necessary for me to state at this time why I have chosen not to call them.

"Mr. Fuster knows the reasons, and that's what's important.

"I don't know if Mr. Fuster is going to insist that they be called as witnesses. I advised him that, if he did so insist, the court could not stop him from putting them on, but that I would not participate in that, nor would I further participate if he insisted in putting on any other witnesses. . . ."

Richard Shiffrin, the silent member of the prosecution team who hovered over each legal entanglement with a fistful of statutes, prepared to cover the appellate rear.

"Before Mr. Shiffrin responds," said Samek, "maybe Mr. Fuster wishes to be heard in this matter?"

This, everyone knew, was a rhetorical query, given Frank's legendary attempts to fill the court record with as many of his own words as possible, as if, by repetition, black might actually become white.

"In reference to this matter?" Judge Newman inquired cautiously, for he knew there were innumerable matters upon which Frank Fuster might expound for days on end, should his leash be the least bit loosened.

"I like to express myself, Your Honor. You know, I have been trying to talk to this court for the past two days on this issue," said Frank Fuster with customary disregard for reality.

Judge Newman had had about enough. There was probably no witness in the Eleventh Judicial Circuit who had been given more latitude of speech in the courtroom than Frank Fuster.

"Excuse me, sir," the judge cut in abruptly. "I'm concerned with *one* matter—the matter Mr. Samek just brought to the attention of this court. . . ."

"Your Honor, excuse me," said the persistent but ever-respectful child molester. "I am concerned with that matter, but I also like to point out to the court that you promised me when I testified, that was my time to talk.

"And yesterday I testified . . . that was *not* my time to talk.

"It seems to me this court does not want to hear what I have to say."

Judge Newman's voice raised perceptibly for the first time in fifteen months. "You are absolutely correct. Absolutely clear. We do not wish to hear from you at this point in time. You are correct, sir. . . ."

Frank would not be still.

"I like to make some complaint, and I like to establish some complaints that are important for Your Honor to know about and to know what's going on."

"Sir, what's important for *your honor,* as you call me, is to see that this case proceeds in a proper and legal manner. . . ."

"OK, Your Honor. If you don't allow me to talk, I cannot go above your authority."

"Nothing for me to hear from you at this point in time," said the judge. "We are in the middle of a trial, and I would like to continue. . . ."

"OK," said Frank, Judge Newman's words alternately bouncing off or passing through his one functional ear. "I am going to talk on the subject of the witness," he lied.

"OK," nodded the resigned magistrate.

"Before I go into that, I like to ask you a question.

"Will I be able to speak in this courtroom before my trial finish, as Your Honor has promise me in the past?"

"If there is anything that you want to say in the form of testimony and it is pertinent to whatever your attorney wants to do, before the jury, you may. That situation may present itself. . . ."

"Your Honor, I am having—I am still having a lot of difficulty with Mr. Samek, and we still have lot of difference. As you very well know, Mr. Samek is not in this case because he wants to be, but because you practically put him here. Ordered him to be here.

"He is not in this case, also, because I want him to be.

"We are having difficulty with this witness. There is one particular witness that I'm going to mention—"

Jeffrey Samek looked liked canned rage. "Don't *mention* that person," he said through gritted teeth. "Frank, I don't want you to say *anything* to *anybody*."

But Frank was already off and running.

"There are several witness that are very important in my defense. Two of them are my son, Jaime, and my wife—ex-wife—Martha. And he refuses to. Or he tells me that if I want to put them on myself I could. I don't know what to do. I mean, I called them here, and he says he is going to sit there, and he's not going to do anything. I called them here. I don't know what to ask. I am not an attorney.

"So what am I to do?

"I want to bring in my son so that my son tells the truth to Mr. Hogan, to Mr. Casey, to Mr. Shiffrin, and to the eight members of the jurors.

"And to the nation that is listening.

"This is the purpose of bring—that is why I want to bring my son in. My son has never been sexually assaulted by me, and I don't believe that he has been sexually assaulted by anyone.

"I think he's an important witness in my case, but due to the brainwashing that my son was subjected to, my attorney is afraid that the damage that was done to him is so big that he is not going to be able to undone the harm in a matter of fifteen or twenty minutes.

"For similar reason, he does not want to bring that other—uh, uh, my ex-wife. I requested him to bring Dr. Hugo Lopez, and he didn't either. Now, I find out by the newspaper that the State is bringing Dr. Hugo Lopez. . . . [As it turned out, neither the defense nor the State was willing to gamble as to the content of this particular witness's testimony on any given day.]

"And there are other witness that I don't know at this time if I could be jeopardizing this case by mentioning to you, but some *important* witness. . . .

"I have nothing to do with his defense or any of his decisions he has taken in this case up to this point except for *two* occasions.

"One time I told him to consider not interviewing . . . one of the children because I don't think that in ten minutes or fifteen minutes he could have undone the conditioning that these children have been subjected for an entire year. I was afraid that he may even make the child cry.

"That will hurt me a lot.

"When he said one day he wasn't going to use the tapes, I ask him make sure those tapes you're not going to use are none of the tapes that can possibly . . . help me.

"Up to this point, the State has presented you and the jurors with thirty-four witnesses against me.

"My attorney has presented fifty hours of tape which are practically against me.

"One is a State witness—Dr. Miranda—that was used to prosecute me on my violation of probation and again in this trial. And mother that say she convinced that her child was sexually abused. A person from HRS was practically neutral.

"And then one Dr. Coleman, which is aware of the truth, and he was positive in my case. I think that if the nation were to listen to *him,* and if the courts would listen to him, perhaps this nation can get somewhere, because Dr. Coleman has *actual knowledge* of the truth and what is happening. . . ."

"Over Mr. Fuster's objection," said the weary Jeffrey Samek, "the defense rests."

Two floors above Courtroom 4-2, where a father demanded that his seven-year-old son be produced to "save" him, Jaime Fuster hovered near John Hogan's office, his mother gripped by one hand.

The year had brought Frank Fuster's son little resolution of his war waged within.

Following his brief but enlightening passage through the "window of disclosure," Jaime had retreated to a state of denial. Having described explicit sexual acts performed between adults and children in the Fuster home, Jaime returned home with his mother and commenced formal therapy, during which he grew increasingly noncommunicative.

No, no, no, no. Nothing happened.

The doctors "forced" him to say what he did.

The hospital must have made a "mistake" about his disease.

He loved his father.

His father was a wonderful human being.

"To Jaime," said Martha, "his father was a god."

And Martha did little to dispel that notion, for she, too, had slammed shut her own "window."

She, too, as she told Dr. Simon Miranda, maintained a bond with Frank Fuster.

As well as a knowledge of his "truths."

She wanted the truth from Jaime's lips, she had begged of the

Bragas before the fourth and final interview—the day her son came to crack wide the window of disclosure.

The truth, Martha apparently decided by the time of the trial, was too terrible to hear.

"I just can't see it," she said. "Are you sure the lab didn't make a mistake?"

No, John Hogan informed her. Petri dishes did not culture gonorrhea spontaneously. There is no such thing as a "false" positive.

Only a false negative.

Still, Martha refused to believe.

Still, she remained in constant contact with the State, via Christina Royo, who called Martha frequently to inquire as to Jaime's progress in the wake of his confusing world turned upside down from every conceivable direction.

Christina wondered often about the future of this child.

She couldn't begin to conceive how he had endured living a seven-year nightmare from which he could not wake.

From which he could not run.

Or hide.

For when the red door closed behind the last babysitting customer, it was *his* turn.

And yet, marveled Christina, Jaime loved his father as deeply as he feared Frank Fuster.

His emotional stamina in the midst of such a war impressed her. Jaime Fuster was a child who had been abused in his short life in ways grown men could never imagine. Yet he functioned as a normal child possessed of a few "quirks," which never caused the only adults he came in contact with outside his father's house to explore the center of his universe—his family—as the source of his irregularities.

Jaime Fuster was smart, but his grades were poor. His teachers had difficulty keeping him in his seat, much less "on task" in the classroom. Jaime was always sharpening his pencil or looking out the window, wandering about. Perpetual motion.

Diagnosis by the school counselor: hyperactive; possibly learning disabled.

Recommended treatment: drugs to extinguish the "undesirable" behaviors.

Twice Iliana conferred with the school counselor and assured him that she would urge her stepson to study harder.

She did not mention that Jaime's energies were more urgently directed toward surviving life with a madman.

Nor did a school bus driver report that one of his young passengers—a handsome brown-eyed *Latino*—would sometimes refuse to get off at his stop, resolutely lashing his arms around the legs of the bolted seat as though anticipating physical ejection.

As the little boy cowered in the school bus, Frank Fuster would angrily board it and curse the driver for "holding" his son "against his will."

And when Jaime relieved himself in a neighbor's bathroom—apparently aiming everywhere except the toilet—he was banished from the house. His best friend's father deemed him a mannerless, "alien creature" not fit to habitate with human beings.

No one paid attention to Jaime Fuster and the signals he emitted regularly.

Not until Jaime Fuster's problem became everyone's.

Nor was his mother paying attention now.

Jaime's doing real well, Martha assured Christina.

No, she was not alarmed that he set a fire in the school bathroom last week. Boys, after all, will be boys.

Are you *sure* the lab didn't make a mistake?

Her son continued to reassure her that it must have.

Eventually, Jaime ceased communicating with his therapists entirely, huddling in a corner, refusing even to speak his name.

Jaime's window was nailed shut.

As was Martha's.

Mother and son were hovering in the sixth-floor corridor when Joe Braga briskly rounded the corner and came face to face with the little boy, who lit up immediately at the sight of his ponytailed friend.

Jaime rushed to Joe, chattering, "Hi! How you doing? Can we talk? Can we play?"

Joe beamed at Frank's son. "I'd like that. But I better check with John and Dan, first, OK? I'll be right back."

Under the circumstances, John Hogan suggested, it might not be a "good idea."

The "circumstances," Joe knew, were complex.

Martha and Jaime were here under Jeffrey Samek's subpoena,

though it remained unclear whether he had ever planned to call them to the stand.

Martha was a close call.

Samek would have to decide whether the benefit of her testifying to the "ideal relationship" between her ex-husband and his son would outweigh the potentially dangerous material the State would most assuredly extract on cross-examination—the profile of a man obsessed with control and rage—who (as she had testified in her deposition) tried on unorthodox and mystical religions in much the way other men shopped for suits.

Samek chose not to open a can filled mostly with worms.

Martha Fuster's testimony would not help his client's case.

Jaime was another story.

Though Frank's son, by now, was more likely to hop off the stand into his father's lap than tell a jury where he got his gonorrhea, Samek could not be sure how the child would react to facing his father.

Frank, on the other hand, was crisply confident that his son would apprise the jury of his father's greatness and correct the "lies" the nation was telling against him.

His son he could count on.

His son would look into his eyes.

The power of the mind, Frank Fuster believed, was "very big."

The state of Florida apparently agreed: it carried a stipulation in its rules of evidence that exluded witnesses who had undergone hypnosis.

As had seven-year-old Jaime Fuster, when his therapist once succeeded in temporarily recracking his window of disclosure by hypnotically "refreshing" his memory.

She did not know, she said, that by doing so she had rendered his testimony inadmissible at the trial.

As Frank Fuster's luck would have it, the law protecting him from the admission of evidence offered by a tampered mind excluded the one witness whose mind he had tampered with for seven years.

Jaime Fuster could not testify at his father's trial.

Still, under the circumstances, Dr. Braga could understand why the State might not consider it a "good idea" for him to spend time with Frank Fuster's son.

Joe returned to the corridor where Jaime still held his mother's hand and explained that today was not a good day.

Next time, OK?

Then we can talk.

Then we can play.

And then it was time for Martha to lead her son away.

Joe's eyes filled with tears as they followed the little boy who retreated sideways down the hall, his one free arm outstretched toward him, his fingers begging to touch.

That was the last time Joe saw Jaime Fuster.

• • •

Dr. Laurie Braga entered Courtroom 4-2 for her second—and final—appearance at the Country Walk trial.

She walked its length in closed-toe pumps.

A tailored suit, hemmed at the knee, had replaced her pastel minis. Dark-tinted hose obscured her disdain for razors.

Her hair was meticulously braided and roped in a bun.

She was sworn in as an expert witness.

Laurie's initial appearance a fortnight ago during the first week of trial had served to supplement her husband's efforts to educate the jury on the principles of child development and the dynamics of interviewing a child suspected to be the victim of sexual abuse.

The State was now offering its rebuttal case—its opportunity to wrap up the loose ends the defense had attempted to unravel over the past two weeks.

It was Laurie's job to refamiliarize the jury members with what they had actually seen on the tapes, as opposed to what Dr. Coleman told them they had seen.

Daniel Casey wore a path around the witness stand for part of the afternoon.

Did you praise the children for telling and disbelieve for not telling?

"No," she said. "What we did was, there are many times when the children would say something; you know, we'd ask them a question. They said, 'No, that didn't happen.' We simply accepted this 'No, that didn't happen.'

"But . . . if you say, 'Did such a thing happen?' or 'Did anything happen to you when you were at Frank and Iliana's house?' and they said 'No,' but behavior showed they were very distressed, then we would give them some encouragement so they would feel comfortable in talking. And if they told, then it was so brave of them if they did talk and did say something, because as I said before when I testified, it is very, very difficult for children to talk about this kind of thing.

"It's difficult for anybody.

"If somebody asked me to talk about what I did with my husband last night, I would be very offended, embarrassed, ashamed."

Samek propelled out of his seat as he would throughout her testimony. "Objection! Nonresponsive."

"Sustain the objection," Judge Newman noted mildly.

What else would you like to say in answer to the question whether you praise the children for telling and disbelieve them for not telling? continued Casey.

"We *do* give them praise for telling because it is important to counteract anything that somebody else may have told them, that they will get in trouble if they tell.

"It's very important by our demeanor, as well as what we say, to let them know they're not going to get in trouble, nobody is going to be mad at them, and that this is very brave of them because it *is* very brave of them. . . .

"I don't consider that a negative. I consider that a very positive and constructive thing for the child. And since our first priority is to first do no harm, and to enable the child to share a burden because a burden shared is no longer a burden, I consider that to be a very positive thing."

Casey then asked her to recall the contents of Jason Harrison's second interview—the one conducted on the red-haired boy's first visit on Abe Laeser's floor. The one that began with Joe asking him, "Can you tell us anything about any masks or anything, or any games that Frank and Iliana played?"

The one in which Jason spilled his guts and Laurie almost lost her lunch.

The one that reduced the jury to tears.

Dr. Coleman has testified, said Casey, *that he has seen that tape and that his review of that tape as reflected in his notes . . says the only significance on that . . . tape is children were "playing." That's the only words in his notes. . . .*

Could you tell me whether that is correct?

"No. . . . Clearly more than playing."

• • •

"The State calls Iliana Fuster."

There was no audible gasp from the gallery, there having been rampant speculation—since the day she pleaded guilty to twelve counts of raping, molesting, and terrorizing children still in diapers—as to whether the State would elect to place Frank Fuster's child bride on the stand.

It would have seemed a most logical strategy in light of this unique addition to the State's case—an adult eyewitness.

But logic had little to do with any aspect of this crime.

And though Iliana's story dovetailed with disturbing precision with the children's in many ways, it deviated sharply in others.

There were masks, she said. And brutality and feces and drugs and sex and terror. Life in the Fuster home was, in fact, more grotesque than even the children had been able to communicate.

But not once, she insisted, had she crossed the line from victim to perpetrator.

The children saw it differently.

Much differently.

The question was, would a jury be able to reconcile Iliana's self-portrait with the one painted by the children on the tapes, in which they described a young woman who did unto them what Frank had done unto them all?

And would the emotionally fragile Iliana be able to face Frank Fuster and the ever-present television camera in the courtroom and tell of the incidents she was willing to acknowledge?

The prosecution team debated for weeks the merits of calling Frank's wife to the stand. Hogan and Casey were inclined to pass. The jury had seen the tapes. It could not possibly acquit.

At least that's what they prayed.

But Richard Shiffrin wasn't concerned about the jury, who had seen not only the children's words but also their actions. He was concerned, he said, about an appeals court, which would see only a transcript of the tapes.

And reading the transcript of children's words as they discussed sexual abuse was akin to listening to ballet on the radio.

"One of the most important parts of the interview is child behavior," Laurie had told the jurors following Dr. Lee Stewart Coleman's error-riddled "recap" of his favored highlights of the children's tapes.

The tapes showed what a transcript could not.

"If you only see the words, then you don't get a good sense at all. . . . You don't see if you asked a child, 'Do you know somebody named Frank and Iliana?' they get very upset.

"You don't see that reaction. . . .

"If you use the dolls and you say, 'Let this be Frank and let this be Iliana,' suddenly the child takes the clothes off, starts putting them in sexual positions.

"I might say, 'Well, did Frank take his clothes off?'

"If you only see the words, you don't realize what happened."

An adult witness who corroborated the children's testimony would carry much weight on appeal, Richard Shiffrin argued. The chief of Janet Reno's legal department agreed that Iliana's testimony would not make or break whatever opinions the jury had formed during five weeks of trial. By now, the shades of grey they brought to court on the first day would no doubt have polarized to either black or white.

Either they understood that the crime had been too terrible for the children to speak initially or they had decided, as Dr. Roland Summit often said, that it was too terrible (for adults) to hear.

Either they believed the children or they didn't.

The appeals court was an entirely different matter.

Iliana's testimony would guard the appellate rear.

Janet Reno agreed.

Frank Fuster's wife gave the defense table a wide berth as she trekked to the stand upon which she perched like a frightened doe, her flawless complexion bare of makeup, her 110-pound frame draped in a pink dress and white jacket with puffed sleeves, her hair braided down the center of her back, clasped in a white ribbon.

John Hogan stood behind the podium, almost as nervous as she was, his back to Frank Fuster, who stared intently at Iliana, pointedly twisting his wedding ring around his finger.

For half an hour Hogan directed her through preliminary testimony, throughout which Jeffrey Samek sputtered objections on behalf of the witness's current husband and former co-defendant.

When the children first started coming to your house, was Frank there?

"Yes. . . ."

Did Frank ever have any contact with the children when they first started coming?

"Yes. . . . He would, like, tell them his name. He would carry them or just be near. Would play with them. . . ."

During the first few months of 1984, did you ever see him take any of the children in a separate room?

"Yes. . . ."

Which child did you see him take into a separate room?

"Andy. . . ."

Did there come a time that you actually saw the defendant kissing the naked body of a child?

"That was the time when I went . . . into Jaime's room. I was passing by—by the hall. And I saw in the room, and Frank was there, and—"

Was Andy in the room?

"Yes."

Where was Andy?

"Andy was laying—was laying on the bed." Iliana's face contorted with great effort as she squeezed the words out, her voice trembling. "And he was *naked*, and Frank was—was kissing his body—"

"You are a *liar!*" Frank's voice cracked like a cannon as he lunged from the defense table and launched an accusatory finger toward his wife, who screamed a blood-curdling scream and grabbed her chest as if pierced by a bullet as she sank like a rock on the stand.

"You are a liar!" Frank screamed, still standing, white with fury. *"God is gonna punish you for this!"*

As a cluster of bailiffs and guards rushed to restrain the raging Frank Fuster, John Hogan stepped instinctively to the stand and awkwardly attempted to calm his witness, who sobbed, "Get me out of here, get me out of here, I told you—I told you what would happen."

"It's OK, it's OK," murmured John Hogan. "I won't leave you."

The stunned Judge Newman barely raised his voice as he calmly but sternly attempted to restore order to his courtroom. "You will refrain—"

"God is gonna punish you!" Frank continued to roar as the guards physically returned him to his seat and Christina Royo briskly slipped his wife off the stand and out a side door.

"God is gonna punish you!"

"I'll have you gagged—locked to your chair," continued Judge Newman, who leaned over the bench toward the defendant. "Now, do you want that? Otherwise, stay where you are and don't—no further outbursts. Mr. Samek, will you please explain to your client what I just said in case he didn't understand me."

Jeffrey Samek, who registered not the slightest degree of surprise at his client's outburst, eyed the eight temporarily forgotten men and women seated in the jury box and hurriedly reminded the court of its audience. "The jury—" he said.

Newman glanced at the stricken faces in the jury box. "Yes," he said quickly, motioning to a bailiff. "Take the jury to the jury room."

Hogan waited for the door to close behind the last juror before he unleashed his own quiet fury. "I'm going to ask the defendant be gagged. I think this is *unconscionable*."

"The court understands what you're saying and does not totally disagree with you. The court made it clear should anything happen even similar to that again, the court will do just that."

"Judge," argued Hogan, "we may not *have* a witness at that time. Justice will be *frustrated*. The man just *disregards* the law."

At that moment "the man" sobbed on the defense table, his head cradled in his arms, where it would remain even after his wife returned to the stand.

At one point, Frank removed his wedding ring and placed it on the defense table.

Undeterred, Iliana completed her testimony, which was, by the rules of evidence, far less expansive than her deposition.

And, compared to her husband's jolting performance, far less dramatic.

Richard Shiffrin rested the State's case for the second and final time.

"Judge," pleaded Jeffrey Samek, "I'm telling you as an officer of the court, I have no questions of him."

But Frank Fuster called himself to the stand anyway.

To "express" his final "truth."

The jurors, Frank complained bitterly, "no longer smile and 'communicate' with me" as he seemed to believe they had up until his wife's testimony.

He particularly despaired over the "defection" of the "young and pretty" one who, he claimed, had been most taken with his charms throughout the trial.

Such were the fantasies of Frank Fuster.

Samek reluctantly unleashed his client.

"Mr. Fuster, if there's anything you wish to tell the jury at this point in rebuttal to the rebuttal testimony the State has presented, please go ahead and tell them."

"Thank you," said the defendant, as he turned to chat with the men and women he had clearly frightened out of their wits just hours before when they witnessed the fury Frank Fuster camouflaged beneath the mask of a reasonable man.

"I requested to speak to you," he told the jurors. "My attorney has just finished—"

Judge Newman was amazed. "Sir, you have to limit your comments. I tried to make that clear to you. . . . [You may] rebut anything that the State has presented in its rebuttal case. You have to limit yourself to that. All right?"

"OK, Your Honor," said the meek Frank. "May I refer to the statement that my attorney just made to the court prior to the jury coming into the room?"

"No. . . ."

"May I bring the jury aware of my disagreement with my own attorney?"

"Definitely not. . . ."

"I see. So I cannot address the jury, human being to eight human beings?"

"You cannot address the jury in any way, shape, or form. All you can do is testify if you so choose as rebuttal to the rebuttal of the State's case."

Undaunted, Frank turned to address the jury.

"OK. Ladies and gentlemen of the jury, there is a lot I want to say . . . My life is in your hands. . . ."

Dan Casey sputtered a string of objections, as he would throughout Frank's rambling address.

"This is not a closing argument," the judge admonished the defendant, who blithely offered one anyway.

"You heard my wife sit in this chair today and tell each one of you that I am guilty of these crimes . . . and you saw me crying in that chair. Because it was painful for me to hear the woman that I love, the woman that I married say these lies against me. . . .

"I have never done none of the crimes. . . . At least you have to give me the benefit of the doubt because I owe the truth. I owe that benefit of that doubt. . . .

"My wife started losing her mind during the month of May 1985. . . ."

Casey continued to sputter.

"My wife is eighteen years old. . . . She does not know the consequences of guilt. And I'm thirty-six years old, and I do.

"I know what guilt is. I know how hard it is for a human being to carry guilt. I'm not able to handle guilt. . . .

"My wife is a good human being. She's not responsible for the things she's saying. She wants to get out of prison. And anytime the system allows a co-defendant to come and accuse a co-defendant, that's not fair.

"That's not justice. . . .

"I'm not worried about the rest because the rest has a very good explanation, and had my wife sat here today and tell you the truth, you would have positively found me not guilty, and I know that.

"I know that only my wife's testimony is hurting me, and you must know why she did it. . . .

"Thirty-five thousand words or more have been used in this courtroom to accuse me, and that is all that the district attorney has presented you with, the words that were used to accuse me. Because they haven't produced you with any evidence.

"No dates, no times, no nothing."

Dan Casey by now had ceased to sputter and begun to plead. "Judge, perhaps maybe a side bar?"

John Hogan was less contained. "Most respectfully, Iliana Fuster was cut off when she tried to testify in narrative. Children were cut off from giving narrative. No *rules* for this man. The rules of evidence are *abandoned* for him. . . ."

"Not abandoned," said Judge Newman, as Frank continued to ramble at will.

"I believe the State—starting with Janet Reno—"

"No," cried the judge. "No, no. Wait. I want you—"

"I'm referring to refuting what they're doing, Your Honor," said the humble defendant.

"What they're *doing*?" said Newman.

"What they're doing," nodded Frank. "Mr. Hogan and Mr. Casey and Mr. Shiffrin and their boss, sitting someplace out there—*Janet Reno*. I believe them to be professional people, and as professional, I believe that they know I am innocent."

"*Judge*," pleaded Casey.

"Mr. Fuster, this is the last time I'm going to tell you. . . ."

"OK," said Frank agreeably as he turned back to the jury. "Human being to eight human beings, I have to be careful with my words. . . . I don't mean to get out of the judge's rules.

"The person that came here today . . . and told you that he saw me wearing mask. . . . He told you that he did business with me and all of that. It is not true that he did business with me. . . . It is not true that that gentleman saw me wearing a mask. It doesn't make sense that a person that comes to my house to do business, that I will go and . . . wear a monster mask and come out like if I was a child. I'm not a child. I was thirty-five years old when that incident took place. . . .

"Coming again to my wife. My wife was seventeen years old when she got arrested. We were practically on our honeymoon. . . . I hope that you have a chance to see at least those few letters in there. . . . Perhaps with some sort of amplifier machine, that you could see them good and read them . . . and when you read them, get inside the human being that wrote those letters to me. . . ."

"Anything from the State?" inquired Judge Newman as Frank prepared to take a bow.

"One question, Judge," said Casey, as he ambled toward the stand.

Mr. Fuster, you've told us that you swear before God everything you're saying is true. You've taken the name of God many times in your statement today.

Could you describe for the ladies and gentlemen, sir, the cross— the cross that Iliana Fuster told us about in her testimony today, the cross that Detective Meznarich found between your mattress and between your springs?

What did that cross look like, sir?

"That cross was built by my son, Jaime, for my wife, Iliana, during Christmas 1983." Frank pulled a rosary from his pocket. "It looked exactly like this, except that it was built of wood . . . symbolizing the same thing—God as a human being in this earth, who came here to teach us how to act, how to behave, and how to be a good human being to one another.

"That's the same cross that my wife, Iliana, accused me of using to insert her on her rectum. By doing that, and by saying that, Brother Casey, she committed a great sin, and when she said those words here, my reaction was to look up and pray to God that he forgive her. . . .

"And that cross was not hiding between the mattress. It was placed there. . . . My mother used to put a cross under my mattress. . . . It was there on purpose for protection—to protect us from committing sins, protect us from any manifestation of evil, of bad dream, for anything bad that is happening on this world. Does that satisfy your question, Brother Casey?"

Mr. Fuster, when your son Jaime gave you that cross—

"He did not give it to me, sir. He gave it as a present to my wife. . . ."

Casey chewed thoughtfully on the tip of his pen.

Do you think he had any idea what you were going to do with that cross at that time?

Daniel Casey ambled back to his seat without asking Frank Fuster about the Santería priest who sat in the gallery wedged between Frank Fuster's mother and uncle.

The jury was unaware that the man who sat in the courtroom was further confirmation of the children's reliability, though this part of the story the prosecutors preferred not to tell.

Despite the assurances of the Santería expert the State had called in when the children began describing peculiar rituals practiced by Frank and Iliana Fuster in the course of defiling their bodies, it was readily apparent from the presence of the man offering "spiritual" support to the defendant's family that Afro-Cuban voodoo was not unfamiliar to the convicted murderer/child molester.

The true nature and intent of the rituals performed by the babysitters would never be known, for Frank would continue to wave rosaries before the jury—and upon the subject of religion, his wife would expand little.

Iliana said she was a devout Catholic. Period.

The Santería expert did, however, recognize the purpose of the cross the Fusters reclined on nightly. It was called "sleeping with the 'incubus,' " she said.

Its purported purpose was to "invoke" a "spirit" that "worked evil" on those who invited it to bed.

The presence of the Santería priest in Courtroom 4-2 as Frank Fuster testified provided for the prosecutors a reminder that the children's concept of truth was *more*, not less, reliable than that of the adult witnesses in the case.

But the jury would never know of the valuable pieces of corroboration that sat in the audience.

For the rituals would not be mentioned at the trial.

The State had to convince a jury that two babysitters had brutalized and terrorized fifteen children who could talk about it— none of whom had gone running home to Mommy with the news at the time. Beyond a reasonable doubt.

The rituals would only take the jurors on a tangent that would divert them from the matters at hand, adding yet another unimaginable dimension to an already unimaginable case.

• • •

Jeffrey Samek approached the jury for the final time.

"It was Dr. Coleman's unequivocal conclusion that the information from the children is completely unreliable because the interviewers have so overwhelmed them with their biases that the children were rendered incapable of telling the difference between what they actually remembered . . . and what someone told them had happened.

"Let me review some of these contaminating techniques with you. . . .

"Now I can go on and on, but the point is this: when somebody says something ridiculous, you have to challenge it with everything else they say. . . .

"Laurie Braga says you don't do that because you don't want to show the child that you didn't believe them. Well, in other situations, they told the children who made completely rational denials, 'I don't believe you.' They said one thing, and they did something else.

"Using anatomically correct dolls, which we've heard aren't really anatomically correct, also taints the results. . . .

"Further, with the dolls, they named them, and that's a damaging technique. . . .

"Well, why did they do this? Laurie Braga told you why they did it. She said if they didn't, it would take too long—longer than they were willing to sit. The judge is going to tell you, if Mr. Fuster is convicted in this case, he'll sit for the rest of his life. That's a long time to sit. It's not too much to have asked for the Bragas to sit a little longer.

"The interviewers also ignored and made no effort to compensate for external influences. Several children said Frank and Iliana are in jail. Several children said Frank and Iliana are bad. Missy Herschel said Frank and Iliana are strangers ' 'cause my mom told me.' Crystal Fletcher said, 'My mom told me they're ugly.' Mrs. Fletcher said she didn't. That either means Crystal was wrong or Mrs. Fletcher was wrong. . . . The Bragas never tried to neutralize these comments to show undocumented communication. We know that there was communication, and we don't know how bad it was. We don't know what else these children were told. . . .

"Now, a technique that everyone agrees is inappropriate, which Dr. Summit said was inappropriate under most of the circumstances, was the use of one child to corrupt another. That was Jason interrogating April. . . .

"Equally inappropriate is confrontational tactics used by Dr. Braga on Jaime Fuster. Laurie Braga and Dr. Summit both said it just was not a good thing to do. Laurie Braga said, not something they would do again. . . .

"All in all, these techniques stink. Children were manipulated. There is no question about that. What they said is unreliable. . . .

"I say, use your common sense. Looking at the tapes, adding it all up, looking at the inconsistencies, how can these answers be reliable?

"These children are tainted forever. . . .

"Counts one, three, and five deal with Jason Harrison. . . .

"What Jason tells us in court about those acts—well, the finished product, the little boy coming in and sitting in the judge's chambers and talking on TV, he said that Frank sucked on his penis one time. Frank touched his penis one time, and he sucked on Frank's penis one time. . . .

"However . . . previously he told the Bragas that it didn't happen. Now you have to decide . . . when he was telling the truth, which time he was right. How can you?

"He said that Frank and Iliana chopped the heads off, threw them away, and ate them for dinner. . . . He talked [on the tapes] about how he rides on sharks, how he rides on whales. Well, you decide if Jason looks to you to be a worldly sea explorer. . . . He said that he threatened Frank with a knife . . . also that he killed a ca-ca demon.

"A person who says these things cannot be believed at all.

"Count eleven is perhaps the most dramatic that Frank is charged with. That's the count that alleges he put his penis in his son Jaime's mouth. Well, Jaime has gonorrhea . . . and the doctors told us you get it from the ejaculate of an infected penis. Well, see that's a problem, because Frank isn't now infected . . . nor has he ever been infected. . . .

"Mr. Casey argued with Frank about Dr. Hugo Lopez, insinuating that Dr. Lopez would come in and testify that Frank had gonorrhea. . . . Well, you can damn well bet your bottom dollar, if that's what Dr. Lopez would have come in here to say, they would have subpoenaed him. . . .

"Now, Iliana Fuster said that she saw it. She saw him, Mr. Fuster, with his penis in his son's mouth. . . . First, I want to call your attention that Iliana Fuster said that, when she saw this, she was weak. She was sick. She was dizzy. She had been drugged. . . .

"Count twenty-four alleges that Mr. Fuster manipulated the vagina of Missy Herschel. . . . She said he and Iliana pulled her private parts.

"Iliana told you that didn't happen. . . .

"According to Andy Pierson, Frank and Iliana pooped on the floor. No testimony we ever saw any stains. There is testimony from Iliana that it didn't happen. She never pooped on the floor. Andy also said he put his finger inside April, not what April says. Andy says that Frank 'ate' him. Well, there's no suggestion that 'ate' is being used as a colloquialism by this young boy. . . . Said the poop came out of Frank's penis . . . that the children broke their necks, that he wasn't scared or hurt, that clothes were on during the playing of games, that clothes were off during the playing of games, that no games were played . . . that Frank wet his pants, that Frank and Iliana threw feces high in the air. . . .

"Bonnie Martinez tells us that Iliana wielded scissors during 'cut your head off,' but that Frank didn't play that game. Iliana says she never played it either. She certainly didn't wield any scissors. . . .

"I find it very interesting that the State's three leading experts did not tell you they concluded any of these children were abused. . . . I don't mean to be betting all your money, but you can bet your bottom dollar, if they had concluded the children were abused, Mr. Hogan would know, and if Mr. Hogan had known, he would have asked, and they would have told you. . . ."

Jeffrey Samek did not, however, mention that the rules of evidence prohibited this testimony.

"Ladies and gentlemen, Mr. Fuster is not an angel. He's been in trouble twice before, just like Bobby Dean, and there were what seemed to be inconsistencies in his testimony. . . .

"Certainly, ladies and gentlemen, I suppose Mr. Hogan will say that . . . Mr. Fuster has every reason in the world to lie—every reason in the world. . . .

"But I submit to you, if you looked at him and you listened to him, and you watched him, that when he tells you he didn't do these things, he was very credible. . . .

"Frank said he has never had any contact with any child, and he also says that he helped some children to their parents' cars.

Obviously one isn't true. He's not an expert witness, ladies and gentlemen. He's nervous. He's got his life on the line. . . . What he's telling you—he's accenting he didn't *molest*. He says he never saw many of the parents who say they saw him. Well, that's not so unusual. He was sitting in a room, a walled-off area . . . working. He wasn't sitting there watching for parents. . . .

"He says he wasn't at home when Iliana was sitting. . . . Again ladies and gentlemen, he's making a point that he wasn't involved with the children. If he was in his home working in his office, he didn't consider that being home. . . .

"There are other conflicts, but if you analyze them, I think you have to conclude that Frank is being truthful because they deal with other things. He has no reason to lie about getting a license in his name, attending or not attending initial interviews with parents, answering or not answering the door. . . .

"On the whole, Mr. Fuster's testimony is credible and contrary to what might be the popular belief expounded to you in this courtroom; you don't have to disbelieve everyone else to believe Frank. . . .

"Speaking of disbelief, that's what Iliana Fuster's testimony is worth. She is a selfish liar. That's as generous as I can be. As I suggested to her, she would tell you, ladies and gentlemen, that the moon was made of green cheese to get out of jail. . . .

"She knows that her one way out is to point a finger. She knows she's facing life in prison as a maximum sentence. She knows she could even get probation if she lies enough. . . . If she says, 'He did it and forced me to do it,' she looks wonderful. . . .

"This may be eighteen, but *this* is cunning. *This* is clever.

"She's lying.

"She's been lying since before she came to this country. She came on a tourist visa when she had every intention in the world to live here.

"She doesn't know what the truth is. Not because she's conditioned, but because she's conditioned herself.

"She's a liar.

"She tells the most fantastic story ever confabulated in Dade County Circuit Court. . . . And she tells us how terrified she was. Well, she should be. . . . terrified of Frank. She's lying to ruin his life.

"Like to show you State's Exhibit No. 3. . . . Shows the Fuster house is like many of the houses in Country Walk. Has a front door. And you have heard testimony not only that the front door opens and closes, but that it was often left unlocked.

"Well, why didn't she use it?

"*Why* didn't she use it?

"If she saw these things, why didn't she use it?

"If she hated him so much, why didn't she use it?

"If she was so terrified . . . why didn't she go to the police? She didn't have to go far. All she would have had to do was go to the front door when Maggie Fletcher and her husband, Peyton Fletcher, came to pick up their child, said, 'Please take me with you; I'm terrified of this man' or 'Please take me with you; he's abusing me, these children.'

"She didn't even have to pick up the phone. . . .

"There are only two possible reasons I can think of. One is that *she* was doing what she says Frank did.

"She's pleaded guilty.

"The other is that it didn't happen. . . .

"Now she's doing what she can to cut the best break she can. . . .

"The defense, like I said before, has no burden to do anything. . . . Why did the State, then, only show you the prepped up . . . end result of all these interviews? Why did they only bring in the children to testify?

"Why didn't *they* show you the tapes?

"Why did I have to show you the rough draft, to show what the children actually were saying before they were manipulated?

"There's a sense of hysteria here. It's not something that's new to the country. . . . You heard testimony about the hysteria in Jordan, Minnesota. . . . We have . . . lived through the hysteria of the McCarthy era . . . and the Salem witch hunts.

"What are they afraid to show you?

". . . Mrs. Vickers' importance to this case is that she didn't believe her son at first, but as she said, after interviews, after reading and studying, and after talking with Joe and Laurie, she believed it, and then she saw the TV with her son, and she believed it. She bought into this the same way as everybody else has bought into it.

"It's a cheap buy. . . .

"Also, many of these children had not been away from their parents. Kyle Maxwell had never been away from his parents outside of his house before. He was anxious. He was fearful. He was angry. . . .

"If there was any video equipment in that house, why didn't they ask Iliana Fuster to tell us all about it? I submit to you, because there was none.

"You promised you would require this government to prove its case beyond, and to the exclusion of, every reasonable doubt. . . . I'm sure you gave us your undivided attention as best as possible under trying circumstances. . . .

"I am sure that you will deliberate deliberately, critically, and that you will return the only *true* verdict possible in this case.

"That verdict is *not guilty*. Thank you."

The jury would not know that, while they were deliberating, Jeffrey Samek was in the corridor, speaking individually to the parents who waited for the verdict.

He was sorry about the kids, he told them.

He hoped they would be "all right."

But he made no apologies for doing his job. The parents had chosen to put their children through the justice process, something that he never would have done.

Had it been his kids, he would later say, he would simply have put them into therapy.

And Frank Fuster would still be running a babysitting service.

Sara Levy sat among the parents who packed the visitors' gallery as Jeffrey Samek explained to a jury that the nightmare the families had lived "didn't happen." It was a "cheap buy" Samek had said of their willingness to believe that it had.

And as Sara sat in Courtroom 4-2, she cradled her new daughter— the child conceived in more innocent times. Chip's mother trembled visibly throughout closing arguments.

For she was just now coming to know that the price of belief was not cheap. Indeed it was very high.

Sara had ridden her roller coaster alone for the past year, her comforting peaks of denial rudely interrupted by moments of stark and panicked doubt, as Chip's behavior grew too ominously "unusual" for his mother to rationalize. Her three-year-old son closed the door to his room and masturbated on his pillow daily—for hours on end. He was aggressive and angry, the slightest circumstance sending him into tantrums of fury. He whined and cried for no apparent reason. And sometimes he woke in the night.

At times Chip's behavior would become too intense to ignore.

And she would "wonder" of him in what she considered a calm and dispassionate tone, whether anything had been done to him at "Frank and Iliana's." Her son would vigorously shake his head and quickly direct his attention to his toys.

Relieved, Sara would return to the comfort of husband Barry's assurances that he might have "seen" something that he couldn't possibly remember or if he did would soon forget. The Fusters' names would be carefully avoided in Chip's presence. He did not know about the trial.

The trial was a turning point for Sara, who had most willingly testified to circumstances that buttressed the State's case. The naked Andy emerging from the master bedroom. The video camera in the Fuster living room. The long waits at the red door. Sara Levy had been a strong and compelling witness, her manner clear and direct, her eyes dry but possessed of a clear and penetrating anger. Not once did she look in Frank Fuster's direction.

It was during closing arguments that Sara's striking composure began to dissolve, as Dan Casey, who preceded Samek, laid out the pieces of the puzzle which neatly conjoined her own. The pieces formed a pattern that she could no longer deny—the mosaic of behavior of the Fuster victims which, she now realized with disturbing clarity, her son had become.

Belief, for Sara Levy, was not a "cheap buy."

• • •

"I think that one of the most difficult things for you to do in this case," began John Hogan, "is to get over what Dr. Summit described as one of the myths that we all work under. . . .

"None of us wants to believe that these horrible things happened . . . that if children who could barely crawl weren't the victims of sex abuse, the world would be a better place, and that cute little kids shouldn't have to carry the burden that they're carrying.

"It would be much easier.

"And there's something almost alluring to say, 'Well, let me just reject all that, and it will be easier to get through the day.'

"But I submit to you, ladies and gentlemen, the facts in this case could not be more clear. . . .

"Mr. Samek began and spent the vast majority of his argument talking about Dr. Coleman, and there was a reason for that. He has what the defendant had to say, and he had what Dr. Coleman had to say, and not much more out of five weeks of testimony. . . .

"I believe the judge is going to tell you that expert witnesses are like other witnesses with one exception. The law permits an expert witness to give his opinion. However, an expert opinion is only reliable when given on a subject about which you believe him to be an expert. . . .

"When Mr. Samek offered Dr. Coleman as an expert, I got up.

"My first question, 'Just so we're clear, he's being offered in psychiatry; is that correct?' Mr. Samek said yes.

"Why is that important? Because he's not an expert in interviewing techniques. He wasn't an expert in child abuse. . . .

"He has testified a lot before . . . not on sex abuse.

"In the area of sex abuse, he testified two or three times. But in his entire career, fifteen, twenty years of private practice, he maybe saw four or five sexually abused children—he's not sure. And that he only became interested in this area in the last six or nine months, depending on which version you want to listen to. He's not an expert on interviewing techniques. He knows nothing about it.

"Couldn't have even told you who has done work in this area. . . .

"Mr. Samek and I and Mr. Casey began work in this case before he . . . even began working in child sex abuse.

"It's all brand-new to him. He simply is not an expert in the areas he's talking about. . . .

"When you consider what he . . . says are appropriate procedures, you're left with only one possibility, and that is that you would . . . ask an open-ended question, the child would be completely forthcoming.

"He admits that will never happen.

"He has painted a little 'catch-22' for himself. That 'catch-22' has allowed him—and will continue to allow him—to testify that no interviewer anywhere knows what they're doing because he has set up something that's logically impossible.

"When asked to say, 'Well, what is the basis for this opinion?' . . . he obviously can't answer. He simply has no background in areas of child memory, child fantasy. He simply—he's started to read.

"He came for his deposition two or three weeks ago. We asked him questions about it. He said, 'I never heard of these people.' He has now come, and admits, those are the leading people in the area.

"He admitted they all disagree with him.

"He has read one or two articles now.

"I think the best way to view Dr. Coleman is maybe someday he'll be an expert within what he's talking about.

"Grandma Moses didn't start painting till she was eighty.

"Maybe someday Dr. Coleman will be an expert in this field. Maybe someday he'll finish the articles he should have read before he charged the citizens of Dade County. Maybe someday he'll know what he's talking about.

"That day is not today. . . .

"We have talked about the fee he charged. Don't get me wrong. Expert witnesses have a right to charge a fee . . . but what you need to do is put the amount of the fee in context.

"The best example is to compare with Dr. Summit. Dr. Summit has been doing this work and lecturing in this area for fifteen years. What did he charge to view a tape?

"Seventy-five dollars.

"Fifteen years' experience, one of the nation's leading experts. The man writes articles for all other experts to rely on.

"What does Dr. Coleman charge based on his six to nine months' experience?

"One hundred and fifty dollars an *hour*.

"His fee is typically twice what Dr. Summit's is with no qualifications. . . . His fee is outrageous.

"Why?

"Supply and demand.

"He's the only man in the country willing to come in and say these outrageous things. . . .

"You have every other mental health professional on one side. You have Dr. Coleman on the other. . . .

"I submit to you, that says something in itself.

"Dr. Coleman defined certain techniques that he said . . . were used to render each of these children incompetent. . . .

"He talks about the idea of the word 'pretend,' that just saying that one word suddenly makes everything a child will ever say unreliable and unbelievable.

"What basis does he have for that?

"His own opinion.

"What do the experts tell us?

"They tell us that when you ask a child to play, that is a basis of child psychiatry and child psychology—that children reflect their life experiences in their play. . . .

"What else do the other experts tell us?

". . . You can't fantasize about something that there is no basis in reality for, that a child may see a doll and . . . may look at the genitals.

"But to dismiss the fact that she takes the male penis and suddenly inserts it in the mouth of a doll that has been labeled to be her—that is not just random play. . . .

"Those children took those dolls—those little three- and four-year-olds, some of them still in diapers and training pants—and sat there and stuck penises in mouths and manipulated penises and manipulated vaginas.

"There had to be a basis for that. . . .

"They had to have a basis and understanding of sex.

"Now, Dr. Laurie Braga explained there's been studies done that would define the expected amount of sexual knowledge of children of different ages. Dr. Coleman admitted he had never heard of those studies, had no basis of understanding them.

"What you saw on those tapes, I submit to you, shows those children were exposed to sex. I ask you what is the common denominator? There's one common denominator. . . .

"Try as you might [to] give him the benefit of every reasonable doubt, but the common denominator of those—we'll call them what they are—those fifteen eyewitnesses, is that they went to *his* house for babysitting. . . .

"Simply using the word 'pretend' doesn't cause that. Why? Well, Dr. Coleman hasn't had the opportunity to do the studies, but Dr. Laurie Braga . . . has had opportunity to do experiments, changing little words and seeing, let's see if we change the variable, what is going to be the result.

"What the result has been, that that word has no effect.

"Dr. Coleman doesn't know any study to the contrary. . . .

"She's actually done it with other children and seen the results. . . .

"Dr. Coleman had nothing to say about that. What is he really saying? You take it to its extreme . . . the ultimate technicality in a court of law, that . . . you say the one word 'pretend' to a three-year-old, suddenly you have to acquit the defendant.

"That's absurd. . . .

"Those children simply aren't going to fantasize about things that have no basis in reality.

"Not to say children don't fantasize.

"I'm not going to try to tell you that Jason ever rode on a shark, or he ever rode on a whale, but how should we treat those things that are apparently not true?

"Dr. Summit told us that . . . first of all, look at it very carefully because some things that you and I might consider fantasy may not be. Why? First of all, sex abusers and people who abuse children simply don't think in normal ways. . . .

"Don't apply your rules to them.

"Don't limit yourself as to what they might do with a child. Good example—Dr. Coleman talked about the fact that it was clearly fantasy that children would talk about using feces or playing with feces. Child after child talked about it.

"Crystal Fletcher thinks it's normal to eat it. . . .

"Dr. Coleman obviously said, 'Well, that's all fantasy,' but luckily, then along comes Iliana Fuster. No testimony she has seen those children or heard what they said. And suddenly what does she talk about? She talks about the defendant taking human excrement and rubbing it all over her body for the children to watch.

"Dr. Coleman—new to this field—he didn't want to believe that there were people in this world who are capable of doing things like that to little children.

"But there are, and one is sitting right *there*.

"He doesn't work by the same rules that the rest of us go by. His mind doesn't work in the same pattern. Because of that, he did things to those children that, at first blush are fantasy, but as all the evidence comes out, it is clear what he did. That is, he abused them in ways that are beyond *imagination*.

"Not fantasy. Just beyond imagination.

"Another reason that we shouldn't necessarily discount what a child says and say it's fantasy—children have trouble describing things that they don't have a word for. . . .

"Just as a child—or probably most of us—would have a problem describing a nuclear reaction . . . children don't have the terms to describe sexual acts. And they have trouble putting it into words. . . .

"That isn't just because it deals with sexual acts, but other things.

"Best example—Dr. Coleman says Jason's clearly fantasizing 'cause he says he broke down a door. We know from other witnesses, there used to be a . . . kiddie accordion door dividing the kitchen from the playroom. Jason broke it. Jason couldn't describe what . . . it was—an accordion door.

"He just knew he broke something.

"Dr. Coleman dismisses all of that.

"Maybe someday he'll understand the significance.

"Finally—I think most importantly—there was some fantasy. I'm not trying to say everything these children said was completely fantasy, but Dr. Summit—again, the expert—tells us how you're supposed to treat that.

"What does he say?

"When you find something that appears to be fantasy, if you'll ask yourself, 'Why is the child fantasizing about that?'

"Why did Jason say he took a knife to Frank? Why does he use that type of fantasy? Well, the answer is fairly clear, I think. It's based in common sense.

"Jason wishes he could have. . . .

"Doesn't mean you discard everything he says. Not at all. . . .

"You also look to everything else he said. You look at the details he gave, the consistency that he gave, and there really is no problem. . . .

"Mr. Samek says when they're given the dolls, obviously they see genitals. Obviously that's not true. The dolls were clothed when they were given. He talks about the fact that the dolls were named, and that's a problem.

"Ladies and gentlemen, I think that Dr. Braga explained these dolls can be used correctly, and they can be misused. If we had a child lying by the side of the road who had been assaulted, and our issue was *who*, it would be improper to name the dolls—I agree.

"But in this case, it was already known that each and every child who was questioned had been in the defendant's custody and had been in his house.

"The only issue is what *happened*, and by simply saying, 'Let this be Frank, and what happened?' does not necessarily cause them to start acting out abuse.

"That makes no sense.

"The key here—as with everything that Dr. Coleman says—is every other national expert simply disagrees with him. . . . He simply doesn't know what he's talking about.

"Mr. Samek argues that the Bragas didn't take enough time with the children and they were too directed. What you saw on those tapes was a very clear pattern. That they began playing with the child, giving him an opportunity to be forthcoming. . . .

"To the extent that the child wasn't, they did what was necessary to focus the child on the issues . . . and there was nothing wrong with that. Obviously, when you evaluate the information that comes back from that, you have to understand, when did the child start talking and how much focusing was necessary? . . .

"That's why the key tape is that [August ninth] tape that says 'Jason and Joshua'—the one Dr. Coleman did not look at.

"I'm not saying he intentionally tried to mislead you all and that he saw that tape and couldn't answer it . . . therefore he lied and said it was 'just playing.' I submit it wasn't an intentional mistake on his part, but just sloppy work.

"If you have any doubts about this case, you ask to look at that tape, because you'll see . . . after Joshua is there with the doctors, Jason comes in, and they say, 'Jason, is there anything else you want to tell us?' . . .

"Jason takes a deep breath and spills his guts. And he describes things that at the time—you look at the Bragas' reaction when he starts talking about playing with ca-ca and smearing ca-ca, and the Bragas are looking at him. 'That didn't really happen, did it?'

" 'Yes, it did.' . . .

"Why was there no leading? Why could it not have been programmed?

"Because the Bragas didn't know anything else about the case other than the fact that kids went to babysitting at Frank and Iliana's out in Country Walk. . . .

"Dr. Coleman basically says a child is so manipulatable—so easily swayed—all you have to do is say, 'You're a good boy' or 'We're proud of you.' Suddenly that child, from then on, will do whatever you want.

"But what he ignores is that the Bragas may have seen them and said that once or twice to each child. But *he* had those children in his home. *He* had them under his power. . . .

"Imagine what he did to their minds.

"Imagine what fears he was able to entrust in them. . . .

"I wish as much as anyone else that these children hadn't gone through that . . . but that simply isn't the way it is.

"The State didn't pick the rules of this game.

"*He* did. . . .

"The Bragas didn't tell Frank Fuster to threaten these children, and I didn't tell Frank Fuster to start screaming in a court of law.

"He shows his colors. He showed his colors here. . . .

"[Dr. Coleman] talks about leading questions or choice questions. . . . This is an example he gave of a leading question:

" 'Crystal, did Frank put his finger inside you?' That's a leading question. . . . Everything else is unreliable.

"First you say, 'Maybe he's got a point there.' What he's doing is taking that statement in a vacuum.

"You look at the tape again.

"What you'll see is Crystal has a little Frank doll. She has a little Crystal doll. She is sticking her finger in the vaginal opening of the doll that's been labeled 'Crystal.'

"That's not a leading question.

"It is simply reflecting in voice what the child is demonstrating. In each of those children, and in each of those interviews, the child could have said, 'no.' . . .

"Whose idea was it to videotape the interviews?

"The Bragas'.

"Any state law requiring it?

"No.

"If they went there and intended to manipulate and brainwash these children, why would they be the ones insisting on having everything videotaped?

"They did it because they have nothing to hide.

"They did it because their procedures are approved; they're recognized all over the country. It is only Dr. Coleman who has a problem with them. . . .

"The key is child memory.

"Dr. Braga testified—Laurie Braga—that a child's memory is different for things they experience and things they're taught. If you tell a child, 'Go upstairs and get your coat, a book, close the door to your sister's room, and get me a pen off my desk,' that . . . child is apt to forget some. . . .

"But ask a child, 'What did you get last Christmas?' you'll get an answer because they are better remembering things they've experienced than things they're taught.

"The reason these children were able to tell you . . . what happened to them is because they remember what they experience.

"I almost wish they didn't—that we could take that memory out of their mind. But for better or worse, we can't.

"They remember it a year later.

"I submit to you they'll remember when they are fifteen or sixteen, and they'll probably remember to their dying day. . . .

"Dr. Coleman doesn't understand memory.

"Mr. Samek doesn't either. . . .

"We get to Crystal Fletcher, and Mr. Samek wants to say,

'Disregard everything she said.' Why? Because she said, 'Laurie Braga "told me" about sex abuse and "told me" what happened.'

"And you saw the tape.

"You realize it didn't happen on the tape.

"But when she said that in [court testimony], I was concerned that you all wouldn't understand. I was concerned that you all would not understand that Crystal and children of this age sometimes have trouble with abstract concepts such as the difference between 'tell' and 'ask.' We all know Laurie Braga 'asked' her about those. She used the word 'tell,' and Crystal . . . cleared that up in the next few seconds.

"Why?

"Because on her own, she turned to Mr. Casey and says, 'Does Mommy like him?' And then she says, 'Tell my Mommy if she likes him.' . . .

"She simply didn't know the difference between 'tell' and 'ask.' Yes, Laurie Braga *asked* her about it. You saw the tape.

"She *never* 'told her.' Not one iota of evidence indicates Laurie Braga interviewed her when it wasn't taped. . . .

"You take the defendant's testimony. . . . It is inconsistent with thirty-eight other witnesses. . . . The key is, he is inconsistent with himself. Why? Because before any of this broke, he said [to Detective Meznarich], 'I was never home when the children were there. . . .'

"We talked about Iliana. He says she is a self-serving liar, that she is cunning and clever. . . .

"You saw her yesterday.

"If you saw anything but dread fear and disgust from that young girl as she described these things, I don't know what it was. We have a number of notes that were written. I think it's important to note we have two Spanish-speaking people. All these are written in English. Makes you wonder whether these notes might have been written for you while you were still at home. That they were written for a jury to see someday, talking about how they're innocent and talking about their love.

"I'm not trying to give an opinion as to whether Iliana Fuster loved this man, despite all the things he did.

"I don't know. I'm not going to try to understand why a woman who goes through this type of thing—how she would feel.

"We know why she wouldn't leave, why she couldn't tell Sergeant Fletcher.

"The same reason the kids couldn't.

"He told the kids, 'I'll hurt you, and I'll hurt your parents.' . . . We know he hurt her. He cut her in front of the kids. We know that she had no place to go. Yes, she came to this country to see her mother. She stayed longer than she should. The fact that she was in this country illegally does not make her fair game.

"Now, when you look at Iliana's testimony, it's true she does not confirm everything that the children say. I think we need to analyze her testimony from the evidence and from the structure that Dr. Summit gave us, because Iliana, I submit to you, is a child who is going through the window of disclosure.

"First, nothing happened. Yes, it happened.

"And she has not yet gotten to the point . . . that afterwards she was able—and she *did*, in fact—abuse the children just as Jason did. Jason was able to talk about how he eventually abused children. Jaime was.

"Iliana isn't. Whether that's because . . . it's very painful for her, she can't accept it, or whether she is concerned about what Judge Newman will do doesn't really concern you. . . .

"More importantly, we know she couldn't have done this by herself. Mr. Samek . . . said in opening, maybe she abused them on her own. . . .

"The kids talked about penises.

"Not *one* child confused the difference between penis and vagina. More importantly, Iliana could not have given Jaime gonorrhea. It takes a penis. . . .

"My job of trying to explain to you might have been difficult if it hadn't been for the defendant. Because when he got up in this courtroom yesterday and screamed and screamed, she grabbed her chest and screamed—screeched—as if she had been shot.

"She demonstrated for you with much more ability than I ever could, the incredible terror she lived under.

"That wasn't fake.

"At the point she was screaming, at the point she was going into a fetal position right in front of you, we were all recovering from what happened. You saw the sincerity of her reaction, the sincerity of her fear.

"You also saw something else.

"You saw how he acts. You saw that in a courtroom filled with police officers in front of a judge, in front of the flag, in one of the most solemn places you will find in our community—this man will get up and scream.

"Imagine what he's like, unleashed, when he's surrounded by his small little wife—his sixteen-year-old wife—and three- and four-year-olds.

"Imagine what he's like when he's got a knife as a tool.

"His genitals as a tool.

"He has his own excrement, and the only other persons there are defenseless little children. I couldn't have ever explained to you what he's like—how Iliana lived—any better than the way he demonstrated for you.

"Mr. Samek alludes to the HRS investigation, alludes to the video, ignoring Jaime's testimony about it, all the other children, all the other parents. When you come down to the fact, we have a pattern here.

"It's a pattern you can't deny.

"It wasn't found by the police just like the masks weren't. Why? Because, as Iliana said, the defendant was smiling, 'I got someone to move all the stuff out of my house.'

"The facts are clear.

"You can take one after another, and there is no conclusion other than the defendant is guilty. . . .

"You can't escape from saying that it happened. . . .

"Listen to the instructions very carefully, because you're going to hear something that's fundamental. That is, that the defendant has a lot of rights, but none of us have the right to violate the law. And as eloquent as Mr. Samek is, as much as the defendant wants to scream, he doesn't have that right, because his time for screaming is over, and his tears that we saw yesterday just came too late.

"The children have told their story, and today is going to be his day of judgment.

"I submit to you that the only true verdict is the defendant is guilty of each and every one of these horrible crimes, and I think that our prayers simply have to be that Mr. Samek is wrong.

"That these children *aren't* tainted for life.

"Thank you."

• • •

At 7:20 P.M., after deliberating for three hours—two hours longer than anyone had anticipated—the jury dispatched a note to Judge Newman asking that they be returned to the refuge of their hotel.

The judge ordered dinner catered to the jury room and instructed them to continue.

At 10:22 P.M., a second scrap of yellow paper wafted from the jurors' tomb, bearing a hand-scrawled plea that caused His Honor no small measure of surprise.

"We'd like to recess for the night. We're making no progress. *Please.*"

Obviously they have paid full attention to what they were told in jury instruction, the judge noted mildly to curious reporters, who had staked out and wired the corridor outside Courtroom 4-2, expecting no less swift and sure a verdict than the parents who lined the walls.

On the floor at Tom Herschel's feet, a satchel bore a magnum of no-longer-iced champagne.

"We're making no progress."

The words seared. Missy and Chad would be waiting for him. And he would have to tell them that the jury had thought about it for six hours and still hadn't decided whether they believed them. Missy was still a little bewildered as to why the trial had continued for another month after her testimony. Why, she asked, hadn't he been found guilty the day she told them what happened?

"Didn't they believe me?"

"Don't worry," John Hogan and Dan Casey told the bedraggled and anxious parents camped out in the hall. "They've got a lot of charges to go through. They're just being careful, that's all." But neither of the grey-faced prosecutors seemed convinced of their own words. The more time that passed, the greater the likelihood of a hung jury—or even acquittal.

Surely no man or woman in that room could be entertaining even a fleeting doubt—they had seen the tapes.

An encouraged Frank beamed at reporters as his jailers led him "home" for the night.

"God," he predicted, "is going to work His miracle."

• • •

Around noon on the second day of deliberations, the jurors ordered a curious combination of lunch and evidence. Along with their sandwiches, they wished the bailiff to bring to them the photograph of the naked Jaime Fuster seated on the toilet, surrounded by excrement hand-smeared all over the floor.

The parents, camped out in the hallway since the building opened, were disintegrating with each passing hour. Yesterday it had seemed impossible that the jury could come back with anything but a conviction.

Now they weren't so sure.

Then the call came.

The jury had reached its verdict.

Virtually the entire contents of the Justice Building emptied onto the fourth floor, where video monitors had been installed to bring the proceedings to the hundreds of spectators who could not gain admittance to the overflowing courtroom.

Inside, the parents filled the wing Christina Royo had reserved for them. A lone woman pushed her way into the courtroom and began to take a seat. Crystal Fletcher's grandmother, seated on the aisle, blocked her progress, saying, "I'm sorry, but these are reserved for the parents of the victims."

The woman looked at her quietly and said, "I am one of the mothers." The Country Walk parents turned to regard her. Who was this woman?

"I am," she said, "the mother of Hilda Gonzalez."

The mother whose nine-year-old daughter had suffered a trial, only to see Frank Fuster walk free on probation.

She had come to see justice done.

Chief Ray Havens wore the only smile in the courtroom. "One hundred percent guilty," he had said to the parents who anguished in the hall. "One hundred percent guilty."

He was sure.

Nearby, Christina Royo stared intently at the court clerk, who had promised, she knew, to glance in John Hogan's direction should the verdict sheets the foreman handed her contain the word *guilty*. Christina would not be satisfied unless she heard that word fourteen consecutive times.

The jury entered. Two of them were crying.

The parents gripped each other's hands, forming a human chain five rows deep—a lifeline.

Judy Prince strained forward, tears streaming down her face. He was her neighbor. And he had raped her little boy.

The court clerk accepted the verdict sheets and began to page through them. Christina was seized by panic. Look at John, she willed her. Look at John. Look at John.

But the court clerk continued paging through the verdict sheets. Christina could barely stay seated. Please, God. Just one count. Please let them have believed just once.

The court clerk began to read from the sheets.

As to count one, sexual battery. Guilty. Count two . . .

The parents went numb. The lifeline went limp. Tears streamed down their faces. Tom Herschel raised his clenched fists above his head in a silent gesture of victory as he looked toward the ceiling, his mouth forming the unspoken words, Thank you.

Outside the courtroom, the masses huddled around the video monitors became one voice—one spontaneous cheer.

Frank Fuster was, as Chief Havens had predicted, "one hundred percent guilty."

All fourteen counts.

Frank Fuster's face remained expressionless.

God, he later told reporters, had instructed him "not to say anything."

Moments later, he gave a forty-five-minute speech before Judge Newman imposed sentence.

"Once more the office of the state attorney has proven to me that they have the legal power to commit legal crimes to put innocent persons and families in prison. . . .

"It is now as in the old times of witch hunt hysteria! It was not until innocent humans got burned alive that these similar crimes came to an end. . . .

"I advise the nation to be very, very, very careful whenever the words of an irresponsible child are going to be used in a court of law to destroy some person's life. . . ."

Then it was John Hogan's turn.

"In front of a police officer, he got out of a car and shot a man repeatedly. He went to prison. He served some time.

"He came to Dade County.

"Within a matter of months, he molested a nine-year-old girl. He went to trial. He was convicted. . . ."

Every jaw on the jury dropped to the floor.

The jurors would later reveal few of the details of their twelve hours of deliberations, attributing their decision to twelve painstaking hours of reviewing the evidence presented on each individual count.

There was no one piece of evidence or testimony that "clinched" their verdict, they said. It was all the evidence put together that formed a compelling "chain of events."

But that didn't lessen the shock of learning afterward that the volatile Cuban "businessman" had murdered and molested twice before.

"He talks about suffering," Hogan continued. "I think the court should be aware that the parents of that nine-year-old girl who was molested by this man a few years ago came to court the other day, but left in tears because, years later, the emotion of what he did to that little girl—the scars—are still there. . . .

"For . . . a number of years, Mr. Casey and I have handled more or less exclusively homicide cases. We always thought that was the ultimate case because you took a person's life.

"What the defendant did to these victims was much worse.

"What he did to those families is so much worse, because they live the pain every day. Whether it's when trying to go to sleep, whether when trying to hug their children, they live the pain because of what he did to them.

"It's true that before this trial started, we offered if he wanted to plead guilty, we would run the sentence concurrently, so we didn't have to put four-year-olds and five-year-olds through the trauma of this. Also, because we felt if the defendant was willing to show some remorse. . . .

"He obviously has no remorse at all. . . .

"We have to make sure he is never able to come in contact with another child again, and the court can do that by running the sentences consecutively."

Judge Newman agreed.

Francisco Fuster Escalona will be eligible for parole in the year 2150.

Part V

LEGACIES

"The purpose of life is not to be happy. The purpose of life is to matter, to be productive, to have it make some difference that you lived at all. Happiness, in the ancient, noble sense means self-fulfillment and is given to those who use to the fullest whatever talents God or luck or fate bestowed upon them. Happiness, to me, lies in stretching to the farthest boundaries of which we are capable, the resources of the mind and heart."

—Rosten, sign posted on wall in bathrooms at Apogee

Epilogue

Judge Robert Newman lost little sleep over his decision that Frank Fuster leave prison in a box.

But this matter of dispensing justice in the case of Iliana Fuster loomed a complex and soul-searching task. For the many faces of Iliana were less easily read than those of her spouse.

Iliana was an enigma.

Her letters to her husband were intricately decorated with commercial quality art sketched by her own hand. For her therapists she drew stick figures.

She *never* would have abused the children if not compelled by Frank, they said. She was sweet. She was gentle. She was kind. And she *never* would have transferred her pain to the children when he wasn't there.

But the fact remained that she did.

The children couldn't have been more clear.

Far more clear than her third and last polygraph at which the esteemed examiner threw up his hands in despair.

November 8, 1985

Dear Mr. Hogan:

Specific polygraph detection of deception examinations were administered to your client, Iliana Fuster, on this date. . . .

Based on the subject's polygraph responses and comments, it is the examiner's opinion she was untruthful as indicated above and was withholding and falsifying information regarding her involvement with other female children at the Country Walk Babysitting Service.

It should be noted that some of her responses during the administering of this examination were inconsistent when compared to previous examinations administered at an earlier date. It was pointed out to the examiner the subject has undergone psychiatric care and the psychiatrist had reported she had previously "blocked" certain

573

information from her mind. The validity of this examination is considered to be contingent upon her mental and psychological normality at this time.

Of all the psychiatrists who sought to unravel the mysteries of Iliana's mind, only one (who was court-appointed and not on Von Zamft's payroll) offered an opinion that in any manner reconciled the differences between the accounts of fifteen young eyewitnesses and her own.

November 15, 1985

Dear Mr. Hogan,

Iliana Fuster was seen at your request at the Women's Annex on November 11, 1985. She was interviewed for a period of almost 2 hours. I had also reviewed my previous evaluation. The defendant was seen so that I might provide a psychiatric assessment of her to your office. You had desired some additional understanding of the defendant and how her mental condition may have affected her behavior at the time of the offenses. The defendant has apparently pled guilty but has not yet been sentenced. . . .

What follows is a description of her functioning during the interview as well as an attempt to provide some understanding as to the defendant's personality structure, adaptive techniques, and to what extent possible, prognosis.

Mrs. Fuster related to me in a friendly and somewhat childlike fashion. There was some enthusiasm expressed by her as to the results of a recent polygraph. She felt that the results were satisfactory. Clearly she was very aware of her current legal situation and noted there was concern as to whether she had independently involved herself with the children when alone with them and without the presence of Frank Fuster. There was certainly an awareness on her part that the children had made these claims and that parents had noted that he was apparently not in the household on a number of occasions when some of the sexual acts with the children had occurred. Considerable skill was displayed on her part in dealing with these. She was not at all flustered and indicated that at times Frank would hide in another room and not let anyone who came to the door know that he was there. Additionally, his car was sometimes said to be in the garage and no one would really know whether he was home or not. Likewise, explanations about how she had initially denied any knowledge of Frank's actions with the children and later acknowledged those acts were offered rather skillfully. It was her view that the continued threats on the part of Frank had caused her to repress recollections and that only through the repeated questioning when polygraphed and by her attorney, did she slowly uncover those recollections. Even though she initially did not tell the truth, it was her belief that she was indeed answering truthfully although the polygraph apparently showed deceptive responses. My own view is that these explanations are less than convincing although not impossible. Her description of Frank's aggressive and threatening behavior towards her and how she was even fearful for her mother's safety, was generally convincing although I feel that she is certainly capable of embellishment.

The most appropriate emotional responses came forth when talking about Frank's son and how she had initially come to like the boy and how this led to her relationship with Frank. I suggested to her that she had indeed chosen Frank and that the son was a vehicle for her to establish the relationship in order to find an alternative to a somewhat unpleasant situation with her mother and stepfather. She agreed that there was some disappointment present after coming to the United States to rejoin her mother. There had always been a strong wish on her part to be with her mother again. When talking about life in Honduras, she described it as comfortable and stable but certainly there seemed to be an emptiness and sadness and she showed some tearfulness when talking about all of this. This made me feel that themes of dependency, loneliness, separation, attachment and fears connected with these are paramount in her dynamics. I could not elicit any previous history of her being molested in Honduras or after coming to the United States. Her denials were firm and consistent.

The defendant is certainly not psychotic and clearly seems to be free of any disorder such as schizophrenia or manic-depressive illness. I would see her as being of well above average intelligence. While only in this country a relatively short time, she has learned to speak English quite well. There is considerable skill demonstrated on her part in terms of her ability to relate to others and respond to their cues. Her particular life experiences have probably allowed for their development. She seems to have a feeling for what one wants to hear and quickly readjusts her responses. Care is taken to avoid offending others and to be accepted. This has been an adaptive style on her part which has probably been, for the most part, quite successful. Certainly the separation from her mother at a relatively early age must have affected her and I believe her statements that she had always dreamed of reuniting with her mother. Certainly she would probably tend to be somewhat passive in terms of relating to others. By being compliant some of her basic security needs could be met. Manipulative adaptations would not be unexpected.

Certainly it would not be unexpected for the defendant to have engaged in some sexual acts with the children without the specific direction or presence of Frank Fuster.

Having been exposed to his domination, assuming that is true, could have generated some identification with the aggressor and it would be reasonable for her to have acted out some of those experiences without his being present. Likewise, there could have been considerable identification with the victims themselves and at times she may indeed honestly perceive herself as being more like the children than an adult. Certainly she could see herself alternately or intermittently in both roles. I see her as being a somewhat chameleon-like individual who takes on the tone of her environment. This is generally consistent with individuals who attach themselves to others utilizing objects to supplement their own deficient egos. While some of her ego functions are well-developed, I do not see her as having a cohesive sense of self. All of this could allow for some degree of fragmentation with attachments to objects who could easily dominate her and whose view she would easily accept. In spite of mistreatment she would certainly find it necessary to continue those relationships in the absence of more suitable replacements.

Her prognosis is, in my opinion, very guarded.

I certainly would not necessarily predict that she would engage in similar activities in the future. I do feel, however, that she is going to be inclined to gravitate towards relationships which will, in fantasy, provide the kind of stability and security that she has probably yearned for since childhood. These relationships in fantasy would serve to meet needs that have been long unfulfilled. Relationships formed on this basis are certainly fraught with problems.

The parents offered their own thoughts on the matter.

November 25, 1985

Your Honor:
For the past 15 months, we, the parents of the children who attended the Country Walk Babysitting Service, have come to identify with the plaque above your bench which reads: "We Who Labor Here Seek

Truth." It is to that end that we respectfully offer comment for your consideration in passing sentence upon Iliana Fuster.

Our conclusions in this matter were not reached without the most soul-searching deliberation as to the facts of the case and the emotions which have inextricably become a part of it.

We are not unaware that a human life is at stake. Nor are we without the compassion to realize that at times even the most malevolent life might be salvaged. However, this can only occur when an individual no longer rejects responsibility for his or her actions. The character disorder must heal before the person can.

The ability to rationalize even the most reprehensible act is a key component in the personality profile of the habitual offender, and a key marker of the most dangerous to society—the sociopath. Rationalization is the process which allows a man to kill in cold blood without a second thought, or a woman to abuse children without remorse. When combined with an aberrant sex drive, it becomes the blueprint for pedophilia. . . .

We are told that Iliana led a double life. We are told that the young woman who cheerfully took our babies from our arms, and who frolicked most amorously and publicly with her husband at the community pool, was in reality a battered bride who felt compelled to marry the man who raped her on her first date. We are told that Iliana Fuster is, herself, a sexually abused child, the only difference between her and our children being a matter of years, not innocence.

Those of us who now face a lifetime of rearing her frightened and confused victims find the analogy insulting.

None of us expect to ever know who Iliana really is, despite her psychiatrists' assertions that she has told them all they need to know.

Our time spent with our former babysitter exceeds that of her therapists ten-fold. Yet we wouldn't venture to say with any measure of assurance precisely what goes on in her mind. Only Frank could tell us that. Or the children.

And they have.

Much of what the children have to say about the Fusters has already entered your court through Frank's trial. Since the proceedings focused on Iliana's husband at the time, the memory of the children's testimony regarding Iliana and her actions independent of Frank may be dim. Our memories remain fresh as to the specifics because we still put the children to bed wondering if it will be another night of purging memories, and fear, and guilt.

The children ask us if we still love them. They wonder how many people know what happened to them and if the ones that do think less of them for it. They worry that they might be put in jail. They feel in some way responsible.

Iliana bears no similar burden. She pled guilty. And then she told the court that she didn't "feel" guilty. And she does not.

Our children don't enjoy the benefits of such a highly evolved defense mechanism. We are grateful they don't, because it reassures us that they have retained the capacity to distinguish right from wrong. But it saddens us to see them so innocently wear someone else's guilt, especially when the woman who raped and degraded them—for whatever reason—refuses to dignify their pain with the truth.

For the better part of a year, we clung to the hope that one day Iliana might give us insight into our children's most deep-seated fears so that we might better defuse them. If we knew what we were dealing with, we would be better equipped to help our children heal.

Instead of providing us with information to that end, she weaves a self-serving tale of abuse in which she, and not the children, is the consummate victim. Despite the fact that this appeared strikingly similar to Frank's long-time career as a professional "victim," which began when he was but two years older than Iliana is now, some of us were willing to give her the benefit of the doubt in the beginning. Then we looked at the facts.

It became increasingly clear that her selective memory was fine-tuned to convert a "straight up" plea of guilty into a more desirable sentence than could be bargained with the State at the time. The handful of "incidents" she offers regarding the children were thrown in to sweeten the pot—a few bones thrown to the State to bolster a couple of the counts against Frank. If Iliana was interested in helping the children or rehabilitating herself, she would make full disclosure. But then, full disclosure might have made the court reach the conclusion that her danger to society might be no less than her husband's. . . .

We cannot even begin to describe the terror our children communicate when they ask us to reassure them that she is still in jail.

It is interesting to note that the children didn't feel secure enough to divulge their most frightening experiences until Iliana was locked safely behind bars. The dated notations of the children's conversations with us, logged at the State's request, clearly demonstrate this phenomenon. . . .

It is most interesting that the woman who taught a child to recite [a prayer to the Devil] as deftly as he recites the "Our Father" holds herself as a devout Catholic.

So does Frank.

In fact, we see many similarities between these two kindred spirits, including what appears to be a shared gift of deceptive charm. Frank has a 15-year history of conning the psychiatrists who have evaluated him. Iliana appears to be following the same course. . . .

Numerous children have told about the video camera which photographed the games. At least one parent had occasion to see the camera in the Fuster home, yet Iliana adamantly denies that there was ever a camera. In fact, she's not entirely sure what home video equipment looks like.

Her therapists suggest that she is "blocking" this information out. We suggest that the videotapes made in the Fuster home are too incriminating for her to even acknowledge. For one thing, it would reveal the Satanic rituals which the children say were recorded and it would support the children's contention that her abuse of them did not occur at knifepoint.

Most telling is the fact that she neglects to inform her therapists of the occasions on which she abused the children in Frank's absence. It would be difficult for her to explain how Frank "forced" her mouth onto penises and vaginas when he was not there.

Frank's psychiatric records indicate that his therapists also chose to disregard fact in favor of their patient's version of reality.

Iliana's version of reality is no less self-serving, and her therapists no less gullible. Both Frank and Iliana are not without acting ability. They fooled us.

We have grave concerns that history is about to repeat itself. In 1969, the State of New York had the opportunity to relieve society of Frank Fuster's presence—permanently. That it did not is now our burden, and our children's, as we try to piece together our shattered lives.

The Court now faces a similar opportunity in deciding the disposition of his wife. It should not fail to consider the striking similarities in the personality make-up of Frank at age 20 and Iliana at age 18. It should be noted that both were at some point in their lives victims of abuse. And that both crossed the line to become the abusers. This is not uncommon in the well-known pattern which perpetuates the child abuse cycle.

We do not question the possibility that Iliana, herself, was abused.

What we question is the "experts'" assertion that her abuse of the children was the result of "duress," not a pathological behavior. . . .

At the age of 18, Iliana's rationalization process appears as highly developed as Frank's. She assumes neither responsibility nor guilt for her actions. This alone would tend to circumvent any attempt at rehabilitation, even if one is to disregard her tendencies toward pedophilia. . . .

Our only certainty is that at some point she crossed the line which separates the abused from the abuser. Frank's influence over her doesn't negate the fact that she not only witnessed, but participated in the brutalization of more than 30 children. . . . We know of no criminals who were not "influenced" by someone at some point in their lives. Some are salvageable. And some are not. . . .

Mental health professionals concur, for the most part, that pedophiles can be "cured" about as readily as practitioners of any other sexual preference. . . . It cannot be known whether any therapist has ever succeeded in "curing" a pedophile because the dispensers of "cure" rates have only the molester's word that he no longer desires and seeks out children. . . .

It is possible that Iliana was once a troubled teenager with family problems who saw Frank as her ticket to a new and affluent life. It is also possible that two "bad seeds" just happened to find each other and formed a malevolent bond. In either case, she is guilty of one of the most heinous crimes of this decade.

Taking all of these circumstances into consideration, it would seem that the interests of the people of the State of Florida would be best served if Iliana Fuster is removed from society for as long as possible. The children of the State of Florida are entitled to be protected from this severely disturbed individual. There exists no guarantee or even likelihood that her destructive behavior patterns will not continue once she is returned to the mainstream. We must ask ourselves if it is worth the risk.

Fifteen months ago we placed our faith and our children in the hands of the justice system. We didn't have to. We could have run for cover as many other parents did, who refuse to even acknowledge that their children were placed in Iliana's care. But we felt a responsibility to ensure that not one family, and not one child would experience the horror we have had to endure.

We have labored for truth. And now we seek justice.

Our most recent and careful consideration has led us to conclude that any sentence less than 30 years would represent a gross indignity to the people of the State of Florida. We are not unfamiliar with the law. Thirty years translates to ten with offenders now earning an average of 20 days of every month off for combined good time/gain time. We are also aware that by statute, a prisoner becomes eligible for work release when 18 months remain of his sentence.

Our children are just now beginning to sleep through the night, assured that Iliana and her demons are locked safely away. If she is unleashed anytime in the near future, their nightmares will become reality once more.

We ask that you give reasonable weight to the children's knowledge of this woman. Their fears are not unfounded.

Clearly they know what we don't. And what they know of Iliana Fuster still sends them screaming in the night.

Thank you for allowing us this opportunity for comment.

Janet Reno was of a much different mind.

MEMORANDUM OF SENTENCING

Five points are critical to the State Attorney's Office in recommending an appropriate sentence for Iliana Fuster. They are:

1. Iliana Fuster is a victim. She was threatened, beaten, tortured and dominated. There is no reason to believe that she would have done what she did had it not been for Frank Fuster;

2. Iliana Fuster cooperated with the State in prosecuting Frank Fuster;

3. Iliana Fuster has the potential for living a law-abiding, productive life;

4. What Iliana Fuster allowed to happen and did herself to the children was horribly, horribly wrong regardless of whether or not she was a victim or acted under duress. There can be no justification for hurting children;

5. Iliana Fuster has never acknowledged or admitted what she did was wrong. When she pled guilty she stated, "I just want you to know that I'm pleading guilty not because I feel or that I know that I'm guilty. I am innocent of all those charges and I would never done anything to harm any child." She had reiterated that point again and again.

Thus, we believe that the sentence should be one that lets Iliana Fuster and others similarly situated know that what she did will not be tolerated or condoned. The punishment must serve as a deterrent to anyone who would do this to children. It must serve as a deterrent to anyone who believes duress justifies harming children. The sentence should also serve as a warning to all that when confronted with a situation like Iliana was, you call the police or seek help from others. Clearly Iliana Fuster had countless opportunities to seek help when Frank Fuster was not present.

On the other hand, the sentence should recognize that Iliana was a seventeen (17)-year-old victim of one of the most horrible criminals this office has ever seen. Despite initial fear, she testified, she made herself available for case preparation, and she cooperated with the State.

She is an intelligent but terribly impressionable, malleable young woman who with proper treatment, structure, and discipline, can have a lawful, productive, and useful life. To achieve that end, the sentence should not be so lengthy as to make her dependent on an institution, while at the same time insuring that she never again hurts a child.

The Youthful Offender Program would be ideal for the rehabilitation of Iliana Fuster. However, due to gain time and credit served, the ultimate period Iliana Fuster would serve under the present system would be insufficient in light of the seriousness of the crimes committed. If Iliana Fuster were committed to rehabilitation and willing to waive credit time served the State would recommend that she be sentenced to ten (10) years in the State Prison. The State would recommend that she be classified as a Youthful Offender. She should be permitted to pursue her education and receive appropriate treatment while incarcerated. This recommendation takes into consideration the present system of gain time and reflects the State's desire that Iliana Fuster spend four (4) to five (5) years in a structured environment. The prison sentence should be followed by a lengthy probation. In order to ensure the structure and discipline necessary for proper supervision, we do not feel she should be deported.

However, should Iliana Fuster not be willing to waive credit time served, the State would recommend that she be sentenced to fifteen (15) years in the State Prison. Under this sentence she would not be eligible for Youthful Offender treatment.

Von Zamft, of course, was looking for probation—a clear and resounding "win" for any attorney whose client had pleaded guilty to four life felonies.

But in the end, there was only one opinion that mattered. On Tuesday, November 26, 1985—two days before Iliana's nineteenth birthday—Judge Robert Newman, whom fate had delivered to preside for fifteen months over this judicial nightmare—rendered it.

He looked not unkindly at the parents who had, as on the day of the trial verdict, gripped each other's hands and strained forward in their seats as if to read from his unreadable face the decision they would bring home to their children, most of whom were aware of what was taking place today.

"I appreciate how you feel," he said. "And I think I know how you feel. It is not an easy matter coming forward—this past year and a half.

"As I've said on other occasions, the scars are there. I only hope and pray that they are healing. . . .

"It is not an easy decision.

"But I have to do what I think is right. . . .

"I feel that Iliana to some extent was a victim—to *some* extent—and that the matters to which she pled guilty . . . would not have occurred had it not been for her actions, along with that of her co-defendant."

"Also," continued Judge Newman, "she did cooperate, to some extent, as a witness for the prosecution in this case.

"No matter what concerns she felt for her own well-being, or her own safety, our society cannot condone the horrid acts visited upon these innocent children. Even if crying out at that time would have imperiled Iliana's own life and own safety.

"I *do* recognize that there is a likelihood that Iliana can become, after time and counseling, a better-adjusted individual, who can, and I hope will, take her place in society. And I feel that a period of incarceration, followed by a term of probation, best satisfy the goals of this court in imposing sentence.

"Incarceration serves as both a punishment for the defendant and a deterrent to those who might consider similar conduct . . . therefore, it is the sentence of this court, that the defendant serve a term of ten years . . . to be followed by a term of ten years' probation. . . .

"It is further recommended that the defendant be classified as a Youthful Offender. . . ."

The three-row lifeline of parents in the visitors' gallery went limp.

Iliana Fuster will be eligible for parole by the year 1990.

Only the children will know whether justice had been done, for Iliana's masks were so many, her truths so few, that only they knew what lay beneath them.

Ironically, the single clear truth to be spoken on this day had come from Iliana herself, as she offered an apology long overdue.

"But still," she said quietly, "the crime was done. . . .

"My own mind refused to believe that it was happening."

Iliana paused, gazed thoughtfully at the parents and said with great deliberation, "But it happened to me.

"It happened to the children.

"And it happened to *you*."

• • •

Jason Harrison sprawled on the living room floor, paging through one of the coloring books Janet Reno had ordered produced to familiarize children with their role in the justice process.

The books had not arrived in time to be used by the children who testified at Country Walk. But Jason didn't mind.

They would be there for other children, just like many things that had not been there for him in August of 1984.

There was a room filled with toys and tiny furniture, instead of Abe Laeser's floor. There was an enlightened state attorney willing to let more children in. There were eight prosecutors in the sexual battery unit, where once there were four, and a witness coordinator had been added to maintain order amidst potential chaos.

County funds had been designated for a Children's Assessment Center, to which HRS immediately tried to lay claim—a circumstance that prompted the parents and Janet Reno to reweave a fragile and tenuous bond, which their opposing views on the matter of Iliana Fuster had left seriously frayed. Though their rift would never be forgotten, the wounds were beginning to heal.

There was work to be done.

Drs. Joseph and Laurie Braga quietly folded their tent and retreated to Apogee shortly after the trial.

The seeds had been planted. The parents of Country Walk were tending them now. The organization J-SAC sponsored a fund-raiser through which to equip the new Child Assessment Center, to which Christina Royo had eagerly accepted assignment.

The politics of bureaucracy no doubt would steepen their road to realizing the justice they wished to carve for children once thought too small. But they were willing to try.

There were still children like Scotty Goldman for whom a shot and an apology remained the only remedy offered for their betrayal and the knowledge they would live with that they were helpless to spare another child their pain.

But there were more pleas of guilty than there once were, as defendants saw on videotape the first moments of disclosure that a jury was now more likely to see.

Though Michael Von Zamft no longer rules the crucial Florida bar committee, standing between the laws that the parents had fought for and won and their use in the courtroom, the state supreme court has not yet (as of the summer of 1986) outlined the rules under which certain provisions of the Child Protection Act will be implemented, but when it does, children's taped statements can be admitted under a new exception of the hearsay rule that acknowledges that the out-of-court statements of a child who had harbored a secret for a long time are not inherently less reliable than those uttered by a child who rushed to report the abuse immediately after the incident. No longer will a child be required to make an "excited utterance" in order to be heard.

The law also acknowledges that children have a right to be questioned during testimony in a language they understand. It is, in fact, the interpreter provision that the state attorney eagerly plans to test. For if a higher court acknowledges the language (and cognitive) barrier that too often impedes truth, it will become case law that extends beyond the Florida peninsula.

Already case law has spawned from the tragedy at Country Walk, a Georgia appeals court having upheld the admissibility of the Child Sexual Abuse Accommodation Syndrome, which Dr. Joseph Braga had introduced in an Atlanta courtroom during the spring of 1985.

Yet another noteworthy landmark occurred in a Miami courtroom in the months after Frank Fuster was granted lifetime admission to Florida State Prison, when a jury convicted the South Miami Police Department's "Officer of the Year."

Officer Harold "Grant" Snowden, whose wife had babysat the children of working mothers in her home for fifteen years, was convicted after his second trial.

The first, well-publicized Snowden trial took place three months prior to Frank Fuster's, when an eleven-year-old girl testified on the stand that her babysitter's husband had molested her at the age of four in a manner she still vividly recalled.

The jury was not impressed with the words of a collected little girl who quietly recounted for them a detailed seven-year-old memory. And the prosecutor handling the case did not believe it necessary to call in an expert on children's memory to explain to them that not only could the little girl remember the details of the trauma experienced at the age of four—she would undoubtedly never forget it.

Harold "Grant" Snowden was acquitted.

The Country Walk parents were despondent over the Snowden acquittal. Shari Herschel wept through the night for the mother who had to tell her daughter (who had received in the mail on Christmas eve an anonymous card out of which fell a used condom and a warning not to testify) that the six men and women she recounted experiences to hadn't believed her.

But the State had other alleged Snowden victims on whom it had withheld the filing of charges in the hope that the testimony of its oldest and most articulate witness would be enough to keep him from walking among the innocent and vulnerable in a police uniform ever again.

Now it was forced to turn to the younger children for another trial, and another and another should that become necessary. For the Snowden babysitting customers could not be encompassed in a single trial like Country Walk, because the activities they described did not involve "group" activities and did not take place in each other's presence. The State filed more charges, this time on behalf of a little girl, now six, whose descriptions—identical in circumstance to the eleven-year-old, whom she'd never met—were corroborated by venereal disease.

Under the "Williams Rule," two additional children (upon whom charges had not yet been filed) were called to testify at Snowden's second trial: one, another little girl, now five; the other, a four-year-old boy who had precipitated the investigation into Officer Snowden's activities in June of 1984 when he greeted his mother one morning with the startling news that "Grant" had "kissed" his "pee-pee" "yesterday."

Although the child gave clear and cogent statements to his father (who was also a policeman), and later to the Bragas, and was found to harbor gonorrhea in his throat, no charges had been filed in the months preceding the opening of Pandora's box.

During the summer of 1984, Grant Snowden's civil attorney collected written character references from other mothers who had paid for Mrs. Snowden's babysitting services, all of whom heartily sympathized with the police officer's suspension from the force.

If they harbored any doubts, Snowden's attorney had urged them upon receiving their testaments to their babysitter's husband's good (though womanizing) ways, "Go home; ask your kids."

One mother, for whom bed-wetting, nightmares, and quiet withdrawal over the past seven years had given her pause, did "go home" and ask for her daughter's reassurance that nothing had occurred.

The girl, then ten, denied that anything "unusual" might have happened to her in the Snowden home and averted her eyes toward the floor. Officer Snowden had been her next-door neighbor for a number of years. His daughter was her best friend. The mother grew anxious for the first time. "Please tell me the truth," she said.

Her daughter burst into tears.

Then smaller, more recent Snowden babysitting customers began to toddle into the State Attorney's Center for Children in the wake of Frank Fuster's arrest. Three of seven, two of whom tested positive for venereal disease, told the Bragas their story, and the interviewers once again became the "force" to which the defense would point to explain the children's collective "fantasy." An argument the Snowden defense hoped would successfully divert the jury's attention from the only other thing the children had in common—Grant Snowden.

The Bragas, having spoken to the eleven-year-old only after she already had given statements to police and prosecutors months before, were not the major focus of the first Snowden trial, though they were characterized by the defense as having "reinforced" (through their brief and belated interview) the "fantasies" the child entertained in testimony.

The jurors were not apprised of these further pertinent circumstances, they being aware only that a lone prepubescent girl had suddenly accused her former babysitter of unspeakable acts committed seven years before. The mother, the defense hinted broadly, was a spurned former lover of the police officer, who used her attention-starved daughter and the recent "community hysteria" to exact revenge. And though no new evidence was produced to support the mother's alleged "motive" (supplied solely by Grant Snowden), there was no evidence offered by the State to explain how an eleven-year-old girl with a seven-year-old memory came to sit on the stand. Nor was mention made of the smaller, diseased babysitting customers who grew older and more verbal with each passing day.

A defendant could not be prejudiced.

Even by the truth.

During the second Snowden trial, which took place a few months after Frank Fuster's, the Bragas' methods were placed on trial once again. Like Jeffrey Samek, the Snowden defense team introduced the interview tapes (of the smaller children) in the hope that a jury might concentrate on the "manipulative techniques" they would attribute to the interviewers instead of the deftness with which the children described and demonstrated details of sexual acts.

The jury that saw the tapes convicted on five counts of sexual battery upon the six-year-old girl and her then-eighteen-month-old brother (which she had witnessed), and Officer Harold "Grant" Snowden was sentenced to life in prison.

Attorney F. Lee Bailey accepted a $40,000 retainer from the court-declared "indigent" Snowden family to handle the appeal, based, he said, "on many years of experience and a strong suspicion that they may have convicted the wrong man."

Bailey noted that the police officer had twice passed polygraphs with flying colors, but failed to note that they had been administered by the same eminent expert who had "tested" Frank Fuster's conscience in 1982 in the matter of Hilda Gonzalez.

F. Lee Bailey told the media following the second—and final—Snowden trial, that many of these kinds of accusations were without merit.

Often, he said, it didn't happen, or perhaps, if it did, the children named the wrong individual.

"Nothing in Mr. Snowden's background is in any way consistent with this kind of conduct. That doesn't mean," he added, "that he didn't do it."

Although Janet Reno had triumphantly embraced the Snowden conviction as further verification that she had, as she told Joe and Laurie before the Country Walk trial, made "the best decision," not "the worst mistake" of her life, the Bragas would long feel the effects of the fifteen-month assault on their prized reputations.

They did not consider it coincidence that, on a night not long after Joe's "resurrection" in Courtroom 4-2 on the eve of his forty-fourth birthday, which marked the "clearing up" of the matter about his untimely 1972 "death," they received a phone call from comic artist Garry Trudeau, informing them that he had just received a phone call from a private eye who wished to bring to his attention that there were "questions" being raised in Miami as to the character and identity of the officers of one of his favorite charities—the National Foundation for Children.

And though Joe and Laurie tried to explain the purpose of similar phone calls being placed to other acquaintances of theirs around the country, Mr. Trudeau's assurances that this, of course, must be the case were followed by his "suggestion" that he had decided to make available to other worthy causes his original comic art, which had previously been offered for "exclusive" sale through the National Foundation for Children.

Trudeau's "Doonesbury" art had become, over the years, the primary source of funds for the programs implemented by the Bragas' foundation. Indeed, the money accrued from "Doonesbury" fund-raisers had made possible the purchase of materials for the children's interview room at the state attorney's office.

The "questions" raised about the Bragas' reputation, though answered, continued to haunt them.

In the spring of 1986, the Bragas were in court again, this time asking that the civil attorneys defending the lawsuits filed against Frank Fuster, Arvida, et al., be required to have their private investigators cease and desist from pawing through the Braga garbage.

Once again, the doctors fielded queries from professional acquaintances who wondered about phone calls they had received asking if they were "aware" that the "real" Joe Braga had died in 1972. Once again, private eyes conducted a fruitless sweep of Boston for skeletons, which existed only in motions filed by Michael Von Zamft that contained the words *fraud* and *child molester*.

In August 1986, Arvida Corporation settled out of court for almost six million dollars to be divided among seven children.

The Bragas continue to consult with the state attorney's office on the more difficult cases that wash up on her shores. And they sometimes speak to children who will speak to no one else. But their most important work is done, although, said Laurie, "We know it takes a long time. We know we won't be shaded by the trees we grow."

But the seeds have been planted.

And though the trials of Country Walk have painted silver slivers in Laurie's chestnut mane, paper rainbows still line her pockets as they did the first day she and Joe came to help the children speak of unspeakable acts.

• • •

The children's nightmares have diminished, though many still harbor fears. They speak little of their former babysitters, though their parents remain braced for unexpected commentary or behavior, which spews from their offspring now and then. The children of Country Walk will have many questions in the years to come, as they deal with their sexuality in a more appropriate context and time.

Only time will tell how scarring are their wounds. That depends largely, say the Bragas, on their parents' willingness to keep cracked the "window of disclosure."

Even after the trial, families continue to learn the lesson of "a burden shared."

None learned so convincingly as Sara Levy, the morning she decided she was ready to hear what caused her son to lock himself in his room with his pillows, day after day.

Chip had experienced a severe asthma attack the night before—an unprecedented occurrence for which his doctors could find no physical cure. He woke that morning medicated and cranky in a state of discontent.

Sara brought him to his bedroom and, with all the equanimity she could muster, inquired of her son, "Did you know that Frank and Iliana are in jail forever?"

"They'll get out," replied Chip, with astonishing conviction.

"No," said Sara, "the judge said they have to stay forever. They can never, *ever* get out."

"They'll get out," Chip continued to insist, as Sara painted images of permanence in terms her son finally understood.

"The judge took the key to the jail and flushed it down the toilet," she said.

Chip grew increasingly agitated and leapt on his bed. Fists clenched, he began to scream at his mother, "Why did you leave me there? Why did you leave me with those bad people?"

Sara, staggered by the intensity of her son's rage, tried desperately to answer the unspoken question that had simmered within him for more than a year.

"I didn't know," said Sara. "They *lied* to me. They told me that they loved you and would take good care of you. They told me they would play games with you and take you for walks."

"But I called for you!" Chip continued to scream. "I cried for you to help me and you never came!"

Sara's heart lurched wildly. "I didn't *know*, Chip," she pleaded. "I couldn't hear you. My work is too far away. If I could've heard you, I would've come right away. But I couldn't hear you. I didn't know. And they *lied* to me, Chip. They told me you were happy there."

Her son would not be consoled.

"What can I do to make you feel better?" she asked him. "Would you like to talk to me about it? Would you rather talk to somebody else?"

"I want to talk to the lady," replied Chip, who became suddenly calm.

"What lady?" asked his bewildered mother.

"Your friend," said Chip. "The lady with the truck."

Sara was struck dumb by the extent to which she had underestimated her son's memory capacity.

Chip was but twenty-one months old at the time of his last visit to the Fuster home. And he was twenty-three months olds on his last—and only—visit to the Metro Justice Building where Laurie Braga had assessed his development while assembling a toy truck and inspired his eyes to widen in stark terror by wondering if he had ever played a game called ring-around-the-rosy.

Now three-and-a-half years old, Chip was asking to speak to the woman to whom, he had gathered, children talked about Frank and Iliana.

Sara called Laurie Braga and arranged to bring Chip to Apogee that very afternoon. From that day, said Sara, her son underwent an abrupt transformation. He no longer passes his days with fists clenched. He is no longer, she said, an angry little boy. And he tells his secrets to her now, not to his pillow.

But for every Chip, there are two others for whom the door is nailed shut. There are Fuster babysitting customers scattered all over the map, from New York to Texas, whose parents continue to deny themselves the dignity of acknowledging the truth. These children might never learn the lessons of "a burden shared" as have the children who were allowed to dignify their pain.

And they might never know that it was for all of them that a husky little red-haired boy spoke of the truth.

Jason Harrison looked up from the coloring book, which was opened to a page that displayed a child on a witness stand.

At the bottom were printed the words:

"I am a _ _ _ _ _ .._ _ ."

The red-haired boy cocked his head thoughtfully.

"Mom?"
"Yes, Jason."
"How do you spell 'hero'?"

• • •

Francisco Fuster Escalona has appealed his conviction and vowed to dedicate the rest of his life to "proving his innocence to the nation."

He currently resides in Florida State Prison, where, it is reported by inmates, he has offered a sizable bounty to anyone who might arrange the death of his soon-to-be-ex-wife, Iliana, whom federal authorities intend to deport when she completes her sentence.

In exchange for his wife's execution, Frank is said to have boasted, he is prepared to offer his most prized possessions.

Videotapes.

Acknowledgments

The author would like to thank the many individuals who opened their lives so their story might be told.

In addition, she extends her gratitude to those who dedicated their time and energies to maintaining its integrity, including publisher Harvey Plotnick, who understood it well enough to title it; senior editor Shari Lesser Wenk, who wielded her blue pencil wisely and sparingly; the kind and caring staff of Contemporary Books, the parent company of Congdon & Weed; literary agent Barbara Markowitz; and the law firm of St. Laurent & St. Laurent, P.A.

A special word of thanks to my husband, whose unwavering support made this work possible.

"It's important," he said.